The Discovery of Drama

Thomas E. Sanders
Miami-Dade Junior College

Scott, Foresman and Company

Acknowledgements

From *Lysistrata* by Aristophanes. From *Lysistrata,* trans. C. T. Murphy, in *Greek Literature in Translation,* ed. C. T. Murphy and W. J. Oates. Used by permission of David McKay Company, Inc. From *The Twelve-Pound Look* by James M. Barrie. Opening stage directions for *The Twelve-Pound Look* are reprinted with the permission of Charles Scribner's Sons from *Half Hours* by James M. Barrie. Copyright 1914 Charles Scribner's Sons; renewal copyright 1942 Cynthia Asquith and Peter Llewelyn Davies. *Orange Soufflé* by Saul Bellow. Copyright © 1965 by Saul Bellow. Reprinted by permission of The Viking Press, Inc. First published in *Esquire* Magazine. *The Latent Heterosexual* by Paddy Chayefsky. © Copyright 1967 by Sidney Productions, Inc. Reprinted by permission of Random House, Inc. From "An Essay of Dramatic Poesy" by John Dryden. Reprinted from *Essays of John Dryden* by permission of the Clarendon Press, Oxford. From *Four Quartets* by T. S. Eliot. From *Four Quartets* by T. S. Eliot, copyright 1936 by Harcourt, Brace & World, Inc. Reprinted by permission. From "Tradition and the Individual Talent" by T. S. Eliot. From *Selected Essays* (New Edition), copyright 1932, 1936, 1950 by Harcourt, Brace & World, Inc.; © 1960 by T. S. Eliot. Reprinted by permission of the publisher. From T. S. Eliot's Introduction to *Shakespeare and the Popular Dramatic Tradition* by S. L. Bethell. Copyright © 1944 by Duke University Press and reprinted by permission. From an interview with William Faulkner in *Writers at Work.* From *Writers at Work,* 1st Series, edited by Malcolm Cowley. All rights reserved. Reprinted by permission of The Viking Press, Inc. From *The Basic Writings of Sigmund Freud.* The material on pp. 128–129 is from *The Basic Writings of Sigmund Freud,* trans. and ed. by Dr. A. A. Brill, Copyright 1938 by Random House, Inc., Copyright renewed 1965 by Gioia Bernheim and Edmund Brill. Reprinted by permission. "Why Verse?" by Christopher Fry. Copyright © 1955 Christopher Fry. Reprinted by permission of the author. From "Catharsis and the Modern Theater" by John Gassner. From *European Theories of the Drama,* ed. Barrett H. Clark. © 1965 by Crown Publishers, Inc. Used by permission of Crown Publishers, Inc. *Sodom and Gomorrah* by Jean Giraudoux. Copyright by Jean Giraudoux and Herma Briffault. Reprinted by permission of Ninon Tallon Karlweis. *Caution:* Professionals and amateurs are hereby warned that *Sodom and Gomorrah* by Jean Giraudoux, being fully protected by copyright, is subject to royalty. All applications for permission to perform the play, including readings, should be made to: Ninon Tallon Karlweis, 250 East 65th Street, New York, N.Y. 10021. From *The Wild Duck* by Henrik Ibsen. Reprinted from *Eleven Plays: An Introduction to Drama,* ed. Gerald Weales, by permission of W. W. Norton & Company, Inc. Copyright © 1964 by W. W. Norton & Company, Inc. "Christopher Fry" by Walter Kerr. From the book *Pieces at Eight* by Walter Kerr. Copyright, ©, 1957 by Walter Kerr. Dutton Paperback Edition (1968). Reprinted by permission of E. P. Dutton & Co., Inc. From "The Tragic Fallacy" by Joseph Wood Krutch. From *The Modern Temper* by Joseph Wood Krutch, copyright 1956 by Harcourt, Brace & World, Inc. Reprinted by permission of the publisher. "Tragedy and the Common Man" by Arthur Miller. Reprinted by permission of Ashley Famous Agency, Inc. and *The New York Times.* Copyright © 1949 by The New York Times Company. From "The Psychology of Tragic Pleasure" by Roy Morrell. Reprinted from *Essays in Criticism* VI (1956) by permission of F. W. Bateson, Publisher of *Essays in Criticism. Desire Under the Elms* by Eugene O'Neill. Copyright 1924 and renewed 1952 by Eugene O'Neill. Reprinted from *Nine Plays by Eugene O'Neill* by permission of Random House, Inc. "The Adventurous Play—Stranger to Broadway" by Tom Prideaux. Tom Prideaux, *Life* Magazine, March 3, 1967 © Time Inc. Reprinted by permission. *Macbeth* by William Shakespeare. *Macbeth* (and accompanying footnotes) is reprinted with the permission of Charles Scribner's Sons from *Shakespeare: Twenty-Three Plays and the Sonnets,* edited by Thomas Marc Parrott. Copyright 1938, 1953 Charles Scribner's Sons: renewal copyright © 1966 Frances M. Parrott Walters. "Phony Fable of a Pop Faust" by Richard Schickel. Copyright © 1967 by Time Inc. Reprinted by permission of The Sterling Lord Agency. *Oedipus Rex* by Sophocles. From *The Oedipus Rex of Sophocles:* An English Version by Dudley Fitts and Robert Fitzgerald, copyright, 1949, by Harcourt, Brace & World, Inc. and reprinted with their permission. *Caution:* All rights, including professional, amateur, motion picture, recitation, lecturing, public reading, radio broadcasting, and television are strictly reserved. Inquiries on all rights should be addressed to Harcourt, Brace & World, Inc., 757 Third Avenue, New York 17, N.Y. *Riders to the Sea* by John Millington Synge. Copyright 1935 by The Modern Library, Inc. Reprinted from *The Complete Works of John M. Synge* by permission of Random House, Inc. From *The Classical Background of English Literature* by J. A. K. Thomson. Copyright © 1948 by George Allen & Unwin Ltd. Reprinted by permission of Barnes & Noble, Inc. and George Allen & Unwin Ltd. "Bad Restoration" from *Time* Magazine. Copyright © 1965 by Time Inc. Reprinted by permission. From "Cartesian Dentist" in *Time* Magazine. Copyright © 1965 by Time Inc. Reprinted by permission. From "Dear Abby," June 1, 1967. Copyright © 1967. Reprinted by permission of Abigail Van Buren. *Camino Real* by Tennessee Williams. Copyright 1948, 1953 by Tennessee Williams. Reprinted by permission of New Directions Publishing Corporation. *Caution:* Professionals and amateurs are hereby warned that *Camino Real,* being fully protected under the copyright laws of the United States, the British Empire including the Dominion of Canada, and all other countries of the Copyright Union, and other countries, is subject to royalty. All rights, including professional, amateur, motion-picture, recitation, lecturing, public reading, radio and television broadcasting, and the rights of translation into foreign languages, are strictly reserved. Particular emphasis is laid on the question of readings, permission for which must be obtained in writing from the author's agents. All enquiries should be addressed to the author's agents: Miss Audrey Wood, Ashley Famous Agency, Inc., 1301 Avenue of the Americas, New York, New York, N.Y. 10019. The amateur acting rights of *Camino Real* are controlled exclusively by the Dramatists Play Service, Inc., 14 East 38th Street, New York 16, N.Y., without whose permission no amateur performances of it may be made. Foreword to *Camino Real* by Tennessee Williams. Reprinted by permission of Ashley Famous Agency, Inc. and *The New York Times.* Copyright © 1953 by The New York Times Company. "The Timeless World of a Play" by Tennessee Williams. From Tennessee Williams, *The Rose Tattoo.* Copyright 1950, 1951 by Tennessee Williams. Reprinted by permission of New Directions Publishing Corporation.

Table of Contents

Preface

Whether "all the world's a stage" or it's all "a chequerboard of nights and days," poets of the past 3000 years have been convinced that an analogy definitely exists between the real and the imagined worlds man inhabits. Man as Self and man as actor so frequently become a single entity that even he doesn't always know when he is living and when he is performing for the infinite amusement of an infinite audience. That his audience may not be infinite, that it may be limited to the tedious confines of his personal theater—these possibilities often make his script confusing, his performance amateurish.

When life becomes a bad script and doubt attends performance, the reality of great plays and professional roles is temporarily comforting. Sophocles, Shakespeare, and Shaw are there, ready to supply instant excellence and allow a brief return to the actual. Of course, after the concrete, man must return to the abstraction he calls "daily life," but it seems somehow saner, somehow sharper in outline before the magic of organized drama wears off and the tedium of a community theater of life overtakes him again. What is the play; what, the playhouse? According to Franklin Hamilton:

> in the playhouse, people wait,
> talk, and appraise each other.
> soon lights dim,
> and players speak their parts.
>
> later the theatre is empty
> and all is as it was before
>
> except the people who saw the play
> and those who spoke their parts,
>
> these have mixed a little together.°

In *The Discovery of Drama,* nine playwrights and 2500 years of scripting offer their services to the reader who will "mix a little together" with them. Beginning with an analysis of dramatic structure, the book attempts to help the student of life explore the nature of dramatic reality as he learns to understand the machinery of poetic faith. It is a literary approach, the techniques of staging left to the technical bu-

° "The Play," from *leaf scar* by Franklin Hamilton. Published by Brookside Press, London; copyright © 1965 by Franklin Hamilton and reprinted by permission.

reaucracy that manipulates and changes the world created by play-wrights. Here, the concern is for the dramatist and the actor of multiple roles, the student of life: the reader.

From misty Athens to the mystic Camino Real, from singular Oedipus to ubiquitous Kilroy, the barriers of space, time, and humanity are leveled as mighty casts are assembled and the play becomes the thing more vital than life because it is the distillation of life. In the final chapter, encouragement to write the play and aid in writing about the play engage the student in more than a passive role. If he leaves the theater of this book and is unchanged by the life he has encountered herein, we can only regret his inability to become involved in life.

Attempting to involve him in the plays, critical analyses and challenging questions stand in close proximity to the playwright's material. Set in two type faces, the script and the textual matter can be read independently of each other without jarring the student's sensibilities. If it pleases the teacher, the interpolations can be ignored completely, can serve as ideas to be argued, or can act as guideposts on the student's journey. Hopefully, they can be helpful in leading the student to under-standing and pleasure.

A large cast of characters has made this book possible. Curt Johnson suggested it; Verne Reaves directed it. The production staff includes such praiseworthies as John Mayahara who gave it visual appeal, Mrs. Pat Parker and Susan Kuc who sent out playbills so untiringly, and Barbara Stewart, a script girl of extraordinary devotion. The angel is Scott, Foresman and Company, a collective producer that deserves my thanks.

And there's a personal cast that deserves listing because their unique contributions have forced my personal drama. Lyle Shupe, Hal Craig, and Graham Cook serve expository function. Grace McAlister, Louise For-shaw, Art Rawlings, and Walter W. Peek are major characters. Phyllis Eisman, Bette Lou Nicolaides, Constance Fleischer, Frank Hester, and Marie Joffre have been dedicated supporting actors. All deserve ovation but must settle for quiet gratitude as this prologue ends and the curtain rises on Act I.

Thomas E. Sanders
Miami, Florida
1968

CHAPTER I

The Theater of the Mind

With the possible exception of the Elizabethan English, no group of people has been as personally captive to the theater as mid-twentieth-century Americans. School groups, amateur groups, little theater groups, experimental theater groups—these bands of pretenders include many thousands of active participants. The legitimate stage (on Broadway, Main Street, and in traveling companies), the motion-picture houses, and the television set in almost every American living room—these media involve the remainder of us in at least a passive way with the theater.

Whether it is spelled *theater* or *theatre,* the word connotes glamour, excitement, entertainment, and escape for the masses. For a smaller number of people, it connotes a reading pleasure second to none. Even the last group, however, is not a tiny segment of our society. Its numbers are large enough to support publication of plays in both soft- and hard-cover editions as well as in magazines of large circulation.

One such magazine, *Esquire,* has been printing plays for more than a decade. The November 1966 issue presented *The Killing of Sister George* by Frank Marcus almost simultaneously with its New York opening on October 5, and Arnold Gingrich wrote in his "Publisher's Page" column:

> There will be some readers of this issue who won't read the play it contains for no better or other reason than that it is a play. These people, from whom we hear every time we print a play, just don't like to read anything that is presented as a form of drama. Fortunately for the state of English literature, such people have always been in the minority, or some of its present chief adornments (Shakespeare for one) would otherwise hardly have been heard of after four centuries.

It is indeed fortunate that such readers constitute a minority, but it is doubly unfortunate—for them—that they constitute a group at all. The living theater—as a geographical, architectural, and artistic entity—is a thrilling and glamorous place. With that statement there can be no argument. But the theater of the mind is even more glamorous, thrilling, and vital, for it suffers none of the limitations of staging, lighting, musical scoring, costuming, and character confinement that are part and parcel of the physical theater.

The terms *the theater* and *the theater of the mind* refer to two distinct and separate theaters. While the stage, movies, and television involve viewers in a passive fashion (as mere spectators), the printed page creates a theater of the imagination for the reader who learns to become a producer, director, set and costume designer, lighting technician, orchestra, choreographer, and actor of multiple roles. Such a wealth of activity is a far cry from the simple involvement of purchasing a ticket and relaxing to receive a playwright's communication second-hand.

In fact, second-hand communication is probably the most confining element of the physical theater for the capable reader. He sits passively and watches the curtain open on a set—for example, the set at the beginning of Henrik Ibsen's *The Wild Duck:*

SCENE—At WERLE'S house. *A richly and comfortably furnished study; bookcases and upholstered furniture; a writing-table, with papers and documents, in the centre of the room; lighted lamps with green shades, giving a subdued light. At the back, open folding-doors with curtains drawn back. Within is seen a large and handsome room, brilliantly lighted with lamps and branching candlesticks. In front, on the right (in the study), a small baize door leads into* WERLE'S *office. On the left, in front, a fireplace with a glowing coal fire, and farther back a double door leading into the dining room.*°

To design this set, the designer for a "live" production of *The Wild Duck* would have to visualize the room, decide what characteristic period furniture to use, utilize only the shades of "green" and "baize" that were in vogue at the time, and establish the acceptable requirements of "richly and comfortably." His elaborate background of study, theatrical knowledge, and personal taste would dictate many of his choices. But those choices would then have to be modified by the demands of the director (who might insist that the furniture be scaled down or rearranged to create more space for the actors' movements), the preferences of the actors (who may feel uncomfortable with certain shades of green and brown or specific arrangements of furniture), and

° Translated by Frances Archer.

the size and shape of the physical stage. And that physical stage itself is a major consideration: it is a room having only three walls; the fourth is like a transparent glass through which the audience views the action. As a result, an added restraint is imposed on an already severely limited setting.

Now the major problem arises: the set designer's concept of "richly and comfortably" (within the limitations of the period) may be at absolute odds with the viewer's idea of rich comfort in decor. *His* taste and sensory reactions may be more (or less) highly developed than any of the "committee's" that has created this setting of a room. Consequently, the first aim of the playwright—the creation of "atmosphere" through a setting—is thwarted. *A* mood, *an* atmosphere will, certainly, be created by the set, but, if it is at odds with the *viewer's* concept, it stands between him and complete enjoyment or understanding of the action that will take place against the backdrop.

Perhaps that is only a small irritation, but compound it with differing concepts in lighting, costuming, and role interpretation, and the viewer may be so frustrated by inconsequentials that he will miss the point of the play entirely, find himself vaguely dissatisfied, and feel somehow cheated of his time. And his complaint will be as old as Aristotle, who was perhaps the first to observe that: "The Spectacle [setting, scenery, etc.] has, indeed, an emotional attraction of its own, but of all the parts, it is the least artistic, and connected least with the art of poetry. . . . the production of spectacular effects depends more on the art of the stage machinist than on that of the poet."*

The theater of the mind, on the other hand, offers no such stumbling blocks. As the reader comes to the play, the screen of his imagination is swept clean and he is ready to visualize sets and costumes, supply mood music and sound effects from his own warehouse of stored memory and experience. What he visualizes may be completely "incorrect" in academic terms. His concept of "richly furnished," for example, may include garish furniture in thoroughly bad taste, but it is *his* concept, and it does not jar his sensibilities. "Comfortable" may suggest chintz and tufted carpets to one reader, brocades and Persian carpets to another. Period styles may be garbled in the reader's mind, but at least his concept will not be at odds with his visual image. Consequently, the action within his set will be of paramount importance. His attention will not be diverted from the subtle implications of a line of dialog by an unfamiliar piece of furniture or an historically accurate but distracting painting which merely completes the set without having a specific function in the performance. Of course, the reader's set will probably not be complete at first. It will

* *Poetics,* tr. S. H. Butcher, p. 25.

contain the essential furniture as suggested by the playwright, but the unfolding of the action may cause him later to visualize a painting on a wall that had previously been bare. And he will supply the painting unobtrusively, almost unaware it had not been a part of the earlier decor. Such is the power of imagination when it has not been blunted by reliance on actual, physical sight.

But, you ask, what if my imagination has been blunted? Well, now is a good time to sharpen it, to hone the edges that have been dulled, to begin once more to see the dragons and giants of childhood's imagination—giants and dragons that can never be technically produced by the limited materials of actuality. For example, you doubtless know the experience of walking to a television set, turning it on, seating yourself comfortably, and forgetting your surroundings, your own personality, your problems and worries. During the two hours you watch a movie, you manage to suspend your awareness of everything but the production. Even the irritation of frequent commercials does not recall you to reality until the end of the performance. The theater of the mind requires the same concentration. And it requires the same exercise of imagination. In other words, before you can participate in the plays which you read, you must learn consciously to do what you already do unconsciously with a click of the television knob: deliberately suspend credulity, be willing to imagine that what you read is not the creation of a playwright but a transcript of reality—a reality that has been pared of all but the basic and necessary ingredients for your understanding of the experience. Moving like a disembodied spirit, you are there, capable of seeing without being seen, hearing without being heard, examining without being examined. You can, at will, enter the minds of people and know the significance of their actions as even they do not. Because you have transcended the flesh, become free in time and in space, you can *be* a person in the play—or *all* of the characters. You can achieve this seeming impossibility because you wish to and because the playwright has afforded you the vehicle to allow your wishes to come true. But *your* willing participation is imperative before *his* vehicle can become effective.

Samuel Taylor Coleridge, addressing himself to his nineteenth-century poetry readers, might as easily have been speaking to you, the play reader, when he stated, in Chapter XIV of *Biographia Literaria,* that his purpose in writing the *Lyrical Ballads* was "to transfer from our inward nature a human interest and a semblance of truth sufficient to procure for these shadows of imagination that willing suspension of disbelief for the moment, which constitutes poetic faith." Poetic faith? In reading plays? Yes, not only because as a reader you must do the work of actors, directors, and all the others who make up a play, but because the important abstractions (friendship, love, fear) which underlie and supply the "meaning" of most plays are neither understandable nor communicable in the scientific logic of the non-poetic or concrete term. Poetic faith is the *ability* to believe in things like the dignity of man, the possibility of justice, or God, as well as to create in your imagination the settings and other trappings of a drama. Poetic faith liberates the play reader's imagination and provides him with, as Coleridge says, "an inexhaustible treasure, but for which, in consequence of the film of familiarity and selfish solicitude, we have eyes yet see not, ears that hear not, and hearts that neither feel nor understand."

Coleridge knew that; so did Sophocles, Shakespeare, and Tennessee Williams. For any play is an analogy. Imitative though it may be, unreal as it may seem, it approximates the *poetic* reality of life and therefore is analogous *to* life. If life is important enough for you to try to understand, you can participate in plays you read, for, no matter how removed they may be from the absolutes of your physical life, they concern the timeless, poetic realities that pervade your every hour. They chronicle your pity, your fear, your aspirations, and your defeats. The playwrights detail your life, but they do so with analogy. And to understand and appreciate the analogies, you must have poetic faith.

Now, consider the *physical* theater again, specifically the beginning of *The Wild Duck.* The set has established a mood for the viewer—a mood in which he has had no active participation. He must merely accept it. Against the backdrop of that set, two actors move and speak:

WERLE'S servant, PETTERSEN, *in livery, and* JENSEN, *the hired waiter, in black, are putting the study in order. In the large room, two or three other hired waiters are moving about, arranging things and lighting more candles. From the dining-room, the hum of conversation and laughter of many voices are heard; a glass is tapped with a knife; silence follows, and a toast is proposed; shouts of "Bravo!" and then again a buzz of conversation.*

PETTERSEN (*lights a lamp on the chimney-place and places a shade over it*). Listen to them, Jensen! Now the old man's on his legs holding a long palaver about Mrs. Sörby.

JENSEN (*pushing forward an armchair*). Is it true, what folks say, that they're—very good friends, eh?

PETTERSEN. Lord knows.

JENSEN. I've heard tell as he's been a lively customer in his day.

PETTERSEN. May be.

JENSEN. And he's giving this spread in honor of his son, they say.

PETTERSEN. Yes. His son came home yesterday.

JENSEN. This is the first time I ever heard as Mr. Werle had a son.

PETTERSEN. Oh, yes, he has a son, right enough. But he's a fixture, as you might say, up at the Höidal works. He's never once come to town all the years I've been in service here.

One of the actors is dressed in the livery of a servant of the period (about 1885). The livery is technically correct, the costume designer having authenticated it down to the last button. The second actor is dressed in a black suit of the period, for, as we are to learn, he is a waiter hired for the occasion. Sounds of a dinner in progress offstage serve as background noise while the servants onstage busy themselves with lighting candles and straightening furniture. They speak their lines—lines designed to give the viewer background information he needs to understand the action which will unfold. Each actor has his own concept of the character he is creating, but that concept has been changed by the director's concept; the actor, given absolute freedom of interpretation, would probably endow the character with more importance than is warranted in the play. The director has, doubtless, seen each character as a plot device, as a supplier of information who must not dominate the stage, for the viewer will erroneously assume the play centers around that character, and an established mood will have to be shattered and rebuilt as the real main character comes on. The director probably insists that a deliberate dehumanization take place so that the conventional device of the physical theater can work.

In the theater of the mind, however, the reader is not confined by such conventions. He has willingly suspended his disbelief on opening the book or magazine. No audience surrounds him as a distracting element, and he can—and will—identify with each character, for he can fancy himself in that role. He has his own concept of the behavioral patterns and thought processes of a "live-in" servant. He can—and does—become (in his mind) that character, for he is not distracted by a flesh-and-blood imitation parading before his eyes. That servant onstage is a man the viewer is watching; the viewer cannot mentally become that man. However, as reader, he *must* briefly become that man—or, at least, the man must become the reader's preconceived idea made flesh. In the reader's mind, the character more nearly approximates the real man than a fleshly actor ever can. The actor is a real man *imitating* another. The created character *becomes* a real man as the reader visualizes him in the theater of the mind. And, because he is a creation of the reader's mind, he is a facet of the reader—their blood, their flesh and bone spring from a shared source. The viewer in the physical theater can never know that sort of unity with a character.

Your concept of "in livery" may spring from a Walt Disney version of *Cinderella* or a Louis XIV movie on the late, late show, but you *do* have a definite picture. If Pettersen is wearing a white wig and silver knee buckles, you may have him confused with the king of a costume movie, but it doesn't make one whit of difference. He fulfills the requirement: you have a satisfactory image, one that you are pleased with, a functional one. If the "hired waiter, in black" is wearing a rented tuxedo and looks like the headwaiter in your favorite nightclub, he will not seem strange in the theater of the mind as he speaks with the bewigged and buckled Pettersen. Your picture is more sharp, more clear than any the physical theater could ever produce, for this is *your* concept, regardless of historical inaccuracy. Such a conglomerate picture, physically presented, would merely approximate a masquerade, but you have not created a costume party. You have visualized a concept, and it is the concept that is important. The physical theater is limited to accuracy because the production is staged for *many* viewers, therefore cannot pander to one. You need not worry about a second viewer in the theater of the mind.

As the waiters speak, you, as a reader, have definite knowledge which a physical theater viewer does not. You know in advance that Pettersen is a retained servant; he lives in the house and therefore has a more personal and intimate knowledge of the family than Jensen does. Jensen is merely a hired hand for the evening. As a human being, you expect Pettersen to possess knowledge of the family that Jensen would not, but you expect him to be loyal to his employer in ways Jensen need not be. And you understand Jensen's curiosity about this wealthy household so removed from his existence. You established your attitudes from the playwright's stage directions; the viewer, however, has no such access to them. He must concentrate on establishing identities, attitudes, and motives from what he sees and hears. His printed program offers some help, but not much:

PETTERSEN, *Werle's servant*
JENSEN, *a hired waiter*

Left to decide which actor is who and what the different costumes mean, the viewer is trying to follow dialog—which involves him in a guessing game. With his attention so divided, he will miss subtlety of inflection and character—even if it be allowed by the director. On the other hand, you as a reader are prepared to hear the characters' words as extensions of your own knowledge. Suddenly, the dialog isn't merely a stage convention used to supply background information; it is the clue which you examine to see if these servants behave in terms acceptable to your ethical code. And, as this play is concerned with ethical codes, you are immediately plunged into the playwright's intention. The viewer is still floundering about, getting the pieces of essential information so he can understand the main characters. It is he, not you, who is at a very real disadvantage.

When Pettersen invites Jensen's attention to "the old man," is he asserting his position in the household to a man who has none? Does he offer the information from a superior position, attempting to make Jensen envious? Is he, in a kind way, attempting to put Jensen at his ease, for would Jensen not be a little nervous? Or is Pettersen making gentle fun of "the old man"—or heavily sarcastic fun? How does he inflect the word *palaver?* What possibilities does his choice of this particular word suggest?

Jensen pushes the armchair forward—an act in the physical theater designed to keep him moving, to sustain action onstage in a reasonably natural fashion. In the theater of the mind, he is doing his job, but does not the act seem to invite confidence? The chair does suggest unguarded conversation, doesn't it? What does the pause after *they're* imply? Is it a deliberate pause, or is Jensen merely groping for words that will not offend Pettersen? Or does the chair become clumsy at this point, diverting attention from the words which continue after he has the chair subdued? The live actor on the physical stage must decide, with the director's approval, which one possible meaning of the line to prefer. With voice inflection, bodily movement, and facial expression, he will color the question. In the theater of the mind, there is no such limitation—one or all of the possibilities can be encompassed, for only the reader assesses the delivery. In the physical theater, it must be telegraphed to many minds at once, and the inflections or movements must be exaggerated enough that everyone will understand the one desired implication.

Pettersen's "Lord knows" may be reverent, disinterested, noncommittal, genuinely perplexed, or simply asserted ignorance. In the reader's mind it may be a combination of any number of the possibilities. If no one possibility seems apparent, the reader can hear the words without inflection, reserving judgment for the moment. In the physical theater, no such delay is possible. One determined character revelation is the viewer's only choice, for it is the only offering.

Pettersen's "May be" will probably give the reader the clue he needs to decide. Does Pettersen answer "*May* be"? or "May *be*"? or "*May be*"? or "Maybe"? Four different attitudes exist in the four possible inflections. Body movements, gestures, and facial expressions extend that number for the reader. Once again, the live actor is limited onstage; the actor in the mind may manage all four possibilities, for his mental reactions are accessible to the reader who can even supply any rationalizations he deems desirable.

And so the play progresses until the curtain descends in the physical theater and the viewer retires to an after-the-theater spot for coffee and discussion of the possible meanings of the play, the quality of the actors, the appropriateness of sets and music. It has probably been a pleasant evening's diversion for him. The reader, on the other hand, may close the book and meditatively reflect on the play, unconcerned with the lighting, the sets, the costumes, or the quality of the acting. They were all perfect. The sets were exactly what he envisioned; the music was superb—even if it was a mixture of opera, rock-and-roll, and outright schmaltz—for it was supplied from the repertoire of memory. The actors? Oh, how wonderfully they performed! Money, commitments, distance— none of these things interfered with the casting. Broadway, Hollywood, the television networks—all supplied the actors. Nor was the reader limited by life and death. He could bring back to life any great actress or actor he fancied to play a role in his production. Therefore, all those things were neither distractions nor problems. The play's the thing!

Perhaps, in the performance, one scene (or even an act) was unclear. In the theater of the mind, it can be reënacted merely by opening the script and beginning to read at any point. Actors are immediately reassembled, mental crews rearrange furniture (at no overtime pay), and the play goes on again, this portion canceling the earlier performance, bringing new insight, depth, and clarity to the total performance.

"All the world's a stage" is a statement that assumes added proportion for the reader of plays. He can move his cast through the rooms of a house, into the garden, down country walks, to exotic lands—all with immediacy and mental dispatch.

Nor is time a problem. It can serve the theater of the mind magnificently. The reader can watch a play in sixth-century B.C. Athens, ring down the curtain, and immediately raise it again on a twentieth-century A.D. treatment of similar material. He may view Aeschylus' *Electra* in the lavender air of Athens, surrounded by such interesting companions as Plato, Pericles, and Aristotle before joining an equally illustrious group of companions from his own time to watch the Mannon family of Eugene O'Neill's *Mourning Becomes Electra* in their stern New England home. And, perhaps, he can answer the anguished question O'Neill asked five years before he completed the Mannon saga: "Is it possible to get modern psychological approximation of the Greek sense of fate into such a play which an intelligent audience of today, possessed of no belief in gods or supernatural retribution, could accept and be moved by?"* In the theater of the mind, anything is possible.

Without his interpreter, the playwright would create a non-work. Only when a play is read or performed by someone does it become a complete work, for it is an attempt to communicate something, and communication does not occur until the sender finds a receiver. The projection is the writer's; the screen on which it may be most intimately flashed is the theater of the mind. In the physical theater, the play is similar to a lecture delivered to a group: it must be universal (therefore general) enough to be received in some way by every viewer. In the theater of the mind, the play may be as personal as a whispered conversation. And when the reader does his half of the job, the play becomes a communication. Spectacular effects become unimportant and the communication itself becomes vital.

CHAPTER II

Of Acts and Scenes— Dramatic Structure

Unfortunately, the lives of few men can qualify as tragedy. Two limitations deny that possibility to most of us. First, *tragedy* can only result when a man involved in a tragic sequence of events is a person of economic or social prestige, nobility of character, and worth to others who may view him as an example. Second, for tragedy to occur, such a man's exemplary Self must be marred by some one human weakness that, perhaps trivial in isolation, nevertheless makes him vulnerable to the tragic sequence of events so that the basic conflict is resolved against him and he is destroyed utterly. Now, few such exemplary humans exist, for most men are so psychologically constituted that they progress from crisis to crisis, seldom encountering one so overwhelming that it can destroy them. In fact, if a man is basically weak enough to be destroyed by a single reversal in life, he is probably far from noble in the first place. As Henry David Thoreau once observed, "The mass of men lead lives of quiet desperation." Unfortunate? Yes. Tragic? Hardly.

On the other hand, equally few of us can be said to lead lives which are a *comedy*. That is, we do not possess one quality or trait that would lend itself to gross exaggeration in our daily lives, thereby enabling a dramatist to reduce us to absurdity. Absurd moments dot our existence, of course; mild psychological shocks create humor; and genuine wit occasionally invests our lives with laughter. But such happy breaks in our desperate routines merely supply relief between crises and are, at best, *comic interludes*.

In short, our lives may fluctuate between the extremes of tragedy and comedy, but it is rare indeed for a life to settle violently or gently at either end of the continuum. Most of the time, we travel between the two extremes on a journey that brings us into any number of conflicts wherein we lose.

Instead of being destroyed, however, we adjust to the new circumstances of life and proceed toward our next conflict. As a result, most of us may be said to live a constant *drama*. Some moments of it are more intense than others, more fraught with danger, suspense, and distress; these are the *dramatic* times of our lives. And, as we adjust from those brief encounters, we laugh a little at fate and at ourselves; we think of the absurd elements of our situation, for laughter is our salvation. In fact, some of us alternate so regularly between the dramatic elements of life and those elements which serve as comic relief that life becomes a *tragicomedy*. Still others of us actually court the dramatic, reveling in it, enjoying it to the point that we become sentimental and maudlin; such lives may be called *melodrama*. Others of us refuse to embroil ourselves in the drama of life; we laugh a little too boisterously at fate and circumstance, reducing it all to *farce* or *burlesque*. A few of us attempt to be impassive, actually to abstract ourselves intellectually and emotionally to see the humor of our foibles. Life then becomes a *comedy of manners*. A smaller number of people not only *attempt* to be impassive, to abstract themselves, but are successful at it. For them, life is a *satire*, brilliant but brittle, for they stand outside the mainstream of the emotions and drift on the currents of the intellect to occupy a rather lonely spiritual geography.

Does life assume such patterns because it is controlled by God or by Nature? Whichever is the answer, the controlling force must be an artist of great scope and depth to allow these infinite variations. And *theatrical drama* (a term here embracing the two extremes of tragedy and comedy with all the intervening gradations) is nothing more or less than an attempt to emulate the wide range of these possibilities of a man's life. For the playwright too is an artist emulating God or Nature; or, as Leonardo da Vinci once said, "Every artist has two subjects: Man and hopes of his soul." In short, those "hopes of his soul" provide the basic themes of drama, themes that are constant in all literature, whether in poetry or in prose, the short story, essay, or novel. They include considerations of love, hate, fear, greed, sexual need, and spiritual fulfillment—in short, any concern in the life of man.

Because life *is* man's greatest concern, the drama has always been patterned on his concept of life. Man knows his activities are bounded by time and take place within a framework of physical geography. That awareness creates the *set* of his play—the background in time against which the action of his life will occur. So too with the setting of a stage production. It may be an artist's apartment in San Francisco in the year 1968, or a hermit's cave in the Black Forest in the year 1283. The geographical locale of a play sets the immediate *atmosphere* (the mood created in the viewer or reader with visual effects), for the reader arbitrarily adopts a set response if the curtains open on a clean, tastefully furnished room; he adopts quite a different one if the room is littered, filthy, and furnished with cast-off furniture.

This immediate acceptance, this willingness to participate in the illusion of the play is basically an acceptance of certain *conventions* or agreements between reader and writer. A suggestion is given by the playwright, and the reader cooperates by supplying his half of the material of credibility. We are quite willing to allow a character in a play to deliver a *soliloquy* (a speech comprised of spoken thoughts) in full hearing of other characters who, for the moment, are arrested in time with their five senses suspended so the thoughts of the speaking character may be verbalized. The soliloquy may go on at some length (Hamlet's "To be or not to be" soliloquy, for instance) or be shortened to an *aside* (a very brief soliloquy or statement directed from the player to the reader) without disturbing us, for we have agreed in advance to honor this particular ground rule of drama. Nor do most of us experience any great difficulty in honoring conventions, for both we and the playwright have started with a basic agreement about language. The word *chair,* for example, means "furniture intended for seating" merely because we have all arbitrarily agreed that it does. We could as easily agree that *snig* means "furniture intended for seating" and respond immediately to the command "Put the book on the red snig before you leave." But the conventions of our language dictate otherwise. Conventions occupy so much of our lives that they create no problems as we read plays.

The geography of the set, then, supplies basic atmosphere; the playwright's selection of characters, words, and general attitude supply the *tone* of the play as characters move and speak against that background. The Beverly Hillbillies are far more humorous in a mansion than they are in their Ozark cabin. A king becomes infinitely more or less regal as he dominates a hideout cave or is dominated by the inconveniences of it. Humorous, pathetic, ironic—these words describe tone, for tone is the attitude created for the reader which he must share if he is to understand the meaning of a line. For this reason, a reader who lacks a sense of humor cannot read comedy with pleasure. And an immature intellect will not respond to a controlled and disciplined, intellectually conceived play.

With the set furnishing the time and place of action, characters move through time and place. Each time a major character enters or leaves the set, a *scene* begins, for, as in life, brief incidents occur when people come into contact with a place or with other people. In isolation, any incident or scene in a play may have little meaning; but, because it is affected by scenes which have occurred before it and itself will affect scenes which come after it, the scene or incident forms a part of the total pattern that is the larger action. In life, you may walk into a room, find it unsatisfactory to your purpose, and rearrange the furniture slightly. In isolation, that scene would suggest you are fastidious, bored, or changeable—if a hidden observer were to assess it. However, if another person then knocked at the door, was admitted to the room, and examined it with a careful eye, the action would become more meaningful. Your rearrangements now would suggest that you knew your caller would be critical of the room; so something would be revealed about both of you. If, on the other hand, the caller came in and was completely unaware of the room, something would *still* be revealed about both of you. And the complete action, with two characters, would be a scene.

In the course of a day, we act out many scenes, all meaningful in some way as they contribute to the total effect of the day. Ordinarily, our multiple scenes are undramatic, merely routine, but they are still a part of the pattern of the whole. A playwright carefully considers the importance of his scenes, assesses their value in making the total picture (his play) clear to the reader, and chooses those scenes which contain the most intense dramatic possibilities. Of course, scenes may serve any one of many functions: to present explanations the reader needs (*expository scenes*); to introduce complicating matter in an easy fashion (*messenger scenes*—including verbal messages, letters read aloud, telephone conversations); to bridge two important scenes that would otherwise seem unrelated (*transition scenes*); to reveal the impact of one complication on another as they are joined together (*development scenes*); or to contain the point of highest interest of the larger unit (*climax scenes*). These scenes are then woven into larger units of action—units which reveal their meaning as the pattern of related scenes emerges.

The larger unit to which each scene makes its unique contribution is called an *act*. An act is, basically, analogous to the days, months, and years in a human life. An act is a measured space of time; the period between acts (marked by an intermission, a falling curtain, or some other device) allows time to be abridged or passed over—a convention the reader accepts as preferable to being bored by tedious scenes which would have to do the job otherwise.

An act may consist of only one scene, or several scenes may be employed—the playwright decides how best to involve the reader, present the problem, reveal complications of the problem, reach a climax which demands resolution, and polish off the work. This decision creates the number of time divisions in the play that make it a one-, three-, or five-act work. While these are the most common numbers of acts, a playwright is not limited to them. He may prefer two, four, or six acts; but readers and viewers are so accustomed to the conventional groupings that problems are created with the use of any other kind of structure. Greek plays set the original pattern for five-act plays, a pattern in which each act fulfills a particular function leading to the success of the larger unit. For example, in a typical five-act play, Act I serves as an introduction (sometimes called *exposition*); it presents the setting, the characters, and the background action needed by the reader if he is to understand the present action, and it also creates the atmosphere and tone of the play. In Sophocles' *Oedipus Rex,* for example, Act I opens with the citizens of Thebes supplicating Zeus and Oedipus to remove the plague from their city. Thus, the basic conflict is established immediately since the reader intuits that a man and a god must eventually collide in some way. Furthermore, since the play begins *in medias res* (in the middle of things), background information must be supplied and the reader prepared to *want* to follow the action. All of this and more is accomplished in Act I of *Oedipus.* Similarly, in Shakespeare's *Hamlet,* the ghostly hour, the dank castle, and the ghost supply the tragic reality, and Horatio's conversation with the watchers supplies background matter.

Act II in a typical five-act play presents *rising action* (also called *complication*), the present action we are concerned with once we have adequate background to hold our interest. For this purpose, an *exciting force* may often be employed. In *Oedipus,* the exciting force is the charge made by Teiresias that Oedipus is the cause of the plague. In *Hamlet,* it is the ghost's revelation of murder. Actually, the exciting force usually closes Act I, paving the way for our concern in Act II. The second act, then, is devoted to creating a series of complicating acts or mental conflicts between the dominant characters of the play. Oedipus and Creon become enemies as suggestions of political intrigue complicate Oedipus' ability to act decisively. Hamlet's love of Ophelia and Queen Gertrude, as well as his concern for his own indecisiveness, encourage the reader's interest.

Action continues to rise in such plays until, usually in Act III, a *turning point* (sometimes called a *crisis*) is reached. Up to this point, the main character has probably managed to succeed in whatever he is attempting without too much hindrance. In fact, he probably seems destined to achieve his ends with happy dispatch. However, suddenly the turning point is reached and he overreaches his good fortune. Oedipus insists, against Iocastê's urging, that the shepherd be brought to him. He will have the truth. Hamlet fails to kill the king at his prayers.

Falling action is the dominant influence, usually late in Act III or early in Act IV, of the forces in opposition to the central character. Suspense must be maintained at this point and any weakness of the play will manifest itself here. The term *falling action* should not suggest a decline of dramatic interest; in fact, interest intensifies at this time. In *Hamlet,* for instance, the young prince begins his descent to death as he sets in motion the *tragic force* (an event bearing the same relation to falling action that the exciting force does to rising action) by stabbing Polonius and forcing his own withdrawal from the court just as he seems destined to succeed in his plans. Oedipus forces truth from the shepherd and *knows* the horror of his life. The *climax* (that point of highest reader interest) usually occurs in this act.

The *catastrophe* occupies Act V as the punishment or the death of the central character and/or opposing characters comes about. In Greek plays, violence is usually offstage; in Shakespearean, it is usually onstage. The action of the play comes to a logical conclusion, and the reader is satisfied with the restored order of life. Shakespeare offers a glimpse of the future in *Hamlet* as the young prince proposes that Fortinbras be crowned the new king. Sophocles offers no such restoration in *Oedipus,* suggesting instead, because *moire* (fate) is in control, that no man should be judged happy until after his death.

The five-act play originated with the Greeks and remained current through 1880, not because the Greeks had originated it, but because the Roman Seneca had emulated it and he served as the model for later dramatists. At the end of the nineteenth century, however, plays with fewer acts gained in popularity until, today, three acts is the accepted standard for artistic as well as economic reasons rising out of theater production costs. The basic plan of introduction, rising action, turning point, falling action, and catastrophe retains currency, however, even in the three-act play, simply because it is artistically sound.

Contemporary three-act plays are written to be acted in approximately two hours, give or take ten minutes. In Act I, the setting is revealed and the mood is established as quickly as possible. The principal characters are introduced and their motives suggested. The *protagonist* is the main character, for his problem is the audience's chief concern. The protagonist may be a *hero* (a person of superior moral qualities except for one fatal weakness or *flaw*). On the other hand, the protagonist may be merely *heroic* (possessing a preponderance of morally desirable characteristics but flawed in several areas). Or, the protagonist may be quite an *ordinary* man to whom fate has been unkind or one who is basically weak (a convict, a failure in life, a neurotic misfit) but who excites our interest because we sympathize with him for any of a number of reasons. Or, finally, the protagonist may be an *anti-hero* (a person of predominantly undesirable characteristics who is "flawed" by a few redeeming good features and, therefore, excites our compassion or sympathy because we are an underdog-oriented people).

The protagonist's opponent in the play is called the *antagonist* (the person intent on defeating or destroying the protagonist). The conflict between antagonist and protagonist is one which is created by opposing wills, moral codes, ambitions, and so on. Each of them desires to attain his own end or to realize his own ambition, and attaining that eventual goal is his or her *motivation*. In Act I, that motivation is either revealed or suggested, and the reader is forced to choose sides in the promised conflict.

Act II in a three-act play reveals the subtleties of both the conflict and the characters, often containing both the exciting force and the tragic force—the first near the beginning of the act, the second near the end. Most modern playwrights include the exciting force in Act I, however, as part of the initial presentation of conflict. Act II then serves the primary function of revealing the principal characters with greater insight, with more elaborate detail than was earlier presented. The conflict and any complication which contribute to the interest generated by that conflict are intensified in this act and it usually closes with the presentation of the climax, allowing the theater audience to speculate during the second intermission and allowing the reader to heighten suspense for himself as he takes a break before beginning to read the third act.

Act III of a three-act play opens on the suspense generated by the climax which ends Act II, or it may present the climax near its own beginning and then resolve the outcome. On the other hand, if the play is designed to build steadily from opening to climax without resolution, the climax and catastrophe will come simultaneously at the end of this act and its resolution will be left to the reader.

In short, whether in five- or three-act form, a play begins with exposition, continues on concentrated refinement, and closes on intensified response, anticipation, or outright resolution. At that time, the *theme* (the basic overall statement of purpose of the play) should either suggest itself or be offered in such a way that the reader can apprehend it. For example, he should be able to say to himself, "Because of this experience, I now know more fully the truth of the statement 'Love is blind' or 'Crime does not pay'" or some such cliché. However, because the play has dramatized the theme, the truism, whatever it is, should also assume meaning for the reader that it has lacked before. Once the reader experiences the truth of the cliché, it assumes new dimensions—it becomes a reality rather than a meaningless, repetitive truism.

Playwrights manage to reveal truth, to make it meaningful, by creating a set of circumstances, peopling those circumstances with characters, giving those characters carefully controlled speeches (*dialog*), and bringing their created world to a conclusion that, in its powerful, directed climax, forces us to understand truth even though we may be psychologically disposed to evade or ignore it. These rules of playwrighting were all examined and listed by Aristotle in his *Poetics* 2300 years ago and we shall return to some of them later. Now, however, let us examine a play to see how a talented playwright works, free of technical language, free of anything but the script of a play itself.

Such an examination may best be accomplished if we employ a one-act play, a remarkably easy-to-read form since it shares so much in common with the short story. Brevity, a single incident illuminating a character's total life, one dominant effect, and a revealed change in the major character—these are the goals aspired to by one-act playwrights and short-story authors alike. Richard Watts, Jr., writing an introduction to a collection of one-act plays, once noted of the form:

> On the whole I think there is more sheer pleasure in reading a one-act play than is to be found in perusing full-length dramas. It is a form which tends to set free the imagination and the spirit of the playwright and to send it bounding through time and space, ignoring the customary fetters of convention and of length. Almost any playwright can say what he wants to say in less time than the full-length play requires, and the one-act work is joyously free of the usual padding.°

As you read Saul Bellow's *Orange Soufflé*, skip the textual discussion that has been interpolated into the script. Read for enjoyment and understanding, not consciously analyzing on your first reading. At the conclusion of the play, write a one-paragraph statement of the theme or a casual statement of what you think the author was attempting. Then, reread the play, pausing at the textual breaks and examining the parts of the work. If you accomplish this reading, rereading, and examination with thoroughness and understanding, you will find the plays that follow much easier to read and comprehend, for they will all, in some way, have much in common with this delightful one-act work.

ORANGE SOUFFLÉ

by Saul Bellow

SCENE: HILDA'S *apartment, a kitchenette-bedroom, in Indiana Harbor, Indiana. A counter or room divider separates the kitchen from the sleeping quarters-cum-living room. The furniture is old-fashioned; by contrast, what can be seen of the kitchen is quite modern. It is a wintry afternoon.* HILDA, *a middle-aged prostitute, is dressing old*

° *Thirty Famous One-Act Plays*, eds. Bennet Cerf and Van H. Cartmell (New York, 1943), pp. xiv, xv.

PENNINGTON, *a very ancient millionaire. At curtain she has already gotten him into his long johns. She is treating him with special care; he is evidently puzzled by this unusual solicitude, and as he sits on the bed, tousled and feeble, he tries to penetrate her motive with his sharp, clear eyes.*

The title offers the first indication of the nature and tone of the play. Titles serve this important function for any literary work from the shortest poem to the longest novel. If the work bears a character's name (*Elmer Gantry,* for example) the reader knows that the work centers or hinges on the life or behavior of that character. The title *Gone With the Wind* establishes the prevailing mood of the novel: nostalgia, homesickness for an unknown but romantic past. *Paradise Lost* suggests the importance of the work and the inevitable tragic ending when Adam and Eve are driven from Eden. *A Streetcar Named Desire* indicates transience, passion, and a trip to the end of the line—all major elements within the work.

Bellow employs his title, *Orange Soufflé,* to focus attention on several subtleties. A *soufflé* is one of a variety of dishes made light and high by the addition of beaten egg whites before baking. The word is the past participle of the French verb *souffler* (to blow) and becomes ironically ambiguous in the play as Hilda "blows her chances" by aspiring to a more exotic possibility than her basic ingredients will accommodate. Soufflés are, usually, either plain or spiced with bland meats such as fish, veal, or chicken, or with equally bland vegetables such as asparagus. Orange soufflés were created by the citrus industry as a promotional idea and are particularly desirable as a dessert when the hostess wishes to impress her guests. Because soufflés are high and light, they create their own problems between oven and table. Undercooked, they fall in the middle because the raw liquid will not support the upper weight. Overcooked, they fall apart because the egg whites have lost too much moisture. Timing, then, becomes the most important consideration if the soufflé is to be successful. The soufflé must be mixed and put into the oven immediately before trapped air can escape from the beaten egg whites. The oven temperature must be constant and correct or the whites will bake too fast and fall. The cooking time must be accurate so the center will be done before the outside is overdone. The final product must be served as soon as it comes from the oven. In short, a sense of timing is of the essence if the basically simple, therefore elegant, dish is to make an impression.

Hilda lacks the delicate touch, the sense of timing required for the simplicity of the soufflé.

Attempting to embellish the quiet elegance of the bland dish (and blandness creates its own charm for the sophisticated palate), Hilda employs the unsubtle, for oranges suggest Florida, and as the play continues her motives become as transparent as her soufflé is heavy. Because nothing exhibits gaucherie as much as an effort to impress, Hilda becomes the personified explanation of her unsuitability as a Palm Beach hostess.

The caustic quality of citric acid (oranges) and the suggestion of blandness in the word *soufflé* create the contrasts of the play. Humor and tragedy combine to form pathos; the common and the exotic fail to mix in the dish; vulgarity and restraint are in conflict. The title suggests many possibilities which the reader will understand later, and, when he has finished reading the play, the title illuminates those understandings brilliantly.

The "scene" emphasizes the contrasts in tone, contrasts which will extend constantly throughout the play. *Indiana* is a middle-western state landlocked except for the northwest corner which borders on Lake Michigan. *Harbor* suggests access to water or a haven from storms, so the locale is a small city with a harbor located somewhere between Chicago, Illinois, and Gary, Indiana. The name creates any number of ambivalences. And these same ambivalences are further revealed in the description of the apartment, *a kitchenette-bedroom.* Supplying one of the basic needs of man (shelter), the apartment minimizes the most important other need (food) in the word *kitchenette* (a little kitchen) and maximizes the least important need (sex) in the word *bedroom.* The word *counter* suggests "service" (certainly Hilda is a "servant"), while *room divider* suggests the separation of needs (it also indicates their associative qualities as the word *wall* could not). Basic irony pervades the term *sleeping quarters-* (with its suggestion of the vernacular "sleeping with") *cum-* (that dignified Latin "with," suggesting degrees) *living room* (that room in which one "lives" as opposed to rooms in which one meets the basic requirements of food, sleep, sex, and excretion). Through such irony, Bellow centralizes all of man's elemental features in one location. Sex-needs remain constant in time (the bedroom furniture is *old-fashioned*) but food-needs change—or at least they assume larger, newer proportions (the kitchenette furniture is *quite modern*).

Time is indicated but obfuscated in the scene: a *wintry afternoon* can occur in any season; *a winter afternoon* or *an afternoon in winter* would have been more exact. Hilda is "a prostitute"; Pennington is "a millionaire." The contrast is sharper than the words *pauper* and *millionaire* could produce. A prostitute (*pro*—before; *statuere*—to cause to stand) stands before *everyone* and is therefore outside the continuum but precedes the lower end. The ages of the prostitute and the millionaire are also in sharp contrast. If Hilda were *middle-aged* and Pennington merely *old,* the difference would not be so apparent. However, Hilda is *middle-aged* while Pennington is *ancient,* and that great age is intensified by the adverb of degree *very.*

From Hilda's position of superior physical strength, she maneuvers Pennington's body, a body his age has partially removed from his control. Still Pennington controls those portions which symbolize strength to him. And his eyes are *sharp* and *clear*.

The names Bellow has chosen for his characters also indicate a great deal about the conflicts the reader can expect in the play. *Hilda,* which you can, as a good reader, discover from a dictionary is Germanic in origin, born of *hild-,* means "battle" or "war." Hilda is, therefore, a battler, a fighter. Her nature is emotionally charged, passionate, willing to do physical violence. *Pennington* suggests *penny* in its Germanic form (*pfennig*) and indicates base form as well as stinginess. The suffix *-ton* is a combining form meaning "in the style or tone of." Therefore, Pennington is a man of stingy tone. *Penni-* is also a combining form of *penna* (Latin) meaning "feather," "featherlike," or "quill" (a feather which serves as a pen). Implicit in the names, then, is the aphorism "The pen is mightier than the sword" and careful consideration on the reader's part will suggest the victor even before the battle lines are drawn.

Reading so carefully may seem, at first, too much work. If it does, remember Henry David Thoreau's assertion that "it takes two to speak the truth—one to speak, and another to hear." Truth is never easily come by; perhaps it is an abstraction that doesn't even exist. But if you are to learn what may at least pass for truth under careful, honest scrutiny, you will have to learn to read, listen, and see with far greater attention, with more work than the person who is willing to deal in surface life only because deeper study is too demanding.

HILDA. Please sit straight, Mr. Pennington. How can I button your chest if you slump. I know you get so relaxed, you droop.

PENNINGTON. Ha!

HILDA. Yes, relaxed. Up, chin, till I get the top button. That's it. I often wondered, Mr. Pennington, do you import these garments?

PENNINGTON. Italian.

HILDA. You have them tailored overseas. A far cry from Montgomery Ward. (*Feels the collar with her finger first from the left, then the right.*) Silk trim. All your accessories are so elegant.

PENNINGTON. Talkative?

HILDA. Oh, why not? Why be so formal after all these years. Ten years.

PENNINGTON. Since my seventy-eighth birthday.

HILDA. Once a month. A hundred and twenty times. If I were one of your regular employees, I'd have plenty of seniority by now. (*Rising, she takes whisk broom and begins to brush his jacket.*)

PENNINGTON. Brushing?

HILDA. I've always been extra attentive. You just never noticed.

PENNINGTON. My powers of observation are famous throughout the financial world.

HILDA. Then maybe you've seen how good I've been for you. Why, the first time you had to be carried up the stairs.

PENNINGTON. Carried? Nonsense. Helped a little. My trick knee was acting up. I was the only man hurt in the Battle of Manila Bay. As I ran along the deck with a message for Admiral Dewey I fell on a winch.

HILDA. Poor Monty! (*She opens an ironing board and begins to iron his necktie.*)

PENNINGTON (*stiffly*). Monty? Monty?

HILDA. What was the message?

PENNINGTON. You've never called me Monty.

HILDA. Well, Christ's sake, ain't it about time? You get very familiar with me.

PENNINGTON. That's another thing.

HILDA. The things you expect me to do—and say. The old-fashioned expressions you made me learn.

PENNINGTON (*fairly proud of himself*). I get carried away.

HILDA. Such a woman in my position is supposed to hold back nothing, allow anything. Here, put your arm into this shirt.

PENNINGTON. You see what I mean? Usually you just pull it over my head.

HILDA. What? I never. You're mistaken. You always get the most classy treatment here.

PENNINGTON. Madame Hilda, during the first year you behaved like a member of the bomb squad with a suspicious parcel.

HILDA. That's not true.

PENNINGTON. Would I forget it? When I said, "Undress me," you bit your lip and had tears in your eyes.

HILDA. The pollen count is the real explanation.

PENNINGTON. And treated me like a mummy afterward. You couldn't wrap me up fast enough. When I got home, my valet couldn't understand how I got so screwed up.

HILDA. It was only a matter of practice.

Expository matter (background) occupies the opening dialog, but character revelation is carefully interwoven. The one-act play is so brief that economy becomes the playwright's major concern, for he does not have space to waste. The opening action reveals Hilda dressing Mr. Pennington, and we are immediately caught up in that action. Her serving him in this intimate fashion suggests the more intimate moments before the play opened. Now, however, her function is that of a nursemaid or a mother, but her formal use of his name suggests the dual nature of their relationship. She speaks as a mother would to a child, coaxingly, as she buttons "your chest" rather than "the front of your drawers." When she wants him to lift his head, she speaks to the chin as if it were a unique entity, as toes are in "This little piggy went to market."

Respect for money is inserted easily as Hilda comments on the old-fashioned long johns and they are revealed as Italian imports rather than practical, dated undergarments. The change in Hilda's attitude allows transition into expository matter of their ten-year relationship, her mathematical mind, and her awareness that he is her eighty-eight year old employer. Hilda is a practical woman who assesses elegance by sensory means. Her fingers serve as agent.

That this incident is to be different from the earlier one hundred and nineteen visits becomes apparent as Mr. Pennington comments on Hilda's unusual attentions, breaking the obviousness of exposition yet allowing it to proceed on his recollection of youth. His delightfully ambiguous "I fell on a winch" precipitates Hilda's sympathy and her use of his first name. And, from this point on, double-entendre is to be an integral element of humor. Pennington has, of course, been "familiar" with Hilda, but she is an employee. He has purchased her services and given orders he expected to be obeyed. Her protestations that his treatment has always been "classy" is not refuted; rather it is demolished as the featherlike old man reveals a dignified but rapier-sharp wit in his "bomb squad" appraisal. At the same time, he reveals his knowledge that he *is* something of a fragile item delivered by a messenger, unwrapped and rewrapped after use.

PENNINGTON. Perhaps my physique took some getting used to. Honestly, did my big bones scare you? (*No answer.*) Pressing a tie with a hot iron makes the silk shiny. It'll smell peculiar, too. Hand it over. (*She gives it to him. He passes the tie near-sightedly before his eye.*)

HILDA (*sitting beside him and helping him into the shirt*). The first time the chauffeur brought you in his arms and put you on this bed. It wasn't a weak knee, you were weak all over.

PENNINGTON (*joyously, almost hooting*). Not all over! Not all over!

HILDA. If you're still going strong ten years later, it's no accident. Even you must admit it.

Silences play a significant part in any play. Here, you must assess Hilda's refusal or failure to answer Pennington's question: *did* his "big bones" scare her? Does she refuse to say "Yes" to save him embarrassment? To hide her fears? Might her answer be "No," revealing she is not one to be frightened by big bones? Or does she recognize a double-entendre which she prefers to ignore, thereby withholding a satisfying, ego-building moment from her aged client? The possibilities are so numerous that the playwright would have been foolish to limit them by allowing Hilda to respond.

That Hilda may have recognized a male-centered ambiguity becomes apparent as she delights in pointing out Pennington's infirmities that long-ago day, but he reveals his mental agility again, using her own statement to top her in their little game of one-upmanship: "Not all over!" Hilda's rejoinder would obviously afford Pennington more satisfaction than she can take in it herself. That he neither must nor will "admit it" closes the expository section.

PENNINGTON (*looks about as she puts in his cuff links*). You're like me. You don't want to change or move. It's a nice little place, for what it is. Except the location.

HILDA. Surrounded by the steel mills, the coke ovens, the gas refineries, the brewery on the right and the soap factory behind. It's bright as day at midnight, and I hear the freights and cattle cars. And I never once even asked you . . . whether you're a major stockholder in any of these companies.

PENNINGTON (*surprised*). What do you know about such things?

HILDA. Why shouldn't I? I read the papers, and that includes the society page, the financial section.

PENNINGTON. Aren't you peculiar today.

HILDA. I never asked you—you should've asked me.

PENNINGTON. What?

HILDA. Like, did I need advice. Like, do I have a problem. I got my problems, like anyone else. Taxes. Savings. You never gave me a tip on something. You know what I mean. I could always use a little capital gains, a little depreciation.

PENNINGTON. What about my socks?

HILDA. Don't get in an uproar. What's it any skin off your nose if I ask a plain question. I read up on politics, too. I wrote a letter to Congress about reapportionment. (*Starts toward copy of the letter.*) I kept a copy.

PENNINGTON (*angry*). No! Don't pester me. I come here for certain things and not other things.

HILDA. But why keep everything in pigeonholes? Breakfast in Libertyville. Business on La Salle Street. Golf one place, social life another place, and sex once every thirty days between three-thirty and five P.M. out in the dirty slums, between the lousy swamps and bulrushes and soap factories. You could swing a whole lot more.

PENNINGTON. That's just the way it happens to be. (*Pause.*) The first eight or nine years you didn't get personal at all.

HILDA (*taking his stiff leg on her lap and putting on one garter*). No, you didn't encourage it.

PENNINGTON. And I don't encourage it now.

HILDA (*her nostrils flaring*). No, you pay good dough. You even up the fee.

PENNINGTON. One hundred, in cash, and you don't have to report it.

HILDA. Neither do you. (*She buckles the second garter.*)

Action has kept the play from becoming static to this point. The act of dressing Mr. Pennington is designed to create continuity at the physical level while chronology is manipulated for background material. You should be seeing the movements of the characters in their present situation while comparing and contrasting it with a similar scene reënacted one hundred and nineteen times before. The small differences between this one day and all of those days creates the exciting force of the play. You know that a revelation is being made in the contrast.

The rising action of the play begins in this portion as Pennington seems to recognize the importance of Hilda's behavior. Instead of taking the bait she has offered in her oblique reference to his preserved potency, he abruptly changes the subject. Still, he is answering her suggestion. If his potency remains strong, he would not endanger the circumstances that have kept it so. His "powers of observation" are still at work.

Complications begin to dominate the scene as Hilda, prepared for battle, charges into that area that is Pennington's province: finance. Her attempt to prove her interest in politics, in finance, in society is rather pathetic. Pennington obviously sees her as a physical gratifier, an ego bolsterer for himself. Beyond that, she has no function. Again he reminds her she is attempting to change things. And, old war horse that she is, Hilda reacts ("her nostrils flaring") visibly, and the reader sees her character more clearly. From hand (cuff links) to foot (the two garters) she manipulates Pennington's physical body, cares for his physical needs, but that is her only function. He pays her for that in cash, and it is a private transaction—even the ever-present government has no knowledge of it. A social comment pervades the final lines of dialog, but it is subservient to the psychological implication: both Hilda and Pennington are aware of their "crime," which she commits by failing to report income, which he commits by failing to report involvement in this socially unacceptable situation. Hilda's action of buckling the second garter punctuates the exchange with an exclamation point. The battle lines are drawn between the valkyrie and the featherweight.

PENNINGTON. Aren't we running a little early this afternoon?

HILDA (*putting on his socks*). It's the same as always.

PENNINGTON. No, it isn't. (*Betrays some agitation.*) You've got me all twisted around today, and I don't like it. I've never been a troublemaker. I never asked for anything unusual. Did I ever make one single peculiar request? (*She is silent.*) And I know what people are. Me, I only need a little assistance. . . . Don't rush things.

Again Pennington changes the subject, once more placing Hilda on the defensive. Her challenge to his secretive conduct has seemed masterly, but he does not allow her to enjoy the advantage for any length of time.

Pennington suggests she is manipulating time, is creating change in a routine he values. In some way, she has brought the one hundred twentieth visit around full circle: the first time, he left "screwed up"; now he is "twisted around," and the synonymous phrases should be noticeable to the reader even if Pennington and Hilda seem unaware of the connection. Pennington feels, at this moment, that Hilda is breaking off their relationship. His reminder that he has "never been a troublemaker" and his agitated need of reassurance ("Did I ever make one single peculiar request?") reveal his fear.

Here again, a double-entendre works advantageously for the playwright. Had Bellow been forced to spell out the various meanings of *peculiar request* in terms of the prostitute-client relationship, vulgarity would overlay the scene. The subtlety of implication is restrained, and that very restraint forces explosive tensions into the scene. The conflicts are mounting steadily, and the reader, by now torn between his curious attachment to these two unlikable people, must assess his attachment. Any ancient theme, poetically stated, creates an identifying response in the reader. That is a truism. Certainly the theme of prostitution is ancient. Certainly the theme of a servant in conflict with his economic master is ancient. Certainly the theme of a man in conflict with a woman is ancient. And certainly Bellow's treatment is poetic. That is, he employs the terse, abbreviated one-act play form; he deals with big themes; he creates rhythmical dialog that could be poetically measured with scansion marks. As a result, vulgarity does not emerge; charm does. Dame Edith Sitwell once commented on modern vulgarity, defining it as a descendant of the goddess Dullness. Bellow is not vulgar here, for this play is not dull.

Hilda's silence after Pennington's request for reassurance is another eloquent pause. It hangs on the scene heavily, forcing Pennington to assert his weakness, to admit to his dependence on her: "Me, I only need a little assistance. . . ."

HILDA. I never can get your long underwear to lie flat under your stockings.
PENNINGTON. My mother had the same problem.

Hilda, a woman again in control, intensifies the advantage intuitively with her comment about Pennington's long underwear, and he associates her with his mother. The reader begins to understand Pennington a little better at this point. Financial tycoon he may be; a male buying satisfaction of his male needs he surely is. But he is also a little boy, returning to the changeless security of Hilda and her apartment for the satisfaction of needs remembered from that distant time of childhood when his mother dressed and undressed him, possibly creating erotic arousal in the young animal. Psychologists are generally in agreement that such is the nature of mother-infant relationships at one stage of any child's development. Utilizing such suggestion, Bellow adds dimension to the play, lifting it from the realm of comedy (for it has seemed humorous to this point) and overlaying it with an Ibsenesque possibility. The reader now knows that Pennington fears an end of the affair or a change in its conduct because it is not primarily a base sexual satisfaction Pennington achieves—it is an understandable psychological one. And, however prudish the reader may be, he is a human with similar human needs. He cannot help reacting to this ancient theme: it is a part of his heritage.

At this point, the advantage is Hilda's. Pennington is almost helpless as she ministers to his emotional needs.

(HILDA *quickly wriggles on the second sock, her hair falling over her eyes, and hurries to the counter, on the kitchen side. There she opens a large French cook-book.*)

HILDA. Flour, salt, sugar, baking powder.

PENNINGTON. What are you doing?

HILDA. Shortening, eggs, orange rind.

PENNINGTON. You rushed me through it. You think I didn't notice.

HILDA. Measuring spoons, and cups. All laid out. (*Rubs her hands.*)

PENNINGTON. The timetable's off by as much as twenty minutes. Well, at least finish dressing me.

HILDA. I'm making something nice. You get your money's worth.

PENNINGTON. What are you pulling, Madame!

HILDA. It's time you got wise to the "what's really what," sir. You take too much for granite. I don't take you for granite. To me, you're not just some wham-bam-thank-you-ma'am kind. I know who you are, so why shouldn't you know me, who I am, finally?

PENNINGTON. Oh, God!

HILDA. What, I'm just on the hook all month like a telephone? I'm a person. When you're coming, I dust, I clean up, I spray a nice flavor all around. I never pester you about how I put out for you. It just proves I'm a true, honest-to-God personality! (*Calms herself.*) I'm cooking you something.

PENNINGTON. Cooking! I'm freezing. Come here and put on my pants.

HILDA. Just hold your horses. The stove is heating. That's so pleasant on a winter day.

It is at this moment that the turning point occurs. Hilda's plans are not yet fully revealed, but she precipitates the crisis that will reverse her scheme, leaving her hopelessly caught in the circumstances of her life. Pennington is dangerously close to realizing his dependence on Hilda and the nature of that dependence. Were she to soothe him, to offer emotional reassurance, she might win the battle and the war. Instead of taking advantage of the moment, however, she proceeds doggedly with her original plan. And the psychological implications are too strong for Pennington. Hilda rejects him as mothers reject their children's emotional needs—to fix food, to attend to immediate physical needs. Another ancient truth emerges: man cannot live by bread alone. Pennington becomes petulant, as a child might. Seizing on his earlier accusation, he repeats it: she is rushing him when his greatest need is to be assisted with patience, without haste. She has failed him.

Pennington is utterly selfish. Hilda's needs are of no concern to him. He buys her services; she has no claim to him as one who should understand her. But Hilda is selfish too in a thoroughly human fashion. She made a bargain ten years earlier, but she now wants more than was included in that agreement. She wants recognition. Prior to this one hundred twentieth time, she has been relatively silent, allowing the featherweight whatever fantasies he wishes. Now she shatters all the illusions. No woman out of Pennington's emotional recesses would confuse *granted* and *granite*. Hilda is ignorant! No such woman would allude to the rabbit joke of excessive vulgarity from which "wham-bam-thank-you-ma'am" is the refrain and punch line. Unfortunately, Hilda *does* finally reveal who she is. As long as Pennington did not know, their association was satisfactory. Robbing him of the fantasy (and rubbing her hands gleefully the while!), she forces him to the despairing plea "Oh, God!"

Double-entendre functions at many levels in Hilda's "telephone" speech. She *is,* in Pennington's fantasies, very like a telephone: an instrument which allows access without involvement at the personal level. Unfortunately, each statement after Hilda's "I'm a person" has some sexual reference that is lacking in dignity and decorum, that would be utterly offensive to the ancient millionaire.

PENNINGTON. If it's for me, I don't want any. What do people cook in Indiana Harbor—pig's knuckles and kapusta? I can't digest cabbage.

HILDA. Something you might enjoy—very, very light. An orange soufflé.

PENNINGTON (*trying feebly to rise, his voice somewhat stifled*). Soufflé! I won't eat it! I'll clench my teeth! Where is my chauffeur? He should be back. What time is it?

Pennington responds with a slur on Hilda's national origin. To this point, the reader has been unaware that she might be anything other than, generally speaking, an American. His "pig's knuckles and kapusta" reduces her to the indignity of being less than a "true, honest-to-God personality." Hilda is merely representative of something Pennington obviously considers distasteful: a minority group. Bellow artfully creates a new conflict at this point: the struggle between a powerful economic figure and an exploited minority group. The play assumes additional social-problem proportions from this point on.

Before the possibility becomes oppressive, however—social problem plays do have that tendency—Bellow returns to the psychological. Like a baby, Pennington tries "feebly to rise" and his voice is "stifled" with rage as he becomes the child who will not eat. But he expects to be force-fed. The hateful-mother image has completely overlaid his wonderful-mother fantasy. His financial security (symbolized by the chauffeur) will save him.

> HILDA. Otto will be back at five P.M. as usual. I know what you must be thinking, what does an Indiana Harbor Polack whore know from soufflé? You think I spend my whole life in the sack with teamsters and rough trade? Well, try to adjust your mind to the reality situation. I have dozens and dozens of interests. I got a certificate from the Cordon Bloo school.
>
> PENNINGTON. When were you in Paris?
>
> HILDA. Paris? I ain't even been to Warsaw. But I'm learning how to be from Paris. The Cordon Bloo has a branch in Gary, Indiana. Only one thing now, where's the bottle of Cointreau? Orange soufflé without Cointreau you can't make. This is real Paris Cointreau—costs $9.35. (*Pause.*) Where's that little dish. . . . (*Rattling sheets of wax paper.*) Where the Christ is it . . . excuse me. Ah, here.

Hilda senses the process at work in Pennington's mind. Her self-description summarizes many minority groups: *Indiana Harbor* (slumdweller) *Polack* (Polish mill-workers exploited by millionaires) *whore* (woman forced by lack of training and economic necessity into an evil social service). Furthermore, *know from soufflé* is a Yiddish grammatical construction suggesting discrimination directed at a religious-philosophical-national group. In short, language is combined and lifted to its highest connotative possibilities in this speech. Then, as if to polish off a little of everything, Bellow adds *rough trade* in the next sentence, employing the jargon of homosexual groups to tie in their removal from the realm of approved people and *foreshadow* (suggest in advance) the nephew-niece change, indicating a deeper involvement in the twilight world of deviation than Hilda's usual speech implies.

The sophistication of Paris is far removed from Hilda who "ain't even been to Warsaw." The misspelling of *Cordon Bleu* indicates her pronunciation, her lack of finesse, and, quite possibly, the tortured change that name would undergo in being adopted as a culinary school name in

Gary, Indiana. The reference to *Cointreau* provides another gentle hint that Hilda is a Polish Jew: notice the construction "Orange soufflé without Cointreau you can't make." The pause after her concern for price as an indicator of value and the rattle of waxed paper bridge the speech into her apology for using Christ's name so casually in the presence of the featherweight WASP.

PENNINGTON. What do you know about kitchens, baking, eggs! It's winter. Hand me my pants. Soufflé!

HILDA. I go shopping like other women. You think they don't let whores in the supermarket? Or maybe they've got separate steel carts marked "for whores only"? Go and look at all those broads in pale lipstick, smoking, and figure out who's the married woman. To make ends meet some of those little married chicks do a trick or two and the husband sits for the kids and knows all about it. If wives can hustle, whores can bake. (*Rapidly beats the eggs.*)

For his part, Pennington grows more and more irritated with Hilda's concern for soufflé rather than sex, especially since he is restrained by the absence of his trousers. She, probably unconsciously, irritates him further by attacking the sacrosanct American motherhood image, ending on a triumphant analogy that makes a marvelously funny kind of sense because it is as absurd as the whole situation. She rounds out the ludicrous statement of philosophy by rapidly beating the eggs—an act of aggression that practically screams "So there!"

PENNINGTON (*wrapping his legs in the blanket*). For ten years everything was smooth.

HILDA. Ten years, but only twelve days in each year.

PENNINGTON. I do the best I can.

HILDA. And the rest of the time?

PENNINGTON. I don't interfere with *you.*

HILDA (*making angry noises with the bowls*). You don't bother yourself about me. If you got enough dough, you can make the world stand still. You can tie it up like a horse and it'll be waiting when you get back. You never took any personal interest in me.

PENNINGTON. Is that so bad? People want to be *seen.* Sometimes they're better off invisible. Anyhow, that's what I think. I'm old enough to be myself. In fact, too old to be anybody else.

Pennington is momentarily defeated. Cold (even though the room seems warm), he wraps his legs in the blanket, indicating his knowledge of defeat. Then, querulously, he withdraws into musings as a child or a senile old man will do when he has lost a verbal battle.

Hilda is not without her poetic moments. An aptness pervades her metaphorical horse-world as completely as it did her telephone-self. And both metaphors indicate the patiently waiting servant of man. Apt she is; aware she is; impatient with waiting she also is. "Making angry noises with the bowls" is a homely and interesting sound. You might examine your response to the noises. Angry noises made with bowls sound like what? Does Hilda break, chip, or crack any of them in the process? Notice, as you think about the line, you are also aware of her face, her body, her hands. You see many things, in addition to hearing bowls hitting each other. Pennington's observation ("People want to be *seen*. Sometimes they're better off invisible") is now meaningful. Perhaps you've never seen a prostitute, but you've seen women making noises with bowls in kitchens, and, as a result, you may have *seen* Hilda for the first time in this play. Attention is refocused on your image by Pennington's words.

HILDA. And rich enough so you don't have to be a hypocrite. —That is a nice thing about you. I appreciate your character.

PENNINGTON (*interested now*). Do you?

HILDA. What's a whore good for if you can't be yourself with her either? What's the whole point of a whore? Her opinions don't worry you. She frees your mind. If you flunk, she doesn't get sore. She doesn't cripple you with a lot of stupid love.

PENNINGTON. Till today, you've been perfect. (*He seems moved.*) You may not know it, but these visits mean a lot to me. Sometimes I count the days. So why spoil things?

HILDA. Why, because I bake you something nice? You don't want to expand a little? I want you to know I have a lot of sides to me. I can cook and bake and serve and keep up a conversation with anybody. Wait until you see what kind of china I've got and linen and silverware. To you a soufflé belongs in the Pump Room where the colored wear a turban. Why shouldn't we know each other better?

PENNINGTON. I know you plenty.

HILDA. Because of sex? I ought to know best how important it is. I never bum-rap it. But. . . . (*She shakes her head, studies the oven thermometer.*)

The traditional gambit of flattery works well for Hilda. She is knowledgeable about men—her business has taught her to be. She is especially knowledgeable about Pennington as a man very selfishly concerned with himself. He would respond to "I appreciate your character," never hearing the second possibility of the ambiguous line: "I *understand* your character."

Hilda's frankness is transparent but effective as she states her whore's philosophy. That she equates a whore with the geisha concept may not be readily apparent, but it becomes more so as she imposes food, conversation, and correct table appointments onto the original idea that a man "can be himself" with a whore. Pennington's defenses are strong. The double-entendre of "I know you plenty" returns Hilda to her sexual role. She recognizes what he has done even though she could probably not explain how (her biblical knowledge is doubtless scanty at best, and her awareness of words is intuitive rather than academic; that *know,* in biblical language, means "to have sexual relations with" might even surprise her). Hilda does understand Pennington's intention, however, and assures him, with magnificent ambiguity, that she can play the game too. *Bum-rap* is criminal jargon for "convicted though innocent." *Bum* also refers to the buttocks (from Middle English *botem*—bottom) and *rap* refers to the worthless or the counterfeit, therefore a minimizing term. *Rap* also suggests striking or knocking, and knocking suggests the slang form of minimizing, as in "If you can't afford it, knock it." The conjunction *But* in "I never bum-rap it. But. . . ." seems to overwhelm Hilda; she has gone beyond her intellectual depth without realizing the scope of her response. She turns her attention to that with which she can cope—the oven thermometer.

> PENNINGTON. What I was as a captain of industry, what I was on the stock market, what I've been in real estate, that's what I've been here. That's the best of me there is, the truest anyway. Not what I was with my wife and sons. With them I did what I had to do, not what I wanted. (*With a strange emotion.*) Why do people have to pry! The secret truth is the best, and let it to hell alone!
>
> HILDA. Let me check now. The rind, the Cointreau, the nutmeg, the stiffener.
>
> PENNINGTON. Stiffener?
>
> HILDA. In she goes. (*Puts dish in oven, sets timer.*) I'm really famous for my soufflé.
>
> PENNINGTON (*too weak to sound tart*). In the gas-tank set.

Pennington has withdrawn deeper into his emotional blanket, for he is moved by "a strange emotion" to express a startling truth: "The secret truth is the best." He would prefer not to know why he comes to Hilda, what she represents. He just wants things to stay as they are, but he is dangerously close to awarenesses that are better "let to hell alone!"

Intensity has now mounted to a sharp point. Hilda cannot comment, so she fills the space with idle chatter about her temporary occupation. And she falls into a built-in trap as she names the ingredients, and the ambiguous *stiffener* reminds Pennington of the virility he prizes and is in danger of losing because she persists in disturbing his fantasy. Time is so important to him; Hilda has rushed him today; she sets the oven timer. Pennington is overcome with his "strange emotion" and outrage at the affront to his $100 hour (Hilda is more expensive than psychiatrists would be though they serve the same function). The economic superior snidely puts Hilda in her place with *gas-tank set.*

HILDA. Don't be upset. You look so ruffled. You've got your feathers up. Let's put on your pants. (*She brushes his trousers.*)

PENNINGTON. I liked it better when things were businesslike. It's upsetting this way.

HILDA. Who knows, things might become even better.

PENNINGTON. Or I might lose something valuable by tampering. I know what works. As long as it works, let it be.

Irony has many functions in literature. It is nowhere more effective than in plays, however, and it is delightfully effective at this point. *Verbal irony* occurs when words either state the opposite of what they mean (such as the response "Why, thank you" to an outrageous insult) or when a statement is actually negated by the suggestions within the words (as "God is not dead; he's alive and well in Mexico City"). *Dramatic irony* occurs when a situation indicates the reverse of what the characters think (Oedipus thinks Teiresias is evil as well as blind, but it is Oedipus who is, in actuality, evil and blind to truth). Dramatic irony becomes even more dramatic when the reader realizes the true state of affairs and the characters are as yet unaware of it. Their words then can be assessed in terms of what they will eventually mean rather than what they mean at the moment. Dramatic irony overlays such statements as the account from "Matthew" in the New Testament:

When Pilate saw that he could prevail nothing, but that rather a tumult was made, he took water, and washed his hands before the multitude, saying, I am innocent of the blood of this just person: see ye to it. Then answered all the people, and said, His blood be on us, and on our children.

As the reader re-creates the scene today, two thousand years of anti-semitism overlay the line, and he shudders at the dramatic irony. Sure in their emotional moment that Christ will be a forgotten figure six weeks after his death, the mob calls down a curse upon themselves and their descendants that will not be lifted easily. Such irony is an ingredient of daily life: the fool frequently reveals that which is profound and wise; the liar unknowingly reveals the truth as truthful men cannot, for they see unclearly.

This is the kind of irony which overlays Hilda's efforts to soothe Pennington. She tells the featherweight, "You've got your feathers up." He has indeed! Small and insignificant physically, the proud little bantam is strong and determined in a fight. When his feathers fluff up, he is prepared for battle, prepared to defend his domain. Irony is added to irony as Hilda urges, "Let's put on your pants." At the obvious level, she, dominant mother-figure, encourages him to dress. However, wrapped in the blanket (like a baby) he has grown stronger. Hilda forces him to put on his long pants now, becoming the rejective mother again, but also psychologically offering to "wear the pants" with him. As a financial wizard, Pennington wears the pants—he has shared them with no one. Nor will he start to now.

The subtleties are not detailed in Pennington's mind (he would be horrified if they were!), but the conflicts are so great that he is upset. He understands that which is "businesslike," and this situation has become too intimate, too personal.

Hilda's reassurance does not work. Pennington knows they trespass on dangerous territory.

HILDA. Mr. Pennington, what's my name? What's the address here?

PENNINGTON. Your name is Hilda. . . . (*He hesitates.*)

HILDA. Hilda what? Come on. If you can't pronounce it, spell it. You can't. You don't know what street this is. You couldn't get here if Otto quit. Lots of people would try to find out who am I, Hilda Schzlepanowski, where do I come from, did I have a father or mother or a husband or a kid, and how did I ever get into this racket!

PENNINGTON. But not me.

HILDA. You should have asked once, anyway, even if you didn't listen to the answer. Do you think I'm just a poor tramp? Well, I want to tell you something. When I first moved in here, I couldn't pay the rent. And now this building belongs to me.

PENNINGTON (*struck by this*). This is your own property?

HILDA. From the cellar to the tar paper. The mortgage is paid off, too.

PENNINGTON. Then why do you . . . ?

HILDA. Financially, I've been independent since 1959. For six years you've been my only client.

PENNINGTON (*as she puts on his pants, he gives a cry from the soul, or its neighborhood*). Oh Lord, Lord, Lord! I've always wanted things so simple.

To this point, the conflict has grown steadily between Hilda and Pennington. The crisis of the play occurs at this point. The trousers symbolize so many things to Pennington. When Hilda removed them before the play opened, she was the erotic mother-figure. Retaining possession of them and attempting to impose her will on him, she has become the social force exerting its will, cutting the umbilical cord and forcing maturity. With the promised return of his trousers, Pennington begins to assume his full dominance again. He knows who he is; he could not possibly care less who Hilda is, for she is not a "who" in his pattern of needs. She is a "what" (mother-figure, supplier of comfort, shielder from harsh business practice, and so on). Attempting to force him to see her as a human, she precipitates the crisis and reverses her possibility of success.

After answering Hilda's question with her first name, Pennington hesitates. Hilda is not "named." She is nomenclatured. And Pennington becomes aware of his attitude toward her.

Demandingly, she does greater damage to her cause. First she attacks Pennington's dependence on Otto; then she asserts her own personality. But personal interest in Hilda has never been Pennington's concern. His personal needs have concerned him, have been his business here, and he has assumed Hilda was a businesswoman in those terms. Now she reveals herself. She is *Hilda Schzlepanowski:* doer of battle, valkyrie-figure, Polish Jew. But even more, she is a *schlepp* (a flunkie, a doer of tedious jobs, an insignificant hireling). Hilda has reduced herself to a level slightly beneath contempt.

Revealing a second facet, however, she retrieves some of her loss. This *schlepp* has been financially busy, moderately successful, and Pennington sees her as a businesswoman in more respectable terms. Even now Hilda's cause is not lost.

But, as Hilda returns Pennington's symbol of dominance, his pants, as she covers his nakedness, she reduces herself to a *schlepp* again: she has served him for six years when she did not have to! And Pennington cries out from "his soul, or its neighborhood." He becomes an afflicted Job.

HILDA. What's so simple? To arrive on this street in a Rolls-Royce? What do you think I tell the neighbors?

PENNINGTON. You tell them I'm your fairy godfather?

HILDA. *They* don't think I'm a dumb Polack. I have a lot of refined friends. I go all over. At the Cordon Bloo I rubbed elbows with the best people on the South Shore, country-club people, politicians' wives. You think I hang around with scrubwomen?

PENNINGTON. I knew you were discreet.

HILDA. We had one conversation the first time. That was all I needed.

PENNINGTON. I knew you wouldn't blab. I thought if I died in your bed, naked, a heart attack. . . .

HILDA (*bringing up a little table and starting to set it for tea*). Did you think I'd phone the gossip columns? I'd say, "Mr. Montgomery G. Pennington of Lake Shore Drive, Eagle River, and Palm Beach, President of the Tower Town Club, Chairman of the Board, and once a member of President Wilson's Cabinet . . . just croaked in my bed—come take my picture."

Hilda is not sensitive to Job's boils, however. Grimly, she pursues him and he adopts a facetious attitude as his agile old brain reduces her. She is no Cinderella to be transformed. She is merely the girl among the industrial cinders that surround her in this ugly neighborhood.

Pennington's *sarcasm* (heavy-handed irony) is wasted on Hilda. She argues her worth, her value, failing to realize that value is an attitude, not a reality to be created by words. Her discretion has been her value to him. Now, indiscreetly, Hilda attempts to usurp the role of a wife. A tea table in a whore house? That ironic contrast is sharpened as the refinement of the socially correct and acceptable *diction* (language at its most correct and acceptable level) is shattered on the jagged edges of Hilda's *idiom* (the unique, personal language revealing the user's thinking processes): the cheap, ugly "just croaked in my bed—come take my picture" paints Pennington's death and Hilda's pretentions.

PENNINGTON. Stop, stop. I felt we should talk it over.

HILDA. I had to promise to dress you and call the chauffeur.

PENNINGTON. Yes. For some reason I wouldn't want him to see me naked. And I still say. . . .

HILDA. The idea of scandal bothers you.

PENNINGTON. Scandal? Nonsense! I was thinking of my wife. She'd have given my body to a medical school. She'd let the students cut me up. She was insanely jealous.

HILDA. But she passed away first.

PENNINGTON. Yes. (*Brief silence.*) You read it in the papers?

HILDA. Four years ago. You miss her?

PENNINGTON (*hesitant*). She's much missed by everybody.

HILDA. I'm sure the Garden Club misses her. The zoo. The museum.

PENNINGTON. Sure, they miss her. She gave them that great collection of South American lizards. Caught every one of them herself. Parachuted out of a plane over Patagonia with a survival kit. Didn't survive.

HILDA. Do you believe in an afterlife?

PENNINGTON. I worry about it. . . . What's that I smell?

Bellow adds the burlesque of a Mystery Play with delightful references to Noah and his shrewish wife. Pennington (Noah) would not like Otto (Ham) to look on his nakedness because that emasculation (a naked body is devoid of financial covering) would make him vulnerable to the shrewish wife who would take her revenge by imposing some indignity on him (Mrs. Noah had slapped Noah about in the Mystery Plays, creating hearty laughter in the viewers).

Hilda's solicitous "But she passed away first" creates Pennington's "brief silence." Her "You miss her?" creates a hesitancy as he formulates verbal ambiguity: "She's much missed by everybody," which becomes rich sarcasm in the *understatement* (restraint designed to intensify meaning) of "Didn't survive." Pennington's worry about the afterlife may very well be less concern for his soul than for the possibility of his having to spend eternity with the shade of his civic-minded spouse.

HILDA (*starting violently*). My soufflé! Where's your watch? (*Finds his large old-fashioned gold watch which hangs on a thick chain. Darts to the timer.*) It's only halfway. (*Her heart is beating. She presses it with both hands.*)

PENNINGTON. Hilda, why did you give up all your clients except me? Am I . . . am I so special? (*Leans toward her.*)

HILDA (*smiling to herself*). You don't have to ask.

PENNINGTON (*taking her hand*). Terrific, eh? I hoped it was like that. Everything about me is wearing out, except. With other men, *it* goes first, they say. Not me. But sometimes I worried that you didn't care about me, really.

HILDA. No!

PENNINGTON. I was like an Indian when I was young, up in Wisconsin—strong, husky, big, straight, tanned.

HILDA. Were you actually in the Battle of Manila?

PENNINGTON. I'm not a hundred percent sure.

HILDA. But you were in the Navy?

PENNINGTON. It seems so, often. I've had so many lives. But I believe I can remember how it was as a young sailor in Hong Kong. And Admiral Dewey was a sportsman. He played golf. Ike wasn't the first. Then I think I can smell the battle—the explosives. Dewey steamed away from the Spanish fleet. He thought he had only fifteen rounds left. A miscount! I was sent with the message. There were forty-five. It started to be dawn, with one of those tropical flashes. But the deck was like a coal tunnel. It smelled like a mine. And suddenly, when I fell, the sun, like sparkling spumoni, chocolate, green, white, and orange, like flamingos. (HILDA, *on the bed, has drowsed off during this reminiscence. He is annoyed.*) Nobody sleeps while I'm talking! (*He goes on.*) I never liked old age. And now I'm it. It's loathsome. Eyes coated, ears filled with old hair, big hollow knee bones, paunch and shanks, veins like bayous. (*Raises his chin.*)

HILDA. You don't realize how a woman looks at things. I've seen guys come and go, all kinds. I know what counts.

PENNINGTON. A strange thing. I was always virile. It showed in business, too.

HILDA. You break all the records.

PENNINGTON. You don't mean it!

HILDA. I mean, a man like you can do what he likes, write his own ticket.

PENNINGTON. You're clever, Hilda. I wouldn't have known it.

The solid, substantial businessman has begun to emerge from the welter of intrigue and the rumpled bed. Now partially dressed, Pennington has reclaimed the major portion of his identity as it exists outside this apartment. The old-fashioned gold watch and its thick chain are indicative of the successful financial figure. As Hilda concentrates her attention on the soufflé, the reader realizes why timing is so vital to the soufflé. Exact ingredients, exact timing. A soufflé waits for no one. Regardless of stiffener (whether flour or cream of tartar or both), wrong timing makes it fall. Hilda's ten-year relationship with Pennington has been dependent on timing, and, in his words, "Till today, you've been perfect." Suddenly, her timing could not possibly be worse. Any good cook knows a soufflé requires a minimum of twenty-five minutes baking time. Because time and patience are vital to Pennington, she has erred in rushing him; she errs further in rushing the soufflé. Her emotions (her beating heart and anguished hands in the stage directions) are off in their timing also.

As Pennington seeks reassurance of his virility, he comes close to being emotional rather than businesslike with Hilda. His reminiscences should engross her, but, with the worst kind of timing, Hilda drowses off! The emotional mood is shattered; Pennington returns to the harsh, present reality.

Seeking to appeal to his vanity, Hilda says the things she knows he wants to hear. But timing has tripped her. Pennington has been recalled to reality, and he will not be lulled into false security again. He recognizes Hilda's cleverness for the first time. But cleverness in a woman, once recognized by a man, is ineffectual—he quietly tells her a truth she fails to recognize.

HILDA (*setting out dishes*). Did you ever see more beautiful bone china? And look at the napkins. (PENNINGTON *looks nearsightedly.*) I put a lot of time into thinking to myself. . . .

PENNINGTON (*catching at watch*). Otto should be here. (*Tries to rise.*)

HILDA (*forcing him back on bed*). Hold still, I'll put on your necktie.

PENNINGTON. Just knot it. I'll pull it into place myself. I couldn't breathe when you did it last time. And I couldn't loosen it.

HILDA. There we are. (*Stands back to admire her work.*) Look, Mr. Pennington . . . why should we see each other only a dozen times a year?

PENNINGTON. I might be able to manage every two weeks. I heard of a fellow who gives injections.

Almost as if to justify Pennington's assessment of her cleverness (which she didn't understand), Hilda commits another tactical timing blunder: she returns to a discussion of her social accomplishments, emphasizing the price. Pennington responds quietly by catching at time—it is very precious to the ancient millionaire. Hilda returns to the doting mother image as she knots the tie, and he speaks to her as a child would to a domineering mother. Satisfied, Hilda is ready to get on to more practical matters. Still hoping to retain the relationship, Pennington mistakes her meaning, offering to seek medical aid to increase his virility.

HILDA. It's not what I have in mind.

PENNINGTON. All this . . . egg-beating, brushing, silverware. (*Startled.*) Marriage?

HILDA. No, what do you think I am, a lousy schemer?

PENNINGTON. I'm a little reassured. But some complicated idea is rotting your mind. I can tell.

HILDA. Why should I lie? There is something.

PENNINGTON (*exclaiming*). I guessed! I guessed! I guessed!

HILDA. Wouldn't it be swell if we could richen our relationship?

PENNINGTON. Relationship!

HILDA. There's a side to me you haven't seen.

PENNINGTON. I haven't seen both sides of the moon, either, and it's all right with me. It's just more craters, I'm sure of it.

Hilda shatters Pennington's dream of virility rudely, precipitating his suspicions. Some scheme is "rotting" her mind. Her confirmation delights him—not because she is scheming but because he is still intellectually aware. That sharpness is humorously revealed when Pennington insults Hilda with man's most cutting reference: he utilizes contemporary imagery in "craters of the moon" but the joke is old. If you fail to see the humor of such cruelty, remember that almost all laughter has its roots in cruelty. The funniest jokes are often those in which someone "gets his." As Will Rogers once said, "Almost everything is funny so long as it happens to somebody else." Nor does a joke of this sort reduce the play to the vulgar, the merely pornographic. As it is written, it has wit and charm that only the masterfully humorous can achieve.

HILDA. When I say there is something, why do you think it's a scheme?

PENNINGTON. Listen, my dear, you read the papers, you say?

HILDA. Sure I do, and the magazines too.

PENNINGTON. Then you know about the Gemini capsule.

HILDA. Those two Russians going up together, you mean?

PENNINGTON. That doesn't count. Americans. Listen: When they reach outer space, they're going to open the hatch. Then one of them will sit in the doorway and let his feet hang. Then, if conditions are right, he'll float outside on a wire or something. He'll glide along with the ship. Oh, imagine! Hundreds of miles above the earth. Hundreds of degrees below zero. (*He strikes his chest with the back of his fist.*) That's what I've been through in my spirit. Floating on a tether through empty space, and each time making it back inside the capsule after my visit to death and nothing. So don't bug me.

HILDA. I never bugged you once in ten years, but now I'm in a squeeze. I have this sister, she lives in a slum, in urban renewal.

PENNINGTON. What's that to me?

The return to a contemporary idiom ("So don't bug me") will be self-explanatory if you examine *bugger* and *buggery* in the dictionary.

Either by accident or design, Hilda misses the import of the space-age discussion. Had she laughed at Pennington's cleverness, her timing would have been served, but, wishing to use him to her own ends, she forges on into the falling action of the play, introducing the tragic force which will lead to the end of her plans and the play.

HILDA. Sometime back, a truck fell on her, a trailer truck skidded on greasy pavement, it jackknifed, she was at the bus stop and boom!

PENNINGTON. Killed?

HILDA. Pinned. The fire department worked hours to get her out. She got some money out of it. The lawyer took one third, the doctor, plenty, but there was still enough from the settlement so she could be comfortable the rest of her life. However. . . .

PENNINGTON. I knew that was coming.

HILDA. Along comes her son—and says he wants to be a daughter. He wants to be a female out-and-out. He says, I want to have an operation in Denmark. And he takes the twenty thousand dollars she was going to retire on. You follow?

PENNINGTON. I wish I could say no.

HILDA. Now they're opening a dress shop together, in Indiana Harbor.

PENNINGTON. Outer space is better.

HILDA. They made me give them the shop in this building.

PENNINGTON. On the corner?

HILDA. The same. My sister and her former son. Now I appeal to you . . . give me this chance for something normal.

PENNINGTON. What's normal?

HILDA. Not to be hemmed in by freaks. That's not for me. I want to get some class in my life.

PENNINGTON. No, no, leave me out of it. I've got a date at my club.

HILDA. After a little soufflé. You never even asked for a glass of water in this house.

PENNINGTON. Okay, Madame, to the point.

HILDA. Have a little coffee first.

PENNINGTON. I don't want any. Will you finally tell me what you're up to?

Bellow has written a capsule history of the drama in this one-act play. Humorous, tragic, tragically comical, and melodramatic by turns, the play has followed a typical five-act development in its one act. It has dealt with serious material in a frequently outrageous manner, with elements of the classical stage, the Miracle Play, and brilliantly parodied the *well-made play* (that technically constructed, contrived play relying on coincidence, surprise ending, and great attention to casual relationships which often posed the question, "Can a fallen woman create a new, socially acceptable life by marrying a respectable gentleman?" The answer was always, "No!").

At this point in the action, *Orange Soufflé* now embodies the basic elements of the twentieth-century's *theater of the absurd*—a theater that assumes that the ingredients of reality are basically absurd, that the world is a nonsensical illusion where cause and effect merely appear to be related, and that language is a series of sounds inherently devoid of rational meaning (see pp. 517–602). The melodramatic recital of the accident that befell Hilda's urban renewal-dwelling sister is, in itself, absurd. However, it mimics reality in that a bid for sympathy does, in our society, frequently precede a plea for financial help. Pennington's "I knew that was coming" reveals his awareness of the gambit. The extreme absurdity of sex transformations in Denmark reduces the imitation of reality to its most unreal level and forces the realistic Pennington to say he wishes he didn't understand any of this idiocy. That a mother and her son-daughter should open a dress shop in Indiana Harbor makes the multiple symbols of outer space seem infinitely preferable. The freakish cycle comes full circle as the fallen woman pleads for normalcy. Pennington wants to escape the insanity of it all by withdrawing to a male sanctuary—his club—but Hilda forces him to demand the "point" of this fiasco that has bogged down in her mother-wish that he drink something—anything—as long as it is liquid.

HILDA. You have that big place in Palm Beach.
PENNINGTON. What'd you know about it?
HILDA. I seen it.
PENNINGTON. In Florida?
HILDA. In the Sunday supplement.
PENNINGTON. What's it got to do with you?
HILDA. Don't jump now. I'm gonna make you a proposition and I really want you to consider it.
PENNINGTON. What proposition?
HILDA. I want to go down there. That's all I been able to think about. Please, Mr. Pennington, don't just say "no."

PENNINGTON. What? What the hell do you want to do there?

HILDA. I'd be the lady of the house. Like—a hostess, a chatelaine. I'd . . . I'd run it. I'd entertain for you. You think I couldn't do it? I could surprise you. I'm terrific with people. They love me. God, they do! They're happy to see me! Even ladies are happy to see me. Oh, Pennington, get me out of here. They're moving in next month and I'll be trapped—my sister and her daughter Archie.

PENNINGTON. I thought life had no more surprises.

HILDA. I'd run that place like a dream. Soufflé isn't all I can make. Duck with oranges. Bouillabaisse. Karsky Shashlik. Barcelona Paella with lobster claws and capers. Five kinds of mousse. Wine, I know all about. Flower arrangements. Your guests would be wild for me. Us American minorities are the spice of life. And to show I'm on the level I'll sign any kind of paper.

PENNINGTON. I have to go.

HILDA. You have to listen. I'll make over my property so it'll go to your estate when I kick off. I don't want to leave it to my niece.

Hilda's "proposition" reveals a pathetic character indeed. She knows she is no lady ("Even ladies are happy to see me") and that she is trapped between the hope of what she can never become ("a hostess, a chatelaine"—romanticism engulfs the words) and the despair of what she barely escapes being (a "freak" with a freak niece named Archie). Pennington's understatement ("I thought life had no more surprises") reveals his incredulity as nothing else could. The absurdity of the recital is not yet over, however. Hilda would be international in her oral scope; she would be a transplanted freak, turning his Palm Beach home into a circus ring ("Us American minorities are the spice of life"). Then she *really* blows it with the offer to add to Pennington's wealth—presupposing she will outlive him and reminding him of his inevitable death.

PENNINGTON. For once a man works out a good thing. For once! At last! After years of trying. A good thing. Naturally, it has to be ruined. It's not only you I like—it's you plus the squalor.

HILDA. A thing has got to be just the way you want it. Couldn't it be even a little bit the way I want it? Give a guy a little chance, Pennington. Try me at Palm Beach. If I don't work out, what do you lose? You can trust me. No pay, on approval—how's that?

PENNINGTON (*his indignation is so great that he finds the strength to rise and reach for his jacket*). Take this table out of the way. Where's my coat? My stick! (*Finding his cane, he stands straighter.*) Nobody has forced me out of character—not in the last sixty years anyway.

Cause and effect, the characters' lack of relationship in the whole absurd exchange, and the improbable psychology—all collide in Pennington's impassioned plea for the *status quo* (the basic premise of the well-made play which his life has been) and the resolution of psychological realism: "It's not only you I like—it's you plus the squalor."

Melodramatically, Pennington asserts himself in his behavior and in his implied realization that "All the world's a stage" (Bellow works Shakespeare into the play in spirit if not in speech) as he asserts, "Nobody has forced me out of character—not in the last sixty years anyway." Pennington likes the role he has assumed; silently he pleads for Hilda to return to hers.

HILDA. Wait, it's almost ready.

PENNINGTON. My overcoat's there. (*Walks slowly toward closet.*) What is this, February? I'll see you in March.

HILDA (*quickly goes to closet and takes out his fur-collared coat*). Here, put it on and sit down. You've just got to sit down.

PENNINGTON. I don't want to sit. I want to go.

HILDA (*as timer buzzes*). Sit. It's ready, it's ready. (*She drapes coat over him, runs to stove. He leans on cane, waiting. She bends out of sight as he peers over counter. Then she rises, wearing asbestos oven mitts. In the round baking dish is nothing resembling a soufflé.*)

PENNINGTON. Is that it?

HILDA. I can't understand what went wrong.

PENNINGTON. You couldn't get it up. (*After a short pause the rich tones of a Rolls-Royce horn are heard.*) Ah, there's Otto with the car. (*Sets homburg on his head with trembling hands, puts on gloves.*) About time, too. (*Leans on counter, the better to point at* HILDA *with his cane.*) Stick to what you know, Madame. (*Exit.*)

HILDA. Once they get you down, they never let you up. (*Striking the oven with the skillet.*) Never, never!

CURTAIN

Hilda cannot return to her old role. She *will* be the hostess rather than the madame. Desperately Pennington attempts to reëstablish their roles; he will be back on schedule next month. Equally desperately, Hilda forces the issue and creates the catastrophe as the timer buzzes in the best tradition of the well-made play. Of course the soufflé is a flop, and Hilda, in one of the most pathetic but hilariously understated ambiguities of all literature observes, "I can't understand what went wrong." Tragedy too attends the line. She *can't* understand what went wrong!

Once again master of all he surveys, Pennington employs a double-entendre of harsh vulgarity and extreme self-satisfaction ("You couldn't get it up") as the well-made play continues on the rich tones of the Rolls-Royce horn and Pennington's very correct "Ah, there's Otto with the car." Deliverance is at hand. Delivering his didactic parting shot, Pennington leaves as, surrounded by her failures, Hilda speaks as a woman dominated by men, a prostitute serving customers, a minority figure at the merciless discrimination of the majority, and as an economic inferior exploited by the ruling monetary class. And she becomes a comic-strip Maggie who has lost her Jiggs as she lashes out with the classical instrument of housewifery and shrewishness—the skillet—suggesting that she will fry in her own hell!

Orange Soufflé is a delightful play, capable of being read on any of a number of levels—or on all of them simultaneously. The mood of the reader will change those levels; the wonderful thing remains, however: the play is always available for a new reading and a fresh interpretation.

CHAPTER III

Classical Tragedy—
The Tears of the Muses

Although drama developed in a relatively unbroken line from ancient Greece, its general outline contains three major time divisions. Each time division includes tragedy and comedy, which are subdivided again and again until the outline includes such specific minor forms as skits, dramatic monologs, and television situation comedies.

The major time divisions during which drama has developed are: (1) the *Classical* period (the age of Greece and Rome), (2) the *Romantic* period (the age of Shakespeare), and (3) the *Modern* period (the twentieth century). Originally, tragedy and comedy were both composed in poetry, prose becoming an acceptable dramatic medium only relatively recently. However, because prose predominates in modern plays, *drama* and *poetic drama* exist as subdivisions in the contemporary period and must be considered separately in the effects each achieves. Further, while two distinct forms may coexist in time, the nature of man demands some merging of all forms. Tragedy and comedy did merge after the classical period, their offspring being called *tragicomedy*. The remainder of this book, then, is divided into chapters, each to contain period representatives of the dramatic form considered in that chapter. First, we will consider classical tragedy.

Since classical tragedy was the earliest type of drama to achieve permanency of form and intention, it must somehow be basic to man's most primitive needs and instincts, since it is in the nature of man to attend to his most urgent needs first. Viewing man in conflict with his gods, his fears, his ambitions, his contemporaries, and himself, classical tragedy originally sprang from a chorus which danced as it chanted hymns—a religious service satisfying man's need to communicate with authority greater than his own. With the addition of the *episode* (spoken lines), tragedy, as a dramatic form, was born.

Its form and the great amphitheater where it was performed imposed certain limitations; yet those limitations added power and greatness to it. Because the amphitheater was large, the production could not be intimate as it can today in a small theater where the actors' facial expressions, voice modulations and inflections, and bodily movements add dimension and depth of characterization simply because the audience can *see* and *hear* those embellishments of the lines. In the great Greek theaters, the greater part of the audience was seated too far away from the stage for such refinements to be of value. As a result, members of the Chorus and the actors were padded and draped in loose-flowing garments, and they were elevated on *cothurni* (boots with high, platform soles) to make them larger than life-size so that they would be visible to the spectators in the last high tiers of seats. Such bulky costumes and clumsy footgear restrained the actors' natural movements, creating the need for stylized posturing (as in ballet), symbolic gestures (such as may be seen in Medieval and Renaissance paintings), and conventional pantomime (so successfully used in the twentieth century by Charlie Chaplin and Marcel Marceau).

So that the distant members of the audience could hear the spoken lines, Greek actors wore masks with built-in megaphones. Obviously, subtlety has never been a characteristic of megaphone or bullhorn delivery. As a result, the lines themselves had to bear the full burden of involving the hearer. Vocabulary, syntax, rhythm—in short, literary *style*—had to be so pronounced that the loss of visual and aural embellishments did not create a hardship for the reader.

Did we say the "reader"? Precisely! The fact is that Greek audiences had much more in common with today's reader than with today's theater or movie-goer. Books as we know them did not exist and would not exist for many centuries, so dramatizations in the amphitheaters of Greece can more accurately be compared to recorded readings of books than to theatrical productions as we think of them. The Greek audiences listened not only with their ears but also with the full force of their retentive memories. In the disastrous wars that eventually destroyed Greece, certain captured Athenian soldiers were awarded special slave status and freed of demeaning and servile tasks because they could entertain their masters with complete recitations of the plays they had heard. That they had heard them only one time makes this sound incredible to us; however, were you suddenly deprived of television, radio, and all printed matter, you would, as the Greeks did, cherish the few intellectual offerings available to you. Your memory, now neglected because it is not vitally needed, would become much more acute if necessity demanded.

Aware of the limitations of their stage, Greek dramatists knew that familiar stories would serve their purpose best. Their purpose was clear to them: while they did wish to entertain their audiences, they also wished to enlighten them, to make them aware of the role of man—as the dramatists saw that role. For this purpose, a wealth of material was at the dramatists' immediate disposal. Everyone in their audiences knew the great religious accounts (which we call *mythology*), the literary-historical material of Homer's *The Iliad* and *The Odyssey,* as well as the Homeric tales containing accounts of the lives of all characters before and after the Trojan War.

Now, because whatever story the Greek dramatist chose was so well-known to his audience, *suspense,* as we understand the word, did not concern him. Instead of listening for plot, the viewer would focus his attention on the subtlety of revealed character, of character response to that which the viewer already knew. The *significance* of the action rather than the action itself became the focal point of the viewer's attention. *Irony* lies at the very heart of tragedy (since man is the only animal that prays, for instance, is it not ironic that he is also the only one that needs to pray?), and irony is meaningful only when the viewer (or reader) recognizes it and knows the significance of *when* it is employed in the play. Because Greek audiences knew the plot and outcome of the plays they saw, they could be exposed to irony piled on irony if such a structure pleased the dramatist. Furthermore, since the characters and incidents were removed in time, the audience could view them with a historical perspective and, at the same time, be spared extensive exposition (background). From the opening words the audience knew the background material, so the dramatist could begin *in medias res* ("in the middle of the action") without fear of confusing the viewer.

Actors padded and elevated to be larger than life-size could be seen and heard; characters from legend and history automatically became larger than life-size because their established importance magnified them. Consequently, the dramatist's lines had to be written in a *language* which was larger than life-size. And poetry *is* "larger" than prose. More intensely emotional, poetry is capable of communicating ideas which prose, lacking essential rhythms and harmonies of sound, cannot communicate. Subjects which prose reduces to pretentious mouthings or to outright insincerity lend themselves to the poetic line. God and love and sexual need, for example, are all intensely personal—so personal, indeed, that we become embarrassed if we are deeply concerned with them and they enter the conversation. On the other hand, when we are not involved in them, we can be somewhat objective. Poetic lines allow a gap to come between us and those things in which we are involved. Because poetry is language removed from the ordinary, because it is language lifted to hypersensitivity, we can be involved in the material it discusses because we can say, "This is no part of me; this is a more aware, articulate analysis than my everyday problem warrants." Analogously, however, the material bears a distinct relationship to our own lives. Removed and seemingly impersonal, the poetic line allows analogous relationships to become meaningful. As we assess the problems of Oedipus or Macbeth or Ephraim Cabot, we are assessing *ourselves,* for we realize we would probably behave and react as they do, or perhaps we would—we think—react differently at some specific point. Since the possibility of our encountering the same or an analogous situation has embroiled us in the first place, we are, then, either reassessing our own past behavioral experience or storing vicarious behavioral patterns against future need. This removal from the personal, which the use of poetry accomplishes so well, is called *aesthetic distance.* Any good dramatist will try to exhibit aesthetic distance as he writes; for example, if he is involved in a hopeless love, he probably should not write about hopeless love because he would be too subjective as a result of his close involvement. The reader (viewer) may be involved in a similar set of circumstances, but the poetic line allows him the distance he needs to become objective *enough* for the experience to become meaningful. So Greek dramatists employed poetic lines—rolling hexameters in which the language sounds proud and seems to become a mighty chorus speaking for all men rather than words spoken by one voice.

Another limitation claimed the Greek dramatist too: the Chorus could not be dismissed from the stage. It functioned as a local group of townsmen or elders or, collectively, as a single character representing all of mankind. Its constant presence on the stage limited action, time, and place, for twelve to fifteen people could not be shuffled about as one body. Out of this need rose the concept of the *unities* (the three limitations of the Chorus which gave coherence to the play). Aristotle in his *Poetics* suggested one of these—the unity of *action,* for, he said, tragedy is an imitation of an action that is both complete and whole, possessing a beginning, a middle, and an end. Causal relationships should bind those parts together. The second unity—that of *time*—grew out of Aristotle's statement that tragedy confines itself to a single revolution of the sun or a little longer span. The third unity—that of *place*—was not mentioned by Aristotle. It grew from the cohesiveness achieved by the first two. If action and time are to be restricted, it is simply easier to limit them to one location. Greek tragedy had limited itself to one setting for practical rather than aesthetic reasons, imposing the unity on itself.

Almost two thousand years after Aristotle wrote his *Poetics,* John Dryden discussed the three unities in his "An Essay of Dramatic Poesy" (1688). He speaks so well it would be folly to paraphrase him:

'The Unity of Time they [the Greeks] comprehend in twenty-four hours, the compass of a natural day, or as near as it can be contrived; and the reason of it is obvious to every one,—that the time of the feigned action, or fable of the play, should be proportioned as near as can be to the duration of that time in which it is represented: since therefore, all plays are acted in the theatre in a space of time much within the compass of twenty-four hours, that play is to be thought the nearest imitation of nature, whose plot or action is confined within that time; and, by the same rule which concludes this general proportion of time, it follows, that all the parts of it are to be equally subdivided; as namely, that one act take not up the supposed time of half a day, which is out of proportion to the rest; since the other four are then to be straitened within the compass of the remaining half: for it is unnatural that one act, which being spoke or written is not longer than the rest, should be supposed longer by the audience; 'tis therefore the poet's duty, to take care that no act should be imagined to exceed the time in which it is represented on the stage; and that the intervals and inequalities of time be supposed to fall out between the acts.

'This rule of time, how well it has been observed by the Ancients, most of their plays will witness; you see them in their tragedies, (wherein to follow this rule, is certainly most difficult,) from the very beginning of their plays, falling close into that part of the story which they intend for the action or principal object of it, leaving the former part to be delivered by narration: so that they set the audience, as it were, at the post where the race is to be concluded; and, saving them the tedious expectation of seeing the poet set out and ride the beginning of the course, you behold him not till he is in sight of the goal, and just upon you.

'For the second Unity, which is that of Place, the Ancients meant by it, that the scene ought to be continued through the play, in the same place where it was laid in the beginning: for the stage on which it is represented being but one and the same place, it is unnatural to conceive it many; and those far distant from one another. I will not deny but, by the variation of painted scenes, the fancy, which in these cases will contribute to its own deceit, may sometimes imagine it several places, with some appearance of probability; yet it still carries the greater likelihood of truth, if those places be supposed so near each other, as in the same town or city; which may all be comprehended under the larger denomination of one place; for a greater distance will bear no proportion to the shortness of time which is allotted in the acting, to pass from one of them to another; for the observation of this, next to the Ancients, the French are to be most commended. They tie themselves so strictly to the Unity of Place, that you never see in any of their plays, a scene changed in the middle of an act: if the act begins in a garden, a street, or chamber, 'tis ended in the same place; and that you may know it to be the same, the stage is so supplied with persons, that it is never empty all the time: he that enters the second, has business with him who was on before; and before the second quits the stage, a third appears who has business with him. This Corneille calls *la liaison des scènes*, the continuity or joining of the scenes; and 'tis a good mark of a well-contrived play, when all the persons are known to each other, and everyone of them has some affairs with all the rest.

'As for the third Unity, which is that of Action, the Ancients meant no other by it than what the logicians do by their *finis*, the end or scope of any action; that which is the first in intention, and last in execution: now the poet is to aim at one great and complete action, to the carrying on of which all things in his play, even the very obstacles, are to be subservient; and the reason of this is as evident as any of the former.

'For two actions, equally laboured and driven on by the writer, would destroy the unity of the poem; it would be no longer one play, but two: not but that there may be many actions in a play, as Ben Jonson has observed in his *Discoveries*; but they must be all subservient to the great one, which our language happily expresses in the name of *under-plots*: such as in Terence's *Eunuch* is the difference and reconcilement of Thais and Phædria, which is not the chief business of the play, but promotes the marriage of Chærea and Chremes's sister, principally intended by the poet. There ought to be but one action, says Corneille, that is, one complete action which leaves the mind of the audience in a full repose; but this cannot be brought to pass but by many other imperfect actions, which conduce to it, and hold the audience in a delightful suspence of what will be.'

As Dryden observes, only one complex situation was presented in each play. The play began at a point of great interest with complications already rife because the reader-viewer knew the story. Crisis was, automatically, impending from the beginning, and that crisis was developed quickly and artfully to expose it and to allow its full force to whirl the reader-viewer's emotions into confusion that, as he left the theater, settled into a realization of the universal meaning of what he had heard and seen. He could then apply the universal message to his particular needs. It was, analogously, as if he went into the theater with the same mental conditioning one might use to view an oncoming storm. Prepared and anticipating the violent winds, he watched them gather into a growing force to buffet the dramatic victims in its path, level their homes and futures, and depart, leaving shattered wreckage in its wake. In the calm aftermath, stunned by the awesome power of the emotional storm, the reader-viewer considered the awful powers ready to be unleashed at any moment, and he sorrowed for its victims, relieved that, for the moment at least, he personally had been merely a spectator rather than a participant. However, new winds constantly form in man's emotional life, new storms are imminent. The next raging violence might sweep through the reader-viewer's life, leaving him as debris in its passing. Determination attends such realization—determination to be grateful for present sparings, to live more intelligently, to prepare for future possibilities.

Aristotle called the audience's participation, response, and realization *catharsis* (a cleansing of the emotions through pity and fear, a purgative action ridding the emotional body of mental poisons and wastes). Later critics were to argue about his meaning, but those arguments need not concern you here. If you should, at some future time, wish to explore the many interpretations, you have a ready-made subject for a research paper. Suffice it here to say, Aristotle, like Dryden, speaks best for himself; you should acquaint yourself with his *Poetics* at your earliest opportunity.

In sum, it would seem that the author of a tragedy could best achieve his intention if he followed the basic rules outlined above. This is not to say that a modern tragedian has to follow these rules assiduously, or that many of them do; modern writers may, in fact, violate them completely, finding their own best way to attain their ends. But that the rules do lend form, coherence, and unity to a play is beyond dispute. Nor can it be denied a knowledge of them is a great aid to the reader who wishes to understand fully and enjoy completely a tragedy as he reads. Not knowing them will not prohibit your comprehension; it will merely cause you to work harder to achieve understanding.

But before you can hope to read a play such as *Oedipus Rex* with interest and insight, there is even more that it would be profitable for you to know: the plot. In fact, you should have the same information the original Greek reader possessed when he came to see the play. Of course, because it was a part of his heritage, you can not possess it as he did. He *knew* it as you *know* "The Lord's Prayer," "The Ten Commandments," or the life of Christ. In short, he could remember no time when he did *not* know the story of Oedipus. Furthermore, if this is your first exposure to it, you may find the story repellent, shocking, even offensive. It should, in one sense, be all of those things, for *Oedipus Rex* is the story of an abandoned child who lives to be guilty of unintentional patricide and incest which produces his daughters who are also his sisters and his sons who are also his brothers. Your moral and cultural background doubtless cries out against all of those elements. "Nice people" don't do such things! Yet Laïos and Iocastê were "nice"; Oedipus was noble except for that flawed portion of his character which precipitated his tragedy. In summary, the story is as follows:

An ancient king of Tyre, Agenor, was descended from both Zeus and Poseidon. His son Kadmos distinguished himself by bringing the alphabet to Greece, siring Semele, the mother of Dionysus—thus incurring the everlasting hatred of Hera—and founding the city of Thebes, populating it with warriors who sprang from the planted teeth of a great serpent he killed there. (One of the warriors was Menoikeus, the father of Creon and Iocastê.) Kadmos was succeeded by his son Polydoros, father of Labdacos. Early death came to Labdacos before his son, Laïos, was old enough to govern Thebes. Lycos, Laïos' uncle, acted as regent, ruling so unwisely that he lost the city to Amphion who expelled Laïos and built the walls of Thebes with their seven mighty gates.

Laïos eventually found his way to the court of Pelops in Pisa and there became enamored of Pelops' son, Chrysippus. Some time later, Amphion died and the Thebans, now a great people, invited Laïos to reclaim the throne. Abducting Chrysippus, Laïos brought the boy to Thebes, married Iocastê, and ascended the throne. The marriage was a condition set by the Thebans, for it united the descendant of Kadmos and a descendant of one of the original "sown-men," ensuring a powerful royal line.

Dallying with his young catamite, Laïos neglected Iocastê, and, when she failed to present him an heir within a year, went secretly to the oracle of Apollo at Delphi. There, the oracle told Laïos he was lucky to be childless, for any son born to Iocastê would murder him. Frightened, Laïos returned to Thebes and, without explaining the reason, told Iocastê he was putting her away (the Greek equivalent of divorce). Enraged that Laïos should prefer Chrysippus' bed to hers, angered that she should lose her position as queen, Iocastê controlled herself and pleaded for one last evening with Laïos. He, grateful that she had been acquiescent, granted the request, drinking excessively at her urging. In the depths of a drunken stupor, Laïos sired Oedipus.

Iocastê had thus succeeded in binding Laïos to her and in securing the throne. She could not now be put aside, and, in due time, Oedipus, the heir of Thebes, was born. When Iocastê presented her son to Laïos, however, he snatched the child from her arms and revealed the prophecy of the oracle. Then, piercing the child's ankles with a thorn to hobble him, Laïos dispatched a herdsman to his distant fields on Mount Kithaeron with instructions to expose the baby. Custom decreed that unwanted children could not be killed (Greeks incurred the wrath of the avenging Furies if they spilled blood of kinsmen), but they could be exposed in deserted places. If the gods ordained, they arranged circumstances to allow the child to live.

Iocastê had at no time been given reason to love Laïos. Now she had ample reason to hate him. For the rest of their married life, he avoided her bed, denying her that part of womanhood she most desired: motherhood. Nor was Laïos a good ruler. Inept, suspicious, he whiled away his days with Chrysippus, refusing to free Iocastê, for, he feared, if she were to bear a son by someone else, that son would fulfill the oracle. Hera, still smarting from Semele's involvement with Zeus, was further angered by the abduction of Chrysippus, for she was also the patroness of married women. Because Thebes did nothing to force Laïos to return the boy to Pisa, she sent the Sphinx to plague the city. This fabulous monster settled just outside the walls and demanded the answer to a riddle of everyone who entered or left the city. The riddle was: "What, having one voice, goes on four legs in the morning, two at noon, and three in the evening, being weakest when it has the most?" All who could not answer were devoured on the spot.

Many Thebans dared the Sphinx, Haeman, son of Creon and nephew of Iocastê, among them. Eventually, Chrysippus either committed suicide or was mysteriously slain, and Laïos, now loathed by all Thebes, slipped out of the city by night to journey once more to Delphi where he hoped the oracle would reveal the answer that would satisfy the Sphinx.

Oedipus had, however, during these unhappy years, grown to young manhood. As bidden, a herdsman had taken the child to the distant borders of Thebes and there, where Thebes' land met the land of Corinth, had disobeyed orders by giving the child to a shepherd from the royal household of Corinth. The king and queen of that city-state, Polybos and Meropê, had grown old without an heir. They took the child from the shepherd and, swearing him to secrecy, proclaimed the infant their natural son. Corinth rejoiced and loved Oedipus (the name meaning "swollen foot," because of the damage done by the thorn). He grew to young manhood, constantly disturbed because, unlike other children, he in no way resembled his parents. One day, after a young Corinthian friend had taunted him about his alien looks, he went to Delphi to ask questions of the oracle.

A strange reception awaited him there. "Leave the shrine immediately," the oracle hissed, "lest you defile it with your presence. You are destined to kill your father and marry your mother!" Shocked, frightened, the youth fled, determined never to go near Corinth again. If he avoided Polybos and Meropê, he reasoned, he could circumvent the oracle.

Taking the nearest road, he followed it to Phokis where it forked into three roads, one leading to Delphi, one to Daulis, and one to Thebes. There, in a sharp defile, he met a man accompanied by four serving-men. The road was too narrow for the chariot of the man to pass unless Oedipus stood aside. Ordered to do so, Oedipus felt his suppressed horror and anger boil up. It had accompanied him from the shrine, and he could now lash out at someone, releasing his youthful frustration. "I stand aside for none save the gods and my parents," Oedipus asserted. Laïos, for such was the imperious man, ordered his charioteer to run the impudent traveler down.

Refusing to be run over, Oedipus killed the man and three of his attendants, not even noticing in his rage that a fifth man had escaped. Then, leaving the corpses for scavengers, Oedipus continued on his way, taking the road to Thebes. There, outside the city, the Sphinx challenged him and finally met her match. "It is man," Oedipus replied. "He has only human speech; he crawls on hands and knees in the morning or babyhood of life, walks upright on two feet as an adult, and supports himself with a staff of old age when he is most weak."

The Sphinx thereupon destroyed herself and Oedipus entered Thebes a hero. Seeing the jubilant mood of the people, Iocastê urged Creon to ask the elders to declare Oedipus king, his right to the deserted throne being assured by his act of deliverance and his acceptance of the existing queen as his wife. Sorrowing for Haeman and hating Laïos, Creon did as Iocastê suggested. The elders, happy to be rid of the effeminate king who had brought them only misery, agreed, and Oedipus accepted the offer.

News of the death of Laïos eventually came to Creon and Iocastê from the king of Plataeae in whose territory the Phokan defile lay. They were indifferent, of course, and, preferring to keep the Thebans content, held the information in secret. The Thebans, unconcerned because they thought Laïos had abandoned them in their hour of need, never bothered to mourn him, giving lip service to his memory instead, for national pride demanded they conceal the scandals of his reign.

Iocastê, still a vigorous woman, bore Oedipus two sons (Polyneices and Eteocles) and two daughters (Antigone and Ismene). Her life had become happy as her role as a mother was fulfilled. Oedipus too was happy, for he had proved himself as a prince, protecting his parents and himself at the same time. And Thebes was happy, for years of prosperity ensued. Whatever rumors drifted to Theban ears were ignored. Whatever rumors Oedipus heard, he ignored, for, if Laïos had been the victim of a Theban plot, the plotters had served Oedipus' ambition.

And so the years passed.

An old aphorism suggests the mills of the gods grind slowly but they grind exceedingly fine. Eventually, a plague descended on Thebes and, acting as a good king, Oedipus dispatched Creon to Delphi to consult the oracle. "Expel the murderer of Laïos," Apollo commanded. Oedipus, ignorant of his guilt, called down a curse on Laïos' murderer, sentencing him to exile.

Summoning Teiresias, the most renowned prophet and seer in all Greece, Oedipus heard himself branded as that murderer. Remembering the old rumors, he concluded Creon had been the plotter and now was plotting again. Enraged, Teiresias revealed the truth, a truth verified by the two herdsmen who had kept the infant Oedipus alive so many years before. The Theban herdsman had been the fifth man with Laïos at Phokis, and, returning to Thebes many months after the arrival of Oedipus, had recognized the murderer-now-king. Fearing Oedipus would also recognize him, the herdsman had pleaded to be stationed far from the city. Iocastê, grateful that the herdsman did not want to spread his tale in Thebes, had sent him away happily.

Discovering the horrible truth that her husband was her son, that her four children by him were the offspring of black incest, Iocastê fled into her chambers and hanged herself. As the truth came fully to him, Oedipus rushed to the side of his dead mother-wife and, with the brooches from her clothing, gouged out his own eyes.

Honoring his own pronouncement, Oedipus relinquished the city to Creon and was led away to the long night of exile.

And now, with full knowledge of the horrible story, read *Oedipus Rex* (Oedipus the King), not to follow the plot but, knowing the story, to understand the greater pleasure of participating in that most awful moment when Oedipus learns the truths that you now know in advance.

OEDIPUS REX

by Sophocles
An English Version
by Dudley Fitts and Robert Fitzgerald

CHARACTERS

OEDIPUS	MESSENGER
A PRIEST	SHEPHERD OF LAÏOS
CREON	SECOND MESSENGER
TEIRESIAS	CHORUS OF THEBAN ELDERS
IOCASTÉ	

THE SCENE—*Before the palace of* OEDIPUS, *King of Thebes. A central door and two lateral doors open onto a platform which runs the length of the façade. On the platform, right and left, are altars; and three steps lead down into the "orchestra," or chorus-ground. At the beginning of the action these steps are crowded by suppliants who have brought branches and chaplets of olive leaves and who lie in various attitudes of despair.* OEDIPUS *enters.*

The cast contains nine speaking roles, the ninth being the Chorus or *choragos* (leader of the Chorus). However, the Greek theater allowed only three actors in each play (the *choragos* not being counted as one of them since he represents the audience). Thus at no time are more than three actors onstage at any one time in the play, and masks so effectively disguise their faces that the same three speak all parts. In your reading of the play, this technicality is of little or no importance, but an awareness of it helps you place yourself in time as both a member of the Greek audience and as a present-day participant.

The characters are all familiar to you from the summary. You should visualize the scene: The palace is a building of simple Greek architecture with a peaked roof. Looking at the front, you see large central doors flanked by a smaller one on each side. At each side of the façade, wings of the building jut forward and a "front porch" stretches between them to create a stage. Steps lead from that stage to the "orchestra," a half-circle extending into the center of the tiers of seats where the audience sits. As the play opens, suppliants bearing symbols sacred to Athena (the goddess of wisdom) wait on the steps for Oedipus, their wise king, to appear and hear their petitions. A priest of Zeus attends the sacred altars at each side of the stage. Burnt offerings send smoke spiraling up into the soft Greek air as the priest and the suppliants pray soundlessly. Oedipus appears in his Greek royal clothing, a noble and respected king who has ruled them wisely and well for many years since that long-ago day when he arrived as a young man to deliver them from the Sphinx.

PROLOGUE

    OEDIPUS. My children, generations of the living
In the line of Kadmos, nursed at his ancient hearth:
Why have you strewn yourselves before these altars
In supplication, with your boughs and garlands?
The breath of incense rises from the city   *5*
With a sound of prayer and lamentation.
                                 Children,
I would not have you speak through messengers,
And therefore I have come myself to hear you—
I, Oedipus, who bear the famous name.
(To a PRIEST.) You, there, since you are eldest in the company,   *10*
Speak for them all, tell me what preys upon you,
Whether you come in dread, or crave some blessing:
Tell me, and never doubt that I will help you
In every way I can; I should be heartless
Were I not moved to find you suppliant here.   *15*
    PRIEST. Great Oedipus, O powerful King of Thebes!
You see how all the ages of our people

Cling to your altar steps: here are boys
Who can barely stand alone, and here are priests
By weight of age, as I am a priest of God,   *20*
And young men chosen from those yet unmarried;
As for the others, all that multitude,
They wait with olive chaplets in the squares,
At the two shrines of Pallas, and where Apollo
Speaks in the glowing embers.

                  Your own eyes   *25*
Must tell you: Thebes is in her extremity
And can not lift her head from the surge of death.
A rust consumes the buds and fruits of the earth;
The herds are sick; children die unborn,
And labor is vain. The god of plague and pyre   *30*
Raids like detestable lightning through the city,
And all the house of Kadmos is laid waste,
All emptied, and all darkened: Death alone
Battens upon the misery of Thebes.
You are not one of the immortal gods, we know;   *35*
Yet we have come to you to make our prayer
As to the man of all men best in adversity
And wisest in the ways of God. You saved us
From the Sphinx, that flinty singer, and the tribute
We paid to her so long; yet you were never   *40*
Better informed than we, nor could we teach you:
It was some god breathed in you to set us free.

Therefore, O mighty King, we turn to you:
Find us our safety, find us a remedy,
Whether by counsel of the gods or men.   *45*
A king of wisdom tested in the past
Can act in a time of troubles, and act well.
Noblest of men, restore
Life to your city! Think how all men call you
Liberator for your triumph long ago;   *50*
Ah, when your years of kingship are remembered,
Let them not say *We rose, but later fell*—
Keep the State from going down in the storm!
Once, years ago, with happy augury,
You brought us fortune; be the same again!   *55*
No man questions your power to rule the land:
But rule over men, not over a dead city!

Ships are only hulls, citadels are nothing,
When no life moves in the empty passageways.

In his first speech (1-9), Oedipus reveals his paternal attitude, a formal but kind attitude not unmixed, however, with an awareness of his own importance. Without braggadocio, he acknowledges his value but assures them he does not hold himself too important to speak directly with them. Choosing a spokesman from among them (10), Oedipus indicates the Greek regard for age rather than for the priesthood. He further indicates his ignorance of their reason for appearing at the palace. This suggests he will hear *any* petition from his people.

The priest of Zeus speaks with great respect to Oedipus, pointing out that all Thebes is represented in the suppliant group, the remainder of the city waiting at the shrines of Apollo and Athena (patrons of wisdom) to add the weight of their prayers to those of their representatives. No motley mob has been sent; a select few are representative. Briefly recapitulating that which Oedipus knows full well, the priest respectfully suggests that the people hold Oedipus in awe as one almost divine in his great wisdom (35-42), a wisdom bestowed by "some god," thereby elevating Oedipus above other men. That Oedipus is favored by "some god" is ironic, an irony *you* can understand but which is not apparent to Oedipus or the priest. Reminding Oedipus of his victory over the Sphinx, the priest carefully and respectfully challenges the king to be as diligent in protecting Thebes now as he was in gaining its throne.

    OEDIPUS. Poor children! You may be sure I know   60
All that you longed for in your coming here.
I know that you are deathly sick; and yet,
Sick as you are, not one is as sick as I.
Each of you suffers in himself alone
His anguish, not another's; but my spirit   65
Groans for the city, for myself, for you.

I was not sleeping, you are not waking me.
No, I have been in tears for a long while
And in my restless thought walked many ways.
In all my search, I found one helpful course,   70
And that I have taken: I have sent Creon,
Son of Menoikeus, brother of the Queen,
To Delphi, Apollo's place of revelation,
To learn there, if he can,
What act or pledge of mine may save the city.   75

I have counted the days, and now, this very day,
I am troubled, for he has overstayed his time.
What is he doing? He has been gone too long.
Yet whenever he comes back, I should do ill
To scant whatever hint the god may give.   80
    PRIEST. It is a timely promise. At this instant
They tell me Creon is here.

Oedipus' response is wrung from a mighty heart, and irony is indicated
a second time in line 66: his spirit groans "for the city, for myself, for
you." Oedipus has no idea how closely related are the three; yet, notice
the order of grief: first for city, second for Self, finally for subjects. In
the progression from most important to least important, Oedipus reveals
the Greek mind: first allegiance is owed to the city (in our terms, country),
second allegiance is owed to oneself, final allegiance is to others. That
order of allegiance will become a mighty force, demanding that Oedipus
sacrifice himself for the city when Creon returns with the message from
Delphi. And Oedipus reveals his greatness and his flaw (for they are,
paradoxically, the same) as he says (79–80) that he will meet his obligation
to duty—whatever it may be. Ambitious for the throne of Thebes, he
is automatically ambitious for the city. Duty lies first to the city, but
in assuming responsibility for that duty, he will assure his duty to himself:
retention of the throne. However, only in doing his duty can Oedipus
lose everything. The irony of these irreconcilables is dramatically apparent
to you; that it is concealed from Oedipus gives us pause. Do our own
words indict us as damagingly?

    The priest accepts the words as "a timely promise" (81): Oedipus has
pledged himself.

    OEDIPUS.   O Lord Apollo!
May his news be fair as his face is radiant!
    PRIEST. It could not be otherwise: he is crowned with bay,
The chaplet is thick with berries.
    OEDIPUS.   We shall soon know;   85
He is near enough to hear us now.
    (*Enter* CREON.)   O Prince:
Brother: son of Menoikeus:
What answer do you bring us from the god?
    CREON. It is favorable. I can tell you, great afflictions
Will turn out well, if they are taken well.   90
    OEDIPUS. What was the oracle? These vague words
Leave me still hanging between hope and fear.

CREON. Is it your pleasure to hear me with all these
Gathered around us? I am prepared to speak,
But should we not go in?
    OEDIPUS.   Let them all hear it.   *95*
It is for them I suffer, more than for myself.
    CREON. Then I will tell you what I heard at Delphi.
In plain words
The god commands us to expel from the land of Thebes
An old defilement that it seems we shelter.   *100*
It is a deathly thing, beyond expiation.
We must not let it feed upon us longer.
    OEDIPUS. What defilement? How shall we rid ourselves of it?
    CREON. By exile or death, blood for blood. It was
Murder that brought the plague-wind on the city.   *105*
    OEDIPUS. Murder of whom? Surely the god has named him?
    CREON. My lord: long ago Laïos was our king,
Before you came to govern us.
    OEDIPUS.   I know;
I learned of him from others; I never saw him.
    CREON. He was murdered; and Apollo commands us now   *110*
To take revenge upon whoever killed him.
    OEDIPUS. Upon whom? Where are they? Where shall we find a clue
To solve that crime, after so many years?
    CREON. Here in this land, he said.
                    If we make enquiry,
We may touch things that otherwise escape us.   *115*
    OEDIPUS. Tell me: Was Laïos murdered in his house,
Or in the fields, or in some foreign country?
    CREON. He said he planned to make a pilgrimage.
He did not come home again.
    OEDIPUS.   And was there no one,
No witness, no companion, to tell what happened?   *120*
    CREON. They were all killed but one, and he got away
So frightened that he could remember one thing only.
    OEDIPUS. What was that one thing? One may be the key
To everything, if we resolve to use it.
    CREON. He said that a band of highwaymen attacked them,   *125*
Outnumbered them, and overwhelmed the King.
    OEDIPUS. Strange, that a highwayman should be so daring—
Unless some faction here bribed him to do it.
    CREON. We thought of that. But after Laïos' death
New troubles arose and we had no avenger.   *130*

OEDIPUS. What troubles could prevent your hunting down the killers?
    CREON. The riddling Sphinx's song
Made us deaf to all mysteries but her own.
    OEDIPUS. Then once more I must bring what is dark to light.
It is most fitting that Apollo shows,   *135*
As you do, this compunction for the dead.
You shall see how I stand by you, as I should,
To avenge the city and the city's god,
And not as though it were for some distant friend,
But for my own sake, to be rid of evil.   *140*
Whoever killed King Laïos might—who knows?—
Decide at any moment to kill me as well.
By avenging the murdered king I protect myself.

Come, then, my children: leave the altar steps,
Lift up your olive boughs!
                One of you go   *145*
And summon the people of Kadmos to gather here.
I will do all that I can; you may tell them that.   (*Exit a* PAGE.)
So, with the help of God,
We shall be saved—or else indeed we are lost.
    PRIEST. Let us rise, children. It was for this we came,   *150*
And now the King has promised it himself.
Phoibos has sent us an oracle; may he descend
Himself to save us and drive out the plague.
  (*Exeunt* OEDIPUS *and* CREON *into the palace by the central door. The* PRIEST *and the* SUPPLIANTS *disperse R and L. After a short pause the* CHORUS *enters the orchestra.*)

Unity of time is as artful here as it will be at other points in the play. Creon's arrival might be suspiciously coincidental and contrived had Oedipus not revealed (71–75) that he had earlier dispatched Creon—an indication of his sense of obligation.

Creon is something of a politician; he would reveal the oracle to Oedipus in private, allowing the king to think on the matter before revealing his plans to the populace. Oedipus, on the other hand, would have the people know straightaway. His assertion that he suffers for them more than for himself is true *at this moment,* but irony is piling on irony: they suffer for him because he has not self-knowledge enough to suffer for himself.

Oedipus is truthful to himself and others when (109) he asserts that he never saw Laïos. *You,* of course, recognize his innocence in the untruth. Lines 119–143 reveal several things about Oedipus. On assuming the throne of Thebes, he should have cleared up the matter of Laïos' murder as the first order of business. That he did not testifies to his personal ambitions. Revelation at that time might have jeopardized his position. Nor in all of the intervening years has he pursued such an investigation. He has been content to "let sleeping dogs lie." Now he begins to wonder if internal plotters might not dispatch him at the instigation of the faction which hired the robbers (128). Aware that he protects himself in avenging Laïos, Oedipus utters two ironic truths as he vows to "bring what is dark to light" and "protect myself." The scene *foreshadows* (hints in advance) the king's accusation of Creon. Suspicion lies in this confrontation and will grow stronger, but Oedipus certainly knows that Creon, as Iocastê's brother, would be next in line if she did not remarry. Irony overlays line 149 as you realize that, in saving the city, Oedipus must destroy himself and lift Creon to the eminence Oedipus here begins to suspect Creon of seeking.

The Prologue has revealed the dramatic story that will now unfold. The Chorus was notably absent, for the action of the play begins with the entry of that musical body which has not heard the Prologue. It will enter in the *Párodos* (or processional entry) and, with stylized dance steps, take its place in the orchestra, that circle extending into and surrounded by the audience. From that geographical point, the Chorus is both within and without the dramatic action. Serving as a group of Theban elders, it is a part of the action, providing a stable group of "friends and neighbors" as well as offering a cross-section of the populace to give advice and consent to its king. Standing between you the reader (or audience) and the actors, it is both in the audience and in the play. It is as if the most sensitive readers (viewers) had been chosen to weld the audience to the action, serving as a spokesman for *you.* You are, then, a member of the Chorus, if not the *choragos* (the leader of the chorus who speaks for the group in the dialog and is, therefore, not considered one of the three actors allowed on stage). In addition to the *choragos,* the Chorus consists of two antiphonal groups of seven each who will sing the *Odes* (poems expressing wonder, passion, or admiration—usually in honor of gods or the tragic hero). Introducing each of the five sections of the play, the Odes are divided into *Strophes* (the call of seven of the Chorus members as they create a dance pattern) and *Antistrophes* (the response by the other seven members as they repeat the dance pattern). The first Ode sets the tone of the whole play and provides the emotional atmosphere as the dramatic winds begin to rise.

PÁRODOS

CHORUS. What is the god singing in his profound   (STROPHE 1.)
Delphi of gold and shadow?   *155*
What oracle for Thebes, the sunwhipped city?

Fear unjoints me, the roots of my heart tremble.
Now I remember, O Healer, your power, and wonder:
Will you send doom like a sudden cloud, or weave it
Like nightfall of the past?   *160*

Ah no: be merciful, issue of holy sound:
Dearest to our expectancy: be tender!

This Párodos Ode is addressed first to Zeus, the oracular god who speaks in riddles ("gold and shadow") at Delphi. The people plead for good tidings rather than ill in the first Strophe.

Let me pray to Athenê, the immortal daughter of Zeus,   (ANTISTROPHE 1.)
And to Artemis her sister
Who keeps her famous throne in the market ring,   *165*
And to Apollo, bowman at the far butts of heaven—

O gods, descend! Like three streams leap against
The fires of our grief, the fires of darkness;
Be swift to bring us rest!

As in the old time from the brilliant house   *170*
Of air you stepped to save us, come again!

The first Antistrophe invokes the three patron gods of Thebes: Athenê, Artemis, and Apollo. Children of Zeus, theirs is a mighty protection that has been given to the city in other cases.

Now our afflictions have no end,   (STROPHE 2.)
Now all our stricken host lies down
And no man fights off death with his mind;

The noble plowland bears no grain,   *175*
And groaning mothers can not bear—

See, how our lives like birds take wing,
Like sparks that fly when a fire soars,
To the shore of the god of evening.

The plague burns on, it is pitiless,   *180*   (ANTISTROPHE 2.)
Though pallid children laden with death
Lie unwept in the stony ways,

And old gray women by every path
Flock to the strand about the altars

There to strike their breasts and cry   *185*
Worship of Zeus in wailing prayers:
Be kind, God's golden child!

    Strophe 2 and Antistrophe 2 are addressed to Phoibos Apollo (the
sun god, healer of illness and disease), pleading for his medicinal inter-
cession.

There are no swords in this attack by fire,   (STROPHE 3.)
No shields, but we are ringed with cries.

Send the besieger plunging from our homes   *190*
Into the vast sea-room of the Atlantic
Or into the waves that foam eastward of Thrace—

For the day ravages what the night spares—

Destroy our enemy, lord of the thunder!
Let him be riven by lightning from heaven!   *195*

    Strophe 3 again turns its appeal to Zeus, the mightiest of the gods.
He, with thunder and lightning, can drive dark plague from the land,
sending it out to sea where it will do no harm.

Phoibos Apollo, stretch the sun's bowstring,   (ANTISTROPHE 3.)
That golden cord, until it sing for us,
Flashing arrows in heaven!
                        Artemis, Huntress,
Race with flaring lights upon our mountains!

O scarlet god, O golden-banded brow,   *200*
O Theban Bacchos in a storm of Maenads,

(*Enter* OEDIPUS, CHORUS.)
Whirl upon Death, that all the Undying hate!
Come with blinding cressets, come in joy!

Antistrophe 3 implores the sun (Apollo), the moon (Artemis), and alcohol (Bacchos, another name for Dionysus, god of wine) to bring joy again into now-joyless Thebes.

Visualize the dance patterns as you read these stately and respectful lines. Remember: a dance pattern is traced in the Strophe by seven of the Chorus members; the same pattern is retraced in the Antistrophe by the second group. Strophe 2 creates a second pattern and so on.

As the first *Episode* (here modernized to the word *Scene*) follows the Párodos, Oedipus comes onstage through the large central doors of the palace.

SCENE I

OEDIPUS. Is this your prayer? It may be answered. Come,
Listen to me, act as the crisis demands,   *205*
And you shall have relief from all these evils.

Until now I was a stranger to this tale,
As I had been a stranger to the crime.
Could I track down the murderer without a clue?
But now, friends,   *210*
As one who became a citizen after the murder,
I make this proclamation to all Thebans:
If any man knows by whose hand Laïos, son of Labdakos,
Met his death, I direct that man to tell me everything,
No matter what he fears for having so long withheld it.   *215*
Let it stand as promised that no further trouble
Will come to him, but he may leave the land in safety.

Moreover: If anyone knows the murderer to be foreign,
Let him not keep silent: he shall have his reward from me.
However, if he does conceal it; if any man   *220*
Fearing for his friend or for himself disobeys this edict,
Hear what I propose to do:

I solemnly forbid the people of this country,
Where power and throne are mine, ever to receive that man
Or speak to him, no matter who he is, or let him   *225*

Join in sacrifice, lustration, or in prayer.
I decree that he be driven from every house,
Being, as he is, corruption itself to us: the Delphic
Voice of Zeus has pronounced this revelation.
Thus I associate myself with the oracle   230
And take the side of the murdered king.

As for the criminal, I pray to God—
Whether it be a lurking thief, or one of a number—
I pray that that man's life be consumed in evil and wretchedness.
And as for me, this curse applies no less   235
If it should turn out that the culprit is my guest here,
Sharing my hearth.
                        You have heard the penalty.
I lay it on you now to attend to this
For my sake, for Apollo's, for the sick
Sterile city that heaven has abandoned.   240
Suppose the oracle had given you no command:
Should this defilement go uncleansed for ever?
You should have found the murderer: your king,
A noble king, had been destroyed!
                        Now I,
Having the power that he held before me,   245
Having his bed, begetting children there
Upon his wife, as he would have, had he lived—
Their son would have been my children's brother,
If Laïos had had luck in fatherhood!
(But surely ill luck rushed upon his reign)—   250
I say I take the son's part, just as though
I were his son, to press the fight for him
And see it won! I'll find the hand that brought
Death to Labdakos' and Polydoros' child,
Heir of Kadmos' and Agenor's line.   255
And as for those who fail me,
May the gods deny them the fruit of the earth,
Fruit of the womb, and may they rot utterly!
Let them be wretched as we are wretched, and worse!

For you, for loyal Thebans, and for all   260
Who find my actions right, I pray the favor
Of justice, and of all the immortal gods.

In his opening speech from the porch of the palace, Oedipus obliquely suggests his belief in a philosophy that has allowed Man to progress when he follows it, caused him to stagnate when he doesn't: God helps him who helps himself. Prayers alone are insufficient; action alone brings about results. That Oedipus himself has procrastinated for many years (his sons by Iocastê are grown) is dismissed—even glossed over (207–211). The proclamation comes about twenty years late. *Hubris* (pride) is an integral part of Oedipus' nature, but is it a flaw? If so, *every* man is flawed, for it is pride that forces reason—and reason lifts man above the other animals of Earth. Oedipus may, admittedly, possess an excess of *hubris,* but that excess makes some men leaders and kings. Thrones inherited by men lacking *hubris* are rickety furniture indeed. Ambition may cause man to rein in hard on his strong pride. Oedipus here dismisses pride, merely passing over those long years as if they were a few seconds. Had he, on marrying his queen, begun to right all the wrongs of Thebes, much that has happened could have been so easily avoided. When pride collides with ambition, when one accompanies the other—now there's a flaw: the inability to master a dominant trait can lead to serving two masters. So here begins the exposure of that tragic flaw in Oedipus that leads to doom.

Ambition overcame the pride Oedipus felt as early king. Establishing his dynasty, repairing his immediate throne, he let the dead past bury its dead—which now returns to haunt him. As long as Laïos' death did not affect the city, it posed no threat to Oedipus. The plague, then, came to precipitate the present king to action. Had it been visited on Thebes alone, it would have come a generation earlier. The crisis is the same to Thebes if it be now or in the past. The intervening twenty years have made it Oedipus' crisis. He acts when action seems to serve his own vaulting ambition. If it does not, he does not act. Therein is Oedipus' flaw.

Now moved to act, he reveals the intellectual power that makes him a good ruler. In lines 212–276, a masterful politician speaks. Informer or confessor may speak out. The informer will be rewarded; the murderer (whether informed against or self-confessed) will be banished rather than slain. The Delphic oracle allowed such a choice; Oedipus uses the choice well. However, if a potential informer or the murderer still conceals his knowledge, Oedipus will call down a violent oath. Suspicion grows within his thoughts as he refers again to treachery (233). With the dramatic flair of a clever politician, he also calls the curse down on himself (an act he has no present reason to fear)—for Creon may be guilty of conspiracy. Creon's exile might inflame the State unless the way is surely paved. And here, the paving stones are laid—and mortared in with irony.

Deflecting guilt, bold Oedipus seeks out the patriots (237–244) and pledges them: "For my sake" (he is Thebes personified as well as a loved ruler), "for Apollo's" (religion too must be observed but it is patriotic too—Apollo protects the city), and "for the sick/Sterile city" (a direct appeal). It is a rousing speech. But passionate speeches are forgot when men are abstractly implored. Oedipus then lays the blame right at the door of every Theban citizen: "You should have found the murderer: your king,/A noble king, had been destroyed!" He fails to say that the responsibility became his own the day he assumed the dead king's throne. And now, since the citizens have failed to meet the duty that they surely own, Oedipus will, outsider though he is, again fight battles for them. Before they can recover from the heavy guilt he has laid on them, however, he plays upon their emotions and assumes "the son's part." And then he binds them to *his* cause, the holy crusade he creates: "For you, for *loyal* Thebans, and for all/*Who find my actions right,* I pray the favor/Of justice, and of all the immortal gods." Remember, Oedipus *is* incarnate Thebes; so to be disloyal to him is to be disloyal to the city. For those who are *not* loyal Thebans the implication is: May you *not* find the favor of justice; may you not find the favor of the immortal gods. Implicit curse? Indeed it is. Directed to a frightened mob aroused to passion by a great speech, it works a present magic.

CHORUS. Since I am under oath, my lord, I swear
I did not do the murder, I can not name
The murderer. Might not the oracle   265
That has ordained the search tell where to find him?
   OEDIPUS. An honest question. But no man in the world
Can make the gods do more than the gods will.
   CHORUS. There is one last expedient—
   OEDIPUS.   Tell me what it is.
Though it seem slight, you must not hold it back.   270
   CHORUS. A lord clairvoyant to the lord Apollo,
As we all know, is the skilled Teiresias.
One might learn much about this from him, Oedipus.
   OEDIPUS. I am not wasting time:
Creon spoke of this, and I have sent for him—   275
Twice, in fact; it is strange that he is not here.
   CHORUS. The other matter—that old report—seems useless.
   OEDIPUS. Tell me. I am interested in all reports.
   CHORUS. The King was said to have been killed by highwaymen.
   OEDIPUS. I know. But we have no witnesses to that.   280

CHORUS. If the killer can feel a particle of dread,
Your curse will bring him out of hiding!
    OEDIPUS.   No.
The man who dared that act will fear no curse.

The *choragos* speaks as the voice of Theban citizens *en masse:* none can name the murderer, and, since none can, does this not mean the gods must name him for them? Oedipus states an obvious truth: man can't coerce his gods. But is it a mere asserted truth or a veiled implication that, once again, Oedipus feels that a man must do for himself, the gods being either uninterested or impotent? However, once moved to action, Oedipus has, in addition to sending Creon to Delphi, twice requested the presence of the blind prophet Teiresias who is reputed, lacking physical vision, to have psychic vision—in short, to be able to see that to which most men are blind because they rely too heavily on their eyes, too little on their spirit or intellect.

The irony of this exchange is almost too obvious to warrant comment. Seeing only with his eyes (and they are dimmed by pride of intellect and ambition), Oedipus pronounces his own doom with a chilling curse. If that curse is even stronger because he does already suspect Creon, a member of his own household, of duplicity, the irony is even more intense. Ignorance of fate alone creates a rich overlay of irony; deliberate formulation of a plan to exile Creon adds an even greater depth to the already rich layer of irony. The closing statement (283–284) becomes almost cloying as Oedipus (who *did* dare "that act") must bear the full force of the curse when the time comes.

    (*Enter the blind seer* TEIRESIAS, *led by a* PAGE.)
    CHORUS. But there is one man who may detect the criminal.
This is Teiresias, this is the holy prophet   *285*
In whom, alone of all men, truth was born.
    OEDIPUS. Teiresias: seer: student of mysteries,
Of all that's taught and all that no man tells,
Secrets of Heaven and secrets of the earth:
Blind though you are, you know the city lies   *290*
Sick with plague; and from this plague, my lord,
We find that you alone can guard or save us.

Possibly you did not hear the messengers?
Apollo, when we sent to him,
Sent us back word that this great pestilence   *295*

Would lift, but only if we established clearly
The identity of those who murdered Laïos.
They must be killed or exiled.
                              Can you use
Birdflight or any art of divination
To purify yourself, and Thebes, and me   *300*
From this contagion? We are in your hands.
There is no fairer duty
Than that of helping others in distress.

When Teiresias enters, you should visualize him: very old, feeble in body but not in mind. A young boy, sharply contrasting physically, leads him. The boy is his eyes, but youth and age have much in common: they see things as they are, untinged by personal ambition. The Chorus again speaks for the people: they will believe whatever Teiresias says, for they believe he was born knowing truth—a rare gift of the gods to some few mortals. Oedipus receives Teiresias kindly, asking the favor of him by reminding him of the Greek concept of duty. Because Teiresias is a seer, *his* first duty is to truth; as a receptacle of that truth, his first duty is then to purification of Self. Since he is a Theban by birth and therefore owes the city his allegiance, as long as it is defiled, he, as a Theban, is also defiled. If he is so defiled, he is defiled as a receptacle of truth. Again Oedipus reveals the clever workings of his mind—the cleverness that serves his ambition well. Still, the city observes it all in the persons of the Chorus; so Oedipus tempers his cleverness by appealing to the humanitarian instincts of the aged prophet.

TEIRESIAS. How dreadful knowledge of the truth can be
When there's no help in truth! I knew this well,   *305*
But did not act on it: else I should not have come.

Teiresias is, indeed, humanitarian. Knowing that "the truth" can bring shame to Thebes through its king, he must decide which is better for his native state: plague that will continue until Oedipus' natural death removes the cause, or eternal shame to the noble house of Thebes which sprang from Poseidon and progressed through the generations of Agenor (King of Tyre): his son Kadmos who brought the first letters to Greece and established Thebes; his son Polydoros; his son Labdakos; his son Laïos; his son Oedipus; and his sons Etiocles and Polyneices. Greatness such as is represented in that line should not be sacrificed on the altars of patricide and incest. Teiresias may feel that Thebes could well afford to bear the plague before such a ruin is pronounced by him. This decision prompts his agonized statement in lines 304 and 305. Truth should, at times, remain concealed if greater harm lies in its revelation. And that statement is its own greatest truth—a wisdom that can be borne only by such men as Teiresias. His face, his body, his feeble hands mirror his agitation as he speaks. The young boy stands wordless beside him, but he is a part of the action, reacting to what he hears—as does the Chorus.

OEDIPUS. What is troubling you? Why are your eyes so cold?

TEIRESIAS. Let me go home. Bear your own fate, and I'll
Bear mine. It is better so: trust what I say.

OEDIPUS. What you say is ungracious and unhelpful   *310*
To your native country. Do not refuse to speak.

TEIRESIAS. When it comes to speech, your own is neither temperate
Nor opportune. I wish to be more prudent.

OEDIPUS. In God's name, we all beg you—

TEIRESIAS.   You are all ignorant.
No; I will never tell you what I know.   *315*
Now it is my misery; then, it would be yours.

OEDIPUS. What! You do know something, and will not tell us?
You would betray us all and wreck the State?

TEIRESIAS. I do not intend to torture myself, or you.
Why persist in asking? You will not persuade me.   *320*

OEDIPUS. What a wicked old man you are! You'd try a stone's
Patience! Out with it! Have you no feeling at all?

TEIRESIAS. You call me unfeeling. If you could only see
The nature of your own feelings . . .

OEDIPUS.   Why,
Who would not feel as I do? Who could endure   *325*
Your arrogance toward the city?

TEIRESIAS.   What does it matter!
Whether I speak or not, it is bound to come.

OEDIPUS. Then, if "it" is bound to come, you are bound to tell me.

TEIRESIAS. No, I will not go on. Rage as you please.

OEDIPUS. Rage? Why not!
                           And I'll tell you what I think: *330*
You planned it, you had it done, you all but
Killed him with your own hands: if you had eyes,
I'd say the crime was yours, and yours alone.

TEIRESIAS. So? I charge you, then,
Abide by the proclamation you have made: *335*
From this day forth

Never speak again to these men or to me;
You yourself are the pollution of this country.

    OEDIPUS. You dare say that! Can you possibly think you have
Some way of going free, after such insolence?   *340*

    TEIRESIAS. I have gone free. It is the truth sustains me.

    OEDIPUS. Who taught you shamelessness? It was not your craft.

    TEIRESIAS. You did. You made me speak. I did not want to.

    OEDIPUS. Speak what? Let me hear it again more clearly.

    TEIRESIAS. Was it not clear before? Are you tempting me?   *345*

    OEDIPUS. I did not understand it. Say it again.

    TEIRESIAS. I say that you are the murderer whom you seek.

    OEDIPUS. Now twice you have spat out infamy. You'll pay for it!

    TEIRESIAS. Would you care for more? Do you wish to be really angry?

    OEDIPUS. Say what you will. Whatever you say is worthless.   *350*

    TEIRESIAS. I say that you live in hideous love with her
Who is nearest you in blood. You are blind to the evil.

    OEDIPUS. It seems you can go on mouthing like this for ever.

    TEIRESIAS. I can, if there is power in truth.

    OEDIPUS.   There is:
But not for you, not for you,   *355*
You sightless, witless, senseless, mad old man!

    TEIRESIAS. You are the madman. There is no one here
Who will not curse you soon, as you curse me.

    OEDIPUS. You child of endless night! You can not hurt me
Or any other man who sees the sun.   *360*

    TEIRESIAS. True: it is not from me your fate will come.
That lies within Apollo's competence,
As it is his concern.

Unable to comprehend truth himself, Oedipus persists, calling Teiresias unfriendly to his native State—an ugly accusation for a Greek. A less wise Theban than Teiresias would take immediate offense; he tempers anger and requests more moderate speech of Oedipus. But Oedipus will not be moderate. Pride and ambition conspire against him. Is he not Thebes? Thebes he'll remain! He accuses the seer of betrayal and subversion. Still Teiresias contains himself, knowing that the truth will hurt them all. Oedipus' rage is great. He accuses the seer of arrogance toward Thebes (326) for he, Oedipus, *is* Thebes. Rage blinds Oedipus now. He accuses Teiresias of being the planner of the interests that murdered Laïos. Though he has not yet said so, he is building a case against Creon—a case that began to form in the Prologue.

No Greek could stand silent against the charge of betraying his city. Again, remember: the king is the city personified. Love of city supplanted all other loves for the classic Greek. In anger Teiresias speaks the guilt of Oedipus. Stunned, Oedipus goads Teiresias to repeat the charge, and, as the seer's anger waxes, he adds the veiled charge of incest, commenting on Oedipus' spiritual blindness just as Oedipus had commented on Teiresias' physical blindness. And that comment leads Oedipus to call the seer blind of mind (356). The irony of lines 359–360 lies in the fact that Teiresias' gift of "sight" comes from Apollo, the god of the sun—an irony Oedipus is cruelly conscious of, his play on words almost an affront to Apollo himself.

Teiresias recognizes the jibe and turns the two-edged pun against its originator: Apollo is the "far-darter," the avenging god. He will avenge the affront to his prophet as he punishes Oedipus for his harsher crimes in due course.

OEDIPUS.   Tell me:
Are you speaking for Creon, or for yourself?
    TEIRESIAS. Creon is no threat. You weave your own doom.   *365*
    OEDIPUS. Wealth, power, craft of statesmanship!
Kingly position, everywhere admired!
What savage envy is stored up against these,
If Creon, whom I trusted, Creon my friend,
For this great office which the city once   *370*
Put in my hands unsought—if for this power
Creon desires in secret to destroy me!
He has bought this decrepit fortune-teller, this
Collector of dirty pennies, this prophet fraud—
Why, he is no more clairvoyant than I am!
                                Tell us: *375*
Has your mystic mummery ever approached the truth?
When that hellcat the Sphinx was performing here,
What help were you to these people?
Her magic was not for the first man who came along:
It demanded a real exorcist. Your birds—   *380*
What good were they? or the gods, for the matter of that?
But I came by,
Oedipus, the simple man, who knows nothing—
I thought it out for myself, no birds helped me!
And this is the man you think you can destroy,   *385*
That you may be close to Creon when he's king!

Well, you and your friend Creon, it seems to me,
Will suffer most. If you were not an old man,
You would have paid already for your plot.

    CHORUS. We can not see that his words or yours   *390*
Have been spoken except in anger, Oedipus,
And of anger we have no need. How can God's will
Be accomplished best? That is what most concerns us.

And now Oedipus speaks the thoughts that have been growing in
his mind since first the Prologue hinted them: Creon has perpetrated
this fraudulent confrontation to conceal his own treachery as the plotter
of Laïos' murder. This intemperate accusation builds into greater
intemperance: Teiresias is a fraud; his divinations are a fraud; his god's
a fraud. As proof, Oedipus declares that neither Teiresias nor the god
could outwit the Sphinx. *Hubris* rises to its most wicked height here.
Oedipus now brags he was more clever than the gods themselves!

    Such impious speech moves the *choragos* to interfere. Serving his capacity
of advising rather than consenting, he seeks to soothe the irate king with
a reminder of the purpose of this meeting.

    TEIRESIAS. You are a king. But where argument's concerned
I am your man, as much a king as you.   *395*
I am not your servant, but Apollo's.
I have no need of Creon to speak for me.

Listen to me. You mock my blindness, do you?
But I say that you, with both your eyes, are blind:
You can not see the wretchedness of your life,   *400*
Nor in whose house you live, no, nor with whom.
Who are your father and mother? Can you tell me?
You do not even know the blind wrongs
That you have done them, on earth and in the world below.
But the double lash of your parents' curse will whip you   *405*
Out of this land some day, with only night
Upon your precious eyes.
Your cries then—where will they not be heard?
What fastness of Kithairon will not echo them?
And that bridal-descant of yours—you'll know it then,   *410*
The song they sang when you came here to Thebes
And found your misguided berthing.
All this, and more, that you can not guess at now,
Will bring you to yourself among your children.

Be angry, then. Curse Creon. Curse my words.   *415*
I tell you, no man that walks upon the earth
Shall be rooted out more horribly than you.

Teiresias' anger will not be soothed, however. He avers he is the equal
of the king. As Apollo's servant, Teiresias needs no mortal to intercede
for him (397). And, to prove his claim, the prophet foretells that moment
when, as physically sightless as himself, Oedipus shall leave Thebes to
wander Kithairon's woods—those mountain fastnesses where rage the
violent Furies, avenging blood let by a family member. Pursued by those
avenging spirits, Oedipus will be the most heavily punished man of all
who live.

OEDIPUS. Am I to bear this from him?—Damnation
Take you! Out of this place! Out of my sight!
    TEIRESIAS. I would not have come at all if you had not asked me.   *420*
    OEDIPUS. Could I have told that you'd talk nonsense, that
You'd come here to make a fool of yourself, and of me?
    TEIRESIAS. A fool? Your parents thought me sane enough.
    OEDIPUS. My parents again!—Wait: who were my parents?
    TEIRESIAS. This day will give you a father, and break your heart.   *425*
    OEDIPUS. Your infantile riddles! Your damned abracadabra!
    TEIRESIAS. You were a great man once at solving riddles.
    OEDIPUS. Mock me with that if you like; you will find it true.
    TEIRESIAS. It was true enough. It brought about your ruin.
    OEDIPUS. But if it saved this town?
    TEIRESIAS (*to the* PAGE).   Boy, give me your hand.   *430*
    OEDIPUS. Yes, boy; lead him away.
                    —While you are here
We can do nothing. Go; leave us in peace.
    TEIRESIAS. I will go when I have said what I have to say.
How can you hurt me? And I tell you again:
The man you have been looking for all this time,   *435*
The damned man, the murderer of Laïos,
That man is in Thebes. To your mind he is foreign-born,
But it will soon be shown that he is a Theban,
A revelation that will fail to please.
                  A blind man,
Who has his eyes now; a penniless man, who is rich now;   *440*
And he will go tapping the strange earth with his staff.
To the children with whom he lives now he will be
Brother and father—the very same; to her

Who bore him, son and husband—the very same
Who came to his father's bed, wet with his father's blood.   *445*

Enough. Go think that over.
If later you find error in what I have said,
You may say that I have no skill in prophecy.

> (*Exit* TEIRESIAS, *led by his* PAGE. OEDIPUS *goes into the palace.*)

Again Oedipus' unleashed tongue goads the blind seer to angry insinuation (423). Oedipus' clever ability to solve riddles is impuned, and Teiresias virtually tells Oedipus the answer to this latest puzzle. Blinded to reason by his wrath, however, Oedipus allows the prophet to be led away and then withdraws into the palace, enraged but shaken by the dark words of the old prophet. Too, he has, in anger, assailed the gods, and man denies the power of deity at his own risk, for centuries of training lie behind him. No matter how right he may consider his disbelief, he is without means to prove the nonexistence or impotency of the gods. He hurls his challenges with inward misgivings, regardless of his seeming assurance and outward calm.

ODE I

CHORUS. The Delphic stone of prophecies   (STROPHE 1.)
Remembers ancient regicide   *450*
And a still bloody hand.
That killer's hour of flight has come.
He must be stronger than riderless
Coursers of untiring wind,
For the son of Zeus armed with his father's thunder   *455*
Leaps in lightning after him;
And the Furies follow him, the sad Furies.

The Chorus now reveals the confusion of the people. Torn between their regard for Oedipus (the city) and their respect for Teiresias (the gods), they consider the angry dispute they have just witnessed—a dispute more knowledgeable politicians would have conducted in private. Again, however, Oedipus has insisted on having no secrets from the people. His honesty (how ironic the word is!) continues to create problems that could so easily be avoided if, as other statesmen have learned, the people were allowed access to final results only rather than made privy to the course of the conduct of state business.

Tracing a pattern symbolizing their confusion, their torn allegiances, the seven members who chant Strophe 1 in the first Ode (called a *Stasimon* in some translations) express their belief in the avenging power of the gods and the Furies—a statement indicating their faith that right will triumph, for those dread Furies, no matter how physically real, represent the conscience of man. Relentless, they cannot be escaped. Wherever the guilty one goes, they follow, for they may reside on the slopes of Kithairon but they also dwell in the dark caves of the human mind.

Holy Parnassos' peak of snow	(ANTISTROPHE 1.)
Flashes and blinds that secret man,	
That all shall hunt him down:	460
Though he may roam the forest shade	
Like a bull gone wild from pasture	
To rage through glooms of stone.	
Doom comes down on him; flight will not avail him;	
For the world's heart calls him desolate,	465
And the immortal Furies follow, for ever follow.	

The second half of the antiphonal group retraces the pattern as it agrees with the Strophe singers by intensifying their observation. A blind awareness (or unstated suspicion) pervades lines 462–463. Was not the young "bull" Oedipus brought from the "wild" pastures of Kithera to "rage" now through the "glooms of stone" (the royal palace)? Within these walls, there is no escape, for the Furies are in the mind. Not a statement about Oedipus specifically, the suggestion however is strong.

But now a wilder thing is heard	(STROPHE 2.)
From the old man skilled at hearing Fate in the wingbeat of a bird.	
Bewildered as a blown bird, my soul hovers and can not find	
Foothold in this debate, or any reason or rest of mind.	470
But no man ever brought—none can bring	
Proof of strife between Thebes' royal house,	
Labdakos' line, and the son of Polybos;	
And never until now has any man brought word	
Of Laïos' dark death staining Oedipus the King.	475

Strophe 2 creates mounting tension and doubt as the first group responds. The people are divided in their loyalties. Teiresias speaks for the gods but his words are riddles to them—as meaningless as the flights of birds. Still, those flights of birds are messages from the gods to Teiresias who can read them correctly. However, prophet, priest, and seer though he may be, Teiresias is a man; and no man has brought or can bring proof that Oedipus' hands are stained with Laïos' blood. If battle lines must be drawn, the people's loyalty to Oedipus is stronger than their loyalty to the gods. Him, as the city, they love; the gods they fear. At this moment, love is stronger than fear.

Divine Zeus and Apollo hold   (ANTISTROPHE 2.)
Perfect intelligence alone of all tales ever told;
And well though this diviner works, he works in his own night;
No man can judge that rough unknown or trust in second sight,
For wisdom changes hands among the wise.   *480*
Shall I believe my great lord criminal
At a raging word that a blind old man let fall?
I saw him, when the carrion woman faced him of old,
Prove his heroic mind! These evil words are lies.

Antistrophe 2 contributes a rationalization that allows the citizens to continue to choose love over fear. Teiresias is the spokesman of the gods, but he is still a man, and man is limited by his mortal mind. Teiresias' blindness was assailed by Oedipus; that blindness does exist. With their own eyes, Thebes saw Oedipus' mind at work as he outwitted the Sphinx. Trusting that knowledge rather than their blind belief in Teiresias who has proved nothing, the people can, because they have "reasoned," state unequivocally: "These evil words are lies." Irony pervades this Ode, for is it not the same intellectual rationalization that Oedipus revealed in the Scene it concludes? That is, the gods cannot be forced to speak; Teiresias is the spokesman of the gods; Oedipus forces him (therefore the gods) to speak; therefore, Oedipus has outwitted the gods just as he did the Sphinx. And if a mortal man can so defeat the gods, their words are less believable than his. Oedipus, therefore, is truthful, and Teiresias lies. Thus, the tragic flaw (ambition served by pride) of Oedipus infects his people.

Notice, this Ode or Stasimon marks a reflective pause in the dramatic action of the play. It summarizes by suggesting to the reader (or viewer) the direction the dramatic action is taking. It tells you, in short, what you should feel at the moment.

Act I (whether called a *Scene* or an *Episode,* it is still an *act* in our terms) closes, having supplied you with all the necessary background establishing the basic conflicts, and having created the general tone of the play through *exposition.* Act II will now present the *rising action* or *complication* by magnifying the existing conflicts between major characters and by adding new complications.

SCENE II

CREON. Men of Thebes: *485*
I am told that heavy accusations
Have been brought against me by King Oedipus.

I am not the kind of man to bear this tamely.

If in these present difficulties
He holds me accountable for any harm to him   *490*
Through anything I have said or done—why, then,
I do not value life in this dishonor.
It is not as though this rumor touched upon
Some private indiscretion. The matter is grave.
The fact is that I am being called disloyal   *495*
To the State, to my fellow citizens, to my friends.

Complication of Oedipus' ordered life follows rapidly in Scene II. Creon's opening speech reveals an angry man ready to defend himself against the worst charge possible—disloyalty to the State. His anger is understandable if you remember it is this very suggestion that enraged Oedipus and made him so intemperate of speech. The two men are alike in their indignation. Creon's "I am not the kind of man to bear this tamely" is practically a restatement of Oedipus' words concerning Teiresias in Scene I: "Am I to bear this from him?" Creon's words reinforce the equation: Oedipus = Thebes. Nevertheless, outraged though he may be, Creon's bearing is dignified, his words tempered with careful selection.

CHORUS. He may have spoken in anger, not from his mind.
CREON. But did you not hear him say I was the one
Who seduced the old prophet into lying?
CHORUS. The thing was said; I do not know how seriously.   *500*
CREON. But you were watching him! Were his eyes steady?
Did he look like a man in his right mind?
CHORUS.   I do not know.
I can not judge the behavior of great men.
But here is the King himself.
(*Enter* OEDIPUS.)

The *choragos'* response reveals the timelessness of great literature. Evasive, equivocal, he refuses to commit himself (remember, he is the voice of the people) and employs ambiguity. The Chorus has praised Oedipus'

clear thinking; it has understood his anger. Now Creon comes, second
in line of succession to the throne, brother of Iocastê, the queen, brother-
in-law of the king. The citizens' respect for Creon almost matches their
respect for Oedipus. Caught between two noble men, the *choragos* can be
disloyal to one or the other—or he can be evasive. Just as you would
probably choose, so he chooses: he will equivocate. Equivocation allows
him to refrain from commitment as he assures Creon, "I can not judge
the behavior of great men" (503). And before he can be pressed further,
Oedipus' arrival rescues him. Can you not feel his relief, see him exhale
silently, gratefully?

OEDIPUS.   So you dared come back.
Why? How brazen of you to come to my house,   *505*
You murderer!
                    Do you think I do not know
That you plotted to kill me, plotted to steal my throne?
Tell me, in God's name: am I coward, a fool,
That you should dream you could accomplish this?
A fool who could not see your slippery game?   *510*
A coward, not to fight back when I saw it?
You are the fool, Creon, are you not? hoping
Without support or friends to get a throne?
Thrones may be won or bought: you could do neither.

Oedipus is still out of control of himself. Indignation colors his speech,
an ill-considered diatribe that he cannot support with proof. Reason tells
Oedipus that Creon alone stands to profit if he is dethroned. Intellectually,
Oedipus' thinking is sound. *If* he is dethroned, Creon will ascend. However, reason and intellect do not make Oedipus right in his assumption
that Creon is plotting evil against him. And his intemperate speech
makes him hopelessly wrong.

CREON. Now listen to me. You have talked; let me talk, too.   *515*
You can not judge unless you know the facts.
OEDIPUS. You speak well: there is one fact; but I find it hard
To learn from the deadliest enemy I have.
CREON. That above all I must dispute with you.
OEDIPUS. That above all I will not hear you deny.   *520*
CREON. If you think there is anything good in being stubborn
Against all reason, then I say you are wrong.
OEDIPUS. If you think a man can sin against his own kind
And not be punished for it, I say you are mad.
CREON. I agree. But tell me: what have I done to you?   *525*

OEDIPUS. You advised me to send for that wizard, did you not?

CREON. I did. I should do it again.

OEDIPUS.   Very well. Now tell me:

How long has it been since Laïos—

CREON.   What of Laïos?

OEDIPUS. Since he vanished in that onset by the road?

CREON. It was long ago, a long time.

OEDIPUS.   And this prophet,   *530*

Was he practicing here then?

CREON.   He was; and with honor, as now.

OEDIPUS. Did he speak of me at that time?

CREON.   He never did;

At least, not when I was present.

OEDIPUS.   But . . . the enquiry?

I suppose you held one?

CREON.   We did, but we learned nothing.

OEDIPUS. Why did the prophet not speak against me then?   *535*

CREON. I do not know; and I am the kind of man

Who holds his tongue when he has no facts to go on

OEDIPUS. There's one fact that you know, and you could tell it.

CREON. What fact is that? If I know it, you shall have it.

OEDIPUS. If he were not involved with you, he could not say   *540*

That it was I who murdered Laïos.

CREON. If he says that, you are the one that knows it!—

But now it is my turn to question you.

OEDIPUS. Put your questions. I am no murderer.

CREON. First, then: You married my sister?

OEDIPUS.   I married your sister.   *545*

CREON. And you rule the kingdom equally with her?

OEDIPUS. Everything that she wants she has from me.

CREON. And I am the third, equal to both of you?

OEDIPUS. That is why I call you a bad friend.

CREON. No. Reason it out, as I have done.   *550*

Think of this first: Would any sane man prefer

Power, with all a king's anxieties,

To that same power and the grace of sleep?

Certainly not I.

I have never longed for the king's power—only his rights.   *555*

Would any wise man differ from me in this?

As matters stand, I have my way in everything

With your consent, and no responsibilities.

If I were king, I should be a slave to policy.

How could I desire a scepter more   *560*

Than what is now mine—untroubled influence?
No, I have not gone mad; I need no honors,
Except those with the perquisites I have now.
I am welcome everywhere; every man salutes me,
And those who want your favor seek my ear,   *565*
Since I know how to manage what they ask.
Should I exchange this ease for that anxiety?
Besides, no sober mind is treasonable.
I hate anarchy
And never would deal with any man who likes it.   *570*

Test what I have said. Go to the priestess
At Delphi, ask if I quoted her correctly.
And as for this other thing: if I am found
Guilty of treason with Teiresias,
Then sentence me to death! You have my word   *575*
It is a sentence I should cast my vote for—
But not without evidence!
               You do wrong
When you take good men for bad, bad men for good.
A true friend thrown aside—why, life itself
Is not more precious!
              In time you will know this well: *580*
For time, and time alone, will show the just man,
Though scoundrels are discovered in a day.

Creon, on the other hand, is magnificently in control. His dignified
rebuke ("I am the kind of man/Who holds his tongue when he has no
facts to go on") is calculated irony, but Oedipus fails to hear it. Pursuing
his quarry, Oedipus becomes the pursued. Creon reaffirms his belief in
the vision of Teiresias, indirectly accusing Oedipus ("If he says that, you
are the one who knows it!") and assuming the role of intellectual reasoner.
Honesty pervades his speech, for he states undeniable truths. Nor does
he minimize his capacity for manipulation. Those who seek kingly favor
seek Creon's ear "Since I know how to manage what they ask" (566).
Does Creon not admit here he can be crafty? Ironic ambiguity closes
Creon's reasoned speech: "scoundrels are discovered in a day." The unity
of time is strictly observed in this play. From its opening line to the
last one, less than twenty-four hours transpires.

CHORUS. This is well said, and a prudent man would ponder it.
Judgments too quickly formed are dangerous.

OEDIPUS. But is he not quick in his duplicity?   585
And shall I not be quick to parry him?
Would you have me stand still, hold my peace, and let
This man win everything, through my inaction?
    CREON. And you want—what is it, then? To banish me?

Creon's bearing, quiet reproach, and unassailable reasoning may leave Oedipus unmoved, but the citizenry are swayed and, in their capacity of advising body, observe obliquely that Oedipus is exhibiting imprudence.

A successful ruler, Oedipus is quick to sense the shift of sympathy within the people. His questions to them are rhetorical, a self-defense that elicits no response from the *choragos,* whose silence is more eloquent than *any* response could be.

Creon may or may not wait for the *choragos* to answer. He may press on immediately, not allowing the *choragos* to answer, thus forcing Oedipus to stand unsupported. Stage directions have not survived—if ever they existed, which is doubtful. Greek dramatists not only wrote their plays, they also composed the music, served as the choreographer and director, and acted roles. They were versatile—as a few theatrical figures (Charlie Chaplin, Orson Welles, and Mike Nichols) are in our day. You must assess the action and decide how such lines are to be read as well as what action should accompany them.

OEDIPUS. No, not exile. It is your death I want,   590
So that all the world may see what treason means.
    CREON. You will persist, then? You will not believe me?
    OEDIPUS. How can I believe you?
    CREON.   Then you are a fool.
    OEDIPUS. To save myself?
    CREON.   In justice, think of me.
    OEDIPUS. You are evil incarnate.
    CREON.   But suppose that you are wrong?   595
    OEDIPUS. Still I must rule.
    CREON.   But not if you rule badly.
    OEDIPUS. O city, city!
    CREON.   It is my city, too!
    CHORUS. Now, my lords, be still. I see the Queen,
Iocastê, coming from her palace chambers;
And it is time she came, for the sake of you both.   600
This dreadful quarrel can be resolved through her.
    (*Enter* IOCASTÊ.)

Creon presses the issue, forcing Oedipus to greater excesses of language. When Oedipus reveals that his greatest concern lies in the potential loss of his throne (594), Creon appeals to "justice." That abstraction is the special province of Zeus; therefore, no greater appeal can be made, no higher power invoked.

Oedipus recognizes the clever ploy, his answer ("You are evil incarnate") ambiguously revealing his knowledge that he has been politically out-maneuvered and establishing blind hatred for the man who has proved his intellectual superior before the people. Still, Creon persists until Oedipus states his ambition. "Still I must rule" can mean only one thing: I shall continue to rule even if I am wrong.

Visualize the impact of such words on the Chorus. Oedipus here asserts, to their Greek ears—ears sensitive to any such suggestion—that he will be a tyrant before he will relinquish the throne. No people ever prided themselves on a working democracy as did the Athenians for whom this play was written. The facts of the story dictate the locale to be Thebes, so that the Chorus, standing as horrified spectators, is, in the dramatic action, a group of Theban citizens; standing as horrified spectators, they are, in their position as representatives of the audience outside the dramatic action, citizens of Athens. Thus, with this speech, Oedipus loses the support of his people and of the audience; they could not accede to such determination on the part of any man.

Creon challenges Oedipus with Greek logic: "But not if you rule badly." And Oedipus realizes his tactical blunder even as he loathes the flaw that led him to make the statement. "O city, city!" he cries in anguish, for he has trespassed against the most important thing in his life—in thought if not in deed.

Creon seizes the advantage and endears himself to Thebes with his passionate assertion, "It is my city, too!" In the eyes of a horrified populace, he, more than Oedipus, loves the city, but, before the populace can be forced to take sides in this contest of wills and politics, Iocastê enters from the palace. Wife to Oedipus, sister to Creon, she holds allegiance to both. Her greatest allegiance, however, is to the city, for she is its queen. The confused citizenry, divided by love of Oedipus and loyalty to Creon, welcome her arrival because, from her unique vantage point of total involvement, she alone can resolve the quarrel.

IOCASTÊ. Poor foolish men, what wicked din is this?
With Thebes sick to death, is it not shameful
That you should rake some private quarrel up?
(To OEDIPUS.) Come into the house.
       —And you, Creon, go now: *605*

Let us have no more of this tumult over nothing.
    CREON. Nothing? No, sister: what your husband plans for me
Is one of two great evils: exile or death.
    OEDIPUS. He is right.
                    Why, woman I have caught him squarely
Plotting against my life.
    CREON.   No! Let me die   *610*
Accurst if ever I have wished you harm!
    IOCASTÊ. Ah, believe it, Oedipus!
In the name of the gods, respect this oath of his
For my sake, for the sake of these people here!

Nor is Iocastê's reaction disappointing. Regardless of her personal loyalty, Thebes occupies her first thought. She berates the two men for their lack of consideration in this desperate hour in the city's life. Her voice is loud and clear so that all may hear her words. Notice the implied stage directions. You can hear her lower her voice as she, a woman, commands her husband quietly so that the Chorus may not hear. With equally soft voice, she bids her brother go home. Her arrival is timely; her advice is sound. But, with a woman's logic, she presses her luck too far: "Let us have no more of this tumult over nothing."

It is not "nothing" to Oedipus or to Creon! The tumult is over a throne and personal vindication. Each of them considers both things considerably more than "nothing." In desperate combat, these men have fought. Momentarily they join ranks to find their first and last mutuality of the play as they band together against Iocastê.

It is Creon who knows Iocastê best. Before the people, at least, she observes religious form. Creon has called down an oath on himself if he lies. The people believe that Zeus enforces the uttered oath. In firm command again, Iocastê subtly warns Oedipus that he must accept that oath because the people are listening.

                              (STROPHE 1.)
    CHORUS. Open your mind to her, my lord. Be ruled by her, I beg you!   *615*
    OEDIPUS. What would you have me do?
    CHORUS. Respect Creon's word. He has never spoken like a fool,
And now he has sworn an oath.
    OEDIPUS. You know what you ask?
    CHORUS.   I do.
    OEDIPUS.   Speak on, then.
    CHORUS. A friend so sworn should not be baited so,   *620*
In blind malice, and without final proof.

OEDIPUS. You are aware, I hope, that what you say
Means death for me, or exile at the least.

    CHORUS. No, I swear by Helios, first in Heaven!   (STROPHE 2.)
    May I die friendless and accurst,   625
The worst of deaths, if ever I meant that!
      It is the withering fields
        That hurt my sick heart:
      Must we bear all these ills,
        And now your bad blood as well?   630

Iocastê's reasoning is immediately proven sound. To indicate the emotional tensions generated by the exchange, Sophocles here inserts a *Kommos* (615–630) into the Scene. Unlike the Ode ending each Scene, the *Kommos* does not mark a break in the action; it intensifies the emotionally tense moment, lifting it to a peak and extracting the greatest dramatic possibility from it.

While the *choragos* speaks as the voice of the people, the Chorus creates the dance pattern symbolizing its plea to the king. Strophe 1 pleads for Creon. Iocastê's inclination was correct. The people respect the power of the oath; Oedipus should respect it too. He has, in their eyes, wronged Creon. This oath allows him to recall his words without loss of pride. However, Oedipus reminds the *choragos* that for him to withdraw the charge against Creon is to place the same charge on himself.

Strophe 2 reveals the anguish of the people in this unresolvable situation. Calling down a mighty oath, they assure Oedipus they did not mean to indict him. In a choral lyric (627–630), the *choragos* cries out: my heart breaks between love of my plague-ridden city and love of my strife-torn king.

OEDIPUS. Then let him go. And let me die, if I must,
Or be driven by him in shame from the land of Thebes.
It is your unhappiness, and not his talk,
That touches me.
            As for him—
Wherever he is, I will hate him as long as I live.   635
    CREON. Ugly in yielding, as you were ugly in rage!
Natures like yours chiefly torment themselves.
      OEDIPUS. Can you not go? Can you not leave me?
      CREON.   I can.
You do not know me; but the city knows me,
And in its eyes I am just, if not in yours.   640   (*Exit* CREON.)

And in his hopeless statement, Oedipus finds his greatness again. The voice of helpless Thebes decides him. Whatever the outcome, Thebes must not suffer. But (and how human is the mighty king at this point) he will hate Creon forever.

Nor is Creon charitable in victory. He tells Oedipus that he is his own worst enemy: "Natures like yours chiefly torment themselves." From this point on, these words are a prophecy if not a curse. Creon has been honest.

(ANTISTROPHE 1.)

CHORUS. Lady Iocastê, did you not ask the King to go to his chambers?

IOCASTÊ. First tell me what has happened.

CHORUS. There was suspicion without evidence; yet it rankled
As even false charges will.

IOCASTÊ. On both sides?

CHORUS.   On both.

IOCASTÊ.   But what was said?   *645*

CHORUS. Oh let it rest, let it be done with!
Have we not suffered enough?

The city does see Creon as honest and just, but, as the second *Kommos,* immediately following Creon's exit, suggests, it loves Oedipus. The just are respected for their uncompromising objectivity, but the imaginative and adventurous are loved. Oedipus proved his youthful, adventurous spirit many years before. They love him still for that. He is their symbol.

Concerned for Oedipus, the *choragos* suggests to Iocastê that Oedipus needs rest, implying that the people feel Oedipus' much-vaunted verbal wit and intellectual acumen have deserted him. Iocastê allows the impertinence, for she must know the details of the quarrel. That she does not ask Oedipus, even though he still stands there, indicates her desire for unbiased truth as well as her power as queen. Characterization is skillfully handled here as she ignores her husband, subtly re-creating some of the lost empathy between Oedipus and the *choragos.* The reader must decide for himself if she does this deliberately and why she does it at all. Does she, for instance, merely seek unbiased truth? Does she attempt to force the *choragos* to see unbiased truth? Does she attempt to regain for Oedipus some of the sympathy he has lost? By minimizing him in public, does she not cause men to resent her action, thus allying themselves with Oedipus against her? While it might be easy for you to consider Iocastê's role scarcely more than a plot device, this *Kommos* presents her as a complex character.

The *choragos* attempts to evade Iocastê's question with a generality that removes explicit blame (643–644). But she will not accept evasion. "On *both* sides?" she asks, forcing a commitment: "On both." Still unsatisfied, she asks for details, but the *choragos* equivocates. To report the argument would demand examination. Which words to recall, how to inflect them, what to report, and what to omit—these choices reveal partiality. Objectivity is almost impossible under ordinary circumstances; it is impossible when we are emotionally involved. Being so involved, the *choragos* evades in a thoroughly natural fashion: he sees *himself* as the offended one. Oedipus and Creon have subjected the *choragos* to this mental confusion; now Iocastê, the last of the ruling triumvirate, would extract the last ounce. In human selfishness, the *choragos* cries out, "Have we not suffered enough?"

> OEDIPUS. You see to what your decency has brought you: 648
> You have made difficulties where my heart saw none.

Oedipus is emotionally selfish too. Ruler he may be, but he is no wiser, no more detached at this moment than the *choragos* (the people as a whole). As he upbraids the *choragos,* he reveals knowledge of his own culpability, but, ironically, he is too emotional to realize it. If the *choragos* has been "decent" and that decency has led to this unpleasantness, "decency" forced the *choragos* to be fair to Creon. Fairness to Creon has created the problem. Had the people supported Oedipus with blind loyalty, Creon could, even now, be on his way into exile. That would have been the edict of Oedipus' "heart" (emotion), an edict that would have secured the throne. Clarence W. Mendell* translates this line: "Seest thou then thy zeal / Whither it leads?" John Gassner° translates it: "But do you see where your good purpose has now carried you in blunting my anger?" This same loyalty, zeal, or intellectual honesty (call it what you will) pervades Oedipus' conduct in all his dealings with life except for this one day. Fear of loss weakens him now and, with great dishonesty, he accuses the *choragos* of that which he himself ordinarily holds most important. Many critics have held Oedipus' tragic flaw to be his persistent seeking after truth from this point on. Close reading suggests that this morning's action reveals his flaw: a denial of his strongest character trait—honesty—as he is, briefly, more concerned with ambition than with truth. In these episodes, Oedipus suffers the tragic reversal. From this episode forward, he redeems himself as a man, though he loses a kingdom.

---

* Yale University Press, 1941.
° *A Treasury of the Theatre* (New York, 1951).

For that reason, we can experience catharsis, for nobility is greater than loss because it is purchased at greater price.

CHORUS. Oedipus, it is not once only I have told you—   (ANTISTROPHE 2.)
You must know I should count myself unwise   *651*
To the point of madness, should I now forsake you—
    You, under whose hand,
      In the storm of another time,
    Our dear land sailed out free.   *655*
      But now stand fast at the helm!

The *choragos* is emotionally sundered. Loyalty to Oedipus on the one hand is at odds with loyalty to the State on the other. Rationalization pervades the anguished response of Antistrophe 2. Because Oedipus has been the savior of the State up to this time, loyalty to both can allow the plea that he be the savior again—regardless of personal cost.

So ends the second *Kommos,* a choral intensification containing many clues to the dramatic power of this play.

IOCASTÊ. In God's name, Oedipus, inform your wife as well:
Why are you so set in this hard anger?
OEDIPUS. I will tell you, for none of these men deserves
My confidence as you do. It is Creon's work,   *660*
His treachery, his plotting against me.
    IOCASTÊ. Go on, if you can make this clear to me.
    OEDIPUS. He charges me with the murder of Laïos.
    IOCASTÊ. Has he some knowledge? Or does he speak from hearsay?
    OEDIPUS. He would not commit himself to such a charge,   *665*
But he has brought in that damnable soothsayer
To tell his story.
    IOCASTÊ.   Set your mind at rest.
If it is a question of soothsayers, I tell you
That you will find no man whose craft gives knowledge
Of the unknowable.
             Here is my proof: *670*

An oracle was reported to Laïos once
(I will not say from Phoibos himself, but from
His appointed ministers, at any rate)
That his doom would be death at the hands of his own son—
His son, born of his flesh and of mine!   *675*
Now, you remember the story: Laïos was killed
By marauding strangers where three highways meet;

But his child had not been three days in this world
Before the King had pierced the baby's ankles
And had him left to die on a lonely mountain.   680

Thus, Apollo never caused that child
To kill his father, and it was not Laïos' fate
To die at the hands of his son, as he had feared.
This is what prophets and prophecies are worth!
Have no dread of them.
                    It is God himself   685
Who can show us what he wills, in his own way.

OEDIPUS. How strange a shadowy memory crossed my mind,
Just now while you were speaking; it chilled my heart.

IOCASTÊ. What do you mean? What memory do you speak of?

OEDIPUS. If I understand you, Laïos was killed   690
At a place where three roads meet.

IOCASTÊ.   So it was said;
We have no later story.

OEDIPUS.   Where did it happen?

IOCASTÊ. Phokis, it is called: at a place where the Theban Way
Divides into the roads toward Delphi and Daulia.

OEDIPUS. When?

IOCASTÊ.   We had the news not long before you came   695
And proved the right to your succession here.

OEDIPUS. Ah, what net has God been weaving for me?

Iocastê is as confused as any Theban. Her life with Oedipus has not
prepared her for this day. Had his conduct been such as to foreshadow
this excess, it would not create the mental chaos for her that it does.
Dramatically, such confusion must exist in Iocastê's thinking, for her
response to his denunciation of Teiresias is a masterpiece of confusion.
Soothsayers are unreliable (668–670), as she can prove. Other priests
foretold the death of Laïos at the hands of his own son (674), which
caused Laïos to expose the child and avert the danger. He was killed
by the hands of others. Because he believed the oracle's ministers, he
averted violent death by his son's hands. Iocastê does not consider the
obvious basic truth: the oracle foretold murder; Laïos was murdered.
Challenging the human ministers of the god, she does not challenge
the god himself, however (685–686). She assures Oedipus that Zeus wills
and his will is done. Her reassurance stirs a dim memory in Oedipus,
a memory that flashes into revelatory brilliance as he begins to suspect
that the plan of Zeus is indeed working (697), that the oracle had indeed
spoken truth, to Creon at least.

IOCASTÊ. Oedipus! Why does this trouble you?

OEDIPUS.   Do not ask me yet.
First, tell me how Laïos looked, and tell me
How old he was.

IOCASTÊ.   He was tall, his hair just touched   *700*
With white; his form was not unlike your own.

OEDIPUS. I think that I myself may be accurst
By my own ignorant edict.

IOCASTÊ.   You speak strangely.
It makes me tremble to look at you, my King.

The irony of Iocastê's description ("his form was not unlike your own") may be lost on the two of them; you, of course, understand it. Oedipus merely sees, in memory, the man he slew that long-ago day at Phokis; however, as the scales of blindness (the blindness of ambition) are beginning to fall away, Oedipus may be unconsciously seeing even more than he realizes. Such is mere speculation, however. Iocastê trembles for Oedipus—but, as he is her son as well as her husband, this (speculatively) may well be her first stirring of knowledge also. Certainly, she understands horror in the play long before Oedipus.

OEDIPUS. I am not sure that the blind man can not see.   *705*
But I should know better if you were to tell me—

IOCASTÊ. Anything—though I dread to hear you ask it.

OEDIPUS. Was the King lightly escorted, or did he ride
With a large company, as a ruler should?

IOCASTÊ. There were five men with him in all: one was a herald;   *710*
And a single chariot, which he was driving.

OEDIPUS. Alas, that makes it plain enough!
                              But who—
Who told you how it happened?

IOCASTÊ.   A household servant,
The only one to escape.

OEDIPUS.   And is he still
A servant of ours?

IOCASTÊ.   No; for when he came back at last   *715*
And found you enthroned in the place of the dead king,
He came to me, touched my hand with his, and begged
That I would send him away to the frontier district
Where only the shepherds go—
As far away from the city as I could send him.   *720*
I granted his prayer; for although the man was a slave,
He had earned more than this favor at my hands.

The ambiguities of lines 705–706 ("I am not sure that the blind man can not see . . .") intensify the irony again because *you* know that Oedipus is more blind than Teiresias; also, Oedipus' words are broad: "the blind man" refers to Teiresias, but it is also the general noun "any blind man." To *know* is to possess knowledge; therefore, Oedipus not only can better assess Teiresias' sight from Iocastê's words, he can also be possessed of self-knowledge by them. Line 707 provides the speculative line again: "Anything—though I dread to hear you ask it." Does Iocastê merely dread the possibility of revealing Oedipus to himself as the murderer of Laïos, or does she dread the awful complete fulfillment of the prophecies—prophecies she has so recently denigrated? Line 712 affirms Oedipus' dark suspicion, and he begins that relentless pressing after the truth that he so lately criticized in the *choragos*. Iocastê's answer contains the implication that she is making certain mental connections. Were she not, she would have no reason to include line 716: "And found you enthroned in the place of the dead king." Without the line, her whole speech assumes a different shading; this line lifts the passage from mere exposition into character revelation. Were she as willing to avoid truth as she later *seems* to be, this line would not escape her lips.

> OEDIPUS. Can he be called back quickly?
> IOCASTÊ.   Easily.
> But why?
> OEDIPUS. I have taken too much upon myself
> Without enquiry; therefore I wish to consult him.   *725*

Oedipus confirms the judgment of the people (the *choragos*) in lines 724–725. He has been emotional, ambitious. In this line he redeems himself. His tragic flaw has caused his downfall, but from this point on, he recovers his nobility and begins to build the stature that will allow him to meet his fate as a man, however miserable it may be.

> IOCASTÊ. Then he shall come.
>   But am I not one also
> To whom you might confide these fears of yours?
> OEDIPUS. That is your right; it will not be denied you,
> Now least of all; for I have reached a pitch
> Of wild foreboding. Is there anyone   *730*
> To whom I should sooner speak?
>
> Polybos of Corinth is my father.
> My mother is a Dorian: Meropê.

I grew up chief among the men of Corinth
Until a strange thing happened—   735
Not worth my passion, it may be, but strange.

At a feast, a drunken man maundering in his cups
Cries out that I am not my father's son!

I contained myself that night, though I felt anger
And a sinking heart. The next day I visited   740
My father and mother, and questioned them. They stormed,
Calling it all the slanderous rant of a fool;
And this relieved me. Yet the suspicion
Remained always aching in my mind;
I knew there was talk; I could not rest;   745
And finally, saying nothing to my parents,
I went to the shrine at Delphi.

The god dismissed my question without reply;
He spoke of other things.
                          Some were clear,
Full of wretchedness, dreadful, unbearable: 750
As, that I should lie with my own mother, breed
Children from whom all men would turn their eyes;
And that I should be my father's murderer.

I heard all this, and fled. And from that day
Corinth to me was only in the stars   755
Descending in that quarter of the sky,
As I wandered farther and farther on my way
To a land where I should never see the evil
Sung by the oracle. And I came to this country
Where, so you say, King Laïos was killed.   760

I will tell you all that happened there, my lady.

There were three highways
Coming together at a place I passed;
And there a herald came towards me, and a chariot
Drawn by horses, with a man such as you describe   765
Seated in it. The groom leading the horses
Forced me off the road at his lord's command;
But as this charioteer lurched over towards me

I struck him in my rage. The old man saw me
And brought his double goad down upon my head   770
As I came abreast.

                   He was paid back, and more!
Swinging my club in this right hand I knocked him
Out of his car, and he rolled on the ground.

                              I killed him.

I killed them all.
Now if that stranger and Laïos were—kin,   775
Where is a man more miserable than I?
More hated by the gods? Citizen and alien alike
Must never shelter me or speak to me—
I must be shunned by all.

                   And I myself
Pronounced this malediction upon myself!   780

Think of it: I have touched you with these hands,
These hands that killed your husband. What defilement!

Am I all evil, then? It must be so,
Since I must flee from Thebes, yet never again
See my own countrymen, my own country,   785
For fear of joining my mother in marriage
And killing Polybos, my father.

                     Ah,
If I was created so, born to this fate,
Who could deny the savagery of God?

O holy majesty of heavenly powers!   790
May I never see that day! Never!
Rather let me vanish from the race of men
Than know the abomination destined me!

    Unstated fears lie heavily on lines 726–813 as the king and queen
approach realization again and again, always withdrawing from it with
deliberate logic. Could anyone be closer to Oedipus (730–731) than his
mother, his wife, and mother of his children, all bound up in one woman?
Doubtful parentage (738) attaches itself to possible murder (753) but
the will to disbelieve the remainder keeps the lines far apart. Oedipus
believes that he "killed them *all*" (774); he *wishes* to believe that the
shepherd who will come cannot report this murder, for no survivors exist.

And yet, does he not, in the depths of his being, fear the full truth? Lines 781–782 reveal his belief that he is the murderer of Laïos. Line 783 asks, "Am I *all* evil, *then?*" If flight can keep him from the ultimate evil (incest and patricide), as lines 784–789 suggest, is he *all* evil? Yet Oedipus brands himself as such either consciously or unconsciously. In line 793, he declares his belief in all oracles: he is *destined* to abomination. Belief is based on emotion, however; knowledge is based on intellect. Did the puzzling Sphinx not play at such games too?

CHORUS. We too, my lord, have felt dismay at this.
But there is hope: you have yet to hear the shepherd.   *795*
  OEDIPUS. Indeed, I fear no other hope is left me.
  IOCASTÊ. What do you hope from him when he comes?
  OEDIPUS.   This much:
If his account of the murder tallies with yours,
Then I am cleared.
  IOCASTÊ.   What was it that I said
Of such importance?
  OEDIPUS.   Why, "marauders," you said,   *800*
Killed the King, according to this man's story.
If he maintains that still, if there were several,
Clearly the guilt is not mine: I was alone.
But if he says one man, singlehanded, did it,
Then the evidence all points to me.   *805*
  IOCASTÊ. You may be sure that he said there were several;
And can he call back that story now? He can not.
The whole city heard it as plainly as I.
But suppose he alters some detail of it:
He can not ever show that Laïos' death   *810*
Fulfilled the oracle: for Apollo said
My child was doomed to kill him; and my child—
Poor baby!—it was my child that died first.

No. From now on, where oracles are concerned,
I would not waste a second thought on any.   *815*
  OEDIPUS. You may be right.
                    But come: let someone go
For the shepherd at once. This matter must be settled.
  IOCASTÊ. I will send for him.
I would not wish to cross you in anything,   *819*
And surely not in this. —Let us go in.   (*Exeunt into the palace.*)

Hope has been said to spring eternal in the human breast, and the *choragos* hopes, as does Oedipus, that a small technicality will prove him free of any guilt. Iocastê alone reveals lost hope; determination replaces it. If you did not read *can* (line 807) with the accent so deliberately placed, you cannot hear her determination, and the line becomes rhetoric rather than revelation. As that determination grows into knowledge, knowledge grows into self-delusion. Eventually (815), self-delusion grows into a refusal to consider. Iocastê closes her mind and, once it is firmly closed, she can acquiesce to any wish of her husband. She has decided the outcome and can return to the palace with Oedipus.

ODE II

CHORUS. Let me be reverent in the ways of right,   (STROPHE 1.)
Lowly the paths I journey on;
Let all my words and actions keep
The laws of the pure universe
From highest Heaven handed down.   *825*
For Heaven is their bright nurse,
Those generations of the realms of light;
Ah, never of mortal kind were they begot,
Nor are they slaves of memory, lost in sleep:
Their Father is greater than Time, and ages not.   *830*

The tyrant is a child of Pride   (ANTISTROPHE 1.)
Who drinks from his great sickening cup
Recklessness and vanity,
Until from his high crest headlong
He plummets to the dust of hope.   *835*
That strong man is not strong.
But let no fair ambition be denied;
May God protect the wrestler for the State
In government, in comely policy,
Who will fear God, and on His ordinance wait.   *840*

The second Ode reveals the mounting fears of the people. Tracing the first dance pattern, the Chorus offers a declaration and a prayer, indicating its collective disapproval of Oedipus' and Iocastê's conduct. Heaven and the gods decree; man obeys. The immutable laws are above and beyond mere mortals. The first Antistrophe traces, as do the symbols of the dance, the attitudes of Oedipus from the beginning of the play. When it opened, ambitious and proud Oedipus was a tyrant, willing to exile Creon to save himself. Because of that weakness, he began to learn truth which dashed him to the dust where now he clings to one weak possibility of deliverance. *If* Oedipus' ambition is for the good of the State (837), the Chorus prays for him. *If* Creon's ambition is good, the prayer is for him. Whichever man it may be, he will honor Zeus and his laws. At this moment, either Oedipus or Creon can be that "wrestler for the State."

Haughtiness and the high hand of disdain   (STROPHE 2.)
Tempt and outrage God's holy law;
And any mortal who dares hold
No immortal Power in awe
Will be caught up in a net of pain: 845
The price for which his levity is sold.
Let each man take due earnings, then,
And keep his hands from holy things,
And from blasphemy stand apart—
Else the crackling blast of heaven   850
Blows on his head, and on his desperate heart;
Though fools will honor impious men,
In their cities no tragic poet sings.

Strophe 2 states firm reservations. Those who would challenge the gods (and, by extension, their prophets) are in mortal danger. Impiety breeds disaster and, if the people pledge their allegiance to the impious, sadness will live in their city. Through the *choragos,* the people have pledged their love to Oedipus.

Shall we lose faith in Delphi's obscurities,   (ANTISTROPHE 2.)
We who have heard the world's core   855
Discredited, and the sacred wood
Of Zeus at Elis praised no more?
The deeds and the strange prophecies
Must make a pattern yet to be understood.
Zeus, if indeed you are lord of all,   860
Throned in light over night and day,
Mirror this in your endless mind:
Our masters call the oracle
Words on the wind, and the Delphic vision blind!
Their hearts no longer know Apollo,   865
And reverence for the gods has died away.

Antistrophe 2 advances distress to its final peak. Oedipus and Iocastê have denied that the gods speak through their prophets. The citizenry is torn. Their allegiance to Oedipus makes them co-doubters, and they are dismayed at their participation. But they recognize the truth of this evil reality, and the last line indicts them as well as their leaders. Obviously, Creon has doubted neither the oracle nor its priests; the people, then, are moved in their support of Oedipus simply because of his performance in the past.

SCENE III

(*Enter* IOCASTÊ.)
IOCASTÊ. Princes of Thebes, it has occurred to me
To visit the altars of the gods, bearing
These branches as a suppliant, and this incense.
Our King is not himself: his noble soul   *870*
Is overwrought with fantasies of dread,
Else he would consider
The new prophecies in the light of the old.
He will listen to any voice that speaks disaster,
And my advice goes for nothing.   (*She approaches the altar, R.*)
                    To you, then, Apollo,   *875*
Lycean lord, since you are nearest, I turn in prayer.
Receive these offerings, and grant us deliverance
From defilement. Our hearts are heavy with fear
When we see our leader distracted, as helpless sailors
Are terrified by the confusion of their helmsman.   *880*

The turning point in Oedipus' life was reached when he sent for the shepherd. Suspense alone must now cement the action if it is to hold your emotions at their present level. You will notice a marked shortening of episodes beginning with Scene III, for Sophocles knows that suspense may not be maintained indefinitely in tragedy any more than in life. Numbness supersedes suspense in both cases.

Iocastê comes onstage from the right door of the palace. Bearing offerings to the Lycean Apollo (whose province is households and family life), she comes suppliant to his altar. Her tone is almost apologetic ("it has occurred to me"), as if she has reconsidered her hasty words at the close of Scene II. Speaking to the "Princes of Thebes," she is addressing those priests whom she so recently minimized. Humble pie is no dish for such a queen as Iocastê. Instead of apologizing or recanting, she attempts dismissal of her earlier words. Oedipus is "not himself" or he would "consider / The new prophecies in the light of the old." Is it strange that Iocastê should so reverse herself? Not if you consider lines 874–875 carefully. The priests at the altars speak for the gods. Should they address hopeful words to Oedipus, he would listen. Bribery? What woman (be she queen or commoner) is not capable of *any* act to protect home and husband? Iocastê's behavior may be spiritually indefensible, but it is humanly understandable.

As she prays directly to Apollo, offering her gifts, she apologizes obliquely to Zeus whose altar is across the porch. That she would attempt to outwit the all-father of the gods with such an obvious gambit may seem strange to you, but Greeks of ancient Athens understood their anthropomorphic gods more intimately, perhaps, than you understand your more abstract concept. Even the gods could understand and forgive the dissembler if he provided an acceptable excuse. Iocastê's "grant us deliverance / From defilement" is markedly ambiguous. "Us" can be both the king and queen as well as the citizens of Thebes. The altar of the Lycean Apollo serves that ambiguity well, for he is the patron of Thebes and, in his Lycean capacity, the patron of this private household. "Defilement" then can mean everything from harboring Laïos' murderer publicly to living incestuously privately. Or it can encompass both. "Our hearts" can be the collective hearts of Thebes or it can be the royal heart of Iocastê preceded by the royal pronoun, or it can be both. Whatever her meaning, you must decide.

(*Enter* MESSENGER.)

MESSENGER. Friends, no doubt you can direct me:
Where shall I find the house of Oedipus,
Or, better still, where is the King himself?

CHORUS. It is this very place, stranger; he is inside.
This is his wife and mother of his children.   *885*

MESSENGER. I wish her happiness in a happy house,
Blest in all the fulfillment of her marriage.

IOCASTÊ. I wish as much for you: your courtesy
Deserves a like good fortune. But now, tell me:
Why have you come? What have you to say to us?   *890*

MESSENGER. Good news, my lady, for your house and your husband.

IOCASTÊ. What news? Who sent you here?

MESSENGER.   I am from Corinth.
The news I bring ought to mean joy for you,
Though it may be you will find some grief in it.

IOCASTÊ. What is it? How can it touch us in both ways?   *895*

MESSENGER. The people of Corinth, they say,
Intend to call Oedipus to be their king.

IOCASTÊ. But old Polybos—is he not reigning still?

MESSENGER. No. Death holds him in his sepulchre.

IOCASTÊ. What are you saying? Polybos is dead?   900

MESSENGER. If I am not telling the truth, may I die myself.

IOCASTÊ (*to a* MAIDSERVANT). Go in, go quickly; tell this to your master.

O riddlers of God's will, where are you now!
This was the man whom Oedipus, long ago,
Feared so, fled so, in dread of destroying him—   905
But it was another fate by which he died.

The *choragos* introduces Iocastê to the messenger with traditional form, but irony overlays that tradition because a more important tradition (the taboo of incest) has been broken. She is indeed "his wife and mother of his children," but note the conjunction *and*. It compounds *wife* and *mother* so that they are both modified by the possessive *his*. This kind of subtlety is, frankly, remarkable in a translation. The messenger's greeting to Iocastê is also traditional—as is her response. To understand irony completely, compare the multiplicity of possibilities in his words, the lack of any but accepted surface meaning in hers. Because you know nothing about his life, her words are endowed with the blandness of uninvolved response. Line 890 is no mere formality, however. Iocastê is almost abrupt in her demand that he state his business. Nor does his preamble immediately set her mind at rest. She has had much already of ambiguities and riddles; here, he offers still another. News of the death of Polybos brings no grief to Iocastê. Oedipus must know immediately. Sending the maidservant may seem merely a dramatic device to keep Iocastê on stage (and it is that, certainly), but it also serves to remind us of Iocastê's opening statement before the altar. Oedipus will listen to any damaging news; he rejects her reassurances. Now he will hear reassuring news from one he could expect to bring further disastrous news. Nor is the maidservant told to bring Oedipus; she is ordered to reveal the news.

Turning then to the priests, Iocastê insults them. So recently humble, she seems utterly inconsistent until you realize the great weight that has been lifted. If one part of an oracle is wrong, will not all parts be wrong? And she does not affront the god, only his priests. This is consistency, for has she not repeatedly separated the gods and their ministers throughout the play, suggesting corruption, if not stupidity, among the priesthood? Perhaps such an attack makes you uncomfortable, but, you should consider, it is these priests to whom the people turn for guidance and interpretation of the will of the gods. Any politically ambitious or motivated priest could do great damage to the reigning king. Intrigue has always attended power.

(*Enter* OEDIPUS, CHORUS.)

OEDIPUS. Dearest Iocastê, why have you sent for me?

IOCASTÊ. Listen to what this man says, and then tell me
What has become of the solemn prophecies.

OEDIPUS. Who is this man? What is his news for me?   *910*

IOCASTÊ. He has come from Corinth to announce your father's death!

OEDIPUS. Is it true, stranger? Tell me in your own words.

MESSENGER. I can not say it more clearly: the King is dead.

OEDIPUS. Was it by treason? Or by an attack of illness?

MESSENGER. A little thing brings old men to their rest.   *915*

OEDIPUS. It was sickness, then?

MESSENGER.   Yes, and his many years.

OEDIPUS. Ah!
Why should a man respect the Pythian hearth, or
Give heed to the birds that jangle above his head?
They prophesied that I should kill Polybos,   *920*
Kill my own father; but he is dead and buried,
And I am here—I never touched him, never,
Unless he died of grief for my departure,
And thus, in a sense, through me. No. Polybos
Has packed the oracles off with him underground.   *925*
They are empty words.

The arrival of Oedipus through the great center doors cuts short the queen's tirade. The maidservant has told him nothing, only summoned him, a natural enough disobedience. Careful reading reinforces, then, the possibility that Iocastê is amazingly aware of her husband's reactions. She does not now summarize the message; she directs Oedipus to speak with the messenger, but she adds her own "I told you so, didn't I?" (908–909). As soon as Oedipus has assured himself that Polybos died peacefully in bed and did not meet a violent end, he can echo Iocastê's sarcasm. While many critics mark 917–926 as the height of *hubris* in Oedipus, scant pride resides in the line. Relief—yes. Anguish and fear have weighed heavily on Oedipus these many years; he has absented himself from Corinth, refused to come into the presence of Polybos, made every effort to avoid the prophesied murder. Now Polybos is dead, and he died of old age. Pride in having evaded a destructive possibility may be a part of Oedipus' relief, but relief is the dominant reaction. Even that relief, however, is tempered by the intellectual reasoning that grief in long separation could have hastened Polybos' death. *Hubris* does not accompany such realizations however. Gentle guilt—yes. Pride—no.

IOCASTÊ.   Had I not told you so?
OEDIPUS. You had; it was my faint heart that betrayed me.
IOCASTÊ. From now on never think of those things again.
OEDIPUS. And yet—must I not fear my mother's bed?
IOCASTÊ. Why should anyone in this world be afraid,   *930*
Since Fate rules us and nothing can be foreseen?
A man should live only for the present day.
Have no more fear of sleeping with your mother:
How many men, in dreams, have lain with their mothers!
No reasonable man is troubled by such things.   *935*

Iocastê's "Had I not told you so?" cannot remain unstated. She too is relieved, and, with a woman's logic, she assures her husband that he can dismiss all prophecies from his mind. That she may be referring to the present problem (that Oedipus is the murderer of Laïos) does not occur to him. His belief in oracles is stronger than he cares to admit, for he does not assume that because one part is wrong both parts are annulled (929). Iocastê's response that each day should be lived for itself is an understandable philosophy—as is her statement that "Fate rules us." The Greeks believed in a power called *Moira* or *Heimarmene* (Roman *Fatum*) which ruled over gods as well as men. Roughly equivalent to "the necessary connection of things" or "necessity itself," *Moira* was not a god; it was a power greater than the god concept. Zeus himself was subject to *Moira*. The attendants of *Moira* were the Parcae (the three Fates) who measure man's mortal life. Iocastê's assurance is, then, one of the most ironic speeches in the play. Stating that the gods cannot foretell things because even they are ruled by Fate (*Moira*), she unwittingly speaks the truth of what is happening. As Fate is "the necessary connection of things," those "things" in Oedipus' life that must of necessity be connected are now in process of connection. "*Moira* moves in a mysterious way, its wonders to perform" to paraphrase William Cowper's observation. Lines 933–935 indicate the early wisdom of the Greeks—a wisdom recognized by Sigmund Freud and instrumental in his formulation of modern psychology. In modern paraphrase, the lines state, "Sleeping with one's mother is a normal fear or desire, released in dreams. Well-adjusted men do not become obsessive about it."

OEDIPUS. That is true; only—
If only my mother were not still alive!
But she is alive. I can not help my dread.
   IOCASTÊ. Yet this news of your father's death is wonderful.
   OEDIPUS. Wonderful. But I fear the living woman.   *940*

Sound psychology is not reassurance. Taboo is older than man's memory. Oedipus remains fearful. As well he might: do mothers not often lie to their children in an effort to comfort them? The child in Oedipus knows truth which Oedipus the man does not understand: "I fear the living woman." If one line can be said to signal the falling action of *Oedipus Rex,* it is this line. Between it and line 1001, Iocastê does not speak. To appreciate the full import of the lines, you must try to visualize her face, her tensing hands, her body movements as she follows the flow of questions and answers between Oedipus, the messenger, and the *choragos.* At first, she will be anxious for the messenger to speak, for what he tells can soothe Oedipus. Slowly, however, the "necessary connection of things" begins to take shape in her mind. As the full horror is revealed to her, she is a stricken woman.

To create the growing awareness in Iocastê, Sophocles employs *stichomythia* (a question-answer exchange of one line per speaker, creating a verbal fencing match wherin motives are revealed simultaneously with the expository matter). The lines are spoken rapidly, allowing the opponents in the match no time to formulate their answers.

MESSENGER. Tell me, who is this woman that you fear?
OEDIPUS. It is Meropê, man; the wife of King Polybos.
MESSENGER. Meropê? Why should you be afraid of her?
OEDIPUS. An oracle of the gods, a dreadful saying.
MESSENGER. Can you tell me about it or are you sworn to silence?   *945*
OEDIPUS. I can tell you, and I will.
Apollo said through his prophet that I was the man
Who should marry his own mother, shed his father's blood
With his own hands. And so, for all these years
I have kept clear of Corinth, and no harm has come—   *950*
Though it would have been sweet to see my parents again.
MESSENGER. And is this the fear that drove you out of Corinth?
OEDIPUS. Would you have me kill my father?
MESSENGER.   As for that
You must be reassured by the news I gave you.
OEDIPUS. If you could reassure me, I would reward you.   *955*

MESSENGER. I had that in mind, I will confess: I thought
I could count on you when you returned to Corinth.

OEDIPUS. No: I will never go near my parents again.

MESSENGER. Ah, son, you still do not know what you are doing—

OEDIPUS. What do you mean? In the name of God tell me!   *960*

MESSENGER. —If these are your reasons for not going home.

OEDIPUS. I tell you, I fear the oracle may come true.

MESSENGER. And guilt may come upon you through your parents?

OEDIPUS. That is the dread that is always in my heart.

MESSENGER. Can you not see that all your fears are groundless?   *965*

OEDIPUS. How can you say that? They are my parents, surely?

MESSENGER. Polybos was not your father.

OEDIPUS.   Not my father?

MESSENGER. No more your father than the man speaking to you.

OEDIPUS. But you are nothing to me!

MESSENGER.   Neither was he.

OEDIPUS. Then why did he call me son?

MESSENGER.   I will tell you: *970*
Long ago he had you from my hands, as a gift.

OEDIPUS. Then how could he love me so, if I was not his?

MESSENGER. He had no children, and his heart turned to you.

OEDIPUS. What of you? Did you buy me? Did you find me by chance?

MESSENGER. I came upon you in the crooked pass of Kithairon.   *975*

OEDIPUS. And what were you doing there?

MESSENGER.   Tending my flocks.

OEDIPUS. A wandering shepherd?

MESSENGER.   But your savior, son, that day.

OEDIPUS. From what did you save me?

MESSENGER.   Your ankles should tell you that.

OEDIPUS. Ah, stranger, why do you speak of that childhood pain?

MESSENGER. I cut the bonds that tied your ankles together.   *980*

OEDIPUS. I have had the mark as long as I can remember.

MESSENGER. That was why you were given the name you bear.

OEDIPUS. God! Was it my father or my mother who did it?
Tell me!

MESSENGER. I do not know. The man who gave you to me
Can tell you better than I.   *985*

OEDIPUS. It was not you that found me, but another?

MESSENGER. It was another shepherd gave you to me.

OEDIPUS. Who was he? Can you tell me who he was?

MESSENGER. I think he was said to be one of Laïos' people.

OEDIPUS. You mean the Laïos who was king here years ago?   *990*

MESSENGER. Yes; King Laïos; and the man was one of his herdsmen.

The messenger was dispatched to bring news of Polybos' death. However, ambition motivated him to anticipate being rewarded for the mission (956–957). Oedipus' unwillingness to return to Corinth while Meropê lives threatens that ambition. Seeing further advantage to himself, however, the messenger reveals his knowledge of Oedipus' arrival in Corinth as a baby. Assuring himself that Oedipus will be further indebted when he comes to Corinth, the messenger bluntly states that he saved the baby's life. Insinuatingly, he uses the familiar "son." To prove his contention, he speaks of the deformity which resulted from the pinned ankles. *Oedipus* means "swollen foot." Iocastê by this time becomes exceedingly nervous. With line 991, she pieces together the connecting links. Do not let your attention to the dialog and the speakers distract your attention from her face. She is the most dramatic figure in this action.

OEDIPUS. Is he still alive? Can I see him?

MESSENGER. These men here
Know best about such things.

OEDIPUS. Does anyone here
Know this shepherd that he is talking about?
Have you seen him in the fields, or in the town? 995
If you have, tell me. It is time things were made plain.

CHORUS. I think the man he means is that same shepherd
You have already asked to see. Iocastê perhaps
Could tell you something.

OEDIPUS. Do you know anything
About him, Lady? Is he the man we have summoned? 1000
Is that the man this shepherd means?

IOCASTÊ. Why think of him?
Forget this herdsman. Forget it all.
This talk is a waste of time.

The *choragos* supplies the identification that Iocastê would probably deny, given a choice. Her silence indicates she does not want to speak. Asked directly and seeing no escape from the truth, she dissembles. Lines 1001–1003 present her hopeless confusion. Under no circumstances could a man "forget it all" when doubted parentage can be revealed.

OEDIPUS. How can you say that,
When the clues to my true birth are in my hands?

IOCASTÊ. For God's love, let us have no more questioning! 1005
Is your life nothing to you?
My own is pain enough for me to bear.

OEDIPUS. You need not worry. Suppose my mother a slave,
And born of slaves: no baseness can touch you.

IOCASTÊ. Listen to me, I beg you: do not do this thing!　　　*1010*

OEDIPUS. I will not listen; the truth must be made known.

IOCASTÊ. Everything that I say is for your own good!

OEDIPUS.　　　　　　　　　　　　　　　My own good
Snaps my patience, then; I want none of it.

IOCASTÊ. You are fatally wrong! May you never learn who you are!

OEDIPUS. Go, one of you, and bring the shepherd here.　　　*1015*
Let us leave this woman to brag of her royal name.

IOCASTÊ. Ah, miserable!
That is the only word I have for you now.
That is the only word I can ever have.　　　　　(*Exit into the palace.*)

Misunderstanding his "wife's" motives (1008–1009), Oedipus thinks she fears to find her "husband" of less than noble rank. His "no baseness can touch you" crackles with irony. No greater baseness, in *his*, a man's eyes, *can* touch her. But in a woman's eyes, one more can: knowledge in Oedipus—knowledge that will make him loathe and fear Iocastê. To be rejected by a husband is more than most women can bear; to be rejected by a son is almost impossible for any woman. Iocastê sees rejection at both levels, but from one and the same person. Line 1010 ("Listen to me, I beg you: do not do this thing!") is Iocastê the wife pleading with her husband. Line 1012 ("Everything that I say is for your own good!") is Iocastê the mother pleading with her son. Oedipus is deaf to both Iocastês, hearing both as the queen of Thebes, possibly more highborn than he. Line 1014 ("May you never learn who you are!") is Iocastê the woman speaking to Oedipus the man. In learning *who* he is, he will also learn *what* he is. As a woman, Iocastê knows Oedipus the man. As a wife, she knows Oedipus the husband. As a mother, she knows Oedipus the son. As a queen, she knows Oedipus the king. From this multiplicity of roles, Iocastê knows Oedipus well enough to know him as representative of all men in his human responses. And she knows that men and women do not respond alike to that which Oedipus must learn. This multiplicity of relationships binds Oedipus closer to Iocastê's heart. Bearing the child, she bore the father of her children. Twice loved to her Oedipus became. Twice bound to her was he by bonds that, individually, are the strongest ties of love a woman knows. What woman, free of moral law, would not willingly perpetuate such a crime? It makes her the ultimate woman biologically. Men, on the other hand, turn from the possibility with a sickened heart. They cannot revel in the flesh that first created their present flesh. The seeds of children they must plant bear fruit that will, in time, replace them on the Earth. They cannot plant those seeds in the same soil wherein *they* were nurtured. Instinct demands that a man plant the seeds; he husbands in a field that yields the youth to murder age. The flesh that gave him birth was tilled by still another farmer. This he must do; he has no choice. But seed bears much of parent Self. To plant it in that selfsame field that gave him birth is to bring forth a second Self to do the deed of murder when the time shall come. And murder by a second Self is suicide, a twice-dread death, true murder at one's own hands.

No woman knows man's fear of death by the hand of a child. Her role in life is procreative; she need not fear what she has borne; she bears no second Self. She is the land receiving seed. Land does not reproduce itself from seed. It creates a protective child to keep it fertile, seed it back, renew it with new plantings. When a father's son tills his father's field, the father's usefulness is done. The field goes on productively, each generation's sons new-bound by love to the timeless field.

This, any woman knows, Iocastê knows. She bears the knowledge and can bear it—if her son is ignorant. She dies as a woman, a mother, and a wife if her husband learns it. And if he persists, he needs must learn. *Miserable* is "the only word" Iocastê can ever have. True, it applies to Oedipus, but it applies to all men who would know the reasons for their fears.

Fifth century B.C. Athenian women knew these truths; twentieth century A.D. American women know them too. Though cultures change and nations die, such truths are as timeless as man. Our knowledge of such truths does not make them more pleasant nor does it explain our fear of them. Neither Sophocles, nor Freud, nor any man can allay the fears attending truth. Each generation fears anew the age-old fears and, unaware that the fears are old, the young ask age-old questions.

"Dear Abby" is a newspaper columnist read widely in America. She chooses to answer letters "of a certain magnitude," for the questions must concern a large percentage of her audience and create broad reader identification. The following letter and response reveal a curious bond between the mother and the columnist—a bond that will, one day, include the now-Embarrassed Daughter. Only the son will never know, unless he is a Sophocles, the drama that surrounds him now each time his mother dresses.

Dear Abby

Quietly Close Door When Mom Dresses

Dear Abby: What do you think of a widowed mother who dresses and undresses with her bedroom door wide open? That's exactly what our mother does.

She has a small, but beautiful figure, and we all know it, but does she have to show it off in front of her children?

When I remind her she has a 20-year-old son in the house, she says, "So what? He doesn't pay any attention to me!" I am 14 and have much more modesty than my mother.

Please tell me what I can do about this terrible situation as it is getting worse every day. Embarrassed Daughter

DEAR DAUGHTER: Your obvious annoyance over the possibility that Big Brother might catch a glimpse of Mamma's "small but beautiful figure" gives me more cause for alarm than anything else.

Quietly close Mamma's bedroom door while she's dressing and don't make a federal case out of an attractive nuisance.

Is Abby's answer honest? No! It is not honest, for the truth lies in the lines Iocastê speaks to her grown son: "OEDIPUS: . . . must I not fear my mother's bed?" "IOCASTÊ: Why should anyone in this world be afraid, / Since Fate rules us and nothing can be foreseen? / A man should live only for the present day." Sons fear the act; mothers do not. Dear Abby and Iocastê both refuse to answer from the heart; instead, they equivocate.

> CHORUS. Why has she left us, Oedipus? Why has she gone   *1020*
> In such a passion of sorrow? I fear this silence:
> Something dreadful may come of it.
>   OEDIPUS.   Let it come!
> However base my birth, I must know about it.
> The Queen, like a woman, is perhaps ashamed
> To think of my low origin. But I   *1025*
> Am a child of Luck; I can not be dishonored.
> Luck is my mother; the passing months, my brothers,
> Have seen me rich and poor.
>   If this is so,
> How could I wish that I were someone else?
> How could I not be glad to know my birth?   *1030*

The *choragos* represents the *men* of Thebes, the citizens, and *as a man* he states, "I fear this silence" when Iocastê leaves, but Oedipus is as deaf to him as he was to Iocastê. He deems himself "a child of Luck," that fickle lady, friend of Chance. "The passing months" are his brothers —so he thinks. Iocastê, though, knows his brothers are his children who must finish what he started with the riddling Sphinx that distant day before the walls of seven-gated Thebes.

Foolish though his words may be, or vain the hopes he strings on sparkling words, Oedipus is a timeless man. Sheer desperation rides the storm: "However base my birth, I must know about it." This is a man, and a man must know his parentage so he can, in some way, exceed the mark his father set. However base the birth may be, however noble be the name, the king must know his father's fame to place it in eclipse. So now he whistles in the wind: "I am a child of Luck; I can not be dishonored." This is the kind of defense that all men make when they most fear the outcome. It is not pride, or stupid men would be most proud of all. It is that dull, unstated fear that "the necessary connection of things" is working. It is the prayer pride offers up that connections will be propitious.

The well-born man expects the outcome to be in favor of his name; the self-made man works doubly hard to insure it will be. Now, shriven of the mighty name, now possibly debased, self-made has Oedipus become. To be a man, he has to know how *Moira* makes connections.

ODE III

CHORUS. If ever the coming time were known   (STROPHE.)
To my heart's pondering,
Kithairon, now by Heaven I see the torches
At the festival of the next full moon,
And see the dance, and hear the choir sing   *1035*
A grace to your gentle shade:
Mountain where Oedipus was found,
O mountain guard of a noble race!
May the god who heals us lend his aid,
And let that glory come to pass   *1040*
For our king's cradling-ground.

Of the nymphs that flower beyond the years,   (ANTISTROPHE.)
Who bore you, royal child,
To Pan of the hills or the timberline Apollo,
Cold in delight where the upland clears,   *1045*
Or Hermês for whom Kyllenê's heights are piled?
Or flushed as evening cloud,
Great Dionysos, roamer of mountains,
He—was it he who found you there,
And caught you up in his own proud   *1050*
Arms from the sweet god-ravisher
Who laughed by the Muses' fountains?

Commenting on the disclosures of the third Scene, Ode III also reveals Thebes' love of Oedipus, joy at the prospect of finding him a countryman, and one of the most ironic passages of the play. Kithairon is the boundary of Thebes' land-holdings; as such it is the "mountain guard of a noble race." It is also the dividing barrier between Thebes and Corinth. In that mountain fastness, Oedipus was to be exposed and allowed to die. *Moira* deemed that he should live; so he passed into the house of Polybos. This much the Thebans know at this point. One other thing is also known to them, but they love Oedipus too much to think of it at all: Kithairon is the traditional home of the *Erinnyes* or Furies. The Furies were, in the beginning, the personification of curses pronounced on guilty criminals (and Oedipus is not only a guilty criminal, he has pronounced his own curse). They also punished those who shed the blood of their own kin (Oedipus is guilty of patricide), of rulers of cities (Oedipus is guilty of regicide), and those disrespectful to old age (Oedipus was unforgivably rude to the ancient and respected Teiresias). Their punishments on cities were wars, pestilence, dissension (all visited on Thebes), and, on humans, the stings of inescapable and unrelenting conscience. "That glory . . . /For our king's cradling-ground" must, at one and the same time, be the glory of Thebes and the unalterable punishments of the Furies! In an excess of hope, the citizens who love Oedipus reinforce the curse he has called down upon himself. The Antistrophe intensifies the irony as, still excessive, the Thebans grant the possibility that Oedipus sprang from a god. It might have been Pan (the god of natural, wondrous things—unnatural is the guilt of Oedipus), or Apollo (that god clear-sighted as the sun—how blind is Oedipus!), or Hermes (god of clever thieves—did Oedipus not steal the throne of Thebes?), or even Dionysus (god of wine; a favored patron of Thebes, so hated by Hera that she sent the riddling Sphinx to plague its gates; a god whose nocturnal rites were held on the night of the full moon on Kithairon's slopes by torch-light, for torches were sacred to the Furies who used their light to search out crime and wickedness). A passage of more controlled and concentrated irony can not be found in all literature. Oedipus has conquered pride and ambition, existing now as a man anxious to understand his birth and his life in relation to that birth. When he has arrived at his most human moment, his supporters would elevate him to near-godhood. *Hubris* is theirs, not his.

SCENE IV

OEDIPUS. Sirs: though I do not know the man,
I think I see him coming, this shepherd we want:

He is old, like our friend here, and the men   *1055*
Bringing him seem to be servants of my house.
But you can tell, if you have ever seen him.
  (*Enter* SHEPHERD *escorted by servants.*)
  CHORUS. I know him, he was Laïos' man. You can trust him.
  OEDIPUS. Tell me first, you from Corinth: is this the shepherd
We were discussing?
  MESSENGER.   This is the very man.   *1060*
  OEDIPUS (*to* SHEPHERD). Come here. No, look at me. You must answer
Everything I ask.—You belonged to Laïos?
  SHEPHERD. Yes: born his slave, brought up in his house.
  OEDIPUS. Tell me: what kind of work did you do for him?
  SHEPHERD. I was a shepherd of his, most of my life.   *1065*
  OEDIPUS. Where mainly did you go for pasturage?
  SHEPHERD. Sometimes Kithairon, sometimes the hills near-by.
  OEDIPUS. Do you remember ever seeing this man out there?
  SHEPHERD. What would he be doing there? This man?
  OEDIPUS. This man standing here. Have you ever seen him before?   *1070*
  SHEPHERD. No. At least, not to my recollection.
  MESSENGER. And that is not strange, my lord. But I'll refresh
His memory: he must remember when we two
Spent three whole seasons together, March to September,
On Kithairon or thereabouts. He had two flocks;   *1075*
I had one. Each autumn I'd drive mine home
And he would go back with his to Laïos' sheepfold.—
Is this not true, just as I have described it?
  SHEPHERD. True, yes; but it was all so long ago.
  MESSENGER. Well, then: do you remember, back in those days,   *1080*
That you gave me a baby boy to bring up as my own?
  SHEPHERD. What if I did? What are you trying to say?
  MESSENGER. King Oedipus was once that little child.
  SHEPHERD. Damn you, hold your tongue!
  OEDIPUS.   No more of that!
It is your tongue needs watching, not this man's.   *1085*
  SHEPHERD. My King, my Master, what is it I have done wrong?
  OEDIPUS. You have not answered his question about the boy.
  SHEPHERD. He does not know. . . . He is only making trouble. . . .
  OEDIPUS. Come, speak plainly, or it will go hard with you.
  SHEPHERD. In God's name, do not torture an old man!   *1090*
  OEDIPUS. Come here, one of you; bind his arms behind him.
  SHEPHERD. Unhappy King! What more do you wish to learn?
  OEDIPUS. Did you give this man the child he speaks of?

SHEPHERD.   I did.
And I would to God I had died that very day.
OEDIPUS. You will die now unless you speak the truth.   *1095*
SHEPHERD. Yet if I speak the truth, I am worse than dead.
OEDIPUS. Very well; since you insist upon delaying—
SHEPHERD. No! I have told you already that I gave him the boy.
OEDIPUS. Where did you get him? From your house? From somewhere else?
SHEPHERD. Not from mine, no. A man gave him to me.   *1100*
OEDIPUS. Is that man here? Do you know whose slave he was?
SHEPHERD. For God's love, my King, do not ask me any more!
OEDIPUS. You are a dead man if I have to ask you again.
SHEPHERD. Then . . . Then the child was from the palace of Laïos.
OEDIPUS. A slave child? or a child of his own line?   *1105*
SHEPHERD. Ah, I am on the brink of dreadful speech!
OEDIPUS. And I of dreadful hearing. Yet I must hear.
SHEPHERD. If you must be told, then . . .
                                        They said it was Laïos' child;
But it is your wife who can tell you about that.
OEDIPUS. My wife!—Did she give it to you?
SHEPHERD.   My lord, she did.   *1110*
OEDIPUS. Do you know why?
SHEPHERD.   I was told to get rid of it.
OEDIPUS. An unspeakable mother!
SHEPHERD.   There had been prophecies . . .
OEDIPUS. Tell me.
SHEPHERD.   It was said that the boy would kill his own father.
OEDIPUS. Then why did you give him over to this old man?
SHEPHERD. I pitied the baby, my King,   *1115*
And I thought that this man would take him far away
To his own country.
                   He saved him—but for what a fate!
For if you are what this man says you are,
No man living is more wretched than Oedipus.
OEDIPUS. Ah God!   *1120*
It was true!
         All the prophecies!
                          —Now,
O Light, may I look on you for the last time!
I, Oedipus,
Oedipus, damned in his birth, in his marriage damned,   *1124*
Damned in the blood he shed with his own hand!   (*He rushes into the palace.*)

Stichomythia is employed throughout this brief, intense scene. *Tempo* (the speed of the play) has been increasing steadily from the beginning, and it becomes most rapid now as the climax occurs.

Possibly unsure of the reason he has been summoned, the shepherd is escorted (which may suggest he comes against his will) by servants. The messenger recognizes and identifies him immediately, a recognition not shared by the shepherd. However, his "What would he be doing there? This man?" indicates he does, indeed, recognize the man and is stalling, hopeful that some evasive possibility will present itself. None does, for the messenger, ambition still driving him, pursues his unknowing course and elicits the harsh "Damn you, hold your tongue!" Oedipus recognizes the evasions then. What might otherwise be cruelty on his part is necessary firmness. The old shepherd is unwilling to be cooperative, but he recognizes Oedipus' refusal to be robbed of the truth. Still, unwilling to divulge any more than is necessary, he forces Oedipus to extract the truth, slow bit by painful bit. Before he hears the truth, however, Oedipus knows it (1107), but he has presumed too much already. He will assume nothing now. Hear it he does and, hearing, recognizes his own blindness. Verbal ambiguity overlays line 1122. Oedipus has failed to see "Light" (truth) because what his eyes beheld (his throne, his pleasant life) blinded him to spiritual truth. He resolves to cancel physical sight as he rushes into the palace.

ODE IV

CHORUS. Alas for the seed of men. (STROPHE 1.)

What measure shall I give these generations
That breathe on the void and are void
And exist and do not exist?

Who bears more weight of joy   1130
Than mass of sunlight shifting in images,
Or who shall make his thoughts stay on
That down time drifts away?

Your splendor is all fallen.

O naked brow of wrath and tears,   1135
O change of Oedipus!
I who saw your days call no man blest—
Your great days like ghósts góne.

That mind was a strong bow.   (ANTISTROPHE 1.)

Deep, how deep you drew it then, hard archer,   *1140*
At a dim fearful range,
And brought dear glory down!

You overcame the stranger—
The virgin with her hooking lion claws—
And though death sang, stood like a tower   *1145*
To make pale Thebes take heart.

Fortress against our sorrow!

Divine king, giver of laws,
Majestic Oedipus!
No prince in Thebes had ever such renown,   *1150*
No prince won such grace of power.

And now of all men ever known   (STROPHE 2.)
Most pitiful is this man's story:
His fortunes are most changed, his state
Fallen to a low slave's   *1155*
Ground under bitter fate.

O Oedipus, most royal one!
The great door that expelled you to the light
Gave at night—ah, gave night to your glory:
As to the father, to the fathering son.   *1160*

All understood too late.

How could that queen whom Laïos won,
The garden that he harrowed at his height,
Be silent when that act was done?

But all eyes fail before time's eye,   *1165*   (ANTISTROPHE 2.)
All actions come to justice there.
Though never willed, though far down the deep past,
Your bed, your dread sirings,
Are brought to book at last.

Child by Laïos doomed to die,   *1170*
Then doomed to lose that fortunate little death,
Would God you never took breath in this air
That with my wailing lips I take to cry:

For I weep the world's outcast.

Blind I was, and can not tell why;   *1175*
Asleep, for you had given ease of breath;
A fool, while the false years went by.

Appalled at the truth, the Chorus sees in Oedipus the fate of all men.
The seeming realities of life are shadows. Oedipus seemed the ideal man:
intelligent, happy, fortunate. Now he has been reduced to the lowest
station a man may hold; he is accursed of gods, of men, of himself.
Antistrophe 1 traces Oedipus' service to men. He was a good king.
Strophe 2 removes the blame from Oedipus, placing it on Iocastê. Lines
1162–1164 indicate that the people think Iocastê either should have known
the truth or that she did know and still allowed the act. The reasoning:
seed of seed (Oedipus, son of Laïos) would not recognize the field, the
second seed being new-born of that field and removed before a time
of knowledge. The field (Iocastê) would know seed that it had seen.
Lines 1167–1169 again acknowledge that Oedipus is free of intentional
guilt, but brand him guilty nonetheless. He could have escaped *Moira*
only if he had been stillborn, only if he had not breathed the same
air which the Chorus uses to weep "the world's outcast." Close analysis
of that thought suggests that Oedipus and the Chorus are, at least
spiritually, one. The same "breath" suffices for both. Both, then, become
"the world's outcast." As such, Oedipus is all men. Reverting to their
role as Theban citizens, they blame Oedipus for lulling them into false
security, thus blinding them. *Moira* must have willed their blindness too;
Oedipus has been blind; they have returned to the statement of Strophe 1,
creating the application of the play.

ÉXODOS

(*Enter, from the palace,* SECOND MESSENGER.)
SECOND MESSENGER. Elders of Thebes, most honored in this land,
What horrors are yours to see and hear, what weight
Of sorrow to be endured, if, true to your birth,   *1180*
You venerate the line of Labdakos!
I think neither Istros nor Phasis, those great rivers,
Could purify this place of the corruption
It shelters now, or soon must bring to light—
Evil not done unconsciously, but willed.   *1185*

The greatest griefs are those we cause ourselves.

In this final episode of three definite divisions, the *catastrophe* occurs. A second messenger opens the first division in the role of an announcer or expositor. He is not a messenger in the traditional sense. Greek drama ordinarily allowed no violence to be depicted onstage, for Spectacle was not the function of tragedy. In short, the emotions of man were not titillated with the superficial. Poetry rises to its greatest height in this scene. The enforced discipline of poetic restraint removes the scene from salaciousness, intensifying its emotional power as the reader is forced to "see" a scene twice-removed. He must first visualize the impact of the scene on the messenger, then re-create it for himself through the messenger's description. Two emotions blend in the recital (the messenger's and the reader's) to create a third: the revealed horror as an experience compounded from the two views.

In a brief preamble, the messenger prepares the reader for the line "The greatest griefs are those we cause ourselves." For a twentieth-century audience, it may be difficult to see Oedipus as the author of his own grief. Pause here, then, and reflect for one moment. How much of your personal life has been foretold by sources in which you have some faith? Oedipus was warned he would kill his father and marry his mother. To avoid that awful fate, he had to do but two things: kill no man old enough to be his father, regardless of provocation; marry no woman old enough to be his mother, regardless of proffered reward. In headstrong anger, he refused to stand aside at Phokis, lashing out in anger at one he felt had violated his right of way. For no defensible reason, he killed a man who was old enough to be his father. Arriving at Thebes, he answered the riddling Sphinx and accepted the hand of Iocastê (who was old enough to be his mother) in marriage because it held the throne of Thebes. He could have refused to marry Iocastê had he been willing to reject the throne. Proud of himself for outwitting the Sphinx, he wished ambition's reward. Willingly he married a woman old enough to be his mother. Believing in oracles, he fled Corinth. Believing in oracles, he slew a man and married a woman. Understanding *Moira,* he allowed two necessary connections to be made. It is difficult to hold him innocent of causing his own grief. Yet, you plead, he was *fated* to behave as he did. But *Moira,* remember, was "the necessary connection of things." And Oedipus *was* the connector. The doctrines of freedom of the will and predestination in Christian theology rest on the same subtle similarities and differences and are, in essence, the same.

CHORUS. Surely, friend, we have grief enough already;
What new sorrow do you mean?
SECOND MESSENGER.   The Queen is dead.

CHORUS. Iocastê? Dead? But at whose hand?

SECOND MESSENGER.   Her own.
The full horror of what happened you cannot know,   *1190*
For you did not see it; but I, who did, will tell you
As clearly as I can how she met her death.

When she had left us,
In passionate silence, passing through the court,
She ran to her apartment in the house,   *1195*
Her hair clutched by the fingers of both hands.
She closed the doors behind her; then, by that bed
Where long ago the fatal son was conceived—
That son who should bring about his father's death—
We heard her call upon Laïos, dead so many years,   *1200*
And heard her wail for the double fruit of her marriage,
A husband by her husband, children by her child.
Exactly how she died I do not know:
For Oedipus burst in moaning and would not let us
Keep vigil to the end: it was by him   *1205*
As he stormed about the room that our eyes were caught.
From one to another of us he went, begging a sword,
Cursing the wife who was not his wife, the mother
Whose womb had carried his own children and himself.
I do not know: it was none of us aided him,   *1210*
But surely one of the gods was in control!
For with a dreadful cry
He hurled his weight, as though wrenched out of himself,
At the twin doors: the bolts gave, and he rushed in.
And there we saw her hanging, her body swaying   *1215*
From the cruel cord she had noosed about her neck.
A great sob broke from him, heartbreaking to hear,
As he loosed the rope and lowered her to the ground.

I would blot out from my mind what happened next!
For the King ripped from her gown the golden brooches   *1220*
That were her ornament, and raised them, and plunged them down
Straight into his own eyeballs, crying, "No more,
No more shall you look on the misery about me,
The horrors of my own doing! Too long you have known
The faces of those whom I should never have seen,   *1225*
Too long been blind to those for whom I was searching!
From this hour, go in darkness!" And as he spoke,

He struck at his eyes—not once, but many times;
And the blood spattered his beard,
Bursting from his ruined sockets like red hail.   *1230*

So from the unhappiness of two this evil has sprung,
A curse on the man and woman alike. The old
Happiness of the house of Labdakos
Was happiness enough: where is it today?
It is all wailing and ruin, disgrace, death—all   *1235*
The misery of mankind that has a name—
And it is wholly and for ever theirs.
    CHORUS. Is he in agony still? Is there no rest for him?
    SECOND MESSENGER. He is calling for someone to lead him to the gates
So that all the children of Kadmos may look upon   *1240*
His father's murderer, his mother's—no,
I can not say it!
          And then he will leave Thebes,
Self-exiled, in order that the curse
Which he himself pronounced may depart from the house.
He is weak, and there is none to lead him,   *1245*
So terrible is his suffering.
          But you will see:
Look, the doors are opening; in a moment
You will see a thing that would crush a heart of stone.

The recital of Iocastê's suicide and Oedipus' self-blinding with the
brooches from her dress is far more graphic than an enactment would
be. Dramatic grandeur pervades the lines—melodrama would ruin the
scene.

    (*The central door is opened;* OEDIPUS, *blinded, is led in.*)
    CHORUS. Dreadful indeed for men to see
Never have my own eyes   *1250*
Looked on a sight so full of fear.

Oedipus!
What madness came upon you, what daemon
Leaped on your life with heavier
Punishment than a mortal man can bear?   *1255*
No; I can not even
Look at you, poor ruined one.
And I would speak, question, ponder,

If I were able. No.
You make me shudder.   *1260*
   OEDIPUS. God.   God.
Is there a sorrow greater?
Where shall I find harbor in this world?
My voice is hurled far on a dark wind.
What has God done to me?   *1265*
    CHORUS. Too terrible to think of, or to see.
    OEDIPUS. O cloud of night,   (STROPHE 1.)
Never to be turned away: night coming on,
I can not tell how: night like a shroud!

My fair winds brought me here.
                 O God. Again   *1270*
The pain of the spikes where I had sight,
The flooding pain
Of memory, never to be gouged out.
    CHORUS. This is not strange.
You suffer it all twice over, remorse in pain,   *1275*
Pain in remorse.
    OEDIPUS. Ah dear friend   (ANTISTROPHE 1.)
Are you faithful even yet, you alone?
Are you still standing near me, will you stay here,
Patient, to care for the blind?
             The blind man!   *1280*
Yet even blind I know who it is attends me,
By the voice's tone—
Though my new darkness hide the comforter.
    CHORUS. Oh fearful act!
What god was it drove you to rake black   *1285*
Night across your eyes?
    OEDIPUS. Apollo. Apollo. Dear   (STROPHE 2.)
Children, the god was Apollo.
He brought my sick, sick fate upon me.
But the blinding hand was my own!   *1290*
How could I bear to see
When all my sight was horror everywhere?
    CHORUS. Everywhere; that is true.
    OEDIPUS. And now what is left?
Images? Love? A greeting even,   *1295*
Sweet to the senses? Is there anything?
Ah, no, friends: lead me away.

Lead me away from Thebes.

                   Lead the great wreck

And hell of Oedipus, whom the gods hate.

    CHORUS. Your fate is clear, you are not blind to that.   *1300*

Would God you had never found it out!

    OEDIPUS. Death take the man who unbound   (ANTISTROPHE 2.)

My feet on that hillside

And delivered me from death to life! What life?

If only I had died,   *1305*

This weight of monstrous doom

Could not have dragged me and my darlings down.

    CHORUS. I would have wished the same.

    OEDIPUS. Oh never to have come here

With my father's blood upon me! Never   *1310*

To have been the man they call his mother's husband!

Oh accurst! Oh child of evil,

To have entered that wretched bed—

                          the selfsame one!

More primal than sin itself, this fell to me.

    CHORUS. I do not know how I can answer you.   *1315*

You were better dead than alive and blind.

    OEDIPUS. Do not counsel me any more. This punishment

That I have laid upon myself is just.

If I had eyes,

I do not know how I could bear the sight   *1320*

Of my father, when I came to the house of Death,

Or my mother: for I have sinned against them both

So vilely that I could not make my peace

By strangling my own life.

                  Or do you think my children,

Born as they were born, would be sweet to my eyes?   *1325*

Ah never, never! Nor this town with its high walls,

Nor the holy images of the gods.

                For I,

Thrice miserable!—Oedipus, noblest of all the line

Of Kadmos, have condemned myself to enjoy

These things no more, by my own malediction   *1330*

Expelling that man whom the gods declared

To be a defilement in the house of Laïos.

After exposing the rankness of my own guilt,

How could I look men frankly in the eyes?

No, I swear it,   *1335*

If I could have stifled my hearing at its source,
I would have done it and made all this body
A tight cell of misery, blank to light and sound:
So I should have been safe in a dark agony
Beyond all recollection.
                  Ah Kithairon!   *1340*
Why did you shelter me? When I was cast upon you,
Why did I not die? Then I should never
Have shown the world my execrable birth.

Ah Polybos! Corinth, city that I believed
The ancient seat of my ancestors: how fair   *1345*
I seemed, your child! And all the while this evil
Was cancerous within me!
                For I am sick
In my daily life, sick in my origin.

O three roads, dark ravine, woodland and way
Where three roads met: you, drinking my father's blood,   *1350*
My own blood, spilled by my own hand: can you remember
The unspeakable things I did there, and the things
I went on from there to do?
              O marriage, marriage!
The act that engendered me, and again the act
Performed by the son in the same bed—
                    Ah, the net   *1355*
Of incest, mingling fathers, brothers, sons,
With brides, wives, mothers: the last evil
That can be known by men: no tongue can say
How evil!
       No. For the love of God, conceal me
Somewhere far from Thebes; or kill me; or hurl me   *1360*
Into the sea, away from men's eyes for ever.

Come, lead me. You need not fear to touch me.
Of all men, I alone can bear this guilt.

The second division of the Exodus begins as Oedipus is led onstage, blood streaming from the sockets that so lately held his eyes. The *choragos* asks the question he would not have answered, for dark incest does exist in dreams, and dreams are but desires held in a self-blinded human heart.

The Strophes and Antistrophes (1267–1316) were chanted to musical accompaniment on the Greek stage. These two old friends, the ruler and his people, say their goodbyes within these lines. As old friends will, they reaffirm their depth of love. Here light and dark, the sun and night, the gods and man—all synonyms—are interchanged. To see what one wills to see is blindness. To close one's eyes to self-delusion is sight. Oedipus still has not regained full sight, though now he is as blind as old Teiresias. He calls a curse upon the shepherd who delivered him from death. Had the shepherd thwarted fate, blind Oedipus would not have sinned in that dark bed. Still, Oedipus does not try to pass off all the blame for his misery. Humbled, he laments his fate and pleads for help.

(*Enter* CREON.)

CHORUS. We are not the ones to decide; but Creon here
May fitly judge of what you ask. He only   1365
Is left to protect the city in your place.

OEDIPUS. Alas, how can I speak to him? What right have I
To beg his courtesy whom I have deeply wronged?

CREON. I have not come to mock you, Oedipus,
Or to reproach you, either.
(*To* ATTENDANTS.)   —You, standing there: 1370
If you have lost all respect for man's dignity,
At least respect the flame of Lord Helios:
Do not allow this pollution to show itself
Openly here, an affront to the earth
And Heaven's rain and the light of day. No, take him   1375
Into the house as quickly as you can.
For it is proper
That only the close kindred see his grief.

OEDIPUS. I pray you in God's name, since your courtesy
Ignores my dark expectation, visiting   1380
With mercy this man of all men most execrable:
Give me what I ask—for your good, not for mine.

CREON. And what is it that you would have me do?

OEDIPUS. Drive me out of this country as quickly as may be
To a place where no human voice can ever greet me.   1385

CREON. I should have done that before now—only,
God's will had not been wholly revealed to me.

OEDIPUS. But his command is plain: the parricide
Must be destroyed. I am that evil man.

CREON. —That is the sense of it, yes; but as things are,   1390
We had best discover clearly what is to be done.

OEDIPUS. You would learn more about a man like me?

CREON. You are ready now to listen to the god.

OEDIPUS. I will listen. But it is to you
That I must turn for help. I beg you, hear me. *1395*

The woman in there—
Give her whatever funeral you think proper:
She is your sister.
       —But let me go, Creon!
Let me purge my father's Thebes of the pollution
Of my living here, and go out to the wild hills, *1400*
To Kithairon, that has won such fame with me,
The tomb my mother and father appointed for me,
And let me die there, as they willed I should.
And yet I know
Death will not ever come to me through sickness *1405*
Or in any natural way: I have been preserved
For some unthinkable fate. But let that be.

As for my sons, you need not care for them.
They are men, they will find some way to live.
But my poor daughters, who have shared my table, *1410*
Who never before have been parted from their father—
Take care of them, Creon; do this for me.
And will you let me touch them with my hands
A last time, and let us weep together?
Be kind, my lord, *1415*
Great prince, be kind!
       Could I but touch them,
They would be mine again, as when I had my eyes.
   (*Enter* ANTIGONE *and* ISMENE, *attended.*)
Ah, God!
Is it my dearest children I hear weeping?
Has Creon pitied me and sent my daughters? *1420*

   CREON. Yes, Oedipus: I knew that they were dear to you
In the old days, and know you must love them still.

   OEDIPUS. May God bless you for this—and be a friendlier
Guardian to you than he has been to me!

Children, where are you? *1425*
Come quickly to my hands: they are your brother's—
Hands that have brought your father's once clear eyes
To this way of seeing—

Ah dearest ones,
I had neither sight nor knowledge then, your father
By the woman who was the source of his own life!   *1430*
And I weep for you—having no strength to see you—,
I weep for you when I think of the bitterness
That men will visit upon you all your lives.
What homes, what festivals can you attend
Without being forced to depart again in tears?   *1435*
And when you come to marriageable age,
Where is the man, my daughters, who would dare
Risk the bane that lies on all my children?
Is there any evil wanting? Your father killed
His father; sowed the womb of her who bore him;   *1440*
Engendered you at the fount of his own existence!

That is what they will say of you.
                                  Then, whom
Can you ever marry? There are no bridegrooms for you,
And your lives must wither away in sterile dreaming.

O Creon, son of Menoikeus!   *1445*
You are the only father my daughters have,
Since we, their parents, are both of us gone for ever.
They are your own blood: you will not let them
Fall into beggary and loneliness;
You will keep them from the miseries that are mine!   *1450*
Take pity on them; see, they are only children,
Friendless except for you. Promise me this,
Great Prince, and give me your hand in token of it.
    (CREON *clasps his right hand.*)
Children:
I could say much, if you could understand me,   *1455*
But as it is, I have only this prayer for you:
Live where you can, be as happy as you can—
Happier, please God, than God has made your father!
        CREON. Enough. You have wept enough. Now go within.
        OEDIPUS. I must; but it is hard.
        CREON.   Time eases all things.   *1460*
        OEDIPUS. But you must promise—
        CREON.   Say what you desire.
        OEDIPUS. Send me from Thebes!
        CREON.   God grant that I may!

OEDIPUS. But since God hates me . . .

CREON.   No, he will grant your wish.

OEDIPUS. You promise?

CREON.   I can not speak beyond my knowledge.

OEDIPUS. Then lead me in.

CREON.   Come now, and leave your children.   *1465*

OEDIPUS. No! Do not take them from me!

CREON.   Think no longer
That you are in command here, but rather think
How when you were, you served your own destruction.

(*Exeunt into the house all but the* CHORUS; *the* CHORAGOS *chants directly to the audience.*)

    CHORUS. Men of Thebes: look upon Oedipus.
This is the king who solved the famous riddle   *1470*
And towered up, most powerful of men.
No mortal eyes but looked on him with envy,
Yet in the end ruin swept over him.

Let every man in mankind's frailty
Consider his last day; and let none   *1475*
Presume on his good fortune until he find
Life, at his death, a memory without pain. ☐

Creon's entry cuts short the lamentations of Oedipus. He is the ruler of Thebes through no choice of his own. Assuring Oedipus that he bears him no ill will, he proves his words and would withdraw the blind one back into the palace. His present words recall his words when he came late from Delphi: some things are best said out of hearing of the masses. But Oedipus forces speech in public just as he had forced it earlier. And Creon answers as the king; he would have exiled Oedipus long, long ago had he not been as blind as any Theban (1386). Harboring no resentment against the man who demanded his death, Creon is magnanimous and prudent. He will not act in haste (1390–1391). Perhaps he remembers too well the outcome of such action on a ruler's part. The god again must be implored (1393) before there can be action. Nor will Creon, like Oedipus, reject the suppliant or refuse him hospitality (1453), for these two crimes are also the province of the dread Furies. Lines 1460–1468 are chanted, each half-line balancing the other. If Creon seems harsh as he leads Oedipus into the palace, consider what he says. Oedipus refused to hear the god; Oedipus wrought his own destruction. Now, blind, he still wants to give orders to his king and brother, Creon. But Creon has seen the fruits of haste. Decisions must wait on the god, and if blind

Oedipus cannot see why, Creon, as king, commands it. Thebes will be served, but so will he who sought to serve himself.

As Creon leads the way into the palace, the *choragos* speaks directly to the audience, making the general application of the play. Didactic though the chant may seem, it serves to summarize the action in one clear statement any man should be able to hear and understand. Presumption is not the right of man, for envy itself is blind. Humility results if we can share in this sad truth.

The Meaning of the Play—Oedipus Rex *in Application*

Now that you have finished reading the play, you are probably temporarily overwhelmed with the power of fate, the awesome destruction of Oedipus, and the fearful results of his incestuous marriage. As you emerge from the cathartic state induced by the tragedy, you are ready to decide whether or not the play has meaning for you. Comfort may demand that you simply refuse to think about it, that you dismiss it from further consideration, but such a dismissal would defeat your intention in learning to read drama. *Escape reading* (or viewing) flourishes in such scripts as are regularly presented on television ("The Beverly Hillbillies" or "Doctor Kildare" or "Peyton Place," for instance) and in musical comedies (such as *Hello, Dolly!* or *Annie Get Your Gun*). Tragedy is not meant for escape; in fact, it allows you to see your own life with greater vision and clarity than you could in daily living.

What then might *Oedipus Rex* mean to you? Several possibilities exist, each intimately associated with twentieth-century life:

1. *Oedipus as any man.* Born into a culture already formed from material of the past, Oedipus is both victim and victor in his life. Denied his own parents, he was reared by another set, particularly loving and grateful because they had been denied children of their own. At that age when life becomes a major problem (the late teen years), Oedipus was forced to evaluate the past and confront the future. Cutting himself adrift from his home and his family, he sought his fortune. Prepared by his background (which would have afforded him an adequate if not an excellent education), he was mentally gifted and could answer the riddling Sphinx, but his emotional responses were immature and subject to violent displays. His killing of Laïos was no more or less horrifying as an act than any murder on any highway. And is not an automobile in immature hands as lethal a weapon as any that was available to Oedipus? Do not dragracers, refusing to yield the road, frequently kill the innocent in much the same irresponsible fashion that Oedipus killed Laïos? And with as little regret?

That Oedipus married an "older woman" to gain economic and social position is certainly not unusual in your time when "marrying the boss's daughter" is as common in practice as it is in jokes. The rich widow, the widow of a political figure, the widow of a socially prominent man—all are desirable marriage objects for ambitious young men. Because the life span of a woman is longer than a man's, marriage counselors, psychologists, and actuaries encourage such liaisons in our time. And, we are told, every man seeks something of a mother figure in his wife; therefore, Oedipus' conduct is scarcely reprehensible or difficult to understand.

In his twenty years' reign in Thebes, Oedipus did not pursue the murderers of Laïos; procrastination is less a human weakness than it is a human behavioral pattern. Whoever had dispatched the king had done Oedipus a service, allowing him access to the throne. Had Oedipus been inclined to avenge Laïos, he would have exhibited a curious nature. Too, had the citizens of Thebes demanded such an inquiry, Oedipus would have acceded to their wishes; that he allowed the years to pass before acting indicates a general Theban indifference. Laïos had been king—seemingly quite an ordinary, utterly undistinguished ruler. His death was overshadowed by the Sphinx, a thorny problem he had been incapable of solving; so he went relatively unmourned. Even Iocastê seems to have been singularly uncurious; neither she nor Creon had encouraged investigation. Surrounded by such deterrents, Oedipus would have been markedly foolish to have created problems.

Subtle warning signs were much easier for Oedipus to read than boldly pronounced ones. What teen-ager has not been warned "If you do that, these results will follow"? Youth almost feels obligated to ignore such advice (even after seeking it), preferring to court disaster and, hopefully, to avert it through personal cleverness. Oedipus could have avoided murder, incest, and self-destruction had he acted on sought advice. That he did not welds him firmly to the family of man and makes him its representative son.

Immediacy creates the need of imperative action—for Oedipus and all men. Nor does strangeness attend Oedipus' accusation that Thebes had been negligent in seeking Laïos' murderer. If others have failed to do a job, we are seldom anxious to repair the damage of their omission unless we will personally gain from the act. But when action was necessary, Oedipus exhibited a degree of organizational ability that would appeal to any mayor of a city, president of a corporation, or king of a country. And that provokes a paradox and the tragedy: in failing to assume full responsibility for his actions, Oedipus became embroiled in the horrors of his life; in assuming full responsibility, he discovered the richness of the horror. What, then, is a man to do when either course leads to nightmare? "Shall I enlist and fulfill my military obligation now or go to college and wait to be drafted?" is just as great a problem for young men today. The answer? Fate lies somewhere ahead. To go now might ensure one's keeping an appointment with death in some distant jungle. To wait may be to bypass stateside duty and keep an appointment with death later. To weigh and consider is, finally, to chance a guess. Destiny does not reveal when we must die (if there is a specific time), but it does reveal that we must die sooner or later. Our choices may only speed or delay the moment.

Religion, God, the spokesmen of God (rabbis, priests, ministers)— what do they offer by way of help? Oedipus had been taught reverence for the gods; he had been taught respect for their earthly voices and interpreters. In short, he had been thoroughly acquainted with the rules of convention in his society. Early in his life, he ran from destiny; in later years, he adopted his own defenses against the voices of destiny, though he could not ignore destiny itself. Then, denied parents a third time in his life, he accepted chance or luck as a substitute for destiny, relying on the fickle, rejecting the certain. Certainty does not accept rejection; it merely ignores the possibility of it and follows its own chosen (if tortured) path. When destiny and Oedipus met at that inevitable fork in his road, he was not prepared to die (as Iocastê had been) nor yet to live physically untouched. Choosing a middle ground, Oedipus assumed a kind of death in life (blinded, he would live in the darkness imposed by death) but, through that assumption, he granted himself the greater gift of life in death, for, out of physical darkness he found the gift of inward sight. Understanding of his Self still lies ahead of Oedipus as the play closes, but it is as sure as if destined. Man can scarcely ask for more than Oedipus is promised. That the Chorus assesses the immediate, failing to anticipate the future, suggests that the citizens of Thebes (therefore the common man) live in that perpetual mid-region from which Oedipus has just emerged. All men possess the possibility of emerging; crisis opens the way, and response to crisis suggests the road downward to defeat or upward to some distant possibility.

2. *Oedipus as a psychological symbol.* Dr. Sigmund Freud speaks so well of this that his words can scarcely be improved upon:

If the *Oedipus Rex* is capable of moving a modern reader or playgoer no less powerfully than it moved the contemporary Greeks, the only possible explanation is that the effect of the Greek tragedy does not depend upon the conflict between fate and human will, but upon the peculiar nature of the material by which this conflict is revealed. There must be a voice within us which is prepared to acknowledge the compelling power of fate in the Oedipus . . . And there actually is a motive in the story of King Oedipus which explains the verdict of this inner voice. His fate moves us only because it might have been our own, because the oracle laid upon us before our birth the very curse which rested upon him. It may be that we were all destined to direct our first sexual impulses toward our mothers, and our first impulses of hatred and resistance toward our fathers; our dreams convince us that we were. King Oedipus, who slew his father Laius and wedded his mother Jocasta, is nothing more or less than a wish-fulfillment—the fulfillment of the wish of our childhood. But we, more fortunate than he, in so far as we have not become psychoneurotics, have since our childhood succeeded in withdrawing our sexual impulses from our mothers, and in forgetting our jealousy of our fathers. We recoil from the person for whom this primitive wish of our childhood has been fulfilled with all the force of the repression which these wishes have undergone in our minds since childhood. As the poet brings the guilt of Oedipus to light by his investigation, he forces us to become aware of our own inner selves, in which the same impulses are still extant, even though they are suppressed . . . Like Oedipus, we live in ignorance of the desires that offend morality, the desires that nature has forced upon us and after their unveiling we may well prefer to avert our gaze from the scenes of our childhood.°

3. *Oedipus as a religious symbol.* Whether he be pagan, Christian, Jew, or atheist, man is constantly aware of the world in which he lives. That world is controlled by forces he calls time and nature, forces that create the recurring, changeless pattern of birth, growth, maturing, and death. Spring begins the annual cycle, summer speeds it into autumn, autumn gives way to winter. In the process, we envision the new year as a baby, innocent but anxious to search through the months until, by December, he has become an ancient graybeard, anxious to be replaced by the new infant of next year. Man has been aware of the pattern since the days of unwritten history. He long ago saw the baby kill its father, mate with its mother, and, in turn, be slain by its father. From this observation grew the myths that led to the growth of enactments of the recurring drama. The ritual: the young king kills his father (time: new and old year) to marry his mother (the wife who is nature) who bears his children. In that pattern, the years give way to new ones which grow out of the old; nature, however, remains constant and singular. Time is male; nature is female; incest is inevitable.

What man does not grow weary of the long, sterile months of winter when leaden skies close out the sun, when the earth lies frozen underfoot? Held impotent in time by ice, he waits for spring. When the sun strikes heat against the ground, when snows slowly melt and the earth grows soft, man reaches down and turns the soil and loves it with his fingers.

° From *The Basic Writings of Sigmund Freud*, tr. A. A. Brill (New York, 1938).

He takes his seed and plants it then; he waters it with tender care; he harvests the fruit of his own toil, and gives his land again to winter. Time ravages the life of man; eventually he leaves his land by passing it on to willing hands—his sons who will pass it on to theirs. This is the timeless act. Man loves his land; he sprang from it; he dies and asks to be returned to it. Each man emerges from that womb to which his death returns him. That land is his "good earth" a while before he too becomes good earth. And suns pass overhead the while as the sons of man sow seeds and dream their gods into existence.

Suggested Assignments. Sophocles' *Oedipus at Colonus* recounts the blind wanderings of Oedipus twenty years after his departure from Thebes. Time has allowed the horror of his life to fade; guilt does not pursue him, for his transgressions were innocent of intent. Now, a beggar in body, he is a nobleman in spirit. Approaching death, he achieves complete tranquility before his mysterious disappearance from the living. The play may be found in any number of books in the library.

1. In a carefully considered paper, compare and contrast the Oedipus who confronts Creon in *Oedipus Rex* with the Oedipus who confronts Creon in *Oedipus at Colonus*. Using the two plays as illustrative material and sources for examples, defend your belief that time does or does not bring understanding or maturity from a series of experiences rather than from learned facts.

2. The Creon of *Oedipus Rex* grows into the Creon of *Oedipus at Colonus*. Carefully documenting your ideas, prove or disprove the following statement: Creon is a more noble man in *Oedipus Rex* than in *Oedipus at Colonus*.

3. Several notable Americans have become unpopular because they loved their country too well to dishonor her merely to please the populace. Read the sketches of Daniel Webster or Robert Taft in John F. Kennedy's *Profiles in Courage* (available in paperback) and compare Oedipus' conduct in *Oedipus Rex* with the decisive conduct of either of those men. How does drama mirror reality in such instances?

CHAPTER IV

Shakespearean Tragedy—
The World As a Stage

The Elizabethan Englishman and the Athenian Greek
of Sophocles' audience were brothers in more ways
than can be chronicled here. Both lived in exciting
worlds made rich by trade, made intellectually stimulating by a growing concern for man, and made casual
by the absence of worry about economic necessity.
Capable, clever rulers (albeit a little ruthless) had
brought both empires to brilliance by establishing
the power of the state, stabilizing the economy, and
encouraging mental stimulation of the masses by
patronizing the artists of the day. However, because
long centuries of Church domination separated the
worlds of Pericles and Elizabeth, the Englishman of
Shakespeare's time did not recognize his debt to or
his alliance with Greece. Instead, he looked back to
Rome which, because it had been the seat of the
Church, seemed to be his cultural ancestor. Still, in
retrospect, the similarities remain, for Rome was an
intermediary, in a sense, between Greece and England.
Tragedy itself reveals that role as well as any other
agent. As J. A. K. Thomson observes in *The Classical
Background of English Literature:*

There are remarkable and significant resemblances between Attic and Shakespearean tragedy. Take this matter
of tragic irony as it was produced by the Greek tragedians
in the manner we have been describing. It is employed by
Shakespeare too. Thus in *Macbeth* he takes occasion at the
very beginning of the play to bring in the witches, who prophesy all that is to befall Macbeth in the sequel. The story was
not, like that of Hamlet, already familiar to Shakespeare's
audience, and so he makes a point of telling them beforehand
what it is. And, as one prophecy after another is fulfilled in
the course of the action, the artistic purpose becomes plain.
The audience has been moved from the state of mind in which
it would simply have wondered what next would happen to
that in which it watches a man struggling vainly in a net of

destiny. In other words the dramatic interest is not in what will happen but in how it will happen; and this is exactly the dramatic interest of the *Oedipus Rex* or the *Agamemnon*. The same may be said of *Hamlet*. There is no doubt that Hamlet will kill and be killed. But how and where? From this it will be seen how mistaken is the view of those who think Hamlet's delays are undramatic. They are on the contrary the very thing that makes the suspense almost unbearable.

There are other similarities due in the main to resemblances in the structure of the Greek and the Elizabethan theatre. Neither had any scenery worth mentioning; neither possessed a drop-curtain. The first deficiency made it necessary for Shakespeare as for the Greeks to indicate the scene of the action by allusions or even set descriptions put in the mouths of the persons of the play. The second deficiency raised technical problems of a kind that may be illustrated by an example. In the *Ajax* of Sophocles, where (by a remarkable exception to the Greek rule) the hero kills himself upon the stage, the dramatist contrives a scene in which the body is carried off to honourable burial. The same situation is found at the end of *Hamlet,* and the problem is solved in the same way. Shakespeare is not here imitating Sophocles, of whom he knew nothing, but adopting like his predecessor an obvious way of getting the corpse removed from the stage. The modern dramatist lowers the curtain—an easy device, which has done more harm than good to dramatic poetry. The particular difficulty in the *Ajax* is normally resolved in Attic tragedy by having the death of the hero reported by a messenger instead of enacted before the audience. The method is adopted once at least by Shakespeare, in *Macbeth,* where the killing of Duncan occurs off the stage. Many critics have thought the scene between Macbeth and Lady Macbeth when the deed is doing or done the most powerful even in Shakespeare. At any rate it is a complete refutation of the notion that a death that is unseen is necessarily less dramatic than one that is thrust upon the eyes. Consider how much more disturbing is the reported murder of Duncan than the public murder of Julius Caesar in Shakespeare's play. It will be seen that the Greek dramatists knew their business.

It has sometimes been thought that there must have been some direct influence upon Shakespeare from the Greeks. That is excessively improbable. Indirect influence is another matter. This came, so far as tragedy is concerned, through the Roman poet Seneca. He was a very distinguished person in more ways than one; but we are not here concerned with his political career or with any of his voluminous writings except some eight or nine tragedies written in his youth, at least with all the marks of youth upon them. They were hardly meant for the stage, but most probably were composed with an eye partly to future readers and partly to their representation in some large Roman house in what used to be called 'private theatricals'. The subjects were all drawn from the Attic tragedians, chiefly Euripides, who ever since his death four centuries and a half before had been by far the most popular and influential of the Greek tragic dramatists. The plays of Seneca are not translations, and he writes freely enough out of his own mind. But if they are not translations they are imitations. In other words the Senecan drama is just Greek drama in a Latin dress. That is why we must begin our study of him with the Greeks.

The faults of the Senecan tragedies are gross and palpable. They are full of blood, cruelty, natural, unnatural and supernatural horrors. There is hardly any truth to life either in the incidents or in the character-drawing, and there is a great deal of rant and bombast in the style. These vices reappear in the 'Senecan' plays of the Elizabethan theatre, such as *Titus Andronicus*, and the result has been a tendency to regard the influence of Seneca upon English drama as mainly if not wholly bad. But there are things to be said in palliation and even in commendation. It might indeed be argued that it did not need a Roman playwright to make the groundlings of an Elizabethan theatre fond of melodramatic horrors; they had that taste already. But that, while it mitigates the effects of Seneca's offence, does not excuse the offence itself. On the other hand it is a thing positively in his favour that he had an unexpected vein of lyrical inspiration, not very abundant or original but genuine enough, which is revealed in the choral odes that divide in the Greek manner the acts of his dramas—a vein worked later with considerable effect by writers like Fulke Greville and Sir William Alexander. It might even be maintained that his characters, though mere types and shadows, move and express themselves with a certain tragic sublimity. But the best way to appreciate what Seneca did for English drama is to think of the mysteries and moralities and miracle plays which he helped so much to supersede. The mediaeval drama has merits which Seneca could never have attained or even perceived, because he was too sophisticated for that. But no one could fairly deny that it tends, broadly speaking, to be formless, and that the ideas it contains are few and of an elementary simplicity. Seneca more than anyone else changed all that.

In the first place he influenced dramatists in the direction of constructing a regular plot worked out through a series of compact, organically connected acts and scenes. That was no small service, although Seneca must share the credit here with the Roman comic poets. His other services were even more important. He raised the intellectual level of the drama. The undeniable fact that early imitations of the Senecan manner, such as *Gorboduc*, are dull is not the fault of Seneca, who was not only a very clever man but had a brilliant gift of aphorism. The Elizabethans admired the 'sentences' of Seneca at least as much as his fustian. What it all led to may be seen in *Hamlet*, which, though its subject is not classical, is a 'Senecan' play improved out of all recognition. There is a ghost crying for revenge and, at the end, an orgy of blood-shedding. But there is also a more than Senecan play of mind. The *To be or not to be* soliloquy is not less in Seneca's way than the ghost; to the classical scholar it reads like a poet's rendering of a typical Stoic—and Seneca was a Stoic—discourse on suicide. Such boldness and freedom of thought on such a theme is not mediaeval but classical. Even in point of style the influence of Seneca was by no means wholly bad. He taught correctness—impeccable grammar, impeccable metre, in neither of which could our native drama be regarded as strong. And, although he overcharged his own style with rhetoric, he taught us that a tragedy must be composed in language of appropriate grandeur.

The extent of Shakespeare's classical education is generally conceded by his contemporaries to be limited, Ben Jonson recording it as "small Latin and less Greek" in a dedicatory poem "To the Memory of Shakespeare." Another contemporary, Frances Meres, on the other hand, writing a book comparable to a modern English textbook, appraised Shakespeare's total output:

> The sweet witty soul of Ovid lies in mellifluous and honey-tongued Shakespeare, witness his *Venus and Adonis*, his *Lucrece,* his sugared sonnets among his private friends. As Plautus and Seneca are accounted the best for comedy and tragedy among the Latins, so Shakespeare among the English is the most excellent in both kinds for the stage.

It is unimportant, actually, whether Shakespeare did or did not know the Greek tragedies. He was not an imitator, nor was he an academician. He was a writer wanting to reach larger audiences, more people than the limited few who read the formal "important" publications or the larger group more-or-less restricted to the "do-it-yourself" texts that were as fashionable in Elizabethan England as they are in contemporary America. That largest group (and how little times change is apparent here) read little more than necessity demanded, preferring to gain their knowledge painlessly through the visual-aural medium of the theater.

The masses then were analogous, in every way, to the largest group of Americans today who scan their newspapers and a favored but undemanding magazine, but gain their literary experience from motion pictures or television. Accustomed to the language of their time, the Elizabethan English exhibited no great depth of intelligence or literary acumen in their warm reception of the "great" plays of Shakespeare. And that those same plays must be footnoted for your understanding now is no more strange than that any popular television script would have to be elaborately footnoted for an Elizabethan reader. Current language and contemporary allusions are certainly not constant. But other elements are.

If, on the one hand, you find it absurd that Hamlet should converse with his father's ghost or that Macbeth should give a willing ear to three witches, consider your own eager perusal of such prophets as Jean Dixon or the daily newspaper horoscope for your zodiacal sign. Adolf Hitler decided the fate of our world with the help of his staff of soothsayers and astrologers. Recent American Presidents have made the White House a hospitable place to seers, possibly because of their entertainment value, possibly for more serious reasons. Daily, we dwellers in a scientifically oriented world knock wood, avoid ladders, skirt black cats, and wish on stars. Our houses of religion have, it is said, never enjoyed greater patronage, and our latter-day priests, the searchers of the psyche, can hardly find enough couch room or hours in the day to soothe anxieties, wash the stained souls of patients, and help their Hamlets learn to make instant but sound decisions.

Possibly our sophisticated attitudes help explain our lack of enthusiasm for Shakespearean productions today. A dedicated few turn out for the legitimate presentation or the motion-picture adaptation of *Hamlet, Macbeth, The Taming of the Shrew,* or *The Merchant of Venice,* but many of the "dedicated" are there to be seen rather than to enjoy the production. Certainly few moments are as entertaining as those spent in lobbies while audiences "discuss" the presentation. Sophistication and ignorance of the play, of dramaturgy, and of staging techniques—all combine to create a magnificent critical farce that is just the comic relief one needs after the often tragic performance one has just witnessed.

But in all candor, Shakespeare reads far better today than he acts. And that is by no means a statement of denigration; rather, it is a testament to Shakespeare's power, an assessment that proves Ben Jonson's contention that "He was not of an age, but for all time." Jonson's poem appeared in the first authorized edition of the plays, Heminge's and Condell's *First Folio,* a collection salvaged for readers through time. But as early as 1811, Charles Lamb, an English essayist of great wit and charm, decided that Shakespeare should not be presented on the stage for a variety of good and sufficient reasons which he set forth in his essay entitled "On Shakspeare's Stage Productions." Many if not most of Lamb's strictures still warrant serious consideration today:

. . . [S]uch is the instantaneous nature of the impressions which we take in at the eye and ear at a play-house, compared with the slow apprehension oftentimes of the understanding in reading, that we are apt not only to sink the play-writer in the consideration which we pay to the actor, but even to identify in our minds, in a perverse manner, the actor with the character which he represents. It is difficult for a frequent play-goer to disembarrass the idea of Hamlet from the person and voice of Mr. K[emble]. We speak of Lady Macbeth, while we are in reality thinking of Mrs. S[iddons]. Nor is this confusion incidental alone to unlettered persons, who, not possessing the advantage of reading, are necessarily dependent upon the stage-player for all the pleasure which they can receive from the drama, and to whom the very idea of *what an author is* cannot be made comprehensible without some pain and perplexity of mind: the error is one from which persons otherwise not meanly lettered, find it almost impossible to extricate themselves.

Never let me be so ungrateful as to forget the very high degree of satisfaction which I received some years back from seeing for the first time a tragedy of Shakspeare performed, in which those two great performers sustained the principal parts. It seemed to embody and realise conceptions which had hitherto assumed no distinct shape. But dearly do we pay all our life after for this juvenile pleasure, this sense of distinctness. When the novelty is past, we find to our cost that instead of realising an idea, we have only materialised and brought down a fine vision to the standard of flesh and blood. We have let go a dream, in quest of an unattainable substance.

How cruelly this operates upon the mind, to have its free conceptions thus cramped and pressed down to the measure of a strait-lacing actuality, may be judged from that delightful sensation of freshness, with which we turn to those plays of Shakspeare which have escaped being performed, and to those passages in the acting plays of the same writer which have happily been left out in the performance. How far the very custom of hearing anything *spouted*, withers and blows upon a fine passage, may be seen in those speeches from *Henry the Fifth*, etc., which are current in the mouths of schoolboys, from their being to be found in *Enfield's Speaker*, and such kind of books! I confess myself utterly unable to appreciate that celebrated soliloquy in *Hamlet*, beginning "To be or not to be," or to tell whether it be good, bad or indifferent, it has been so handled and pawed about by declamatory boys and men, and torn so inhumanly from its living place and principle of continuity in the play, till it is become to me a perfect dead member.

It may seem a paradox, but I cannot help being of opinion that the plays of Shakspeare are less calculated for performance on a stage, than those of almost any other dramatist whatever. Their distinguishing excellence is a reason that they should be so. There is so much in them, which comes not under the province of acting, with which eye, and tone, and gesture, have nothing to do.

The glory of the scenic art is to personate passion, and the turns of passion; and the more coarse and palpable the passion is, the more hold upon the eyes and ears of the spectators the performer obviously possesses. For this reason, scolding scenes, scenes where two persons talk themselves into a fit of fury, and then in a surprising manner talk themselves out of it again, have always been the most popular upon our stage. And the reason is plain, because the spectators are here most palpably appealed to, they are the proper judges in this war of words, they are the legitimate ring that should be formed round such "intellectual prize-fighters." Talking is the direct object of the imitation here. But in all the best dramas, and in Shakspeare above all, how obvious it is, that the form of *speaking*, whether it be in soliloquy or dialogue, is only a medium, and often a highly artificial one, for putting the reader or spectator into possession of that knowledge of the inner structure and workings of the mind in a character, which he could otherwise never have arrived at *in that form of composition* by any gift short of intuition. We do here as we do with novels written in the *epistolary form*. How many improprieties, perfect solecisms in letter-writing, do we put up with in *Clarissa* and other books, for the sake of the delight which that form upon the whole gives us! . . .

The character of Hamlet is perhaps that by which, since the days of Betterton, a succession of popular performers have had the greatest ambition to distinguish themselves. The length of the part may be one of their reasons. But for the character itself, we find it in a play, and therefore we judge it a fit subject of dramatic representation. The play itself abounds in maxims and reflections beyond any other, and therefore we consider it as a proper vehicle for conveying moral instruction. But Hamlet himself—what does he suffer meanwhile by being dragged forth as the public schoolmaster, to give lectures to the crowd! Why, nine parts in ten of what Hamlet does, are transactions between himself and his moral sense; they are the effusions of his solitary musings, which he retires to holes and corners and the most sequestered parts of the palace to pour forth; or rather, they are the silent meditations with which his bosom is bursting, reduced to *words* for the sake of the reader, who must else remain ignorant of what is passing there. These profound sorrows, these light-and-noise-abhorring ruminations, which the tongue scarce dares utter to deaf walls and chambers, how can they be represented by a gesticulating actor, who comes and mouths them out before an audience, making four hundred people his confidants at once! I say not that it is the fault of the actor so to do; he must pronounce them *ore rotundo;* he must accompany them with his eye; he must insinuate them into his auditory by some trick of eye, tone or gesture, or he fails. *He must be thinking all the while of his appearance, because he knows that all the while the spectators are judging of it.* And this is the way to represent the shy, negligent, retiring Hamlet!

It is true that there is no other mode of conveying a vast quantity of thought and feeling to a great portion of the audience, who otherwise would never earn it for themselves by reading, and the intellectual acquisition gained this way may, for aught I know, be inestimable; but I am not arguing that Hamlet should not be acted, but how much Hamlet is made another thing by being acted. . . .

The truth is, the characters of Shakspeare are so much the objects of meditation rather than of interest or curiosity as to their actions, that while we are reading any of his great criminal characters,—Macbeth, Richard, even Iago,—we think not so much of the crimes which they commit, as of the ambition, the aspiring spirit, the intellectual activity, which prompts them to overleap these moral fences. Barnwell [a character in a mediocre play of Lamb's time] is a wretched murderer; there is a certain fitness between his neck and the rope; he is the legitimate heir to the gallows; nobody who thinks at all can think of any alleviating circumstances in his case to make him a fit object of mercy. . . . Whereas in corresponding characters in Shakspeare, so little do the actions comparatively affect us, that while the impulses, the inner mind in all its perverted greatness, solely seems real and is exclusively attended to, the crime is comparatively nothing. But when we see these things represented, the acts which they do are comparatively everything, their impulses nothing. The state of sublime emotion into which we are elevated by those images of night and horror which Macbeth is made to utter, that solemn prelude with which he entertains the time till the bell shall strike which is to call him to murder Duncan,—when we no longer read it in a book, when we have given up that vantage ground of abstraction which reading possesses over seeing, and come to see a man in his bodily shape before our eyes actually preparing to commit a murder, if the acting be true and impressive, as I have witnessed it in Mr. K[emble]'s performance of that part, the painful anxiety about the act, the natural longing to prevent it while it yet seems unperpetrated, the too close pressing semblance of reality, give a pain and an uneasiness which totally destroy all the delight which the words in the book convey, where the deed doing never presses upon us with the painful sense of presence: it rather seems to belong to history,—to something past and inevitable, if it has anything to do with time at all. The sublime images, the poetry alone, is that which is present to our minds in the reading.

So to see Lear acted,—to see an old man tottering about the stage with a walking-stick, turned out of doors by his daughters in a rainy night, has nothing in it but what is painful and disgusting. We want to take him into shelter and relieve him. That is all the feeling which the acting of Lear ever produced in me. But the Lear of Shakspeare cannot be acted. The contemptible machinery by which they mimic the storm which he goes out in, is not more inadequate to represent the horrors of the real elements, than any actor can be to represent Lear; they might more easily propose to personate the Satan of Milton upon a stage, or one of Michael Angelo's terrible figures. The greatness of Lear is not in corporal dimension, but in intellectual: the explosions of his passion are terrible as a volcano; they are storms turning up and disclosing to the bottom that sea, his mind, with all its vast riches. It is his mind which is laid bare. This case of flesh and blood seems too insignificant to be thought on; even as he himself neglects it. On the stage we see nothing but corporal infirmities and weakness, the impotence of rage; while we read it, we see not Lear, but we are Lear,—we are in his mind, we are sustained by a grandeur which baffles the malice of daughters and storms; in the aberrations of his reason, we discover a mighty irregular power of reasoning, immethodised from the ordinary purposes of life, but exerting its powers, as the wind blows where it listeth, at will upon the corruptions and abuses of mankind. What have looks, or tones, to do with that sublime identification of his age with that of the *heavens themselves*, when, in his reproaches to them for conniving at the injustice of his children, he reminds them that "they themselves are old"? What gesture shall we appropriate to this? What has the voice or the eye to do with such things? But the play is beyond all art, as the tamperings with it show: it is too hard and stony; it must have love-scenes, and a happy ending. It is not enough that Cordelia is a daughter, she must shine as a lover too. Tate has put his hook in the nostrils of this Leviathan, for Garrick and his followers, the show-men of the scene, to draw the mighty beast about more easily. A happy ending!—as if the living martyrdom that Lear had gone through,—the flaying of his feelings alive, did not make a fair dismissal from the stage of life the only decorous thing for him. If he is to live and be happy after, if he could sustain this world's burden after, why all this pudder and preparation,—why torment us with all this unnecessary sympathy? As if the childish pleasure of getting his gilt robes and sceptre again could tempt him to act over again his misused station—as if, at his years and with his experience, anything was left but to die.

Lear is essentially impossible to be represented on a stage. But how many dramatic personages are there in Shakspeare, which though more tractable and feasible (if I may so speak) than Lear, yet from some circumstance, some adjunct to their character, are improper to be shown to our bodily eye! Othello for instance. Nothing can be more soothing, more flattering to the nobler parts of our natures, than to read of a young Venetian lady of the highest extraction, through the force of love and from a sense of merit in him whom she loved, laying aside every consideration of kindred, and country, and colour, and wedding with a *coal-black Moor*—(for such he is represented, in the imperfect state of knowledge respecting foreign countries in those days, compared with our own, or in compliance with popular notions, though the Moors are now well enough known to be by many shades less unworthy of a white woman's fancy)—it is the perfect triumph of virtue over accidents, of the imagination over the senses. She sees Othello's colour in his mind. But upon the stage, when the imagination is no longer the ruling faculty, but we are left to our poor unassisted senses, I appeal to every one that has seen Othello played, whether he did not, on the contrary, sink Othello's mind in his colour; whether he did not find something extremely revolting in the courtship and wedded caresses of Othello and Desdemona; and whether the actual sight of the thing did not overweigh all that beautiful compromise which we have in reading;—and the reason it should do so is obvious, because there is just so much reality presented to our senses as to give a perception of disagreement, with not enough of belief in the internal motives,—all that which is unseen,—to overpower and reconcile the first and obvious prejudices. What we see upon a stage is body and bodily action; what we are conscious of in reading is almost exclusively the mind, and its movements; and this I think may sufficiently account for the very different sort of delight with which the same play so often affects us in the reading and the seeing.

It requires little reflection to perceive, that if those characters in Shakspeare which are within the precincts of nature, have yet something in them which appeals too exclusively to the imagination, to admit of their being made objects to the senses without suffering a change and a diminution,—that still stronger the objection must lie against representing another line of characters, which Shakspeare has introduced to give a wildness and a supernatural elevation to his scenes, as if to remove them still farther from that assimilation to common life in which their excellence is vulgarly supposed to consist. When we read the incantations of those terrible beings the Witches in *Macbeth*, though some of the ingredients of their hellish composition savour of the grotesque, yet is the effect upon us other than the most serious and appalling that can be imagined? Do we not feel spellbound as Macbeth was? Can any mirth accompany a sense of their presence? We might as well laugh under a consciousness of the principle of Evil himself being truly and really present with us. But attempt to bring these things on to a stage, and you turn them instantly into so many old women, that men and children are to laugh at. Contrary to the old saying, that "seeing is believing," the sight actually destroys the faith; and the mirth in which we indulge at their expense, when we see these creatures upon a stage, seems to be a sort of indemnification which we make to ourselves for the terror which they put us in when reading made them an object of belief,—when we surrendered up our reason to the poet, as children to their nurses and their elders; and we laugh at our fears as children, who thought they saw something in the dark, triumph when the bringing in of a candle discovers the vanity of their fears. For this exposure of supernatural agents upon a stage is truly bringing in a candle to expose their own delusiveness. It is the solitary taper and the book that generates a faith in these terrors: a ghost by chandelier light, and in good company, deceives no spectators,— a ghost that can be measured by the eye, and his human dimensions made out at leisure. . . .

. . . Spirits and fairies cannot be represented, they cannot even be painted,—they can only be believed. But the elaborate and anxious provision of scenery, which the luxury of the age demands, in these cases works a quite contrary effect to what is intended. That which in comedy, or plays of familiar life, adds so much to the life of the imitation, in plays which appeal to the higher faculties positively destroys the illusion which it is introduced to aid. A parlour or a drawing room,—a library opening into a garden—a garden with an alcove in it,—a street, or the piazza of Covent Garden, does well enough in a scene; we are content to give as much credit to it as it demands; or rather, we think little about it,—it is little more than reading at the top of a page, "Scene, a garden"; we do not imagine ourselves there, but we readily admit the imitation of familiar objects. But to think by the help of painted trees and caverns, which we know to be painted, to transport our minds to Prospero, and his island and his lonely cell, or by the aid of a fiddle dexterously thrown in, in an interval of speaking, to make us believe that we hear those supernatural noises of which the isle was full: the Orrery Lecturer at the Haymarket might as well hope, by his musical glasses cleverly stationed out of sight behind his apparatus, to make us believe that we do indeed hear the crystal spheres ring out that chime, . . .

The subject of Scenery is closely connected with that of the Dresses, which are so anxiously attended to on our stage. I remember the last time I saw *Macbeth* played, the discrepancy I felt at the changes of garment which he varied,—the shiftings and re-shiftings, like a Romish priest at mass. The luxury of stage improvements, and the importunity of the public eye, require this. The coronation robe of the Scottish monarch was fairly a counterpart to that which our King wears when he goes to the Parliament-house,—just so full and cumbersome, and set out with ermine and pearls. And if things must be represented, I see not what to find fault with in this. But in reading, what robe are we conscious of? Some dim images of royalty—a crown and sceptre—may float before our eyes, but who shall describe the fashion of it? Do we see in our mind's eye what Webb or any other robe-maker could pattern? This is the inevitable consequence of imitating everything, to make all things natural. Whereas the reading of a tragedy is a fine abstraction. It presents to the fancy just so much of external appearances as to make us feel that we are among flesh and blood, while by far the greater and better part of our imagination is employed upon the thoughts and internal machinery of the character. But in acting, scenery, dress, the most contemptible things, call upon us to judge of their naturalness.

Perhaps it would be no bad similitude, to liken the pleasure which we take in seeing one of these fine plays acted, compared with that quiet delight which we find in the reading of it, to the different feelings with which a reviewer, and a man that is not a reviewer, reads a fine poem. The accursed critical habit,—the being called upon to judge and pronounce, must make it quite a different thing to the former. In seeing these plays acted, we are affected just as judges. When Hamlet compares the two pictures of Gertrude's first and second husband, who wants to see the pictures? But in the acting, a miniature must be lugged out; which we know not to be the picture, but only to show how finely a miniature may be represented. This showing of everything levels all things: it makes tricks, bows, and curtseys, of importance. Mrs. S[iddons] never got more fame by anything than by the manner in which she dismisses the guests in the banquet-scene in *Macbeth:* it is as much remembered as any of her thrilling tones or impressive looks. But does such a trifle as this enter into the imaginations of the readers of that wild and wonderful scene? Does not the mind dismiss the feasters as rapidly as it can? Does it care about the gracefulness of the doing it? But by acting, and judging of acting, all these non-essentials are raised into an importance, injurious to the main interest of the play. . . .

With Lamb's words in mind, let us turn now to *Macbeth*. A rewarding play in itself, it takes on added dimension viewed in close proximity to *Oedipus Rex,* for, the shortest of Shakespeare's tragedies, it is powerful and compelling for many of the same reasons *Oedipus Rex* is. The story was as familiar to Elizabethan audiences as the story of Oedipus was to the Greeks. Shakespeare's probable source of usable material was a history of Britain called the *Chronicles,* written by Raphael Holinshed. Popular in that time, it was read and discussed extensively, so the basic story-line, like that of *Oedipus,* was known to the audience. Suspense is generated, then, in the unfolding of character rather than in the disclosure of outcome. Of course, in building his dramatic structure, Shakespeare did not literally recreate Holinshed's story. Combining the account of Macbeth with the account of an earlier Scottish king, Duff, and Donwald, Shakespeare neatly rearranged history, telescoped ideas, and created a new approach to old accounts.

THE TRAGEDY OF MACBETH

by William Shakespeare

DRAMATIS PERSONAE

DUNCAN, *King of Scotland.*

MALCOLM,
DONALBAIN, } *his sons.*

MACBETH,
BANQUO, } *generals of the King's army.*

MACDUFF,
LENNOX,
ROSS,
MENTEITH,
ANGUS,
CAITHNESS, } *noblemen of Scotland.*

FLEANCE, *son to* BANQUO.

SIWARD, *earl of Northumberland.*

Young SIWARD, *his son.*

SEYTON, *an officer attending on* MACBETH.

Boy, *son to* MACDUFF.

An English Doctor.

A Scotch Doctor.

A Captain.

A Porter.

An Old Man.

LADY MACBETH.

LADY MACDUFF.

Gentlewoman attending on LADY MACBETH.

HECATE.

Three Witches.

The Ghost of BANQUO.

Apparitions.

Lords, Gentlemen, Officers, Soldiers, Murderers, Attendants, and Messengers.

SCENE: *Scotland; England*

ACT I

SCENE I. *A heath.*

(*Thunder and lightning. Enter three* WITCHES.)

FIRST WITCH. When shall we three meet again
In thunder, lightning, or in rain?

SECOND WITCH. When the hurlyburly's done,
When the battle's lost and won.

THIRD WITCH. That will be ere the set of sun.   *5*

The notes and text for "Macbeth" are from *Shakespeare, Twenty-three Plays and the Sonnets,* revised edition, pp. 828–858, edited by Thomas Marc Parrott. Copyright 1938, 1953 Charles Scribner's Sons. Used by permission of the publisher. (The line number at the end of each prose passage corresponds to the standard numbering in all modern Shakespeare texts. Line numbers of blank verse are always standard.)

3. **hurlyburly's,** turmoil's.

FIRST WITCH. Where the place?
SECOND WITCH.   Upon the heath.
THIRD WITCH. There to meet with Macbeth.
FIRST WITCH. I come, Graymalkin!
SECOND WITCH. Paddock calls.
THIRD WITCH. Anon!   *10*
ALL. Fair is foul, and foul is fair;
Hover through the fog and filthy air.   (*Exeunt.*)

Macbeth immediately presents a very different atmosphere and tone
if compared with *Oedipus*. Much of the horror of *Oedipus* results from
the bright presence of Phoebos Apollo, a symbolic sun bathing the dark
recesses of Oedipus' mind and actions with its illumination, leaving no
shadows, either physical or mental, where ignorance, ambition, or guilt
can hide. Whereas *Macbeth* begins in gloom and then proceeds on a
series of scenes dominated by darkness, only breaking into light in the
last four scenes as good triumphs over evil. Hellish fire and clinging-blood
images provide scant but horrible illumination for the first twenty-two
gloom-heavy scenes. Hecate (the goddess of darkness, the queen of the
dead, and the patroness of families with children) hovers over all of *Macbeth,* actually appearing or simply materializing in the three weird sisters
(each possibly suggesting one of her aspects, for she was a triple-faced
deity worshipped where three roads meet). Witches the sisters surely are,
for Hecate had become queen of all witches by the time of King James
during whose reign *Macbeth* was written. But the sisters are more than
mere witches; they recall the three fates of the Greeks, though they are
not the identical three. The witches are, in short, personifications of evil,
awful creatures who can reveal the *possible* future—possible because man,
gifted with freedom of will, can change that future. He is not destined to
any eventuality. Each man's nature being what it is, however, the weird
sisters *can* forecast probability. They *warn* quite as much as they *foretell;*
man is free to heed the warning, to hasten the prophesy, or to circumvent it utterly if such be his will. Macbeth can and must make his own
choices.

Stage settings are easy to visualize in this play. The heaths of Scotland
are desolate, fog-shrouded wastelands supporting no large vegetation.
Heather and other hardy shrubs cling to the storm-blasted face of the
land, withstanding the excesses of rain, sun, and wind through sheer
determination to survive. Lichens and mosses, the lowliest of plants, claim

---

8. **Graymalkin,** gray cat, a common familiar spirit of the witch.   9. **Paddock,** toad.   10. **Anon,**
coming.

the heath with their leech-like networks of hair roots. Life is difficult on these lonely stretches—difficult and unfriendly, for social amenities are luxuries which the bitter, determined life forms have not had time to cultivate. Kindness requires effort, and all effort of life on a heath must go toward simple survival. Yet a wild, excessive beauty dwells here. Gnarled by wind, stunted by time, heath plants bloom in fierce pastels, contrasting sharply with the dark earth from which they rise. Strange forms and weird imaginings lurk in the misty distances; every sound rides the lonely winds and seems the anguished cry of nature's neglected exiles threatening the very existence of those who intrude themselves in this unhappy place, bringing memory and suggestion of a less precarious existence to taunt these lonely land swells.

Set in this place of contrasts, Scene I intensifies the eerie atmosphere with heavy thunder and jagged lightning. And out of the ugly beauty come three witches—creatures neither human nor divine, dwellers in the evil beauty that exists between the world of man and his envisioned heaven. Free of their fleshy confines, they can ride the air, but it is always heavy with their presence, nor can it buoy them up to God nor drop them into Hell. Unchained from earth, denied the sky, the witches symbolize the dreams of men who, wanting faith, find flesh a curse in constant utterance. Confusion clouds their every word, these oracles of some nether-god, and, like the voice of Phoebos' snake, they speak a promise that's a lie when it's received with hope.

Three in number, the witches even mock the sacred trinity and suggest the very contradictions of man's faith. "When the battle's lost and won" —a battle lost is a battle won by the opponent; still, who presumes to fight and lose? The witches' answer is a riddle: "Fair is foul, and foul is fair." What seems open and sporting often is, in actuality, dishonest. What seems harsh and gives offense is often the most honest. Hypocrisy veils its acts in words of dark intent, and man is always willing to be devious in his means, *if* the final end is desirable enough. Macbeth is a man of noble grain, a grain that is flawed by his human needs. What he is now and what he will become seem to reside in the powerful words of these three sisters: so fair he is; so foul he'll be. And fair and foul do make up Macbeth's soul. His soul is, like that of any man, and like this god-blasted heath, a mid-region of strange contrasts—contrasts extended to the final lines of this first scene wherein the witches' familiars (their intimate spiritual servants) summon them. Implicit is the suggestion that evil serves that which is served by evil, or, in an evil situation, the master becomes the slave to the slave in return for services rendered.

SCENE II. *A camp near Forres.*

(*Alarum within.* Enter KING DUNCAN, MALCOLM, DONALBAIN, LENNOX, *with Attendants, meeting a bleeding* CAPTAIN.)

DUNCAN. What bloody man is that? He can report,
As seemeth by his plight, of the revolt
The newest state.

  MALCOLM. This is the sergeant
Who like a good and hardy soldier fought
'Gainst my captivity. Hail, brave friend!   *5*
Say to the King the knowledge of the broil
As thou didst leave it.

  CAPTAIN.   Doubtful it stood,
As two spent swimmers that do cling together
And choke their art. The merciless Macdonwald—
Worthy to be a rebel, for to that   *10*
The multiplying villainies of nature
Do swarm upon him—from the Western Isles
Of kerns and gallowglasses is suppli'd;
And Fortune, on his damned quarrel smiling,
Show'd like a rebel's whore: but all's too weak; *15*
For brave Macbeth—well he deserves that name—
Disdaining Fortune, with his brandish'd steel,
Which smok'd with bloody execution,
(Like Valour's minion) carv'd out his passage
Till he fac'd the slave;   *20*
Which ne'er shook hands, nor bade farewell to him,
Till he unseam'd him from the nave to th' chaps,
And fix'd his head upon our battlements.

  DUNCAN. O valiant cousin! worthy gentleman!

  CAPTAIN. As whence the sun gins his reflection *25*
Shipwrecking storms and direful thunders break,
So from that spring whence comfort seem'd to come
Discomfort swells. Mark, King of Scotland, mark!
No sooner justice had, with valour arm'd,
Compell'd these skipping kerns to trust their heels, *30*

---

6. **broil,** battle. 9. **choke,** render useless. 10. **for to that,** because. 13. **kerns,** light-armed Irish foot-soldiers. **gallowglasses,** heavily armed retainers of Irish chiefs. 19. **minion,** favorite. 21. **Which,** who, i.e., Macbeth. 22. **unseam'd,** ripped up. **nave,** navel. **chaps,** jaws. 24. **cousin,** a common form of address from a king to a noble, but Duncan and Macbeth were really first cousins. 25. **gins his reflection,** the new danger came from the East.

But the Norweyan lord, surveying vantage,
With furbish'd arms and new supplies of men
Began a fresh assault.
    DUNCAN.   Dismay'd not this
Our captains, Macbeth and Banquo?
    CAPTAIN.   Yes;
As sparrows eagles, or the hare the lion.   *35*
If I say sooth, I must report they were
As cannons overcharg'd with double cracks;
So they doubly redoubled strokes upon the foe.
Except they meant to bathe in reeking wounds,
Or memorize another Golgotha,   *40*
I cannot tell.
But I am faint, my gashes cry for help.
    DUNCAN. So well thy words become thee as thy wounds;
They smack of honour both. Go get him surgeons.   (*Exit* CAPTAIN, *attended.*)

Exposition (background) and details of character occupy the first half of Scene II. Envisioning a military camp's drab tents beneath brilliant oriflammes should create no great problem for the reader who has seen Hollywood's epic re-creations. Soldiers garbed in battle dress, horses pawing at the turf, a lowering sky—all build the scene within the mind. And over all, the clank of metal, the sound of oaths muttered softly in the gathering dark. Then add the fumes of food blown on the wind, the moist heat of horses ridden hard, the dark leather waxed and stained by sweat, and the cloying, sweet, rich smell of blood let flow in manly fight, and you will have the scene. It all seems so clean, so washed of filth in contrast to Scene I.

You should note the dignity attending these men, this king, these princes, these nobles, and their officers. You should hear greatness standing proud as only it can stand in gratitude. You should hear battles being waged in the words the Captain speaks. Staunch, bold, and fearless, he says, was Macbeth with Banquo at his side. Outnumbered, tired, but undismayed, they fought like eagles, like proud lions. But now Scene I intrudes a thought; what rendezvous could evil hags have with this mighty captain named Macbeth? Surely his world is valiant; surely theirs is vile. Can even a heath with its sharp contrasts bridge Macbeth's world and theirs?

---

31. **surveying vantage,** seeing a good opportunity.   32. **furbish'd,** burnished, fresh.   37. **cracks,** charges.   40. **memorize,** make memorable.

(*Enter* ROSS *and* ANGUS.)
Who comes here?
    MALCOLM.   The worthy thane of Ross.   *45*
    LENNOX. What a haste looks through his eyes!
So should he look that seems to speak things strange.
    ROSS.   God save the King!
    DUNCAN. Whence cam'st thou, worthy thane?
    ROSS.   From Fife, great king;
Where the Norweyan banners flout the sky
And fan our people cold.   *50*
Norway himself, with terrible numbers,
Assisted by that most disloyal traitor,
The thane of Cawdor, began a dismal conflict;
Till that Bellona's bridegroom, lapp'd in proof,
Confronted him with self-comparisons,   *55*
Point against point, rebellious arm 'gainst arm,
Curbing his lavish spirit; and, to conclude,
The victory fell on us;—
    DUNCAN.   Great happiness!
    ROSS.   That now
Sweno, the Norway's king, craves composition;
Nor would we deign him burial of his men   *60*
Till he disbursed at Saint Colme's inch
Ten thousand dollars to our general use.
    DUNCAN. No more that thane of Cawdor shall deceive
Our bosom interest. Go pronounce his present death,
And with his former title greet Macbeth.   *65*
    ROSS. I'll see it done.
    DUNCAN. What he hath lost, noble Macbeth hath won.   (*Exeunt.*)

Fresh from the battlefield at Fife come Ross and Angus bringing news. The traitorous thane of Cawdor has been vanquished, Norway's Sweno has sued for peace and, meeting the terms presented to him, has accepted his defeat. King Duncan's ears still ring with the brave words the bleeding Captain spoke. Comparing Cawdor's villainy with the valorous actions

---

45. **thane,** Scottish title equivalent to earl.   47. **seems,** seems about.   49. **flout,** mock.
54. **Bellona,** Roman goddess of war.   **lapp'd in proof,** clad in armor.   55. **Confronted . . .**
self-comparisons, showed prowess equal to his own.   57. **lavish,** arrogant.   59. **composition,**
terms of peace.   61. **Saint Colme's inch,** Inchcolm, the Isle of St. Columba, in the Firth of
Forth.   64. **bosom interest,** loving confidence.   **present,** instant.

of Macbeth, the grateful Duncan grants Macbeth the title lately sullied. Now it is that evil (Cawdor) begins to serve the good (Macbeth): "foul is fair." And yet the implication is there for those who can see it: evil corrupts that which it serves. *Macbeth* begins to take its form, suggesting in two closely-knit scenes the theme to be unravelled.

SCENE III. *A heath near Forres.*

> (*Thunder. Enter the three* WITCHES.)
> FIRST WITCH. Where hast thou been, sister?
> SECOND WITCH. Killing swine.
> THIRD WITCH. Sister, where thou?
> FIRST WITCH. A sailor's wife had chestnuts in her lap,

And munch'd, and munch'd, and munch'd. "Give me!" quoth I.   *5*
"Aroint thee, witch!" the rump-fed ronyon cries.
Her husband's to Aleppo gone, master o' th' Tiger;
But in a sieve I'll thither sail,
And, like a rat without a tail,
I'll do, I'll do, and I'll do.   *10*

> SECOND WITCH. I'll give thee a wind.
> FIRST WITCH. Thou 'rt kind.
> THIRD WITCH. And I another.
> FIRST WITCH. I myself have all the other,

And the very ports they blow,   *15*
All the quarters that they know
I' th' shipman's card.
I'll drain him dry as hay:
Sleep shall neither night nor day
Hang upon his pent-house lid;   *20*
He shall live a man forbid.
Weary sev'nights nine times nine
Shall he dwindle, peak, and pine.
Though his bark cannot be lost,
Yet it shall be tempest-tost.   *25*
Look what I have.

> SECOND WITCH. Show me, show me.

---

6. **Aroint,** be gone.   **rump-fed ronyon,** mangy creature fed on refuse.   7. **Aleppo,** city in Syria.   8. **sieve,** a traditional vehicle of witches.   9. **rat . . . tail,** witches could change themselves into the form of animals, but could sometimes be recognized by a physical defect, such as the lack of a tail.   14. **other,** others.   15. **blow,** blow upon.   17. **card,** compass card or chart.   20. **pent-house lid,** eyelid.   21. **forbid,** accursed.

FIRST WITCH. Here I have a pilot's thumb,
Wreck'd as homeward he did come. *(Drum within.)*
   THIRD WITCH. A drum, a drum! *30*
Macbeth doth come.
   ALL. The weird sisters, hand in hand,
Posters of the sea and land,
Thus do go about, about;
Thrice to thine, and thrice to mine, *35*
And thrice again, to make up nine.
Peace! the charm's wound up.

Evil thrives on petty deeds and takes its pleasure in the telling of them. The witches gather on the heath, sharing their tales of mischief done: of killing swine or venting wrath on those who have aroused their anger. Unable to predetermine destiny ("Though his bark cannot be lost"), they work enchantments on the mind; they weaken the will with pressure plied against the brain. The sailor's wife who would not share the wealth of chestnuts in her lap enraged the witch who will now make her pay through that which is important: her husband will be wracked with the pain of sleeplessness and shall live accursed. The first witch has a pilot's thumb to guide with guile the victim's course *if* he prefers to follow. If such an unimportant man supplies the witches with such fun, how great the pleasure Macbeth will bring as they wind up the charm!

   (Enter MACBETH *and* BANQUO.*)*
   MACBETH. So foul and fair a day I have not seen.
   BANQUO. How far is 't call'd to Forres? What are these
So wither'd and so wild in their attire, *40*
That look not like th' inhabitants o' th' earth,
And yet are on 't? Live you? or are you aught
That man may question? You seem to understand me,
By each at once her choppy finger laying
Upon her skinny lips: you should be women, *45*
And yet your beards forbid me to interpret
That you are so.
   MACBETH. Speak, if you can. What are you?
   FIRST WITCH. All hail, Macbeth! hail to thee, thane of Glamis!
   SECOND WITCH. All hail, Macbeth! hail to thee, thane of Cawdor!

---

32. **weird sisters,** sisters of destiny.   33. **Posters of,** travelers over.   44. **choppy,** chapped.

THIRD WITCH. All hail, Macbeth, that shalt be King hereafter!   *50*
BANQUO. Good sir, why do you start, and seem to fear
Things that do sound so fair?—
                                        I' th' name of truth,
Are ye fantastical, or that indeed
Which outwardly ye show? My noble partner
You greet with present grace and great prediction   *55*
Of noble having and of royal hope,
That he seems rapt withal; to me you speak not.
If you can look into the seeds of time,
And say which grain will grow and which will not,
Speak then to me, who neither beg nor fear   *60*
Your favours nor your hate.
    FIRST WITCH. Hail!
    SECOND WITCH. Hail!
    THIRD WITCH. Hail!
    FIRST WITCH. Lesser than Macbeth, and greater.   *65*
    SECOND WITCH. Not so happy, yet much happier.
    THIRD WITCH. Thou shalt get kings, though thou be none;
So all hail, Macbeth and Banquo!
    FIRST WITCH. Banquo and Macbeth, all hail!
    MACBETH. Stay, you imperfect speakers, tell me more.   *70*
By Sinel's death I know I am thane of Glamis;
But how of Cawdor? The thane of Cawdor lives,
A prosperous gentleman; and to be king
Stands not within the prospect of belief
No more than to be Cawdor. Say from whence   *75*
You owe this strange intelligence, or why
Upon this blasted heath you stop our way
With such prophetic greeting. Speak, I charge you.   (WITCHES *vanish.*)
    BANQUO. The earth hath bubbles, as the water has,
And these are of them. Whither are they vanish'd?   *80*
    MACBETH. Into the air; and what seem'd corporal melted
As breath into the wind. Would they had stay'd!
    BANQUO. Were such things here as we do speak about,
Or have we eaten on the insane root
That takes the reason prisoner?   *85*
    MACBETH. Your children shall be kings.

---

53. fantastical, creatures of the imagination.   **54. show,** appear to be.   **56. having,** possessions,
rank.   **57. rapt,** in a trance.   **67. get,** beget.   **71. Sinel's,** Macbeth's father.   **76. owe,**
have.   **84. on,** of.   **insane root,** root that causes insanity.

BANQUO.   You shall be King.
MACBETH. And thane of Cawdor too; went it not so?
BANQUO. To th' self-same tune and words.
Who's here?

As sunlight parts the shrouding clouds, it glints upon the horses' flanks and twinkles on the studded mail worn by Macbeth and Banquo. But briefly do the rays come down to chase away the gloom of a stormy evening; the clouds regroup to shut out the light, intensifying beauty: "So foul and fair a day I have not seen," Macbeth observes. Foul gloom and fair sun alternate this day, just as the desires of man may alternate. Macbeth's noble nature is clouded by the gloom of his deep longings. The battle is done, the glory is gone, and now must follow long and boring days of anticlimax. So fair our hero's actions in the fray, so foul the daily life to come. Dramatic irony thus illuminates the dark wisdom of Macbeth's first line. This day has seen his sun of fame break through, but now it seems to die as spiritual storm-clouds gather. Briefly it shone upon a man of deeds; it dies before his human needs. So foul and fair it is.

Brave Banquo points out three ancient crones, the withered witches gazing on the flesh of two men upright before their drooling presence. Chapped fingers on their skinny lips, their rags blown back by heath-wild winds, the witches pick at the facial hair which sprouts from the brown, round moles on their chins. The drama of this eerie scene builds on the fears each man knew as a child when, looking at an October moon, he fled his Halloween pumpkins.

Suddenly, hearing the future shaped on these skinny, slobbering lips, Macbeth at first "starts" and then "seems to fear" before he grows entranced. What visions flicker through the heath of his noble mind? What makes him grow so silent at the words the three witches breathe into the foul heath air? Does future hope hold him in thrall so quickly that he is struck dumb? Or is he noble at this point and caught amazed by the evil in the words he hears? His bravery in the recent fight now seems part of the distant past as, in the fog-filled twilight heath, Banquo allies himself in haste with the witches.

Do the waiting horses shy and paw the turf? Do they softly whinny in the gloom? Is this what makes Macbeth finally regain his speech, demanding proof? Or is it merely that he hears the hope the witches' words seem to have planted in Banquo's willing heart? At any rate, he demands "whence" and "why," but as he asks, the witches melt away; their dirt-encrusted rags turn pale; diaphanous, they blend into the wind and vanish in its quick-tortured course across the heath. Lest it be thought merely a dream or a deranged thought, Macbeth and Banquo hastily verify the words they each heard, each of their fancies caught on future promise.

(*Enter* ROSS *and* ANGUS.)

ROSS. The King hath happily receiv'd, Macbeth,
The news of thy success; and when he reads   90
Thy personal venture in the rebels' fight,
His wonders and his praises do contend
Which should be thine or his. Silenc'd with that,
In viewing o'er the rest o' th' self-same day,
He finds thee in the stout Norweyan ranks,   95
Nothing afeard of what thyself didst make,
Strange images of death. As thick as hail
Came post with post; and every one did bear
Thy praises in his kingdom's great defence,
And pour'd them down before him.

    ANGUS.   We are sent   100
To give thee from our royal master thanks;
Only to herald thee into his sight,
Not pay thee.

    ROSS. And, for an earnest of a greater honour,
He bade me, from him, call thee thane of Cawdor;   105
In which addition, hail, most worthy thane!
For it is thine.

    BANQUO (*aside*). What, can the devil speak true?

    MACBETH. The thane of Cawdor lives; why do you dress me
In borrowed robes?

    ANGUS.   Who was the thane lives yet;
But under heavy judgement bears that life   110
Which he deserves to lose. Whether he was combin'd
With those of Norway, or did line the rebel
With hidden help and vantage, or that with both
He labour'd in his country's wreck, I know not;
But treasons capital, confess'd and prov'd,   115
Have overthrown him.

    MACBETH (*aside*). Glamis, and thane of Cawdor!
The greatest is behind.

96. **Nothing afeard,** not at all afraid.   104. **earnest,** advance payment.   106. **In . . . addition,** under which title.   112. **line,** support.

(*To* ROSS *and* ANGUS.)   Thanks for your pains.
(*To* BANQUO.) Do you not hope your children shall be kings,
When those that gave the thane of Cawdor to me
Promis'd no less to them?

      BANQUO.   That trusted home   120
Might yet enkindle you unto the crown,
Besides the thane of Cawdor. But 't is strange;
And oftentimes, to win us to our harm,
The instruments of darkness tell us truths,
Win us with honest trifles, to betray 's   125
In deepest consequence.
Cousins, a word, I pray you.

      MACBETH (*aside*).   Two truths are told,
As happy prologues to the swelling act
Of the imperial theme.—I thank you, gentlemen.
(*Aside.*) This supernatural soliciting   130
Cannot be ill, cannot be good. If ill,
Why hath it given me earnest of success.
Commencing in a truth? I 'm thane of Cawdor.
If good, why do I yield to that suggestion
Whose horrid image doth unfix my hair   135
And make my seated heart knock at my ribs,
Against the use of nature? Present fears
Are less than horrible imaginings.
My thought, whose murder yet is but fantastical,
Shakes so my single state of man that function   140
Is smother'd in surmise, and nothing is
But what is not.

      BANQUO.   Look, how our partner's rapt.

      MACBETH (*aside*). If chance will have me King, why, chance may crown me,
Without my stir.

      BANQUO.   New honours come upon him
Like our strange garments, cleave not to their mould   145
But with the aid of use.

      MACBETH (*aside*).   Come what come may,
Time and the hour runs through the roughest day.

      BANQUO. Worthy Macbeth, we stay upon your leisure.

---

120. **home,** to the full.   129. **imperial theme,** theme of sovereignty.   130. **soliciting,**
temptation.   140. **single state of man,** the harmonious kingdom of my mind.   140-2. **function . . . not,** the power to act is lost in one overpowering image, that of the crown, which is
for me the only reality.   144. **my stir,** action on my part.   145. **strange,** new.

MACBETH. Give me your favour; my dull brain was wrought
With things forgotten. Kind gentlemen, your pains   *150*
Are register'd where every day I turn
The leaf to read them. Let us toward the King.
(*To* BANQUO.) Think upon what hath chanc'd, and, at more time,
The interim having weigh'd it, let us speak
Our free hearts each to other.
    BANQUO.   Very gladly.   *155*
    MACBETH. Till then, enough. Come, friends.   (*Exeunt.*)

It would take a Sophocles to improve the unity of *Macbeth*. This scene supplies that unity and brings it to the exposition of the play as the pieces begin to fall into place to shape the form of Macbeth's mind. Bright Banquo quickly sees the truth, and quickly he accepts the hope. But slower in his hour of triumph here, Macbeth is more disturbed. Again he asks for further proof—a proof the messengers *can* give, for they confirm and do not confound as the witches sought to do.

Coincidence or destiny? Should a man know the future? Can he live with his knowledge of it and yet not move to make it be as promised? Banquo is cautious, knowing that hope is but a snare for weak-willed men; an evil promise brings swift doom if we demand fulfillment. Macbeth, less cautious now, knows the pain of promise that unfolds ahead; immediacy is harder borne than distant hopes not readily attained. Banquo can wait—*his* children reap the promised future which he can not. Yet Duncan has two sons in line; Macbeth has none. If Glamis and Cawdor move to bring the evil hags' fair words to foul, will not the sons of Banquo be moved nearer their crowns by Macbeth's act? What holds the tongue of Banquo dumb? Does he here serve two masters?

SCENE IV. *Forres. The palace.*
(*Flourish. Enter* KING DUNCAN, MALCOLM, DONALBAIN, LENNOX, *and Attendants.*)
    DUNCAN. Is execution done on Cawdor? Are not
Those in commission yet return'd?
    MALCOLM.   My liege,
They are not yet come back. But I have spoke
With one that saw him die; who did report
That very frankly he confess'd his treasons,   *5*
Implor'd your Highness' pardon, and set forth
A deep repentance. Nothing in his life

---

149. **favour,** pardon. **wrought,** disturbed. 153. **at . . . time,** when we have more time. 155. **Our free hearts,** our hearts freely. 2. **in commission,** deputed to carry it out.

Became him like the leaving it. He died
As one that had been studied in his death
To throw away the dearest thing he ow'd,   *10*
As 't were a careless trifle.
    DUNCAN.   There's no art
To find the mind's construction in the face.
He was a gentleman on whom I built
An absolute trust.

    Suddenly trumpets blare, harsh sounds ricochet off chiseled stones and down drafty halls. The Scottish palace, bleak and bare, sits hard by the peat-bogged heath. Down the gloomy walls of mossing stone, up the battlements haze-hung and dim, a dying light beclouds the air, concealing all but a few sharp outlines as bodies move through the sick light that struggles through the gloom. Tall torches, high up on the walls, and a cavernous fireplace filled with flame lend sooty smoke to cancel the light they create in the room. King Duncan speaks with dark-edged words requesting that Cawdor's death be told to him. Malcolm's report is bright with the praise of reclaimed dignity. Dark blends with light as Duncan sadly notes how seldom a man's face reveals his heart (11–12)—what slight foundations we mortals make for edifices as great as trust! Still, what else can man found his trust upon? The king now trusts Macbeth. This irony is stronger than all men, all trust, and all time between the hour Shakespeare first set it down and now.

    (*Enter* MACBETH, BANQUO, ROSS, *and* ANGUS.)
                    O worthiest cousin!
The sin of my ingratitude even now   *15*
Was heavy on me. Thou art so far before
That swiftest wing of recompense is slow
To overtake thee. Would thou hadst less deserv'd,
That the proportion both of thanks and payment
Might have been mine! only I have left to say,   *20*
More is thy due than more than all can pay.
    MACBETH. The service and the loyalty I owe,
In doing it, pays itself. Your Highness' part
Is to receive our duties; and our duties
Are to your throne and state children and servants,   *25*
Which do but what they should, by doing everything
Safe toward your love and honour.

---

11. **careless,** not cared for.   12. **construction,** interpretation.   27. **Safe toward,** with sure regard for.

DUNCAN.   Welcome hither!
I have begun to plant thee, and will labour
To make thee full of growing. Noble Banquo,
That hast no less deserv'd, nor must be known   30
No less to have done so, let me infold thee
And hold thee to my heart.
     BANQUO.   There if I grow,
The harvest is your own.
          DUNCAN.   My plenteous joys,
Wanton in fulness, seek to hide themselves
In drops of sorrow. Sons, kinsmen, thanes,   35
And you whose places are the nearest, know
We will establish our estate upon
Our eldest, Malcolm, whom we name hereafter
The Prince of Cumberland; which honour must
Not unaccompanied invest him only,   40
But signs of nobleness, like stars, shall shine
On all deservers. From hence to Inverness,
And bind us further to you.
     MACBETH. The rest is labour, which is not us'd for you.
I'll be myself the harbinger and make joyful   45
The hearing of my wife with your approach;
So humbly take my leave.
          DUNCAN.   My worthy Cawdor!
     MACBETH (*aside*). The Prince of Cumberland! That is a step
On which I must fall down, or else o'erleap,
For in my way it lies. Stars, hide your fires;   50
Let not light see my black and deep desires;
The eye wink at the hand; yet let that be
Which the eye fears, when it is done, to see.   (*Exit.*)
          DUNCAN. True, worthy Banquo; he is full so valiant,
And in his commendations I am fed;   55
It is a banquet to me. Let's after him,
Whose care is gone before to bid us welcome.
It is a peerless kinsman.   (*Flourish. Exeunt.*)

King Duncan's words are sincere speech; a man needs new walls when
his old bastions fall. Cawdor has failed to merit trust; that trust must

37-9. The Prince of Cumberland was the official title of the heir to the Scottish throne, like that
of the Prince of Wales. This nomination of Malcolm blocks Macbeth's chance of succession.
Cf. ll. 48-50.   45. **harbinger,** officer who went ahead to arrange lodging for the king.
52. **wink at,** refuse to see.

now be cemented in new walls—and Macbeth's seem strongest. Proud Duncan looks upon the face Macbeth wears in the flickering gloom. It seems a fine and noble face, firmed up by battle's measure. So fair it seems; so foul it hides—dishonor shapes veneer of form. Macbeth's duty may be to his king and to his heirs (25), but loyalty *does* pay itself (22–23) when evil serves corruptly.

Banquo too presents a noble face, soft-touched with firelight in the gloom. As Duncan sets his deeds to words and embraces him, Banquo replies with ironic ambiguity: "There if I grow [planted in your heart]/The harvest is your own." Duncan, indeed, has planted thorns; they will now grow and fester on their need to see the witches' words fulfilled; and the harvest will be bloody. If Banquo should speak now and tell Duncan about the prophecies upon the heath, that heart that holds its generals so willingly might be a little more guarded. So Banquo stands dumb as Duncan names his eldest son as his heir and grants him title to the throne of Scotland that has been, by evil, promised to Macbeth.

Macbeth's "mind's construction in the face" is hidden now in the murky hall, guarded in the murky depths of himself stirred by King Duncan's words. Still, as he leaves the stately hall, the glow of flames outlines his form, and like the fires of Hell flamed up, his thoughts are darkly brimstone-tinged: he knows he'll kill to gain the throne late promised him.

Still Banquo stands on silent form and lets the king approach his doom, for in the dancing shadows cast on Forres' walls, he sees his line ascending thrones, he hears his name in Scotland's rolls, he knows his destiny is barred if Macbeth is not left free to act. So Banquo stands on silent form; Macbeth's *his* "peerless kinsman"!

SCENE V. *Inverness. Macbeth's castle.*

(*Enter* MACBETH'S WIFE, *alone, with a letter.*)

LADY MACBETH (*reads*). "They met me in the day of success; and I have learned by the perfect'st report, they have more in them than mortal knowledge. When I burned in desire to question them further, they made themselves air, into which they vanished. Whiles I stood rapt in the wonder of it, came missives from the King, who 5 all-hailed me 'Thane of Cawdor'; by which title, before, these weird sisters saluted me, and referred me to the coming on of time, with 'Hail, King that shalt be!' This 10 have I thought good to deliver thee, my dearest partner of greatness, that thou mightst not lose the dues of rejoicing by being ignorant of what greatness is promised thee. Lay it to thy heart, and farewell." 15

Glamis thou art, and Cawdor; and shalt be

5. **missives,** messengers.

What thou art promis'd. Yet do I fear thy nature;
It is too full o' th' milk of human kindness
To catch the nearest way. Thou wouldst be great,
Art not without ambition, but without   20
The illness should attend it. What thou wouldst highly,
That wouldst thou holily; wouldst not play false,
And yet wouldst wrongly win. Thou 'dst have, great Glamis,
That which cries, "Thus thou must do, if thou have it";
And that which rather thou dost fear to do   25
Than wishest should be undone. Hie thee hither
That I may pour my spirits in thine ear,
And chastise with the valour of my tongue
All that impedes thee from the golden round
Which fate and metaphysical aid doth seem   30
To have thee crown'd withal.
    (*Enter a* MESSENGER.)
                    What is your tidings?
    MESSENGER. The King comes here to-night.
    LADY MACBETH.   Thou 'rt mad to say it!
Is not thy master with him? who, were 't so.
Would have inform'd for preparation.
    MESSENGER. So please you, it is true; our thane is coming.   35
One of my fellows had the speed of him,
Who, almost dead for breath, had scarcely more
Than would make up his message.
    LADY MACBETH.   Give him tending;
He brings great news.   (*Exit* MESSENGER.)
              The raven himself is hoarse
That croaks the fatal entrance of Duncan   40
Under my battlements. Come, you spirits
That tend on mortal thoughts, unsex me here,
And fill me from the crown to the toe top-full
Of direst cruelty! make thick my blood;
Stop up th' access and passage to remorse,   45
That no compunctious visitings of nature
Shake my fell purpose, nor keep peace between
Th' effect and it! Come to my woman's breasts

---

17. **fear,** fear for.   18. **milk of human kindness,** gentleness of human nature.   21. **illness,** evil.   29. **golden round,** the crown.   30. **metaphysical,** supernatural.   36. **had . . . of,** outstripped.   41-2. **spirits . . . thoughts,** evil spirits that inspire murderous thoughts.   45. **remorse,** pity.   46. **compunctious . . . nature,** natural feelings of pity.

And take my milk for gall, you murd'ring ministers,
Wherever in your sightless substances   *50*
You wait on nature's mischief! Come, thick night,
And pall thee in the dunnest smoke of hell,
That my keen knife see not the wound it makes,
Nor heaven peep through the blanket of the dark
To cry, "Hold, hold!"

Now the action moves to Inverness, the Scottish castle, seat of Glamis. Its halls, like those at Forres, are of stone—dark massive stone piled up to bar the savage winds blown from the sea, the foggy damp, and the evil breath of the night-winds from the heath. Gaunt battlements peer down through the mists, high walks cross the air where witches ride, slit windows let in air and light in skinny bits, and jealously. Great wooden doors studded with iron hold nature out; great blazing fires on massive hearths urge heat and light into the rooms, but hand-hewn beams hold the ceilings high, dark corners seem to flee the flames, and heavy hangings hug the walls, protecting them from light.

Outside, the wind moans on the heath, its distant anguish weaving through the gorse and heather crouching down, bent hard against the wind. Heath birds cry out in loneliness in the mists. A dismal sun tries fitfully to part the dull clouds that press the land and hold it in their dew-spawned grasp and shade the mossy fungus growths, slow-spreading spores in shadow.

Deep in the dark and waiting hulk of Inverness, Macbeth's wife reads, in a solitude that she has learned to bear, a letter from her husband. She holds its inked face to the light, and by the flickering tongues of flame, breathes out each word in wonderment at the weird sisters' knowledge. Dwarfed by the massive, stone-walled hall, her tiny figure wreathed in silk embroidered thick with golden threads, she seems so small against the fire that gives her light. Though slight her figure, she looms large in her will-to-win and in her love of him who wrote the letter she here reads. Her words are as dark as any hall that winds its way to the deepest depths beneath the castle at Inverness, but her love gleams and glitters on the surface of her words. Ambition, like a torch, lights up the dark deeds festering in her opening speech, but it is all for her husband—not once does she think the word "queen." She knows Macbeth's nature—or so she thinks—knows he will wait to claim the crown, knows he will do only that which is fair and refuse to do the

---

49. murd'ring ministers, instruments of murder.   **50. sightless,** invisible.   **52. pall,** wrap.

foul. So she will serve his nature fairly by furnishing him with the foulness he needs. Again the implication shines through the flickering words: when evil serves, it masters with the evil of its service.

Suddenly the great doors open, winds sweep in, and the letter flutters in Lady Macbeth's lap. Recalled from her dark revery, she hears the news: Macbeth and the king are coming. Does she spring up to cry "Thou'rt mad"? Or does she sit huddled by the fire? Or does she, with sudden guilt, hold the letter closer to her brocaded thigh? Then, when the messenger leaves, what is her stance? Does she stand looking into the flames? Or does she cross to a window slit and gaze upon the teeming air, there seeing things men cannot see and thinking unnamed names? Whichever way, her words (41-55) now begin to wind up the charm of hate that only a woman knows when she wants to serve the man she loves. Though removed from them by class, by nobility, by love, and by morality, Lady Macbeth nevertheless is wedded to those three sisters dancing on the heath. She is one of their company as she here asks the dark, dread powers (and are they not the powers Hecate rules?) to make her capable of the deed Macbeth needs do and cannot do himself.

Is Lady Macbeth full vile? Ambition-mad? Does she not fear the consequences? Can she, a Christian, flee from God and contemplate dark murder? Not so; if such were her reasons, would she need to plead with the spirits she calls upon? Would she not find herself already possessed of the power to do the dreadful deed? Her woman's nature cries out "Shame!" against her female nature. Dark strength she asks to do the deed; dark strength she asks to hold back light; dark strength she asks to make her dark. She is a noble woman—one who knows that a strength which is given weakens one to pay; still, she asks the dark powers to serve her now—she knows she'll serve them later.

(Enter MACBETH.)

Great Glamis! worthy Cawdor!   *55*
Greater than both, by the all-hail hereafter!
Thy letters have transported me beyond
This ignorant present, and I feel now
The future in the instant.

MACBETH.   My dearest love,
Duncan comes here to-night.

LADY MACBETH.   And when goes hence?   *60*

MACBETH. To-morrow, as he purposes.

LADY MACBETH.   O, never
Shall sun that morrow see!
Your face, my thane, is as a book where men

May read strange matters. To beguile the time,
Look like the time; bear welcome in your eye,   65
Your hand, your tongue; look like th' innocent flower,
But be the serpent under 't. He that's coming
Must be provided for; and you shall put
This night's great business into my dispatch,
Which shall to all our nights and days to come   70
Give solely sovereign sway and masterdom.

    MACBETH. We will speak further.

    LADY MACBETH.   Only look up clear;
To alter favour ever is to fear.
Leave all the rest to me.   *(Exeunt.)*

Lady Macbeth greets her husband with the same words the witches used: "Great Glamis! worthy Cawdor!" Is her speech defiant? Did Macbeth catch her unawares and break her charm midway? To ward off his questioning what he heard or saw as he came softly in, does she engage him willingly with a formal "hail"? Lines 55–56 differ in tone from 57–59. The latter are a plea of love; no formal pattern sets their tone; they are ripped from a loving heart. Does Lady Macbeth not run into his arms? Does she not lift her face to his? And does he not answer her with a kiss? Still, the first two lines preclude that which is so personal in the latter two lines. And Macbeth hears the latter first; his love is more strongly stated here than anywhere else in the play. She is his "dearest love." Never again will she be; never again will his love be the vibrant thing he here declares: "My *dearest* love."

Still, time grows short; the greeting waits. Macbeth supplies his wife with a cue (61) which she, still seeing him as "fair," reacts to without knowledge. Revealing then that she is of a mind to match his earlier, darkest thoughts as hinted at in his letter, she now reads his face and finds it fair, then pleads he make it foul. If he can manage to wear a face that smiles and does not show "the mind's construction," *she* will construct the evil plan: "Leave all the rest to me."

SCENE VI. *Before Macbeth's castle.*

    (Hautboys and torches. Enter KING DUNCAN, MALCOLM, DONALBAIN, BANQUO, LENNOX, MACDUFF, ROSS, ANGUS, *and Attendants.)*

    DUNCAN. This castle hath a pleasant seat; the air
Nimbly and sweetly recommends itself
Unto our gentle senses.

---

72. **clear,** untroubled.   73. **alter favour,** change countenance.   S. d. **Hautboys,** wind instruments.   3. **gentle senses,** senses made gentle.

BANQUO.   This guest of summer,
The temple-haunting martlet, does approve,
By his loved mansionry, that the heaven's breath   *5*
Smells wooingly here; no jutty, frieze,
Buttress, nor coign of vantage, but this bird
Hath made his pendent bed and procreant cradle:
Where they most breed and haunt, I have observ'd
The air is delicate.

In the evening dusk, King Duncan comes. He is ushered in with sounding brass. His retinue, in equine rank, attend his progress, happy in the new-found peace their Scotland knows. Their gentle laughter fills the dusk; their horses' hooves are muffled by the mossy peat they prance across; and martins twitter in the gathering gloom, clearing the air of insects. A pretty sight as night comes on, it draws approval from the king—his defenses all are down.

General Banquo rides beside the king in an honored place. He finds the martins bode him well: his talk is all of children. Here in the lofty halls of Glamis, the king shall rest with his two sons. That rest may be eternal sleep, and Inverness may this night be procreant cradle for the line that the witches promised Banquo.

(*Enter* LADY MACBETH.)
DUNCAN.   See, see, our honour'd hostess!   *10*
The love that follows us sometime is our trouble,
Which still we thank as love. Herein I teach you
How you shall bid God 'ield us for your pains,
And thank us for your trouble.

LADY MACBETH.   All our service
In every point twice done and then done double   *15*
Were poor and single business to contend
Against those honours deep and broad wherewith
Your Majesty loads our house: for those of old,
And the late dignities heap'd up to them,
We rest your hermits.

DUNCAN.   Where's the thane of Cawdor?   *20*
We cours'd him at the heels, and had a purpose

---

4. **martlet,** martin.   **approve,** prove.   5. **mansionry,** nest-building.   6. **jutty,** projection.
7. **coign of vantage,** convenient corner.   8. **procreant cradle,** nest where the young are
hatched.   11–14. **The love . . . trouble,** the love that attends us is troublesome sometimes,
but we always thank it because it is prompted by love.   13. **'ield,** yield, reward.   16. **single,**
small.   16–17. **to contend/Against,** in comparison with.   20. **rest . . . hermits,** will pray
for you, like hermits or beadsmen.

To be his purveyor; but he rides well,
And his great love, sharp as his spur, hath holp him
To his home before us. Fair and noble hostess,
We are your guest to-night.
    LADY MACBETH.   Your servants ever   *25*
Have theirs, themselves, and what is theirs, in compt,
To make their audit at your Highness' pleasure,
Still to return your own.
    DUNCAN.   Give me your hand;
Conduct me to mine host; we love him highly,
And shall continue our graces towards him.   *30*
By your leave, hostess.   (*Exeunt.*)

Lady Macbeth sweeps out from the pile of stone the king has stopped before. She prettily curtsies: the king dismounts and lifts her up. Chivalrous speech and pleasant form mask well this woman's face that "looks up clear"; Duncan is pleased with her favour and with her pious blessing. Escorting her with courtly grace, King Duncan leads his retinue into his final slumbering place.

SCENE VII. *Within Macbeth's castle.*
    (*Hautboys and torches. Enter a* SEWER, *and divers* SERVANTS *with dishes and service, over the stage. Then enter* MACBETH.)
    MACBETH. If it were done when 't is done, then 't were well
It were done quickly: if the assassination
Could trammel up the consequence, and catch
With his surcease success; that but this blow
Might be the be-all and the end-all here,   *5*
But here, upon this bank and shoal of time,
We'd jump the life to come. But in these cases
We still have judgement here, that we but teach
Bloody instructions, which, being taught, return
To plague th' inventor. This even-handed justice   *10*
Commends th' ingredients of our poison'd chalice
To our own lips. He 's here in double trust:
First, as I am his kinsman and his subject,
Strong both against the deed; then, as his host,
Who should against his murderer shut the door,   *15*

---

22. **purveyor,** officer who went ahead to provide food for the king.   26. **in compt,** subject to account.   28. **Still,** always.   S. d. **Sewer,** butler.   3. **trammel up,** entangle, as in a net.
4. **with his surcease,** with the cessation of consequences.   7. **jump,** risk.

Not bear the knife myself. Besides, this Duncan
Hath borne his faculties so meek, hath been
So clear in his great office, that his virtues
Will plead like angels, trumpet-tongued, against
The deep damnation of his taking-off;   *20*
And pity, like a naked new-born babe
Striding the blast, or heaven's cherubin hors'd
Upon the sightless couriers of the air,
Shall blow the horrid deed in every eye,
That tears shall drown the wind. I have no spur   *25*
To prick the sides of my intent, but only
Vaulting ambition, which o'erleaps itself
And falls on the other—

Castle Inverness is now as bright as smoking torches and candles can make its ancient beam-topped walls and sooty ceilings. The dark woods glint dully in the light of the roaring fires in every fireplace. Again the sounding brasses herald lines of servants carrying food. Great joints of beef and venison, a suckling pig, bay-covered fish—all the things that the kitchens can provide for Scotland's reigning monarch are supplied. The sound of distant laughter swells, then fades into the hangings of the passageway Macbeth now paces, grim-faced, drawn, a troubled man who sees the night blown back against the walls of his treason-tainted castle. A muted lute in the background sings a tale of Scottish kings, the valorous and the shriven of heaven. The winds outside add their mournful moan to the scene as Macbeth stops and gazes through a slit on a murky, cloud-hid heaven. Does he lean on one hand against the cold, damp wall? Does he clench both hands at his sides? Does he lift one hand to rub his brow, as the other grasps his firm-sheathed dagger? Now in velvets and brocades, does he still seem the tall, staunch man who fought for Duncan and his throne? Or is he bowed now beneath their weight and the thoughts that ride the night winds of his mind and seek out its dark corners?

His heart grown faint, Macbeth thinks on the guilt that will attend his deed, shudders in advance at the anguish of conscience that only good men need fear. Actually, his Scottish reasons for hesitating are Greek-born: the Greek gods proclaimed that hosts could kill their guests only on peril of their own dear lives. They further proclaimed a curse on those who shed the blood of kinsmen—a curse to be carried out

17. **faculties**, royal authority.   20. **taking-off**, murder.   23. **sightless couriers**, invisible messengers.   28. **the other**, the other side.

by those awful Furies of the mind who lived on Kithairon. First cousin to the king as well as his subject, Macbeth knows that his deed would be more than an assassin's shame, more than just dark regicide. And, as the willing host to a blameless king, Macbeth knows he lacks any claim to justify the act except his high ambition. Yet even that ambition leaps so high it overleaps itself and leaves him with no stomach for the ugly deed.

(*Enter* LADY MACBETH.)
How now! what news?

LADY MACBETH. He has almost supp'd. Why have you left the chamber?

MACBETH. Hath he ask'd for me?

LADY MACBETH.   Know you not he has?   *30*

MACBETH. We will proceed no further in this business.
He hath honour'd me of late; and I have bought
Golden opinions from all sorts of people,
Which would be worn now in their newest gloss,
Not cast aside so soon.

LADY MACBETH.   Was the hope drunk   *35*
Wherein you dress'd yourself? Hath it slept since?
And wakes it now, to look so green and pale
At what it did so freely? From this time
Such I account thy love. Art thou afeard
To be the same in thine own act and valour   *40*
As thou art in desire? Wouldst thou have that
Which thou esteem'st the ornament of life,
And live a coward in thine own esteem,
Letting "I dare not" wait upon "I would,"
Like the poor cat i' th' adage?

MACBETH.   Prithee, peace!   *45*
I dare do all that may become a man;
Who dares do more is none.

LADY MACBETH.   What beast was 't, then,
That made you break this enterprise to me?
When you durst do it, then you were a man;
And, to be more than what you were, you would   *50*
Be so much more the man. Nor time nor place
Did then adhere, and yet you would make both.
They have made themselves, and that their fitness now

---

37. **green,** sick.   45. **th' adage:** "The cat would eat fish, and would not wet her feet."   **48. break,** propose.   52. **Did then adhere,** were suitable.

Does unmake you. I have given suck, and know
How tender 't is to love the babe that milks me;   55
I would, while it was smiling in my face,
Have pluck'd my nipple from his boneless gums
And dash'd the brains out, had I so sworn as you
Have done to this.
    MACBETH.   If we should fail?
    LADY MACBETH.   We fail?
But screw your courage to the sticking-place,   60
And we'll not fail. When Duncan is asleep—
Whereto the rather shall his day's hard journey
Soundly invite him—his two chamberlains
Will I with wine and wassail so convince
That memory, the warder of the brain,   65
Shall be a fume, and the receipt of reason
A limbeck only: when in swinish sleep
Their drenched natures lie as in a death,
What cannot you and I perform upon
Th' unguarded Duncan? what not put upon   70
His spongy officers, who shall bear the guilt
Of our great quell?
    MACBETH.   Bring forth men-children only;
For thy undaunted mettle should compose
Nothing but males. Will it not be receiv'd,
When we have mark'd with blood those sleepy two   75
Of his own chamber and us'd their very daggers,
That they have done 't?
    LADY MACBETH.   Who dares receive it other,
As we shall make our griefs and clamour roar
Upon his death?
    MACBETH.   I am settled, and bend up
Each corporal agent to this terrible feat.   80
Away, and mock the time with fairest show;
False face must hide what the false heart doth know.   (*Exeunt.*)

    Macbeth's soliloquy (his spoken thoughts) is interrupted by his wife.
She finds him ill and sick at heart in horror of the work this night.

60. **But,** only.   64. **wassail,** carousing, liquor.   **convince,** overpower.   **65-7. That . . . only,**
according to old anatomists memory was stationed in the back of the head, like a warder to the
brain. Drunkenness turns memory into a fume or smoke which rises into the part of the brain
(receptacle) where reason is placed, as vapor from a retort rises into the cap (limbeck) of a still.
71. spongy, drunken.   **72. quell,** murder.   **74. receiv'd,** believed.   **77. other,** otherwise.
78. As, since.

He would undo their present plans, but Lady Macbeth has forseen this hour and she has planned against it. She has three arguments at hand: (1) your love of me will be revealed in future deed; (2) are you a coward? (3) are you a man? She then proves, by example, that he must carry through the deed: (1) in first proposing the act to her, he raised her expectations; (2) he was no coward at that time; (3) he'll be a greater man when he completes the deed (47-54). And then she caps the argument, comparing Macbeth's resolve with hers (54-59): though they are childless, they have had a male child, who died. Had *she* been false in *that* important enterprise (getting a son to inherit his name), she would have killed the child she'd borne to fulfill his expectations. But she had not played his hopes so false; still *he* now dares to play *hers* false. An implicit threat veils her every word: Fail me now and I'll bear no children to replace the son who died.

Between the two wishes and the two deeds (to get life, he must take life), Macbeth is caught up on the horns of her debate. He pleads for reassurance that they can meet both deed and expectation: "If *we* should fail?" He begs her to swear that if *he* aids death, *she* will bring forth life. Her answer is ambiguous; all women seem oracular when the time demands. Her plan is made to bring forth death; Macbeth leaps the thought and considers life: "Bring forth men-children only." His need of an heir, her unstated pledge—both serve structurally as an exciting force which closes out Act I.

Do they seal the bargain with a kiss? Can this cold plan support that warmth, or do they go their separate ways, each feeling a subtle loss? The love Lady Macbeth bears her husband is great; he needs her love and firm eye to hold him in its steady gaze and find him manly. Ambition fled before his manly fear that a murderous deed would weaken him; his wife's love played on that manly need and brought him back to action. In serving him, she makes him weak. In being served, he serves her now. Who is the master of this house? The heath winds moan outside.

The exposition (background) completely given, we now know the conflicts that beset Macbeth and his small lady. His manly form, his noble height have dwarfed her tiny, fragile form; but she is larger than he in resolve. When Macbeth grows weak, entertaining doubt, his wife lends him her strength or forces him with logic that she knows will work to serve his purpose. That she is his *wife* is paramount. Deprived of a child, she has no other object to which to offer up her female Self except to her husband. To him she offers it entire, knowing full well she calls down heaven to witness here at Inverness her loathsome act. Nor does she ask a pardon of the brightest powers; she damns herself to aid Macbeth—Macbeth the man and husband who needs her strength.

Macbeth is ambitious, but he needs approval more than he needs power. That others see him as being noble now, and that they would see him lessened by this deed—these serve as his first deterrents. That he would see *himself* as being ignoble further lessens his resolve. But Lady Macbeth above all others must have a good opinion of him, so, pleasing her, he will do the deed. But how much does Macbeth need an excuse? How accurately did his wife assess his nature in Act I?

ACT II

Scene I. *The Court of Macbeth's castle.*
  (*Enter* BANQUO, *and* FLEANCE *with a torch before him.*)
  BANQUO. How goes the night, boy?
  FLEANCE. The moon is down; I have not heard the clock.
  BANQUO. And she goes down at twelve.
  FLEANCE.   I take 't, 't is later, sir.
  BANQUO. Hold, take my sword. There 's husbandry in heaven;
Their candles are all out. Take thee that too.   5
A heavy summons lies like lead upon me,
And yet I would not sleep. Merciful powers,
Restrain in me the cursed thoughts that nature
Gives way to in repose!
  (*Enter* MACBETH, *and a* SERVANT *with a torch.*)
                        Give me my sword.
Who's there?   10
  MACBETH. A friend.
  BANQUO. What, sir, not yet at rest? The King 's a-bed.
He hath been in unusual pleasure, and
Sent forth great largess to your offices.
This diamond he greets your wife withal,   15
By the name of most kind hostess; and shut up
In measureless content.
  MACBETH.   Being unprepar'd,
Our will became the servant to defect;
Which else should free have wrought.
  BANQUO.   All 's well.
I dreamt last night of the three weird sisters: 20
To you they have show'd some truth.
  MACBETH.   I think not of them;
Yet, when we can entreat an hour to serve,

4. **husbandry,** economy.   5. **that,** his dagger.   14. **largess,** gifts.   **offices,** servants' quarters.

We would spend it in some words upon that business,
If you would grant the time.

BANQUO.   At your kind'st leisure.

MACBETH. If you shall cleave to my consent, when 't is,   *25*
It shall make honour for you.

BANQUO.   So I lose none
In seeking to augment it, but still keep
My bosom franchis'd and allegiance clear,
I shall be counsell'd.

MACBETH.   Good repose the while!   *29*

BANQUO. Thanks, sir; the like to you!   (*Exeunt* BANQUO *and* FLEANCE.)

Act II follows hard, in time, on Act I. The hour of midnight has
come and gone. The castle sleeps in utter dark. The moon has crossed
the Scottish sky and left it to the stars. Then they have, one by one,
blinked out. Unbroken darkness reigns. Now, flickering in the chilly dark,
a torch lights Banquo's restless form. Fleance, his son, accompanies him,
supplying light. Banquo is tired, he should be at rest, but weighty fears
keep him awake. If he should sleep, then he would dream, then he would
have to face the thoughts he holds just free of consciousness. Like Hamlet,
he finds dreams "the rub"—if he sleeps, perchance he'll dream.

Suddenly, a second torch reveals a human form that could be ripped
from Banquo's dream. It is Macbeth, who receives his friend's words
spoken fair—or are they spoken foul? The answer lies in what dreams
alone could reveal: Banquo's dark nights are peopled by the witches and
by their promises to him which Macbeth may, this night, help to make
real. In guarded words, Macbeth extends a promise (25-26) which finds
willing ears: Banquo will reap his own reward by failing now to sow
the seeds of warning to the king. Banquo need not act in villainy; he
simply need not act at all. He has only to remain a silent guest and then
eat at the victor's table.

MACBETH. Go bid thy mistress, when my drink is ready,
She strike upon the bell. Get thee to bed.   (*Exit* SERVANT.)
Is this a dagger which I see before me,
The handle toward my hand? Come, let me clutch thee.
I have thee not, and yet I see thee still.   *35*
Art thou not, fatal vision, sensible
To feeling as to sight? or art thou but
A dagger of the mind, a false creation,

---

25. If . . . 't is, if you are loyal to me when the time comes.   **28. franchis'd,** free from guilt.
36. fatal, prophetic.   **sensible,** perceptible.

Proceeding from the heat-oppressed brain?
I see thee yet, in form as palpable   40
As this which now I draw.
Thou marshall'st me the way that I was going,
And such an instrument I was to use.
Mine eyes are made the fools o' th' other senses,
Or else worth all the rest: I see thee still,   45
And on thy blade and dudgeon gouts of blood,
Which was not so before. There 's no such thing.
It is the bloody business which informs
Thus to mine eyes. Now o'er the one half-world
Nature seems dead, and wicked dreams abuse   50
The curtain'd sleep: witchcraft celebrates
Pale Hecate's offerings, and wither'd Murder,
Alarum'd by his sentinel, the wolf,
Whose howl's watch, thus with his stealthy pace,
With Tarquin's ravishing strides, towards his design   55
Moves like a ghost. Thou sure and firm set earth,
Hear not my steps, which way they walk, for fear
The very stones prate of my whereabout,
And take the present horror from the time,
Which now suits with it. Whiles I threat, he lives: 60
Words to the heat of deeds too cold breath gives.   (*A bell rings.*)
I go, and it is done; the bell invites me.
Hear it not, Duncan; for it is a knell
That summons thee to heaven or to hell.   (*Exit.*)

The promise to Banquo made, Macbeth's way is clear. Banquo and Fleance light their way to dream-filled sleep—and silence. But in silence, Banquo will conspire in the dark deed; Banquo—who could prevent the flow of blood—has disengaged himself from all immediately concerned; he has gone to occupy himself with a sullen sleep wherein his eyes are closed, his mouth sealed shut, to see not, hear not, know not of the things that will transpire this night.

Macbeth sends a signal to his wife. But as he waits there in the dark, as night owls moan and crickets call, as the heath winds surge through the stunted gorse and the night-damp gathers on the stones of Inverness, Macbeth, alone, is not alone. His other self (the fair half) wars with the half so murderously foul, in thrall to dark ambition.

---

46. **dudgeon,** hilt.   **gouts,** drops.   48. **informs,** takes this shape.   50. **abuse,** deceive.
52. **Hecate's,** Hecate (here a dissyllable) was goddess of the underworld, and hence of witchcraft.
54. **howl's watch,** murder's signal.   55. **Tarquin's,** Sextus Tarquin, who ravished Lucretia.

Macbeth's words (a soliloquy) rise on the night-fouled air like vapors to an evil god. His brain supplies the sign he fears—a dagger, the sign of murder. At this moment his conscience might still free him of the deed he must do; his brain teems with revulsion at the knowledge of his act. Yet his words sound hollow in the dark, blown back on winds of direst hope. Decision rides the echoes of Macbeth's heels on the stones, and like an answer to his fading voice, Lady Macbeth's bell calls him in to finish what ambition began on the fair-foul heath. Now, like a Donne parishioner, Macbeth thinks that the bell tolls for the king, one little sleep away from death—but he is wrong. For if he could ask his conscience now, "For whom does this bell toll?" it would not answer "Duncan." No. It would ring out "It tolls for thee."

SCENE II. *The hall of the castle.*

(*Enter* LADY MACBETH.)

LADY MACBETH. That which hath made them drunk hath made me bold;
What hath quench'd them hath given me fire. Hark! Peace!
It was the owl that shriek'd, the fatal bellman
Which gives the stern'st good-night. He is about it.
The doors are open; and the surfeited grooms   5
Do mock their charge with snores. I have drugg'd their possets,
That death and nature do contend about them,
Whether they live or die.

No flickering torch lights this long hall which leads the way to chambered death. Here Macbeth and his lady walk, but as they walk their muffled steps echo their heartbeats. Her heart is buoyed up on wine; she lacked the will to do the deed without the aid of the grape. Still she is afraid; the wine strengthens her but it cannot make her fearless when, alone, she needs no outward mask such as she must wear to cheer Macbeth. An owl's cry cuts the night apart, startles her from her self-encouraging speech. Her "explanation" shows that her heart (3-4) is a pitying one, not evil-hardened nor quite drugged by wine. Lady Macbeth shares the guilt, even in her heart, and seeks no excuse for her small hand that paved the way to Duncan's death. And she absolves the grooms.

(*Enter* MACBETH.)

MACBETH. Who's there? What, ho!

LADY MACBETH. Alack, I am afraid they have awak'd,   10

---

3. **bellman,** the night watchman sent to condemned persons the night before their execution.
5. **grooms,** servants.   6. **charge,** business, i.e., care of the king.   **possets,** hot drinks composed of wine, milk, etc.

And 't is not done. Th' attempt and not the deed
Confounds us. Hark! I laid their daggers ready;
He could not miss 'em. Had he not resembled
My father as he slept, I had done 't.—My husband?

MACBETH. I have done the deed. Didst thou not hear a noise?   *15*

LADY MACBETH. I heard the owl scream and the crickets cry.
Did not you speak?

MACBETH.   When?

LADY MACBETH.   Now.

MACBETH.   As I descended?

LADY MACBETH. Ay.

MACBETH. Hark!
Who lies i' th' second chamber?

LADY MACBETH.   Donalbain.   *20*

MACBETH. This is a sorry sight.   (*Looking on his hands.*)

LADY MACBETH. A foolish thought, to say a sorry sight.

MACBETH. There 's one did laugh in 's sleep, and one cried, "Murder!"
That they did wake each other: I stood and heard them;
But they did say their prayers, and address'd them   *25*
Again to sleep.

LADY MACBETH. There are two lodg'd together.

MACBETH. One cried, "God bless us!" and "Amen" the other,
As they had seen me with these hangman's hands.
List'ning their fear, I could not say "Amen,"
When they did say, "God bless us!"

LADY MACBETH.   Consider it not so deeply.   *30*

MACBETH. But wherefore could not I pronounce "Amen"?
I had most need of blessing, and "Amen"
Stuck in my throat.

LADY MACBETH.   These deeds must not be thought
After these ways; so, it will make us mad.

MACBETH. Methought I heard a voice cry, "Sleep no more!   *35*
Macbeth does murder sleep,"—the innocent sleep,
Sleep that knits up the ravell'd sleave of care,
The death of each day's life, sore labour's bath,
Balm of hurt minds, great nature's second course,
Chief nourisher in life's feast,—

LADY MACBETH.   What do you mean?   *40*

---

12. **Confounds,** ruins.   21. **sorry,** wretched.   25. **address'd them,** composed themselves.
28. **hangman's hands,** the Elizabethan hangman was accustomed to cut up the bodies of traitors;
hence "bloody hands."   29. **List'ning,** listening to.   37. **sleave,** coarse unwrought silk.
39. **second course,** main course of a dinner.

MACBETH. Still it cried, "Sleep no more!" to all the house;
"Glamis hath murder'd sleep, and therefore Cawdor
Shall sleep no more; Macbeth shall sleep no more."
  LADY MACBETH. Who was it that thus cried? Why, worthy thane,
You do unbend your noble strength, to think   45
So brainsickly of things. Go get some water,
And wash this filthy witness from your hand.
Why did you bring these daggers from the place?
They must lie there: go carry them; and smear
The sleepy grooms with blood.
  MACBETH.   I 'll go no more.   50
I am afraid to think what I have done;
Look on 't again I dare not.
  LADY MACBETH.   Infirm of purpose!
Give me the daggers. The sleeping and the dead
Are but as pictures; 't is the eye of childhood
That fears a painted devil. If he do bleed,   55
I 'll gild the faces of the grooms withal;
For it must seem their guilt.   (*Exit. Knocking within.*)
  MACBETH.   Whence is that knocking?
How is 't with me, when every noise appals me?
What hands are here? Ha! they pluck out mine eyes.
Will all great Neptune's ocean wash this blood   60
Clean from my hand? No, this my hand will rather
The multitudinous seas incarnadine,
Making the green one red.
  (*Re-enter* LADY MACBETH.)
  LADY MACBETH. My hands are of your colour; but I shame
To wear a heart so white. (*Knocking.*) I hear a knocking   65
At the south entry: retire we to our chamber.
A little water clears us of this deed;
How easy is it then! Your constancy
Hath left you unattended. (*Knocking.*) Hark! more knocking.
Get on your nightgown, lest occasion call us   70
And show us to be watchers. Be not lost
So poorly in your thoughts.
  MACBETH. To know my deed, 't were best not know myself.   (*Knocking.*)
Wake Duncan with thy knocking! I would thou couldst!   (*Exeunt.*)

---

46. brainsickly, madly.   62. incarnadine, make red.   68-9. constancy . . . unattended,
your firmness has deserted you.   70. nightgown, dressing gown.   73. To . . . myself, it
would be better to lose consciousness of my being than to realize what I have done.

Their bodies share the night-dark hall, but they are both cloaked in their thoughts. His wife fears Macbeth has failed to act, regrets she did not do his work, but knows her heart was sickened by King Duncan's countenance. So like her father's, it became her father's and withheld her hand. Such sentiment is not for those who would be ruthless in their deeds. Still, when Macbeth needs strength, she masks the thoughts she has so lately held; the "fatal bellman" was "an owl"; no fancy here endows the word; she must be strong.

Macbeth stares at his bloody hands, those murderer's hands that killed the king. His soul is sickened by the fear that God will punish him upon the spot and banish him from heaven. There is a fatal irony in Macbeth's fear (35-43) that he has murdered sleep: "Uneasy lies the head that wears a crown," as Shakespeare wrote in *King Henry IV*. His wife has also known fear this fatal night. Too, she knows her husband's weakness and she recognizes the need to still his weakening resolve with present action. "Think not; fear not" might be her creed—and yet, soon, she too must sleep and her dreams, in time, will make her mad. Macbeth, though, shares his guilt with her and thus frees his mind of the night-born horror.

Now present action serves Lady Macbeth well, however: take back the daggers, smear the grooms, and wash your hands. But Macbeth has used up all his strength for evil deeds. Now his wife must act his part for him. The "knocking" as she leaves the hall is a hollow echo of their hearts. Macbeth thus seems to inherit the same fear of strange sounds that his wife had as she stood in this same dark hall, waiting for him. Also he fears that water will not wash this deed from him—but it is a fear he voices, thus saving his mind from inner sickness.

As Lady Macbeth returns, her hands are red; but she minimizes the symbol's power and she closets her sickness in her heart that will give it lodging until her brain is ready to receive the guest that will slowly drive her mad. Macbeth cannot hide his sickened heart; he states his fears, again lets loose the fatal urgings that, bound up, increase in prison. His festering sores are lanced in time to let their poison drain away. But his wife must present an unblemished front, and so she imprisons the poison of guilt.

SCENE III. *The courtyard of the castle.*

(*Enter a* PORTER. *Knocking within.*)

PORTER. Here 's a knocking indeed! If a man were porter of hell-gate, he should have old turning the key. (*Knocking.*) Knock, knock, knock! Who 's there, i' th' name

2. **old,** a colloquial intensive (cf. "high old time").

of Belzebub? Here 's a farmer, that hanged himself on the expectation of plenty. *5*
Come in time; have napkins enow about you; here you 'll sweat for 't. (*Knocking.*)
Knock, knock! Who's there, in th' other devil's name? Faith, here's an equivocator,
that could swear in both the scales against either scale; who committed treason *10*
enough for God's sake, yet could not equivocate to heaven. O, come in, equivocator.
(*Knocking.*) Knock, knock, knock! Who 's there? Faith, here 's an English tailor come
hither, for stealing out of a French hose. Come in, tailor; here you may roast your *15*
goose. (*Knocking.*) Knock, knock; never at quiet! What are you? But this place is
too cold for hell. I'll devil-porter it no further: I had thought to have let in some of *20*
all professions that go the primrose way to th' everlasting bonfire. (*Knocking.*) Anon,
anon. I pray you, remember the porter.   (*Opens the gate.*)

(*Enter* MACDUFF *and* LENNOX.)

MACDUFF. Was it so late, friend, ere you went to bed,
That you do lie so late?   *25*

PORTER. Faith, sir, we were carousing till the second cock; and drink, sir, is a
great provoker of three things.

MACDUFF. What three things does drink especially provoke?   *30*

PORTER. Marry, sir, nose-painting, sleep and urine. Lechery, sir, it provokes, and
unprovokes; it provokes the desire, but it takes away the performance. Therefore,
much drink may be said to be an equivocator with lechery: it makes him, and it mars *35*
him; it sets him on, and it takes him off; it persuades him, and disheartens him;
makes him stand to, and not stand to; in conclusion, equivocates him in a sleep,
and, giving him the lie, leaves him.   *40*

MACDUFF. I believe drink gave thee the lie last night.

PORTER. That it did, sir, i' the very throat on me. But I requited him for his lie;
and, I think, being too strong for him, though he took up my legs sometime, yet I
made a shift to cast him.   *46*

In all literature, probably no scene rises to greater artistry than lines
1–46. To this point in the play, our complete attention has been directed
to noble figures in ignoble circumstances, good in the grip of evil, passions
born of supernatural need sundered by unnatural deed. Transported to
a world of kings, of thanes, and ladies as great as portraits from a mighty
past, we have been removed from the common dust that makes us ordinary. In darkness we have seen dark deeds, in darkness we have shared dark
thoughts, in darkness we have allied ourselves with murderers. Think:
have we known Duncan as a man who bleeds just as we do? Have we

---

5. **farmer . . . plenty,** the farmer who hoarded his grain had been ruined by the prospect of a
large harvest and low prices.   6. **napkins,** handkerchiefs.   15. **French hose,** short and tight,
from the material of which it would be hard to steal anything.   16. **goose,** pressing iron.
26. **second cock,** 3 a.m.   46. **cast,** throw, throw up.

seen him except as a king who is mightily pleased and therefore lordly and gracious? Was he brought to life as a man before he was slaughtered as a symbol of worldly rank, merely a barrier in Macbeth's path? Has our sympathy been granted to Duncan, or was he, dimly, only a symbol for that which stands in our own paths as we seek goals without the aid of a helper comparable to Lady Macbeth?

Unsexed she's been; unmanned, Macbeth. Our primal passions have been roused till we are stripped of moral pride in making our alliance with them. We have stood out on the open heath; we have shared, with Banquo, silent sin; we have been parties to the deed of murder. The sun-filled days of the ordinary life we know have been abandoned for a while—and now, somehow, we must be recalled. Inverness Castle has become a brooding pile of evil rocks where evil walks the night-doomed halls, and we, in the same evil retinue, have felt its stones beneath our feet. Now we must be returned to daylight, to a world that is neither good nor bad, but merely imperfect and touched with laughter.

How shall we be drawn back to real life, to living in a world of ordinary men? The porter of the castle allows us access to it on his words. He is a marvelous caricature of everything we are. His words are spoken in the fumes of last night's wine; he has no thought of ambition or desire to rise above his rank. He lives on food, knows how to dwell with work that lacks a challenge to unlock his mind as he unlocks these mighty-timbered portals. So the porter merely exists throughout his days, makes light of his work, and cares not one whit if he shall do it well or ill—as long as he is employed. The people outside can stand and wait; he will please himself with daydreams first; then he will suggest they tip him for the inconvenience they have caused him.

The hollow knocking punctuates the porter's lines to tie this scene to all those we have seen up to this point. His words ("Knock, knock!") weld him to scenes that could not hold his comic form; his lumbering gait is the perfect foil to noble Macduff's figure. Macduff and Lennox enter into raillery with the bleary porter who offers them sage comments on the state of drink and drunken men, but here again a symbol appears in the words he speaks: Ambition, too, is a heady drink; it "makes" Macbeth and "mars" him too. So fair drink seems, so foul it is, it turns our stomachs as we strive to hold it and contend with it. Then, when we are sick and banish it, it has conquered us by its reduction of our dignity.

(*Enter* MACBETH.)

MACDUFF. Is thy master stirring?
Our knocking has awak'd him; here he comes.

LENNOX. Good morrow, noble sir.

MACBETH.   Good morrow, both.

MACDUFF. Is the King stirring, worthy thane?

MACBETH.   Not yet.   *50*

MACDUFF. He did command me to call timely on him.

I have almost slipp'd the hour.

MACBETH.   I'll bring you to him.

MACDUFF. I know this is a joyful trouble to you;

But yet 't is one.

MACBETH. The labour we delight in physics pain.   *55*

This is the door.

MACDUFF.   I'll make so bold to call.

For 't is my limited service.   (*Exit.*)

LENNOX. Goes the King hence to-day?

MACBETH.   He does; he did appoint so.

LENNOX. The night has been unruly: where we lay,

Our chimneys were blown down; and, as they say,   *60*

Lamentings heard i' th' air; strange screams of death,

And prophesying with accents terrible

Of dire combustion and confus'd events

New hatch'd to th' woeful time. The obscure bird

Clamour'd the livelong night; some say, the earth   *65*

Was feverous and did shake.

MACBETH.   'T was a rough night.

LENNOX. My young remembrance cannot parallel

A fellow to it.

The patterned language now bridges our attention to the horror we know sleeps upstairs in Duncan's chamber. It is the same ritual we all employ: "Good morning, how are you?" "I'm fine. I hope you rested well?" It is meaningless, designed to fill our inconvenient vacuums. But this vacuum is a trying space. No friendship fills it. Soft, guarded words are spoken without a hint of warmth. Lennox, alone, must carry on the conversation at some length. He speaks of dire portents which the night has shown as if he is grateful he can speak impersonally.

Macbeth's brief irony, " 'Twas a rough night," reveals that he has assessed Lennox's words as one who has spoken with witches—with knowledge of their meaning. A painful passage, this, designed to bridge a brief time and yet add suspense, it works its wiles, for we now await Macduff's

---

51. **timely**, early.   55. **physics**, cures.   57. **limited**, appointed.   63. **combustion**, tumult.
64. **obscure bird**, owl.

return. Will Macbeth hear the news as if it were, indeed, news to his ears?

(*Re-enter* MACDUFF.)

MACDUFF. O horror, horror, horror! Tongue nor heart
Cannot conceive nor name thee!

MACBETH. ⎱
LENNOX. ⎰   What's the matter?   *70*

MACDUFF. Confusion now hath made his masterpiece!
Most sacrilegious murder hath broke ope
The Lord's anointed temple, and stole thence
The life o' th' building!

MACBETH.   What is 't you say? The life?

LENNOX. Mean you his Majesty?   *75*

MACDUFF. Approach the chamber, and destroy your sight
With a new Gorgon. Do not bid me speak;
See, and then speak yourselves.   (*Exeunt* MACBETH *and* LENNOX.)
      Awake, awake!

Ring the alarum-bell. Murder and treason!
Banquo and Donalbain! Malcolm! awake!   *80*
Shake off this downy sleep, death's counterfeit,
And look on death itself! Up, up, and see
The great doom's image! Malcolm! Banquo!
As from your graves rise up, and walk like sprites,
To countenance this horror! Ring the bell!   *85*   (*Bell rings.*)

(*Enter* LADY MACBETH.)

LADY MACBETH. What 's the business,
That such a hideous trumpet calls to parley
The sleepers of the house? Speak, speak!

MACDUFF.   O gentle lady,
'T is not for you to hear what I can speak;
The repetition in a woman's ear   *90*
Would murder as it fell.

(*Enter* BANQUO.)

      O Banquo, Banquo,
Our royal master 's murder'd!

LADY MACBETH.   Woe, alas!
What, in our house?

---

71. **Confusion,** destruction.   77. **Gorgon,** Medusa, one of the three monstrous Gorgons, turned people who saw her face into stone.   83. **great doom's image,** image of the Day of Judgment. 85. **countenance,** be in keeping with.

BANQUO.   Too cruel anywhere.

Dear Duff, I prithee, contradict thyself,

And say it is not so.   *95*

   (*Re-enter* MACBETH *and* LENNOX, *with* ROSS.)

   MACBETH. Had I but died an hour before this chance,

I had liv'd a blessed time; for, from this instant,

There 's nothing serious in mortality.

All is but toys; renown and grace is dead;

The wine of life is drawn, and the mere lees   *100*

Is left this vault to brag of.

   (*Enter* MALCOLM *and* DONALBAIN.)

   DONALBAIN. What is amiss?

   MACBETH.   You are, and do not know 't.

The spring, the head, the fountain of your blood

Is stopp'd; the very source of it is stopp'd.

   MACDUFF. Your royal father 's murder'd.

   MALCOLM.   O, by whom?   *105*

   LENNOX. Those of his chamber, as it seem'd, had done 't.

Their hands and faces were all badg'd with blood;

So were their daggers, which unwip'd we found

Upon their pillows.

They star'd, and were distracted; no man's life   *110*

Was to be trusted with them.

   MACBETH. O, yet I do repent me of my fury,

That I did kill them.

   MACDUFF.   Wherefore did you so?

   MACBETH. Who can be wise, amaz'd, temp'rate and furious,

Loyal and neutral, in a moment? No man.   *115*

Th' expedition of my violent love

Outrun the pauser, reason. Here lay Duncan,

His silver skin lac'd with his golden blood,

And his gash'd stabs look'd like a breach in nature

For ruin's wasteful entrance; there, the murderers,   *120*

Steep'd in the colours of their trade, their daggers

Unmannerly breech'd with gore. Who could refrain,

That had a heart to love, and in that heart

Courage to make 's love known?

   LADY MACBETH.   Help me hence, ho!

   MACDUFF. Look to the lady.

---

98. **mortality,** human life.   107. **badg'd,** marked.   116. **expedition,** haste.   122. **breech'd,** clothed.

MALCOLM (*aside to* DONALBAIN). Why do we hold our tongues,   *125*
That most may claim this argument for ours?

DONALBAIN (*aside to* MALCOLM). What should be spoken here, where our fate,
Hid in an auger-hole, may rush and seize us?
Let 's away;
Our tears are not yet brew'd.

MALCOLM (*aside to* DONALBAIN). Nor our strong sorrow   *130*
Upon the foot of motion.

BANQUO.   Look to the lady;   (LADY MACBETH *is carried out.*)
And when we have our naked frailties hid,
That suffer in exposure, let us meet
And question this most bloody piece of work,
To know it further. Fears and scruples shake us: *135*
In the great hand of God I stand, and thence
Against the undivulg'd pretence I fight
Of treasonous malice.

MACDUFF.   And so do I.

ALL.   So all.

MACBETH. Let 's briefly put on manly readiness,
And meet i' th' hall together.

ALL.   Well contented.   *140*

                    (*Exeunt all but* MALCOLM *and* DONALBAIN.)

MALCOLM. What will you do? Let 's not consort with them;
To show an unfelt sorrow is an office
Which the false man does easy. I 'll to England.

DONALBAIN. To Ireland, I; our separated fortune
Shall keep us both the safer: where we are,   *145*
There 's daggers in men's smiles; the near in blood,
The nearer bloody.

MALCOLM.   This murderous shaft that 's shot
Hath not yet lighted, and our safest way
Is to avoid the aim. Therefore, to horse;
And let us not be dainty of leave-taking,   *150*
But shift away. There's warrant in that theft
Which steals itself, when there 's no mercy left.   (*Exeunt.*)

The part Macbeth must now play is one which too many words might
well betray. He chooses few, but chooses well. Lady Macbeth's seem less
capable, and Banquo's are surely the merest form and poorly executed.

126. **argument**, subject.   128. **an auger-hole**, obscure place.   131. **Upon . . . motion**,
ready to be translated into action.   137. **pretence**, purpose.   139. **manly readiness**, male
equipment, armor.   146-7. **the near . . . bloody**, the nearer the relationship, the more danger.
148. **lighted**, spent its force.   150. **dainty**, ceremonious.

As Macbeth, Ross, and Lennox come from seeing death's most bloody face, Macbeth's words (96–101) have the sincerest ring: "Had I died but an hour before. . . ." But as Duncan's sons hear the grisly news, Macbeth "protests too much" and resorts to melodrama—a speech a bit too pat, too pure, too proper for such an unexpected occasion. And before he has his full speech out (there is doubtless more; he is scarcely half-done), Lady Macbeth knows he is overacting and interrupts by fainting.

Macduff and Lennox are diverted; Banquo gives his attention. But Duncan's sons have seen the act, have heard the hollow ring of lies in Macbeth's words. They know that to speak their fears could mean their instant deaths. As servants support their mistress out, Banquo adjourns the suspicious group. His words are double-edged to serve his own ambitions. He saves Macbeth from further speech; he grants Macbeth a little time to stand concealed from those who would judge his present act. The throne is Cumberland's to claim; should oracles prove to be false, Banquo is safe for he has sworn to fight the purpose of treasonous malice. This oath makes him an ally to whoever wears the crown—whatever king shall ride to Scone for Scotland's coronation.

The princes know their peril here and plan in haste how best to meet the emergency that well may rise. They ride to self-imposed exile in nearby lands.

SCENE IV. *Outside Macbeth's castle.*

(*Enter* ROSS *and an* OLD MAN.)

OLD MAN. Threescore and ten I can remember well;
Within the volume of which time I have seen
Hours dreadful and things strange; but this sore night
Hath trifled former knowings.

ROSS.   Ah, good father,
Thou seest the heavens, as troubled with man's act,   5
Threatens his bloody stage: by th' clock 't is day,
And yet dark night strangles the travelling lamp.
Is 't night's predominance or the day's shame
That darkness does the face of earth entomb,
When living light should kiss it?

OLD MAN.   'T is unnatural,   10
Even like the deed that 's done. On Tuesday last,
A falcon, tow'ring in her pride of place,
Was by a mousing owl hawk'd at and kill'd.

4. Hath . . . knowings, has made former experiences seem trivial.   7. lamp, the sun.   8. predominance, astrological influence.   12. tow'ring . . . place, circling upward to the highest point in her flight.

ROSS. And Duncan's horses—a thing most strange and certain—
Beauteous and swift, the minions of their race,   15
Turn'd wild in nature, broke their stalls, flung out,
Contending 'gainst obedience, as they would make
War with mankind.

    OLD MAN.   'T is said they eat each other.

    ROSS. They did so, to th' amazement of mine eyes
That look'd upon 't.

    (*Enter* MACDUFF.)

                Here comes the good Macduff.   20
How goes the world, sir, now?

    MACDUFF.   Why, see you not?

    ROSS. Is 't known who did this more than bloody deed?

    MACDUFF. Those that Macbeth hath slain.

    ROSS.   Alas, the day!
What good could they pretend?

    MACDUFF.   They were suborned.
Malcolm and Donalbain, the King's two sons,   25
Are stolen away and fled; which puts upon them
Suspicion of the deed.

    ROSS.   'Gainst nature still!
Thriftless ambition, that will ravin up
Thine own life's means! Then 't is most like
The sovereignty will fall upon Macbeth.   30

    MACDUFF. He is already nam'd, and gone to Scone
To be invested.

    ROSS.   Where is Duncan's body?

    MACDUFF. Carried to Colmekill,
The sacred storehouse of his predecessors,
And guardian of their bones.

    ROSS.   Will you to Scone?   35

    MACDUFF. No, cousin, I'll to Fife.

    ROSS.   Well, I will thither.

    MACDUFF. Well, may you see things well done there,—adieu!—
Lest our old robes sit easier than our new!

    ROSS. Farewell, father.

    OLD MAN. God's benison go with you; and with those   40
That would make good of bad, and friends of foes!   (*Exeunt.*)

---

24. **pretend,** intend.   **suborned,** set on by others.   **28. ravin up,** devour ravenously.   **31.**
Scone, the ancient royal town where Scottish kings were crowned.   **33. Colmekill,** Iona, one
of the western isles, the burial place of Scottish kings.   **40. benison,** blessing.

The times are stranger than they seem. By Inverness an old man speaks; he can remember seventy years, but these days are the strangest he has seen. Macduff hears the strangest tale of all: the princes fled, suspicion travels in their wake. Macbeth is gone to gain the crown at Scone, but Macduff decides he will not follow; he speaks his fear that Macbeth may drop old nobles out of favor. Respectful Ross takes a blessing from the old man's (old Scotland's) hand and rides to Scone.

ACT III

SCENE I. *Forres. The palace.*

(*Enter* BANQUO.)

BANQUO. Thou hast it now: King, Cawdor, Glamis, all,
As the weird women promis'd, and, I fear,
Thou play'dst most foully for 't: yet it was said
It should not stand in thy posterity,
But that myself should be the root and father   5
Of many kings. If there come truth from them—
As upon thee, Macbeth, their speeches shine—
Why, by the verities on thee made good,
May they not be my oracles as well,
And set me up in hope? But hush! no more.   10

(*Sennet sounded. Enter* MACBETH, *as King,* LADY MACBETH, LENNOX, ROSS, LORDS, *and Attendants.*)

MACBETH. Here 's our chief guest.

LADY MACBETH.   If he had been forgotten,
It had been as a gap in our great feast,
And all-thing unbecoming.

MACBETH. To-night we hold a solemn supper, sir,
And I 'll request your presence.

BANQUO.   Let your Highness   15
Command upon me; to the which my duties
Are with a most indissoluble tie
For ever knit.

MACBETH. Ride you this afternoon?

BANQUO. Ay, my good lord.   20

MACBETH. We should have else desir'd your good advice,
(Which still hath been both grave and prosperous)
In this day's council; but we 'll take to-morrow.
Is 't far you ride?

---

7. **shine,** are conspicuously verified.   10. S. d. **Sennet,** signal on a trumpet.   13. **all-thing,**
altogether.   14. **solemn,** formal.

BANQUO. As far, my lord, as will fill up the time   25
'Twixt this and supper. Go not my horse the better,
I must become a borrower of the night
For a dark hour or twain.
    MACBETH.   Fail not our feast.
    BANQUO. My lord, I will not.
    MACBETH. We hear our bloody cousins are bestow'd   30
In England and in Ireland, not confessing
Their cruel parricide, filling their hearers
With strange invention. But of that to-morrow,
When therewithal we shall have cause of state
Craving us jointly. Hie you to horse; adieu,   35
Till you return at night. Goes Fleance with you?
    BANQUO. Ay, my good lord. Our time does call upon 's.
    MACBETH. I wish your horses swift and sure of foot;
And so I do commend you to their backs.
Farewell.   40   (*Exit* BANQUO.)
Let every man be master of his time
Till seven at night. To make society
The sweeter welcome, we will keep ourself
Till supper-time alone; while then, God be with you.
                  (*Exeunt all but* MACBETH *and a* SERVANT.)
                         Sirrah,
A word with you. Attend those men our pleasure?   45
    SERVANT. They are, my lord, without the palace gate.
    MACBETH. Bring them before us.   (*Exit* SERVANT.)
                To be thus is nothing;
But to be safely thus. Our fears in Banquo
Stick deep; and in his royalty of nature   50
Reigns that which would be fear'd. 'T is much he dares;
And, to that dauntless temper of his mind,
He hath a wisdom that doth guide his valour
To act in safety. There is none but he
Whose being I do fear; and, under him,   55
My Genius is rebuk'd, as, it is said,
Mark Antony's was by Cæsar. He chid the sisters
When first they put the name of king upon me,
And bade them speak to him; then prophet-like

---

30. **are bestow'd,** have taken refuge.   48. **thus,** a king.   51. **would,** should.   **56-7. My Genius . . . Caesar,** Shakespeare got this story from Plutarch; cf. *Antony and Cleopatra,* II, iii, 18–22.

They hail'd him father to a line of kings.   60
Upon my head they plac'd a fruitless crown,
And put a barren sceptre in my gripe,
Thence to be wrench'd with an unlineal hand,
No son of mine succeeding. If 't be so,
For Banquo's issue have I fil'd my mind;   65
For them the gracious Duncan have I murder'd;
Put rancours in the vessel of my peace
Only for them; and mine eternal jewel
Given to the common enemy of man,
To make them kings, the seeds of Banquo kings!   70
Rather than so, come fate into the list,
And champion me to th' utterance! Who's there?
    (*Re-enter* SERVANT, *and two* MURDERERS.)
Now go to the door, and stay there till we call.   (*Exit* SERVANT.)
Was it not yesterday we spoke together?
    FIRST MURDERER. It was, so please your Highness.
    MACBETH.   Well then, now   75
Have you consider'd of my speeches? Know
That it was he in the times past which held you
So under fortune, which you thought had been
Our innocent self. This I made good to you
In our last conference, pass'd in probation with you,   80
How you were borne in hand, how cross'd, the instruments,
Who wrought with them, and all things else that might
To half a soul and to a notion craz'd
Say, "Thus did Banquo."
    FIRST MURDERER.   You made it known to us.
    MACBETH. I did so, and went further, which is now   85
Our point of second meeting. Do you find
Your patience so predominant in your nature
That you can let this go? Are you so gospell'd
To pray for this good man and for his issue,
Whose heavy hand hath bow'd you to the grave   90
And beggar'd yours for ever?
    FIRST MURDERER.   We are men, my liege.
    MACBETH. Ay, in the catalogue ye go for men,

---

62. gripe, grasp.   **65. fil'd,** defiled.   **68-9. mine . . . man,** sold my soul to the devil.   **71. list,** lists, place of combat.   **72. champion me,** fight for me.   **to th' utterance,** to the death.
80. pass'd in probation, proved clearly.   **81. borne in hand,** led on by deceitful promises.
83. notion craz'd, feeble mind.   **88. gospell'd,** full of the spirit of the gospel.

As hounds and greyhounds, mongrels, spaniels, curs,
Shoughs, water-rugs, and demi-wolves, are clept
All by the name of dogs; the valued file   95
Distinguishes the swift, the slow, the subtle,
The housekeeper, the hunter, every one
According to the gift which bounteous nature
Hath in him clos'd; whereby he does receive
Particular addition, from the bill   100
That writes them all alike; and so of men.
Now, if you have a station in the file,
Not i' th' worst rank of manhood, say 't;
And I will put that business in your bosoms,
Whose execution takes your enemy off,   105
Grapples you to the heart and love of us,
Who wear our health but sickly in his life,
Which in his death were perfect.
    SECOND MURDERER.   I am one, my liege,
Whom the vile blows and buffets of the world
Hath so incens'd that I am reckless what   110
I do to spite the world.
    FIRST MURDERER.   And I another
So weary with disasters, tugg'd with fortune
That I would set my life on any chance,
To mend it, or be rid on 't.
    MACBETH.   Both of you
Know Banquo was your enemy.
    BOTH MURDERERS.   True, my lord.   115
    MACBETH. So is he mine; and in such bloody distance,
That every minute of his being thrusts
Against my near'st of life; and though I could
With barefac'd power sweep him from my sight
And bid my will avouch it, yet I must not,   120
For certain friends that are both his and mine,
Whose loves I may not drop, but wail his fall
Who I myself struck down; and thence it is,
That I to your assistance do make love,

---

94. **Shoughs, water-rugs,** shaggy dogs, water-dogs.   **demi-wolves,** half dog, half wolf.   **clept,** called.   95. **valued file,** list based on value.   97. **housekeeper,** watch-dog.   100–1. **Particular . . . alike,** special value apart from the generic qualities of dogs.   107. **in his life,** while he lives.   112. **tugg'd with,** pulled about by.   116. **distance,** enmity.   118. **near'st of life,** most vital parts.   120. **avouch,** warrant, affirm.   122. **wail,** pretend to lament.

Masking the business from the common eye   *125*
For sundry weighty reasons.
   SECOND MURDERER.   We shall, my lord,
Perform what you command us.
   FIRST MURDERER.   Though our lives—
   MACBETH. Your spirits shine through you. Within this hour at most
I will advise you where to plant yourselves;
Acquaint you with the perfect spy o' th' time,   *130*
The moment on 't; for 't must be done tonight,
And something from the palace; always thought
That I require a clearness: and with him—
To leave no rubs nor botches in the work—
Fleance his son, that keeps him company,   *135*
Whose absence is no less material to me
Than is his father's, must embrace the fate
Of that dark hour. Resolve yourselves apart;
I'll come to you anon.
   BOTH MURDERERS.   We are resolv'd, my lord.
   MACBETH. I'll call upon you straight; abide within.   (*Exeunt* MURDERERS.)
It is concluded. Banquo, thy soul's flight,   *141*
If it find heaven, must find it out to-night.   (*Exit.*)

Act III finds Macbeth king—his plans have worked with steady ease.
From Forres he rules all Scotland with his bloody hand. It is a troubled
land, however, for Macbeth is made anxious by uneasy thoughts of what
has happened and of what may come from Banquo's issue.

Banquo himself, here walking in the grounds of Forres, thinks on
his life as it unfolds according to the witches' words. Morality, good
Duncan's death, concern him less than promises made to his line on
that wild heath.

A royal trumpet ushers in Macbeth and all his retinue. Macbeth speaks
with two pronoun forms, the royal *we,* the personal *I,* revealing his attitudes
as he does so. Banquo is the royal guest tonight; "the king" will honor
him at court; "Macbeth" requests his presence too. The first is merely
a command; the second an attempt to show warm, personal friendship.
"Macbeth" asks after Banquo's present plans; "the king" has missed
Banquo's advice. "The king" has heard "rumors" spread by Duncan's
sons in other courts; "Macbeth" commends Banquo to his horse—and
to his death.

---

130. **perfect . . . time,** exact knowledge of Banquo's arrival.   132. **something,** some distance.
thought, it being remembered.   133. **require a clearness,** am not to be suspected.   134. **rubs,**
hindrances, slips.   138. **Resolve yourselves,** make up your minds.

That death is planned with savage ease by King Macbeth who, as a thane, found murder foul, but, served well by it, now deems it fair for present gain. Macbeth fears Banquo for two reasons: (1) he can blow with all prevailing winds; and (2) he may beget the future line bought with Macbeth's own soul. To circumvent that oracle delivered on the windy heath, Macbeth has hired murderers who may or may not have been brought to their present low state by Banquo. At any rate, Macbeth has convinced them that Banquo has so fouled their lives. They are a mangy, cur-cursed pair whom Macbeth loathes with little grace. He weaves his hatred into their strong hate for Banquo. Serving their ends (which are revenge), he serves them as they both serve him. Again the master is the slave when evil is the common goal. Nor is Macbeth alone tinged with such evil. That blot he does, with bitterness, assign to those who serve at court (116 – 126). Fleance must also be struck down; Macbeth gives the order without a hint of the conscience that once overtook his high-vaulting ambition. Now is Macbeth truly sold to darkest doom; he cannot lose any more of his soul than he has already lost. He can send Banquo's soul to God (Macbeth's final words betray his own fear), but Banquo's name will perish.

SCENE II. *The palace.*

(*Enter* LADY MACBETH *and a* SERVANT.)

LADY MACBETH. Is Banquo gone from court?

SERVANT. Ay, madam, but returns again to-night.

LADY MACBETH. Say to the King, I would attend his leisure
For a few words.

SERVANT.   Madam, I will.   (*Exit.*)

LADY MACBETH.   Nought 's had, all 's spent,
Where our desire is got without content: *5*
'T is safer to be that which we destroy
Than by destruction dwell in doubtful joy.

(*Enter* MACBETH.)

How now, my lord! why do you keep alone,
Of sorriest fancies your companions making,
Using those thoughts which should indeed have died   *10*
With them they think on? Things without all remedy
Should be without regard; what 's done is done.

MACBETH. We have scorch'd the snake, not kill'd it;
She 'll close and be herself, whilst our poor malice
Remains in danger of her former tooth.   *15*

13. **scorch'd**, scored, gashed.   14. **close**, reunite.

But let the frame of things disjoint, both the worlds suffer,
Ere we will eat our meal in fear, and sleep
In the affliction of these terrible dreams
That shake us nightly. Better be with the dead
Whom we, to gain our peace, have sent to peace,   20
Than on the torture of the mind to lie
In restless ecstasy. Duncan is in his grave;
After life's fitful fever he sleeps well.
Treason has done his worst; nor steel, nor poison,
Malice domestic, foreign levy, nothing,   25
Can touch him further.
    LADY MACBETH.   Come on,
Gentle my lord, sleek o'er your rugged looks;
Be bright and jovial among your guests tonight.
    MACBETH. So shall I, love; and so, I pray, be you.
Let your remembrance apply to Banquo;   30
Present him eminence, both with eye and tongue—
Unsafe the while, that we
Must lave our honours in these flattering streams,
And make our faces vizards to our hearts,
Disguising what they are.
    LADY MACBETH.   You must leave this.   35
    MACBETH. O, full of scorpions is my mind, dear wife!
Thou know'st that Banquo and his Fleance lives.
    LADY MACBETH. But in them nature's copy 's not eterne.
    MACBETH. There 's comfort yet; they are assailable:
Then be thou jocund; ere the bat hath flown   40
His cloister'd flight, ere to black Hecate's summons
The shard-borne beetle with his drowsy hums
Hath rung night's yawning peal, there shall be done
A deed of dreadful note.
    LADY MACBETH.   What 's to be done?
    MACBETH. Be innocent of the knowledge, dearest chuck,   45
Till thou applaud the deed. Come, seeling night,
Scarf up the tender eye of pitiful day,
And with thy bloody and invisible hand

---

16. **frame of things,** the universe.   **both the worlds,** heaven and earth.   22. **ecstasy,** frenzy.
31. **Present him eminence,** show him special favor.   32. **Unsafe . . . that,** we are unsafe so
long as.   34. **vizards,** masks.   38. **nature's . . . eterne,** their lease (copy) of life is not everlasting.   41. **cloister'd,** in the cloisters.   42. **shard-borne,** borne on horny wings.   43. **yawning,** drowsy.   46. **seeling,** eye-closing. Hawks were tamed by having their eyelids "seeled"
or sewn shut.

Cancel and tear to pieces that great bond
Which keeps me pale! Light thickens, and the crow   *50*
Makes wing to th' rooky wood;
Good things of day begin to droop and drowse,
Whiles night's black agents to their preys do rouse.
Thou marvell'st at my words, but hold thee still;
Things bad begun make strong themselves by ill.   *55*
So, prithee, go with me.   (*Exeunt.*)

This exchange between husband and wife is as near a love scene as Shakespeare can come in the play without violating the characterization he has built so carefully to this point.

The setting is, obviously, the royal bedchamber—a room inviting the greatest intimacy possible between two people. Lady Macbeth understands her husband. She knows that Banquo's presence serves to distract Macbeth so completely that communication with him is impossible unless Banquo is gone. She knows, further, that Banquo's departure will leave her husband anxious of mind, in need of comforting. Sending the servant to fetch Macbeth, she admits to herself they have gained nothing, that they have even lost what they earlier had. Prior to lines 4–7, she has exhibited no unhappiness in her marriage. Now joy is doubtful—and marriage can survive anything but doubt. It is less harmful, she says, to die physically than to live with harmed love.

Macbeth's arrival, however, forces her to closet these thoughts in her heart. She encourages her husband to disregard those very thoughts which she finds most dismaying. "What's done is done," she says, and yet she privately thinks on their deeds, regretting a greater loss than gain. Love is not declared at any point throughout the play. But no greater proof exists than this that Lady Macbeth does love her king. No matter what her private griefs, regardless of her own great doubts, she will be his true helpmate without betraying her own state of mind.

Does Macbeth love her? Surely their minds work in the selfsame veins with the selfsame thoughts. Lady Macbeth fears "to dwell in doubtful joy"; her husband fears "to lie in restless ecstasy." Their two hearts may not beat as one, but their two minds converge as one to find communication. And yet the few signs of their earlier love have already lessened, for "my dearest love" (I:v, 59) has now softened to simple "love" (29), "dear wife" (36), and "dearest chuck" (45). Macbeth's wife will never

49. **great bond,** both Banquo's lease of life and the promise made to Banquo by the witches.
51. **rooky,** inhabited by rooks.

be "my dearest love" again. No new loved one usurps her place, but when lovers conspire, not to love, but to hate, then love is weakened. Still, here, they try to love.

For reasons he does not disclose by word or deed, Macbeth keeps fast within his heart his plan to murder Banquo. Does he still rankle at his wife's charge of unmanliness? Does he prefer, now a powerful king, to prove that he can achieve his ends alone, without her tiny woman's hand? Not so. Rather, he bares his hatred of Banquo and of Fleance. He brushes past his wife's assurances that they cannot live forever. Then, hopeful the deed will be done, knowing he has disturbed her thoughts, he commands "Then be thou jocund." A bold hint dropped, he leaves her free of any part of this dark deed. She has already stained her hands with blood for him, but not again will she be asked to share in his anguished conscience. "Be innocent of the knowledge, dearest chuck," Macbeth pleads. Twice now he has used a lover's term in speaking to the wife he loves. Lines 29 and 45 have brought Macbeth back from the brink of the utter evil he could be, for evil cannot love. In loving his wife, he is a man, regardless of his other acts; and, as his wife looks upon his face, her face aflame with love of him, he knows the burden her heart bears. He knew that burden earlier, but, not as strong as he is now, he let her share it. Still, is he stronger now that he is king? Has his whole Self changed with the crown? Actually, his head alone wears that gold ring, but his character is unchanged. Macbeth's new strength, then, is the strength of love, a strength he always had but could not always use, for other needs sapped him of strength in his dark hour. Lady Macbeth's love of her husband made her give what strength she had to him. Macbeth's love of her now lets him return the lover's act. He will bear the full weight of this deed because he loves her.

No subtler statement of love could be found, no matter where one sought it. With understatement in each line, Shakespeare shows how true love will shine in darkest corners, in foulest deeds, and with its dim light keep men good even when they have surrendered willingly the remainder of their manhood. As long as Macbeth can descend from pride, from greed, from dark ambition, to think of her who shares his throne in this hour, so long will he remain the man love lets him be. Such greatness stamps the hero with a noble mark which men of lesser passion seldom know at any point in their lives. But that hero's mark is tragic too, for its counterpart, the hero's flaw, is made uglier by contrast than it would be in a common man who lacks excessive peaks and pits but, bound by his much smaller Self, swings back and forth on shorter lines of weaker passions.

SCENE III. *A park near the palace.*

(*Enter three* MURDERERS.)

FIRST MURDERER. But who did bid thee join with us?

THIRD MURDERER.   Macbeth.

SECOND MURDERER. He needs not our mistrust, since he delivers
Our offices and what we have to do
To the direction just.

FIRST MURDERER. Then stand with us;
The west yet glimmers with some streaks of day.   *5*
Now spurs the lated traveller apace
To gain the timely inn; and near approaches
The subject of our watch.

THIRD MURDERER.   Hark! I hear horses.

BANQUO (*within*). Give us a light there, ho!

SECOND MURDERER.   Then 't is he; the rest
That are within the note of expectation   *10*
Already are i' th' court.

FIRST MURDERER.   His horses go about.

THIRD MURDERER. Almost a mile; but he does usually,
So all men do, from hence to th' palace gate
Make it their walk.

(*Enter* BANQUO, *and* FLEANCE *with a torch.*)

SECOND MURDERER. A light, a light!

THIRD MURDERER.   'T is he.

FIRST MURDERER. Stand to 't.   *15*

BANQUO. It will be rain to-night.

FIRST MURDERER.   Let it come down.   (*They set upon* BANQUO.)

BANQUO. O, treachery! Fly, good Fleance, fly, fly, fly!
Thou mayst revenge. O slave!   (*Dies,* FLEANCE *escapes.*)

THIRD MURDERER. Who did strike out the light?

FIRST MURDERER.   Was 't not the way?

THIRD MURDERER. There's but one down; the son is fled.

SECOND MURDERER.   We have lost   *20*
Best half of our affair.

FIRST MURDERER. Well, let 's away, and say how much is done.   (*Exeunt.*)

Day dwindles in the west, and in the park great trees spread wide
their shielding limbs to shut out even the twilight. In the dew-hung

---

2. **He,** the third murderer.   3. **offices,** duties.   4. **To . . . just,** exactly as Macbeth directed
us.   6. **lated,** belated.   10. **within . . . expectation,** on the list of expected guests.

undergrowth, two men, dark hulks with darker hearts, wait for Banquo and his young son. Hidden in the shadows, they seem shunned, rejected by revealing light. Perhaps some thinly-smiling ray finds out the daggers at their belts and twinkles on the cross-shaped hilts, then flickers out as if in dread of the ugly deed these crosses hold in their blades. Suddenly a third shade joins the two murderers in the dark; they question him with suspicious fear. Has Macbeth sent the third man to murder the first two once they have dispatched Banquo? Two mouths unsealed can spread dark deeds with greater speed than one that stops those mouths when they have done their work. Then that last mouth can be closed by one king who hears the last report.

A flickering light held by Fleance lights Banquo into this dark glen. Leading their horses, as custom is, they walk their final mile. No thought of treachery walks with them; their talk is small: "It will be rain tonight." Darker and darker grow the clouds that gather over Scotland's throne. No moon shines bright as daggers find the heart of Banquo. Still, Fleance lives, and Fleance flies. Banquo lies dead in his final glade. For him no sun will ever shine. But his son lives and will give life to new, young kings.

SCENE IV. *A hall in the palace.*

(*A banquet prepared. Enter* MACBETH, LADY MACBETH, ROSS, LENNOX, LORDS, *and* Attendants.)

MACBETH. You know your own degrees; sit down: at first
And last, the hearty welcome.

  LORDS.   Thanks to your Majesty.

  MACBETH. Ourself will mingle with society
And play the humble host.
Our hostess keeps her state, but in best time   *5*
We will require her welcome.

  LADY MACBETH. Pronounce it for me, sir, to all our friends,
For my heart speaks they are welcome.

  (*Enter First* MURDERER *at the door.*)

  MACBETH. See, they encounter thee with their hearts' thanks.
Both sides are even; here I 'll sit i' th' midst.   *10*
Be large in mirth; anon we 'll drink a measure
The table round.   (*Approaching the door.*)
    —There 's blood upon thy face.

  MURDERER. 'T is Banquo's then.

---

1. **degrees,** rank, order of precedence.   1–2. **at . . . last,** once for all.   5. **state,** chair of state.
6. **require,** ask for.   11. **large,** free.

MACBETH. 'T is better thee without than he within.
Is he dispatch'd?   15
    MURDERER. My lord, his throat is cut; that I did for him.
    MACBETH. Thou art the best o' th' cut-throats; yet he 's good
That did the like for Fleance. If thou didst it,
Thou art the nonpareil.
    MURDERER.   Most royal sir,
Fleance is scap'd.   20
    MACBETH. Then comes my fit again. I had else been perfect,
Whole as the marble, founded as the rock,
As broad and general as the casing air;
But now I am cabin'd, cribb'd, confin'd, bound in
To saucy doubts and fears. But Banquo 's safe?   25
    MURDERER. Ay, my good lord; safe in a ditch he bides,
With twenty trenched gashes on his head,
The least a death to nature.
    MACBETH.   Thanks for that;
There the grown serpent lies: the worm that 's fled
Hath nature that in time will venom breed,   30
No teeth for th' present. Get thee gone; tomorrow
We 'll hear ourselves again.   (*Exit* MURDERER.)
    LADY MACBETH.   My royal lord,
You do not give the cheer: the feast is sold
That is not often vouch'd, while 't is a-making,
'T is given with welcome. To feed were best at home;   35
From thence, the sauce to meat is ceremony;
Meeting were bare without it.

Outside, clouds gather overhead as evil rides the upper air and rushes on toward Forres. Inside the castle, torches smoke their flickering way up the lofty walls. The banquet is spread; the fires are laid. Macbeth leads in the royal band and makes short work of welcome. His lady bears a heavy heart; he spares her with a modest speech; she rallies briefly, asking aid, for dread sits on her.

A vacant chair divides the group. Macbeth will sit between two even halves. His favor equals everyone. But business must be done. The blood-stained murderer enters in the same door the group has entered by. The guests face front and do not see the murderer who waits on

14. thee . . . within, on the outside of thee than inside him.   23. casing, surrounding.   24. cribb'd, hampered.   25. saucy, insolent.   32. hear ourselves, discuss the matter.   33. give the cheer, act as a proper host.   the feast is sold, like a meal at an inn.   36. From thence, away from home.

Macbeth. Does the faint queen now find fresh heart and bring attention to herself? She sits apart, in her accustomed place; her face is to that door and she can watch the parley of her lord. This stratagem Macbeth arranged with his early welcome. Does Lady Macbeth regain her strength now and bind all eyes at the table to her lips with her queenly talk? She surely must or else the speech of the murderers and Macbeth at the banquet door would stop all food and be a cause for all to shudder at the bloody words soft-spoken there.

At what great price does Lady Macbeth thus hold attention on her tiny self? As soon as she perceives a need, she speaks out to Macbeth. Again her action reveals her as one who times her passions well. The news was bad; Macbeth's wife reads his face and knows he needs to be led with words back to the table. If she does not call, he will stand apart and brood on the news. Lady Macbeth may not know the message given, but she knows Macbeth's needs.

(Enter the Ghost of BANQUO, and sits in MACBETH'S place.)

MACBETH.   Sweet remembrancer!
Now, good digestion wait on appetite,
And health on both!
    LENNOX.   May 't please your Highness sit.
    MACBETH. Here had we now our country's honour roof'd,   40
Were the grac'd person of our Banquo present,
Who may I rather challenge for unkindness
Than pity for mischance.
    ROSS.   His absence, sir,
Lays blame upon his promise. Please 't your Highness
To grace us with your royal company?   45
    MACBETH. The table 's full.
    LENNOX.   Here is a place reserv'd, sir.
    MACBETH. Where?
    LENNOX. Here, my good lord. What is 't that moves your Highness?
    MACBETH. Which of you have done this?
    LORDS.   What, my good lord?
    MACBETH. Thou canst not say I did it; never shake   50
Thy gory locks at me.
    ROSS. Gentlemen, rise: his Highness is not well.
    LADY MACBETH. Sit, worthy friends; my lord is often thus,
And hath been from his youth. Pray you, keep seat;
The fit is momentary; upon a thought   55

40. **roof'd**, under one roof.   41. **grac'd**, gracious, honored.   55. **upon a thought**, in a moment.

He will again be well. If much you note him,
You shall offend him and extend his passion.
Feed, and regard him not. (*Aside to* MACBETH.) Are you a man?

    MACBETH. Ay, and a bold one, that dare look on that
Which might appal the devil.

    LADY MACBETH (*aside to* MACBETH). O proper stuff!   *60*
This is the very painting of your fear;
This is the air-drawn dagger which, you said,
Led you to Duncan. O, these flaws and starts,
(Impostors to true fear) would well become
A woman's story at a winter's fire,   *65*
Authoriz'd by her grandam. Shame itself!
Why do you make such faces? When all 's done,
You look but on a stool.

    MACBETH. Prithee, see there! behold! look! lo! how say you?
Why, what care I? If thou canst nod, speak too.   *70*
If charnel-houses and our graves must send
Those that we bury back, our monuments
Shall be the maws of kites.   (GHOST *vanishes.*)

    LADY MACBETH (*aside to* MACBETH). What, quite unmann'd in folly?

    MACBETH. If I stand here, I saw him.

    LADY MACBETH (*aside to* MACBETH). Fie, for shame!

    MACBETH. Blood hath been shed ere now, i' th' olden time,   *75*
Ere humane statute purg'd the gentle weal;
Ay, and since too, murders have been perform'd
Too terrible for the ear. The times has been,
That, when the brains were out, the man would die,
And there an end; but now they rise again,   *80*
With twenty mortal murders on their crowns,
And push us from our stools. This is more strange
Than such a murder is.

    LADY MACBETH.   My worthy lord,
Your noble friends do lack you.

    MACBETH.   I do forget.
Do not muse at me, my most worthy friends;   *85*
I have a strange infirmity, which is nothing
To those that know me. Come, love and health to all;

---

57. extend, prolong.   60. **O proper stuff**, what utter nonsense.   63. **flaws**, gusts of passion.
66. **Authoriz'd . . . grandam**, on the authority of her grandmother.   72–3. **our . . . kites**,
let us be buried in the stomachs of hawks, in which case ghosts could not rise.   76. **purg'd, . . .
weal**, made the nation gentle by purging it of violence.   81. **mortal murders**, fatal wounds.
84. **lack**, miss.   85. **muse**, wonder.

Then I 'll sit down. Give me some wine; fill full.
I drink to th' general joy o' the whole table,
And to our dear friend Banquo, whom we miss;   *90*
Would he were here! to all and him we thirst,
And all to all.
    LORDS.   Our duties, and the pledge.

Recalled to duty by his queen, Macbeth assumes his social face, and
with the cheer of form-born words, becomes the host. But in that chair
he said he would use, a bloody spectre now shakes its head in bloody
accusation at its murderer. No one else can see the silent ghost—as no
one else could see the dagger that appeared to Macbeth on the night
he murdered Duncan. Are these, then, visions? Are they Macbeth's
conscience damning him? Whatever their state truly is, they are real to
him.

Macbeth draws back in the smoky hall, addresses the chair—a mad
scene this for those who watch his fearful form and hear his words. *They*
hear his words; his lady hears the anguish she once heard before when
her small hand and her great heart supplied her husband strength. Again
she finds her secret store of love's strength, offering it to him. He has
been subject to such seizures from his youth, she pleads; do not question
him. For, if anyone should offer aid, should ask Macbeth to speak the
cause, might he not blurt out "Banquo's ghost," thus betraying his
knowledge of the death? Lady Macbeth now knows full well what she
has only guessed before this hour. For this occasion she has watched,
and now she rallies to her husband's aid.

The arguments she used with Macbeth before worked well; now
whispering into his ear, perhaps now clinging to his arm, she uses them
again. "Are you a man?" she asks again. Does his child's eye still fear
"painted devils"? As those at the table occupy themselves with food at
her request, she brings Macbeth to grips with himself, then smooths
the way for him to lead the discussion once again. If Macbeth can be
diverted, perhaps his mind will clear. Again his wife finds the key to
lock his passions back within his breast. Again she's been his only strength
when he has had none.

(*Re-enter* GHOST.)
    MACBETH. Avaunt! and quit my sight! let the earth hide thee!
Thy bones are marrowless, thy blood is cold;

---

91. **thirst,** offer a toast.   92. **all to all,** all good health to all.

Thou hast no speculation in those eyes   *95*
Which thou dost glare with!
    LADY MACBETH.   Think of this, good peers,
But as a thing of custom; 't is no other,
Only it spoils the pleasure of the time.
    MACBETH. What man dare, I dare.
Approach thou like the rugged Russian bear,   *100*
The arm'd rhinoceros, or th' Hyrcan tiger;
Take any shape but that, and my firm nerves
Shall never tremble. Or be alive again,
And dare me to the desert with thy sword;
If trembling I inhabit then, protest me   *105*
The baby of a girl. Hence, horrible shadow!
Unreal mockery, hence!   (GHOST *vanishes.*)
                Why, so; being gone,
I am a man again. Pray you, sit still.
    LADY MACBETH. You have displac'd the mirth, broke the good meeting,
With most admir'd disorder.
    MACBETH.   Can such things be,   *110*
And overcome us like a summer's cloud,
Without our special wonder? You make me strange
Even to the disposition that I owe,
When now I think you can behold such sights,
And keep the natural ruby of your cheeks,   *115*
When mine is blanch'd with fear.
    ROSS.   What sights, my lord?
    LADY MACBETH. I pray you, speak not; he grows worse and worse;
Question enrages him. At once, good-night.
Stand not upon the order of your going,
But go at once.
    LENNOX.   Good-night; and better health   *120*
Attend his Majesty!
    LADY MACBETH.   A kind good-night to all!   (*Exeunt* LORDS.)

So firm has been the queen's guiding hand that, when the ghost appears again, she holds the group, but Macbeth regains his composure when the ghost is gone without her aid. In fact, so naturally does he

---

95. **speculation,** light of intelligence.   101. **Hyrcan,** of Hyrcania, near the Caspian Sea.
105. **trembling I inhabit,** dwell, continue, in a state of trembling.   106. **baby of a girl,** a girl's doll.   110. **admir'd,** causing wonder.   119. **Stand . . . going,** do not take formal leave.

become himself again that he chastises his wife for not sharing his concern. Then Lady Macbeth knows the night must end. Too close to truth are her husband's soft words; she sends the guests away, abandoning form. The guests go in haste, their tongues in check, but on their faces one can read strange wonderings, strange fears, strange doubts which all will speak excitedly about when they are free to speak.

MACBETH. It will have blood, they say; blood will have blood.
Stones have been known to move and trees to speak;
Augures and understood relations have
By maggot-pies and choughs and rooks brought forth   *125*
The secret'st man of blood. What is the night?
    LADY MACBETH. Almost at odds with morning, which is which.
    MACBETH. How say'st thou, that Macduff denies his person
At our great bidding?
    LADY MACBETH.   Did you send to him, sir?
    MACBETH. I hear it by the way; but I will send.   *130*
There 's not a one of them but in his house
I keep a servant fee'd. I will to-morrow,
(And betimes I will) to the weird sisters.
More shall they speak; for now I am bent to know,
By the worst means, the worst. For mine own good   *135*
All causes shall give way. I am in blood
Stepp'd in so far that, should I wade no more,
Returning were as tedious as go o'er.
Strange things I have in head, that will to hand,
Which must be acted ere they may be scann'd.   *140*
    LADY MACBETH. You lack the season of all natures, sleep.
    MACBETH. Come, we 'll to sleep. My strange and self-abuse
Is the initiate fear that wants hard use;
We are yet but young in deed.   (*Exeunt.*)

Reflectively, as to himself, Macbeth acknowledges a truth that all men in history have known—a little late: "blood will have blood." The evil

---

123. **Stones . . . speak,** possibly an allusion to the superstition that stones refused to cover the body of a murdered man. Speaking trees may be a reminiscence of a passage in Reginald Scot's *Discovery of Witchcraft,* or of the incident in the *Aeneid,* where a tree reveals a murder.   124. **Augures,** auguries, interpretation of omens.   **understood relations,** a continuation of the idea of auguries, the perception of significance in omens.   125. **maggot-pies,** magpies.   **choughs,** jackdaws.   139. **will to hand,** must be acted.   141. **season,** seasoning, preservative.   142. **self-abuse,** self-delusion.   143. **initiate fear,** fear of a novice in crime.

deed begets its own dark brood of deeds—all evil. Each new one, sprung from blood, demands new blood. Then, shaking off the grisly thought, abruptly Macbeth moves back to real life and, even as a common man, thinks of time. His lady answers, pleased, it seems, that he has turned his mind from thoughts that lead to fears and offer no way to cancel the truth that they have held.

To think leads nowhere for Macbeth; to act is quite another thing. A warrior transplanted to a throne grows sickly, like an untamed vine root-pruned and potted. He seeks deeds to cancel thought. Macbeth will visit the witches again, they who can say the hell-charmed words that he must know if he is to act with wisdom. But act he will; that much he swears: "Strange things I have in head, that will to hand,/ Which must be acted ere they may be scann'd." Plans *will* be acted, plans that must be acted before they *may* be examined. Until the deeds are done, they cannot be examined. This is no ruler's mind at work; it is a man of bold action speaking. To act, not to plan, is Macbeth's way—unfortunately. *If* plans are called for, they must be the work of women. Their minds see the shape of things that are not done, before they're done.

What passions move across the face the queen allows her king to see? Does she thank him for freeing her of planning? Is she pleased that he will seek the advice of the witches on the misty heath? Does her heart ache because he has turned away from her? Is "doubtful joy" more doubtful now when he withholds his present plans from her, and does not ask her to share them as fully as he had once asked before he gained the crown?

Whatever passions prod Lady Macbeth's mind, she sends them back to distant cells. She invites sleep that seems to keep such thoughts imprisoned. Macbeth agrees and finds release by steeping himself in the ugly truth, "Blood will have blood." He here accepts his depravity as his wife seeks out the long, dark halls of sleep that lead to madness. This is the crisis of their married lives; the turning point is in these words they have lifted up, like common stones, between them. Had they moved on as they have come, with reasoned hope and full-shared plans, their road might lead a different way; they would at any rate travel it together. Now each will walk a single road: Macbeth's leads to action; his wife's leads to guilt. Together the two of them were strong enough to stand before disaster. But each on his solitary way will lack the other's willing help, and (as they are, together, one) their separateness will lead back to Macbeth's earlier fear (III, ii:15–19): their universe of love disjoint, they both will suffer.

SCENE V. *A heath.*

    (*Thunder. Enter the three* WITCHES, *meeting* HECATE.)

    FIRST WITCH. Why, how now, Hecate! you look angerly.

    HECATE. Have I not reason, beldams as you are,

Saucy and overbold? How did you dare

To trade and traffic with Macbeth

In riddles and affairs of death;   *5*

And I, the mistress of your charms,

The close contriver of all harms,

Was never call'd to bear my part,

Or show the glory of our art?

And, which is worse, all you have done   *10*

Hath been but for a wayward son,

Spiteful and wrathful, who, as others do,

Loves for his own ends, not for you.

But make amends now; get you gone,

And at the pit of Acheron   *15*

Meet me i' th' morning; thither he

Will come to know his destiny.

Your vessels and your spells provide,

Your charms and everything beside.

I am for the air; this night I 'll spend   *20*

Unto a dismal and a fatal end;

Great business must be wrought ere noon.

Upon the corner of the moon

There hangs a vaporous drop profound;

I 'll catch it ere it come to ground;   *25*

And that distill'd by magic sleights

Shall raise such artificial sprites

As by the strength of their illusion

Shall draw him on to his confusion.

He shall spurn fate, scorn death, and bear   *30*

His hopes 'bove wisdom, grace, and fear;

And, you all know, security

Is mortals' chiefest enemy.

    (*Music, and a song.*)

Hark! I am call'd; my little spirit, see,

Sits in a foggy cloud, and stays for me.   *35*   (*Exit.*)

Scene V. An unShakespearean scene.   **15. Acheron,** river in Hades.   **24. profound,** having deep and hidden qualities.   **32. security,** overconfidence.

(*Sing within:* "Come away, come away," etc.)

FIRST WITCH. Come, let 's make haste; she 'll soon be back again.   (*Exeunt.*)

The wild and windy heath is gray beneath the clattering thunder-clouds; bright lightning flames like Hell's own fire sent down from Heaven. The angry goddess Hecate berates her followers. How dared they play the game she loves—and almost botch it? They've set a snare to catch a bird that can't be caged. Macbeth's love is not completely base: he "Loves for his own ends, not for you." Evil is not the end he serves, nor has he lost all his humanity in serving it for this brief time. He is, right now, as Evil speaks, a "wayward son" still tied to Man, and Man is the son of God. Macbeth acts like men ("Loves for his own ends") "as others [all men] do." Nobility still finds his brow a likely place to find the sun. But Hecate knows that all men share in Adam's sin. Confidently, he ate the fruit; he disobeyed the highest rule; and that overwhelming confidence brought him to ruin. Macbeth is Adam's latest child; he too has eaten of the fruit of power. If overconfidence can be allowed time to grow, he will be defeated. But should Macbeth stop to think a while, he would find the flaw within the fatal plan. Dark Hecate is theatrical: she understands illusion. "Go set the stage," she urges now (14–19). Macbeth's eyes must continue to overwhelm his brain. If what he sees negates the words he hears, he will be lost. To think is to win. Macbeth must not think. His mind must be diverted. Then he can be destroyed on the earth and caged in eternal darkness.

SCENE VI. *Forres. The palace.*
    (*Enter* LENNOX *and another* LORD.)
    LENNOX. My former speeches have but hit your thoughts,
Which can interpret farther; only, I say,
Things have been strangely borne. The gracious Duncan
Was pitied of Macbeth; marry, he was dead:
And the right-valiant Banquo walk'd too late;   *5*
Whom, you may say (if 't please you) Fleance kill'd,
For Fleance fled; men must not walk too late.
Who cannot want the thought how monstrous
It was for Malcolm and for Donalbain
To kill their gracious father? Damned fact!   *10*
How it did grieve Macbeth! Did he not straight
In pious rage the two delinquents tear,
That were the slaves of drink and thralls of sleep?
Was not that nobly done? Ay, and wisely too;

8. **cannot . . . thought,** can help thinking.

For 't would have anger'd any heart alive   *15*
To hear the men deny 't. So that, I say,
He has borne all things well; and I do think
That had he Duncan's sons under his key—
As, an 't please Heaven, he shall not—they should find
What 't were to kill a father; so should Fleance.   *20*
But, peace! for from broad words, and 'cause he fail'd
His presence at the tyrant's feast, I hear
Macduff lives in disgrace. Sir, can you tell
Where he bestows himself?

LORD.   The son of Duncan
(From whom this tyrant holds the due of birth)   *25*
Lives in the English court, and is receiv'd
Of the most pious Edward with such grace
That the malevolence of Fortune nothing
Takes from his high respect. Thither Macduff
Is gone to pray the holy king, upon his aid   *30*
To wake Northumberland and warlike Siward;
That, by the help of these—with Him above
To ratify the work—we may again
Give to our tables meat, sleep to our nights,
Free from our feasts and banquets bloody knives,   *35*
Do faithful homage and receive free honours;
All which we pine for now: and this report
Hath so exasperate their king that he
Prepares for some attempt of war.

LENNOX.   Sent he to Macduff?

LORD. He did; and with an absolute "Sir, not I,"   *40*
The cloudy messenger turns me his back,
And hums, as who should say, "You 'll rue the time
That clogs me with this answer."

LENNOX.   And that well might
Advise him to a caution, t' hold what distance
His wisdom can provide. Some holy angel   *45*
Fly to the court of England and unfold
His message ere he come, that a swift blessing
May soon return to this our suffering country
Under a hand accurs'd!

LORD.   I 'll send my prayers with him.   (*Exeunt.*)

---

21. **from,** because of.   **broad,** plain.   27. **Edward,** Edward the Confessor.   30. **upon his aid,** in aid of Malcolm.   36. **free,** due to free men.   38. **their king,** the king of England.   40. **absolute,** positive.   41. **cloudy,** sullen.

In the gathering dusk at Castle Forres, Lennox and a friend walk in the light that dwindles on the western rim of heaven. Irony and rage tear at the words young Lennox speaks into the gloom. How noble seem Macbeth's base acts through half-closed eyes! But opened wide, those eyes can see the truth that veils each sullen act. Lennox pleads for news of those who might deliver Scotland. In England, Edward hears the plea of Malcolm, rightful heir of Scone, and sends Macduff his audience if he will have it. Have it he will, he hastens now to weld the ranks of noblemen who hold their armies ready to defend true, rightful kings. Lennox prays that deliverance will come—as do all true lords symbolized by this one beside him who is nameless for that reason.

ACT IV

SCENE I. *A cavern. In the middle, a boiling cauldron.*

(*Thunder. Enter the three* WITCHES.)

FIRST WITCH. Thrice the brinded cat hath mew'd.

SECOND WITCH. Thrice, and once the hedge-pig whin'd.

THIRD WITCH. Harpier cries; "'T is time, 't is time."

FIRST WITCH. Round about the cauldron go;

In the poison'd entrails throw.   *5*

Toad, that under cold stone

Days and nights has thirty-one

Swelter'd venom sleeping got,

Boil thou first i' th' charmed pot.

ALL. Double, double, toil and trouble;   *10*

Fire burn and cauldron bubble.

SECOND WITCH. Fillet of a fenny snake,

In the cauldron boil and bake;

Eye of newt and toe of frog,

Wool of bat and tongue of dog,   *15*

Adder's fork and blind-worm's sting,

Lizard's leg and howlet's wing,

For a charm of powerful trouble,

Like a hell-broth boil and bubble.

ALL. Double, double, toil and trouble;   *20*

Fire burn and cauldron bubble.

THIRD WITCH. Scale of dragon, tooth of wolf,

---

1. **brinded,** brindled.   3. **Harpier,** the familiar of the third witch, in the form of a harpy. 12. **fenny,** inhabiting swamps.   16. **fork,** forked tongue.   **blind-worm's,** small lizard thought to be poisonous.   17. **howlet's,** owl's.

Witches' mummy, maw and gulf
Of the ravin'd salt-sea shark,
Root of hemlock digg'd i' th' dark,   25
Liver of blaspheming Jew,
Gall of goat, and slips of yew
Sliver'd in the moon's eclipse,
Nose of Turk and Tartar's lips,
Finger of birth-strangled babe   30
Ditch-deliver'd by a drab,
Make the gruel thick and slab.
Add thereto a tiger's chaudron,
For th' ingredients of our cauldron.
> ALL. Double, double, toil and trouble;   35
Fire burn and cauldron bubble.
> SECOND WITCH. Cool it with a baboon's blood,
Then the charm is firm and good.
> (*Enter* HECATE *and the other three* WITCHES.)
> HECATE. O, well done! I commend your pains;
And every one shall share i' th' gains.   40
And now about the cauldron sing,
Like elves and fairies in a ring,
Enchanting all that you put in.   (*Exit* HECATE.)
> (*Music and a song:* "Black spirits," *etc.*)
> SECOND WITCH. By the pricking of my thumbs,
Something wicked this way comes.   45
> > Open, locks,
> > Whoever knocks!

Deep in a cavern on the dim heath, flames caught in Hell and transported hither heat the great iron pot that bubbles lethargically in the center of the subterranean room. In the dark shadows veiling the walls, water squeezed from the misty heath gathers on the rocks and, drop by caustic drop, falls with a muffled metallic "tlark" to form foul rivulets that gargle muddily away through jagged fissures to some night-haunted river. The spongy floor, with lichen spread, dulls footfalls into whispered oaths as, chanting their black hymn of hate, the witches brew Macbeth's dark charm out of their evil larder. Hecate lends her presence and her hellish blessing to the rite. What is done is done—and now Macbeth comes. Without the shared love of his queen, he is "Something wicked." Did he, then,

23. **mummy,** medicine made from mummies.   **gulf,** gullet.   24. **ravin'd,** ravenous.   32. **slab,** sticky.   33. **chaudron,** entrails.

leave his human self in that long hall where Banquo's ghost mocked him last night? Or, sleeping, did his soul steal out across the heath and leave him free of the fear that keeps a good man earth-bound?

(*Enter* MACBETH.)

MACBETH. How now, you secret, black, and midnight hags!
What is 't you do?

ALL.   A deed without a name.

MACBETH. I conjure you, by that which you profess,   *50*
Howe'er you come to know it, answer me!
Though you untie the winds and let them fight
Against the churches; though the yesty waves
Confound and swallow navigation up;
Though bladed corn be lodg'd and trees blown down;   *55*
Though castles topple on their warders' heads;
Though palaces and pyramids do slope
Their heads to their foundations; though the treasure
Of nature's germen tumble all together,
Even till destruction sicken; answer me   *60*
To what I ask you.

FIRST WITCH.   Speak.

SECOND WITCH.   Demand.

THIRD WITCH.   We'll answer.

FIRST WITCH. Say, if thou 'dst rather hear it from our mouths,
Or from our masters'?

MACBETH.   Call 'em; let me see 'em.

FIRST WITCH. Pour in sow's blood, that hath eaten
Her nine farrow; grease that 's sweaten   *65*
From the murderer's gibbet throw
Into the flame.

ALL.   Come, high or low;
Thyself and office deftly show!

Yes, Macbeth is fearless. He speaks his words across the cauldron where the charm coats each passing sound with its steam and purifies each word with filth in this cold, evil chapel. Macbeth is given a choice and he chooses to speak directly to the witches' fearful masters. How could any

---

53. **yesty,** foamy.   55. **bladed,** in the blade, green.   **lodg'd,** beaten down.   57. **pyramids,** steeples.   59. **nature's germen,** seeds of matter.   60. **sicken,** be surfeited.   65. **farrow,** litter of pigs.

man ask, face-to-face, for a grim confrontation with the powers that feed
on souls, denying them a passage into Heaven? Despair alone can make
a man so bold, when, losing all, he can but hope to regain whatever
it is he has lost if only he can face the last, the ultimate terror.

> (*Thunder. First* APPARITION, *an armed Head.*)
> MACBETH. Tell me, thou unknown power,—
> FIRST WITCH.   He knows thy thought.

Hear his speech, but say thou nought.   *70*

> FIRST APPARITION. Macbeth! Macbeth! Macbeth! beware Macduff;

Beware the thane of Fife. Dismiss me. Enough.   (*He descends.*)

> MACBETH. Whate'er thou art, for thy good caution, thanks;

Thou hast harp'd my fear aright. But one word more,—

> FIRST WITCH. He will not be commanded. Here 's another,   *75*

More potent than the first.

> (*Thunder. Second* APPARITION, *a bloody Child.*)
> SECOND APPARITION. Macbeth! Macbeth! Macbeth!
> MACBETH. Had I three ears, I 'd hear thee.
> SECOND APPARITION. Be bloody, bold, and resolute; laugh to scorn

The power of man; for none of woman born   *80*

Shall harm Macbeth.   (*Descends.*)

> MACBETH. Then live, Macduff: what need I fear of thee?

But yet I'll make assurance double sure,

And take a bond of fate: thou shalt not live;

That I may tell pale-hearted fear it lies,   *85*

And sleep in spite of thunder.

> (*Thunder. Third* APPARITION, *a Child crowned, with a tree in his hand.*)
>   What is this

That rises like the issue of a king,

And wears upon his baby-brow the round

And top of sovereignty?

> ALL.   Listen, but speak not to 't.
> THIRD APPARITION. Be lion-mettled, proud, and take no care   *90*

Who chafes, who frets, or where conspirers are.

Macbeth shall never vanquish'd be until

---

68. S. d. **armed Head,** representing the severed head of Macbeth (cf. V, viii, 54–55). But it may
also suggest the rising of Scotland, led by Macduff; cf. the warning "beware Macduff," and "Rebellious head" (l. 97 below). "Head" is frequent in Shakespeare for a rebellion.   74. **harp'd,**
touched.   76. S. d. **bloody Child,** a glance at the manner of Macduff's birth (cf. V, viii, 15–16).
86. S. d. **a Child crowned, with a tree in his hand,** Malcolm, whose device it was that his
soldiers should carry boughs before them (cf. V, iv, 4 ff.).   88. **round,** crown.

Great Birnam wood to high Dunsinane hill
Shall come against him.   *(Descends.)*

MACBETH.   That will never be.

Who can impress the forest, bid the tree   95
Unfix his earth-bound root? Sweet bodements! good!
Rebellious head, rise never till the wood
Of Birnam rise, and our high-plac'd Macbeth
Shall live the lease of nature, pay his breath
To time and mortal custom. Yet my heart   100
Throbs to know one thing: tell me, if your art
Can tell so much, shall Banquo's issue ever
Reign in this kingdom?

ALL.   Seek to know no more.

MACBETH. I will be satisfied! Deny me this,
And an eternal curse fall on you! Let me know.   105
Why sinks that cauldron? And what noise is this?   *(Hautboys.)*

FIRST WITCH. Show!

SECOND WITCH. Show!

THIRD WITCH. Show!

ALL. Show his eyes, and grieve his heart;   110
Come like shadows, so depart!

(*A show of Eight* KINGS *and* BANQUO, *the last with a glass in his hand.*)

MACBETH. Thou art too like the spirit of Banquo; down!
Thy crown does sear mine eye-balls. And thy hair,
Thou other gold-bound brow, is like the first.
A third is like the former. Filthy hags!   115
Why do you show me this? A fourth! Start, eyes!
What, will the line stretch out to th' crack of doom?
Another yet! A seventh! I'll see no more.
And yet the eighth appears, who bears a glass
Which shows me many more; and some I see   120
That twofold balls and treble sceptres carry.
Horrible sight! Now, I see, 't is true;
For the blood-bolter'd Banquo smiles upon me,
And points at them for his. (APPARITIONS *vanish.*) What, is this so?

FIRST WITCH. Ay, sir, all this is so; but why   125

---

95. **impress,** force into military service.   96. **bodements,** prophecies.   97. **Rebellious head,** army of rebels.   99. **lease of nature,** natural term.   100. **mortal custom,** human custom of dying.   106. **noise,** music.   121. **twofold balls and treble sceptres carry,** a reference to King James's being crowned at Scone and at Westminster, and assuming the title of King of Great Britain, France and Ireland.   123. **blood-bolter'd,** having hair matted with blood.

Stands Macbeth thus amazedly?
Come, sisters, cheer we up his sprites,
And show the best of our delights.
I 'll charm the air to give a sound,
While you perform your antic round;   *130*
That this great king may kindly say,
Our duties did his welcome pay.   *(Music. The* WITCHES *dance, and vanish.)*
   MACBETH. Where are they? Gone? Let this pernicious hour
Stand aye accursed in the calendar!
Come in, without there!
   (Enter LENNOX.)
   LENNOX.   What 's your Grace's will?   *135*
   MACBETH. Saw you the weird sisters?
   LENNOX.   No, my lord.
   MACBETH. Came they not by you?
   LENNOX.   No, indeed, my lord.
   MACBETH. Infected be the air whereon they ride;
And damn'd all those that trust them! I did hear
The galloping of horse; who was 't came by?   *140*
   LENNOX. 'T is two or three, my lord, that bring you word
Macduff is fled to England.
   MACBETH.   Fled to England!
   LENNOX. Ay, my good lord.
   MACBETH. Time, thou anticipat'st my dread exploits:
The flighty purpose never is o'ertook   *145*
Unless the deed go with it. From this moment
The very firstlings of my heart shall be
The firstlings of my hand. And even now,
To crown my thoughts with acts, be it thought and done:
The castle of Macduff I will surprise;   *150*
Seize upon Fife; give to th' edge o' th' sword
His wife, his babes, and all unfortunate souls
That trace him in his line. No boasting like a fool;
This deed I'll do before this purpose cool.
But no more sights!—Where are these gentlemen?   *155*
Come, bring me where they are.   *(Exeunt.)*

Out of the cauldron's hissing steam, a disembodied head streams up
the silent vapors, wavers there prepared to prophesy. Such sight would
terrify and hold the tongue of almost any man, but Macbeth speaks with

---

130. **antic round,** grotesque circular dance.   145. **flighty,** fleeting.   153. **trace,** follow.

a fearless voice and receives the answer, "Beware Macduff." Next a bloody child screams up the steam; Macbeth hears words that seem to negate those he heard from the disembodied head. Still, he will take the safer way: he will slay Macduff. The third steam-borne unholy sight speaks of an act no man can fear. Trees do not walk across the land—of reason. Then, blaring trumpets ricochet their brazen notes against the rocks that build these walls to evil height, and Banquo's line is shown. That hateful line is the foulest possible sight to Macbeth as he stands aghast. His fears are real; Banquo *will* live eight lives or more in glory!

The sisters pass away into the air, the cauldron sinks, and the cave is suddenly bare of everything save King Macbeth when Lennox enters. He brings the news he earlier knew and gazes on his maddened king who swears to act without a thought from this fixed moment. The Thane of Fife may flee the land; his hostages to fate are left. Dull rage fills the dark vaulted cave as Macbeth proclaims their deaths.

SCENE II. *Fife. Macduff's castle.*

(*Enter* LADY MACDUFF, *her* SON, *and* ROSS.)

LADY MACDUFF. What had he done, to make him fly the land?

ROSS. You must have patience, madam.

LADY MACDUFF.   He had none;
His flight was madness: when our actions do not,
Our fears do make us traitors.

ROSS.   You know not
Whether it was his wisdom or his fear.   5

LADY MACDUFF. Wisdom! to leave his wife, to leave his babes,
His mansion and his titles, in a place
From whence himself does fly? He loves us not,
He wants the natural touch; for the poor wren,
The most diminutive of birds, will fight,   10
Her young ones in her nest, against the owl.
All is the fear and nothing is the love;
As little is the wisdom, where the flight
So runs against all reason.

ROSS.   My dearest coz,
I pray you, school yourself; but for your husband,   15
He is noble, wise, judicious, and best knows
The fits o' th' season. I dare not speak much further;
But cruel are the times when we are traitors
And do not know ourselves; when we hold rumour

7. **titles**, estates. 9. **touch**, affection. 15. **school**, control. 17. **fits . . . season**, disorders of the time. 19. **hold**, accept.

From what we fear, yet know not what we fear, 20
But float upon a wild and violent sea
Each way and move. I take my leave of you;
Shall not be long but I 'll be here again.
Things at the worst will cease, or else climb upward
To what they were before. My pretty cousin, 25
Blessing upon you!

LADY MACDUFF. Father'd he is, and yet he 's fatherless.

ROSS. I am so much a fool, should I stay longer,
It would be my disgrace and your discomfort.
I take my leave at once. (*Exit.*)

LADY MACDUFF. Sirrah, your father 's dead; 30
And what will you do now? How will you live?

SON. As birds do, mother.

LADY MACDUFF. What, with worms and flies?

SON. With what I get, I mean; and so do they.

LADY MACDUFF. Poor bird! thou 'dst never fear the net nor lime,
The pitfall nor the gin. 35

SON. Why should I, mother? Poor birds they are not set for.
My father is not dead, for all your saying.

LADY MACDUFF. Yes, he is dead. How wilt thou do for a father?

SON. Nay, how will you do for a husband?

LADY MACDUFF. Why, I can buy me twenty at any market. 40

SON. Then you 'll buy 'em to sell again.

LADY MACDUFF. Thou speak'st with all thy wit; and yet, i' faith,
With wit enough for thee.

SON. Was my father a traitor, mother?

LADY MACDUFF. Ay, that he was. 45

SON. What is a traitor?

LADY MACDUFF. Why, one that swears and lies.

SON. And be all traitors that do so?

LADY MACDUFF. Every one that does so is a traitor, and must be hanged. 50

SON. And must they all be hanged that swear and lie?

LADY MACDUFF. Every one.

SON. Who must hang them?

LADY MACDUFF. Why, the honest men. 55

SON. Then the liars and swearers are fools; for there are liars and swearers enow
to beat the honest men and hang up them.

---

22. **Each . . . move,** every way and toss to and fro.   29. **It . . . discomfort,** i.e., I should weep.
34. **lime,** lime used for catching birds.   35. **gin,** snare.   47. **swears and lies,** takes an oath
and breaks it.

LADY MACDUFF. Now, God help thee, poor monkey!
But how wilt thou do for a father?   60
    SON. If he were dead, you 'd weep for him; if you would not, it were a good sign
that I should quickly have a new father.
    LADY MACDUFF. Poor prattler, how thou talk'st!
    (*Enter a* MESSENGER.)
    MESSENGER. Bless you, fair dame! I am not to you known,   65
Though in your state of honour I am perfect.
I doubt some danger does approach you nearly.
If you will take a homely man's advice,
Be not found here; hence, with your little ones.
To fright you thus, methinks, I am too savage;   70
To do worse to you were fell cruelty,
Which is too nigh your person. Heaven preserve you!
I dare abide no longer.   (*Exit* MESSENGER.)
    LADY MACDUFF.   Whither should I fly?
I have done no harm. But I remember now
I am in this earthly world, where to do harm   75
Is often laudable, to do good sometime
Accounted dangerous folly. Why then, alas,
Do I put up that womanly defence,
To say I have done no harm?
    (*Enter* MURDERERS.)
                    What are these faces?
    FIRST MURDERER. Where is your husband?   80
    LADY MACDUFF. I hope, in no place so unsanctified
Where such as thou mayst find him.
    FIRST MURDERER.   He 's a traitor.
    SON. Thou liest, thou shag-ear'd villain!
    FIRST MURDERER.   What, you egg! (*Stabbing him.*)
Young fry of treachery!
    SON.   He has kill'd me, mother:
Run away, I pray you!   (*Dies.*)   85
    (*Exit* LADY MACDUFF *crying "Murder!" Exeunt* MURDERERS, *following her.*)

The castle at Fife seems warm and bright and friendly as Lady Macduff
and her son enter with Ross. Distraught by her husband's actions, she
speaks ill of him to her cousin. Calling him a coward and a traitor, she
doubts that he loves her and their son. Her distress would be commonplace
if she were speaking with herself. But she calls her husband a coward

66. in . . . perfect, know your rank.   84. fry of treachery, child of a traitor.

to Ross as her son listens! True, love will often doubt, but would love curse the loved one where he most is hurt? Would Macbeth's wife have spoken these harsh lines were she in Lady Macduff's place? Ross takes his leave, for he is shocked that she should wear her rank so ill to give way to unseemly speech before her son.

How ugly seems Lady Macduff's vengeance now! She sorely abuses her own child with wicked words which the lad cannot stop though he is his father's child. And yet the boy's wit is quick; his presence, great. He honors his mother with adult poise, but honor is his father's due and that he gives too. Why could Macduff not tell his wife his mission in this fitful time? If Ross is any judge of character at all, Macduff is "noble, wise, judicious." Did Macduff then know his wife too well, distrust her nature, and feel that in anger she might speak her mind and betray Scotland's secret? Her wrath is not a noble wrath; she speaks as one not schooled to hold a position that demands restraint or diplomacy. A peasant woman might upbraid a father's son with better grace—and still reveal her peasant blood and peasant breeding. At Forres, a tiny lady waits who, steeped in blood, retains her rank in every word and every deed though she has reason to cry out against the husband that she loves. Instead, *she* keeps her counsels still, locks horror in her tiny breast, and plays at the role of steady wife—and all for love.

Shakespeare thus paints, on a little canvas, a perfect foil for Lady Macbeth. Comparing these two (as we must), we find our preference for the one whose hands are bloody. Though she has seen ignoble deeds, though she has aided in dark crimes, Lady Macbeth still remains a woman free of selfish motives. Her interest is in her husband's heart—though it now seems he has closed it to her.

The messenger (surely sent by Lennox) grants some grace to Lady Macduff; she sees and speaks of reality once at least before she dies. And in that moment prior to death, she stands a Lady in her height and pledges her allegiance to Macduff.

SCENE III. *England. Before the King's palace.*

(*Enter* MALCOLM *and* MACDUFF.)

MALCOLM. Let us seek out some desolate shade, and there
Weep our sad bosoms empty.

MACDUFF.　　　　　　　Let us rather
Hold fast the mortal sword, and like good men
Bestride our down-fall'n birthdom. Each new morn
New widows howl, new orphans cry, new sorrows　　　　5

---

3. **mortal**, deadly.　4. **Bestride**, stand over as defenders.　**birthdom**, native land.

Strike heaven on the face, that it resounds
As if it felt with Scotland, and yell'd out
Like syllable of dolour.

MALCOLM.　　　　　What I believe I 'll wail,
What know believe, and what I can redress,
As I shall find the time to friend, I will.　　　　　*10*
What you have spoke, it may be so perchance.
This tyrant, whose sole name blisters our tongues,
Was once thought honest; you have lov'd him well.
He hath not touch'd you yet. I am young; but something
You may deserve of him through me, and wisdom　　　　　*15*
To offer up a weak poor innocent lamb
To appease an angry god.

MACDUFF. I am not treacherous.

MALCOLM.　　　　　But Macbeth is.
A good and virtuous nature may recoil
In an imperial charge. But I shall crave your pardon;　　　　　*20*
That which you are my thoughts cannot transpose.
Angels are bright still, though the brightest fell.
Though all things foul would wear the brows of grace,
Yet grace must still look so.

MACDUFF.　　　　　I have lost my hopes.

MALCOLM. Perchance even there where I did find my doubts.　　*25*
Why in that rawness left you wife and child,
Those precious motives, those strong knots of love,
Without leave-taking? I pray you,
Let not my jealousies be your dishonours,
But mine own safeties. You may be rightly just,　　　　　*30*
Whatever I shall think.

MACDUFF.　　　　　Bleed, bleed, poor country!
Great tyranny! lay thou thy basis sure,
For goodness dare not check thee; wear thou thy wrongs;
The title is affeer'd! Fare thee well, lord:
I would not be the villain that thou think'st　　　　　*35*
For the whole space that 's in the tyrant's grasp,
And the rich East to boot.

MALCOLM.　　　　　Be not offended;
I speak not as in absolute fear of you.

---

8. syllable of dolour, cry of anguish.　　**10. the time . . . friend,** good occasion.　　**12. sole,** mere.　　**15. wisdom,** it were wisdom.　　**19-20. recoil . . . charge,** act dishonorably under a king's orders.　　**21. transpose,** alter.　　**25. doubts,** of your honor, doubts awakened by Macduff's leaving his family.　　**26. rawness,** haste.　　**29. jealousies,** suspicions.　　**34. affeer'd,** confirmed.

I think our country sinks beneath the yoke;
It weeps, it bleeds; and each new day a gash   *40*
Is added to her wounds. I think withal
There would be hands uplifted in my right;
And here from gracious England have I offer
Of goodly thousands. But, for all this,
When I shall tread upon the tyrant's head,   *45*
Or wear it on my sword, yet my poor country
Shall have more vices than it had before,
More suffer and more sundry ways than ever,
By him that shall succeed.
> MACDUFF.   What should he be?
> MALCOLM. It is myself I mean; in whom I know   *50*
All the particulars of vice so grafted
That, when they shall be open'd, black Macbeth
Will seem as pure as snow, and the poor state
Esteem him as a lamb, being compar'd
With my confineless harms.
> MACDUFF.   Not in the legions   *55*
Of horrid hell can come a devil more damn'd
In evils to top Macbeth.
> MALCOLM.   I grant him bloody,
Luxurious, avaricious, false, deceitful,
Sudden, malicious, smacking of every sin
That has a name; but there 's no bottom, none,   *60*
In my voluptuousness: your wives, your daughters,
Your matrons, and your maids, could not fill up
The cistern of my lust, and my desire
All continent impediments would o'erbear
That did oppose my will. Better Macbeth   *65*
Than such an one to reign.
> MACDUFF.   Boundless intemperance
In nature is a tyranny; it hath been
Th' untimely emptying of the happy throne
And fall of many kings. But fear not yet
To take upon you what is yours: you may   *70*
Convey your pleasures in a spacious plenty,
And yet seem cold, the time you may so hoodwink.
We have willing dames enough; there cannot be

---

55. confineless harms, unlimited evil-doing.   **58. Luxurious,** lustful.   **59. Sudden,** violent.
64. continent, restraining.   **69. yet,** however.   **71. Convey,** obtain secretly.   **72. cold,**
chaste.

That vulture in you, to devour so many
As will to greatness dedicate themselves,   *75*
Finding it so inclin'd.

    MALCOLM.   With this there grows
In my most ill-compos'd affection such
A stanchless avarice that, were I King,
I should cut off the nobles for their lands,
Desire his jewels and this other's house;   *80*
And my more-having would be as a sauce
To make me hunger more, that I should forge
Quarrels unjust against the good and loyal,
Destroying them for wealth.

    MACDUFF.   This avarice
Sticks deeper, grows with more pernicious root   *85*
Than summer-seeming lust, and it hath been
The sword of our slain kings: yet do not fear;
Scotland hath foisons to fill up your will,
Of your mere own. All these are portable,
With other graces weigh'd.   *90*

    MALCOLM. But I have none. The king-becoming graces,
As justice, verity, temp'rance, stableness,
Bounty, perseverance, mercy, lowliness,
Devotion, patience, courage, fortitude,
I have no relish of them, but abound   *95*
In the division of each several crime,
Acting it many ways. Nay, had I power, I should
Pour the sweet milk of concord into hell,
Uproar the universal peace, confound
All unity on earth.

    MACDUFF.   O Scotland, Scotland!   *100*

    MALCOLM. If such an one be fit to govern, speak.
I am as I have spoken.

    MACDUFF.   Fit to govern!
No, not to live. O nation miserable,
With an untitled tyrant bloody-sceptred,
When shalt thou see thy wholesome days again,   *105*
Since that the truest issue of thy throne
By his own interdiction stands accurs'd,

---

77. **affection,** disposition.   78. **stanchless,** insatiable.   86. **summer-seeming,** belonging only to early life.   88. **foisons,** plenty.   89. **mere own,** your absolute possessions.   **portable,** endurable.   95. **relish,** savor, trace.   96. **division,** variation (musical term).   104. **untitled,** usurping.   106. **truest issue,** rightful heir.   107. **interdiction,** decree of exclusion.

And does blaspheme his breed? Thy royal father
Was a most sainted king; the queen that bore thee,
Oftener upon her knees than on her feet,   110
Died every day she liv'd. Fare thee well!
These evils thou repeat'st upon thyself
Hath banish'd me from Scotland. O my breast,
Thy hope ends here!
  MALCOLM. Macduff, this noble passion,
Child of integrity, hath from my soul   115
Wip'd the black scruples, reconcil'd my thoughts
To thy good truth and honour. Devilish Macbeth
By many of these trains hath sought to win me
Into his power, and modest wisdom plucks me
From over-credulous haste: but God above   120
Deal between thee and me! for even now
I put myself to thy direction, and
Unspeak mine own detraction; here abjure
The taints and blames I laid upon myself,
For strangers to my nature. I am yet   125
Unknown to woman, never was forsworn,
Scarcely have coveted what was mine own,
At no time broke my faith, would not betray
The devil to his fellow, and delight
No less in truth than life; my first false speaking   130
Was this upon myself. What I am truly,
Is thine and my poor country's to command;
Whither indeed, before thy here-approach,
Old Siward, with ten thousand warlike men,
Already at a point, was setting forth.   135
Now we 'll together; and the chance of goodness
Be like our warranted quarrel! Why are you silent?
  MACDUFF. Such welcome and unwelcome things at once
'T is hard to reconcile.
  (*Enter a* DOCTOR.)
  MALCOLM. Well; more anon.—Comes the King forth, I pray you?   140
  DOCTOR. Ay, sir; there are a crew of wretched souls
That stay his cure: their malady convinces
The great assay of art; but at his touch—
Such sanctity hath Heaven given his hand—

---

111. Died . . . liv'd, lived a life of daily mortification. 118. trains, plots. 135. at a point,
ready. 136. goodness, success. 142. stay his cure, wait to be cured by him. convinces,
is proof against. 143. assay of art, skill of doctors.

They presently amend.

MALCOLM.   I thank you, doctor.   (*Exit* DOCTOR.)

MACDUFF. What 's the disease he means?

MALCOLM.   'T is call'd the evil: *146*

A most miraculous work in this good king;

Which often, since my here-remain in England,

I have seen him do. How he solicits Heaven,

Himself best knows; but strangely-visited people, *150*

All swollen and ulcerous, pitiful to the eye,

The mere despair of surgery, he cures,

Hanging a golden stamp about their necks,

Put on with holy prayers; and 't is spoken,

To the succeeding royalty he leaves *155*

The healing benediction. With this strange virtue,

He hath a heavenly gift of prophecy,

And sundry blessings hang about his throne,

That speak him full of grace.

(*Enter* ROSS)

MACDUFF.   See, who comes here?

MALCOLM. My countryman; but yet I know him not. *160*

MACDUFF. My ever-gentle cousin, welcome hither.

MALCOLM. I know him now. Good God, betimes remove

The means that makes us strangers!

ROSS.   Sir, amen.

MACDUFF. Stands Scotland where it did?

ROSS.   Alas, poor country!

Almost afraid to know itself. It cannot *165*

Be call'd our mother, but our grave; where nothing,

But who knows nothing, is once seen to smile;

Where sighs and groans and shrieks that rend the air

Are made, not mark'd; where violent sorrow seems

A modern ecstasy: the dead man's knell *170*

Is there scarce ask'd for who; and good men's lives

Expire before the flowers in their caps,

Dying or ere they sicken.

MACDUFF.   O, relation

Too nice, and yet too true!

MALCOLM.   What 's the newest grief?

---

146. **the evil,** scrofula was called "the king's evil." Belief in the healing power of the royal touch lasted down into the 18th century. 153. **stamp,** coin. 166. **nothing,** no one. 167. **once,** ever. 170. **modern ecstasy,** commonplace emotion. 174. **nice,** minute.

ROSS. That of an hour's age doth hiss the speaker; *175*
Each minute teems a new one.

MACDUFF.   How does my wife?

ROSS. Why, well.

MACDUFF.   And all my children?

ROSS.   Well too.

MACDUFF. The tyrant has not batter'd at their peace?

ROSS. No; they were well at peace when I did leave 'em.

MACDUFF. Be not a niggard of your speech; how goes 't? *180*

ROSS. When I came hither to transport the tidings,
Which I have heavily borne, there ran a rumour
Of many worthy fellows that were out;
Which was to my belief witness'd the rather,
For that I saw the tyrant's power a-foot. *185*
Now is the time of help; your eye in Scotland
Would create soldiers, make our women fight,
To doff their dire distresses.

MALCOLM.   Be 't their comfort
We 're coming thither. Gracious England hath
Lent us good Siward and ten thousand men; *190*
An older and a better soldier none
That Christendom gives out.

ROSS.   Would I could answer
This comfort with the like! But I have words
That would be howl'd out in the desert air,
Where hearing should not latch them.

MACDUFF.   What concern they? *195*
The general cause? Or is it a fee-grief
Due to some single breast?

ROSS.   No mind that 's honest
But in it shares some woe; though the main part
Pertains to you alone.

MACDUFF.   If it be mine,
Keep it not from me, quickly let me have it. *200*

ROSS. Let not your ears despise my tongue for ever,
Which shall possess them with the heaviest sound
That ever yet they heard.

MACDUFF.   Hum! I guess at it.

---

175. **hiss,** bring hissing upon (for repeating an old story).   176. **teems,** brings forth.   182. **heavily,** sadly.   183. **out,** in arms.   192. **gives out,** tells of.   195. **latch,** catch.   196. **fee-grief,** private grief.   202. **possess,** fill.

ROSS. Your castle is surpris'd; your wife and babes
Savagely slaughter'd. To relate the manner,   205
Were, on the quarry of these murder'd deer,
To add the death of you.
    MALCOLM.   Merciful heaven!
What, man! ne'er pull your hat upon your brows;
Give sorrow words: the grief that does not speak
Whispers the o'er-fraught heart and bids it break.   210
    MACDUFF. My children too?
    ROSS.   Wife, children, servants, all
That could be found.
    MACDUFF.   And I must be from thence!
My wife kill'd too?
    ROSS.   I have said.
    MALCOLM.   Be comforted.
Let 's make us med'cines of our great revenge,
To cure this deadly grief.   215
    MACDUFF. He has no children.—All my pretty ones?
Did you say all? O hell-kite! All?
What, all my pretty chickens and their dam
At one fell swoop?
    MALCOLM. Dispute it like a man.
    MACDUFF.   I shall do so;   220
But I must also feel it as a man.
I cannot but remember such things were,
That were most precious to me. Did heaven look on,
And would not take their part? Sinful Macduff,
They were all struck for thee! Naught that I am,   225
Not for their own demerits, but for mine,
Fell slaughter on their souls. Heaven rest them now!
    MALCOLM. Be this the whetstone of your sword; let grief
Convert to anger; blunt not the heart, enrage it.
    MACDUFF. O, I could play the woman with mine eyes   230
And braggart with my tongue! But, gentle heavens,
Cut short all intermission: front to front
Bring thou this fiend of Scotland and myself;
Within my sword's length set him; if he scape,
Heaven forgive him too!
    MALCOLM.   This time goes manly.   235

---

206. **quarry,** heap of dead game. 220. **Dispute,** fight. 225. **naught,** worthless. 229. **Convert,** change. 232. **intermission,** delay. 235. **time,** tune.

Come, go we to the King; our power is ready;
Our lack is nothing but our leave. Macbeth
Is ripe for shaking, and the powers above
Put on their instruments. Receive what cheer you may;
The night is long that never finds the day.   (*Exeunt*.)   240

In England, plans are readied. Edward the Confessor (how Shakespeare played the royal tune with this intrusion, weakening the scene already dull to tedium!) will give aid to Malcolm.

Ross brings the news from Scotland's shores that tragedy stalks everywhere and rests in Fife. The irony of his early words (177–179) gives way to woeful news at last (204–216) and makes Macduff share Macbeth's grief in childlessness. The tragic force of this dull act precedes the brilliant final act. If you found your attention eased, don't be disturbed. Few plays are perfect; most will drag somewhere before the action is done. In *Macbeth*, Act IV could be cut in half without much damage.

The witches' scene (I) is overdrawn; spectacular, it lacks the fire of luster we expect by now. It is bright in words but dull in form, creating only a brief diversion. Scene II serves a purpose, but that is all: it creates tension in Act V as Macduff and Macbeth cross swords for more than Scotland. Scene III rounds out the lackluster act and makes Act V seem more tense than it otherwise might be.

ACT V

SCENE I. *Dunsinane. A room in the castle.*
(*Enter a* DOCTOR *of Physic and a Waiting* GENTLEWOMAN.)
DOCTOR. I have two nights watched with you, but can perceive no truth in your report. When was it she last walked?   3
GENTLEWOMAN. Since his Majesty went into the field, I have seen her rise from her bed, throw her nightgown upon her, unlock her closet, take forth paper, fold it, write upon 't, read it, afterwards seal it, and again return to bed; yet all this while in a most fast sleep.   9
DOCTOR. A great perturbation in nature, to receive at once the benefit of sleep, and do the effects of watching! In this slumb'ry agitation, besides her walking and other actual performances, what, at any time, have you heard her say?   15
GENTLEWOMAN. That, sir, which I will not report after her.
DOCTOR. You may to me: and 't is most meet you should.
GENTLEWOMAN. Neither to you nor any one; having no witness to confirm my speech.   21

---

237. **Our . . . leave,** we have only to take leave.   239. **Put . . . instruments,** urge us on as their agents.   11. **do . . . watching,** act as if awake.

(*Enter* LADY MACBETH, *with a taper*.)

Lo you, here she comes! This is her very guise; and, upon my life, fast asleep. Observe her; stand close.

DOCTOR. How came she by that light? 2

GENTLEWOMAN. Why, it stood by her: she has light by her continually; 't is her command.

DOCTOR. You see, her eyes are open.

GENTLEWOMAN. Ay, but their sense are shut.

DOCTOR. What is it she does now? Look, how she rubs her hands. 3

GENTLEWOMAN. It is an accustomed action with her, to seem thus washing her hands. I have known her continue in this a quarter of an hour.

LADY MACBETH. Yet here 's a spot. 3

DOCTOR. Hark! she speaks. I will set down what comes from her, to satisfy my remembrance the more strongly. 3

LADY MACBETH. Out, damned spot! out, I say!—One: two: why, then 't is time to do't.—Hell is murky!—Fie, my lord, fie! a soldier, and afeard? What need we fear who knows it, when none can call our power to account?—Yet who would have thought the old man to have had so much blood in him? 4

DOCTOR. Do you mark that?

LADY MACBETH. The thane of Fife had a wife; where is she now?—What, will these hands ne'er be clean?—No more o' that, my lord, no more o' that; you mar all with this starting. 5

DOCTOR. Go to, go to; you have known what you should not.

GENTLEWOMAN. She has spoke what she should not, I am sure of that; Heaven knows what she has known. 5

LADY MACBETH. Here 's the smell of the blood still; all the perfumes of Arabia will not sweeten this little hand. Oh, oh, oh!

DOCTOR. What a sigh is there! The heart is sorely charged. 6

GENTLEWOMAN. I would not have such a heart in my bosom for the dignity of the whole body.

DOCTOR. Well, well, well,—

GENTLEWOMAN. Pray God it be, sir. 6

DOCTOR. This disease is beyond my practice; yet I have known those which have walked in their sleep who have died holily in their beds.

LADY MACBETH. Wash your hands, put on your nightgown; look not so pale.—I tell you yet again, Banquo 's buried; he cannot come out on 's grave. 7

DOCTOR. Even so?

LADY MACBETH. To bed, to bed! there 's knocking at the gate. Come, come, come, come, give me your hand. What 's done cannot be undone.—To bed, to bed, to bed! 7

(*Exit*.)

DOCTOR. Will she go now to bed?

GENTLEWOMAN. Directly.

DOCTOR. Foul whisp'rings are abroad; unnatural deeds
Do breed unnatural troubles; infected minds   *80*
To their deaf pillows will discharge their secrets.
More needs she the divine than the physician.
God, God, forgive us all! Look after her;
Remove from her the means of all annoyance,
And still keep eyes upon her. So, good-night!   *85*
My mind she has mated, and amaz'd my sight.
I think, but dare not speak.
    GENTLEWOMAN.   Goodnight, good doctor.   (*Exeunt*)

Catastrophe hangs heavy on each scene as it now unfolds with a speed Act IV prepared the reader to anticipate. Macbeth has moved his court from Forres to Dunsinane where he feels safe, for woods cannot move to this high hill. Here he reigns, waiting. In the deep of night, dark Dunsinane broods on the hill and turns its blind eyes, its unlighted windows, to the woods it watches. These long, dark halls have heard sharp mail clank through their ancient stones by day, but night-time silence chills the sounds to memory at rest. No quickened pulse announces love; no laughter lights bright friendship's walk; no movement stirs the fungoid dark—but wait! Two figures creep into the silent hall. Their whispered counsel stirs the air. Lady Macbeth's acts are an alarm to call them from their slumber.

Her doctor and her lady-in-waiting share a vigil they have shared three nights, and he is plainly skeptical, demanding proof that his loss of sleep will be rewarded. The gentlewoman's words are strange; they echo words which she could not have heard: "Get on your nightgown, lest occasion call us/And show us to be watchers" (II:ii, 69–70). Lady Macbeth watches now when occasion calls and she cannot answer. What does she write in the depth of the night? The letter that she did not write, but waited for Macbeth to come to Inverness and seek her words in person (I:v, 26–50)? Does she write "Be content with Glamis; with Cawdor let our lives be glad"? Or does she plead with Macbeth to seek her counsel once again? Whatever doubts and fears she has held, locked in her heart, unseen by him, she still clasps to her tiny breast by day. The misty night betrays her fears and sends her here to seek "A little water" which, she once said, "clears us of this deed" (II:ii, 67). Her urgings trace the death of love: first, Duncan; next, Banquo; then Lady Macduff. She knows where Fife's wife is, of course, but where (implied) is Macbeth's wife? She has bloodied her own hands and stained their power to soothe her husband's

84. **annoyance,** self-injury.   86. **mated,** bewildered.

fears. Where is the wife of Glamis and Cawdor? Will he give her his hand again? No! "What's done cannot be undone."

The doctor prays that she may survive the death she has already died, and live in life, but constantly be heaven-protected. An irony pervades his words: the means of her self-injury may be, to him, a physical weapon, but the actual weapon is Macbeth's love—which has already been removed. Were it returned, her mind would hold. The gentlewoman cannot return Macbeth's emotional self to the queen; nor yet can God at this late hour; and so the words, addressed to both, must go unheeded.

SCENE II. *The country near Dunsinane.*

(*Drum and colours. Enter* MENTEITH, CAITHNESS, ANGUS, LENNOX, *and* SOLDIERS.)

MENTEITH. The English power is near, led on by Malcolm,
His uncle Siward, and the good Macduff.
Revenges burn in them; for their dear causes
Would to the bleeding and the grim alarm
Excite the mortified man.

ANGUS.   Near Birnam wood   5
Shall we well meet them; that way are they coming.

CAITHNESS. Who knows if Donalbain be with his brother?

LENNOX. For certain, sir, he is not; I have a file
Of all the gentry: there is Siward's son,
And many unrough youth that even now   10
Protest their first of manhood.

MENTEITH.   What does the tyrant?

CAITHNESS. Great Dunsinane he strongly fortifies.
Some say he 's mad, others that lesser hate him
Do call it valiant fury; but, for certain,
He cannot buckle his distemper'd cause   15
Within the belt of rule.

ANGUS.   Now does he feel
His secret murders sticking on his hands;
Now minutely revolts upbraid his faith-breach;
Those he commands move only in command,
Nothing in love. Now does he feel his title   20
Hang loose about him, like a giant's robe
Upon a dwarfish thief.

MENTEITH.   Who then shall blame
His pester'd senses to recoil and start,

---

3. **dear,** deeply felt.   4. **bleeding . . . alarm,** bloody battle.   5. **mortified,** deadened, strengthless.   8. **file,** list.   10. **unrough,** beardless.   11. **Protest,** assert.   15. **distemper'd cause,** disordered party.   18. **minutely,** occurring every minute.

When all that is within him does condemn
Itself for being there?
    CAITHNESS.   Well, march we on   25
To give obedience where 't is truly ow'd.
Meet we the med'cine of the sickly weal,
And with him pour we in our country's purge
Each drop of us.
    LENNOX.   Or so much as it needs
To dew the sovereign flower and drown the weeds.   30
Make we our march towards Birnam.   (*Exeunt, marching.*)

In early morning, at a predawn hour, the hosts of Malcolm bear down on great Birnam Wood where they will join with him to march on Dunsinane and vanquish Scotland's tyrant king. They speak of his deeds with hate, for he has made men hate throughout the land. His followers stay on in fear—not out of love for him who bears no love in his black heart.

Four scenes, half of the final act, reveal the physical defeat Macbeth will suffer for his deeds; the other four (I, III, V, VII) reveal his spiritual decay. Scene I showed Lady Macbeth dead in spirit even if, in body, well. Scene II shows Scotland sickened from Macbeth's black hate.

The doctor seeks to find a cure for Scotland's queen, but he knows that God alone can cleanse a heart betrayed by deed and loss of love. Scene II reveals the military doctors who, with steadfast hearts and tempered steel, will cure the land of ill by purging it of Macbeth.

SCENE III. *Dunsinane. A room in the castle.*
    (*Enter* MACBETH, DOCTOR, *and* ATTENDANTS.)
    MACBETH. Bring me no more reports; let them fly all;
Till Birnam wood remove to Dunsinane
I cannot taint with fear. What 's the boy Malcolm?
Was he not born of woman? The spirits that know
All mortal consequences have pronounc'd me thus: 5
"Fear not, Macbeth; no man that 's born of woman
Shall e'er have power upon thee." Then fly, false thanes,
And mingle with the English epicures!
The mind I sway by and the heart I bear
Shall never sag with doubt nor shake with fear.   10
    (*Enter a* SERVANT.)

27. med'cine, i.e., Malcolm. weal, commonwealth. 1. them, cf. line 7. 3. taint, be infected by. 5. mortal consequences, human destinies. 8. epicures, unwarlike gluttons. 9. sway by, am swayed by.

The devil damn thee black, thou cream-fac'd loon!
Where got'st thou that goose look?

SERVANT. There is ten thousand—

MACBETH.   Geese, villain?

SERVANT.   Soldiers, sir.

MACBETH. Go prick thy face and over-red thy fear,
Thou lily-liver'd boy. What soldiers, patch?   *15*
Death of thy soul! those linen cheeks of thine
Are counsellors to fear. What soldiers, whey-face?

SERVANT. The English force, so please you.

MACBETH. Take thy face hence. (*Exit* SERVANT.) Seyton!—I am sick at heart
When I behold—Seyton, I say!—This push   *20*
Will chair me ever, or disseat me now.
I have liv'd long enough: my way of life
Is fall'n into the sear, the yellow leaf;
And that which should accompany old age,
As honour, love, obedience, troops of friends,   *25*
I must not look to have; but, in their stead,
Curses, not loud but deep, mouth-honour, breath
Which the poor heart would fain deny, and dare not.
Seyton!

(*Enter* SEYTON.)

SEYTON. What 's your gracious pleasure?

MACBETH.   What news more?   *30*

SEYTON. All is confirm'd, my lord, which was reported.

MACBETH. I 'll fight till from my bones my flesh be hack'd.
Give me my armour.

SEYTON.   'T is not needed yet.

MACBETH. I 'll put it on.
Send out moe horses; skirr the country round;   *35*
Hang those that talk of fear. Give me mine armour.
How does your patient, doctor?

DOCTOR.   Not so sick, my lord,
As she is troubled with thick-coming fancies,
That keep her from her rest.

MACBETH.   Cure her of that.
Canst thou not minister to a mind diseas'd,   *40*
Pluck from the memory a rooted sorrow,
Raze out the written troubles of the brain,

---

14. **over-red,** redden with blood.   17. **Are . . . fear,** cause fear.   20. **push,** test, crisis.   21.
chair, enthrone.   **disseat,** dethrone.   35. **skirr,** scour.

And with some sweet oblivious antidote
Cleanse the stuff'd bosom of that perilous stuff
Which weighs upon the heart?
DOCTOR.   Therein the patient   45
Must minister to himself.
MACBETH. Throw physic to the dogs; I 'll none of it.
Come, put mine armour on; give me my staff.
Seyton, send out. Doctor, the thanes fly from me.
Come, sir, dispatch. If thou couldst, doctor, cast   50
The water of my land, find her disease,
And purge it to a sound and pristine health,
I would applaud thee to the very echo,
That should applaud again.—Pull 't off, I say.—
What rhubarb, senna, or what purgative drug,   55
Would scour these English hence? Hear'st thou of them?
DOCTOR. Ay, my good lord; your royal preparation
Makes us hear something.
MACBETH.   Bring it after me.
I will not be afraid of death and bane,
Till Birnam forest come to Dunsinane.   60
DOCTOR. Were I from Dunsinane away and clear,
Profit again should hardly draw me here.   (*Exeunt.*)

In Dunsinane, the sun cannot pierce the embattled walls that have withstood the onslaught of rebellious thanes before this time. Dark messages come to Macbeth: his thanes desert him to enlist in Malcolm's fast approaching ranks. He will hear no more! Safe here within these thick, dark walls, he knows that no man of a woman's womb shall vanquish him. Why should he need deserting thanes?

But is Macbeth so assured, so free of doubt, so calm, so unafraid? What king is this who shows his power to a simple servant boy? Where is the nature, once "too full o' th' milk of human kindness" (I:v, 18)? Gone. Gone. All gone. And in its place, despair sits heavy on the heart that knows it has failed to earn old age's noble courtiers. Honor and love, obedience, friends—Macbeth will never have these wondrous things. Still, he does *not* lack courage! Beneath the suns of other days he fought rebellion in the land. He will now fight again beneath the sun of this new day. His darker nature is revealed when night lies heavy on the land; sun finds him manful, noble, strong in his simple, virile virtues.

43. **oblivious,** causing forgetfulness.   48. **staff,** lance.   50. **dispatch,** hurry.   50-1. **cast/The water,** analyze the urine, a common medical method of diagnosis.   58. **it,** the armor.

In this excess of manliness, Macbeth reveals only his strong concern. He does not feel love, for that he has lost—for both his wife and his country. Dramatic irony overlays each line as ambiguity brings its full power to every word the two men speak. Lady Macbeth is sick to death; Scotland too is overrun with alien bodies in the corpus of the land. Love does not motivate the king: his once "dearest love" is now called "your patient." Scotland has become "my land": not "country," just land, the earth possessed. Macbeth wants each to be cured of the ills he has brought but cannot own as being his infections. "Cure her" of memory, he commands, memory of her ugly deeds and of her loss resulting from those ugly deeds. No doctor can grant such a cure; the body itself must reject the ill that festers there. And that the queen cannot do. Macbeth will not pursue the cure. He turns his attention to the land; but "Scotland too must cleanse itself," the doctor says ambiguously. That ambiguity becomes caught in the turmoil Macbeth knows. "If you cannot cure the human land, then diagnose the ills of the earth you stand on," Macbeth seems to plead. That land and Lady Macbeth share the ability to grant Macbeth the one thing that he desperately wants: a long rule by issue. Lady Macbeth and Scotland's soil are *one* field where he wants to plant his seed. This need was shared by Oedipus and will be shared by all future men as long as there are men. Too close the blood of Iocastê's land; troubled the mind of Scotland's queen. Plagues fill the land of both these kings (the land of wife and the land of soil) and, in each case, the land is cursed by the taint of the husband—a taint sought and nurtured by the soil in its weakest hour.

The doctor hears more than he cares to admit he hears. He would leave his patient if he could—regardless of his ethical bond—for she is lost without the love that kept her whole. Who is the patient in this hour? The one who must herself hire cure. The purge that cures can also kill, and patients ministering to the Self do not need doctors.

SCENE IV. *Country near Birnam wood.*

(*Drum and colours. Enter* MALCOLM, *old* SIWARD *and his* SON, MACDUFF, MENTEITH, CAITHNESS, ANGUS, *and* SOLDIERS, *marching.*)

MALCOLM. Cousins, I hope the days are near at hand
That chambers will be safe.

MENTEITH.   We doubt it nothing.

SIWARD. What wood is this before us?

MENTEITH.   The wood of Birnam.

MALCOLM. Let every soldier hew him down a bough
And bear 't before him; thereby shall we shadow   5

---

2. **chambers,** bed-rooms, such as Duncan's.

The numbers of our host and make discovery
Err in report of us.
    SOLDIERS.   It shall be done.
    SIWARD. We learn no other but the confident tyrant
Keeps still in Dunsinane, and will endure
Our setting down before 't.
    MALCOLM.   'T is his main hope;   *10*
For where there is advantage to be given,
Both more and less have given him the revolt,
And none serve with him but constrained things
Whose hearts are absent too.
    MACDUFF.   Let our just censures
Attend the true event, and put we on   *15*
Industrious soldiership.
    SIWARD.   The time approaches
That will with due decision make us know
What we shall say we have and what we owe.
Thoughts speculative their unsure hopes relate,
But certain issue strokes must arbitrate;   *20*
Towards which advance the war.   (*Exeunt, marching.*)

The secret is out; young Malcolm knows the throne of Scotland is unmanned by any but "constrained things whose hearts are absent too." The prophecy begins to seek its present end as camouflage is ordered by the rightful heir to Scotland. Here darkness passes from the land; here darkness passes from the scenes; night now is gone—concealment comes from moving wood.

SCENE V. *Dunsinane. Within the castle.*
    (*Enter* MACBETH, SEYTON, *and* SOLDIERS, *with drum and colours.*)
    MACBETH. Hang out our banners on the outward walls;
The cry is still, "They come!" Our castle's strength
Will laugh a siege to scorn; here let them lie
Till famine and the ague eat them up.
Were they not forc'd with those that should be ours,   *5*
We might have met them dareful, beard to beard,
And beat them backward home.   (*A cry within of women.*)
               What is that noise?
    SEYTON. It is the cry of women, my lord.   (*Exit.*)

---

6. **discovery,** Macbeth's scouts.   11. **advantage to be given,** opportunity afforded, i.e., chance of desertion in the field.   12. **more and less,** high and low.   14. **censures,** verdicts.   15. **Attend . . . event,** await the actual outcome.   5. **forc'd,** reinforced.

MACBETH. I have almost forgot the taste of fears.
The time has been, my senses would have cool'd   *10*
To hear a night-shriek, and my fell of hair
Would at a dismal treatise rouse and stir
As life were in 't. I have supp'd full with horrors;
Direness, familiar to my slaughterous thoughts,
Cannot once start me.
          (*Re-enter* SEYTON.)   Wherefore was that cry?   *15*
          SEYTON. The Queen, my lord, is dead.
          MACBETH. She should have died hereafter;
There would have been a time for such a word.
To-morrow, and to-morrow, and to-morrow,
Creeps in this petty pace from day to day   *20*
To the last syllable of recorded time;
And all our yesterdays have lighted fools
The way to dusty death. Out, out, brief candle!
Life 's but a walking shadow, a poor player
That struts and frets his hour upon the stage   *25*
And then is heard no more. It is a tale
Told by an idiot, full of sound and fury,
Signifying nothing.
          (*Enter a* MESSENGER.)
Thou com'st to use thy tongue; thy story quickly.
          MESSENGER. Gracious my lord,   *30*
I should report that which I say I saw,
But know not how to do it.
          MACBETH.   Well, say, sir.
          MESSENGER. As I did stand my watch upon the hill,
I look'd toward Birnam, and anon, methought,
The wood began to move.
          MACBETH.   Liar and slave!   *35*
          MESSENGER. Let me endure your wrath, if 't be not so.
Within this three mile may you see it coming:
I say, a moving grove.
          MACBETH.   If thou speak'st false,
Upon the next tree shalt thou hang alive,
Till famine cling thee; if thy speech be sooth,   *40*
I care not if thou dost for me as much.

---

11. **fell of hair,** hair of the scalp.   12. **dismal treatise,** horrible story.   14. **slaughterous,**
murderous.   15. **start,** startle.   17. **should have,** would inevitably have.   18. **such a word,**
i.e., as death.   40. **cling,** shrivel up.   **sooth,** truth.

I pull in resolution, and begin
To doubt the equivocation of the fiend
That lies like truth: "Fear not, till Birnam wood
Do come to Dunsinane;" and now a wood   45
Comes toward Dunsinane. Arm, arm, and out!
If this which he avouches does appear,
There is nor flying hence nor tarrying here.
I gin to be aweary of the sun,
And wish th' estate o' th' world were now undone.   50
Ring the alarum-bell! Blow, wind! come, wrack!
At least we 'll die with harness on our back.   (*Exeunt.*)

A gallant but an empty show brings King Macbeth onto Dunsinane's walls. The castle is prepared for seige and will outlast the mighty band of Malcolm's men—and Macbeth's too who have gone to join the prince.

The cry of anguish from within leaves Macbeth unafraid, unstirred. He has lost his human fear. No longer is he, as he was, "afraid to think what I have done" (II:ii, 51). Nor does he question what he has done on hearing that his queen is dead. Had he more time, he would mourn her death. Now there's no time. Yet, unaware of any change, Macbeth reveals a growing urge to find this life mere trivia. Before the death of Duncan, life to Macbeth was a noble task. He fought for his country, he loved his wife, and he acquitted himself in sunshine. With Duncan's death, all life became "but toys" (II:iii, 99) to Macbeth, a desperate game he played to win, knowing full well that there was no prize even if he should. In the desperate play, he used the crown of Scotland as a tarnished prize, bought dearly with the blood of those most close. First Duncan, then Banquo, and now his wife who, unloved, finds no love of life to sustain living; so she dies by her own hand.

Before her death, life was mere toys, but toys have a concrete form which man can perceive. But now life is an abstract shadow. When all is gone, when nothing is left, life counts for little, Macbeth says; but Birnam Wood moves to the hill and Macbeth moves into the sun. Out of dark Dunsinane he goes to face his own destruction. He may be weary of the sun (49) and he may know that he seeks his death, but he *will* seek it in the rays of that bright star. In darkness, he lacks nobleness; in sunshine, he is valiant, brave. He will die, in the sun, a noble death "with harness on our back."

51. **wrack,** wreck, destruction.

SCENE VI. *Dunsinane. Before the castle.*

(*Drum and colours. Enter* MALCOLM, *old* SIWARD, MACDUFF, *and their Army, with boughs.*)

MALCOLM. Now near enough; your leavy screens throw down,
And show like those you are. You, worthy uncle,
Shall, with my cousin, your right noble son,
Lead our first battle. Worthy Macduff and we
Shall take upon 's what else remains to do,   *5*
According to our order.

    SIWARD.   Fare you well.
Do we find the tyrant's power to-night,
Let us be beaten, if we cannot fight.

    MACDUFF. Make all our trumpets speak; give them all breath,   *9*
Those clamorous harbingers of blood and death.   (*Exeunt. Alarums continued.*)

The battle orders are read out; the young prince shows himself a man well fit to lead the country from its dark days back into sunlight. Green boughs of Birnam Wood fill the mind as far as the camera of the brain can sweep across the imagined plains converging on the hill. The sound of drums beats in the mind; men march with steady pace behind the colors of their oriflammes like blossoms in the leaves. A steady pulse moves thousands on across the stage your mind has become. How grimly silent are the men; how loud the rustle of the leaves; how martial are the drums!

SCENE VII. *Another part of the field.*

(*Enter* MACBETH.)

MACBETH. They have tied me to a stake; I cannot fly,
But, bear-like, I must fight the course. What 's he
That was not born of woman? Such a one
Am I to fear, or none.

(*Enter young* SIWARD.)

    YOUNG SIWARD. What is thy name?

    MACBETH.   Thou 'lt be afraid to hear it.   *5*

    YOUNG SIWARD. No; though thou call'st thyself a hotter name
Than any is in hell.

    MACBETH.   My name 's Macbeth.

    YOUNG SIWARD. The devil himself could not pronounce a title
More hateful to mine ear.

    MACBETH.   No, nor more fearful.

4. **battle,** division.   2. **course,** a round in bear-baiting.

YOUNG SIWARD. Thou liest, abhorred tyrant; with my sword   10
I'll prove the lie thou speak'st. (*They fight and young* SIWARD *is slain.*)
    MACBETH.   Thou wast born of woman.
But swords I smile at, weapons laugh to scorn,
Brandish'd by man that 's of a woman born.   (*Exit.*)

Below the hill of Dunsinane, in its broad shadow, Macbeth waits and watches as the mighty wood moves on the land. False valor lifts his spirits up. No man born from a woman's womb can kill him. Young Siward, filled with love of life, gives up that life, bleeds in the sun as Macbeth's confidence soars upward on the witches' chant. The couplet (12–13) might be lifted from Hecate's speech (III:v) for it follows the pattern set by that dread queen of night. Did you hear steel swords clash and clang, see age and youth locked in combat? How easy was the victory Macbeth won here? How nobly did young Siward die in the line *They fight and young* SIWARD *is slain?* Did you hear music? Or feel the sun burn on the arms the two men wear? Did clouds blot out the golden sun as Siward died and Macbeth laughed, crazed with his own charmed life? If not, read lines 1–13 once again; then close your eyes and see if you can set the scene and see it. What music do you hear? How blows the wind? How can you tell?

    (*Alarums. Enter* MACDUFF.)
    MACDUFF. That way the noise is. Tyrant, show thy face!
If thou be'st slain and with no stroke of mine,   15
My wife and children's ghosts will haunt me still.
I cannot strike at wretched kerns, whose arms
Are hir'd to bear their staves; either thou, Macbeth,
Or else my sword with an unbattered edge
I sheathe again undeeded. There thou shouldst be;   20
By this great clatter, one of greatest note
Seems bruited. Let me find him, Fortune!
And more I beg not.   (*Exit. Alarums.*)
    (*Enter* MALCOLM *and old* SIWARD.)
    SIWARD. This way, my lord; the castle 's gently render'd:
The tyrant's people on both sides do fight;   25
The noble thanes do bravely in the war;
The day almost itself professes yours,
And little is to do.

22. **bruited,** announced with noise.   24. **gently render'd,** tamely surrendered.   27. **itself professes,** declares itself.

MALCOLM.　　　We have met with foes
That strike beside us.
　　SIWARD.　　　　　Enter, sir, the castle.　　　　　(*Exeunt. Alarums.*)

In still another part of the plain, Macduff seeks Macbeth for his own. Not love of Scotland but the loss of his family moves him to vengeance. Around him rings the sound of swords, above him shines the brilliant sun, within him lies the need to kill his personal enemy.

Across the plain, the castle falls. The battle is won as Malcolm takes old Siward into Dunsinane and trumpets blare.

SCENE VIII. *The same.*
　　(*Enter* MACBETH.)
　　MACBETH. Why should I play the Roman fool, and die
On mine own sword? Whiles I see lives, the gashes
Do better upon them.
　　(*Enter* MACDUFF.)
　　MACDUFF.　　　　　Turn, hell-hound, turn!
　　MACBETH. Of all men else I have avoided thee:
But get thee back; my soul is too much charg'd　　　　　5
With blood of thine already.
　　MACDUFF.　　　　　　I have no words,
My voice is in my sword, thou bloodier villain
Than terms can give thee out!　　　　　(*They fight. Alarum.*)
　　MACBETH.　　　　　Thou losest labour.
As easy mayst thou the intrenchant air
With thy keen sword impress as make me bleed.　　　　　10
Let fall thy blade on vulnerable crests;
I bear a charmed life, which must not yield
To one of woman born.
　　MACDUFF.　　　　　Despair thy charm;
And let the angel whom thou still hast serv'd
Tell thee, Macduff was from his mother's womb　　　　　15
Untimely ripp'd.
　　MACBETH. Accursed be that tongue that tells me so,
For it hath cow'd my better part of man!
And be these juggling fiends no more believ'd
That palter with us in a double sense,　　　　　20

---

29. **strike . . . us,** fight along with us, or, deliberately avoid striking us.　　1. **Roman fool,** possibly Cato, the traditional example of Roman stoicism, but Shakespeare may be thinking also of Brutus, Cassius, and Antony.　　9. **intrenchant,** that cannot be cut.　　14. **angel,** evil genius.　　18. **cow'd . . . man,** broken my spirit.

That keep the word of promise to our ear,
And break it to our hope. I 'll not fight with thee.
  MACDUFF. Then yield thee, coward,
And live to be the show and gaze o' th' time.
We 'll have thee, as our rarer monsters are,   *25*
Painted upon a pole, and underwrit,
"Here may you see the tyrant."
  MACBETH.   I will not yield,
To kiss the ground before young Malcolm's feet
And to be baited with the rabble's curse.
Though Birnam wood be come to Dunsinane,   *30*
And thou oppos'd, being of no woman born,
Yet I will try the last. Before my body
I throw my warlike shield. Lay on, Macduff,
And damn'd be him that first cries, "Hold, enough!"   (*Exeunt fighting. Alarums.*)

Does Macbeth see himself entire in this last scene? Does he reject the stoic path, preferring to take blood and die "with harness on our back"? Or does he see the traitors who slew Caesar and then took their lives when all was lost before they could, by other hands, be punished? Macduff's arrival forces on Macbeth an open, clean avowal. He wants no further blood of clan Macduff on his lost soul—he knows it is lost. What moves him then to such compassion? Would not true evil glory in new evil since it could not lose more than is already lost?

Cold agony is on the brow Macduff turns toward his hated foe; sun glistens on his sharp-edged sword that thirsts for Macbeth's blood. As they cross swords, the battle brass sounds out across the bloody plain; Macbeth's voice lifts above the din to proclaim the immortality revealed to him.

Charms which evil bears may not be charms. The servant has become the served. Macbeth has traded his own soul for an empty promise. Macduff was from no woman's womb delivered into air and life. Caesarian birth brought him to breath out of his mother's side.

Oracles speak with double tongue; a man hears the tongue he wants to hear. Macbeth now knows he can be impaled on Macduff's sword. His spirit broken, he becomes the servant to the master, fate. He drops his sword arm, says he will live, surrenders up his dignity, becomes, at last, less than a man. Evil has won.

Visions enough Macbeth has had for any man. A mind-drawn dagger long ago (II:i, 33–61) stayed his hand before he killed his guest-king;

---

26. **Painted,** with your picture.

then, he saw the ghost of Banquo mock him at his feast. "Life's but a walking shadow" now; it signifies, for him, nothing. It pauses, moves across the stage, and leaves. But does Macbeth believe his words? What fears still linger from the time he held some part of his dark soul and called it his? When fear of the bloody sight refused his feet access to Duncan's room (II:ii, 50–53), Lady Macbeth called him "infirm," compared him to a child. She said that night: "The sleeping and the dead/Are but as pictures; 't is the eye of childhood/That fears a painted devil." Her words now seem echoed in Macduff's cold promise: "We'll have thee . . . painted upon a pole." Posters shall draw crowds to see Macbeth, the tyrant-monster rare, cast down at Malcolm's feet. And *that* painted devil terrifies the eye of childhood Macbeth turns upon the vision Macduff conjures up in the sunny air. *That* vision lights his way to death, for in it lie all his yesterdays—and all his tomorrows if he live. Uncharmed his life; dead, his love and his queen; lost, his throne and his country—what is left? Firmness of purpose is Macbeth's at last: "Lay on, Macduff,/ And damn'd be him that first cries, 'Hold, enough!'"

Does Macbeth, with proferred curse, lend strength to Macduff's arm? Is he not damned already—damned by his admission earlier given? Or is salvation his at last? By choice to die a manly death, does Macbeth find some small grace at last?

That choice is yours; here, *you* are God as Macbeth fights his final fight. What moved him to call down the curse in these last moments?

(*Retreat and Flourish. Enter, with drum and colours,* MALCOLM, *old* SIWARD, ROSS, THANES, *and* SOLDIERS.)

    MALCOLM. I would the friends we miss were safe arriv'd.   *35*

    SIWARD. Some must go off; and yet, by these I see,
So great a day as this is cheaply bought.

    MALCOLM. Macduff is missing, and your noble son.

    ROSS. Your son, my lord, has paid a soldier's debt.
He only liv'd but till he was a man;   *40*
The which no sooner had his prowess confirm'd
In the unshrinking station where he fought,
But like a man he died.

    SIWARD.   Then he is dead?

    ROSS. Ay, and brought off the field. Your cause of sorrow
Must not be measur'd by his worth, for then   *45*
It hath no end.

    SIWARD.   Had he his hurts before?

36. **go off,** be killed.   42. **unshrinking station,** the post he did not desert.

ROSS. Ay, on the front.

SIWARD.   Why then, God's soldier be he!
Had I as many sons as I have hairs,
I would not wish them to a fairer death.
And so, his knell is knoll'd.

MALCOLM.   He's worth more sorrow,   *50*
And that I'll spend for him.

SIWARD.   He's worth no more.
They say he parted well, and paid his score;
And so, God be with him! Here comes newer comfort.

With mighty brass and unfurled flags, with drums that echo from the
wings, the victors gather on the stage here in your mind. Old Siward
hears of his son's death—a noble death, the kind *men* die. He lived to
be a man and died the death he chose. Old Siward wants to know if
his son died from wounds received as brave men's are—in front—not
as a coward's, whose wounds are in the back. Assured his son died *facing*
death, he finds the day still cheaply bought: "God's soldier be he!" Siward
declares the rule of battle. All cultures share this firm belief: if warriors
die with nobleness, they pay their passage to the land (removed from
life) where warriors find their highest reward. Young Siward "parted
well," so he thus "paid his score" and is with God. What father could
ask for more?

This seems a sentimental scene, a cloying scene that makes us glad
old Siward finds his comfort in his son's good death. If that is the only
reason for the scene, however, it weakens Shakespeare's firm control. He
has built a steady structure up to this point, strong in its restraint of
sentiment. Then why this scene? Does it just fill the space that Shakespeare
needs between the off-stage battle taking place about this time and the
next? Or are old Siward's comments true of Macbeth also as he dies?
His childhood's eye made him the man who faced his death in this same
hour. Will Macbeth die well and pay *his* score and be with God?

(*Re-enter* MACDUFF *with* MACBETH'S *head.*)

MACDUFF. Hail, king! for so thou art. Behold, where stands
The usurper's cursed head: the time is free.   *55*
I see thee compass'd with thy kingdom's pearl,
That speak my salutation in their minds;

52. parted, died.   54–5. stands . . . head, Macbeth's severed head fixed on a pole stands in
the ground.   55. the time, the world.   56. compass'd . . . pearl, surrounded by the best
men of your kingdom.

Whose voices I desire aloud with mine:
Hail, King of Scotland!

ALL.   Hail, King of Scotland!   (*Flourish.*)

MALCOLM. We shall not spend a large expense of time   60
Before we reckon with your several loves,
And make us even with you. My thanes and kinsmen,
Henceforth be earls, the first that ever Scotland
In such an honour nam'd. What 's more to do,
Which would be planted newly with the time,   65
As calling home our exil'd friends abroad
That fled the snares of watchful tyranny;
Producing forth the cruel ministers
Of this dead butcher and his fiend-like queen,
Who, as 't is thought, by self and violent hands   70
Took off her life; this, and what needful else
That calls upon us, by the grace of Grace,
We will perform in measure, time, and place.
So, thanks to all at once and to each one,   74
Whom we invite to see us crown'd at Scone.   (*Flourish. Exeunt omnes.*)

Macduff strides on with Macbeth's head impaled as proof of the tyrant's death. He makes short work of offering it to Malcolm. Would it not please him to speak of Macbeth's cowardice had he turned, had he been killed, his wounds behind, and died ignobly? But no such speech suggests an ignoble death for Macbeth. He fought out his final time. He therefore parted well, it seems. Did this, then, pay his final score? Can God be with him? You must judge. Where is Macbeth—in Heaven or in Hell?

The restoration of the world, this world of Scotland long ago, comes quickly as Malcolm invites all to see him crowned at Scone.

The Meaning of the Play—Macbeth As Any Man

The curtain is down; the play is done. "What's done is done," we were lately told. But you will never be the same again: *Macbeth* has changed too many things, now that you have read it.

Who is Macbeth—a Scottish king, a Shakespearean tragic hero caught and held for his hour upon some stage, a distant figure fighting life and losing love? Yes, he is every one of those delimiting things. And yet,

---

63. earls, an English title.   **68. Producing forth,** bringing to justice.   **70. self and violent,** her own violent.

he is more. Like Oedipus, Macbeth is any man you know—your friend, your neighbor, your enemy, yourself. Remove his robe and crown, and he becomes a stock-clerk facing life, a student in a lecture hall, an engineer who sees reward in his firm if he can plot and finally reach the top.

Each has his own ambitious dreams; each fights some battles well because he has equipment for those fights and knows that he can win. Each also hears the evil call of witches in his teeming brain. Do they not urge the shorter way that leads to instant glory? When you sit in some silent hall where tension rides the nervous air, as test sheets crackle in your ear and monitors creep, like grey heath moss, down aisles that light your dreary way to failure—do you not hear the witches' call to take from your neighbor what is his? To use his answer to your end that you may gain what you've not won? And if you take that broader way, attain the grade but lose the fight for knowledge which you one day may need, are you not *your* own Macbeth?

Or are you Banquo in that hour? Do you see some student Macbeth take gain from someone's paper, and then say: "I won't get involved. I'll *know* but I'll stand detached. I can't lose, for if they're caught, the curve will lower; I will gain. If they aren't caught, I haven't lost their friendship; I've gained their gratitude, for I've kept still. But I am clean, all uninvolved and righteous."

A false analogy? Not so! We are not, for the greater part, born to the upper ruling class. We seek our smaller, lesser worlds and find them quite as large as Scottish thrones, for they are all we have. Within the confines of our worlds, we play our lives out on the stage set with the trappings of our days—then find the candle that will light our dusty way to death. If our aspirations lead to gain of any sort, that gain is our concept of a crown—for crowns are merely symbols of the power that rulers have. A crown is merely physical—bright gold, some jewels—on which to look, to *see* the power it signifies. Diplomas, bank accounts, and such make up the crowns we ourselves are apt to wear. They must suffice and we may sell our souls for them as surely as Macbeth sold his to gain control of Scotland.

However, once we have attained the crown to which we aspired, do we not find it lacking in the rewards it earlier promised? Macbeth gained what he had been told he would surely gain—not one bit more. Did that attainment satisfy him? Not at all. He wanted more but could not see that new ambition met.

As envy overpowered Macbeth, as he saw Banquo's issue becoming kings, he moved to circumvent those heirs, supplanting them with—what? And here Macbeth is any man. An able man when he can act, what happens when his acts depend on careful planning? Had he succeeded and killed Fleance, what future line would wear the crown? Not his. Then whose? That would have been a new-found problem he would face "tomorrow" in its petty pace. How human is Macbeth!

His wife is every woman too. She owns her female destiny. She bears a child and sees it die; she loves a man and sees him lose that which had made her love him at first: his milk of human kindness. As it dries up, his old love dies. She knows the truth which some women find and fear, once found: her love kills love. As she goes mad, what terrors does her mind embrace? Why does she brood on bloody deeds? Are they the agents serving her within her slow decay? Or do those deeper, darker depths contain the knowledge that she has *failed* to do one deed—hold Macbeth's love—as she accomplished other deeds requiring her "unsexing"? Unsexed, a woman cannot be loved by a man who loves those things her sex supplies: trust, honor, warm companionship. Those she abandoned with her vow to be her husband's firmness of purpose.

Lady Macbeth may live next door; she may be the mother in your house; she may be a wife to you one day; she may be you. Confined to her own smaller world, she markets, cleans the house, or goes off daily to her office job, but she still functions like that queen who, loving her husband, reduced him with dark ambition for his power. As any woman's husband grows, becomes the man that pleases her, she risks the damage that is done by her own urgings. Should this be so? Who can say? And is it so? Too frequently. And other thanes have other wives: Fife also has her counterparts.

Macbeth looms larger than our lives. Thanes, kings, and castles are removed from that daily existence we know. But we also know man's emotions. There, themes are ancient—as is man. Old Adam in his distant glade aspired to something that was just out of his reach but still within his grasp. He, the father of the race of man, was born to sit upon a chair above mere earthly thrones. Eve, given to enrich his life by sharing its long, golden hours, heard urgings in the silken voice of promises oracular. They held the truth, those promises, but truth is what one wants to hear if he has mortal ears. Eve urged Adam to aspire to the knowledge which man had been denied—his thrones were there in that globed fruit. He ate, and founded many thrones for men to sit upon. A later son, Macbeth, sat on one throne for such a little while. And in his mortal doubts and fears, he is all men.

Eve's little hand had held the fruit, had been directed by the snake. It had held love and promises, before it held ambition. A human hand is a tiny thing that can hold things great beyond belief, but it cannot hold, simultaneously, great love and great ambition. Lady Macbeth was Eve's own child; she re-created that old role. And in that pattern, she is indeed all women.

Could Sigmund Freud and you conspire to seek out the reasons for the name psychology would give to these heath-haunted hearts, the task would send you down those psychic roads man's dreams hedge dark; but on that field where Macbeth died, you would draw up, caught by hope. Death waits for man on some dim field. He seeks it out and finds it where it has waited till he finds the place to meet it. Man knows the place is there, and one day he will find it out, and if he can say "Lay on" then, not turning his back and dying unwell, he is a *Man*—that one word transcending race and sex, returning him to Adam's chair and to his own concept of his god.

Suggested Assignments. 1. Throughout *Macbeth,* symbols and images create themes and motifs of rich and varied patterns. In a carefully considered paper, trace Shakespeare's use of one of the following: blood, darkness, masks, tattered clothes, dreams, sleep, hair, or stones.

2. Lady Macbeth and Iocastê have more in common as wives than you might now think. Isolate the speeches of each and, in a well-written paper, compare their attitudes toward their husbands as their words reveal those attitudes.

3. The similarities between Oedipus and Macbeth are readily apparent. In a brief paper, compare them in one of the following areas:

   a. Each is a plague on his land.
   b. Each clings to hope until hope destroys him.
   c. Each redeems himself through an overt act that is logical.
   d. Witches and oracles speak double-edged words upon which both Macbeth and Oedipus cut themselves fatally.

CHAPTER V

Modern Tragedy—
Reaping the Whirlwind

Probably no term in the long history of the theater is more impossible of definition than "modern tragedy." Beyond arbitrarily setting 1890 as its beginning date, we can say little about it that is not immediately refutable. Unlike classical or romantic tragedy, modern tragedy is not *of* a tradition. Nor has it, like its predecessors, established a definite tradition of its own.

Born in violent revolt against "dead" tradition, modern tragedy rejected the relatively absolute limits of its forebears. The "reality" of Sophocles, of Shakespeare, of Racine dismayed dramatic innovators as the nineteenth century moved headlong toward the twentieth—a century that would expand realities, challenge old "truths," and reject many of man's blindly accepted concepts. God or gods had, until the 1890's, been comfortably close or disastrously removed from the tragic hero—that which was least godlike in his nature was his essential flaw. The flaw made him a little lower than the angels and, growing progressively stronger, dropped him into the hell of his unique catastrophe.

As the machine created economic and social changes in the world, tragedy reflected those changes, moving away from a spiritual concept of morality to a secular social attitude. Oedipus or Macbeth, Medea or Hamlet, no matter how unique, represented every man in their tragic larger-than-life passions. Catharsis attended their ultimate destruction, for they were expansive enough to incorporate the identity of the most insignificant participant in their tragedy. And that tragedy became the participant's tragedy.

Such group participation irritated the new thinkers. Sigmund Freud, Soren Kierkegaard, and Henrik Ibsen saw each man as a distinct individual toiling in a mutual vineyard but heir to his own unique harvest. That his grapes had been planted by others, ripened by an impartial and finite sun merely intensified his realities—realities which loomed larger for him because they were not symbols or collective possibilities. While the mechanical age reduced him to a number, man enlarged himself to important proportions. He became an individual in his own eyes, however distorted his view as he turned inward to see an object held too close.

In the old myth plays, a god or a concept of "good" influenced the tragic hero as he worked out his own destruction by opposing it. That fatal opposition, so human and so universal, reflected the average viewer's obstinacy and created his intense identification with the dramatic character. The tragic hero's lofty station and noble character created further identifications, for the viewer, knowing he lacked those attributes, aspired to them and, finding the flaw a common denominator, multiplied other small similarities until he "became" the tragic hero—at least vicariously. After 1890, the new role of man reduced even that possibility to the realm of naivete, and the epic man became anachronistic in plays. On the other hand, gods as protagonists had always lacked verisimilitude, their entrances and exits reducing them to human proportions, their lofty speeches elevating them to Olympic heights, and bombastic dwarfs resulting. Only in the Passion Plays did God assume credibility, but that dramatic form left the viewer outside the action, for, though he may have known pity and fear as he viewed the Crucifixion, he could achieve no catharsis: the figure nailed to the Cross was really no part of him. No matter what the grace of God, he could never be that figure.

Somewhere between these two extremes, modern tragedy exists. Oedipus was, basically, the mirror of his gods: god and myth-hero somehow merged in him. Macbeth was the failure of his god, a distortion of what man should reflect; so god and myth-hero-turned-villain somehow merged in him, only the passion of personal dignity in death affording him his ultimate salvation. As the twentieth century's new sciences, psychology, existentialism, and social awareness removed God from man's behavioral patterns, man lost his heroic qualities. Free of myth and the comfort of religion, he became a non-hero, no matter how virtuous he might be, for his virtue was not collectively symbolic. It was a personal value lacking the absolute delineations imposed by moral (that is, religious) restraints. Incapable of evil in a spiritual sense, man could not be a villain either, for his dark nature sprang from no mystical alliance; it was a manifestation of his ego, his libido, his id, his existential presence, or a revolt against his culture, his environment, or his social milieu. Man became a cabbage, a misfit, a victim, or a social phenomenon. And it is difficult, if not impossible, to create heroes from those categories.

We will, however, continue to watch these protagonists. They afford a limited peep show into our world, but its horizons are those established by the limits of the experience in progress. Application of these plays to "any man" becomes difficult, for the uniqueness of the protagonist's life sets him apart—reclaiming for him some small semblance of the god's passion but isolating the viewer and making identification impossible. And we will certainly continue to attempt to understand these protagonists. Desiring our own measure of understanding and tolerance, we feel obligated by training to be empathetic—no matter where our sympathies may lie. As the protagonist becomes a clinical study, we are further removed and our emotions undergo less catharsis than sanitizing. And we may even find ourselves converted to the cause of these protagonists—not necessarily if it is just but if it has enough in common with our personal cause to allow us to see it as a step in our own right direction.

Medea is a tragic figure transplanted to alien soil by love, betrayed by another's ambition, and magnified by her own decisiveness. Her excesses are her strengths, and her vengeance is the viewer's hour of triumph as he too grows large enough to meet the exigencies of existence. Moral right or wrong becomes, at that moment, subservient to the reality that he has acted without equivocation, without vacillation, without remorse. Whatever horror might engulf him later, he has known his one supreme moment. Blanche DuBois (in Tennessee Williams' *A Streetcar Named Desire*) is a pathetic figure transplanted to alien soil by the failure of love, betrayed by another's avarice, and reduced to psychologically-shocked pulp that is led away to a madhouse as her betrayers withdraw into their auto-erogenous comfort-station, the bedroom.

As the Greek viewer left the theater, he was overwhelmed with the realization, "This must be." The mythical hero as a representative of the race could not escape the dictates of fate if he could not control his flawed Self—nor, analogously, could the viewer. *Moira* (fate) willed, and human attempts to manipulate or circumvent *moira* created irony that, multiplying itself, merely hastened inevitable death.

Romantic or Shakespearean tragedy lessened the impact of the myth as a basic plot device, adulterating it, hybridizing it with created dramatic incidents so that the viewer was held in suspense by the unfolding plot as well as by the destruction of the tragic hero. The irony of his two or more natures (Macbeth as a mythical hero, as any man, and Macbeth as a unique historical person, for instance) reduces the inevitable to the probable, for irony is so theatrically compelling that Shakespeare and other romantic dramatists could not resist its lure. And when the tragic hero died, his death was less inevitable than spectacular, achieving its effect in the act rather than in the significance of the act. The viewer was less overwhelmed than sated with the possibility that "This very well might be."

Modern tragedy, dismissing the mythical hero and utilizing the common man, turned to new "truths," those supplied by psychology, social awareness, class conflict, and so on, deliberately employing irony in all its dramatic intensity to create arbitrary (even if academically logical) or senseless catastrophes. Inevitability and probability were abandoned for dramatic possibilities which explored the causes of a catastrophe rather than the catastrophe itself. God is out of his heaven; all is *not* right with the world. The protagonist's disoriented soul clashes with a reactionary world, and death now becomes ironic rather than tragic. The viewer is fascinated by the clinical treatment of a fellow human out of control, but propinquity alone binds the viewer and the protagonist together. As the viewer leaves the play, he knows intellectually, "This much at least *is*." The god-concept that found its meaningful birth on some distant Attic stage as it created a collective consciousness in the spectator-participants eventually expired on the modern stage as, isolated in their collective self-consciousness, the viewers watched the dramatic protagonist in his ironic death-throes through the microscopes of their clinical detachment.

One of the most eloquent of our modern playwrights, Tennessee Williams, laments this very fact in the Preface to the published text of his play *The Rose Tattoo:*

. . . Plays in the tragic tradition offer us a view of certain moral values in violent juxtaposition. Because we do not participate, except as spectators, we can view them clearly, within the limits of our emotional equipment. These people on the stage do not return our looks. We do not have to answer their questions nor make any sign of being in company with them, nor do we have to compete with their virtues nor resist their offenses. All at once, for this reason, we are able to see them! Our hearts are wrung by recognition and pity. . . .

[Yet] so successfully have we disguised from ourselves the intensity of our own feelings, the sensibility of our own hearts, that plays in the tragic tradition have begun to seem untrue. For a couple of hours we may surrender ourselves to a world of fiercely illuminated values in conflict, but when the stage is covered and the auditorium lighted, almost immediately there is a recoil of disbelief . . . we have convinced ourselves once more that life has as little resemblance to the curiously stirring and meaningful occurrences on the stage as a jingle has to an elegy of Rilke.

This modern condition of his theater audience is something that an author must know in advance. The diminishing influence of life's destroyer, time, must be somehow worked into the context of his play. Perhaps it is a certain foolery, a certain distortion toward the grotesque, which will solve the problem for him. Perhaps it is only restraint, putting a mute on the strings that would like to break all bounds. But almost surely, unless he contrives in some way to relate the dimensions of his tragedy to the dimensions of a world in which time is *included*—he will be left among his magnificent debris on a dark stage, muttering to himself: "Those fools . . ."°

Other contemporary playwrights, attempting to find the easy answer, or at least the acceptable one, to such questions as "Must the viewer be clinical? Can he not be involved?" employ a new kind of facile myth that suggests that sacrifice and simplicity can negate tragedy in life even if the negation rewrites the cast and ending of the old Damon and Pythias legend. The heroine of Robert Anderson's *Tea and Sympathy,* for instance, sacrifices her sexual honor to a young man proving his masculinity—a masculinity challenged by a latent homosexual, her husband, protecting his own terrified ego. Her happiness becomes a warm hope that her sex partner will be raised to instant manhood and will "be kind" in later years as he thinks back on the experience. This pop-tragedy finds its counterpart in the Charles Schulz *Peanuts* attitude that *Happiness Is a Warm Puppy* or the Joan Walsh Anglund belief that *A Friend Is Someone Who Likes You.*

Although no one can say for certain what happiness *is* in the twentieth century, tragedy seems, of a certainty, to be the absence of it. To die of unhappiness is, however, almost impossible, nor is it common to be killed because of one's own unhappiness. Unhappiness is ubiquitous nevertheless—and modern tragedies grow more scarce each year. That scarcity was noted and possibly explained by Arthur Miller in an essay defending his play *Death of a Salesman,* considered by many critics to be a modern drama that can be defined as a tragedy even though the classical tragic hero is nowhere evident. Such a hero is not necessary, argues Miller in "Tragedy and the Common Man":

In this age few tragedies are written. It has often been held that the lack is due to a paucity of heroes among us, or else that modern man has had the blood drawn out of his organs of belief by the skepticism of science, and the heroic attack on life cannot feed on an attitude of reserve and circumspection. For one reason or another, we are often held to be below tragedy—or tragedy above us. The inevitable conclusion is, of course, that the tragic mode is archaic, fit only for the very highly placed, the kings or the kingly, and where this admission is not made in so many words it is most often implied.

I believe that the common man is as apt a subject for tragedy in its highest sense

° Tennessee Williams, from "The Timeless World of a Play," *The Rose Tattoo* (New York, 1951), pp. viii-ix.

as kings were. On the face of it this ought to be obvious in the light of modern psychiatry, which bases its analysis upon classific formulations, such as the Oedipus and Orestes complexes, for instance, which were enacted by royal beings, but which apply to everyone in similar emotional situations.

More simply, when the question of tragedy in art is not at issue, we never hesitate to attribute to the well-placed and the exalted the very same mental processes as the lowly. And finally, if the exaltation of tragic action were truly a property of the high-bred character alone, it is inconceivable that the mass of mankind should cherish tragedy above all other forms, let alone be capable of understanding it.

As a general rule, to which there may be exceptions unknown to me, I think the tragic feeling is evoked in us when we are in the presence of a character who is ready to lay down his life, if need be, to secure one thing—his sense of personal dignity. From Orestes to Hamlet, Medea to Macbeth, the underlying struggle is that of the individual attempting to gain his "rightful" position in his society.

Sometimes he is one who has been displaced from it, sometimes one who seeks to attain it for the first time, but the fateful wound from which the inevitable events spiral is the wound of indignity, and its dominant force is indignation. Tragedy, then, is the consequence of a man's total compulsion to evaluate himself justly.

In the sense of having been initiated by the hero himself, the tale always reveals what has been called his "tragic flaw," a failing that is not peculiar to grand or elevated characters. Nor is it necessarily a weakness. The flaw, or crack in the character, is really nothing—and need be nothing—but his inherent unwillingness to remain passive in the face of what he conceives to be a challenge to his dignity, his image of his rightful status. Only the passive, only those who accept their lot without active retaliation, are "flawless." Most of us are in that category.

But there are among us today, as there always have been, those who act against the scheme of things that degrades them, and in the process of action everything we have accepted out of fear or insensitivity or ignorance is shaken before us and examined, and from this total onslaught by an individual against the seemingly stable cosmos surrounding us—from this total examination of the "unchangeable" environment—comes the terror and the fear that is classically associated with tragedy.

More important, from this total questioning of what has been previously unquestioned, we learn. And such a process is not beyond the common man. In revolutions around the world, these past thirty years, he has demonstrated again and again this inner dynamic of all tragedy.

Insistence upon the rank of the tragic hero, or the so-called nobility of his character, is really but a clinging to the outward forms of tragedy. If rank or nobility of character was indispensable, then it would follow that the problems of those with rank were the particular problems of tragedy. But surely the right of one monarch to capture the domain from another no longer raises our passions, nor are our concepts of justice what they were to the mind of an Elizabethan king.

The quality in such plays that does shake us, however, derives from the underlying fear of being displaced, the disaster inherent in being torn away from our chosen image of what and who we are in this world. Among us today this fear is as strong, and perhaps stronger, than it ever was. In fact, it is the common man who knows this fear best.

Now, if it is true that tragedy is the consequence of a man's total compulsion to evaluate himself justly, his destruction in the attempt posits a wrong or an evil in his environment. And this is precisely the morality of tragedy and its lesson. The discovery of the moral law, which is what the enlightenment of tragedy consists of, is not the discovery of some abstract or metaphysical quantity.

The tragic right is a condition of life, a condition in which the human personality is able to flower and realize itself. The wrong is the condition which suppresses man, perverts the flowing out of his love and creative instinct. Tragedy enlightens—and it must, in that it points the heroic finger at the enemy of man's freedom. The thrust for freedom is the quality in tragedy which exalts. The revolutionary questioning of the stable environment is what terrifies. In no way is the common man debarred from such thoughts or such actions.

Seen in this light, our lack of tragedy may be partially accounted for by the turn which modern literature has taken toward the purely psychiatric view of life, or the purely sociological. If all our miseries, our indignities, are born and bred within our minds, then all action, let alone the heroic action, is obviously impossible.

And if society alone is responsible for the cramping of our lives, then the protagonist must needs be so pure and faultless as to force us to deny his validity as a character. From neither of these views can tragedy derive, simply because neither represents a balanced concept of life. Above all else, tragedy requires the finest appreciation by the writer of cause and effect.

No tragedy can therefore come about when its author fears to question absolutely everything, when he regards any institution, habit or custom as being either everlasting, immutable or inevitable. In the tragic view the need of man to wholly realize himself is the only fixed star, and whatever it is that hedges his nature and lowers it is ripe for attack and examination. Which is not to say that tragedy must preach revolution.

The Greeks could probe the very heavenly origin of their ways and return to confirm the rightness of laws. And Job could face God in anger, demanding his right, and end in submission. But for a moment everything is in suspension, nothing is accepted, and in this stretching and tearing apart of the cosmos, in the very action of so doing, the character gains "size," the tragic stature which is spuriously attached to the royal or the high born in our minds. The commonest of men may take on that stature to the extent of his willingness to throw all he has into the contest, the battle to secure his rightful place in this world.

There is a misconception of tragedy with which I have been struck in review after review, and in many conversations with writers and readers alike. It is the idea that tragedy is of necessity allied to pessimism. Even the dictionary says nothing more about the word than that it means a story with a sad or unhappy ending. This impression is so firmly fixed that I almost hesitate to claim that in truth tragedy implies more optimism in its author than does comedy, and that its final result ought to be the reinforcement of the onlooker's brightest opinions of the human animal.

For, if it is true to say that in essence the tragic hero is intent upon claiming his whole due as a personality, and if this struggle must be total and without reservation, then it automatically demonstrates the indestructible will of man to achieve his humanity.

The possibility of victory must be there in tragedy. Where pathos rules, where pathos is finally derived, a character has fought a battle he could not possibly have won. The pathetic is achieved when the protagonist is, by virtue of his witlessness, his insensitivity, or the very air he gives off, incapable of grappling with a much superior force.

Pathos truly is the mode for the pessimist. But tragedy requires a nicer balance between what is possible and what is impossible. And it is curious, although edifying, that the plays we revere, century after century, are the tragedies. In them, and in them alone, lies the belief—optimistic, if you will—in the perfectibility of man.

It is time, I think, that we who are without kings, took up this bright thread of our history and followed it to the only place it can possibly lead in our time—the heart and spirit of the average man.°

Attempting to find "the heart and spirit of the average man," Arthur Miller (like most modern playwrights) employs the vocabulary and sentence patterns of contemporary speech. The lofty hexameters of Sophocles, the iambic blank verse of Shakespeare are suited to larger-than-life-size plots and the passions of larger-than-life tragic heroes because those poetic lines have nobility and grandeur at their metrical hearts. The language and sentence structure of modern tragedy, on the other hand, are closer to verbal reality (therefore life-size) because the characters and plots are taken from ordinary life.

Plots of classical and romantic tragedies are very much like great paintings. The artistry of composition, the balanced masses, and the careful color usage is so apparent that the viewer may, unless he consciously guards against it, become more aware of the component parts than of the total canvas. Modern tragedy is more analogous to art photography— not candid or professional photography (except as the "slice-of-life" play or the musical comedy resemble those forms), but that careful photography which results from the artist's having rearranged nature in the photograph by blocking out areas, having added chiaroscuro to the negative with brush work before the final printing, and having utilized lenses to

° *The New York Times*, February 27, 1949, Section 2.

juxtapose sharp images against blurred backgrounds. A deceptive "natural" quality results. Barns, trash heaps, and deformities become "interesting" because they are seen with fresh vision rather than through stereotyped response. In plays, using the same process, plot becomes more important than character development. "What will happen" dominates the work; "why or how the character will grow or decay" becomes secondary.

The reader is always aware after reading *Death of a Salesman,* for example, that Willy Loman is an unchanged man from the opening to the closing lines. Happy, Linda, Biff—they all are *static* (unchanging) rather than *dynamic* (changing) characters. Interesting theatrical effects are substituted for more traditional dramatic devices. The soliloquy is replaced by memory sequences and the reader analyzes the Freudian possibilities for himself. He is not told how the character assesses incidents; he must, by imagining himself in the realistic situation, evaluate the possibilities from his own viewpoint. In this one respect, modern tragedy is more personal, more involving than classical or romantic works.

Yet Willy Loman remains a drab little man—a "loser" in contemporary terms. And Linda fails so completely as a wife that her insistence that "Attention, attention must be finally paid to such a person" seems sociologically correct (because Willy is a human being) but humanly irrelevant because our lives are as brief as Willy's, and Linda speaks to us with no authority. Willy has failed to make her life fuller, richer than it might otherwise have been, so how can he enlarge ours?

Speaking on "The Psychology of Tragic Pleasure," Roy Morrel points out the need of the reader to participate in "a fuller life" through tragedy:

To enable us to live more complexly and to persuade us that what we are getting is true to life—for it is important that we should not feel that the dramatist is either cheating us or sparing us, treating us as children who cannot be told the truth—we are invited to empathize in a hero of a certain type. We feel more deeply and subtly, act more courageously, more passionately, in him, and all the time with the conviction that it is true to life, a fuller life than our own. We may add that as drama has to work quickly, superficial superiorities, such as those of rank and fortune mentioned by classical critics, may predispose some of us to empathize, though modern class-conscious audiences may prefer other qualities. Whatever else the tragic hero is, however, he should not be dull: some conscientiously proletarian modern writers make a mistake, I think, when they solemnly present a drab little hero—unless they succeed in making out of him a twentieth-century Everyman. That may be as successful occasionally as the great character who lifts our imaginations, and it may invite our empathy no less.

Edith Sitwell has remarked that tragedy always opens on a question, "Who?"—

Who is the tragic hero? what is his significance? The answer is seldom given as explicitly as in the closing lines of *The Great God Brown:* the Police Captain, you may remember, has given Cybel a few minutes alone with the dying Brown to make him talk; he then comes in and asks, "Well, what's his name?" Cybel answers, "Man," and the Police Officer, his notebook open, asks "How d'yuh spell it?"

The spelling is not difficult: it is either "Everyman," ourselves, whose fate we must endure; or it is "Potential Man," whose powers of living it would be well for the species if we could assimilate.°

"Everyman" is "Potential Man" and therein lies most of the would-be tragedian's problem. Because man has not reached his potential, he strives for whatever constitutes his personal concept of his "just deserts" if not of his ultimate capability. Empty monarchies are inherited; dictators aren't noble; world leaders may be as glamorous as America's young assassinated President, but political power-struggles involving millions of people are conducted by committee or junta, and they are certainly not the material of tragedy. Contemporary playwrights seem incapable of finding tragic figures because the myth of the hero has been replaced by the myth of the common man. Heroes attain their title because they are unique; the common man inherits his because he is undistinguished by problems important enough to arouse our interest. He is a type without an archetype. He is a representative of the masses; yet no one character is undistinguished enough to be representative, for the masses are numbered in the billions.

American authors seek to deal with the common man more desperately than European writers do, probably because we have yet to produce the great American poem comparable to Italy's *Divine Comedy,* England's *Beowulf,* or Germany's *Nibelungenlied.* We have yet to write the great American novel comparable to Russia's *War and Peace,* France's *Les Misérables,* or Spain's *Don Quixote.* Nor have we achieved one drama that can, without qualification, be called a tragedy in the sense of Greece's *Oedipus Rex,* Germany's *Faust,* or England's *Macbeth.*

Walt Whitman and Hart Crane are probably the two greatest poets to have emerged from America, but neither is The American Poet. Theodore Dreiser found a struggling Clyde Griffiths seeking success through murder to be the hero of his novel *An American Tragedy;* but his book is not *The* American Tragedy. Arthur Miller's Willy Loman is an unsuccessful Jewish salesman, and Tennessee Williams' Tom Wingfield (*The Glass Menagerie*) is an itinerant poet equally unsuccessful.

Oedipus was not a typical Greek king of Sophocles' or of any other time, but he did represent the Greek ideal of potential. Macbeth is the

° *Essays in Criticism VI* (New York, 1956).

archetype of leaders in whom the milk of human kindness has curdled. What contemporary archetype of man (noble, ignoble, or common) exists in America? Possibly the ubiquitous "Kilroy" of World War II, but he was a symbol rather than a model, and his proper province is the Theater of the Absurd where he exists in Tennessee Williams' *Camino Real* (pp. 526–602).

Eugene O'Neill was always concerned with Potential Man, and it was he who moved American drama to the international stage. Before 1915, ours had been a provincial extension of the European theater which had fought the literary battles of Ibsen's realism and Strindberg's expressionism while America saw the traditional plays or contented itself with the melodramatic, often spectacular but seldom challenging offerings of Broadway. After 1915, however, the "little theater" movement came to America with its interest in art rather than profit. O'Neill became the darling of these groups, for he was a native dramatist of obvious talent. The son of a famous actor, O'Neill had studied classical drama extensively and become enchanted with Strindberg's experimental plays such as *The Spook Sonata*. *Bound East for Cardiff* was produced by the newly formed Provincetown Players in 1916, and O'Neill quickly moved into the commercial theaters of New York City, his first full-length tragedy, *Beyond the Horizon,* being produced in 1920.

From that time on, O'Neill went from success to success, experimenting continuously with realism, naturalism, expressionism (bringing Greek masks back to the stage in *The Great God Brown*), a nine-act drama (*Strange Interlude*—a novel in dramatic form), and finally moving back to the Greek concept with his monumental trilogy, *Mourning Becomes Electra.* In the process, he was to garner three Pulitzer Prizes (1920, 1922, 1928) and the Nobel Prize in 1936, becoming the first and only American dramatist to establish an international reputation. (It is yet too early to predict Miller's and Williams' reputations.) O'Neill's *Desire Under the Elms* (1924) is a realistic tragedy—or, more properly perhaps, a psychological drama—indebted to the author's Greek studies and rooted in Freud. Always lacking the poetic rhythms of the classical playwrights, O'Neill did possess their concern for man whom he saw as the inheritor of the earth, a legacy that imprisoned him. His common men were sailors, the members of an aristocratic New England family, his own neurosis-ridden relatives, or the dirt farmers of *Desire Under the Elms*—unrepresentative of anything but the tragic waste of man's potential when it is misdirected by passion. The recording of such wasted potential does not create catharsis but rather what has been called "limited catharsis," wherein the reader's emotional responses of pity and fear are divided between the protagonist and his victim. We cannot identify completely with the protagonist in such dramas because, though we admire his determination, we are appalled at its misdirection.

Attempting to define the cathartic effects of modern drama, John Gassner believes "many serious modern plays are not tragedies at all but a new form of tragicomedy for which no term has yet been found." In support of his contention, he says:

Has it not always been recognized that the superiority of the great tragedies, if we exclude purely stylistic differences, has resided in their powerful blending of passion with enlightenment? This is what we mean when we attribute their superiority to the significance of their content, the depth and scope of their conflict, or the relevance of their action to the major aspects and problems of humanity. In tragedy there is always a precipitate of final enlightenment—some inherent, cumulatively realized, understanding. We have seen an experience enacted on the stage, and have externalized its inner counterpart in ourselves by the process of vibrating to the acted passions; or possibly by some other means, since unconscious processes are open to infinite debate. Then, ensuring the externalization of the inner drives, we have given them form and meaning—that is, understood their causes and effects, which brings us to the furthest point from the unconscious, or from nebulous emotion, ever reached by the individual. Enlightenment is, therefore, the third component of the process of purgation.

It exists in perfect harmony with the components of "pity and fear," and it is even supported by them. "Pity and fear," (using these terms to cover the emotional experience) are the *fixatives* of tragic enlightenment, for without their agency the meaning of a play would be superficial and fleeting; enlightenment unrooted in the emotions or unsupported and unevoked by them would be something imposed from without, unprecipitated from the struggle of the drama, and devoid of persuasive growth or cumulative effect. Moreover, pity and terror have mnemonic values which the drama cannot dispense with, because of its rapid course of action. Who would remember the significances of *Hamlet* without its anguish?

Finally, but keeping the above qualifications strictly in mind, we can maintain that enlightenment is not only the third element in catharsis, but the decisive one. The ultimate relief comes when the dramatist brings the tragic struggle to a state of rest. This cannot occur so long as we are left in a state of tension. No matter how well the action or the main character's destiny is resolved and concluded, the anarchic forces, "the pity and fear," evoked by the tragedy cannot establish a suitable inner equilibrium. Only enlightenment, a clear comprehension of what was involved in the struggle, an understanding of cause and effect, a judgment on what we have witnessed, and an induced state of mind that places it above the riot of passion—can effect this necessary equilibrium. And it is a necessary one if there is to be purgation, and if for the moment we are to be healed of the wounds self-inflicted in the unconscious, inflicted on us from without by external circumstance before they settle our inmost self, then inflicted once more by the tragic story enacted before our eyes on the stage. Only enlightenment can therefore round out the esthetic experience in tragedy, can actually ensure complete esthetic gratification. True tragic exaltation, which we require of a tragedy, also lies in this. For the exaltation comes only if we have prevailed over the anarchy of our inner life and the ever present and ever pressing life around us; and how can we master this anarchy without understanding it, without putting order into this house of disorder?°

Eugene O'Neill attempted such pity, fear, and illumination in *Desire Under the Elms* by extracting dramatic elements from the *Medea* and the *Hippolytus* of Euripides, refining them through an Elizabethan poetic ear for dialog that is neither realistic nor poetic, and presenting them in a New England farm setting in 1850. Realism at its best, the play employs an expressionistic technique in setting. Opening on a front view of the Cabot farmhouse, the play moves into the house and back outside with the removal of the walls. We may be outside, inside one room, or in several at one time, a device that creates the intimacy of omniscient eavesdropping.

DESIRE UNDER THE ELMS

by Eugene O'Neill

CHARACTERS

EPHRAIM CABOT

SIMEON ⎫
PETER ⎬ *His sons*
EBEN ⎭

ABBIE PUTNAM

Young Girl, Two Farmers, The Fiddler, A Sheriff, and other folk from the neighboring farms.

The action of the entire play takes place in, and immediately outside of, the Cabot farmhouse in New England, in the year 1850. The south end of the house faces front

---

° "Catharsis and the Modern Theater," *European Theories of the Drama,* Barrett H. Clark, ed. (New York, 1964).

to a stone wall with a wooden gate at center opening on a country road. The house is in good condition but in need of paint. Its walls are a sickly grayish, the green of the shutters faded. Two enormous elms are on each side of the house. They bend their trailing branches down over the roof. They appear to protect and at the same time subdue. There is a sinister maternity in their aspect, a crushing, jealous absorption. They have developed from their intimate contact with the life of man in the house an appalling humaneness. They brood oppressively over the house. They are like exhausted women resting their sagging breasts and hands and hair on its roof, and when it rains their tears trickle down monotonously and rot on the shingles.

There is a path running from the gate around the right corner of the house to the front door. A narrow porch is on this side. The end wall facing us has two windows in its upper story, two larger ones on the floor below. The two upper are those of the father's bedroom and that of the brothers. On the left, ground floor, is the kitchen—on the right, the parlor, the shades of which are always drawn down.

The surname *Cabot* immediately suggests New England; the given names of the family just as quickly suggest the stern puritanism of those rock-bound coasts; and you, as the reader, already know a great deal about the play from such associations. The setting intensifies this first response by repeating the name Cabot, stating that it is indeed New England, and focusing attention on the *stone wall.* Stones and their hard quality dominate the play in actuality and symbolically, for Nature (of the universe and of man) is hard. The word *wall* creates a complex response in man—a response not generated by the word *fence* which, theoretically, this stone wall is. A wall separates and prohibits entry. It cannot be climbed over, for a barrier exists at the top. Whether that barrier is the sky or a ceiling, it defies scaling. Walls create rooms, physical or mental compartments where a man is imprisoned or imprisons himself. Fortunately, walls have doors and *door* here equals *gate.* In this setting, the gate is *wooden,* a word implying both the weakness of wood as opposed to stone and the unemotional. Gates too keep creatures in as well as out, however, for they are, like doors, intended to be kept closed. This attention to fine detail reveals O'Neill's realism, expressionism, symbolism, and poetry working smoothly and harmoniously together to create an atmosphere that is almost palpable.

Romanticism is also present in the setting—a psychological romanticism that becomes almost melodramatic in the description of the house and trees. "Sickly grayish" walls, faded green shutters create a cancerous, festering growth—which is the house—attended by the maternal trees, ministering but also keeping the house prisoner. Four rooms—one closed against the world—seem a small space for breathing life into souls, a possibility suggested in the title.

PART ONE

SCENE ONE

Exterior of the farmhouse. It is sunset of a day at the beginning of summer in the year 1850. There is no wind and everything is still. The sky above the roof is suffused with deep colors, the green of the elms glows, but the house is in shadow, seeming pale and washed out by contrast.

A door opens and EBEN CABOT *comes to the end of the porch and stands looking down the road to the right. He has a large bell in his hand and this he swings mechanically, awakening a deafening clangor. Then he puts his hands on his hips and stares up at the sky. He sighs with a puzzled awe and blurts out with halting appreciation.*

EBEN. God! Purty! (*His eyes fall and he stares about him frowningly. He is twenty-five, tall and sinewy. His face is well-formed, good-looking, but its expression is resentful and defensive. His defiant, dark eyes remind one of a wild animal's in captivity. Each day is a cage in which he finds himself trapped but inwardly unsubdued. There is a fierce repressed vitality about him. He has black hair, mustache, a thin curly trace of beard. He is dressed in rough farm clothes. He spits on the ground with intense disgust, turns and goes back into the house.*)

Sunset is a time of rest, a time of dying. The vibrant, great elms seem to nurse the house in this pastel hour. The bell, clangorous and alien in a place of sickness, seems hostile, shocking; its wielder, brutal. But his opening words dispel that attitude, forcing ambivalence on us. His sensitivity to the sky, his rangy good looks predispose us to like him, a predisposition strengthened as we learn he is a caged thing, "trapped but inwardly unsubdued." We know that feeling; we too have rattled the bars of our cages clangorously at beautiful moments. Then, as if to lessen our sympathy, as if anxious to alienate us, Eben "spits on the ground," a loutish act in our presence (however unknown it is to him) and our ambivalence grows. We want to like this boy; his physical features and his reaction to beauty are appealing; his uneducated speech, his noisy desecration, his disgusting personal habits are appalling. And so that attitude of ambivalence is set; it will not change throughout the play until we know why we must be of two minds about Eben—even as he seems to be of two minds about his surroundings.

(SIMEON *and* PETER *come in from their work in the fields. They are tall men, much older than their half-brother [*SIMEON *is thirty-nine and* PETER *thirty-seven], built on a squarer, simpler model, fleshier in body, more bovine and homelier in face, shrewder and more practical. Their shoulders stoop a bit from years of farm work. They clump*

heavily along in their clumsy thick-soled boots caked with earth. Their clothes, their
faces, hands, bare arms and throats are earth-stained. They smell of earth. They stand
together for a moment in front of the house and, as if with the one impulse, stare
dumbly up at the sky, leaning on their hoes. Their faces have a compressed, unresigned
expression. As they look upward, this softens.)

SIMEON (*grudgingly*). Purty.

PETER. Ay-eh.

SIMEON (*suddenly*). Eighteen years ago.

PETER. What?

SIMEON. Jenn. My woman. She died.

PETER. I'd fergot.

SIMEON. I rec'lect—now an' agin. Makes it lonesome. She'd hair long's a hoss'
tail—an' yaller like gold!

PETER. Waal—she's gone. (*This with indifferent finality—then after a pause*)
They's gold in the West, Sim.

SIMEON (*still under the influence of sunset—vaguely*). In the sky!

PETER. Waal—in a manner o' speakin'—thar's the promise. (*Growing excited*) Gold
in the sky—in the West—Golden Gate—Californi-a!—Goldest West!—fields o' gold!

SIMEON (*excited in his turn*). Fortunes layin' just atop o' the ground waitin' t' be
picked! Solomon's mines, they says! (*For a moment they continue looking up at the
sky—then their eyes drop.*)

PETER (*with sardonic bitterness*). Here—it's stones atop o' the ground—stones
atop o' stones—makin' stone walls—year atop o' year—him 'n' yew 'n' me 'n' then
Eben—makin' stone walls fur him to fence us in!

SIMEON. We've wuked. Give our strength. Give our years. Plowed 'em under in the
ground,—(*He stamps rebelliously*)—rottin'—makin' soil for his crops! (*A pause*)
Waal—the farm pays good for hereabouts.

PETER. If we plowed in Californi-a, they'd be lumps o' gold in the furrow!

SIMEON. Californi-a's t'other side o' earth, a'most. We got t' calc'late—

PETER (*after a pause*). 'Twould be hard fur me, too, to give up what we've 'arned
here by our sweat. (*A pause.* EBEN *sticks his head out of the dining-room window,
listening.*)

SIMEON. Ay-eh. (*A pause*) Mebbe—he'll die soon.

PETER (*doubtfully*). Mebbe.

SIMEON. Mebbe—fur all we knows—he's dead now.

PETER. Ye'd need proof.

SIMEON. He's been gone two months—with no word.

PETER. Left us in the fields an evenin' like this. Hitched up an' druv off into the
West. That's plum onnateral. He hain't never been off this farm 'ceptin' t' the village
in thirty year or more, not since he married Eben's maw. (*A pause. Shrewdly*) I
calc'late we might git him declared crazy by the court.

SIMEON. He skinned 'em too slick. He got the best o' all on 'em. They'd never b'lieve him crazy. (*A pause*) We got t' wait—till he's under ground.

EBEN (*with a sardonic chuckle*). Honor thy father! (*They turn, startled, and stare at him. He grins, then scowls*) I pray he's died. (*They stare at him. He continues matter-of-factly*) Supper's ready.

SIMEON *and* PETER (*together*). Ay-eh.

EBEN (*gazing up at the sky*). Sun's downin' purty.

SIMEON *and* PETER (*together*). Ay-eh. They's gold in the West.

EBEN. Ay-eh. (*Pointing*) Yonder atop o' the hill pasture, ye mean?

SIMEON *and* PETER (*together*). In Californi-a!

EBEN. Hunh? (*Stares at them indifferently for a second, then drawls*) Waal— supper's gittin' cold. (*He turns back into kitchen.*)

SIMEON (*startled—smacks his lips*). I air hungry!

PETER (*sniffing*). I smells bacon!

SIMEON (*with hungry appreciation*). Bacon's good!

PETER (*in same tone*). Bacon's bacon! (*They turn, shouldering each other, their bodies bumping and rubbing together as they hurry clumsily to their food, like two friendly oxen toward their evening meal. They disappear around the right corner of house and can be heard entering the door.*)

CURTAIN

The entrance of Simeon and Peter is, seemingly, a simple entrance. But is it? Rearrange the order of their names: *Peter and Simeon come in from their work in the fields.* A subtle change occurs. In O'Neill's order, their names together create *Simon Peter,* a name rich in Christian symbolism, a name suggesting a rock ("For thou art Peter, and upon this rock will I build my church"). The stone wall is recalled briefly and, before reading further, you know that these men are somehow a part of the cage in which Eben is trapped. Instinctively, you dislike them. That dislike becomes more intense as details are supplied: They are half-brothers, older than Eben. He is outnumbered; he is youth in conflict with age. They are bovine, shrewd, and hulking. Standing, looking at the sky, they are the personification of Edwin Markham's "The Man with the Hoe," but *their* threat is not to an uncaring world—it is directed at Eben. Simeon's "Purty" is grudging; Eben's was a testament to God, freely given. Jenn's death is merely a passing thought and you know Simeon misses creature comfort rather than the human creature, so it is impossible to be sympathetic.

By popular consensus, dreams seem to be for the young, so Simeon and Peter lack even the stability of plodders as they see California as the El Dorado they've never known.

The image of cattle clings to them, cattle turned greedy. Their resentment against their father (the nameless "he") is distasteful, not because their words are unbelievable but because grown men should not be as weak, as snivelling as these. Their grievance, rather than enlisting our sympathy, reminds us again of the caged Eben, especially when "him 'n' yew 'n' me 'n' then Eben" seems to bury Eben under the stone walls everyone has built. His young cooperation is forgivable, but their older bitterness is unmanly. Greed, not man, binds them to this earth. Greed, not love of the earth itself, holds them captive. That they should wish their father's death, then consider having him declared insane reveals their weak, calculating natures, and the expository background material becomes an integral part of our dislike for the men, making us unaware of the dramatic structure that is giving us the information.

Eben's reappearance is almost a relief after our brief exposure to the ugly natures of the half-brothers. His sarcastic "Honor thy father" seems at first a reprimand until it is followed with his bitter "I pray he's died." Then we know the father is Eben's jailor. The half-brothers are also prisoners, but theirs is a voluntary servitude. Eben's is not. How we know this is uncertain, but we are sure of it. His concern for the gold of nature as contrasted to their concern for material gold supplies the answer. Eben loves this land! Love imbues his "Yonder atop o' the hill pasture" with a kind of wonder. The gold that Eben sees on the crest of the hill is the gold that man's spirit responds to. Simeon and Peter's greed is forcefully made plain when they virtually slobber at the mention of food and lumber along like "oxen" to the stalls where immediate demands take precedence over anything else, no matter how important.

O'Neill has created four characters in this scene, forced your response to them, and suggested the conflict that will result in tragedy. With deft precision, he planted the lines "He skinned 'em too slick. He got the best o' all on 'em" when your attention was focused on the half-brothers' ugly plottings. Those lines are crucial in the play, foreshadowing the motives of Eben. At the proper time you will remember them. Now they seem merely a character device to reveal Simeon and Peter. Such dramaturgy is the mark of a masterful playwright. No line is wasted by having one function only.

SCENE TWO

The color fades from the sky. Twilight begins. The interior of the kitchen is now visible. A pine table is at center, a cookstove in the right rear corner, four rough wooden chairs, a tallow candle on the table. In the middle of the rear wall is fastened a big advertizing poster with a ship in full sail and the word "California" in big letters.

Kitchen utensils hang from nails. Everything is neat and in order but the atmosphere is of a men's camp kitchen rather than that of a home.

Places for three are laid. EBEN *takes boiled potatoes and bacon from the stove and puts them on the table, also a loaf of bread and a crock of water.* SIMEON *and* PETER *shoulder in, slump down in their chairs without a word.* EBEN *joins them. The three eat in silence for a moment, the two elder as naturally unrestrained as beasts of the field,* EBEN *picking at his food without appetite, glancing at them with a tolerant dislike.*

The dimness of twilight filters through the great elms and into the kitchen through the large window in the wall that is removed so we can see inside. At no time do the elms not dominate the set. The poster serves a triple function: first, it symbolizes the half-brothers' ambition; second, it foreshadows their lack of transportation; third, it raises the question of decoration. Simeon and Peter are unimaginative, oxen-like men. The poster is a dreamer's touch. No woman has lived in this house for some years; yet the poster is decorative even as it serves as a constant reminder to the half-brothers. Eben has inherited the household duties, obviously, for it is he who cooks and waits on the table. Therefore, the poster is Eben's doing. He is sensitive to impressions (you saw that in his mistaking *gold* to mean sunshine), yet he is not an effeminate interior decorator. The poster, then, is a shrewd maneuver: he wants the brothers to leave. His preoccupation, his sensitivity both become apparent as, like cattle, the brothers eat in the neat and orderly kitchen while he picks at his food.

SIMEON (*suddenly turns to* EBEN). Looky here! Ye'd oughtn't t' said that, Eben.

PETER. 'Twa'n't righteous.

EBEN. What?

SIMEON. Ye prayed he'd died.

EBEN. Waal—don't yew pray it? (*A pause*)

PETER. He's our Paw.

EBEN (*violently*). Not mine!

SIMEON (*dryly*). Ye'd not let no one else say that about yer Maw! Ha! (*He gives one abrupt sardonic guffaw.* PETER *grins.*)

EBEN (*very pale*). I meant—I hain't his'n—I hain't like him—he hain't me!

PETER (*dryly*). Wait till ye've growed his age!

EBEN (*intensely*). I'm Maw—every drop o' blood! (*A pause. They stare at him with indifferent curiosity.*)

PETER (*reminiscently*). She was good t' Sim 'n' me. A good stepmaw's curse.

SIMEON. She was good t' everyone.

EBEN (*greatly moved, gets to his feet and makes an awkward bow to each of them—stammering*). I be thankful t' ye. I'm her—her heir. (*He sits down in con-fusion.*)

PETER (*after a pause—judicially*). She was good even t' him.

EBEN (*fiercely*). An' fur thanks he killed her!

SIMEON (*after a pause*). No one never kills nobody. It's allus some thin'. That's the murderer.

EBEN. Didn't he slave Maw t' death?

PETER. He's slaved himself t' death. He's slaved Sim 'n' me 'n' yew t' death—on'y none o' us hain't died—yit.

SIMEON. It's somethin'—drivin' him—t' drive us!

EBEN (*vengefully*). Waal—I hold him t' jedgment! (*Then scornfully*) Somethin'! What's somethin'?

SIMEON. Dunno.

The half-brothers are characterized as chronic irritants. They do not hate Eben. Their passions are not deep enough for that. Animalistic by nature, they have been trained, but the subtleties of training are too aesthetic for them to understand. Eben "prayed" their father would die; they merely "wish" it. Outraged morality is beyond them too—they are merely picking at Eben. He is not brutish. Determined, strong in the delicate way of sensitive people, he is honest. He hates his father, considers him merely his sire. "Oxen" cannot be patiently cruel—their attention span is too short—and like animals, the boys remember kindness. Eben recognizes their short attention span, therefore the poster. The half-brothers are not capable of intellectualizing their hate either. It is easier to accept the drive of their father. They could not explain it, but, like beasts of the field, they accept certain truths—truths Eben cannot accept because he is unlike them.

EBEN (*sardonically*). What's drivin' yew to Californi·a, mebbe? (*They look at him in surprise.*) Oh, I've heerd ye! (*Then, after a pause*) But ye'll never go t' the gold fields!

PETER (*assertively*). Mebbe!

EBEN. Whar'll ye git the money?

PETER. We kin walk. It's an a'mighty ways—Californi·a—but if yew was t' put all the steps we've walked on this farm end t' end we'd be in the moon!

EBEN. The Injuns'll skulp ye on the plains.

SIMEON (*with grim humor*). We'll mebbe make 'em pay a hair fur a hair!

EBEN (*decisively*). But t'aint that. Ye won't never go because ye'll wait here fur yer share o' the farm, thinkin' allus he'll die soon.

SIMEON (*after a pause*). We've a right.

PETER. Two-thirds belong t' us.

EBEN (*jumping to his feet*). Ye've no right! She wa'n't yewr Maw! It was her farm! Didn't he steal it from her? She's dead. It's my farm.

SIMEON (*sardonically*). Tell that t' Paw—when he comes! I'll bet ye a dollar he'll laugh—fur once in his life. Ha! (*He laughs himself in one single mirthless bark.*)

PETER (*amused in turn, echoes his brother*). Ha!

SIMEON (*after a pause*). What've ye got held agin us, Eben? Year arter year it's skulked in yer eye—somethin'.

PETER. Ay-eh.

EBEN. Ay-eh. They's somethin'. (*Suddenly exploding*) Why didn't ye never stand between him 'n' my Maw when he was slavin' her to her grave—t' pay her back fur the kindness she done t' yew? (*There is a long pause. They stare at him in surprise.*)

SIMEON. Waal—the stock's got t' be watered.

PETER. 'R they was woodin' t' do.

SIMEON. 'R plowin'.

PETER. 'R hayin'.

SIMEON. 'R spreadin' manure.

PETER. 'R weedin'.

SIMEON. 'R prunin'.

PETER. 'R milkin'.

EBEN (*breaking in harshly*). An' makin' walls—stone atop o' stone—makin' walls till yer heart's a stone ye heft up out o' the way o' growth onto a stone wall t' wall in yer heart!

SIMEON (*matter-of-factly*). We never had no time t' meddle.

PETER (*to* EBEN). Yew was fifteen afore yer Maw died—an' big fur yer age. Why didn't ye never do nothin'?

EBEN (*harshly*). They was chores t' do, wa'n't they? (*A pause—then slowly*) It was on'y arter she died I come to think o' it. Me cookin'—doin' her work—that made me know her, suffer her sufferin'—she'd come back t' help—come back t' bile potatoes—come back t' fry bacon—come back t' bake biscuits—come back all cramped up t' shake the fire, an' carry ashes, her eyes weepin' an' bloody with smoke an' cinders same's they used t' be. She still comes back—stands by the stove thar in the evenin'—she can't find it nateral sleepin' an' restin' in peace. She can't git used t' bein' free—even in her grave.

SIMEON. She never complained none.

EBEN. She'd got too tired. She'd got too used t' bein' too tired. That was what he done. (*With vengeful passion*) An' sooner'r later, I'll meddle. I'll say the thin's I didn't say then t' him! I'll yell 'em at the top o' my lungs! I'll see t' it my Maw gits some rest an' sleep in her grave! (*He sits down again, relapsing into a brooding silence. They look at him with a queer indifferent curiosity.*)

Eben's campaign to rid the farm of the half-brothers intensifies now. He reveals his knowledge of their California hopes and says why he wants them gone: the farm was his mother's, and the half-brothers did not protect her from their Paw. They share the old man's guilt and would share his ill-gotten gains. Eben wants to avoid the latter. It is too late to change their guilt. He can scarcely cope with his own; it manifests itself in his belief (who can call such beliefs delusion?) that his mother is not at rest, that she returns to the house, uneasy, unable to rest in peace, still a prisoner beneath the great elms.

You must assess Simeon and Peter's failure to be amused, amazed, or incredulous. Do they think Eben unbalanced? Do they too feel an unnatural presence in the house? Are they too bovine to seek reasons for his belief? Curiosity, whether concerned or indifferent, suggests a state of mind; what is theirs as they look at him?

PETER (*after a pause*). Whar in tarnation d'ye s'pose he went, Sim?

SIMEON. Dunno. He druv off in the buggy, all spick an' span, with the mare all breshed an' shiny, druv off clackin' his tongue an' wavin' his whip. I remember it right well. I was finishin' plowin', it was spring an' May an' sunset, an' gold in the West, an' he druv off into it. I yells "Whar ye goin', Paw?" an' he hauls up by the stone wall a jiffy. His old snake's eyes was glitterin' in the sun like he'd been drinkin' a jugful an' he says with a mule's grin: "Don't ye run away till I come back!"

PETER. Wonder if he knowed we was wantin' fur Californi-a?

SIMEON. Mebbe. I didn't say nothin' and he says, lookin' kinder queer an' sick: "I been hearin' the hens cluckin' an' the roosters crowin' all the durn day. I been listenin' t' the cows lowin' an' everythin' else kickin' up till I can't stand it no more. It's spring an' I'm feelin' damned," he says. "Damned like an old bare hickory tree fit on'y fur burnin'," he says. An' then I calc'late I must've looked a mite hopeful, fur he adds real spry and vicious: "But dont git no fool idee I'm dead. I've sworn t' live a hundred an' I'll do it, if on'y t' spite yer sinful greed! An' now I'm ridin' out t' learn God's message t' me in the spring, like the prophets done. An' yew git back t' yer plowin'," he says. An' he druv off singin' a hymn. I thought he was drunk—'r I'd stopped him goin'.

EBEN (*scornfully*). No, ye wouldn't! Ye're scared o' him. He's stronger—inside— than both o' ye put together!

PETER (*sardonically*). An' yew—be yew Samson?

EBEN. I'm gittin' stronger. I kin feel it growin' in me—growin' an growin'—till it'll bust out—! (*He gets up and puts on his coat and a hat. They watch him, gradually breaking into grins. EBEN avoids their eyes sheepishly.*) I'm goin' out fur a spell—up the road.

PETER. T' the village?

SIMEON. T' see Minnie?

EBEN (*defiantly*). Ay-eh?

PETER (*jeeringly*). The Scarlet Woman!

SIMEON. Lust—that's what's growin' in ye!

EBEN. Waal—she's purty!

PETER. She's been purty fur twenty year!

SIMEON. A new coat o' paint'll make a heifer out of forty.

EBEN. She hain't forty!

PETER. If she hain't, she's teeterin' on the edge.

EBEN (*desperately*). What d'yew know—

PETER. All they is . . . Sim knew her—an' then me arter—

SIMEON. An' Paw kin tell yew somethin' too! He was fust!

EBEN. D'ye mean t' say he . . . ?

SIMEON (*with a grin*). Ay-eh! We air his heirs in everythin'!

EBEN (*intensely*). That's more to it! That grows on it! It'll bust soon! (*Then violently*) I'll go smash my fist in her face! (*He pulls open the door in rear violently.*)

SIMEON (*with a wink at* PETER—*drawlingly*). Mebbe—but the night's wa'm—purty—by the time ye git thar mebbe ye'll kiss her instead!

PETER. Sart'n he will! (*They both roar with coarse laughter.* EBEN *rushes out and slams the door—then the outside front door—comes around the corner of the house and stands still by the gate, staring up at the sky.*)

Simeon's account of Ephraim's departure is the first glimpse we have had of the old man, and it is a reflection of Simeon's viewpoint. Still, it reveals a great deal beyond the simple expository matter which is the dialog's primary function. The taciturn Simeon becomes almost loquacious. His terse speech becomes almost poetic in its vivid biblical imagery— imagery you realize is a heritage from old Ephraim just as the names of the sons are. Driving into the sunset, the old man is ablaze with fire and he speaks like a drunk man, according to Simeon. The image is also of a religiously possessed man. His eyes are "old snake's eyes," an unconscious if dubious compliment within the biblical context of the dialog, and Simeon spells out the need of biological fulfillment, the call of spring, and the stirrings of the land, but the boys are all too filled with their own hate to hear the message. Eben loves this land; Eben is like his father; and Ephraim loves the land more intensely than Eben, for he has had forty years more of love to pour into it than his twenty-five year old son has had. Eben is growing stronger in both his love and his hate, but he is still a boy.

Spring calls Eben too: he feels his growing strength (the strength of Ephraim though Eben does not know it) and it calls him to go into the spring night, to Minnie, to the procreative if thwarted act. Eben is as firmly bound to the soil as Ephraim, and his hate of the old man is the same eternal conflict that, in more symbolic terms, existed in Oedipus. Eben wants the soil of his mother, soil Ephraim wishes to relinquish to no son. Simeon and Peter have known the same urges, have known the same Minnie that Ephraim had known before them. They do not understand she was no inheritance—she was no soil in which seed was sown by their father.

SIMEON (*looking after him*). Like his Paw.

PETER. Dead spit an' image!

SIMEON. Dog'll eat dog!

PETER. Ay-eh (*Pause. With yearning*) Mebbe a year from now we'll be in Californi-a.

SIMEON. Ay-eh. (*A pause. Both yawn.*) Let's git t' bed. (*He blows out the candle. They go out door in rear.* EBEN *stretches his arms up to the sky—rebelliously.*)

EBEN. Waal—thar's a star, an' somewhar's they's him, an' here's me, an' thar's Min up the road—in the same night. What if I does kiss her? She's like t'night, she's soft 'n' wa'm, her eyes kin wink like a star, her mouth's wa'm, her arms're wa'm, she smells like a wa'm plowed field, she's purty . . . Ay-eh! By God A'mighty she's purty, an' I don't give a damn how many sins she's sinned afore mine or who she's sinned 'em with, my sin's as purty as any one of 'em! (*He strides off down the road to the left.*)

CURTAIN

The boys' observation that Eben is "like his Paw" is one of those truths here stated for the first time. Perhaps it accounts for their general dislike of Eben. It is a truth that Eben does not want to know, refuses to consider, but it is a truth that will be explored throughout the play. Old Ephraim's legacy is strong in all his sons. Remember Simeon's "eye for an eye" philosophy as he replied to the threat of Indians? A stern God demands stern justice, and their God-concept was instilled by their father. It is strongest in Eben, however, for he is most like Ephraim.

And in their own brute way, Simeon and Peter know that Eben is more their father's son than they. His determination, his temper, his indomitable will are old Ephraim's, a realization that causes Simeon to predict accurately, "Dog'll eat dog!"

Eben the poet, the afflicted of his father's stern God, stands beneath the giant elms, by the gate that breaks the stone wall, and declares his will to a sky that, in his New England theological background, is the abode of God. His declaration is not calculated to be sacrilegious nor an affront; it is a declaration of intent, of a strong, inherited will.

SCENE THREE

It is the pitch darkness just before dawn. EBEN comes in from the left and goes around to the porch, feeling his way, chuckling bitterly and cursing half-aloud to himself.

EBEN. The cussed old miser! (*He can be heard going in the front door. There is a pause as he goes upstairs, then a loud knock on the bedroom door of the brothers.*) Wake up!

SIMEON (*startedly*). Who's thar?

EBEN (*pushing open the door and coming in, a lighted candle in his hand. The bedroom of the brothers is revealed. Its ceiling is the sloping roof. They can stand upright only close to the center dividing wall of the upstairs.* SIMEON *and* PETER *are in a double bed, front.* EBEN'S *cot is to the rear.* EBEN *has a mixture of silly grin and vicious scowl on his face*). I be!

PETER (*angrily*). What in hell's-fire . . . ?

EBEN. I got news fur ye! Ha! (*He gives one abrupt sardonic guffaw.*)

SIMEON (*angrily*). Couldn't ye hold it 'til we'd got our sleep?

EBEN. It's nigh sunup. (*Then explosively*) He's gone an' married agen!

SIMEON *and* PETER (*explosively*). Paw?

EBEN. Got himself hitched to a female 'bout thirty-five—an' purty, they says . . .

SIMEON (*aghast*). It's a durn lie!

PETER. Who says?

SIMEON. They been stringin' ye!

EBEN. Think I'm a dunce, do ye? The hull village says. The preacher from New Dover, he brung the news—told it t' our preacher—New Dover, that's whar the old loon got himself hitched—that's whar the woman lived—

PETER (*no longer doubting—stunned*). Waal . . . !

SIMEON (*the same*). Waal . . . !

EBEN (*sitting down on a bed—with vicious hatred*). Ain't he a devil out o'hell? It's jest t' spite us—the damned old mule!

PETER (*after a pause*). Everythin'll go t' her now.

SIMEON. Ay-eh. (*A pause—dully*) Waal—if it's done—

PETER. It's done us. (*Pause—then persuasively*) They's gold in the fields o' Californi-a, Sim. No good a-stayin' here now.

SIMEON. Jest what I was a-thinkin'. (*Then with decision*) S'well fust's last! Let's light out and git this mornin'.

PETER. Suits me.

EBEN. Ye must like walkin'.

SIMEON (*sardonically*). If ye'd grow wings on us we'd fly thar!

EBEN. Ye'd like ridin' better—on a boat, wouldn't ye? (*Fumbles in his pocket and takes out a crumpled sheet of foolscap*) Waal, if ye sign this ye kin ride on a boat. I've had it writ out an' ready in case ye'd ever go. It says fur three hundred dollars t' each ye agree yewr shares o' the farm is sold t' me (*They look suspiciously at the paper. A pause.*)

SIMEON (*wonderingly*). But if he's hitched agen—

PETER. An' whar'd yew git that sum o' money, anyways?

EBEN (*cunningly*). I know whar it's hid. I been waitin'—Maw told me. She knew whar it lay fur years, but she was waitin' . . . It's her'n—the money he hoarded from her farm an' hid from Maw. It's my money by rights now.

PETER. Whar's it hid?

EBEN (*cunningly*). Whar yew won't never find it without me. Maw spied on him—'r she'd never knowed. (*A pause. They look at him suspiciously, and he at them.*) Waal, is it fa'r trade?

SIMEON. Dunno.

PETER. Dunno.

SIMEON (*looking at window*). Sky's grayin'.

PETER. Ye better start the fire, Eben.

SIMEON. An' fix some vittles.

EBEN. Ay-eh. (*Then with a forced jocular heartiness*) I'll git ye a good one. If ye're startin' t' hoof it t' Californi-a ye'll need somethin' that'll stick t' yer ribs. (*He turns to the door, adding meaningly*) But ye kin ride on a boat if ye'll swap. (*He stops at the door and pauses. They stare at him.*)

SIMEON (*suspiciously*). Whar was ye all night?

EBEN (*defiantly*). Up t' Min's. (*Then slowly*) Walkin' thar, fust I felt 's if I'd kiss her; then I got a-thinkin' o' what ye'd said o' him an' her an' I says, I'll bust her nose fur that! Then I got t' the village an' heerd the news an' I got madder 'n hell an' run all the way t' Min's not knowin' what I'd do— (*He pauses—then sheepishly but more defiantly*) Waal—when I seen her, I didn't hit her—nor I didn't kiss her nuther—I begun t' beller like a calf an' cuss at the same time, I was so durn mad—an' she got scared—an' I jest grabbed holt an' tuk her! (*Proudly*) Yes, sirree! I tuk her. She may've been his'n—an' your'n, too—but she's mine now!

SIMEON (*dryly*). In love, air yew?

EBEN (*with lofty scorn*). Love! I don't take no stock in sech slop!

PETER (*winking at* SIMEON). Mebbe Eben's aimin t' marry, too.

SIMEON. Min'd make a true faithful he'pmeet! (*They snicker.*)

EBEN. What do I care fur her—'ceptin' she's round an' wa'm? The p'int is she was his'n—an' now she b'longs t' me! (*He goes to the door—then turns—rebelliously*) An' Min hain't sech a bad un. They's worse'n Min in the world, I'll bet ye! Wait'll we see this cow the Old Man's hitched t'! She'll beat Min, I got a notion! (*He starts to go out.*)

SIMEON (*suddenly*). Mebbe ye'll try t' make her your'n, too?

PETER. Ha! (*He gives a sardonic laugh of relish at this idea.*)

EBEN (*spitting with disgust*). Her—here sleepin' with him—stealin' my Maw's farm! I'd as soon pet a skunk 'r kiss a snake! (*He goes out. The two stare after him suspiciously. A pause. They listen to his steps receding.*)

PETER. He's startin' the fire.

SIMEON. I'd like t' ride t' Californi-a—but—

PETER. Min might o' put some scheme in his head.

SIMEON. Mebbe it's all a lie 'bout Paw marryin'. We'd best wait an' see the bride.

PETER. An' don't sign nothin' till we does!

SIMEON. Nor till we've tested it's good money! (*Then with a grin*) But if Paw's hitched we'd be sellin' Eben somethin' we'd never git nohow!

PETER. We'll wait an' see. (*Then with sudden vindictive anger*) An' till he comes, let's yew 'n' me not wuk a lick, let Eben tend to thin's if he's a mind t', let's us jest sleep an' eat an' drink likker an' let the hull damned farm go t' blazes!

SIMEON (*excitedly*). By God, we've 'arned a rest! We'll play rich fur a change. I hain't a-going to stir outa bed till breakfast's ready.

PETER. An' on the table!

SIMEON (*after a pause—thoughtfully*). What d'ye calc'late she'll be like—our new Maw? Like Eben thinks?

PETER. More'n' likely.

SIMEON (*vindictively*). Waal—I hope she's a she-devil that'll make him wish he was dead an' livin' in the pit o' hell fur comfort!

PETER (*fervently*). Amen!

SIMEON (*imitating his father's voice*). "I'm ridin' out t' learn God's message t' me in the spring like the prophets done," he says. I'll bet right then an' thar he knew plumb well he was goin' whorin', the stinkin' old hypocrite!

CURTAIN

The night is dark, but the yard is even darker, shielded by the giant elms from whatever small light stars give. Eben's dual nature is nowhere more evident than in the pleasure and pain with which he reports Ephraim's marriage. On the one hand, he sees an end to the brothers; on the other, he sees the farm slipping away. Still, he has planted the idea of their shipping to California; he knows where the money is. At least the new wife will not have access to it; Eben will have insured his rights as the only blood heir. Time can take care of the rest. Strong wills must be patient wills. He will manage to take the farm as he took Min—by brute force if necessary.

The crude but intuitive Simeon again predicts Eben's future course. Old Ephraim would attempt to seduce Eben's wife were their positions reversed. And as Simeon earlier said, "Dog'll eat dog." If Eben took Min to prove his inheritance, he will as readily take the new wife. Dramatic structure and characterization again and again work cohesive magic as O'Neill draws the net of fate tighter and tighter around Eben.

The half-brothers will sell their share of the farm to Eben. You know it before they do, for they are too dull to realize they would not dare be slugabeds were they to stay on. They fear their father too much to expose themselves to his punishment.

Accusing the old man of hypocrisy, Simeon and Peter "hope" the new wife will make Ephraim's life a living hell. They do not see the wish as a prayer even though it is sealed with a fervent "Amen." "Wifing" and "whoring" are poles apart, but the near-sighted do not make fine distinctions. In their near-sightedness, Simeon and Peter are their father's sons.

SCENE FOUR

Same as Scene Two—shows the interior of the kitchen with a lighted candle on the table. It is gray dawn outside. SIMEON *and* PETER *are just finishing their breakfast.* EBEN *sits before his plate of untouched food, brooding frowningly.*

PETER (*glancing at him rather irritably*). Lookin' glum don't help none.

SIMEON (*sarcastically*). Sorrowin' over his lust o' the flesh!

PETER (*with a grin*). Was she yer fust?

EBEN (*angrily*). None o' yer business. (*A pause*) I was thinkin' o' him. I got a notion he's gittin' near—I kin feel him comin' on like yew kin feel malaria chill afore it takes ye.

PETER. It's too early yet.

SIMEON. Dunno. He'd like t' catch us nappin'—jest t' have somethin' t' hoss us 'round over.

PETER (*mechanically gets to his feet.* SIMEON *does the same*). Waal—let's git t' wuk. (*They both plod mechanically toward the door before they realize. Then they stop short.*)

SIMEON (*grinning*). Ye're a cussed fool, Pete—and I be wuss! Let him see we hain't wukin'! We don't give a durn!

PETER (*as they go back to the table*). Not a damned durn! It'll serve t' show him we're done with him. (*They sit down again.* EBEN *stares from one to the other with surprise.*)

SIMEON (*grins at him*). We're aimin' t' start bein' lilies o' the field.

PETER. Nary a toil 'r spin 'r lick o' wuk do we put in!

SIMEON. Ye're sole owner—till he comes—that's what ye wanted. Waal, ye got t' be sole hand, too.

PETER. The cows air bellerin'. Ye better hustle at the milkin'.

EBEN (*with excited joy*). Ye mean ye'll sign the paper?

SIMEON (*dryly*). Mebbe.

PETER. Mebbe.

SIMEON. We're considerin'. (*Peremptorily*). Ye better git t' wuk.

EBEN (*with queer excitement*). It's Maw's farm agen! It's my farm! Them's my cows! I'll milk my durn fingers off fur cows o' mine! (*He goes out door in rear, they stare after him indifferently.*)

SIMEON. Like his Paw.

PETER. Dead spit 'n' image!

SIMEON. Waal—let dog eat dog! (EBEN *comes out of front door and around the corner of the house. The sky is beginning to grow flushed with sunrise.* EBEN *stops by the gate and stares around him with glowing, possessive eyes. He takes in the whole farm with his embracing glance of desire.*)

EBEN. It's purty! It's damned purty! It's mine! (*He suddenly throws his head back boldly and glares with hard, defiant eyes at the sky.*) Mine, d'ye hear? Mine! (*He turns and walks quickly off left, rear, toward the barn. The two brothers light their pipes.*)

Hypocrisy dotes on quoting Scripture; Simeon and Peter reveal their ability to quote advantageously, at breakfast. Eben's pleasure at the prospect of toiling on his own farm is a desire more deeply rooted in the flesh than was his lust for Min. Again Simeon sees the pattern he has learned to hate in Ephraim, and again he comments on the similarity.

Outside, under the elms, Eben again looks at the sky. Unlike his defensive explanation when he left to "take" Min, his statement now is an oath to that distant, grim God. To achieve his end, Eben will challenge the Almighty Himself.

SIMEON (*putting his muddy boots up on the table, tilting back his chair, and puffing defiantly*). Waal—this air solid comfort—fur once.

PETER. Ay-eh. (*He follows suit. A pause. Unconsciously they both sigh.*)

SIMEON (*suddenly*). He never was much o' a hand at milkin', Eben wa'n't.

PETER (*with a snort*). His hands air like hoofs! (*A pause*)

SIMEON. Reach down the jug thar! Let's take a swaller. I'm feelin' kind o' low.

PETER. Good idee! (*He does so—gets two glasses—they pour out drinks of whisky.*) Here's t' the gold in Californi-a!

SIMEON. An' luck t' find it! (*They drink—puff resolutely—sigh—take their feet down from the table.*)

PETER. Likker don't 'pear t' sot right.

SIMEON. We hain't used t' it this early. (*A pause. They become very restless.*)

PETER. Gittin' close in this kitchen.

SIMEON (*with immense relief*). Let's git a breath o' air. (*They arise briskly and go out rear—appear around house and stop by the gate. They stare up at the sky with a numbed appreciation.*)

PETER. Purty!

SIMEON. Ay-eh. Gold's t' the East now.

PETER. Sun's startin' with us fur the Golden West.

SIMEON (*staring around the farm, his compressed face tightened, unable to conceal his emotion*). Waal—it's our last mornin'—mebbe.

PETER (*the same*). Ay-eh.

SIMEON (*stamps his foot on the earth and addresses it desperately*). Waal—ye've thirty year o' me buried in ye—spread out over ye—blood an' bone an' sweat—rotted away—fertilizin' ye—richin' yer soul—prime manure, by God, that's what I been t' ye!

PETER. Ay-eh! An' me!

SIMEON. An' yew, Peter. (*He sighs—then spits.*) Waal—no use'n cryin' over spilt milk.

PETER. They's gold in the West—an' freedom, mebbe. We been slaves t' stone walls here.

SIMEON (*defiantly*). We hain't nobody's slaves from this out—nor no thin's slaves nuther. (*A pause—restlessly*) Speakin' o' milk, wonder how Eben's managin'?

PETER. I s'pose he's managin'.

SIMEON. Mebbe we'd ought t' help—this once.

PETER. Mebbe. The cows knows us.

SIMEON. An' likes us. They don't know him much.

PETER. An' the hosses, an' pigs, an' chickens. They don't know him much.

SIMEON. They knows us like brothers—an' likes us! (*Proudly*) Hain't we raised 'em t' be fust-rate, number one prize stock?

PETER. We hain't—not no more.

SIMEON (*dully*). I was fergittin'. (*Then resignedly*) Waal, let's go help Eben a spell an' git waked up.

PETER. Suits me. (*They are starting off down left, rear, for the barn when* EBEN *appears from there hurrying toward them, his face excited.*)

Simeon and Peter are creatures of habit. Too long have they been in thrall to this farm to escape its rhythms easily. The unaccustomed leisure, freedom to do as they please are luxuries they are ill-trained to handle. Simeon's desperate statement to the land is regretful. Were he and Peter less hypocritical than they are, they would reveal the thought that plagues them both: they are, like Esau, prepared to sell their birthright for a mess of pottage only to find they do not despise it as much as they thought. Such near-realizations are too powerful to be dealt with now, however, and they turn to the only freedom from thought they know: the bondage of work. Their short-sightedness has played them false again.

EBEN (*breathlessly*). Waal—thar they be! The old mule an' the bride! I seen 'em from the barn down below at the turnin'.

PETER. How could ye tell that far?

EBEN. Hain't I as far-sight as he's near-sight? Don't I know the mare 'n' buggy, an' two people settin' in it? Who else . . . ? An' I tell ye I kin feel 'em a-comin', too! (*He squirms as if he had the itch.*)

PETER (*beginning to be angry*). Waal—let him do his own unhitchin'!

SIMEON (*angry in his turn*). Let's hustle in an' git our bundles an' be a-goin' as he's a-comin'. I don't want never t' step inside the door agen arter he's back. (*They both start back around the corner of the house.* EBEN *follows them.*)

EBEN (*anxiously*). Will ye sign it afore ye go?

PETER. Let's see the color o' the old skinflint's money an' we'll sign. (*They disappear left. The two brothers clump upstairs to get their bundles.* EBEN *appears in the kitchen, runs to window, peers out, comes back and pulls up a strip of flooring in under stove, takes out a canvas bag and puts it on table, then sets the floorboard back in place. The two brothers appear a moment after. They carry old carpetbags.*)

EBEN (*puts his hand on bag guardingly*). Have ye signed?

SIMEON (*shows paper in his hand*). Ay-eh. (*Greedily*) Be that the money?

EBEN (*opens bag and pours out pile of twenty-dollar gold pieces*). Twenty-dollar pieces—thirty of 'em. Count 'em. (*Peter does so, arranging them in stacks of five, biting one or two to test them.*)

PETER. Six hundred. (*He puts them in bag and puts it inside his shirt carefully.*)

SIMEON (*handing paper to* EBEN). Har ye be.

EBEN (*after a glance, folds it carefully and hides it under his shirt—gratefully*). Thank yew.

PETER. Thank yew fur the ride.

SIMEON. We'll send ye a lump o' gold fur Christmas. (*A pause.* EBEN *stares at them and they at him.*)

PETER (*awkwardly*). Waal—we're a-goin'.

SIMEON. Comin' out t' the yard?

EBEN. No. I'm waitin' in here a spell. (*Another silence. The brothers edge awkwardly to door in rear—then turn and stand.*)

SIMEON. Waal—good-by.

PETER. Good-by.

EBEN. Good-by. (*They go out. He sits down at the table, faces the stove and pulls out the paper. He looks from it to the stove. His face, lighted up by the shaft of sunlight from the window, has an expression of trance. His lips move. The two brothers come out to the gate.*)

The far-sighted Eben not only reports the imminent arrival of Ephraim but also extracts the signatures from his near-sighted brothers. For thirty pieces of gold (O'Neill plays the biblical symbolism for all it's worth) the sons sell their one possibility of salvation, the farm. Cut loose from the only important thing in their lives, they will wander out of the play, like Judas, possibly to hang on some distant tree in their dream of El Dorado for which they have betrayed the land.

Eben's lips move as he sits in the kitchen as if in a "trance." What does he say to the restless spirit of the woman who haunts this place? As yet, he is not victorious, he has not defeated Ephraim, but the battle lines are now more even, the odds not quite so great.

PETER (*looking off toward barn*). Thar he be—unhitchin'.

SIMEON (*with a chuckle*). I'll bet ye he's riled!

PETER. An' thar she be.

SIMEON. Let's wait 'n' see what our new Maw looks like.

PETER (*with a grin*). An' give him our partin' cuss!

SIMEON (*grinning*). I feel like raisin' fun. I feel light in my head an' feet.

PETER. Me, too. I feel like laffin' till I'd split up the middle.

SIMEON. Reckon it's the likker?

PETER. No. My feet feel itchin' t' walk an' walk—an' jump high over thin's—an'. . . .

SIMEON. Dance? (*A pause*)

PETER (*puzzled*). It's plumb onnateral.

SIMEON (*a light coming over his face*). I calc'late it's 'cause school's out. It's holiday. Fur once we're free!

PETER (*dazedly*). Free?

SIMEON. The halter's broke—the harness is busted—the fence bars is down—the stone walls air crumblin' an' tumblin'! We'll be kickin' up an' tearin' away down the road!

PETER (*drawing a deep breath—oratorically*). Anybody that wants this stinkin' old rock-pile of a farm kin hev it. 'T ain't our'n, no sirree!

SIMEON (*takes the gate off its hinges and puts it under his arm*). We harby 'bolishes shet gates, an' open gates, an' all gates, by thunder!

PETER. We'll take it with us fur luck an' let 'er sail free down some river.

SIMEON (*as a sound of voices comes from left, rear*). Har they comes! (*The two brothers congeal into two stiff, grim-visaged statues.*)

Simeon and Peter are as rebellious as school boys suddenly set free. The gate represents that freedom; it will never imprison them inside the stone walls again, but they are wrong in assuming that the stone walls are crumbling. Wherever they go, the stones will accompany them, for the stones are representative of more than the farm and Ephraim. They belong to this land, to the cultural tradition of the father, to the stern God represented in the stones. The walls are a creation forced by Ephraim but embodying a part of the sons. Every stone piled on another is a testament, a confession, and a commitment to this land wherein the New England God moved and worked his hard, lonely, but relentless miracle—that of incorporating the worshipper into the godhead, of making him a part of the godhead through his participation in the mass of work with and for the representational stones.

(EPHRAIM CABOT *and* ABBIE PUTNAM *come in.* CABOT *is seventy-five, tall and gaunt, with great, wiry, concentrated power, but stoop-shouldered from toil. His face is as hard as if it were hewn out of a boulder, yet there is a weakness in it, a petty pride in its own narrow strength. His eyes are small, close together, and extremely near-sighted, blinking continually in the effort to focus on objects, their stare having a straining, ingrowing quality. He is dressed in his dismal black Sunday suit.* ABBIE *is thirty-five, buxom, full of vitality. Her round face is pretty but marred by its rather gross sensuality. There is strength and obstinacy in her jaw, a hard determination in her eyes, and about her whole personality the same unsettled, untamed, desperate quality which is so apparent in* EBEN.)

Ephraim has dominated the play through three and a third scenes, though present in none of them. His appearance is much as you have expected, but it is somehow different. Old but strong, hard of face, and proud—these things he is. But he is a true picture, not a romanticized one. There is "a weakness" in his face, "a petty pride." His eyes are "small, close together, and extremely nearsighted, blinking continuously." Abbie Putnam is buxom, vital, strong, determined, and pretty—but she too is marred. Her face possesses a "rather gross sensuality" and she has an "unsettled, untamed, desperate quality." In both characters, strength is tinctured with weakness, the desirable is flawed by the undesirable; good qualities possessed in abundance are minimized by a small excess of evil qualities in tension with the good. In short, the old man and his young wife are realistically conceived and realistically drawn. They seem uncommonly "real" rather than dramatic creations designed merely to forward the plot.

CABOT (*as they enter—a queer strangled emotion in his dry cracking voice*). Har we be t' hum, Abbie.

ABBIE (*with lust for the word*). Hum! (*Her eyes gloating on the house without seeming to see the two stiff figures at the gate*) It's purty—purty! I can't b'lieve it's r'ally mine.

CABOT (*sharply*). Yewr'n? Mine! (*He stares at her penetratingly, she stares back. He adds relentingly*) Our'n—mebbe! It was lonesome too long. I was growin' old in the spring. A hum's got t' hev a woman.

ABBIE (*her voice taking possession*). A woman's got t' hev a hum!

Abbie "lusts" after the word *hum* (home) and sees the decaying house and the giant elms as "purty," a description entailing more than a visual response. Hers is a need for the concept of "home" and you realize immediately why she married an old, near-sighted dirt farmer when her young vitality could have been more ambitious. *This* is her ambition: this house, this land. However, old Cabot is immediately unwilling to relinquish the house, and Abbie is immediately greedy for possession.

From this moment, you know theirs can only be an unhappy life under these great trees.

CABOT (*nodding uncertainly*). Ay-eh. (*Then irritably*) Whar be they? Ain't thar nobody about—'r wukin'—'r nothin'?

ABBIE (*sees the brothers. She returns their stare of cold appraising contempt with interest—slowly*). Thar's two men loafin' at the gate an' starin' at me like a couple o' strayed hogs.

CABOT (*straining his eyes*). I kin see 'em—but I can't make out. . . .

SIMEON. It's Simeon.

PETER. It's Peter.

CABOT (*exploding*). Why hain't ye wukin'?

SIMEON (*dryly*). We're waitin' t' welcome ye hum—yew an' the bride!

CABOT (*confusedly*). Huh? Waal—this be yer new Maw, boys. (*She stares at them and they at her.*)

SIMEON (*turns away and spits contemptuously*). I see her!

PETER (*spits also*). An' I see her!

ABBIE (*with the conqueror's conscious superiority*). I'll go in an' looks at *my* house. (*She goes slowly around to porch.*)

SIMEON (*with a snort*). *Her* house!

PETER (*calls after her*). Ye'll find Eben inside. Ye better not tell him it's *yewr* house.

ABBIE (*mouthing the name*). Eben. (*Then quietly*) I'll tell Eben.

CABOT (*with a contemptuous sneer*). Ye needn't heed Eben. Eben's a dumb fool—like his Maw—soft an' simple!

SIMEON (*with his sardonic burst of laughter*). Ha! Eben's a chip o' yew—spit 'n' image—hard 'n' bitter's a hickory tree! Dog'll eat dog. He'll eat ye yet, old man!

CABOT (*commandingly*). Ye git t' wuk!

SIMEON (*as ABBIE disappears in house—winks at PETER and says tauntingly*). So that thar's our new Maw, be it? Whar in hell did ye dig her up? (*He and PETER laugh.*)

PETER. Ha! Ye'd better turn her in the pen with the other sows. (*They laugh uproariously, slapping their thighs.*)

CABOT (*so amazed at their effrontery that he stutters in confusion*). Simeon! Peter! What's come over ye? Air ye drunk?

SIMEON. We're free, old man—free o' yew an' the hull damned farm! (*They grow more and more hilarious and excited.*)

PETER. An' we're startin' out fur the gold fields o' Californi-a!

SIMEON. Ye kin take this place an' burn it!

PETER. An' bury it—fur all we cares!

SIMEON. We're free, old man! (*He cuts a caper.*)

PETER. Free! (*He gives a kick in the air.*)

SIMEON (*in a frenzy*). Whoop!

PETER. Whoop! (*They do an absurd Indian war dance about the old man who is petrified between rage and fear that they are insane.*)

SIMEON. We're free as Injuns! Lucky we don't skulp ye!

PETER. An' burn yer barn an' kill the stock!

SIMEON. An' rape yer new woman! Whoop! (*He and* PETER *stop their dance, holding their sides, rocking with wild laughter.*)

CABOT (*edging away*). Lust fur gold—fur the sinful, easy gold o' Californi-a! It's made ye mad!

SIMEON (*tauntingly*). Wouldn't ye like us to send ye back some sinful gold, ye old sinner?

PETER. They's gold besides what's in Californi-a! (*He retreats back beyond the vision of the old man and takes the bag of money and flaunts it in the air above his head, laughing.*)

SIMEON. And sinfuller, too!

PETER. We'll be voyagin' on the sea! Whoop! (*He leaps up and down.*)

SIMEON. Livin' free! Whoop! (*He leaps in turn.*)

CABOT (*suddenly roaring with rage*). My cuss on ye!

SIMEON. Take our'n in trade fur it! Whoop!

CABOT. I'll hev ye both chained up in the asylum!

PETER. Ye old skinflint! Good-by!

SIMEON. Ye old blood sucker! Good-by!

CABOT. Go afore I . . . !

PETER. Whoop! (*He picks a stone from the road.* SIMEON *does the same.*)

SIMEON. Maw'll be in the parlor.

PETER. Ay-eh! One! Two!

CABOT (*frightened*). What air ye . . . ?

PETER. Three! (*They both throw the stones, hitting the parlor window with a crash of glass, tearing the shade.*)

SIMEON. Whoop!

PETER. Whoop!

CABOT (*in a fury now, rushing toward them*). If I kin lay hands on ye—I'll break yer bones fur ye! (*But they beat a capering retreat before him,* SIMEON *with the gate still under his arm.* CABOT *comes back, panting with impotent rage. Their voices as they go off take up the song of the gold-seekers to the old tune of "Oh, Susannah!"*)

"I jumped aboard the Liza ship,
And traveled on the sea,
And every time I thought of home
I wished it wasn't me!
Oh! Californi-a,
That's the land fur me!
I'm off to Californi-a!
With my wash bowl on my knee."

Walking into *her* home, Abbie will "tell Eben" it is her house. She will set her will against Eben's, against the restless spirit of Eben's mother. Conflicts are apparent; complications, symbolically massive. And Simeon reminds you again that Eben and Ephraim are equally hard, equally bitter. Their final, rebellious act carries their curse into the house, a rock into the parlor, a god-stone into the realm of the restless dead.

(*In the meantime, the window of the upper bedroom on right is raised and* ABBIE *sticks her head out. She looks down at* CABOT—*with a sigh of relief*).

ABBIE. Waal—that's the last o' them two, hain't it? (*He doesn't answer. Then in possessive tones*) This here's a nice bedroom, Ephraim. It's a r'al nice bed. Is it my room, Ephraim?

CABOT (*grimly—without looking up*). Our'n! (*She cannot control a grimace of aversion and pulls back her head slowly and shuts the window. A sudden horrible thought seems to enter* CABOT'S *head.*) They been up to somethin'! Mebbe—mebbe they've pizened the stock—'r somethin'! (*He almost runs off down toward the barn. A moment later the kitchen door is slowly pushed open and* ABBIE *enters. For a moment she stands looking at* EBEN. *He does not notice her at first. Her eyes take him in penetratingly with a calculating appraisal of his strength as against hers. But under this her desire is dimly awakened by his youth and good looks. Suddenly he becomes conscious of her presence and looks up. Their eyes meet. He leaps to his feet, glowering at her speechlessly.*)

ABBIE (*in her most seductive tones which she uses all through this scene*). Be you—Eben? I'm Abbie—(*She laughs.*) I mean, I'm yer new Maw.

EBEN (*viciously*). No, damn ye!

ABBIE (*as if she hadn't heard—with a queer smile*). Yer Paw's spoke a lot o' yew. . . .

EBEN. Ha!

ABBIE. Ye mustn't mind him. He's an old man. (*A long pause. They stare at each other.*) I don't want t' pretend playin' Maw t' ye, Eben. (*Admiringly*) Ye're too big an' too strong fur that. I want t' be frens with ye. Mebbe with me fur a fren ye'd find ye'd like livin' here better. I kin make it easy fur ye with him, mebbe. (*With a scornful sense of power*) I calc'late I kin git him t' do most anythin' fur me.

EBEN (*with bitter scorn*). Ha! (*They stare again,* EBEN *obscurely moved, physically attracted to her—in forced stilted tones*) Yew kin go t' the devil!

ABBIE (*calmly*). If cussin' me does ye good, cuss all ye've a mind t'. I'm all prepared t' have ye agin me—at fust. I don't blame ye nuther. I'd feel the same at any stranger comin' t' take my Maw's place. (*He shudders. She is watching him carefully.*) Ye must've cared a lot fur yewr Maw, didn't ye? My Maw died afore I'd growed. I don't remember her none. (*A pause*) But yew won't hate me long, Eben. I'm not the wust in the world—an' yew an' me've got a lot in common. I kin tell that by lookin' at ye. Waal—I've had a hard life, too—oceans o' trouble an' nuthin' but wuk fur reward. I was a orphan early an' had t' wuk fur others in other folks' hums. Then I married an' he turned out a drunken spreer an' so he had to wuk fur others an' me too agen in other folks' hums, an' the baby died, an' my husband got sick an' died too, an' I was glad sayin' now I'm free fur once, on'y I diskivered right away all I was free fur was t' wuk agen in other folks' hums, doin' other folks' wuk till I'd most give up hope o' ever doin' my own wuk in my own hum, an' then your Paw come. . . . (CABOT *appears returning from the barn. He comes to the gate and looks down the road the brothers have gone. A faint strain of their retreating voices is heard:* "Oh, Californi-a! That's the place for me." *He stands glowering, his fist clenched, his face grim with rage.*)

EBEN (*fighting against his growing attraction and sympathy—harshly*). An' bought yew—like a harlot! (*She is stung and flushes angrily. She has been sincerely moved by the recital of her troubles. He adds furiously*) An' the price he's payin' ye—this farm—was my Maw's, damn ye!—an' mine now!

ABBIE (*with a cool laugh of confidence*). Yewr'n? We'll see 'bout that! (*Then strongly*) Waal—what if I did need a hum? What else'd I marry an old man like him fur?

EBEN (*maliciously*). I'll tell him ye said that!

ABBIE (*smiling*). I'll say ye're lyin' a-purpose—an' he'll drive ye off the place!

EBEN. Ye devil!

ABBIE (*defying him*). This be my farm—this be my hum—this be my kitchen—!

EBEN (*furiously, as if he were going to attack her*). Shut up, damn ye!

ABBIE (*walks up to him—a queer coarse expression of desire in her face and body—slowly*). An' upstairs—that be my bedroom—an' my bed! (*He stares into her eyes, terribly confused and torn. She adds softly*) I hain't bad nor mean—'ceptin' fur an enemy—but I got t' fight fur what's due me out o' life, if I ever 'spect t' git it. (*Then putting her hand on his arm—seductively*) Let's yew 'n' me be frens, Eben.

EBEN (*stupidly—as if hypnotized*). Ay-eh. (*Then furiously flinging off her arm*) No, ye durned old witch! I hate ye! (*He rushes out the door.*)

ABBIE (*looks after him smiling satisfiedly—then half to herself, mouthing the word*). Eben's nice. (*She looks at the table, proudly.*) I'll wash up my dishes now.

Abbie has not sought the realm of death in the house, however; she is in the bedroom, a place of life and the getting of life. That she must share that life with old Ephraim disgusts her, but such was her bargain. Eben and Abbie are immediately drawn to each other by a lust for life. By her account, they are alike. Each wants to work for his own home; each has been forced into a life of servitude in someone else's home. Now, fate-drawn, they must both work for this home, each claiming it, each seeing the other as the eventual victor. And all the while, there is the magnetic response that suggests that their work could be a mutual effort but for Ephraim to whom they are bound by ties stronger than home, ties as strong and as strange as the rocky land.

(EBEN *appears outside, slamming the door behind him. He comes around corner, stops on seeing his father, and stands staring at him with hate.*)

CABOT (*raising his arms to heaven in the fury he can no longer control*). Lord God o' Hosts, smite the undutiful sons with Thy wust cuss!

EBEN (*breaking in violently*). Yew 'n' yewr God! Allus cussin' folks—allus naggin' 'em!

CABOT (*oblivious to him—summoningly*). God o' the old! God o' the lonesome!

EBEN (*mockingly*). Naggin' His sheep t' sin! T' hell with yewr God! (CABOT *turns. He and* EBEN *glower at each other.*)

CABOT (*harshly*). So it's yew. I might've knowed it. (*Shaking his finger threateningly at him*) Blasphemin' fool! (*Then quickly*) Why hain't ye t' wuk?

EBEN. Why hain't yew? They've went. I can't wuk it all alone.

CABOT (*contemptuously*). Nor noways! I'm wuth ten o' ye yit, old 's I be! Ye'll never be more'n half a man! (*Then, matter-of-factly*) Waal—let's git t' the barn. (*They go. A last faint note of the "Californi-a" song is heard from the distance.* ABBIE *is washing her dishes.*)

CURTAIN

Eben, the dramatic hero, and Ephraim, the tragic hero, come face to face across the tragic force that moves each man to his separate disaster: the hard and lonesome God of the old. Ephraim speaks to that God in an intensely personal way. He is the God of the hills and valleys, the land and the rocks, the barren, lonesome God that grimly demands and ungraciously gives.

From the barn, that God calls the old and the young, locked in their desperate refusal to recognize themselves in each other. In the house, Abbie washes *her* dishes, the dishes from which she will feed these men bread even as her presence feeds their lonely strengths and fears and lusts for life.

PART TWO

Scene One

The exterior of the farmhouse, as in Part One—a hot Sunday afternoon two months later. ABBIE, dressed in her best, is discovered sitting in a rocker at the end of the porch. She rocks listlessly, enervated by the heat, staring in front of her with bored, half-closed eyes.

EBEN *sticks his head out of his bedroom window. He looks around furtively and tries to see—or hear—if anyone is on the porch, but although he has been careful to make no noise,* ABBIE *has sensed his movement. She stops rocking, her face grows animated and eager, she waits attentively.* EBEN *seems to feel her presence, he scowls back his thoughts of her and spits with exaggerated disdain—then withdraws back into the room.* ABBIE *waits, holding her breath as she listens with passionate eagerness for every sound within the house.*

EBEN *comes out. Their eyes meet. His falter, he is confused, he turns away and slams the door resentfully. At this gesture,* ABBIE *laughs tantalizingly, amused but at the same time piqued and irritated. He scowls, strides off the porch to the path and starts to walk past her to the road with a grand swagger of ignoring her existence. He is dressed in his store suit, spruced up, his face shines from soap and water.* ABBIE *leans forward on her chair, her eyes hard and angry now, and, as he passes her, gives a sneering, taunting chuckle.*

EBEN (*stung—turns on her furiously*). What air yew cacklin' 'bout?

ABBIE (*triumphant*). Yew!

EBEN. What about me?

ABBIE. Ye look all slicked up like a prize bull.

EBEN (*with a sneer*). Waal—ye hain't so durned purty yerself, be ye? (*They stare into each other's eyes, his held by hers in spite of himself, hers glowingly possessive. Their physical attraction becomes a palpable force quivering in the hot air.*)

ABBIE (*softly*). Ye don't mean that, Eben. Ye may think ye mean it, mebbe, but ye don't. Ye can't. It's agin nature, Eben. Ye been fightin' yer nature ever since the day I come—tryin' t' tell yerself I hain't purty t'ye. (*She laughs a low humid laugh without taking her eyes from his. A pause—her body squirms desirously—she murmurs languorously*) Hain't the sun strong an' hot? Ye kin feel it burnin' into the earth—Nature—makin' thin's grow—bigger 'n' bigger—burnin' inside ye—makin' ye want t' grow—into somethin' else—till ye're jined with it—an' it's your'n—but it owns ye, too—an' makes ye grow bigger—like a tree—like them elums—(*She laughs again softly, holding his eyes. He takes a step toward her, compelled against his will.*) Nature'll beat ye, Eben. Ye might's well own up t' it fust 's last.

EBEN (*trying to break from her spell—confusedly*). If Paw'd hear ye goin' on. . . . (*Resentfully*) But ye've made such a damned idjit out o' the old devil . . . ! (ABBIE *laughs.*)

ABBIE. Waal—hain't it easier fur yew with him changed softer?

EBEN (*defiantly*). No. I'm fightin' him—fightin' yew—fightin' fur Maw's rights t' her hum! (*This breaks her spell for him. He glowers at her.*) An' I'm onto ye. Ye hain't foolin' me a mite. Ye're aimin' t' swaller up everythin' an' make it your'n. Waal, you'll find I'm a heap sight bigger hunk nor yew kin chew! (*He turns from her with a sneer.*)

ABBIE (*trying to regain her ascendancy—seductively*). Eben!

EBEN. Leave me be! (*He starts to walk away.*)

ABBIE (*more commandingly*). Eben!

EBEN (*stops—resentfully*). What d'ye want?

ABBIE (*trying to conceal a growing excitement*). Whar air ye goin'?

EBEN (*with malicious nonchalance*). Oh—up the road a spell.

ABBIE. T' the village?

EBEN (*airily*). Mebbe.

ABBIE (*excitedly*). T' see that Min, I s'pose?

EBEN. Mebbe.

ABBIE (*weakly*). What d'ye want t' waste time on her fur?

EBEN (*revenging himself now—grinning at her*). Ye can't beat Nature, didn't ye say? (*He laughs and again starts to walk away.*)

ABBIE (*bursting out*). An ugly old hake!

EBEN (*with a tantalizing sneer*). She's purtier'n yew be!

ABBIE. That every wuthless drunk in the country has. . . .

EBEN (*tauntingly*). Mebbe—but she's better'n yew. She owns up fa'r 'n' squar' t' her doin's.

ABBIE (*furiously*). Don't ye dare compare. . . .

EBEN. She don't go sneakin' an' stealin'—what's mine.

ABBIE (*savagely seizing on his weak point*). Your'n? Yew mean—my farm?

EBEN. I mean the farm yew sold yerself fur like any other whore—my farm!

ABBIE (*stung—fiercely*). Ye'll never live t' see the day when even a stinkin' weed on it'll belong t' ye! (*Then in a scream*) Git out o' my sight! Go on t' yer slut—disgracin' yer Paw 'n' me! I'll git yer Paw t' horsewhip ye off the place if I want t'! Ye're only livin' here cause I tolerate ye! Git along! I hate the sight o' ye! (*She stops, panting and glaring at him.*)

EBEN (*returning her glance in kind*). An' I hate the sight o' yew! (*He turns and strides off up the road. She follows his retreating figure with concentrated hate.*)

Part Two develops the greed and lust (or is it love?) between Abbie and Eben. His role as a dramatic hero becomes stronger while Ephraim's role as a tragic hero becomes more difficult to understand because he is removed from most of the action, sundered from life and withdrawn into the lonely world of his God. The tragic element intensifies through his withdrawal from human life, his immersion in the natural life of cattle and the bare rocks of his New England farm.

Scene One opens more on the absence of Ephraim than on the presence of Abbie and Eben, though they are the center of physical action. The awareness of physical proximity has grown between them; they are like animals placed within range of each other but separated by a wall—the stone wall of Ephraim. The "Nature" Abbie feels burning into her through the Sunday sun, the heat of desire she voices—these are the driving forces that sent Ephraim out "t' learn God's message," and they speak loudly now as Abbie assures Eben that "Nature'll beat ye."

Nature wars within both Eben and Abbie. She wants Eben and the farm; he wants the farm and her. That they see no reconciliation in their joint desires indicates a trained restraint if not a basic goodness in them. Abbie is no more jealous of Min than Eben is of his father; still, unable to voice these realities, each spitefully and possessively uses the farm as the apparent battleground until hate actually does exist.

(Old CABOT *appears coming up from the barn. The hard, grim expression of his face has changed. He seems in some queer way softened, mellowed. His eyes have taken on a strange, incongruous dreamy quality. Yet there is not a hint of physical weakness about him—rather he looks more robust and younger.* ABBIE *sees him and turns away quickly with unconcealed aversion. He comes slowly up to her.*)

CABOT (*mildly*). War yew an' Eben quarrelin' agen?

ABBIE (*shortly*). No.

CABOT. Ye was talkin' a'mighty loud. (*He sits down on the edge of porch.*)

ABBIE (*snappishly*). If ye heerd us they hain't no need askin' questions.

CABOT. I didn't hear what ye said.

ABBIE (*relieved*). Waal—it wa'n't nothin' t' speak on.

CABOT (*after a pause*). Eben's queer.

ABBIE (*bitterly*). He's the dead spit 'n' image o' yew!

CABOT (*queerly interested*). D'ye think so, Abbie? (*After a pause, ruminatingly*) Me 'n' Eben's allus fit 'n' fit. I never could b'ar him noways. He's so thunderin' soft—like his Maw.

ABBIE (*scornfully*). Ay-eh! 'Bout as soft as yew be!

CABOT (*as if he hadn't heard*). Mebbe I been too hard on him.

ABBIE (*jeeringly*). Waal—ye're gittin' soft now—soft as slop! That's what Eben was sayin'.

CABOT (*his face instantly grim and ominous*). Eben was sayin'? Waal, he'd best not do nothin' t' try me 'r he'll soon diskiver. . . . (*A pause. She keeps her face turned away. His gradually softens. He stares up at the sky.*) Purty, hain't it?

ABBIE (*crossly*). I don't see nothin' purty.

CABOT. The sky. Feels like a wa'm field up thar.

ABBIE (*sarcastically*). Air yew aimin' t' buy up over the farm too? (*She snickers contemptuously.*)

CABOT (*strangely*). I'd like t' own my place up thar. (*A pause*) I'm gittin' old, Abbie. I'm gittin' ripe on the bough. (*A pause. She stares at him mystified. He goes on.*) It's allus lonesome cold in the house—even when it's bilin' hot outside. Hain't yew noticed?

ABBIE. No.

CABOT. It's wa'm down t'the barn—nice smellin' an' warm—with the cows. (*A pause*) Cows is queer.

ABBIE. Like yew?

CABOT. Like Eben. (*A pause*) I'm gittin' t' feel resigned t' Eben—jest as I got t' feel 'bout his Maw. I'm gittin' t' learn to b'ar his softness—jest like her'n. I calc'late I c'd a'most take t' him—if he wa'n't sech a dumb fool! (*A pause*) I s'pose it's old age a'creepin' in my bones.

ABBIE (*indifferently*). Waal—ye hain't dead yet.

CABOT (*roused*). No, I haint, yew bet—not by a hell of a sight—I'm sound 'n' tough as hickory! (*Then moodily*) But arter three score and ten the Lord warns ye t' prepare. (*A pause*) That's why Eben's come in my head. Now that his cussed sinful brothers is gone their path t' hell, they's no one left but Eben.

Ephraim is a "more robust and younger" man as he comes from the barn. Summer, that fecund, sultry time of excess, hangs heavy under the elms, lies in pools of shadow on the gray porch.

Simeon's charge that Eben is Ephraim's "spit 'n' image" has become Abbie's awareness, an awareness that, voiced, makes Ephraim "queerly interested." Abandoned by Simeon and Peter, Ephraim has seen more virtue in Eben, Eben the soft one, Eben the son of a soft mother. Yet there is a bond Ephraim does not understand. He only knows he grows old, that he does not yet "own my place up thar." How does one buy such a place? For a man, the price is children, children who will carry on the name, who will work the land, who will follow the tradition of their father. Ephraim's house is cold; life does not stir there now; he finds it in the barn where warmth and natural smells accompany the natural actions of the cattle. In the eternal patterns, they violate no natural laws, are possessed of no emotional necessities. Ephraim can understand the ways of Nature without understanding his need to bring those ways into his house. Such near-sightedness has flawed his life. Here, briefly, he seems ready to understand that flaw, but Abbie's needs are powerful. She sees his growing emotional awareness as a threat to her future.

ABBIE (*resentfully*). They's me, hain't they? (*Agitatedly*) What's all this sudden likin' ye've tuk to Eben? Why don't ye say nothin' 'bout me? Hain't I yer lawful wife?

CABOT (*simply*), Ay-eh. Ye be. (*A pause—he stares at her desirously—his eyes grow avid—then with a sudden movement he seizes her hands and squeezes them, declaiming in a queer camp-meeting preacher's tempo*) Yew air my Rose o' Sharon! Behold, yew air fair; yer eyes air doves; yer lips air like scarlet; yer two breasts air like two fawns; yer navel be like a round goblet; yer belly be like a heap o' wheat. . . . (*He covers her hand with kisses. She does not seem to notice. She stares before her with hard angry eyes.*)

ABBIE (*jerking her hands away—harshly*). So ye're plannin' t' leave the farm t' Eben, air ye?

CABOT (*dazedly*). Leave . . . ? (*Then with resentful obstinacy*) I hain't a-givin' it t' no one!

ABBIE (*remorselessly*). Ye can't take it with ye.

CABOT (*thinks a moment—then reluctantly*). No, I calc'late not. (*After a pause— with a strange passion*) But if I could, I would, by the Etarnal! 'R if I could, in my dyin' hour, I'd set it afire an' watch it burn—this house an' every ear o' corn an' every tree down t' the last blade o' hay! I'd sit an' know it was all a-dying with me an' no one else'd ever own what was mine, what I'd made out o' nothin' with my own sweat 'n' blood! (*A pause—then he adds with a queer affection*) 'Ceptin' the cows. Them I'd turn free.

ABBIE (*harshly*). An' me?

CABOT (*with a queer smile*). Ye'd be turned free, too.

Abbie is a sensual, vital woman; Ephraim is a robust, vigorous man still capable of the natural demands. His biblical description of his Rose of Sharon is sensual and filled with the hurtful needs of his flesh. She is his land; she is his possession that he hates to think of leaving as much as any of the rest of his world. The farm could be burned, his inanimate possessions removed from the grasp of the world, but his cattle (those fertile, living creatures of new life) would have to be freed into the natural order of things—as would Abbie. She too is a breeding animal, the flesh wherein new flesh may be seeded and caused to grow.

ABBIE (*furiously*). So that's the thanks I git fur marryin' ye—t' have ye change kind to Eben who hates ye, an' talk o' turnin' me out in the road.

CABOT (*hastily*). Abbie! Ye know I wa'n't. . . .

ABBIE (*vengefully*). Just let me tell ye a thing or two 'bout Eben! Whar's he gone? T' see that harlot, Min! I tried fur t' stop him. Disgracin' yew an' me—on the Sabbath, too!

CABOT (*rather guiltily*). He's a sinner—nateral-born. It's lust eatin' his heart.

ABBIE (*enraged beyond endurance—wildly vindictive*). An' his lust fur me! Kin ye find excuses fur that?

CABOT (*stares at her—after a dead pause*). Lust—fur yew?

ABBIE (*defiantly*). He was tryin' t' make love t' me—when ye heerd us quarrelin'.

CABOT (*stares at her—then a terrible expression of rage comes over his face—he springs to his feet shaking all over*). By the A'mighty God—I'll end him!

ABBIE (*frightened now for* EBEN). No! Don't ye!

CABOT (*violently*). I'll git the shotgun an' blow his soft brains t' the top o' them elums!

ABBIE (*throwing her arms around him*). No, Ephraim!

CABOT (*pushing her away violently*). I will, by God!

ABBIE (*in a quieting tone*). Listen, Ephraim. 'Twa'n't nothin' bad—on'y a boy's foolin'—'twa'n't meant serious—jest jokin' an' teasin'. . . .

CABOT. Then why did ye say—lust?

ABBIE. It must hev sounded wusser'n I meant. An' I was mad thinkin'—ye'd leave him the farm.

CABOT (*quieter but still grim and cruel*). Waal then, I'll horsewhip him off the place if that much'll content ye.

ABBIE (*reaching out and taking his hand*). No. Don't think o' me! Ye mustn't drive him off. 'Tain't sensible. Who'll ye get to help ye on the farm? They's no one here-abouts.

CABOT (*considers this—then nodding his appreciation*). Ye got a head on ye. (*Then irritably*) Waal, let him stay. (*He sits down on the edge of the porch. She sits beside him. He murmurs contemptuously*) I oughtn't t' git riled so—at that 'ere fool calf. (*A pause*) But har's the p'int. What son o' mine'll keep on here t' the farm—when the Lord does call me? Simeon an' Peter air gone t' hell—an' Eben's follerin' 'em.

ABBIE. They's me.

CABOT. Ye're on'y a woman.

ABBIE. I'm yewr wife.

CABOT. That hain't me. A son is me—my blood—mine. Mine ought t' git mine. An' then it's still mine—even though I be six foot under. D'ye see?

ABBIE (*giving him a look of hatred*). Ay-eh. I see. (*She becomes very thoughtful, her face growing shrewd, her eyes studying CABOT craftily.*)

CABOT. I'm gittin' old—ripe on the bough. (*Then with a sudden forced reassurance*) Not but what I hain't a hard nut t' crack even yet—an' fur many a year t' come! By the Etarnal, I kin break most o' the young fellers' backs at any kind o' work any day o' the year!

ABBIE (*suddenly*). Mebbe the Lord'll give us a son.

CABOT (*turns and stares at her eagerly*). Ye mean—a son—t' me 'n' yew?

ABBIE (*with a cajoling smile*). Ye're a strong man yet, hain't ye? 'Tain't noways impossible, be it? We know that. Why d'ye stare so? Hain't ye never thought o' that afore? I been thinkin' o' it all along. Ay-eh—an' I been prayin' it'd happen, too.

CABOT (*his face growing full of joyous pride and a sort of religious ecstasy*). Ye been prayin', Abbie?—fur a son?—t' us?

ABBIE. Ay-eh. (*With a grim resolution*) I want a son now.

CABOT (*excitedly clutching both of her hands in his*). It'd be the blessin' o' God, Abbie—the blessin' o' God Almighty on me—in my old age—in my lonesomeness! They hain't nothin' I wouldn't do fur ye then, Abbie. Ye'd hev on'y t' ask it—anythin' ye'd a mind t'!

ABBIE (*interrupting*). Would ye will the farm t' me then—t' me an' it. . . ?

CABOT (*vehemently*). I'd do anythin' ye axed, I tell ye! I swar it! May I be everlastin' damned t' hell if I wouldn't! (*He sinks to his knees pulling her down with him. He trembles all over with the fervor of his hopes.*) Pray t' the Lord agen, Abbie. It's the Sabbath! I'll jine ye! Two prayers air better nor one. "An' God hearkened unto Rachel"! An' God hearkened unto Abbie! Pray, Abbie! Pray fur him to hearken! (*He bows his head, mumbling. She pretends to do likewise but gives him a side glance of scorn and triumph.*)

CURTAIN

Abbie may not understand Ephraim's needs, but she understands his maleness. He could tolerate another man's lust for his wife—if that man were not his son. But he will not offer his seed-bed to a son's seed. His rage is less anger than fear, a fear Abbie knows she has released and must restrain. Only then does Ephraim frame his fear. Eben is the closest restatement of himself Ephraim has sired; yet that restatement is not a duplicate. Eben is "soft" (at least old Cabot thinks he is) and there is no possibility of another child. "A son is me—my blood—mine. Mine ought t' git mine. An' then it's still mine—even though I be six foot under."

Now Abbie knows the way to her desire. Eben can sire the child to inherit the land, to cut him off, to make her free. And she will have the use of Eben who has moved her so.

The summer air hangs ripely hot beneath the giant elms that hear the prayer old Cabot prays as Abbie plans her action.

SCENE TWO

About eight in the evening. The interior of the two bedrooms on the top floor is shown. EBEN is sitting on the side of his bed in the room on the left. On account of the heat he has taken off everything but his undershirt and pants. His feet are bare. He faces front, brooding moodily, his chin propped on his hands, a desperate expression on his face.

In the other room CABOT and ABBIE are sitting side by side on the edge of their bed, an old four-poster with feather mattress. He is in his night shirt, she in her nightdress. He is still in the queer, excited mood into which the notion of a son has thrown him. Both rooms are lighted dimly and flickeringly by tallow candles.

CABOT. The farm needs a son.

ABBIE. I need a son.

CABOT. Ay-eh. Sometimes ye air the farm an' sometimes the farm be yew. That's why I clove t' ye in my lonesomeness. (*A pause. He pounds his knee with his fist.*) Me an' the farm has got t' beget a son!

ABBIE. Ye'd best go t' sleep. Ye're gittin' thin's all mixed.

CABOT (*with an impatient gesture*). No, I hain't. My mind's clear's a well. Ye don't know me, that's it. (*He stares hopelessly at the floor.*)

ABBIE (*indifferently*). Mebbe. (*In the next room* EBEN *gets up and paces up and down distractedly.* ABBIE *hears him. Her eyes fasten on the intervening wall with concentrated attention.* EBEN *stops and stares. Their hot glances seem to meet through the wall. Unconsciously he stretches out his arms for her and she half rises. Then aware, he mutters a curse at himself and flings himself face downward on the bed, his clenched fists above his head, his face buried in the pillow.* ABBIE *relaxes with a faint sigh but her eyes remain fixed on the wall; she listens with all her attention for some movement from* EBEN.)

Ephraim becomes the voice of Man as he cries out, "Sometimes ye air the farm an' sometimes the farm be yew. That's why I clove t' ye in my lonesomeness. Me an' the farm has got t' beget a son!" Man has the land to plant, the seed to sow. Until he has done his work and left the son, he is a lonely animal without a reason. A wife is only land for urban man; but for rural folk close to the soil, a wife is the land and the land is the land, but both are one. Good fallow land cries out to a man, "Plant me, plant me," and Abbie is a buxom plot for Ephraim's seed, but Ephraim's seed is sterile.

No woman seems to know the need a man has, for hers is a different need. She is not *his* land; she is the land that any man can sow when need lies on that land. Her crop needs no distinctive mark; it need not have a proper name; it need not represent a strain; it just need *be*. But man's crop must bear his likeness stamped into its grain.

Abbie does not know Ephraim—true. She only knows her own urgent need. Old Cabot cannot meet that need, but his son can. Abbie concentrates upon the wall that separates Eben from her; she does not hear old Cabot's words, words wrung from Man.

CABOT (*suddenly raises his head and looks at her—scornfully*). Will ye ever know me—'r will any man 'r woman? (*Shaking his head*) No. I calc'late 't wa'n't t' be. (*He turns away.* ABBIE *looks at the wall. Then, evidently unable to keep silent about his thoughts, without looking at his wife, he puts out his hand and clutches her knee. She starts violently, looks at him, sees he is not watching her, concentrates again on the wall and pays no attention to what he says.*) Listen, Abbie. When I come here fifty odd year ago—I was jest twenty an' the strongest an' hardest ye ever seen—ten times as strong an' fifty times as hard as Eben. Waal—this place was nothin' but fields o' stones. Folks laughed when I tuk it. They couldn't know what I knowed. When ye kin make corn sprout out o' stones, God's livin' in yew! They wa'n't strong enuf fur that! They reckoned God was easy. They laughed. They don't

laugh no more. Some died hereabouts. Some went West an' died. They're all underground—fur follerin' arter an easy God. God hain't easy. (*He shakes his head slowly.*)
An' I growed hard. Folks kept allus sayin' he's a hard man like 'twas sinful t' be hard,
so's at last I said back at 'em: Waal then, by thunder, ye'll git me hard an' see how
ye like it! (*Then suddenly*) But I give in t' weakness once. 'Twas arter I'd been here
two year. I got weak—despairful—they was so many stones. They was a party leavin',
givin' up, goin' West. I jined 'em. We tracked on 'n' on. We come t' broad medders,
plains, whar the soil was black an' rich as gold. Nary a stone. Easy. Ye'd on'y to
plow an' sow an' then set an' smoke yer pipe an' watch thin's grow; I could o' been
a rich man—but somethin' in me fit me an' fit me—the voice o' God sayin': "This
hain't wuth nothin' t' Me. Git ye back t' hum!" I got afeerd o' that voice an' I lit
out back t' hum here, leavin' my claim an' crops t' whoever'd a mind t' take em.
Ay-eh. I actoolly give up what was rightful mine! God's hard, not easy! God's in the
stones! Build my church on a rock—out o' stones an' I'll be in them! That's what He
meant t' Peter! (*He sighs heavily—a pause*) Stones. I picked 'em up an' piled 'em
into walls. Ye kin read the years o' my life in them walls, every day a hefted stone,
climbin' over the hills up and down, fencin' in the fields that was mine, whar I'd
made thin's grow out o' nothin'—like the will o'God, like the servant o' His hand.
It wa'n't easy. It was hard an' He made me hard fur it. (*He pauses.*) All the time
I kept gittin' lonesomer. I tuk a wife. She bore Simeon an' Peter. She was a good
woman. She wuked hard. We was married twenty year. She never knowed me. She
helped but she never knowed what she was helpin'. I was allus lonesome. She died.
After that it wa'n't so lonesome fur a spell. (*A pause*) I lost count o' the years. I
had no time t' fool away countin' 'em. Sim an' Peter helped. The farm growed. It
was all mine! When I thought o' that I didn't feel lonesome. (*A pause*) But ye can't
hitch yer mind t' one thin' day an' night. I tuk another wife—Eben's Maw. Her folks
was contestin' me at law over my deeds t' the farm—my farm! That's why Eben
keeps a-talkin' his fool talk o' this bein' his Maw's farm. She bore Eben. She was
purty—but soft. She tried t' be hard. She couldn't. She never knowed me nor nothin'.
It was lonesomer 'n hell with her. After a matter o' sixteen odd years, she died. (*A
pause*) I lived with the boys. They hated me 'cause I was hard. I hated them 'cause
they was soft. They coveted the farm without knowin' what it meant. It made me
bitter 'n wormwood. It aged me—them coveting what I'd made fur mine. Then this
spring the call come—the voice o' God cryin' in my wilderness, in my lonesomeness—t'
go out an' seek an' find! (*Turning to her with strange passion*) I sought ye an' I
found ye! Yew air my Rose o' Sharon! Yer eyes air like. . . . (*She has turned a blank
face, resentful eyes to his. He stares at her for a moment—then harshly*) Air ye
any the wiser fur all I've told ye?

ABBIE (*confusedly*). Mebbe.

CABOT (*pushing her away from him—angrily*). Ye don't know nothin'—nor never
will. If ye don't hev a son t' redeem ye. . . . (*This in a tone of cold threat.*)

ABBIE (*resentfully*). I've prayed, hain't I?

CABOT (*bitterly*). Pray agen—fur understandin'!

ABBIE (*a veiled threat in her tone*). Ye'll have a son out o' me. I promise ye.

CABOT. How kin ye promise?

ABBIE. I got second-sight mebbe. I kin foretell. (*She gives a queer smile.*)

CABOT. I believe ye have. Ye give me the chills sometimes. (*He shivers.*) It's cold in this house. It's oneasy. They's thin's pokin' about in the dark—in the corners. (*He pulls on his trousers, tucking in his night shirt, and pulls on his boots.*)

ABBIE (*surprised*). Whar air ye goin'?

CABOT (*queerly*). Down whar it's restful—whar it's warm down t' the barn. (*Bitterly*) I kin talk t' the cows. They know. They know the farm an' me. They'll give me peace. (*He turns to go out the door.*)

ABBIE (*a bit frightenedly*). Air ye ailin' tonight, Ephraim?

CABOT. Growin'. Growin' ripe on the bough. (*He turns and goes, his boots clumping down the stairs.*)

Primitive man equates the stones with gods and with their almighty force. If a god so wills, struck stones will yield up water, which is life to man. If a god so wills, stones become seeds that sprout into the race of man. If a god so wills, cathedral stones *are* that god that man erects with the need to have and serve his god. Old Ephraim is all primitive men; his God is hard, the stones of Earth. His God demands that the tribute be hard, as stones are hard and yield with work that is man's faith.

Does woman know primitive man? She yields, like rocks, a living farm. She is the rock from which man comes; that much she understands. She builds man first; he builds his gods. Her need is life—immediate life. Man needs eternity to plead his own stern need. A woman's son need not be strong; he need not have the stamp of a god; a man's son must bear a greater weight, must own the strength to lift the rocks and build his god. This Abbie cannot understand. Each woman in old Cabot's life failed utterly to know the need. Each left him lonelier than the last, and now he seeks the barn. There, cattle *know;* their nature is the knowledge of the God of stones. Women have failed; the first wife helped without knowing what she was helping. Then Eben's mother claimed the farm; Ephraim married her to stop a court of law from claiming the land his hands had built. Now Abbie wants the land for herself, wants it *and* Eben. Ephraim fears her kind of need: "They coveted the farm without knowin' what it meant." He wants her need to be his need, but she isn't any wiser. Her failure underscores the cold that pokes in the corners of the house. Old Cabot goes down to the barn where the cattle know the farm and him and give him peace.

(EBEN *sits up with a start, listening.* ABBIE *is conscious of his movement and stares at the wall.* CABOT *comes out of the house around the corner and stands by the gate, blinking at the sky. He stretches up his hands in a tortured gesture.*) God A'mighty, call from the dark! (*He listens as if expecting an answer. Then his arms drop, he shakes his head and plods off toward the barn.* EBEN *and* ABBIE *stare at each other through the wall.* EBEN *sighs heavily and* ABBIE *echoes it. Both become terribly nervous, uneasy. Finally* ABBIE *gets up and listens, her ear to the wall. He acts as if he saw every move she was making, he becomes resolutely still. She seems driven into a decision—goes out the door in rear determinedly. His eyes follow her. Then as the door of his room is opened softly, he turns away, waits in an attitude of strained fixity.* ABBIE *stands for a second staring at him, her eyes burning with desire. Then with a little cry she runs over and throws her arms about his neck, she pulls his head back and covers his mouth with kisses. At first, he submits dumbly; then he puts his arms about her neck and returns her kisses, but finally, suddenly aware of his hatred, he hurls her away from him, springing to his feet. They stand speechless and breathless, panting like two animals.*)

ABBIE (*at last—painfully*). Ye shouldn't, Eben—ye shouldn't—I'd make ye happy!

EBEN (*harshly*). I don't want t' be happy—from yew!

ABBIE (*helplessly*). Ye do, Eben! Ye do! Why d'ye lie?

EBEN (*viciously*). I don't take t'ye, I tell ye! I hate the sight o' ye!

ABBIE (*with an uncertain troubled laugh*). Waal, I kissed ye anyways—an' ye kissed back—yer lips was burnin'—ye can't lie 'bout that! (*Intensely*) If ye don't care, why did ye kiss me back—why was yer lips burnin'?

EBEN (*wiping his mouth*). It was like pizen on 'em. (*Then tauntingly*) When I kissed ye back, mebbe I thought 'twas someone else.

ABBIE (*wildly*). Min?

EBEN. Mebbe.

ABBIE (*torturedly*). Did ye go t' see her? Did ye r'ally go? I thought ye mightn't. Is that why ye throwed me off jest now?

EBEN (*sneeringly*). What if it be?

ABBIE (*raging*). Then ye're a dog, Eben Cabot!

EBEN (*threateningly*). Ye can't talk that way t' me!

ABBIE (*with a shrill laugh*). Can't I? Did ye think I was in love with ye—a weak thin' like yew? Not much! I on'y wanted ye fur a purpose o' my own—an' I'll hev ye fur it yet 'cause I'm stronger'n yew be!

EBEN (*resentfully*). I knowed well it was on'y part o' yer plan t' swaller everythin'!

ABBIE (*tauntingly*). Mebbe.

EBEN (*furious*). Git out o' my room!

ABBIE. This air my room an' ye're on'y hired help!

EBEN (*threateningly*). Git out afore I murder ye!

ABBIE (*quite confident now*). I hain't a mite afeerd. Ye want me, don't ye? Yes, ye do! An' yer Paw's son'll never kill what he wants! Look at yer eyes! They's lust fur me in 'em, burnin' 'em up! Look at yer lips now! They're tremblin' an' longin' t' kiss me, an' yer teeth t' bite! (*He is watching her now with a horrible fascination. She laughs a crazy triumphant laugh.*) I'm a-goin' t' make all o' this hum my hum! They's one room hain't mine yet, but it's a-goin' t' be tonight. I'm a-goin' down now an' light up! (*She makes him a mocking bow.*) Won't ye come courtin' me in the best parlor, Mister Cabot?

EBEN (*staring at her—horribly confused—dully*). Don't ye dare! It hain't been opened since Maw died an' was laid out thar! Don't ye . . . ! (*But her eyes are fixed on his so burningly that his will seems to wither before hers. He stands swaying toward her helplessly.*)

ABBIE (*holding his eyes and putting all her will into her words as she backs out the door*). I'll expect ye afore long, Eben.

EBEN (*stares after her for a while, walking toward the door. A light appears in the parlor window. He murmurs*). In the parlor? (*This seems to arouse connotations for he comes back and puts on his white shirt, collar, half ties the tie mechanically, puts on coat, takes his hat, stands barefooted looking about him in bewilderment, mutters wonderingly*) Maw! Whar air yew? (*Then goes slowly toward the door in rear*)

CURTAIN

Desire lies heavy on the air. Death haunts the parlor; hate becomes love. Life feeds on need and cannot share this little house with death's unrest. A woman, Abbie wants the house, all of the house, as her domain. She forces Eben through his urgent need to visit his own barn. His weakness is incestuous need: the farm is his mother, a mother who was the wife to the man who holds the land. He will give the land to his wife who will be won in the mother's parlor. There in that room Abbie will be possessed, a wife and a mother. "Whar air yew?" Eben cries and goes down to his Maw.

SCENE THREE

A few minutes later. The interior of the parlor is shown. A grim, repressed room like a tomb in which the family has been interred alive. ABBIE sits on the edge of the horsehair sofa. She has lighted all the candles and the room is revealed in all its preserved ugliness. A change has come over the woman. She looks awed and frightened now, ready to run away.

The door is opened and EBEN appears. His face wears an expression of obsessed confusion. He stands staring at her, his arms hanging disjointedly from his shoulders, his feet bare, his hat in his hand.

ABBIE (*after a pause—with a nervous, formal politeness*). Won't ye set?

EBEN (*dully*). Ay-eh. (*Mechanically he places his hat carefully on the floor near the door and sits stiffly beside her on the edge of the sofa. A pause. They both remain rigid, looking straight ahead with eyes full of fear.*)

ABBIE. When I fust come in—in the dark—they seemed t' be somethin' here.

EBEN (*simply*). Maw.

ABBIE. I kin still feel—somethin' . . . .

EBEN. It's Maw.

ABBIE. At fust I was feered o' it. I wanted t' yell an' run. Now—since yew come— seems like it's growin' soft an' kind t' me. (*Addressing the air—queerly*) Thank yew.

EBEN. Maw allus loved me.

ABBIE. Mebbe it knows I love yew, too. Mebbe that makes it kind t' me.

EBEN (*dully*). I dunno. I should think she'd hate ye.

ABBIE (*with certainty*). No. I kin feel it don't—not no more.

EBEN. Hate ye fur stealin' her place—here in her hum—settin' in her parlor whar she was laid—(*He suddenly stops, staring stupidly before him.*)

ABBIE. What is it, Eben?

EBEN (*in a whisper*). Seems like Maw didn't want me t' remind ye.

ABBIE (*excitedly*). I knowed, Eben! It's kind t' me! It don't b'ar me no grudges fur what I never knowed an' couldn't help!

EBEN. Maw b'ars him a grudge.

ABBIE. Waal, so does all o' us.

EBEN. Ay-eh. (*With passion*) I does, by God!

ABBIE (*taking one of his hands in hers and patting it*). Thar. Don't git riled thinkin' o' him. Think o' yer Maw who's kind t' us. Tell me about yer Maw, Eben.

EBEN. They hain't nothin' much. She was kind. She was good.

ABBIE (*putting one arm over his shoulder. He does not seem to notice—passion-ately*). I'll be kind an' good t' ye!

EBEN. Sometimes she used t' sing fur me.

ABBIE. I'll sing fur ye!

EBEN. This was her hum. This was her farm.

ABBIE. This is my hum! This is my farm!

EBEN. He married her t' steal 'em. She was soft an' easy. He couldn't 'preciate her.

ABBIE. He can't 'preciate me!

EBEN. He murdered her with his hardness.

ABBIE. He's murderin' me!

EBEN. She died. (*A pause*) Sometimes she used to sing fur me. (*He bursts into a fit of sobbing.*)

ABBIE (*both her arms round him—with wild passion*). I'll sing fur ye! I'll die fur ye! (*In spite of her overwhelming desire for him, there is a sincere maternal love in her manner and voice—a horribly frank mixture of lust and mother love.)* Don't cry, Eben! I'll take yer Maw's place! I'll be everythin' she was t' ye! Let me kiss ye, Eben! *(She pulls his head around. He makes a bewildered pretense of resistance. She is tender.)* Don't be afeerd! I'll kiss ye pure, Eben—same 's if I was a Maw t' ye—an' ye kin kiss me back 's if yew was my son—my boy—sayin' good-night t' me! Kiss me, Eben. *(They kiss in restrained fashion. Then suddenly wild passion overcomes her. She kisses him lustfully again and again and he flings his arms about her and returns her kisses. Suddenly, as in the bedroom, he frees himself from her violently and springs to his feet. He is trembling all over, in a strange state of terror.* ABBIE *strains her arms toward him with fierce pleading.)* Don't ye leave me, Eben! Can't ye see it hain't enuf—lovin' ye like a Maw—can't ye see it's got t' be that an' more—much more—a hundred times more—fur me t' be happy—fur yew t' be happy?

EBEN *(to the presence he feels in the room).* Maw! Maw! What d'ye want? What air ye tellin' me?

ABBIE. She's tellin' ye t' love me. She knows I love ye an' I'll be good t' ye. Can't ye feel it? Don't ye know? She's tellin' ye t' love me, Eben!

EBEN. Ay-eh. I feel—mebbe she—but—I can't figger out—why—when ye've stole her place—here in her hum—in the parlor whar she was—

ABBIE *(fiercely).* She knows I love ye!

EBEN *(his face suddenly lighting up with a fierce, triumphant grin).* I see it! I see why. It's her vengeance on him—so's she kin rest quiet in her grave!

ABBIE *(wildly).* Vengeance o' God on the hull o' us! What d'we give a durn? I love ye, Eben! God knows I love ye! *(She stretches out her arms for him.)*

EBEN *(throws himself on his knees beside the sofa and grabs her in his arms— releasing all his pent-up passion).* An' I love yew, Abbie!—now I kin say it! I been dyin' fur want o' ye—every hour since ye come! I love ye! *(Their lips meet in a fierce, bruising kiss.)*

CURTAIN

Only you can decide how much Abbie and Eben believe their own words. Eben's mother has haunted the house from the beginning of the play—at least every Cabot has felt her presence. Whether their awareness of her is actual, a brooding fear engendered by the overhanging elms, or a fiction created by Eben and transferred to the others, her presence has received comment. Abbie too has commented on it, though her motives are also yours to evaluate. In the parlor, passions send spirits soaring whether they exorcise ghosts or not. Eben and Abbie may rationalize their conduct, seek to influence each other with the most convenient tool, or be truthful. You must decide. Whether they are despicable and weak, foolhardy and weak, determined and strong, right or wrong—these are also your decisions. As Ephraim finds solace in the barn, Abbie and Eben find solace in each other's arms.

SCENE FOUR

Exterior of the farmhouse. It is just dawn. The front door at right is opened and EBEN *comes out and walks around to the gate. He is dressed in his working clothes. He seems changed. His face wears a bold and confident expression, he is grinning to himself with evident satisfaction. As he gets near the gate, the window of the parlor is heard opening and the shutters are flung back and* ABBIE *sticks her head out. Her hair tumbles over her shoulders in disarray, her face is flushed, she looks at* EBEN *with tender, languorous eyes and calls softly.*

ABBIE. Eben. (*As he turns—playfully*) Jest one more kiss afore ye go. I'm goin' to miss ye fearful all day.

EBEN. An' me yew, ye kin bet! (*He goes to her. They kiss several times. He draws away, laughingly.*) Thar. That's enuf, hain't it? Ye won't hev none left fur next time.

ABBIE. I got a million o' 'em left fur yew! (*Then a bit anxiously*) D'ye r'ally love me, Eben?

EBEN (*emphatically*). I like ye better'n any gal I ever knowed! That's gospel!

ABBIE. Likin' hain't lovin'.

EBEN. Waal then—I love ye. Now air yew satisfied?

ABBIE. Ay-eh, I be. (*She smiles at him adoringly.*)

EBEN. I better git t' the barn. The old critter's liable t' suspicion an' come sneakin' up.

ABBIE (*with a confident laugh*). Let him! I kin allus pull the wool over his eyes. I'm goin' t' leave the shutters open and let in the sun 'n' air. This room's been dead long enuf. Now it's goin' t' be my room!

EBEN (*frowning*). Ay-eh.

ABBIE (*hastily*). I meant—our room.

EBEN. Ay-eh.

ABBIE. We made it our'n last night, didn't we? We give it life—our lovin' did. (*A pause*)

EBEN (*with a strange look*). Maw's gone back t' her grave. She kin sleep now.

ABBIE. May she rest in peace! (*Then tenderly rebuking*) Ye oughtn't t' talk o' sad thin's—this mornin'.

EBEN. It jest come up in my mind o' itself.

ABBIE. Don't let it. (*He doesn't answer. She yawns.*) Waal, I'm a-goin' t' steal a wink o' sleep. I'll tell the Old Man I hain't feelin' pert. Let him git his own vittles.

EBEN. I see him comin' from the barn. Ye better look smart an' git upstairs.

ABBIE. Ay-eh. Good-by. Don't forget me. (*She throws him a kiss. He grins—then* squares *his shoulders and awaits his father confidently.* CABOT *walks slowly up from the left, staring up at the sky with a vague face.*)

EBEN (*jovially*). Mornin', Paw. Star-gazin' in daylight?

CABOT. Purty, hain't it?

EBEN (*looking around him possessively*). It's a durned purty farm.

CABOT. I mean the sky.

EBEN (*grinning*). How d'ye know? Them eyes o' your'n can't see that fur. (*This tickles his humor and he slaps his thigh and laughs.*) Ho-ho! That's a good un!

CABOT (*grimly sarcastic*). Ye're feelin' right chipper, hain't ye? Whar'd ye steal the likker?

EBEN (*good-naturedly*). 'Tain't likker. Jest life. (*Suddenly holding out his hand—soberly*) Yew 'n' me is quits. Let's shake hands.

CABOT (*suspiciously*). What's come over ye?

EBEN. Then don't. Mebbe it's jest as well. (*A moment's pause*) What's come over me? (*Queerly*) Didn't ye feel her passin'—goin' back t' her grave?

CABOT (*dully*). Who?

EBEN. Maw. She kin rest now an' sleep content. She's quit with ye.

CABOT (*confusedly*). I rested. I slept good—down with the cows. They know how t' sleep. They're teachin' me.

EBEN (*suddenly jovial again*). Good fur the cows! Waal—ye better git t' work.

CABOT (*grimly amused*). Air ye bossin' me, ye calf?

EBEN (*beginning to laugh*). Ay-eh! I'm bossin' yew! Ha-ha-ha! See how ye like it! Ha-ha-ha! I'm the prize rooster o' this roost. Ha-ha-ha! (*He goes off toward the barn laughing.*)

CABOT (*looks after him with scornful pity*). Soft-headed. Like his Maw. Dead spit 'n' image. No hope in him! (*He spits with contemptuous disgust.*) A born fool! (*Then matter-of-factly*) Waal—I'm gittin' peckish. (*He goes toward door.*)

CURTAIN

The parlor has been large enough for breathing life into souls this night. Abbie and Eben are unrepentant; indeed, they gloat over their individual victories. She has claimed the whole house; Eben has avenged his mother by cuckolding his father. The rationale may seem contrived, but a man is seldom rational when he needs to rationalize an act. Again, Ephraim dominates the scene before he arrives. Eben is willing to make his peace ("Yew 'n' me is quits") with Ephraim, to call the score even for both himself and his mother. Ephraim considers the overture a rash act, the behavior of a boy who is the "dead spit 'n' image" of his weak mother. Ironically, Eben's reasoning would be Ephraim's were their positions reversed. Once he had won it, Ephraim would not prolong a battle. He too would call it quits. Closer to a sense of the immediacy of his God than ever before, Ephraim is at last aware of the sky—an awareness that everyone else has had, that he only now achieves. At the darkest hour of his deception, he lifts up his eyes and, like a Psalmist, finds his strength flowing from that source. In this moment, Eben is bound as hopelessly to the land as Ephraim has always been. The irony of fateful actions has come full circle.

PART THREE

SCENE ONE

A night in late spring the following year. The kitchen and the two bedrooms upstairs are shown. The two bedrooms are dimly lighted by a tallow candle in each. EBEN *is sitting on the side of the bed in his room, his chin propped on his fists, his face a study of the struggle he is making to understand his conflicting emotions. The noisy laughter and music from below where a kitchen dance is in progress annoy and distract him. He scowls at the floor.*

In the next room a cradle stands beside the double bed.

In the kitchen all is festivity. The stove has been taken down to give more room to the dancers. The chairs, with wooden benches added, have been pushed back against the walls. On these are seated, squeezed in tight against one another, farmers and their wives and their young folks of both sexes from the neighboring farms. They are all chattering and laughing loudly. They evidently have some secret joke in common. There is no end of winking, of nudging, of meaning nods of the head toward CABOT *who, in a state of extreme hilarious excitement increased by the amount he has drunk, is standing near the rear door where there is a small keg of whisky and serving drinks to all the men. In the left corner, front, dividing the attention with her husband,* ABBIE *is sitting in a rocking chair, a shawl wrapped about her shoulders. She is very pale, her face is thin and drawn, her eyes are fixed anxiously on the open door in rear as if waiting for someone.*

The musician is tuning up his fiddle, seated in the far right corner. He is a lanky young fellow with a long, weak face. His pale eyes blink incessantly and he grins about him slyly with a greedy malice.

ABBIE (*suddenly turning to a young girl on her right*). Whar's Eben?

YOUNG GIRL (*eyeing her scornfully*). I dunno, Mrs. Cabot. I hain't seen Eben in ages. (*Meaningly*) Seems like he's spent most of his time t' hum since yew come.

ABBIE (*vaguely*). I tuk his Maw's place.

YOUNG GIRL. Ay-eh. So I've heerd. (*She turns away to retail this bit of gossip to her mother sitting next to her.* ABBIE *turns to her left to a big stoutish middle-aged man whose flushed face and starting eyes show the amount of "likker" he has consumed.*)

ABBIE. Ye hain't seen Eben, hev ye?

MAN. No, I hain't. (*Then he adds with a wink*) If yew hain't, who would?

ABBIE. He's the best dancer in the county. He'd ought t' come an' dance.

MAN (*with a wink*). Mebbe he's doin' the dutiful an' walkin' the kid t' sleep. It's a boy, hain't it?

ABBIE (*nodding vaguely*). Ay-eh—born two weeks back—purty's a picture.

MAN. They all is—t' their Maws. (*Then in a whisper, with a nudge and a leer*) Listen, Abbie—if ye ever git tired o' Eben, remember me! Don't fergit now! (*He looks at her uncomprehending face for a second—then grunts disgustedly*) Waal—guess I'll likker agin. (*He goes over and joins* CABOT *who is arguing noisily with an old farmer over cows. They all drink.*)

ABBIE (*this time appealing to nobody in particular*). Wonder what Eben's a-doin'? (*Her remark is repeated down the line with many a guffaw and titter until it reaches the* FIDDLER. *He fastens his blinking eyes on* ABBIE.)

FIDDLER (*raising his voice*). Bet I kin tell ye, Abbie, what Eben's doin'! He's down t' the church offerin' up prayers o' thanksgivin'. (*They all titter expectantly.*)

A MAN. What fur? (*Another titter*)

FIDDLER. 'Cause unto him a—(*He hesitates just long enough.*) brother is born! (*A roar of laughter. They all look from* ABBIE *to* CABOT. *She is oblivious, staring at the door.* CABOT, *although he hasn't heard the words, is irritated by the laughter and steps forward, glaring about him. There is an immediate silence.*)

CABOT. What're ye all bleatin' about—like a flock o' goats? Why don't ye dance, damn ye? I axed ye here t' dance—t' eat, drink an' be merry—an' thar ye set cacklin' like a lot o' wet hens with the pip! Ye've swilled my likker an' guzzled my vittles like hogs, hain't ye? Then dance fur me, can't ye? That's fa'r an' squar', hain't it? (*A grumble of resentment goes around but they are all evidently in too much awe of him to express it openly.*)

FIDDLER (*slyly*). We're waitin' fur Eben. (*A suppressed laugh*)

CABOT (*with a fierce exultation*). T'hell with Eben! Eben's done fur now! I got a new son! (*His mood switching with drunken suddenness*) But ye needn't t' laugh at Eben, none o' ye! He's my blood, if he be a dumb fool. He's better nor any o' yew! He kin do a day's work a'most up t' what I kin—an' that'd put any o' yew pore critters t' shame!

FIDDLER. An' he kin do a good night's work too! (*A roar of laughter*)

CABOT. Laugh, ye damn fools! Ye're right jist the same, Fiddler. He kin work day an' night, too, like I kin, if need be!

OLD FARMER (*from behind the keg where he is weaving drunkenly back and forth—with great simplicity*). They hain't many t' touch ye, Ephraim—a son at seventy-six. That's a hard man fur ye! I be on'y sixty-eight an' I couldn't do it. (*A roar of laughter in which* CABOT *joins uproariously*)

CABOT (*slapping him on the back*). I'm sorry fur ye, Hi. I'd never suspicion sech weakness from a boy like yew!

OLD FARMER. An' I never reckoned yew had it in ye nuther, Ephraim. (*There is another laugh.*)

CABOT (*suddenly grim*). I got a lot in me—a hell of a lot—folks don't know on. (*Turning to the* FIDDLER) Fiddle 'er up, durn ye! Give 'em somethin' t' dance t'! What air ye, an ornament? Hain't this a celebration? Then grease yer elbow an' go it!

FIDDLER (*seizes a drink which the* OLD FARMER *holds out to him and downs it*). Here goes! (*He starts to fiddle "Lady of the Lake." Four young fellows and four girls form in two lines and dance a square dance. The* FIDDLER *shouts directions for the different movements, keeping his words in the rhythm of the music and interspersing them with jocular personal remarks to the dancers themselves. The people seated along the walls stamp their feet and clap their hands in unison.* CABOT *is especially active in this respect. Only* ABBIE *remains apathetic, staring at the door as if she were alone in a silent room.*)

FIDDLER. Swing your partner t' the right! That's it, Jim! Give her a b'ar hug! Her Maw hain't lookin'. (*Laughter*) Change partners! That suits ye, don't it, Essie, now ye got Reub afore ye? Look at her redden up, will ye? Waal, life is short an' so's love, as the feller says. (*Laughter*)

CABOT (*excitedly, stamping his foot*). Go it, boys! Go it, gals!

FIDDLER (*with a wink at the others*). Ye're the spryest seventy-six ever I sees, Ephraim! Now if ye'd on'y good eyesight . . . ! (*Suppressed laughter. He gives* CABOT *no chance to retort but roars*) Promenade! Ye're walkin' like a bride down the aisle, Sarah! Waal, while they's life they's allus hope, I've heerd tell. Swing your partner to the left! Gosh A'mighty, look at Johnny Cook high-steppin'! They hain't goin' t'be much strength left fur howin' in the corn lot t'morrow. (*Laughter*)

CABOT. Go it! Go it! (*Then suddenly, unable to restrain himself any longer, he prances into the midst of the dancers, scattering them, waving his arms about wildly.*) Ye're all hoofs! Git out o' my road! Give me room! I'll show ye dancin'. Ye're all too soft! (*He pushes them roughly away. They crowd back toward the walls, muttering, looking at him resentfully.*)

FIDDLER (*jeeringly*). Go it, Ephraim! Go it! (*He starts "Pop Goes the Weasel," increasing the tempo with every verse until at the end he is fiddling crazily as fast as he can go.*)

CABOT (*starts to dance which he does very well and with tremendous vigor. Then he begins to improvise, cuts incredibly grotesque capers, leaping up and cracking his heels together, prancing around in a circle with body bent in an Indian war dance, then suddenly straightening up and kicking as high as he can with both legs. He is like a monkey on a string. And all the while he intersperses his antics with shouts and derisive comments.*) Whoop! Here's dancin' fur ye! Whoop! See that! Seventy-six, if I'm a day! Hard as iron yet! Beatin' the young 'uns like I allus done! Look at me! I'd invite ye t' dance on my hundredth birthday on'y ye'll all be dead by then. Ye're a sickly generation! Yer hearts air pink, not red! Yer veins is full o' mud an' water!

I be the on'y man in the county! Whoop! See that! I'm a Injun! I've killed Injuns in the West afore ye was born—an' skulped 'em too! They's a arrer wound on my backside I c'd show ye! The hull tribe chased me. I outrun 'em all—with the arrer stuck in me! An' I tuk vengeance on 'em. Ten eyes fur an eye, that was my motter! Whoop! Look at me! I kin kick the ceilin' off the room! Whoop!

FIDDLER (*stops playing—exhaustedly*). God A'mighty, I got enuf. Ye got the devil's strength in ye.

CABOT (*delightedly*). Did I beat yew, too? Wa'al, ye played smart. Hev a swig. (*He pours whisky for himself and* FIDDLER. *They drink. The others watch* CABOT *silently with cold, hostile eyes. There is a dead pause. The* FIDDLER *rests.* CABOT *leans against the keg, panting, glaring around him confusedly. In the room above,* EBEN *gets to his feet and tiptoes out the door in rear, appearing a moment later in the other bedroom. He moves silently, even frightenedly, toward the cradle and stands there looking down at the baby. His face is as vague as his reactions are confused, but there is a trace of tenderness, of interested discovery. At the same moment that he reaches the cradle,* ABBIE *seems to sense something. She gets up weakly and goes to* CABOT.)

ABBIE. I'm goin' up t' the baby.

CABOT (*with real solicitation*). Air ye able fur the stairs? D'ye want me t' help ye, Abbie?

ABBIE. No. I'm able. I'll be down agen soon.

CABOT. Don't ye git wore out! He needs ye, remember—our son does! (*He grins affectionately, patting her on the back. She shrinks from his touch.*)

ABBIE (*dully*). Don't—tech me. I'm goin'—up. (*She goes.* CABOT *looks after her. A whisper goes around the room.* CABOT *turns. It ceases. He wipes his forehead steaming with sweat. He is breathing pantingly.*)

CABOT. I'm a-goin' out t' git fresh air. I'm feelin' a mite dizzy. Fiddle up thar! Dance, all o'ye! Here's likker fur them as wants it. Enjoy yerselves. I'll be back. (*He goes, closing the door behind him.*)

FIDDLER (*sarcastically*). Don't hurry none on our account! (*A suppressed laugh. He imitates* ABBIE.) Whar's Eben? (*More laughter*)

A WOMAN (*loudly*). What's happened in this house is plain as the nose on yer face! (ABBIE *appears in the doorway upstairs and stands looking in surprise and adoration at* EBEN *who does not see her.*)

A MAN. Ssshh! He's li-ble t' listenin' at the door. That'd be like him. (*Their voices die to an intensive whispering. Their faces are concentrated on this gossip. A noise as of dead leaves in the wind comes from the room.* CABOT *has come out from the porch and stands by the gate, leaning on it, staring at the sky blinkingly.* ABBIE *comes across the room silently.* EBEN *does not notice her until quite near.*)

EBEN (*starting*). Abbie!

ABBIE. Ssshh! (*She throws her arms around him. They kiss—then bend over the cradle together.*) Ain't he purty?—dead spit 'n' image o' yew!

EBEN (*pleased*). Air he? I can't tell none.

ABBIE. E-zactly like!

EBEN (*frowningly*). I don't like this. I don't like lettin' on what's mine's his'n. I been doin' that all my life. I'm gittin t' the end o' b'arin' it!

ABBIE (*putting her finger on his lips*). We're doin' the best we kin. We got t' wait. Somethin's bound t' happen. (*She puts her arms around him.*) I got t' go back.

EBEN. I'm goin' out. I can't b'ar it with the fiddle playin' an' the laughin'.

ABBIE. Don't git feelin' low. I love ye, Eben. Kiss me. (*He kisses her. They remain in each other's arms.*)

CABOT (*at the gate, confusedly*). Even the music can't drive it out—somethin'. Ye kin feel it droppin' off the elums, climbin' up the roof, sneakin' down the chimney, pokin' in the corners! They's no peace in houses, they's no rest livin' with folks. Somethin's always livin' with ye. (*With a deep sigh*) I'll go t' the barn an' rest a spell. (*He goes wearily toward the barn.*)

FIDDLER (*tuning up*). Let's celebrate the old skunk gittin' fooled! We kin have some fun now he's went. (*He starts to fiddle "Turkey in the Straw." There is real merriment now. The young folks get up to dance.*)

CURTAIN

Scene One may, on first reading, seem merely gross humor, but the characters are juxtaposed in a tense pattern creating a canvas of conflicting masses and needs. An uncouth, hard, primitive man (Ephraim) delights in his accomplishments downstairs. A sensitive, delicate, civilized man (Eben) contemplates his work upstairs—to his mixed satisfaction and dissatisfaction. Youth and age, the old and the new, are sharply compared and contrasted while an eternal woman (Abbie) sits between the two, tied to one by practical necessity, to the other by emotional desire. Coarsely passing judgment, society assumes an attitude suggesting indignation and outrage but reflecting an evil intention darker than any deed done in this house. Ephraim's flight from the house leaves Abbie and Eben in physical possession, society in control. The God of stones glimmers in the moonlight while, shut in by the elms, the house harbors its evil revelry.

Scene Two

*A half-hour later—Exterior—*EBEN *is standing by the gate looking up at the sky, an expression of dumb pain bewildered by itself on his face.* CABOT *appears, returning from the barn, walking wearily, his eyes on the ground. He sees* EBEN *and his whole mood immediately changes. He becomes excited, a cruel, triumphant grin comes to his lips, he strides up and slaps* EBEN *on the back. From within comes the whining of the fiddle and the noise of stamping feet and laughing voices.*

CABOT. So har ye be!

EBEN (*startled, stares at him with hatred for a moment—then dully*). Ay-eh.

CABOT (*surveying him jeeringly*). Why hain't ye been in t' dance? They was all axin' fur ye.

EBEN. Let 'em ax!

CABOT. They's a hull passel o' purty gals.

EBEN. T' hell with 'em!

CABOT. Ye'd ought t' be marryin' one o' 'em soon.

EBEN. I hain't marryin' no one.

CABOT. Ye might 'arn a share o' a farm that way.

EBEN (*with a sneer*). Like yew did, ye mean? I hain't that kind.

CABOT (*stung*). Ye lie! 'Twas yer Maw's folks aimed t' steal my farm from me.

EBEN. Other folks don't say so. (*After a pause—defiantly*) An' I got a farm, anyways!

CABOT (*derisively*). Whar?

EBEN (*stamps a foot on the ground*). Har!

CABOT (*throws his head back and laughs coarsely*). Ho-ho! Ye hev, hev ye? Waal, that's a good un!

EBEN (*controlling himself—grimly*). Ye'll see!

CABOT (*stares at him suspiciously, trying to make him out—a pause—then with scornful confidence*). Ay-eh. I'll see. So'll ye. It's ye that's blind—blind as a mole underground. (EBEN *suddenly laughs, one short sardonic bark:* "Ha." *A pause.* CABOT *peers at him with renewed suspicion.*) Whar air ye hawin' 'bout? (EBEN *turns away without answering.* CABOT *grows angry.*) God A'mighty, yew air a dumb dunce! They's nothin' in that thick skull o' your'n but noise—like a empty keg it be! (EBEN *doesn't seem to hear.* CABOT'S *rage grows.*) Yewr farm! God A'mighty! If ye wa'n't a born donkey ye'd know ye'll never own stick nor stone on it, specially now arter him bein' born. It's his'n, I tell ye—his'n arter I die—but I'll live a hundred jest t' fool ye all—an' he'll be growed then—yewr age a'most! (EBEN *laughs again his sardonic* "Ha." *This drives* CABOT *into a fury.*) Ha? Ye think ye kin git 'round that someways, do ye? Waal, it'll be her'n, too—Abbie's—ye won't git 'round her—she knows yer tricks—she'll be too much fur ye—she wants the farm her'n—she was afeerd o' ye—she told me ye was sneakin' 'round tryin' t' make love t' her t' git her on yer side . . . ye . . . ye mad fool, ye! (*He raises his clenched fists threateningly.*)

EBEN (*is confronting him choking with rage*). Ye lie, ye old skunk! Abbie never said no sech thing!

CABOT (*suddenly triumphant when he sees how shaken* EBEN *is*). She did. An' I says, I'll blow his brains t' the top o' them elums—an' she says no, that hain't sense, who'll ye git t' help ye on the farm in his place—an' then she says yew'n me ought t' have a son—I know we kin, she says—an' I says, if we do, ye kin have anythin' I've got ye've a mind t'. An' she says, I wants Eben cut off so's this farm'll be mine when ye die! (*With terrible gloating*) An that's what's happened, hain't it? An' the farm's her'n! An' the dust o' the road—that's you'rn! Ha! Now who's hawin'?

EBEN (*has been listening, petrified with grief and rage—suddenly laughs wildly and brokenly*). Ha-ha-ha! So that's her sneakin' game—all along!—like I suspicioned at fust—t' swaller it all—an' me, too . . . ! (*Madly*) I'll murder her! (*He springs toward the porch but* CABOT *is quicker and gets in between.*)

CABOT. No, ye don't!

EBEN. Git out o' my road! (*He tries to throw* CABOT *aside. They grapple in what becomes immediately a murderous struggle. The old man's concentrated strength is too much for* EBEN. CABOT *gets one hand on his throat and presses him back across the stone well. At the same moment,* ABBIE *comes out on the porch. With a stifled cry she runs toward them.*)

ABBIE. Eben! Ephraim! (*She tugs at the hand on* EBEN'S *throat.*) Let go, Ephraim! Ye're chokin' him!

CABOT (*removes his hand and flings* EBEN *sideways full length on the grass, gasping and choking. With a cry,* ABBIE *kneels beside him, trying to take his head on her lap, but he pushes her away.* CABOT *stands looking down with fierce triumph*). Ye needn't t've fret, Abbie, I wa'n't aimin' t' kill him. He hain't wuth hangin' fur—not by a hell of a sight! (*More and more triumphantly*) Seventy-six an' him not thirty yit—an' look whar he be fur thinkin' his Paw was easy! No, by God, I hain't easy! An' him upstairs, I'll raise him t' be like me! (*He walks to the porch—then turns with a great grin.*) I don't calc'late it's left in him, but if he gits pesky, Abbie, ye jest sing out. I'll come a-runnin' an' by the Eternal, I'll put him across my knee an' birch him! Ha-ha-ha! (*He goes into the house laughing. A moment later his loud "whoop" is heard.*)

That which Ephraim sensed "droppin' off the elums, climbin' up the roof, sneakin' down the chimney, pokin' in the corners" has worked its evil so thoroughly that not even the peace of the barn has freed him of it. Meeting Eben, the old man attempts to make peace with his son, offering a share of the farm to Eben when he proves he can sire his own line. The implications, the ironic superiority Eben finds in the promise fill his already full heart with hate, a hate that breeds hate in old Cabot and goads him on to threatening Eben with Abbie's harsh strength. Surely the elms drop their centuries of accumulated hate across the shoulders of the two men as, with the prize Abbie a horrified onlooker, a primitive man beats his civilized son in hand-to-hand combat. Ephraim has defeated Eben in the psychological struggle too, for, unknowingly, Ephraim has struck deeply at Eben's most sensitive area. Symbolic of his mother and her struggle against Ephraim, Abbie first became an instrument, then a mother-substitute, then a wife-mother—such a complex symbol that when one part of it crumpled the whole structure fell, leaving Eben a defeated, raging child. The stones have not worked their magic for him; he cannot stand against adversity with the determined strength of his father.

ABBIE (*tenderly*). Eben. Air ye hurt? (*She tries to kiss him but he pushes her violently away and struggles to a sitting position.*)

EBEN (*gaspingly*). T' hell—with ye!

ABBIE (*not believing her ears*). It's me, Eben—Abbie—don't ye know me?

EBEN (*glowering at her with hatred*). Ay-eh—I know ye—now! (*He suddenly breaks down, sobbing weakly.*)

ABBIE (*fearfully*). Eben—what's happened t' ye—why did ye look at me 's if ye hated me?

EBEN (*violently, between sobs and gasps*). I do hate ye! Ye're a whore—a damn trickin' whore!

ABBIE (*shrinking back horrified*). Eben! Ye don't know what ye're sayin'!

EBEN (*scrambling to his feet and following her—accusingly*). Ye're nothin' but a stinkin' passel o' lies! Ye've been lyin' t' me every word ye spoke, day an' night, since we fust—done it. Ye've kept sayin' ye loved me. . . .

ABBIE (*frantically*). I do love ye! (*She takes his hand but he flings her away.*)

EBEN (*unheeding*). Ye've made a fool o' me—a sick, dumb fool—a-purpose! Ye've been on'y playin' yer sneakin', stealin' game all along—gittin' me t' lie with ye so's ye'd hev a son he'd think was his'n, an' makin' him promise he'd give ye the farm and let me eat dust, if ye did git him a son! (*Staring at her with anguished, bewildered eyes*) They must be a devil livin' in ye! T'ain't human t' be as bad as that be!

ABBIE (*stunned—dully*). He told yew . . . ?

EBEN. Hain't it true? It hain't no good in yew lyin'.

ABBIE (*pleadingly*). Eben, listen—ye must listen—it was long ago—afore we done nothin'—yew was scornin' me—goin' t' see Min—when I was lovin' ye—an' I said it t' him t' git vengeance on ye!

EBEN (*unheedingly. With tortured passion*). I wish ye was dead! I wish I was dead along with ye afore this come! (*Ragingly*) But I'll git my vengeance too! I'll pray Maw t' come back t' help me—t' put her cuss on yew an' him!

ABBIE (*brokenly*). Don't ye, Eben! Don't ye! (*She throws herself on her knees before him, weeping.*) I didn't mean t' do bad t' ye! Fergive me, won't ye?

EBEN (*not seeming to hear her—fiercely*). I'll git squar' with the old skunk—an' yew! I'll tell him the truth 'bout the son he's so proud o'! Then I'll leave ye here t' pizen each other—with Maw comin' out o' her grave at nights—an' I'll go t' the gold fields o' Californi-a whar Sim an' Peter be!

ABBIE (*terrified*). Ye won't—leave me? Ye can't!

EBEN (*with fierce determination*). I'm a-goin', I tell ye! I'll git rich thar an' come back an' fight him fur the farm he stole—an' I'll kick ye both out in the road—t' beg an' sleep in the woods—an' yer son along with ye—t' starve an' die! (*He is hysterical at the end.*)

ABBIE (*with a shudder—humbly*). He's yewr son, too, Eben.

EBEN (*torturedly*). I wish he never was born! I wish he'd die this minit! I wish I'd never sot eyes on him! It's him—yew havin' him—a-purpose t' steal—that's changed everythin'!

ABBIE (*gently*). Did ye believe I loved ye—afore he come?

EBEN. Ay-eh—like a dumb ox!

ABBIE. An' ye don't believe no more?

EBEN. B'lieve a lyin' thief! Ha!

ABBIE (*shudders—then humbly*). An' did ye r'ally love me afore?

EBEN (*brokenly*). Ay-eh—an' ye was trickin' me!

ABBIE. An' ye don't love me now!

EBEN (*violently*). I hate ye, I tell ye!

ABBIE. An' ye're truly goin' West—goin' t' leave me—all account o' him being born?

EBEN. I'm a-goin' in the mornin'—or may God strike me t' hell!

ABBIE (*after a pause—with a dreadful cold intensity—slowly*). If that's what his comin 's done t' me—killin' yewr love—takin' yew away—my on'y joy—the on'y joy I ever knowed—like heaven t' me—purtier'n heaven—then I hate him, too, even if I be his Maw!

EBEN (*bitterly*). Lies! Ye love him! He'll steal the farm fur ye! (*Brokenly*) But t'ain't the farm so much—not no more—it's yew foolin' me—gittin' me t' love ye—lyin' yew loved me—jest t' git a son t' steal!

ABBIE (*distractedly*). He won't steal! I'd kill him fust! I do love ye! I'll prove t' ye . . . !

EBEN (*harshly*). T'ain't no use lyin' no more. I'm deaf t' ye! (*He turns away.*) I hain't seein' ye agen. Good-by!

ABBIE (*pale with anguish*). Hain't ye even goin' t' kiss me—not once—arter all we loved?

EBEN (*in a hard voice*). I hain't wantin' t' kiss ye never agen! I'm wantin' t' forgit I ever sot eyes on ye!

ABBIE. Eben!—ye mustn't—wait a spell—I want t' tell ye. . . .

EBEN. I'm a-goin' in t' git drunk. I'm a-goin' t' dance.

ABBIE (*clinging to his arm—with passionate earnestness*). If I could make it—'s if he'd never come up between us—if I could prove t' ye I wa'n't schemin' t' steal from ye—so's everythin' could be jest the same with us, lovin' each other jest the same, kissin' an' happy the same's we've been happy afore he come—if I could do it—ye'd love me agen, wouldn't ye? Ye'd kiss me agen? Ye wouldn't never leave me, would ye?

EBEN (*moved*). I calc'late not. (*Then shaking her hand off his arm—with a bitter smile*) But ye hain't God, be ye?

ABBIE (*exultantly*). Remember ye've promised! (*Then with strange intensity*) Mebbe I kin take back one thin' God does!

EBEN (*peering at her*). Ye're gittin' cracked, hain't ye? (*Then going towards door*) I'm a-goin' t' dance.

ABBIE (*calls after him intensely*). I'll prove t' ye! I'll prove I love ye better'n. . . . (*He goes in the door, not seeming to hear. She remains standing where she is, looking after him—then she finishes desperately*) Better'n everythin' else in the world!

CURTAIN

Eben's destruction is more than Abbie can bear. He is her son, her lover, and her beloved—a mighty combination that overpowers her love for his child. Passion transcends lust when, with the intensity of a Medea, Abbie decides what she must do. Unlike Medea, however, her decision is an emotional response rather than a controlled act of will and intellect. She lacks heroic stature as a dramatic character only because she lacks heroic stature as a human being. It is, perhaps, that very weakness that makes her action so believable.

Scene Three

Just before dawn in the morning—shows the kitchen and CABOT'S *bedroom. In the kitchen, by the light of a tallow candle on the table,* EBEN *is sitting, his chin propped on his hands, his drawn face blank and expressionless. His carpetbag is on the floor beside him. In the bedroom, dimly lighted by a small whale-oil lamp,* CABOT *lies asleep.* ABBIE *is bending over the cradle, listening, her face full of terror yet with an undercurrent of desperate triumph. Suddenly, she breaks down and sobs, appears about to throw herself on her knees beside the cradle; but the old man turns restlessly, groaning in his sleep, and she controls herself, and, shrinking away from the cradle with a gesture of horror, backs swiftly toward the door in rear and goes out. A moment later she comes into the kitchen and, running to* EBEN, *flings her arms about his neck and kisses him wildly. He hardens himself, he remains unmoved and cold, he keeps his eyes straight ahead.*

ABBIE (*hysterically*). I done it, Eben! I told ye I'd do it! I've proved I love ye—better'n everythin'—so's ye can't never doubt me no more!

EBEN (*dully*). Whatever ye done, it hain't no good now.

ABBIE (*wildly*). Don't ye say that! Kiss me, Eben, won't ye? I need ye t' kiss me arter what I done! I need ye t' say ye love me!

EBEN (*kisses her without emotion—dully*). That's fur goodby. I'm a-goin' soon.

ABBIE. No! No! Ye won't go—not now!

EBEN (*going on with his own thoughts*). I been a-thinkin'—an' I hain't goin' t' tell Paw nothin'. I'll leave Maw t' take vengeance on ye. If I told him, the old skunk'd jest be stinkin' mean enuf to take it out on that baby. (*His voice showing emotion in spite of him*) An' I don't want nothin' bad t' happen t' him. He hain't t' blame fur yew. (*He adds with a certain queer pride*) An' he looks like me! An' by God, he's mine! An' some day I'll be a-comin' back an' . . . !

ABBIE (*too absorbed in her own thoughts to listen to him—pleadingly*). They's no cause fur ye t' go now—they's no sense—it's all the same's it was—they's nothin' come b'tween us now—arter what I done!

EBEN (*something in her voice arouses him. He stares at her a bit frightenedly*). Ye look mad, Abbie. What did ye do?

ABBIE. I—I killed him, Eben.

EBEN (*amazed*). Ye killed him?

ABBIE (*dully*). Ay-eh.

EBEN (*recovering from his astonishment—savagely*). An' serves him right! But we got t' do somethin' quick t' make it look 's if the old skunk'd killed himself when he was drunk. We kin prove by 'em all how drunk he got.

ABBIE (*wildly*). No! No! Not him! (*Laughing distractedly*) But that's what I ought t' done, hain't it? I oughter killed him instead! Why didn't ye tell me?

EBEN (*appalled*). Instead? What d'ye mean?

ABBIE. Not him.

EBEN (*his face grown ghastly*). Not—not that baby!

ABBIE (*dully*). Ay-eh?

EBEN (*falls to his knees as if he'd been struck—his voice trembling with horror*). Oh, God A'mighty! A'mighty God! Maw, whar was ye, why didn't ye stop her?

ABBIE (*simply*). She went back t' her grave that night we fust done it, remember? I hain't felt her about since. (*A pause.* EBEN *hides his head in his hands, trembling all over as if he had the ague. She goes on dully.*) I left the piller over his little face. Then he killed himself. He stopped breathin'. (*She begins to weep softly.*)

EBEN (*rage beginning to mingle with grief*). He looked like me. He was mine, damn ye!

ABBIE (*slowly and brokenly*). I didn't want t' do it. I hated myself fur doin' it. I loved him. He was so purty—dead spit 'n' image o' yew. But I loved yew more—an' yew was goin' away—far off whar I'd never see ye agen, never kiss ye, never feel ye pressed agin me agen—an' ye said ye hated me fur havin' him—ye said ye hated him an' wished he was dead—ye said if it hadn't been fur him comin' it'd be the same's afore between us.

EBEN (*unable to endure this, springs to his feet in a fury, threatening her, his twitching fingers seeming to reach out for her throat*). Ye lie! I never said—I never dreamed ye'd—I'd cut off my head afore I'd hurt his finger!

ABBIE (*piteously, sinking on her knees*). Eben, don't ye look at me like that—hatin' me—not after what I done fur ye—fur us—so's we could be happy agen—

EBEN (*furiously now*). Shut up, or I'll kill ye! I see yer game now—the same old sneakin' trick—ye're aimin' t' blame me fur the murder ye done!

ABBIE (*moaning—putting her hands over her ears*). Don't ye, Eben! Don't ye! (*She grasps his legs.*)

EBEN (*his mood suddenly changing to horror, shrinks away from her*). Don't ye tech me! Ye're pizen! How could ye—t' murder a pore little critter—Ye must've swapped yer soul t' hell! (*Suddenly raging*) Ha! I kin see why ye done it! Not the lies ye jest told—but 'cause ye wanted t' steal agen—steal the last thin' ye'd left me—my part o' him—no, the hull o' him—ye saw he looked like me—ye knowed he was all mine—an' ye couldn't b'ar it—I know ye! Ye killed him fur bein' mine! (*All this has driven him almost insane. He makes a rush past her for the door—then turns—shaking both fists at her, violently.*) But I'll take vengeance now! I'll git the Sheriff! I'll tell him everythin'! Then I'll sing "I'm off to Californi-a!" an' go—gold—Golden Gate—gold sun—fields o' gold in the West! (*This last he half shouts, half croons incoherently, suddenly breaking off passionately*) I'm a-goin' fur the Sheriff t' come an' git ye! I want ye tuk away, locked up from me! I can't stand t' luk at ye! Murderer an' thief 'r not, ye still tempt me! I'll give ye up t' the Sheriff! (*He turns and runs out, around the corner of house, panting and sobbing, and breaks into a swerving sprint down the road.*)

ABBIE (*struggling to her feet, runs to the door, calling after him*). I love ye, Eben! I love ye! (*She stops at the door weakly, swaying, about to fall.*) I don't care what ye do—if ye'll on'y love me agen—(*She falls limply to the floor in a faint.*)

CURTAIN

Passion has unhinged Abbie. Killing Ephraim did not occur to her. Eben did not tell her to do that. In her frenzy, her panic at potential loss, she heard Eben's harsh words as a directive to kill their child, to choose between her two loves. Eben is weakest as a man at this point. Seeing only Abbie's guilt, he refuses to see his own participation in this violent act, refuses to accept responsibility for his unguarded speech. Horrified, angry, vengeful, he is reduced to baseness, the disappearing layers of civilization revealing the shell of a primitive man, but a primitive man unrefined by successive generations. Having violated every law of God and man, Eben has no recourse but man's law, and he turns to it blindly.

SCENE FOUR

About an hour later. Same as Scene Three. Shows the kitchen and CABOT'S *bedroom. It is after dawn. The sky is brilliant with the sunrise. In the kitchen,* ABBIE *sits at the table, her body limp and exhausted, her head bowed down over her arms, her face hidden. Upstairs,* CABOT *is still asleep but awakens with a start. He looks toward the window and gives a snort of surprise and irritation—throws back the covers and begins hurriedly pulling on his clothes. Without looking behind him, he begins talking to* ABBIE *whom he supposes beside him.*

CABOT. Thunder 'n' lightin', Abbie! I hain't slept this late in fifty year! Looks 's if the sun was full riz a'most. Must've been the dancin' an' likker. Must be gittin' old. I hope Eben's t' wuk. Ye might've tuk the trouble t' rouse me, Abbie. (*He turns —sees no one there—surprised.*) Waal—whar air she? Gittin' vittles, I calc'late. (*He tiptoes to the cradle and peers down—proudly.*) Mornin', sonny. Purty's a picture! Sleepin' sound. He don't beller all night like most o' 'em. (*He goes quietly out the door in rear—a few moments later enters kitchen—sees* ABBIE—*with satisfaction.*) So thar ye be. Ye got any vittles cooked?

ABBIE (*without moving*). No.

CABOT (*coming to her, almost sympathetically*). Ye feelin' sick?

ABBIE. No.

CABOT (*pats her on shoulder. She shudders*). Ye'd best lie down a spell. (*Half jocularly*) Yer son'll be needin' ye soon. He'd ought t' wake up with a gnashin' appetite, the sound way he's sleepin'.

ABBIE (*shudders—then in a dead voice*). He hain't never goin' t' wake up.

CABOT (*jokingly*). Takes after me this mornin'. I hain't slept so late in . . .

ABBIE. He's dead.

CABOT (*stares at her—bewilderedly*). What. . . .

ABBIE. I killed him.

CABOT (*stepping back from her—aghast*). Air ye drunk—'r crazy—'r . . . !

ABBIE (*suddenly lifts her head and turns on him—wildly*). I killed him, I tell ye! I smothered him. Go up an' see if ye don't b'lieve me! (CABOT *stares at her a second, then bolts out the rear door—can be heard bounding up the stairs—and rushes into the bedroom and over to the cradle.* ABBIE *has sunk back lifelessly into her former position.* CABOT *puts his hand down on the body in the crib. An expression of fear and horror comes over his face.*)

CABOT (*shrinking away—tremblingly*). God A'mighty! God A'mighty. (*He stumbles out the door—in a short while returns to the kitchen—comes to* ABBIE, *the stunned expression still on his face—hoarsely*) Why did ye do it? Why? (*As she doesn't answer, he grabs her violently by the shoulder and shakes her.*) I ax ye why ye done it! Ye'd better tell me 'r . . . !

ABBIE (*gives him a furious push which sends him staggering back and springs to her feet—with wild rage and hatred*). Don't ye dare tech me! What right hev ye t' question me 'bout him? He wa'n't yewr son! Think I'd have a son by yew? I'd die fust! I hate the sight o' ye an' allus did! It's yew I should've murdered, if I'd had good sense! I hate ye! I love Eben. I did from the fust. An' he was Eben's son—mine an' Eben's—not your'n!

CABOT (*stands looking at her dazedly—a pause—finding his words with an effort—dully*). That was it—what I felt—pokin' round the corners—while ye lied—holdin' yerself from me—sayin' ye'd a'ready conceived—(*He lapses into crushed silence—then with a strange emotion*) He's dead, sart'n. I felt his heart. Pore little critter! (*He blinks back one tear, wiping his sleeve across his nose.*)

ABBIE (*hysterically*). Don't ye! Don't ye! (*She sobs unrestrainedly.*)

CABOT (*with a concentrated effort that stiffens his body into a rigid line and hardens his face into a stony mask—through his teeth to himself*). I got t' be—like a stone—a rock o' jedgment! (*A pause. He gets complete control over himself— harshly*) If he was Eben's, I be glad he air gone! An' mebbe I suspicioned it all along. I felt they was somethin' onnateral—somewhars—the house got so lonesome—an' cold—drivin' me down t' the barn—t' the beasts o' the field. . . . Ay-eh. I must've suspicioned—somethin'. Ye didn't fool me—not altogether, leastways—I'm too old a bird—growin' ripe on the bough. . . . (*He becomes aware he is wandering, straightens again, looks at* ABBIE *with a cruel grin.*) So ye'd like t' hev murdered me 'stead o' him, would ye? Waal, I'll live to a hundred! I'll live t' see ye hung! I'll deliver ye up t' the jedgment o' God an' the law! I'll git the Sheriff now. (*Starts for the door*)

ABBIE (*dully*). Ye needn't. Eben's gone fur him.

CABOT (*amazed*). Eben—gone fur the Sheriff?

ABBIE. Ay-eh.

CABOT. T' inform agen ye?

ABBIE. Ay-eh.

CABOT (*considers this—a pause—then in a hard voice*). Waal, I'm thankful fur him savin' me the trouble. I'll git t' wuk. (*He goes to the door—then turns—in a voice full of strange emotion*) He'd ought t' been my son, Abbie. Ye'd ought t' loved me. I'm a man. If ye'd loved me, I'd never told no Sheriff on ye no matter what ye did, if they was t' brile me alive!

ABBIE (*defensively*). They's more to it nor yew know, makes him tell.

CABOT (*dryly*). Fur yewr sake, I hope they be. (*He goes out—comes around to the gate—stares up at the sky. His control relaxes. For a moment he is old and weary. He murmurs despairingly*) God A'mighty, I be lonesomer'n ever! (*He hears running footsteps from the left, immediately is himself again.* EBEN *runs in, panting exhaustedly, wild-eyed and mad looking. He lurches through the gate.* CABOT *grabs him by the shoulder.* EBEN *stares at him dumbly.*) Did ye tell the Sheriff?

EBEN (*nodding stupidly*). Ay-eh.

CABOT (*gives him a push away that sends him sprawling—laughing with withering contempt*). Good fur ye! A prime chip o'yer Maw ye be! (*He goes toward the barn, laughing harshly.* EBEN *scrambles to his feet. Suddenly* CABOT *turns—grimly threatening*) Git off this farm when the Sheriff takes her—or, by God, he'll have t' come back an' git me fur murder, too! (*He stalks off.* EBEN *does not appear to have heard him. He runs to the door and comes into the kitchen.* ABBIE *looks up with a cry of anguished joy.* EBEN *stumbles over and throws himself on his knees beside her—sobbing brokenly.*)

EBEN. Fergive me!

ABBIE (*happily*). Eben! (*She kisses him and pulls his head over against her breast.*)

EBEN. I love ye! Fergive me!

ABBIE (*ecstatically*). I'd fergive ye all the sins in hell fur sayin' that! (*She kisses his head, pressing it to her with a fierce passion of possession.*)

EBEN (*brokenly*). But I told the Sheriff. He's comin' fur ye!

ABBIE. I kin b'ar what happens t' me—now!

EBEN. I woke him up. I told him. He says, wait 'til I git dressed. I was waiting. I got to thinkin' o' yew. I got to thinkin' how I'd loved ye. It hurt like somethin' was bustin' in my chest an' head. I got t' cryin'. I knowed sudden I loved ye yet, an' allus would love ye!

ABBIE (*caressing his hair—tenderly*). My boy, hain't ye?

EBEN. I begun t' run back. I cut across the fields an' through the woods. I thought ye might have time t' run away—with me—an' . . .

ABBIE (*shaking her head*). I got t' take my punishment—t' pay fur my sin.

EBEN. Then I want t' share it with ye.

ABBIE. Ye didn't do nothin'.

EBEN. I put it in yer head. I wisht he was dead! I as much as urged ye t' do it!

ABBIE. No. It was me alone!

EBEN. I'm as guilty as yew be! He was the child o' our sin.

ABBIE (*lifting her head as if defying God*). I don't repent that sin! I hain't askin' God t' fergive that!

EBEN. Nor me—but it led up t' the other—an' the murder ye did, ye did 'count o' me—an' it's my murder, too. I'll tell the Sheriff—an' if ye deny it, I'll say we planned it t'gether—an' they'll all b'lieve me, fur they suspicion everythin' we've done, an' it'll seem likely an' true to 'em. An' it is true—way down. I did help ye—somehow.

ABBIE (*laying her head on his—sobbing*). No! I don't want yew t' suffer!

EBEN. I got t' pay fur my part o' the sin! An' I'd suffer wust leavin' ye, goin' West, thinkin' o' ye day an' night, bein' out when yew was in— (*Lowering his voice*) 'r bein' alive when yew was dead. (*A pause*) I want t' share with ye, Abbie—prison 'r death 'r hell 'r anythin'! (*He looks into her eyes and forces a trembling smile.*) If I'm sharin' with ye, I won't feel lonesome, leastways.

ABBIE (*weakly*). Eben! I won't let ye! I can't let ye!

EBEN (*kissing her—tenderly*). Ye can't he'p yerself. I got ye beat fur once!

ABBIE (*forcing a smile—adoringly*). I hain't beat—s'long's I got ye!

EBEN (*hears the sound of feet outside*). Ssshh! Listen! They've come t' take us!

ABBIE. No, it's him. Don't give him no chance to fight ye, Eben. Don't say nothin'—no matter what he says. An' I won't neither. (*It is* CABOT. *He comes up from the barn in a great state of excitement and strides into the house and then into the kitchen.* EBEN *is kneeling beside* ABBIE, *his arm around her, hers around him. They stare straight ahead.*)

CABOT (*stares at them, his face hard. A long pause—vindictively*). Ye make a slick pair o' murderin' turtle doves! Ye'd ought t' be both hung on the same limb an' left thar t' swing in the breeze an' rot—a warnin' t' old fools like me t' b'ar their lonesomeness alone—an' fur young fools like ye t' hobble their lust. (*A pause. The excitement returns to his face, his eyes snap, he looks a bit crazy.*) I couldn't work today. I couldn't take no interest. T' hell with the farm! I'm leavin' it! I've turned the cows an' other stock loose! I've druv 'em into the woods whar they kin be free! By freein' 'em, I'm freein' myself! I'm quittin' here today! I'll set fire t' house an' barn an' watch 'em burn, an' I'll leave yer Maw t' haunt the ashes, an' I'll will the fields back t' God, so that nothin' human kin never touch 'em! I'll be a-goin' to Californi-a—t' jine Simeon an' Peter—true sons o' mine if they be dumb fools—an' the Cabots'll find Solomon's Mines t'gether! (*He suddenly cuts a mad caper.*) Whoop! What was the song they sung? "Oh, Californi-a! That's the land fur me." (*He sings this—then gets on his knees by the floor-board under which the money was hid.*) An' I'll sail thar on one o' the finest clippers I kin find! I've got the money! Pity ye didn't know whar this was hidden so's ye could steal. . . . (*He has pulled up the board. He stares—feels—stares again. A pause of dead silence. He slowly turns, slumping into a sitting position on the floor, his eyes like those of a dead fish, his face the sickly green of an attack of nausea. He swallows painfully several times—forces a weak smile at last.*) So—ye did steal it!

EBEN (*emotionlessly*). I swapped it t' Sim an' Peter fur their share o' the farm—t' pay their passage t' Californi-a.

CABOT (*with one sardonic*). Ha! (*He begins to recover. Gets slowly to his feet—strangely*) I calc'late God give it to 'em—not yew! God's hard, not easy! Mebbe they's easy gold in the West but it hain't God's gold. It hain't fur me. I kin hear His voice warnin' me agen t' be hard an' stay on my farm. I kin see his hand usin' Eben t' steal t' keep me from weakness. I kin feel I be in the palm o' His hand, His fingers guidin' me. (*A pause—then he mutters sadly*) It's a-goin' t' be lonesomer now than ever it war afore—an' I'm gittin' old, Lord—ripe on the bough. . . . (*Then stiffening*) Waal—what d'ye want? God's lonesome, hain't He? God's hard an' lonesome! (*A pause. The* SHERIFF *with two men comes up the road from the left. They move cautiously to the door. The* SHERIFF *knocks on it with the butt of his pistol.*)

SHERIFF. Open in the name o' the law! (*They start.*)

CABOT. They've come fur ye. (*He goes to the rear door.*) Come in, Jim! (*The three men enter.* CABOT *meets them in doorway.*) Jest a minit, Jim. I got 'em safe here. (*The* SHERIFF *nods. He and his companions remain in the doorway.*)

EBEN (*suddenly calls*). I lied this mornin', Jim. I helped her to do it. Ye kin take me, too.

ABBIE (*brokenly*). No!

CABOT. Take 'em both. (*He comes forward—stares at* EBEN *with a trace of grudging admiration*) Purty good—fur yew! Waal, I got t' round up the stock. Good-by.

EBEN. Good-by.

ABBIE. Good-by. (CABOT *turns and strides past the men—comes out and around the corner of the house, his shoulders squared, his face stony, and stalks grimly toward the barn. In the meantime the* SHERIFF *and men have come into the room.)*

SHERIFF *(embarrassedly).* Waal—we'd best start.

ABBIE. Wait. *(Turns to* EBEN*)* I love ye, Eben.

EBEN. I love ye, Abbie. *(They kiss. The three men grin and shuffle embarrassedly.* EBEN *takes* ABBIE'S *hand. They go out the door in rear, the men following, and come from the house, walking hand in hand to the gate.* EBEN *stops there and points to the sunrise sky.)* Sun's a-rizin'. Purty, hain't it?

ABBIE. Ay-eh. *(They both stand for a moment looking up raptly in attitudes strangely aloof and devout.)*

SHERIFF *(looking around at the farm enviously—to his companion).* It's a jim-dandy farm, no denyin'. Wished I owned it!

CURTAIN

Ephraim attains the tragic heights in the last scene; God is harsh and impersonal—and impersonal forces are lonely forces. The man in Ephraim would have protected Abbie had she loved him; the man in Ephraim allows him to pity her but loathe Eben for his weakness in betraying Abbie. But he is a mortal man; there is some of the child in him. For one moment, he would free himself from the farm, will it back to the ghost of Eben's mother and God, and seek an El Dorado with the sons he let go without a tear. In his one compassionate moment, old Ephraim wept for the dead child—not his son, not his grandson, but the son of Man, the child born in sin, now dead of passion.

Deprived of his escape, knowing that Eben has stolen his wife and child and money, leaving him only the hard stones and his lonesome God, Ephraim accepts the dictates of the stern Jehovah. "I kin feel I be in the palm of His hand, His fingers guidin' me," Ephraim declares. Among the stones, on the hill where the elms spread their massive boughs, Ephraim accepts the necessities of his God ("God's lonesome, hain't He? God's hard an' lonesome!") even though he cannot understand the reason for such necessities. He can never be like God—no man can—but he will not be defeated by that inability. Rather, like Job, he will submit to God without yielding to man. And therein lies his tragic power.

In this final hour, Eben finds a bare minimum of salvation as a tragic figure, but he does achieve great power as a dramatic hero. Accepting his responsibility, recognizing the power of love (that emotion he has never understood till now), he accepts a modern concept of manhood. It is not tragic; it is dramatic. Eben has not been victorious but he has not been defeated. Neither has he accepted God or himself. Instead, he has found the hope of love, however romantic or unrealistic that hope may be, and he has made an irrevocable decision. That is the drama of life: growth toward the ability to make a decision.

O'Neill would have called Ephraim a tragic figure, Eben a "spiritual middle classer." Speaking of another play, *Diff'rent,* O'Neill observed:

I have been accused of unmitigated gloom. Is this a pessimistic view of life? I do not think so. There is a skin deep optimism and another higher optimism, not skin deep, which is usually confounded with pessimism. To me, the tragic alone has that significant beauty which is truth. It is the meaning of life—and the hope. The noblest is eternally the most tragic. The people who succeed and do not push on to a greater failure are the spiritual middle classers. Their stopping at success is the proof of their compromising insignificance. How petty their dreams must have been! The man who pursues the mere attainable should be sentenced to get it—and keep it. Let him rest on his laurels and enthrone him in a Morris chair, in which laurels and hero may wither away together. Only through the unattainable does man achieve a hope worth living and dying for—and so attain himself. He with the spiritual guerdon of a hope in hopelessness, is nearest to the stars and the rainbow's foot.°

Suggested Assignments. 1. Oedipus, Macbeth, and Ephraim love the land they consider their exclusive domain. Each loves it in a different way, however. Modern Americans are relatively free of the land (only seven per cent of our population live on the farm) yet we can understand the ties that bind these men to the soil. Explain, in a brief paper, the primitive response we understand even if we have never owned land.

2. Iocastê, Lady Macbeth, and Abbie Putnam have known motherhood. Defend your choice of the "best" mother of the group, documenting your analysis carefully with textual references.

3. Primitive needs, desires, and fears create a subconscious life seemingly far removed from the surface reality of our days. Tragedy seeks out these subterranean areas and purges the soul through an examination of them, a purgation that can be achieved in no other way. Choose one of the three tragedies you have studied and explain why you consider it a successful play in achieving such purgation for a modern American audience.

4. In *The Tragic Fallacy,* Joseph Wood Krutch noted:

We read but we do not write tragedies. The tragic solution of the problem of existence, the reconciliation to life by means of the tragic spirit is, that is to say, now only a fiction surviving in art. When that art itself has become, as it probably will, completely meaningless, when we have ceased not only to write but to *read* tragic

° *New York Herald Tribune,* February 13, 1921.

works, then it will be lost and in all real senses forgotten, since the devolution from Religion to Art to Document will be complete.°

In a brief paper, state your agreement or disagreement with Krutch's statement, supporting your beliefs with arguments that are as concrete as you can make them.

° Joseph Wood Krutch, "The Tragic Fallacy," *The Modern Temper* (New York, 1956), pp. 79-97.

CHAPTER VI

Of Satyrs and Such—Comedy

If it is ironic that man is the only animal that prays—or needs to—it is also ironic that he is the only animal that laughs—or needs to. It is equally ironic that prayer and laughter seem to serve similar needs under completely dissimilar circumstances.

Possibly every tragedy is a form of collective prayer—a literary Mass read to propitiate unknown gods with the sacrifice of tragic heroes, the celebrants of that Mass finding their souls cleansed in the symbolic destruction of their representative. Certainly, tragedy is always concerned with man's desire to free himself of earthly limitations—whether they are imposed by God, by nature, by other men, or by man's own human nature. As a result, tragedy is a conservative and restraining form that persuades man to idealize himself by aspiring to some kind of perfection. And we weep when we cannot attain it.

It is equally possible that comedy is a raucous hymn of thanksgiving that other men are more arrogant, stupid, foolish, inadequate, or wicked than we, and that *they* are discovered publicly. Accepting the inevitability of man's limitations, comedy suggests that we learn to live with those limitations by being amused by them. Comedy is a revolutionary, permissive form happily urging man to view himself as an imperfect animal chronically blundering into his imperfections—and laughing at his own clumsiness.

Comedy, of course, is always associated with laughter—though "laughter" itself is a process which is difficult to either account for or explain. Psychologists, for example, are as concerned with laughter as they are with tears—and probably in greater disagreement about its purpose. Writers are equally argumentative, each expressing his pet theory with defensive authority and a willingness to do battle for it. Baudelaire, that grim French poet who wrote *Flowers of Evil,* calls laughter the greatest Satanic element in man. W. McDougall, in *The Group Mind*,* says that man's ability to laugh evolved as an "antidote to sympathy," adding that it has a shielding capacity that protects us from "the depressive influence of the shortcomings of our fellow men." A. Bain, one of the pioneers in modern psychology, believed "Not in physical effects alone, but in everything where a man can achieve a stroke of superiority, in surpassing or discomforting a rival, is the disposition of laughter apparent."°

Various writers have argued that humor (and its result, laughter) is broadly based on a variety of elements: physical deformity (Falstaff's obesity or Cyrano de Bergerac's oversized nose); defective senses (especially in such Hollywood comedy teams as Stan Laurel and Oliver Hardy or Bud Abbott and Lou Costello); stock behavioral patterns of such groups as intellectuals (Henry Higgins, for example, in Shaw's *Pygmalion,* which was to become *My Fair Lady*) or traveling salesmen and librarians (*The Music Man*); or affectation resulting from vanity or hypocrisy (which Robert Burns, in "To a Louse," suggested would leave us if God would give us the gift to see ourselves as others see us). But they all agree, aware of it or not, that some degree of cruelty underlies humor and laughter.

The French philosopher Henri Bergson once observed, "Laughter is, above all, a corrective. Being intended to humiliate, it must make a painful impression on the person against whom it is directed. By laughter, society avenges itself for liberties taken with it."* Those "liberties" may run the gamut from crude practical jokes to snobbery. And whether we laugh *at* someone or *with* someone, we are attempting the corrective. Laughing at someone allows us superiority if only for the moment in which his dignity is damaged by our laughter. Laughing with someone, we laugh at ourselves as we share his uncomfortable moment.

Laughter may be a gentle chuckle or uncontrolled hysteria, and between those two extremes are many gradations of the sound created when tensions are relieved with noise. For that is what laughter is, a tension-releaser. Happy people laugh more than unhappy people, of course, and it is axiomatic that happy people are less neurotic than unhappy ones. Laughter seems to be man's emotional steam-valve that blows easily and frequently before any great pressure can accumulate. The smaller the pressure, the more restrained the laughter; the greater the pressure, the more boisterous the mirth.

Puritans and prudes, unfortunately, find little to laugh at or with in life. For them, politics, religion, and sex are deadly serious. Laughter

---

° New York, 1920.

° *Manual of Mental and Moral Science* (London, 1868).

* *Laughter,* tr. Cloudesley Brereton and Fred Rothwell (New York, 1917).

will not relieve their pressures, for laughter cannot be aroused by situations wherein human feelings or involvement are violent. Such situations are already beyond exaggeration and, as Aristotle suggested, comedy shows men to be worse than they are. Puritans and prudes are convinced man is, by nature, already depraved; therefore, it is impossible for them to appreciate an exaggeration of his weaknesses and vices.

Wit and humor do not exist for such people. And that is tragic indeed, for *wit* results from a barbed ability to observe the incongruous and comment on it in a clever, sharp way. Wit creates laughter at the expense of others (and is, therefore, malicious), but it is easily forgivable because its creator must recognize foibles in others from perceived weaknesses in himself. *Humor* is wit gentled by humility. It results from the ability to observe the incongruous or ludicrous in others, become aware of its counterpart in oneself, and temper the comment with self-inclusion. Humor allows us to laugh with others. It is, therefore, lacking in malice and needs no apology.

Generally speaking, *comedy* relies on wit, and no element (such as plot, characters, or dialog) is allowed to interfere with the barbed observations frequently tempered with humor. *Nothing* is sacred in comedy, the form that originated with the Greeks from a happy blending of the most joyous elements of their religion.

The early worship of Dionysus centered in licentious street processions which included revelers in fanciful and ridiculous costumes and masks. Singing and dancing as they went, the revelers carried wine in great jars and a goodly quantity in their stomachs. At the head of the procession a huge phallus indicated the nature of the celebrants: they were satyrs— those half-human, half-beast followers of Dionysus who spent their days in pursuit of nymphs for purely carnal purposes. Called a *comus* (or *Komos*), the procession eventually became a form of drama now designated as the *satyr play*. Satyrs formed the Chorus: men dressed in skins, horns, and tails—with exaggerated phalluses frequently tripping them.

Thoroughly bawdy, delighting in unabashed vulgarity (by our standards), the satyr plays followed high drama in the theater, the licentious hilarity of them releasing the tensions generated by the tragedies. Frequently, the hero of the tragedy was the central figure in the satyr play. A typical such play was a relatively plotless series of indecent skits and dances employing the broadest kind of *burlesque* (an imitation, extremely exaggerated to reveal laughable qualities), *farce* (humor resulting from ludicrous situations such as a man blundering into a women's restroom and attempting to escape undetected), or *slapstick* (farce resulting from physical assault and named after a prop made from two thin slats of wood which, when slapped on an exposed rump, creates a loud noise).

Comedy (named after the *comus*) grew out of the satyr play and went its separate way to be performed at the City Lenaea, the winter celebration in honor of Dionysus. Elevated somewhat, it still retained much of the ribald humor of the satyr plays and combined it with *satire* (the sharpest kind of wit, designed to ridicule and arouse outright contempt). Politics, religion, and sex are, therefore, virtual "naturals" for comedy, for man is most amusing, inane, and ridiculous in any one of these three areas of his life.

Because comedy was an outgrowth of the fertility rites of Dionysus, it is concerned with life and its wonderful moments. Death and unhappiness are not its province. In fact, it celebrates man's ability to defeat the unpleasant vagaries of living. Consequently, *Old Comedy* (the earliest Greek comedy, exemplified by Aristophanes, *circa* 450 B.C.–380 B.C.) combines fantastic elements (clouds, frogs, wasps, and birds as characters) with outrageous situations (sheer farce wherein men are dressed as women, for instance) and rollicking political satire (indicating the strength of Athenian democracy). Lacking the tight dramatic structure of tragedy, Old Comedy followed a loose pattern. Beginning with a prologue, it alternated scenes of hilarious action with lyric interludes of great poetic beauty, the first half of the play providing the exposition of whatever small plot held the buffoonery together. Somewhere around the middle, a *parabasis* was inserted. It consisted of a lengthy speech by the author of the play and could be devoted to any topic or topics he cared to enlarge upon. In the *parabasis* of *The Clouds,* for instance, Aristophanes himself (represented by the Chorus) discussed the literary excellence of his play, persuading the audience that they should adjudge him the winning comedy playwright of that night's contest. The remainder of the play was a series of farcical sketches (not unlike vaudeville acts) which brought the "plot" to a happy conclusion. The play ended in a *comus* (revel) consisting of songs and dances celebrating the victory of joy over unhappiness.

Middle Comedy was a transitional form, examples of which did not survive, so we are unsure of its structure.

New Comedy (exemplified by Menander, *circa* 340 B.C.–290 B.C.) imposed restraints on the licentious elements of Old Comedy and added romance as the basic plot device, strengthening the plot in the process. In Old Comedy, nothing was sacred—not even the gods who frequently appeared onstage, drunk and disorderly. Everything was secondary to the raucous wit of the hilarious lines. New Comedy relegated humor to a secondary position, romance being paramount: boy meets girl, boy loses girl, boy gets girl after many obstacles have been overcome. The Chorus became relatively unimportant and *parabasis* was dismissed entirely as Menander added sentiment and pathos to tender scenes, creating characters that grew, developed, and changed in the course of the play. While no New Comedy is extant, records indicate that Menander was its major exemplar.

Roman comedy developed from imitations of Menander by Terence and Plautus, and *Romantic comedy* (whose greatest exponent is Shakespeare) was modeled on those two Romans. Plautus' *The Menaechmi,* for instance, was adapted by Shakespeare as *Comedy of Errors,* and *Miles Gloriosus* served as the model for all future braggart soldiers such as Shakespeare's Falstaff and Edmund Rostand's Cyrano de Bergerac.

Romantic comedy established and set many of the conventions that remain basic to comedy today. Servants being loyal to sons rather than to their masters, men masquerading as women and women masquerading as men for romantic reasons, women marrying for love rather than for money (as their fathers wished), shrewish wives being humbled by determined husbands—these were standard situations always accepted by Roman audiences and, because New Comedy was well received, borrowed by playwrights as recent as the ones who churn out the situation comedies you may have seen on last night's television screen.

Times have changed, however, and the delights of Aristophanes are almost lost in the contemporary theater except for isolated moments such as vaudeville acts which, if not washed, have been dry-cleaned until they are frayed and dull. An occasional comedy such as *The Moon Is Blue* or *Two for the Seesaw* promises to allow delight in a mature and witty treatment of our real problems; but then the playwrights either reconsider or the producers become wary, and the promise becomes lost in a series of compromises which merely titillate us and seem dirty rather than amuse us and seem honest. Comedy then becomes tragic in a sense, because, as Jean Giraudoux observed, "When the pure do not die but compromise and live on, then, and then only, we have tragedy."°

The ancient Greeks would have found our attitudes both primitive and barbarian, for they viewed the human body as a pagan field rather than as a Christian temple. And pagan fields were flower-strewn and meant to be run through barefooted. In short, sex was not a problem in Greece. Serving two functions (procreation and enjoyment), it was recognized as a necessity and as a pleasure. That it might be "sinful" never occurred to the Greeks, for they saw their gods in the natural phenomena on every hand. And they observed promiscuity in nature. Their major god (Zeus) was, more often than not, dallying in some quiet grove with a maiden who had caught his fancy. His wife, Hera, spent much of her time attempting to circumvent his pleasures—not that she considered such

° Joseph Chiari, *Contemporary French Theater,* p. 119.

pleasures immoral; indeed, his bedside manner was, in her opinion, too good for any lesser personage than herself. She never attempted to limit his sexual activity; she constantly attempted to limit it to her Olympian bed.

The Greeks emulated their gods: every man fancied himself a disseminator of joy; every woman felt that she was *the* deserving recipient. Consequently (because people enjoy others not having what they consider theirs), the Greeks were amused and delighted by stories revealing lovers discovered. For instance, a favorite myth concerned the trysts of Aphrodite and Ares (Venus and Mars) in the home of her husband Haephestos (Vulcan) when he was away. Forging a magnificient golden net, he covered the bed with it, then ostensibly left on a trip, and returned to find the lovers dallying. Releasing a trigger, he hauled the naked pair into the air like carp caught in a fishnet and called the other Olympians in to laugh at the suddenly un-amorous pair. Aphrodite and Ares were not embarrassed by the nude exposure (Greeks enjoyed the naked body, attaching no shame to it) or by the exposure of their illicit romance (all Olympus knew—how do you think Haephestos discovered the affair?). Rather, they were embarrassed because they had been outwitted and their present predicament served as proof of their lack of cleverness. In the sexual game, one-upmanship was the province of the Greeks while Britons (today's masters) were still tattooed naked savages chasing each other through the fog.

The opening scene of Aristophanes' *Lysistrata,* for example, provides a rich overlay of sexual, mythological allusion to the whole play. (And remember, the comedy was written to be performed at a festival honoring a god!) The Prologue is a brief dialog between Lysistrata and Calonice and the *double entendres* are precisely that. Such lines as "they lie abed and don't come" or "What's up? Something big?" can be read at the slangiest possible level—in fact, they must be, for they were written that way. Remember, as these beautiful women (young, curvaceous, and sexy) stand at the gateway to the sacred and the profane, they are unashamed of sex and are delighted by it—as often as possible. Their distress results less from political convictions (which are, ordinarily, the province of men only) than from loneliness and longing for their bed-partners. The opening scene follows:°

SCENE: *In Athens, beneath the Acropolis. In the center of the stage is the Propylaea, or gate-way to the Acropolis; to one side is a small grotto, sacred to Pan. The Orchestra represents a slope leading up to the gate-way.*

It is early in the morning. LYSISTRATA *is pacing impatiently up and down.*

° Translated by Charles T. Murphy.

LYSISTRATA. If they'd been summoned to worship the God of Wine, or Pan, or to visit the Queen of Love, why, you couldn't have pushed your way through the streets for all the timbrels. But now there's not a single woman here—except my neighbour; here she comes.

(*Enter* CALONICE.)

Good day to you, Calonice.

CALONICE. And to you, Lysistrata. (*Noticing* LYSISTRATA'S *impatient air*) But what ails you? Don't scowl, my dear; it's not becoming to you to knit your brows like that.

LYSISTRATA (*sadly*). Ah, Calonice, my heart aches; I'm so annoyed at us women. For among men we have a reputation for sly trickery—

CALONICE. And rightly too, on my word!

LYSISTRATA. —but when they were told to meet here to consider a matter of no small importance, they lie abed and don't come.

CALONICE. Oh, they'll come all right, my dear. It's not easy for a woman to get out, you know. One is working on her husband, another is getting up the maid, another has to put the baby to bed, or wash and feed it.

LYSISTRATA. But after all, there are other matters more important than all that.

CALONICE. My dear Lysistrata, just what is this matter you've summoned us women to consider? What's up? Something big?

LYSISTRATA. Very big.

CALONICE (*interested*). Is it stout, too?

LYSISTRATA (*smiling*). Yes indeed—both big and stout.

CALONICE. What? And the women still haven't come?

LYSISTRATA. It's not what you suppose; they'd have come soon enough for *that*. But I've worked up something, and for many a sleepless night I've turned it this way and that.

CALONICE (*in mock disappointment*). Oh, I guess it's pretty fine and slender, if you've turned it this way and that.

LYSISTRATA. So fine that the safety of the whole of Greece lies in us women.

CALONICE. In us women? It depends on a very slender reed then.

LYSISTRATA. Our country's fortunes are in our hands; and whether the Spartans shall perish—

CALONICE. Good! Let them perish, by all means.

LYSISTRATA. —and the Boeotians shall be completely annihilated.

CALONICE. Not completely! Please spare the eels.

LYSISTRATA. As for Athens, I won't use any such unpleasant words. But you understand what I mean. But if the women will meet here—the Spartans, the Boeotians, and we Athenians—then all together we will save Greece.

CALONICE. But what could women do that's clever or distinguished? We just sit around all dolled up in silk robes, looking pretty in our sheer gowns and evening slippers.

LYSISTRATA. These are just the things I hope will save us: these silk robes, perfumes, evening slippers, rouge, and our chiffon blouses.

CALONICE. How so?

LYSISTRATA. So never a man alive will lift a spear against the foe—

CALONICE. I'll get a silk gown at once.

LYSISTRATA. —or take up his shield—

CALONICE. I'll put on my sheerest gown!

LYSISTRATA. —or sword.

CALONICE. I'll buy a pair of evening slippers.

LYSISTRATA. Well then, shouldn't the women have come?

CALONICE. Come? Why, they should have *flown* here.

LYSISTRATA. Well, my dear, just watch: they'll act in true Athenian fashion—everything too late! And now there's not a woman here from the shore or from Salamis.

CALONICE. They're coming, I'm sure; at daybreak they were laying—to their oars to cross the straits.

LYSISTRATA. And those I expected would be the first to come—the women of Acharnae—they haven't arrived.

CALONICE. Yet the wife of Theagenes means to come: she consulted Hecate about it. (*Seeing a group of women approaching*) But look! Here come a few. And there are some more over here. Hurrah! Where do they come from?

LYSISTRATA. From Anagyra.

CALONICE. Yes indeed! We've raised up quite a stink from Anagyra anyway.

(*Enter* MYRRHINE *in haste, followed by several other women.*)

MYRRHINE (*breathlessly*). Have we come in time, Lysistrata? What do you say? Why so quiet?

LYSISTRATA. I can't say much for you, Myrrhine, coming at this hour on such important business.

MYRRHINE. Why, I had trouble finding my girdle in the dark. But if it's so important, we're here now; tell us.

LYSISTRATA. No. Let's wait a little for the women from Boeotia and the Peloponnesus.

MYRRHINE. That's a much better suggestion. Look! Here comes Lampito now.

(*Enter* LAMPITO *with two other women.*)

LYSISTRATA. Greetings, my dear Spartan friend. How pretty you look, my dear. What a smooth complexion and well-developed figure! You could throttle an ox.

LAMPITO. Faith, yes, I think I could. I take exercises and kick my heels against my bum. (*She demonstrates with a few steps of the Spartan "bottom-kicking" dance.*)

LYSISTRATA. And what splendid breasts you have.

LAMPITO. La! You handle me like a prize steer.

LYSISTRATA. And who is this young lady with you?

LAMPITO. Faith, she's an Ambassadress from Boeotia.

LYSISTRATA. Oh yes, a Boeotian, and blooming like a garden too.

CALONICE (*lifting up her skirt*). My word! How neatly her garden's weeded!

LYSISTRATA. And who is the other girl?

LAMPITO. Oh, she's a Corinthian swell.

MYRRHINE (*after a rapid examination*). Yes indeed. She swells very nicely (*pointing*) here and here.

LAMPITO. Who has gathered together this company of women?

LYSISTRATA. I have.

LAMPITO. Speak up, then. What do you want?

MYRRHINE. Yes, my dear, tell us what this important matter is.

LYSISTRATA. Very well, I'll tell you. But before I speak, let me ask you a little question.

MYRRHINE. Anything you like.

LYSISTRATA (*earnestly*). Tell me: don't you yearn for the fathers of your children, who are away at the wars? I know you all have husbands abroad.

CALONICE. Why, yes; mercy me! my husband's been away for five months in Thrace keeping guard on—Eucrates.

MYRRHINE. And mine for seven whole months in Pylus.

LAMPITO. And mine, as soon as ever he returns from the fray, readjusts his shield and flies out of the house again.

LYSISTRATA. And as for lovers, there's not even a ghost of one left. Since the Milesians revolted from us, I've not even seen an eight-inch dingus to be a leather consolation for us widows. Are you willing, if I can find a way, to help me end the war?

MYRRHINE. Goodness, yes! I'd do it, even if I had to pawn my dress and—get drunk on the spot!

CALONICE. And I, even if I had to let myself be split in two like a flounder.

LAMPITO. I'd climb up Mt. Taygetus if I could catch a glimpse of peace.

LYSISTRATA. I'll tell you, then, in plain and simple words. My friends, if we are going to force our men to make peace, we must do without—

MYRRHINE. Without what? Tell us.

LYSISTRATA. Will you do it?

MYRRHINE. We'll do it, if it kills us.

LYSISTRATA. Well then, we must do without sex altogether. (*General consternation*)

As you read this expository dialog, remember comedians whom you enjoy. Their effect is achieved as much from their timing as from the lines themselves. Hear that timing (the pauses and the hurried words) as you listen to the women of the Aegean world. Notice, for instance: CALONICE: *Why, yes;* (is not *yes* a word here saying "How obvious can you be?") *mercy me!* (great sympathy for herself—hear the inflection?) *my husband's been away for five months in Thrace* (hear five months of frustration as Thrace seems a million miles away—and might as well be!) *keeping guard on—* (the *o*'s slur together to create a longing vulgarity and the dash indicates a pause before a word she prefers not to think about) *Eucrates* (he has a young male sex companion there, while Calonice has no sex partner at home).

Little barbs pass between the women (Lampito's "What about the Athenian rabble?" for instance) but their need is greater than their nationalism. And their greatest barbs lie in the oath they eventually take (how realistic they are!) which reveals their knowledge of the pleasure principle and the various positions most desirable to the men.

The Roman comedy which followed Greek New Comedy abandoned philosophical subjects and, in concentrating on romanticized rather than biological sex, was forced to establish the more tightly-woven, connected series of episodes we call *plot*. As characters and situations became standardized (there are, after all, a limited number of devices whereby boy may love girl, lose girl, and regain girl), the action became swifter. Characters who did not undergo change through revelation (as they do in tragedy) had to achieve or fail to achieve their goals as a result of changing circumstances. So unrealistic is such a process, however, that speed alone allows a reader to accept the necessary conventions. Should he be allowed to pause and consider the possibilities, he would abandon the experience as being "ridiculous." Therefore, he comes to Roman comedy expecting it to be sprightly, racy, and outrageous. If a comic incident fails to satisfy that expectation, another must follow quickly before he can assume a reflective attitude.

Elizabethan or Romantic comedy (Shakespeare's in particular) also races along on swift action. Quite possibly those comedies seem much less humorous today than they did in Shakespeare's time because we have removed a remarkably comic element. In the Elizabethan theater itself, women did not appear onstage. Feminine roles were played by young boys, and, if anything is more ludicrous than a male in "high drag," it is a male in "low drag." The humorous becomes hysterical as a boy plays the part of a girl who, in the play, impersonates a boy. Social points of view become hopelessly tangled and the social viewpoint itself becomes humorous.

After the Puritans had closed England's theaters and Cromwell's rule had run its course, a near-return to Greek comedy occurred in the Restoration comedy exemplified by William Wycherley's *The Country Wife*. In 1965 the Lincoln Center Repertory Company attempted a performance of that enduring classic. *Time* magazine's drama critic viewed the play and the performance, assessing both in relation to the American concept of comedy:

Bad Restoration

The Country Wife, by William Wycherley. Charles II's England shared the obsession of its king—it was sex-mad. From that consuming passion sprang the witty, monomaniacally bawdy drama known as Restoration comedy. If Congreve was the age's greatest theatrical wit, Wycherley (1640–1715) may well have been its most vigorous social chronicler. He was a rake who later reformed, with all the zealotry that implies. In him, the pagan warred with the Puritan, the scandalizer with the sermonizer, and perhaps never more fiercely than in his most durable play, *The Country Wife.*

The plot is carnally direct. Mr. Horner (Stacy Keach), a notorious London lecher, has it bruited about town through his quack doctor that recent sexual misadventures in France have left him impotent. He rightly guesses that this will give him unlimited access to bored wives and unmatched opportunities to cuckold their husbands. The game is at least as important as the score to Horner, and he especially relishes the sight of husbands forcing their wives upon him under the delusion that he is an innocuous companion.

A co-plot might be called Sex and the Country Girl, or how Mrs. Pinchwife (Elizabeth Huddle) is schooled in the sexual duplicities of the big city. The climax is a scene of biting mockery in which Mr. Pinchwife, more jealous jailer than husband, is tricked into delivering his wife, masked, straight to Horner's seduction headquarters.

The satirist in Wycherley never subdued the pornographer, and this bed-drawing-room comedy contains some of the most salaciously funny scenes and speeches known to dramatic literature. But if Wycherley uses, and perhaps abuses, sex to make his point, sex is not his point. His moral intent is to show that ethics are lowest where the prizes are greatest—and sex was the dearest trophy of Restoration society.

With its woefully unseasoned actors, its melting-pot English, and its lack of anything resembling ensemble playing, the Lincoln Center Repertory Company is pitiably overmatched by the play. However, no American company would be likely to carry it off successfully. The heart of this comedy is heartlessness, and its surface is its substance. It demands dry, stylized cynicism. By temperament and training, this is alien to the American actor, who almost invariably tries to humanize his role and to bridle the most outrageous farce with the halter of naturalisitic plausibility. And Wycherley's characters cannot be played as people, since they are monsters in velvet and lace, transparencies of vice through which the playgoer is meant to view his own.

The glacial pace at which Robert Symonds has directed *The Country Wife* is a further handicap. Speed, as well as brevity, is the soul of wit, and *double entendres* go best at the double-quick. Tame Wycherley is lame Wycherley—which is precisely what is wrong at Lincoln Center.°

English comedy manages to survive—even in prose form—as English tragedy does not. Between Shakespeare and the present time, for instance, surviving prose tragedies are relegated to literary histories rather than

° *Time,* December 17, 1965.

to living theater, and they are all too often too dull to perform well in the theater of the mind. On the other hand, *The Country Wife,* William Congreve's *Love for Love* and *The Way of the World,* Oliver Goldsmith's *She Stoops to Conquer,* and Richard Brinsley Sheridan's *The School for Scandal* all act on the stage or in the mind with grace and charm, the wit undiminished and the humor unabated after several centuries. Recent comedy writers have updated the Restoration theater's *comedy of manners* (comedy based on the sophisticated, brittle, conventional manners of acceptable society) in such plays as Wilde's *The Importance of Being Earnest* and *Lady Windermere's Fan,* and George Bernard Shaw single-handedly managed to create a *comedy of ideas* wherein hallowed beliefs and crusty traditions were reduced to virtual ruin with pointed humor, stiletto wit, and logic stretched almost to the breaking point.

American comedy has been a desultory thing at best. We have run to the farcical in such broad humor as *Charley's Aunt,* the *situation comedy* (humor developed from a ridiculous situation wherein one mistake creates another until all is resolved mirthfully) in such romps as *You Can't Take It With You* and *The Man Who Came to Dinner,* or a vitriolic kind of comedy of manners depending on the cult of bitchiness in such plays as Clare Booth Luce's *The Women.*

In the same issue of *Time* that carried *The Country Wife* review, *Cactus Flower* (a French farce adapted by Abe Burrows) was also probed in a characteristic Time-in-chic review. The critic's summation of national humor is breezy enough to be mere drollery, but it is defensible enough to be included here for your evaluation:

Humor is often the puckish shadow cast by national character. English comedy is a running display of one-upmanship, reflecting an indelible class system. The Teutonic cast-ironies of Brecht seem manufactured by Krupp. The classic American comic event is the chase, a drolly tangible version of the pursuit of happiness and the American Dream. And the French sex farce is logic run rampant, reason carried to an unreasonable and absurd extremity. That is why French sex farces are innately sexless: Descartes wrote them all. They begin with *cogito ergo sum,* and they rely not on seduction but sophistry, not on rolled-down beds but revved-up minds, not on fervid matings but frenetic misunderstandings.

As recently as August, 1967, however, the comedy situation in America radically improved with the publication in *Esquire* Magazine of Paddy Chayefsky's *The Latent Heterosexual.* The play will *not* be produced on Broadway, however, for Mr. Chayefsky wrote it for a repertory company he envisions. Speaking of his play in "Backstage With Esquire," Chayefsky said:

"I have a theory about sparseness in theatre. *The Latent Heterosexual* has it; it belongs to the theatre of the joke. In other words, instead of the woven fabric of the drama, it has the straight linear framework of a joke building to the punch line.

"Of course, whether or not this theatre will come about is something else again. Does the theatre have any future at all? We may be lemmings, racing for the sea. Kurt Vonnegut put it well—the only useless things left are people."

And Arnold Gingrich responded on the "Publisher's Page":

Well, Broadway's current loss is our present gain, in this respect, for the joke, as distinguished from the absurd and from so-called black comedy, has long been in dwindling supply. Nor are we the only ones to complain of the scarcity of humor. All editors nowadays find it the hardest thing there is to find.

It's a long time since the funny papers even tried to be funny, and you could go through tons of comic books in a vain search for anything even faintly comical.

Things weren't exactly gay in the Depression days when this magazine was young, but humor was in anything but short supply. There were funny things being said and written and painted and drawn and sung, and we had no trouble getting our fair share. When times were tough, that very fact seemed to afford grist for the humorist's mill. But now that things are better than they have ever been, at least in a material sense, life seems less and less a laughing matter. It's a puzzlement, and we don't profess to know the answer.

Life may, indeed, be less and less a laughing matter. Atomic bombs, class hatred, racial tensions, and affluence that gives a man enriched bread but starves his soul are scarcely humorous. Still, politics and religion and sex are of vital concern to us at the individual level, and, individually, we have a definite social attitude toward them. That social attitude has always been the province of the comedy writer; he, even more than the tragedian, has always presented a social point of view. His moral judgments are seldom tempered with a plea for tolerance or understanding (that is the realm of tragedy). Instead, he holds the characters up to ridicule in one way or another. Either they are so stupid that they deserve what happens, or they are so outrageously intelligent that their come-uppance is pleasing to us—sometimes it is a mixture of both that delights the reader. Abnormality (at least by our standards) distinguishes the laughable: it is not of the norm to be excessively stupid, excessively intelligent, excessively ugly or beautiful—in short, excessively anything. In deciding what is the norm for his audience, the comic writer becomes a worldly philosopher.

In establishing a moral concept—and it seems immoral to deviate from the norm—the comic writer must exaggerate, and exaggeration leads to *caricature* (an elaboration upon dominant features—John F. Kennedy's shock of hair, for instance, which immediately identified him in political cartoons). Such caricature leads away from realism, even as it creates the super-real. And perhaps that is comedy—the super-real. Stripping away the revealing niceties (the name of one form of comedy, *satire,* literally means "I strip the flesh from the bones"), comedy demands that we examine the veiled and the concealed *if* we, rather than nature, have deliberately hidden it. If we are to examine it, however, we must have that steam-valve, laughter, to allow us release when the subject becomes too personal. For this reason, comedy is deliberately directed away from an imitation of real life. It is no mirror of reality; it is, rather, a fun-house mirror that distorts in such a fashion that we can be amused by the distortion.

We have noted that much of what is called humor rests upon some form of cruelty. Cruelty underlies the humor of *The Latent Heterosexual,* but it is a unique cruelty that resides in the social attitudes of Americans rather than in the lines of Chayefsky's play. Our attitudes toward the tax structure of our economy, for example, are ambivalent at best. We are taxed by way of our congressional representation, but we are dissatisfied with the process even though we can offer no alternative method. Our Puritan ethic demands that we be honest in such matters, so we cheat without finding pleasure in our successful evasion of tax laws. That ethic also pervades our sexual attitudes as well as our god concepts. The cruelty is directed primarily at ourselves then, for we are dismayed with the system, but we cannot successfully revolt against it. Caught between our needs and our desires, we are usually uncertain about our social attitudes and become victimized by our resulting resentments.

Taxes (a primary subject in Chayefsky's play) are funny because, like birth and death, they are inescapable. The inescapable *must* be humorous to be bearable. Homosexuals (another subject in the play) are funny because they are living proof of "the shortcomings of our fellow men." We laugh at them and the "antidote to sympathy" is effective. To find God amusing is a little harder because we are uncertain of the deity's role. However, the corporate machine (another subject) has replaced God in our everyday world, for we identify with and become a part of it in much the same way medieval man identified with and became a part of God through the church. And any President (still another subject) is good for a laugh; in fact, Americans feel obligated to find their leaders amusing because they represent our own mismanagement and bad judgment. We elect them; they do our bidding; we are unsure of our desires. In laughing at our leaders, we laugh at ourselves.

The Latent Heterosexual may, on first reading, seem to be *black humor* (sometimes called *sick humor*), a form of humor which consists of masochistic barbs directed at the most sensitive areas of guilt in our lives. Shocking ourselves with a cruel and barbarous forcing of attention to our most indefensible behavior, we laugh because we have no other defense against the focusing action. The minority group (ethnical, religious, or sexual) serves as a frequent butt of black humor because our cruelty to such groups is necessary to our own sense of superiority, but the sense of superiority resulting from abusing the helpless is coarsened into inferiority by the lack of fair play and we become inferior bullies. Because we are psychologically oriented to the superior need, however, we temper our success by cruelly calling attention to our psychic illness. Laughter releases some of the guilt, our rationale being that "that which provokes mirth can't be bad, and laughter is healthy." The guilts arising from our ability to laugh at the abused butt of the joke make the laughter hollow and our sickness is confirmed, but it is better to be aware of our transgressions against humanity than to ignore them utterly. So reasoning, we make the humor self-defeating, therefore *black*.

Chayefsky's play is *not* black humor; it is a comedy resting on *wit* in the French tradition. The most ludicrous elements of our society are first isolated, then combined, and finally spun out to their own illogical end—which is the epitome of logic. Every character is absurd, but, caught in and representative of our absurd society, each becomes a warmly sympathetic representative of large masses of people. It is curiously difficult to laugh at any character in the play, for our laughter becomes self-directed. The identification with characters is rapid because they are so removed from—yet representative of—reality.

THE LATENT HETEROSEXUAL

by Paddy Chayefsky

SCENE ONE

The office of IRVING SPAATZ, a tax consultant: October 11, 1960; afternoon.

At curtain rise, SPAATZ (short, in his fifties, bespectacled, necktied, as serene as a Buddha) ushers in HENRY JADD (a middle-aged intellectual) and JOHN MORLEY (an enormous Bodenheim of a man in his forties, the hero of our play; he wears an ill-fitting suit and is on the verge of tears). JADD and MORLEY carry coats which SPAATZ *takes and drops on the upstage couch.* MORLEY *sinks down onto the couch and stares piteously off.* JADD *hands* SPAATZ *a large envelope and sits in the client's chair facing* SPAATZ *across the desk.*

The title sets the tone of the play and precipitates the reader into the first of a long series of necessary reassessments of his own illogical attitudes. The term *latent homosexual* has become a cliché in our pseudo-Freudian conversation, a cliché we use to minimize the object of our dislike when we have nothing very substantial to use by way of accusation. Because homosexuality is a latent possibility in everyone, the charge becomes almost impossible to deny because denials tend to make the protestor seem too anxious and he damns himself. The phrase is neatly turned by Chayefsky, so we read it as we are predisposed to, smugly assume a superior attitude, then suddenly realize the word is *heterosexual.* We have adopted a superior attitude toward ourself and are suddenly forced to be defensive about our own sexual role, a turnabout that reduces us to ridicule in our own eyes, thereby forcing us to laugh at ourselves—and the French approach to comedy is achieved at the outset.

Nor is the homosexual reader denied amusement in the process either. Long the recipient of the accusation, he has developed his own acceptances and defenses, and they are utterly shattered as he recognizes his inflexible and immediate responses. That he should be so impatiently ready to defend himself against an unmade accusation reduces him to laughter also, and he allies himself with the new victim of a cruelty he has resented. Such sharing creates the humor of mutuality—and he laughs.

Scene One opens on an ordinary enough setting, the words *tax consultant* suggesting an opulent office with thick carpets, expensive furniture, and a couple of good, modern paintings chosen by a decorator rather than by Irving Spaatz. The name is obviously Jewish, a gambit that is also amusing, for it points up the pigeon-hole method of identifications we indulge in regularly. That a Jew should be a tax consultant seems ridiculously fitting. That he should be "as serene as a Buddha" delights the fancy, for the picture is right, the mixing of religious metaphor all wrong. We've been placed in a ludicrous position once again. John Morley is a "Bodenheim of a man," the metaphor creating a recollection of Maxwell Bodenheim, the literary iconoclast of Greenwich Village in the 1920's, the original inhabitant of the state of mind called Bohemia. His ultimate decay and recent death serve as foreshadowing elements for the educated reader. (And here it might be noted that the uneducated reader will probably find this play pointless, or he will find it a sardonic attack upon himself, and therefore humorless.)

JADD (*a man under strain*). We appreciate your seeing us, Irving. We won't take up much of your time. Here's Mr. Morley's royalty statements and the notices the government sent him. Mr. Morley's the author of *A Corporation of Cadis,* which we published on our spring list last year. It's sold over forty thousand in hard cover to date. The paperback version, as of October one—Dell works on the calendar year—at any rate, Lamarchina, the man at Dell, says it should do a million, even a million five—well, you've got all the figures there. Anyway, this grotesque man here has made a potful. . . .

SPAATZ (*studying the papers* JADD *gave him*). Some seventy-two thousand last year.

JADD. Yes, and Stanley Kramer bought the book for the movies, though what he hopes to do with it I can't imagine. The point is, the government's attached Kramer's check, which is in the amount of sixty-seven thousand five hundred, that's less our commission for negotiating the sale. Apparently, Dell's been put on notice as well, attaching all Morley's money there too, you see (MORLEY *breaks into a sob*), because the stupid son of a bitch didn't pay his taxes last year.

SPAATZ (*still studying the papers*). He's apparently not paid his taxes for any year.

Jadd's obvious subservience to Spaatz and his careful analysis of the problem establish Morley as financially important, but he is reduced to the absurd with "this grotesque man here" and "the stupid son of a bitch." Spaatz says little, his priestly mien growing the while, but his laconic understatements reveal his knowledge and his power.

(ARTHUR LANDAU, *lawyer, in his forties, bespectacled, likewise serene, likewise necktied and in shirt sleeves, obviously the canonicals of this priestly caste, enters. He smiles benignly at* JADD, *who waves freely back.* LANDAU *pulls a chair up to the desk, takes the papers which* SPAATZ *holds out to him and silently examines them.*)

JADD. Irving, Mr. Morley here's one of our disenfranchised aesthetes. Such *bürgerlich* rituals as paying taxes are entirely alien to him. I've known him since he was a reedy boy of eighteen, if you can imagine him reedy. I was editing a little magazine in Chicago in those days. He came swishing in with a sheaf of short stories, spinsterly things about sensitive Cincinnati schoolboys whose English teachers turn out to be faggots. His style has changed since then, of course. He is currently one of the leaders of the panic-stricken participle school of writing, and his subject matter is less maidenly. *The New York Review* described his last book as fetid. . . .

MORLEY (*muttering*). Fecaloid. Norman Mailer wrote the review.

JADD. In that case, it was probably fecaloid. At any rate, Morley's book is about the homosexual community in Tangiers. Hot sperm spurting and smooth-skinned Arab boys on every page, some instant upanishad here and there and what is perhaps meant to be Swiftian satire on American middle-classness. This fecaloid pile of prose is presented to us as man's search for serenity, a search presumably conducted with a proctoscope. . . .

MORLEY (*erupting from the couch*). You old fruit! An hour ago you were comparing me to Proust.

JADD (*just as shrilly*). I said you had a Proustian tendency to the agglutinization of detail!

MORLEY. I never agglutinized a detail in my life!

JADD (*in a state*). Irving, I can't tell you what I've been through today! This fruitcake has been trying to slash his wrists with a letter opener all morning. I must explain to you, Irving—this man's a miser. I mean miser in the total caricature of the word. I mean, he actually has a little room on the fourth floor of his house where he keeps two brass-bound coffers—so help me, God!—two little pirate's chests filled with antique gold pieces—doubloons, napoleons, Russian imperials, half-neds and louis d'or; and he sits up there in that little room—I'm not making this up, I've seen it with my own eyes!—he sits up there counting and cackling over these gold pieces. For hours! It's absolutely elemental, Irving, that you grasp this fact about this grotesque man! Well, I called the nut this morning, and I said: "John, Random House has received a note from the government telling us to hold any money we've received for you, because of nonpayment of taxes." There was this long pause. Then Richard, that little flit he has living with him, got on the phone hysterically. In the background, I hear inhuman shrieks. "What the hell's going on, Richard?" I said. "He's lamenting," said Richard. "He's rending his caftan and lamenting." "Rending his caftan?" I said. "Is he wearing a caftan?" "Yes," said Richard, "he's wearing a caftan, green-striped izar and a fringed cashmere girdle." Which gives you some idea of what I mean by grotesque. On top of everything else, this nut's a junkie and, by the time I got up to his place, he was floating around in a narcotic trance. Irving, if you've never seen a faggot junkie poet caparisoned in a yellow caftan, green-striped izar and a fringed cashmere girdle, slashing at his wrists with a letter opener—well, now you know what I've been through all morning. I don't like to trouble you with this kind of nonsense, Irving. . . .

SPAATZ. It's no trouble, Henry.

MORLEY (*screaming at JADD*). You also compared me to Joyce! You said I had revivified poetry in the novel form, not as Wilde and Pater did, by lacquered ornamentation—

JADD. I never said any such thing. It sounds like Alfred Kazin.

MORLEY. Kazin detested my book. He told me so personally.

JADD. Nonsense, he resolutely compared you to Hawthorne.

MORLEY. He compares everyone to Hawthorne! And I wasn't trying to slash my wrists with that letter opener. I was doing with that letter opener what you're supposed to do with letter openers—I was trying to open a goddam letter. That very letter Mr. Spaatz is looking at right now, as a matter of fact, that announcement from my bank that the government has put a lien on my house! Well, goddam! What kind

of depraved despotism is this! I'm not going to pay a penny, Spaatz! I finally hit
with one lousy book which took me twenty-five years to write! What about all those
years I waited on tables and scrubbed floors and scraped for tips guiding tourists
in Marrakesh—

JADD. Oh, for God's sakes!

MORLEY. And you clam up, you papist!

JADD. Papist?

Landau's entry is that of the Buddha as Pope—serene, silent, and almost
omniscient. Jadd's résumé of Morley's rise to literary prominence reveals
a personal style as precious as any disenfranchised aesthete's, obviously
lifting him to the superior, rarefied realm of the tax priests and revealing
Morley as a depraved practitioner of anally aggressive prose while reducing him to the dated cult of psychoanalysis—yesterday's religion. *Fecaloid, instant upanishad,* and *proctoscope* all establish Jadd's self-satisfied
superiority—just in time for Morley to destroy it utterly with "You old
fruit!" The resulting hysterical exchange leaves Jadd standing in the
shattered wreckage of his superiority, and he is so unnerved he babbles
such terms of denigration as *fruitcake, flit, junkie,* and *nut.* In his frenzy,
he has revealed Morley's proclivity for esoteric religions (*caftan, izar,
girdle,* and *trance*), a revelation Morley employs to reduce him to the
role of the ultra-conservative unenlightened (*papist*).

Note also Chayefsky's insertion at this point of an important character
motive for Morley: his latest book deals with, among other things, "man's
search for serenity." Morley's search for "serenity" in the mystical religion
of taxation will be explored more fully as the play progresses. Remember:
a good playwright seldom uses lines which have *one* function only!

LANDAU. Mr. Morley, do you have any records that go to prove you worked
twenty-five years on your novel?

MORLEY. Crates of it.

JADD. As a matter of fact, Random House is considering publishing his journals.

MORLEY. What I try to do, you understand, is capture stylistically the fragments
of terror which is the human condition. Kazin thought the whole thing gibberish.
You son of a bitch, I said, forty thousand in hardback alone isn't gibberish. Kazin,
you understand, has come out strongly for the lyric poetry of William Blake, a
reasonably safe predilection in the middle of the twentieth century. Oh, would all
our lyricism be so orderly. Am I right? Eh? Today, we deal with the plummeting hysteria
of prose. Hyphen. The hell with it. Pussy on the table. Listen, Spaatz, boobie, for
God's sakes, help me. This is the first money I've ever made. Don't let them take
it away. Please, don't let them take it away! For God's sakes, don't make me crawl!
Leave me a shred of dignity!

JADD. My God, will you go back and sit down!

(MORLEY, *who had fallen to his knees in a posture of supplication, returns to the couch, where he sits, moaning softly and occasionally beating his breast.* JADD *leans back in his leather chair, closes his eyes and sighs long-sufferingly.* SPAATZ *and* LANDAU *study the papers of* MORLEY'S *case. A long moment of silence is interrupted by* MORLEY *muttering more or less to* JADD.)

MORLEY. Agglutinization of detail. Jesus Christ! Surrealist association, you fat-assed pimp. I pinched the whole style from Eliot. "Rocks, moss, stonecrop, iron, merds/ Rat's coat, crowskin, crossed staves in field." Eliot, Eliot, you dim, old *fadaise*. Jesus Christ—agglutinization of detail—Jesus Christ—(As MORLEY *drifts off into sullen inaudibility, there is another long silence.*)

Standing between these representatives of religious extremes, the priests of the new god, the tax structure, are as unmoved as distant Greeks surveying the barbarians. The esoterica of Morley's literary revelations are fashionably shallow, indicative of the mentality of an audience that would lift *A Corporation of Cadis* to the ranks of the best-seller. The title (meaning "a corporation composed of minor Moslem judges") summarizes the incongruous combinations that create the basic humor of the play, and a literary barb results from Morley's hysterical confession that he stole his style from T. S. Eliot, the darling of the *fadaise*. Morley himself has assumed a comparable, if less lasting, role, and the humor becomes bitter indeed as the reader recognizes his own delighted involvement in this joke being played on him.

Through it all, the priests of the tax structure sit quietly, watching the antics of these little mortals. Tensions exist between the arts (literature) and the market place (the tax structure) and a bonus feature is supplied for the reader who can be amused by the Arab-Israeli conflicts. If that subject is too emotionally taxing, however, the reader can ignore it completely.

(Then SPAATZ *and* LANDAU *begin a traditional murmured liturgy.*)

SPAATZ. Consistent violator?

LANDAU. Yes, if they want to get nasty about it.

SPAATZ. What are they calling it now, felony or misdemeanor?

LANDAU. They've been leaning toward felony.

SPAATZ. I think we'd better ask for sixty days. On the Fifty-nine, can we throw the spread back thirty-six months?

LANDAU. There's probably a limitation on the year.

SPAATZ. Mel just got a favorable ruling on Victor Loew.

LANDAU. And there's interest charges on the prior twenty-three years.

SPAATZ. No, this is income-splitting.

LANDAU. Maybe you're right at that.

SPAATZ. What'll we throw into Sixty-one? Entertainment?

LANDAU. In my opinion, the government would resist the purchase of narcotics as entertainment.

SPAATZ. Development and Research?

LANDAU. Yes.

SPAATZ. Not dissimilar from the Kurnitz thing.

LANDAU. They're getting rough on joint-ventures, Irving. The government was disagreeable about Kurnitz's leaseholds. We have a holding corporation threat here.

SPAATZ. I think for Sixty though.

LANDAU. It's fragile. I was thinking a foundation. By the way, we'll need a deposition from Leverett.

SPAATZ. Yes. (*To* MORLEY, *who has come out of his despair to stare fascinated through tear-filled eyes at* SPAATZ.) Well, Mr. Morley, you're in one of those technical binds that come up in tax matters now and then, more frequently than you might think, as a matter of fact. Willful failure to file a tax return is punishable by a ten-thousand-dollar fine and a year's imprisonment. In the government's eyes, you've willfully failed to file tax returns since your majority, which was twenty-two years ago. Since the government has no figures on your income other than last year's, they'll assess your delinquencies on a like basis. There are interest charges of six percent on all those years. There's also a twelve-percent assessment on your willful failure to pay your quarterly installments for all those years. With all the fines, penalties and assessments applicable to your case, you're technically liable for—how much do you make it, Arthur?

LANDAU. About five hundred thousand.

SPAATZ. That's what I have. About five hundred thousand dollars, Mr. Morley, and, of course, twenty-two years in a federal prison.

MORLEY. My God, what are you saying?

SPAATZ. The practice in cases like this is to have the client declared incompetent by a reputable psychiatrist, which takes everybody off the hook. The government would just as soon not open that can of beans, as you can readily see—

MORLEY. What can of beans? What the hell is he talking about?

SPAATZ. —and they readily accept these psychiatric depositions. We've had similar cases over the years. We generally refer our clients to a psychiatrist named Leverett, a first-rate man, associated with the Karen Horney Institute. If you'd like, we'll arrange an interview with him. (*He regards* MORLEY *agreeably;* MORLEY *stares back, at first incredulously and then sullenly.*) Are you offended by this, Mr. Morley?

MORLEY. No, I'm not offended. It's just such a tacky gambit, that's all. The old psychiatrist wheeze. Third-rate farce. I mean, after that black mass you and your apprentice just intoned, I'd expected something more occult. Henry said you were a sorcerer in financial matters. The archimage of tax consultants, he said. Conjures up loopholes before your very eyes. I had expected something of a show frankly, all sorts of sinuously complex structures rising in wisps out of inkwells. Hardly this scenario psychiatrist. I don't think it's very clever. I want my money back.

The priests intone their mystic mumbo-jumbo, a Mass that is meaningful to them but which leaves the initiate Morley awe-struck until his own religious rites are incorporated. Now he is on familiar grounds—he understands the liturgy of the couch. His familiarity makes him contemptuous enough to combine his facile prose with his fecaloid style to demand his own money back—an artful allusion to the admission price of theatrical entertainment and the collection plate of the church.

SPAATZ. Well, we're going to turn you into a corporation, how's that?

MORLEY (*considering it, then smiling*). Oh, I'd like that.

SPAATZ. Also a familiar tax device, I'm afraid, lacking in creative invention. The first thing any accountant does with a client of irregular income is incorporate him. So, in a few days, Mr. Morley, you'll sign papers inaugurating your career as a publishing house. Random House will actually publish your next book, your scandalous journals, but only as your agent. You'll reimburse Random House for printing, advertising, and distributing costs, for which your company will receive ten percent of the publisher's profits. You as the author will contract with yourself as the publisher for this book. How's that for sinuous complexity?

MORLEY. The most voluptuous thing I've ever heard.

JADD. There will be some compensation in royalties, of course.

SPAATZ. Of course, Henry. We're not going to do Random House dirty. We represent them too, you know. Now, Mr. Morley, we're also planning on making a charitable foundation out of you as well.

MORLEY. A charitable foundation! My God, may I call you Irving?

SPAATZ. Of course. You endow universities with scholarship funds, that sort of thing.

MORLEY. Oh, my God! Will that save me money?

SPAATZ. Well, if you were a charitable foundation right now, you could save fifteen to twenty thousand dollars on this year alone. What we would do is assign the residual rights of your already published book to your corporation, the publishing house, in exchange for twenty thousand dollars' worth of preferred stock which your corporation would issue for the purpose; which stock you then denote to your charitable foundation—is he all right, Henry?

(*This last is in reference to the fact* MORLEY *seems to be going through some sort of lubricious experience. He is lying sprawled on the Swedish modern couch, eyes closed and murmuring in a way that can only be described as sensual.*)

JADD. He's trying to make the point, I think, that he finds all this talk about money stimulating.

SPAATZ. I see. Well, all this doesn't help us out much for this year's taxes, of course, Mr. Morley. It will take us about a year to get a ruling on your foundation. This year, I'm afraid there's very little we can do. It may please you to know, Mr. Morley, the fee of the psychiatrist who will declare you incompetent is deductible.

As is, of course, our fee here. How much do you spend a year on narcotics, Mr. Morley? We can't very well deduct them as medical expenses or entertainment, at least not in the government's appreciation of the word. But let me ask you, Mr. Morley—

MORLEY (*opening his eyes*). For God's sakes, call me John.

SPAATZ. John, then, is there anything about dope addiction in your book?

MORLEY. Curious you should ask. I'm beginning a book on dope addiction this very evening.

SPAATZ. In that case, we can deduct whatever you paid for narcotics last year as Development and Research.

MORLEY. Development and Research?

SPAATZ. Yes.

MORLEY. I tell you, I'm going to come any minute.

LANDAU. By the way, you won't be able to keep all those antique gold pieces, Mr. Morley. It's against the law to have private gold hoards.

MORLEY. I'll do anything you say. I'm hopelessly in love with both of you. (*He flutters his eyes at the two tax men in shameless flirtation. He stands, flounces happily around the room.*)

Spaatz's suggestion that Morley be incorporated invites the initiate to become a novitiate in this thrilling new religion he has avoided for twenty-two years. As capable of transference as any good psychiatric patient, Morley embraces the tax god, its priests, and its argot simultaneously, reverting to his own sexual group's argot in his ecstasy of conversion. Transference becomes complete with the ritual of first names and an open avowal of complete surrender. Chayefsky's adroit manipulations reveal the tenuous hold man's institutions claim when the novel, the complex-made-simple are offered as blandishments. Mix in a bit of "love" and our vacillations become the gyrations of dervishes.

SPAATZ. I'm also going to suggest, John, that you get married to take advantage of the joint tax declaration.

MORLEY (*whose critical eye had been caught by an Impressionist print on the wall, now turns back to* SPAATZ, *smiling again*). What do you mean?

SPAATZ. You'd have to get married before the end of this calendar year if we're to derive any immediate benefit out of it.

MORLEY (*frowning*). Do you mean to a woman?

SPAATZ. Well, of course to a woman. The marriage must be recognized by law. Do you have some woman friend who would go through the formality of a marriage for you? We might be able to work out something advantageous for the lady as well.

MORLEY. I don't have any women friends. (*He swishes prettily across the room to* SPAATZ'S *desk where he stands, a large unkempt man, his right arm akimbo in the traditional posture of effeminacy. He smiles sweetly.*) I'm a flaming faggot,

Irving. I was sure you were on to that. I don't go around waving the flag, of course, and I definitely do not proselytize. Homosexuality is, to me, an inner satisfaction, a pride in a heritage of greatness. To marry a woman would be an inadmissible rejection of my identity.

SPAATZ. It'll save you about fifteen thousand dollars on your 1960 taxes.

MORLEY. Oh, well, in that case, dig someone up for me.

The new economic religion conflicts with both the psychological and the literary ones from the past when a heterosexual marriage is suggested. Years of training surface on Morley's protestations of self-acceptance in language as ambivalent as "flaming faggot" and "pride in a heritage of greatness." The rebellious cliché and the pompous platitude cannot withstand the promised rewards of the new religion's first test, however. For a tax saving of fifteen thousand dollars, Morley can sacrifice his lofty principles with "Oh, well, in that case, dig someone up for me."

Note, too, Chayefsky's artful inclusion here of information that will become more important as the play proceeds: Morley says, "To marry a woman would be an inadmissible rejection of my identity." You will encounter virtually these same words again—watch for them. They will constitute a structural turning-point in the play.

(*The phone on* SPAATZ'S *desk rings.* SPAATZ *answers, murmurs, hangs up.*)

JADD (*as he stands up*). Well, Irving, we won't take up any more of your time. Set up an appointment with the psychiatrist. I'll see that this lunatic gets there. I'm sorry I had to bother you with this.

SPAATZ (*as he too stands*). Not at all, Henry. It was a very welcome break in the dusty routine.

JADD. Well, let's just be grateful he didn't put on his cosmetics today. He frequently does, you know.

MORLEY (*who has been flouncing about in a growing manic state, suddenly erupts*). My God, this experience has been chilling! I came into this office a shattered soul, and, in a matter of minutes, you people have incarnated me into a publishing house, a charitable foundation and even a married man. It's the most goddam transcendental thing that's ever happened to me. And let me tell you, boobie, I've spent my whole life hunting down transcendental things. Back in 1940, when I was twenty-one, I went off into the Sudanese desert in search of patristic passion. Saint Anthony of Padua sort of thing. I lived entirely alone, subsisting on berries and insects, and abusing myself with the usual practices of mortification. I liked being an anchorite, and I might still be there, Christian as hell, a haggard bag of bones, but, of course, the war started. Battalions of Germans came *ein-zwei-drei*-ing down with their goddam tanks, and the British North African Army came rumbling in from El Alamein. Bang, bang, boom. Well, I'd like to see Saint Anthony operate under those conditions. I hauled my ass back to Cairo, turned myself in to the American Consulate, still wearing my tattered rags and streaming putrescence from hundreds of self-inflicted wounds. Didn't faze anyone in the American Consulate. That sort of thing's a common sight in Cairo. Well, I've spent my life trying to retrieve that serenity in the desert. Not until now have I felt so transfigured!

JADD (*handing* MORLEY *his overcoat*). Yeah, well, let's go, guru.

(JADD *herds* MORLEY *out of the office.* SPAATZ *closes the door after them, shuffles silently back to his desk.* LANDAU, *who had stood, sits again.*)

(*The Curtain begins slowly to descend as the two tax men begin another murmured priestly liturgy.*)

LANDAU. Who've you got outside, Willie Nicholson?

SPAATZ. Yes. Has Mel been keeping you up on that business?

LANDAU. Yes. Who's the lending agency?

SPAATZ. Hanover. I think its premature.

LANDAU. Yes, so do I.

SPAATZ (*picking up phone, murmuring into it*). Send Mr. Nicholson in.

CURTAIN

The conversion complete, Morley's excessive fervor is that of the thoroughly indoctrinated convert. His "testimony" is more literate than Salvation Army street offerings, but it grows from that same gravid condition of the soul seduced to follow a new saving god. He has understood the concept, accepted the tenets, castigated himself through self-sacrifice, and testified in the name of the cleansing power of his new faith. Now he is ready to test his new strength in the world. As he leaves, the priests of the tax structure turn their attention to another potential follower, this one not ready for conversion but a probable acolyte.

That such conversions are not unique in our society is amusing; that they are standard with us is hysterical.

SCENE TWO

SPAATZ'S *office, two weeks later.*

At curtain rise, SPAATZ *enters, wearing a winter coat and hat from which he brushes the snow as he hangs them on the coat-tree. He crosses to his desk.*

SPAATZ (*picking up the phone and murmuring into it*). Lillian, is Mr. Landau in his office? (*He returns the phone to its cradle, crosses to the coat-tree, slips out of his jacket, hangs that up, and is once again restored to his familiar sacerdotal costume of short-sleeved white shirt and necktie. The phone rings. He crosses to his desk to answer it.*) Arthur, that nut's here again. . . . Well, did you see him today? He's wearing makeup. He's wearing orange lipstick and little spots of rouge on his cheeks like a Kewpie doll. Please send him home. (*A secretary enters with sheaves of filing folders, correspondence and messages which she piles on the desk, already awash with documents. She sits, stenographic pad and pencil poised.*) Arthur, I have a note here from you that Lester Freitag's coming up. Is that the nonsense he spoke to me about yesterday? . . . Oh, dear, when's he coming up? . . . No, never mind, I'll call Marty Halloran right now. (*He flashes his phone.*) Lillian, see if Marty Halloran at the Manhattan Regional Office is in, thank you. (*Hangs up, dictates to his secretary in the same breath.*) By hand, attention of Mr. Harry Pfeiffer, re Loan Agreement between Hanover Trust Company and Nicholson and Mayer comma Inc parenthesis Nineteen Sixty close parenthesis underline dear Harry I enclose for your comments copies of a correspondence between the Food and Drug capital F capital D commissioners and myself. Until the F.D.A. rules on the product comma the Loan Committee capital L capital C at the Hanover Trust Company advises me Hanover will insist on a quote uncomfortable clause close quote to the effect that the Hanover Trust Company parenthesis quote the Bank capital B close quote close parenthesis shall have the right comma at any time thereafter and in their sole discretion—(*the phone rings*)—comma to demand—(*He answers the phone, fishing out a paper from among the welter on his desk.*) Marty, Irving Spaatz here. Listen, Marty, I've got one of those sometime things again. Do you know Lester Freitag? . . . Well, he's a tax lawyer, handles mostly show-business accounts. He also handles most of the call girls in the city. . . . Yes, one of those things. He's having a little run-in with your department right now. . . . (MORLEY *appears in the doorway, quite the same as he was last time we saw him except that he is indeed wearing orange lipstick, black circles of Arabian kohl around his eyes and has spots of rouge on his cheeks like a Kewpie doll. Carrying his shabby coat, he shuffles in, an enormous, frightened, painted schoolboy of a man, and sits apprehensively on the edge of the upstage couch.*) Well, the girl's name is Christine Van Dam . . . Van Dam, V-a-n capital D-a-m. Apparently, a rug manufacturer in Detroit deducted this tart as an entertainment expense, deducted her eleven times in fact; and some zealot in your department named Hirschkorn—(*The second phone on his desk rings; the secretary answers in a murmur*)—couldn't help but stub his toe over Miss Van Dam, and this defender of the faith decided to look up Miss Van Dam's Ten-forty; and there she was, a television actress and/or model (which is how Freitag lists these tarts on their returns) who claimed to have earned two thousand three hundred dollars in Fifty-nine, an improbable figure since she had earned something over six thousand dollars from the rug manufacturer alone. Anyway, this Hirschkorn has called the girl for a hearing next Thursday, and Freitag phoned me yesterday to see if I could help nip the silly business. He's coming up in a few minutes. Can I tell him its nipped? . . . Thank you, Marty. (*He hangs up.*)

THE SECRETARY. Mr. Churchill on seven.

SPAATZ (*pressing receiver button*). Jimmie, I've reflected on the matter, and the answer is still no, and, as a friend, I want to say again I think it improper for a law firm of your repute to handle this kind of client. . . . I'm sure of that, and thank

you for having considered me. *(He hangs up and in the same breath dictates)*—from the undersigned comma and forthwith upon such demand comma assign and hypothecate to them as collateral security for the repayment of the Loan capital L comma marketable securities having a readily ascertainable market value and acceptable to them comma equal to at least one hundred thirty percent of the then—*(the phone rings)*—unpaid principal amount of the Loan capital L and —*(he answers the phone, grunts, hangs up)*—shall deliver to them said securities comma together with blank stock powers relating thereto. Helen, tell Mr. Landau Mr. Freitag is here, would he take care of that? I've spoken to Marty Halloran, and the matter is dropped.
(The secretary nods, stands, exits.)

Jokes can make large time jumps (the most common being "nine months later"), so the second scene presupposes character development that you will supply. The ritual and liturgy of the tax religion is more obvious now. Far removed from the puritan ethic of Judeo-Christian theology, the tax-priest reveals that his religion's basic ethos exists—though it boggles the mind to consider the "kind of client" Spaatz would consider outside propriety. Certainly there is no separation of church and state in Spaatz's religious philosophy, for the call to Marty Halloran suggests that priests of one master enlist and receive aid from priests of the other.

Christine Van Dam's name is evocatively rich, serving as a vivid example of the "Proustian tendency to agglutinization of detail." Each of the three words promises, by way of foreshadowing, that her role will be more than that of plot expediency.

(SPAATZ turns his attention to MORLEY who is anxiously wringing his hands.)
MORLEY. Arthur says you're cross with me.
SPAATZ. What'd you expect, coming down here wearing orange lipstick?
MORLEY. It's the current fashion.
SPAATZ. It's calculated mischief to attract my attention.
MORLEY. Well, you've been icy the last few days, Irving.
SPAATZ. You've been making a nuisance of yourself. I told you last week there was no reason to hang around here every day, dogging Arthur's heels as well as my own. And now the clerks complain you've taken over the library.
MORLEY. That happened only once, and I apologized the moment. . . .
SPAATZ. John, go home. There's at least another week before they'll finish filing your corporate charter in Delaware. We've asked for and received a sixty-day extension from the Westchester Board, so we have till December sixteenth to prepare your returns. That's six weeks away, so, for heaven's sakes. . . .
MORLEY *(standing, frantically contrite)*. You're right, of course. Please forgive me. It's just I've never had a corporation before. I know I'm hovering over it like a new mother—

SPAATZ. Yes, exactly.

MORLEY (*with growing panic*).—but I've come to it late in life, a child of my middle years, so to speak, and it's so delicate. It has this holding corporation threat. The joint venture with Random House is an utterly transparent dodge—

SPAATZ. It's entirely supportable.

MORLEY. Can't you give it some net-leaseholds, something like that?

SPAATZ. The government's been getting sticky about these syndication deals.

MORLEY. Some real estate titles—

SPAATZ. And, if Kennedy gets elected, they'll be even stickier.

MORLEY.—apartment houses, that sort of thing, for a ten percent return. I've been reading up, you see, the management corporation retaining of course—

SPAATZ. John, for the past year the government has tended to treat title-buying as an investment and not ownership.

MORLEY (*in near hysteria*). How about mortgaging my house and investing the money in cattle-raising? I don't know how you put up with me, Irving. (*He slips into the client's chair by the desk, smiling the most enchanting smile; it's impossible not to like the man.*) I went for my psychiatric examination with Doctor Leverett yesterday, Irving. I arrived promptly and behaved well throughout. His report will be entirely supportive of our case. I'm an instance of character corrosion, unable to sustain any meaningful relationships with other human beings. I relate only to inanimate things. I think of my own writings, for example, in much the same way other men think of women. This poem is a slattern, that story a bitch, this one a silly little thing but fun for a weekend.

SPAATZ. I don't see anything unusual in that. Artists have been falling in love with their own creations since Pygmalion.

MORLEY. Well, I think the doctor's point is it's one thing to fondle a statue you've sculpted; you're nuts, however, if you expect it to bear children. Dr. Leverett doesn't think I've quite reached that point yet, but I bear watching. (*Stands, moves about with gathering agitation and an increasing spasmodism in his speech and manner.*) He says I'm on the verge of a breakdown. I expect he's right. I have a constant and familiar sensation of hysteria. I've gone mad before, you know. Oh, yes, I've done that turn. Eight months at Rockland State, shock treatments and all. (*He is suddenly shrill and thoroughly hysterical.*) I defend myself, you see, by all these theatrical excesses! I play mad so even my madness will seem a deceit! But I'm terrified it may be my only incontrovertible fragment of reality! Dr. Leverett thinks a breakdown is imminent! He wants me to start therapy tomorrow! For God's sakes, Irving, what do you think?

SPAATZ (*with sober consideration*). Well, I'd rather you didn't incur large medical expenses like that until next year when we can possibly derive some tax benefit from it.

MORLEY (*deprived of his hysteria, goes back to his chair, sits down and regards* SPAATZ *for a long moment*). In that case, of course, I'll put my breakdown off till January.

SPAATZ. Why have it at all?

MORLEY. Good God, you mean it's not even deductible next year?

SPAATZ. Well, only those medical expenses that go beyond three percent of your adjusted gross income. It's not really worth it.

MORLEY. The hell with it, then. I won't have a breakdown at all. (*He flicks a Kleenex from its container on* SPAATZ's *desk and sets about wiping his makeup off.*) You have healing powers, Irving. (*The secretary looks in inquiringly.* SPAATZ *nods to her. She enters and stands in the back, note pad in hand.*) I'm going home and write that book on dope addiction you suggested so we can deduct all last year's heroin as Development and Research.

SPAATZ. Very sensible.

MORLEY (*murmuring*). Development and Research. How goddam purposeful can you get? (*He finishes wiping off his makeup and offers his face for* SPAATZ's *approval.*) All off?

SPAATZ. There's a smudge of black around your eye, but you'll need a mirror for that.

(MORLEY *stands, looks around for his coat, which is on the couch, as the door opens and* LANDAU, *shirt-sleeved and necktied, pokes his head in.*)

LANDAU. Irving, I've got Lester Freitag in my office. Do you have a minute?

SPAATZ. Yes. (*The phone rings.* SPAATZ *answers.*) I'll be with him in a few moments. (*He hangs up.*)

LANDAU. Who's that? Willie Nicholson?

SPAATZ. Yes. (*To secretary.*) Get me the rest of the Loan Agreement between Nicholson and Mayer and Hanover.

(*The secretary exits.*)

LANDAU. How's it going with Hanover?

SPAATZ. They're sticking to their collateral security clause.

LANDAU. Mel says you refused to buy the interim-demand.

SPAATZ. Yes, much too risky.

(*In the background, forgotten,* MORLEY, *clutching his overcoat, slips out the door.*)

Converts invariably know more about their religion than those born and reared in it. Morley is so obsessed with his that he has confused it completely with the remainder of his personality. His need of communion with his new priest is no more complex than the need of any new faddist to ingratiate himself with the expert who originally infected him with his current monomania. Chayefsky does not spare himself in such lines as "I play mad so even my madness will seem a deceit!" If Morley has plagiarized Eliot's style, Chayefsky suggests that his John Morley is patterned a bit on Shakespeare's Hamlet. The old religions cling; their strength is waning more rapidly however. Art can be prostituted (Morley will start his book on dope addiction) and psychology can be dismissed (he will simply not have a breakdown if it is unprofitable). Old religious affiliations die hard but ignominious deaths!

SPAATZ. I'm sorry I had to saddle you with Lester.

LANDAU. Not at all. Lester tells me this particular girl made upward of fifty thousand dollars last year. I had no idea whores made that kind of money. She can't declare any of it, of course, without getting arrested. She lives pretty high, charges at all the good shops, and she just bought herself a four-room co-op in Murray Hill. Lester doesn't know where he can possibly hide all that.

(*The door is suddenly thrust open and* MORLEY, *overcoated now, roars back in.*)

MORLEY. Irving, you haven't forgotten about marrying me off, have you?

LANDAU. As a matter of fact, Irving, that's really why I dropped in just now. Do you think we could sell Lester this curious contract?

SPAATZ (*taking a moment to sort this thought out*). You're being arch, Arthur.

LANDAU. It makes a good mutual shelter. The girl could throw all her posh charge accounts into the joint declaration, and Morley's company would pick up that expensive co-op she just bought as a business expense.

SPAATZ. You're presuming a purely technical arrangement.

LANDAU. The statute doesn't stipulate a single marital domicile.

SPAATZ. Still, if Morley's company's picking up her flat as a business expense, I'd feel a lot better if the girl took up actual residence in Morley's home. We're vulnerable as it is on that income-splitting. I wouldn't want to throw in a totally transparent marriage as well. The examiner may lack the necessary sense of drollery.

LANDAU. Very well. Let the girl move into Morley's place. If the arrangement doesn't work out, they can get divorced January first. Technically, the government still has to recognize the marriage.

SPAATZ. I'd like to hold off on that. I've a hunch we could use the divorce better in Sixty-two or Sixty-three. Have you tried this out on Lester yet?

LANDAU. Yes, he's not unreceptive.

SPAATZ (*turning to* MORLEY, *who hasn't quite caught up yet*). Well, John, Arthur here, usually cautious to a fault, has hit on the abandoned idea of marrying you off to a high-priced whore, a client of one of our colleagues. While the law itself does not insist you and the girl have to live together, anything less, in my opinion, would be patently evasive, and I will not recommend it. At least for a while, I think you and the girl should make a show of a single marital domicile. The marriage, of course, remains a purely technical one, and I understand the girl makes fifty thousand a year; which means she won't be hanging around the house very much anyway. On the plus side, marriage has many tax advantages, principally the possibility of divorce. The property arrangements attendant on divorce proceedings are rife with deductions, and, of course, if you marry, you get the immediate and continuing benefit of the joint declaration which, this year alone, I think, comes to fifteen thousand.

LANDAU. It actually works out to about thirteen four.

SPAATZ. A not insubstantial saving. At any rate, I'd like you to consider this idea of Arthur's—

MORLEY. There's nothing to consider. The idea's radiant. I'd marry a mad dog for thirteen thousand four hundred dollars.

SPAATZ. I don't want you to be headlong about this, John. Marriage is a sacrament—

MORLEY. That's probably what's wrong with it. My God, you boys are on to something ultimate here, don't you know it? I tell you, I felt it the first moment I came in here—a sensation of beatitude, of illuminated innocence. One avoids nervous breakdowns because they are not deductible; one writes books because they are; one marries for the joint tax declaration; one divorces for the property settlement. My God! Don't you recognize the apocalyptic clarity of all that? Of course I'll marry the wretched whore! You'd better find out if she'll marry me. You must make clear to her the totally technical nature of the marriage.

LANDAU. Oh, she understands all that, John.

If ignominy attends the death of old religions, it is also the midwife at the birth of new ones. Morley grows objective about those marvelous evasions demanded in his old houses of worship, but he invests his new dogma with the old trappings of language, and it all assumes "apocalyptic clarity"—a heavy-handed foreshadowing of the tag line of this complex joke. If you read Morley's speech (beginning "That's probably what's wrong with it") casually, reread it carefully. Much of the art of this joke lies in these lines.

SPAATZ. Is she here?

LANDAU. Yes, Lester brought her up. She's in my office. A stunning baggage.

SPAATZ. If she made fifty thousand last year, I would certainly think so. Why don't you bring her in? The two of them might as well meet and see what they think of each other.

MORLEY (*petrified for a moment at the information the girl was just down the hall, now bolts in terror for the door*). I'm getting the hell out of here!

SPAATZ. Take it easy, John.

MORLEY (*panic-stricken*). She won't like me, don't you understand? I mean, look at me, for God's sakes!

LANDAU (*standing*). Maybe we ought to put the meeting off at that, Irving. You've got Willie Nicholson waiting outside.

SPAATZ. Willie's fifteen minutes early as usual. Arthur, go fetch Lester and the girl, and, John, sit down and compose yourself.

(LANDAU *exits.*)

MORLEY (*in a state*). Look, Irving, let's be sensible about this. It was a wonderfully funny idea, of course—ha-ha-ha—but I can't insert some silly slut into my house.

It'll be a circus, for Christ's sake. I have to consider Richard. He's such a dim thing. When I mentioned the idea to him last week, he burst into tears. An operating whore, for Christ's sake! Some big-titted bawd who'll flap around in the kitchen all day reading the *Daily News!* Look, I don't want her in the kitchen, is that clear? She's to stay out of my kitchen! You make that clear to her! First thing!

SPAATZ (*with some asperity*). John, you're only going to meet the girl. There's no commitment involved. If it's impracticable, of course we'll drop the idea. But if you are to get married, it'll have to be an arrangement similar to this. So sit down (MORLEY *sits*) and behave yourself. For all you know, you might like the girl.

MORLEY (*erupting from the couch again*). Oh, my God! Here they come! Tell her to go home!

SPAATZ. Sit down, John!

(MORLEY, *who had started for and whirled away from the now opening door and who for a moment seemed to be about to hurl himself through the twelfth-floor window, jerks to a rigid halt at the penetrating sound of* SPAATZ'S *voice and abruptly sinks into a sitting position on the couch. He just as abruptly stands again as* LANDAU *ushers in* LESTER FREITAG, *a coarser breed of tax lawyer, and* CHRISTINE VAN DAM, *an utterly beautiful girl of twenty-three. They carry their coats over their arms.* MISS VAN DAM *wears a black shantung suit, obviously expensive. A brief flurry of hellos and introductions ensues ("Lester, good to see you—Hi, Irving—Lester, Miss Van Dam, this is John Morley—Irving—this is Miss Van Dam—etc.''). Despite her shyness, there is something predatory in* MISS VAN DAM'S *beauty. She looks at* SPAATZ *when introduced the way a man looks at a woman, seeing him naked on the first glance and considering an affair as she shakes his hand. Throughout this,* MORLEY *has braced himself with his back to the windows, staring down in petrified panic at the floor.*)

LANDAU. John, this is Miss Van Dam, Mr. Freitag—

(MORLEY *manages to nod his head a few abrupt bobs but keeps his gaze resolutely on the floor.*)

FREITAG (*sitting, to* SPAATZ). Listen, Irving, you really serious about this?

SPAATZ. Of course.

(*Slowly,* MORLEY *forces his eyes up from the floor to literally boggle at* MISS VAN DAM, *who is waiting for* LANDAU *to drag a chair up for her.*)

FREITAG (*to* SPAATZ). Because the funny thing is I've been advising Christine here for months to marry one of these big swingers of hers from out of town—(MISS VAN DAM, *aware of* MORLEY'S *attention, turns to look at him across the room.*) One guy, in particular, from Cleveland, he's ready to leave his wife and kids for her. But she's a compulsive whore—(*Suddenly,* MORLEY *sweeps across the room to* MISS VAN DAM *and stands staring at her as he would at a painting, backing off a pace to get better light on her. The girl seems pleased by his intense scrutiny, and she smiles boldly back at him; her eyes rake him up and down with the most shamelessly wayward interest.*) I could get her a studio contract tomorrow, but do you know how much legitimate income she'd have to make as an actress to come out with an adjusted gross of fifty grand a year? She's better off whoring.

MORLEY (*suddenly swishing back to the couch where he flounces down, crosses his legs and pats the hair over his ears in a caricature of effeminacy*). I don't like the suit at all, dear.

CHRISTINE (*turning slowly around as if modeling, pinching in the skirt at the thigh*). It's too loose here, don't you think?

MORLEY. Oh, that too. I mean, you've got a sweet ass, dear, you ought to show it. But the whole thing's much too stark for you. Where'd you get it?

CHRISTINE. Saks.

MORLEY. Oh, they're so contrasty at Saks. I mean, you've got this gorgeous pale face, dear, utterly dramatic in itself, you don't want simple blacks.

CHRISTINE. I think they've tailored the jacket too tight, don't you? It makes my bust bigger than I really am.

MORLEY. They've got you bulging on top like a mother, and the skirt's much too long. You need to be taken in from all directions. If I had some pins here, I could do the whole thing for you in twenty minutes. Now, sit down. I want to talk to you.

CHRISTINE (*sitting*). I told her she was making it too tight on top and too loose on bottom.

FREITAG. Irving, there's a couple of things—

MORLEY. Shut up. Miss Van Dam, you're to stay out of the kitchen. That's paramount. The kitchen is my province. Stay out of it. And I don't want you wandering around the house in tatty kimonos. I'm going to give you one of the guest bedrooms on the third floor. It has a view of the river if you crane your neck a bit. You will keep both room and bath impeccably clean. We have no one in help. You know what it's like getting decent help nowadays. And I don't want stockings, brassieres and garter belts dangling from the shower rods and dripping on the tiles. (FREITAG *chuckles, shakes his head, winks at* SPAATZ.) Shut up. (*To* MISS VAN DAM, *who nods at everything* MORLEY *says like a maid applying for a position.*) During your menstrual weakness, Miss Van Dam, you will simply stay out of the house altogether. I don't want to find half filled boxes of Tampax behind the plumbing in the can. When I have friends in, stay in your room. If, by hazard, you bump into my friends, just stride rudely off without a word. You will not show your transparent tolerance of us poor deviates. Above all, stay away from the boy who lives with me. He's mine. Resist that vanity common to all women that makes each think she alone can straighten out a homosexual. If I catch you near Richard, I'll tear your eyes out, they're lovely, by the way, where do you get that delicious grey eye shadow? No visitors. I assume you will want a television set. Very well, but you will not have the use of the family car. If you have your own car, you may use the garage, but if you scratch up my Chrysler, three lawful cuts of the ground ash, my dear. You may use the telephone, the one in the front hall, not the one in the kitchen, and no more than three times in one day and for no longer than three minutes at any one time. Neither Richard nor I expect cheerful hellos in the morning. We prefer you do not join us at meals. If you have to go into the town of Ardsley, see to it you conduct yourself with decorum. I am well-liked in Ardsley. No soliciting in the streets. I occasionally have the neighbors in for dinner. Mr. Spaatz thinks you should play the mistress on these occasions. Just pass the food around and keep your mouth shut. And, of course, this above all, to thine own self be true, neither a lender nor a borrower be, and he who steals your purse steals trash, Miss Van Dam. (*He smiles his enchanting smile at her. She looks a look of utter longing at him.*)

CHRISTINE. Are you really a poet, Mr. Morley? I never met a living poet.

MORLEY. Oh, there are no living poets, Miss Van Dam. We're not entirely sure there ever were. They've found some sherds of sonnets in England and, embedded in a chalk wall of a cave in France, some yet undetermined thing which might be the legendary inward eye. But all evidence, such as it is, suggests that, if there ever were poets, they were all burned into extinction during the interglacial period of despair. (*They stare at each other, enchanted.*)

FREITAG. Irving, if she's going to maintain residence in Ardsley, why can't we throw off an allocable share of her New York apartment as her studio?

SPAATZ. We're writing it off as Morley's company, Lester. That's a hundred percent write-off. We can't deduct it twice.

(MISS VAN DAM *leans to* FREITAG *and whispers.* FREITAG *nods.*)

FREITAG. Miss Van Dam says the deal is okay with her, Irving. She'd like to get married.

CHRISTINE (*to* MORLEY). I'd like a simple ceremony, wouldn't you?

MORLEY. Yes, a small intimate affair, just a few close accountants and lawyers.

FREITAG. Well, how we going to work this out? I understand you need this for the calendar year.

SPAATZ. The sooner the better.

MORLEY (*leaning toward* MISS VAN DAM). Did you know Proust never dated his letters? What an affectation!

CURTAIN

Confirmed converts have moments of doubt, and Morley panics at meeting his prospective bride. Her predatory appraisal of Spaatz does not distinguish her as an expensive whore; it is a ubiquitous response. Morley, recognizing a sister-under-the-skin, adopts the couturier-cosmetologist-confidante approach, and Christine is captivated because she is, naturally, even more interested in herself than in sex. Then, having outmaneuvered the lady, Morley becomes a bitch, dominating and abusing and captivating Christine. "What an affectation!" is comic misdirection at its best!

A joke is a linear work; that is, it begins, builds to a suspenseful middle, and ends with something of the power of tragedy—the end of a joke being the *punch* or *gag line* (the one line synthesizing the point of the story, the line toward which the whole narrative is directed). Comedy and tragedy of the highest order, then, rest on the Aristotelian concept: the shortest, best way to catharsis is a beginning, a middle, and an end—without diversions. Scenes One and Two of *The Latent Heterosexual* constitute that beginning; Scenes Three, Four, and Five comprise the middle; Scene Six is the end.

The beginning established the basic premise: A homosexual poet seeking fame and fortune had bumbled down many roads, both geographical and emotional, seeking that indefinable thing variously called identification, Self, inner peace, or stability. Poverty, experience, sex, esoteric religions, and drugs had failed to disclose his elusive rainbow's end. One day, however, he awoke rich, famous, and felonious, for his book had been enthusiastically received by an affluent and regressive society which rewarded him with adulation, money, and the threat of incarceration for nonpayment of taxes. The society he had rejected had demanded nothing of him until it accepted him. That acceptance, however, demanded he pay the penalties of acceptance: taxes. Having lived too long outside the law, he decided he could not live within the law *if* the law provided its own exits. A firm of tax consultants had made a blueprint of those exits and happily supplied the escape route—for a fee. Each doorway was marked with a rule, however. "Those who enter here must forfeit leisure," for instance. The first forfeits were difficult for the author, but the third and fourth were easier.

The middle of the joke begins, "In six month's time. . . ." You are now ready to begin threading your own way through the intricacies of the middle.

SCENE THREE

SPAATZ'S *office, six months later.*

At curtain rise, SPAATZ, JIMMIE CHURCHILL, *a grey-haired corporation-type lawyer in his sixties, and* MEL DELANEY, *another lawyer-acolyte in the* SPAATZ *office (and consequently also shirt-sleeved, necktied and benign), are having an impromptu conference lunch (wax-paper sandwich wrappings and plastic coffee containers all over the desk).* CHURCHILL *wears a spring suit.*

The phone rings. SPAATZ *answers.*

SPAATZ. I said, no calls. (*He hangs up.*)

DELANEY. Well, we can't expose your people in this transaction, Jimmie.

CHURCHILL. Christ no. Have you any idea of the punitive action they'd face? (*Scans the front page of the New York* Times *lying on the desk; to* SPAATZ.) Boy, your people are in a lot of trouble!

(*There is a knock on the door and* LANDAU, *shirt-sleeved, necktied, bespectacled, benign, pokes his head in. He smiles to* DELANEY, *waves cheerfully to* CHURCHILL—"Hi, Jimmie"—*and calls softly to* SPAATZ *who is now in deep speculation.*)

LANDAU. Irving, I've got John Morley coming up in a few minutes.

SPAATZ. Who?

LANDAU. Morley. The novelist Henry Jadd brought up last October. You said yesterday you'd like to say hello.

SPAATZ. I'm all jammed up, Arthur. Give him my best.

(LANDAU *smiles, exits, closes the door softly after himself.*)

CHURCHILL (*standing*). Why don't I call my people, see how it sits with them so far?

DELANEY (*rising*). Use my office, Jimmie. I have a direct line outside.

CHURCHILL (*to* SPAATZ). There's no trouble amending the certificate?

SPAATZ (*deep in meditation, murmurs*). It's a family corporation.

DELANEY. I'll be right back, Irving.

(SPAATZ *merely nods.* DELANEY *ushers* CHURCHILL *out. The door closes.* SPAATZ *is alone onstage. He sits, a short, round, Buddha-like man, his hands folded in his lap, his face a mask of meditation. Then he reaches over for the New York* Times *on the desk and rereads a front-page item which apparently concerns a client of his. He picks up his phone.*)

SPAATZ. Ask Arthur if he'd come in, please. (*He hangs up. The door opens, and* MEL DELANEY *returns.*)

DELANEY. They're going to insist on a proprietary interest in any intermediate agency—

SPAATZ. Mel, do you remember this fellow Morley that Arthur was just talking about? He was that nutty novelist who used to hang around here about six months ago. He used to wear lipstick. I think we introduced you once.

DELANEY. Oh, yes.

(*The door opens and* ARTHUR LANDAU *slips silently into the room, closing the door softly behind him. He sinks back on the couch upstage, crossing his legs.* DELANEY *stretches out on one of the client chairs.* SPAATZ *leans back in his swivel chair behind the desk, folds his hands on his Buddha-like belly; and the three shirt-sleeved monks engage in a murmured interchange.*)

SPAATZ. Arthur, let me try something on you. Has Mel been keeping you up on this Nicholson and Mayer business?

LANDAU. I've been reading the papers, of course.

DELANEY. Hanover just blew the whistle on them.

LANDAU. Surely, that's not unexpected.

SPAATZ. They're in the hole for four million dollars plus contracts and commitments for construction and merchandising in the amount of nearly twenty millions. Now, Jimmie Churchill, who's in Mel's office now, approached me some months ago to handle the accounts of a foreign investment syndicate with a lot of accumulated cash in Switzerland.

LANDAU. How foreign is this syndicate?

DELANEY. Let's just say it can't be a principal in the loan.

SPAATZ. It's Mafia money, Arthur. Specifically, it's Frank Tosca's money.

LANDAU. Frank Tosca? Presumably, Irving, this loan would be in the form of convertible debentures. Surely, a reputable drug company like Nicholson and Mayer—

SPAATZ. As Mel says, the syndicate can't be a principal to the loan.

LANDAU. You're suggesting Morley's corporation as intermediary?

DELANEY. It'll throw a hell of a lot of dividend income into it.

LANDAU. They'll want a proprietary interest.

SPAATZ. Fifty percent for, say, fifty thousand—

DELANEY. You'll have to throw in something better than that, Irving, maybe a hundred percent of the Class B.

LANDAU. That'd have to be issued.

DELANEY. You'll need a Swiss subsidiary.

SPAATZ. I think we ought to form in Liechtenstein first.

LANDAU. To hold foreign distribution rights?

SPAATZ. Something like that. Has this publishing company of Morley's published anything yet?

LANDAU. As a matter of fact, we've got a small unreasonable accumulation of capital. They've put out two books of his in conjunction with Random House, and they're both doing well.

SPAATZ. I think we're on firm ground here, don't you, Mel?

DELANEY. Hell, yes.

LANDAU. Let me throw it at Morley when he comes up.

DELANEY. Isn't he the guy you married off to a high-priced whore?

SPAATZ. Yes. How's that working out, Arthur?

LANDAU. Very well, it seems. Irving, I know I told you about the time with the man from White Plains.

SPAATZ (*reflecting for a moment and then beginning to wheeze out a very rusty chuckle*). Oh, dear me, yes, oh yes, that curious library—

DELANEY. What's so funny?

LANDAU. Well, apparently, Mr. and Mrs. Morley have fallen dementedly in love with each other.

DELANEY. You've got to be kidding, Arthur. He was a howling faggot, wasn't he?

LANDAU. Well, perhaps not. (*To* SPAATZ.) Did you ever get a chance to read that psychiatric report Dr. Leverett sent in? (SPAATZ'S *secretary enters to clear away the lunch things on* SPAATZ'S *desk.*) Frances, ask Louise to bring in Mr. Morley's files; they're on my desk. (*The secretary exits bearing paper plates, wrappers and containers.*)

DELANEY. Look at Irving, will you? He's going to bust a binding in a minute. (*Indeed,* SPAATZ *is wheezing, chortling, grunting and chuckling away.*)

LANDAU (*chuckling just a bit himself*). Well, I had to go up to Morley's house last December. By this time, Morley had been turned over to the Collection Division, and I was dealing with a man named Gutman.

DELANEY. Don't know him.

LANDAU. We were claiming income-splitting, and Morley had trunks and crates of journals and diaries which went to our case; so we decided to hold the examination at his house. Accordingly, I picked up this Gutman at the Ardsley depot at ten o'clock in the morning, and we drove out to Morley's house, which is one of those shambling, grey, turn-of-the-century, four-story clapboard buildings with dormers and filigreed balconies; you can see it from the river. Both Mr. and Mrs. Morley were in the driveway waiting to greet us. Morley was wearing a red-checked lumberman's mackinaw and smoking a cigar. Mrs. Morley had her arm linked through his; they were smiling; it seemed strange. I asked Mrs. Morley how long she'd been living up here. She said three weeks. I asked how it was going, and she said, "Great!" She kept hanging on her husband's arm with what I thought a questionable excess of affection. Gutman asked me if they were newly married. I said yes. Then we went into the house, which, I must say, gave Gutman and me quite a start. You walk into almost total darkness and the smell of incense. That incense takes a little getting used to. Morley, who had been under a Turkish influence at the time he bought the house, had achieved a plausible look of Levantine voluptuousness by having knocked out the walls of what had been an entrance foyer, parlor, living room and dining room to make one large inner room, a sort of inner courtyard, and by fringing the whole area with a gallery of Moorish arches. There were divans, yataghans, cushions and rugs everywhere. The walls and windows were covered with hangings and rich baldaquin tapestries on which were hand-painted blue and gold cypress trees and incarnadine peacocks. I had to take Morley's word for that since, as I say, the room was almost black. About now, Gutman was beginning to see this wasn't going to be a run-of-the-mill examination, especially when, as we were going up the dark stairway, Mrs. Morley apparently reached over and fondled him briefly.

(SPAATZ, *whose chortling jag had momentarily subsided, now begins to wheeze and chuckle even more rustily than before.*)

DELANEY. What do you mean?

LANDAU. I mean, she stuck her hand inside his overcoat and gave him a quick tug.

DELANEY. The examining agent?

LANDAU. Yes.

DELANEY. You've got to be kidding, Arthur.

LANDAU. I'm only telling you what Gutman told me. I heard this gasp, and then Gutman grabbed me by the arm in the darkness and said: "What the hell is this?" I said: "What?" He said: "She just give me a feel." Well, we continued up the stairs, but Gutman was clearly put off by the experience. He kept muttering: "What kind of nut-house is this?" Well, then, Morley took us into his library, which was on the second floor and—

DELANEY (*wheezing and chortling*). You mean she just grabbed his pintle, just like that?

LANDAU. Yes.

(*The three tax men are by now all cackling and hissing laughter to beat hell. Indeed, tears stream from* DELANEY'S *eyes, and he has to stand and stomp around a bit, clutching his sides.*)

LANDAU. Well, Morley ushered us into his library, which he warned us was, quote, cluttered. And, if poor Gutman retained any doubts about the eccentricity of this day's work, the library put an end to that. Mel, it was stupefying. It has to be seen to be believed. It took up the whole of the second floor. Here again, Morley had knocked out all the walls of what must have been three bedrooms, and the enormous room that resulted had been turned into one impenetrable jungle of books. Rank, fetid, streaming with books, the floor a matted tangle of them. Stacks, piles of them, some neatly bound, others growing to terrifying heights. Books ramified from the walls and dangled from the ceiling, at least fifty thousand of them, hard cover, soft cover, dust-jacketed, leather-bound, vellum, folios, manuscripts, codices, incunabula, tomes and directories, first editions, texts, manuals, lexicons, thesauri, novels, romances, quartos, octavos, duodecimos, grammars, primers, Bibles, Korans, sutras, scrolls, parchments, megillah, grey, green, brown, blue, red, yellowed with age, black with grime, spotted with coffee and food stains and smelling eternally of what Morley announced to be that most civilized of all smells, the primordial musk of doubt. Morley obviously has a very bad case of book hoarding. He still had primers bearing the imprimatur of the Cincinnati Public School system.

LANDAU'S SECRETARY (*entering with a small pile of manila file folders which she puts on the desk*). Mr. Morley's here.

SPAATZ (*standing*). I'll fetch him. You tell Mel the rest of the story. (SPAATZ *exits with* LANDAU'S *secretary.*)

LANDAU (*leafing through one of the files just brought in*). There's not much more to tell really. Later that afternoon, I asked Morley point-blank what was going on. He suddenly got shy, even reddened, and said: "I'm in love with her. I'm deliriously happy." He turned on his heel and hurried away. And that's all, except a month or two later I bumped into Henry Jadd, who said he had received a mysterious midnight call from Morley. "Listen, Henry," Morley had said, "if Richard Babcock calls, tell him I've been with you all night, going over sales charts. Okay?" The tone of the call had been exactly that of a newly peccant husband, and, in fact, Jadd said he heard a woman giggling in the background, presumably Mrs. Morley. The man seemed to be having a clandestine affair with his wife. Ah, here— (*He has found the page in the file he was looking for.*) This is the psychiatrist's deposition we had to get on Morley. Standard boiler plate, and then, suddenly, at the end, the doctor says he doubts Morley's a homosexual. (*Reads*) "His primary background suggests impotence rather. The patient seems to have had a few shattering adolescent experiences and took for granted he was homosexual. I suggest he had mistaken his terror of sexual impotence for a terror of women, his inability to fulfill the male role for a desire to play the female role."

DELANEY. How about that?

LANDAU (*continuing reading*). "In America, a country whose national lunacy is virility, where a man's measure is the multiplicity of his erections—and where a high officer of our government is said to have interrupted councils of state to unzipper his pants, unleash his beef and flop it on the conference table, saying: "Has Mao Tse-tung got anything like that?"—in such a society, impotence is far more of a stigma than homosexuality, and the patient might well have fancied himself a homosexual all these years just to maintain his self-respect."

DELANEY (*standing*). Or his sanity.

LANDAU. Yes, the doctor makes that point too. (*Reads*) "The patient's theatrical posture of effeminacy seems to be the only socially recognizable identity he can find for himself. In all probability, the patient's ego structure would collapse without this pretense to homosexuality."

(*The door opens, and* SPAATZ *ushers in* MORLEY. LANDAU *closes the file and stands. There is a smiling, murmured flurry of hellos.*)

SPAATZ. You remember Mel Delaney of our office, I'm sure, John.

MORLEY. Yes, of course, how are you, Mr. Delaney?

(*Handshakes, etc. The* MORLEY *we are looking at now is a noticeably different man from the* MORLEY *we last saw. He is neatly groomed in a dark-blue suit and carries his cashmere overcoat neatly folded over his arm. Most striking perhaps is the ten-gallon Stetson hat he's wearing. All traces of effeminacy have disappeared. He seems in excellent spirits.*)

DELANEY. I'd better go see to Jimmie Churchill.

LANDAU. How's Mrs. Morley, John?

MORLEY (*sitting*). She's pregnant. (*This information raises eyebrows on* SPAATZ *and* LANDAU *and causes* DELANEY, *about to leave, to pause.*) Fourth month. It's beginning to show. How do you like them apples, Charlie? (*He extracts a cigar from his jacket pocket, nips off the end.*)

LANDAU (*reaching over to pump* MORLEY'S *hand*). That's wonderful, John.

SPAATZ. Mrs. Morley must be very pleased.

MORLEY. Exuberant. I'm picking her up at the gynecologist's in half an hour, so whatever you got for me to sign, let's get at them.

LANDAU. Actually, John, the only thing that needs any discussion is we'll have to siphon off some of our unreasonable accumulation of surplus in the form of salary to you as president.

DELANEY. Congratulations, Mr. Morley.

MORLEY. Thank you, son.

(DELANEY *exits.*)

LANDAU. However, if we add a large salary to your royalty earnings, it's going to throw you into a hell of a tax bracket.

MORLEY (*suddenly standing, beaming with enthusiasm*). I tell you, men, I'm pretty damned excited about this baby! (*He thumps* LANDAU *a manly thump on the shoulder.*) Well, boy, what you gone do about the tax bracket you just threw me into?

SPAATZ. For heaven's sake, John, are you speaking with a drawl?

MORLEY. A reversion to the Midwestern twang of my youth.

LANDAU. What I want to do, John, is to have the library of yours appraised.

MORLEY (*pauses in the act of lighting his cigar to frown*). My library?

LANDAU. We should take advantage of your charitable foundation. We'll have a ruling on that before the end of the year.

MORLEY. Do you mean to use my library as a charitable donation?

LANDAU. Yes, you donate the library for equivalent shares of nonvoting preferred stock—

MORLEY. The answer's no, thumbs down, *verso pollice*, absolutely not. I'm not like to give away my library.

LANDAU. You only give it away in title, John. The library stays in your house on loan. Not a book leaves your house.

MORLEY. Forget it, Charlie. That library's my one incorruptible vanity. Goddam, you two boys are the blandest bastards I ever like to see. I come walking in here after six months and announce my wife's pregnant, and you boys act like you got queers walking in here all day telling you their wives are pregnant. I tell you, in your most fevered fancies, you ain't never gone conceive the improbable events of the past half year. You boys know the Babcock boy I had living to the house killed himself, don't you?

SPAATZ (*sitting*). No, we didn't know at all. When did this happen?

MORLEY. February fourteenth. He drove my Chrysler over the embankment of the West Side Highway at a Hundred-eighty-first Street. His mother sailed in from Saint Louis in all her battleship grey to claim the body. The Chrysler has been recovered.

SPAATZ. You certainly have had an eventful time of it.

MORLEY. Irving, this has been one long club-footed farce. (*Glances at his watch, takes off his Stetson, sits down, lights his cigar.*) Men, I would like to think of my marriage as an enchanted state and of my wife as a water sprite who resurrected me with a kiss. But I see you have a copy of Dr. Leverett's report here, and so you already know clinically that I'm not the accomplished faggot I thought I was. Lord knows, all that crumbled the first moment my wife unzipped my corduroy trousers. She was the aggressor, of course. I just stood there, mute and trembling like a fawn throughout the whole experience. My wife is a predatory lady. Like so many women who are constantly told how desirable they are, my wife distrusts her beauty and can affirm herself only with the love of incompetent men. She has all sorts of merry ways. She likes to make covert love in public places, the men's room at Idlewild Airport, under the restaurant table while her escort orders dinner. She fancies middle-aged parish priests and has shameless fantasies about her father, a haberdasher in Amsterdam. She's a Dutch girl, by the way, a bit of irrelevance that pleases me. At any rate, twenty minutes after she arrived at my home for her first visit last Thanksgiving, she ravished me ruthlessly in my library; and we've been maniacally in love with each other ever since. And I mean love. I mean, bug-eyed, unbridled, carnivorous love, lyrical exaltation, bottomless despair, jealous rages, volcanic tendernesses, and more flesh-eating sex than I dare to recall. Well, goddam, do you know what it's like to find out after forty years the damn thing works? Men, you talking with the hottest pistol down to the docks! (*Puffs futilely on his cigar which has gone out.*) Well, this outlandish state of affairs would have quickly degenerated into an utterly conventional marriage except for the note of distortion brought in by the Babcock boy living in the house. Now, mind you, Richard and I had never been anything more than companions. Nevertheless, poor Richard found himself in the role of my betrayed wife, while my actual wife was thrust into the posture of my mistress. In this curiously miscast manner, the rest of the wretched drama played itself out. Christine and I now conducted our marriage as if it were a clandestine affair. She maintained the pretense of her own bedroom on the third floor, and we met only in trysts. We soon began, however, to drop broad hints and exchange mysterious glances across the breakfast table. Christine took to brazenly clumping down the stairs on her way to our midnight meetings in the library, for, like all illicit lovers, it was necessary we be caught. We kissed and fondled whenever Babcock briefly left the room, darting away from each other at the sound of his returning footsteps, and sometimes carefully not in time. He must've seen us several times, but he refused to understand. Then—one day in February, when the snow was thick on the ground, Richard was in the kitchen, and I came in from shoveling snow, wearing my red-checked mackinaw, sweating bullets and looking for all the world like something out of Jack London. I slumped into a chair and said: "Man, I'm bushed." Christine came in at that moment, and I whacked her affectionately across the ass. Richard broke into a sweat and ran out of the room. I turned to my wife. "He knows," I said. "What shall we do?" she said. "For God's sakes," I cried, "let's deal with this like adults!" I embraced her. We kissed hotly. I simply can't tell how futilely banal we had all become. I followed Richard up to his room for the confrontation scene. He had already shot some heroin into the deflated vein of his left arm and was beyond understanding anything I said. I plunged inexorably on regardless. "I love her!" I shouted. "I can't live without her!" "Well, baby, that's like crazy, baby," he grunted at me, grinning like an idiot. "I'm helpless in the grip of this passion," I shouted. "If there ever was anything between us, it's over, Richard! For God's sakes, let's behave like intelligent people!" The poor hopped-up son of a bitch, utterly confused, began to cry. "For God's sakes, don't cry!" I caterwauled and stormed out of the room. (MORLEY *relights his cigar.*) Well, I won't go through the whole farce. We spent the rest of the night in a series of familiar emotional scenes until I had convinced Richard grand passions were called for. We were back in the kitchen by then. He was coming off his jag. He was on a twelve-hour cycle. It was nearly midnight. We were all slumped around, drained and drawn. He got up to leave the room. He was only going to the john, but my wife and I both leaped from our chairs and seized the startled boy. "You're not going to do anything foolish?" I hissed. He realized at last something foolish was in fact expected of him, some act that would put an end to this insane play-acting, that would indurate and make credible the incredible feelings Christine and I felt for each other. Somebody had to be hurt. Love, like everything else in the human condition, is perceptible only through pain, do you agree? (*The cigar, which has gone out again, dangles from his limp fingers.* MORLEY, *suddenly saddened, stares at the floor.*) About five minutes later, we heard the front door slam, and a few minutes after that we heard the grind of the Chrysler's motor disappearing into the distance of the still winter night.

SPAATZ. He drove the car over the highway embankment.

MORLEY. Yes. At the emergency parking area near the Washington Bridge. He died suspecting his heart had been broken. The homosexual community still regards his gesture with awe.

SPAATZ. You've made the whole thing up.

MORLEY. No, it happened exactly as I told it to you. It was even in the papers. (*Stands, returns the Stetson to his head.*) Well, I got to get going, men. I got to pick up Maw. (*He starts for the door, but is restrained by* SPAATZ'S *voice, barely more than a murmur, but nevertheless compelling.*)

SPAATZ. One of our corporate clients, John, is Nicholson and Mayer, the well-known pharmaceutical company, specializing in women's medications. The name might mean something to you. They've been all over the papers the last two days. They're the manufacturers of Formalex, the prenatal pill which has caused the deformed birth of seventy-odd babies. Perhaps you've read about it.

MORLEY (*turning*). Yes, I have.

SPAATZ. Well, Nicholson and Mayer embarked on an ambitious expansion program last year, based on the prospects of being the first drug company on the market with an oral contraceptive pill, Contrex, the manufacture of which requires new factories, new laboratories and equipment, new foreign merchandising outlets, especially to such countries as India, China, the South American countries, et cetera. (MORLEY *sits.*) I thought this expansion premature since Contrex was still being tested by the Food and Drug Administration, but they were entirely convinced of their product, and so they went to the banks for a four-million-dollar loan with which to begin construction. Two days ago, the roof fell in on Nicholson and Mayer. The Formalex business. Seventy-three babies, if they lived, would mature into withered, armless or legless creatures, and four young mothers had died of puerperal fever. Within hours, Nicholson and Mayer was gasping for its own life. Lawsuits totaling nearly a billion dollars in damage claims have already been filed against them, and the banks blew the whistle on them. The note, which falls due in ten days' time, is being called up by Hanover Trust. They are also committed to over eighteen million dollars in construction and purchase contracts. They can't raise a nickel from the conventional loan organizations, and they can't go to the sharks like Kimmie Allen without losing control of the company. They're a financially sound company, and they can weather this storm if only they can get Contrex on the market. But for that they need twenty-two million dollars, and they have no place to get it. All this clear so far?

MORLEY (*takes off his Stetson, sets it on the desk*). Yes.

SPAATZ. I know where I can get twenty-two million dollars in a hurry.

MORLEY. I never doubted that for a moment, Irving.

SPAATZ. Some months ago, I was approached by a reputable corporation counsel, Jimmie Churchill of Watts, Fitzgerald, Churchill and Whitcomb, to handle the accounts of an investment syndicate in Switzerland. What Jimmie Churchill was in fact saying was that his client was Frank Tosca, one of the *capo mafiosi*, who is, at this moment, facing deportation proceedings. Needless to say, I wouldn't touch the account with a ten-foot pole. However, I don't see why Tosca's investment syndicate can't lend Nicholson and Mayer twenty-two million dollars. Neither principal would want to expose this deal, of course. A reputable drug company can hardly afford to have it noised about that one of its principal bondholders is a syndicate of racketeers closely bound up with the traffic in illegal drugs. And of course Tosca doesn't want the government to know he's got anything like twenty-two million dollars; the tax bite would be prohibitive, even for him. So we need an intermediary company by which to effect the transfer of the money. So, John, how would you like to be a *gesellschaft?*

MORLEY. A *gesellschaft*—

SPAATZ. The loan would be made in the following way: the foreign investment syndicate would form a Swiss corporation into which they deposit the numbered Swiss bank account. You, John, in your corporate form, will reincarnate in the shape of a Swiss company, the John Morley Gesellshaft A.G. First, however, we will have incorporated you in Liechtenstein as the John Morley Société Anonyme, so that you can take advantage of the fixed tax they have in Liechtenstein. The foreign investment Swiss corporation transfers the twenty-two million dollars to John Morley Gesellschaft A.G. which turns it over to John Morley Société Anonyme, and the John Morley Société Anonyme promptly shoots the money to its parent corporation, the well-known publishing company, Morley House, Inc. in New York. Morley House, Inc. lends the money to Nicholson and Mayer at five percent with a stock option. Morley House, Inc. will immediately exercise its option because you don't want to get stuck with debenture income.

MORLEY. Good God, no.

SPAATZ. The first eighty-five percent of dividend income is not taxed, you see, while debenture income is taxed from the first dollar. The foreign investment syndicate will want some control over their money, of course, so you'll have to sell them, let's say, fifty percent of your company's common stock and a hundred percent of your Class B nonvoting stock.

MORLEY. I don't remember having any Class B nonvoting stock.

SPAATZ. You'll amend your Certificate of Incorporation to issue ten thousand shares of Class B nonvoting stock which you'll sell to the syndicate for the twenty-two million dollars you'll lend Nicholson and Mayer at five percent with an option to buy their Class B nonvoting stock which they will have issued after amending their Certificate of Incorporation; said option being immediately exercised by you in order to get the dividend income rather than the debenture income; in this manner, the foreign investment syndicate will have gotten the legitimate outlet for investment they want, Nicholson and Mayer will be redeemed from bankruptcy, and Morley House, Inc. will be a multimillion-dollar corporation with extensive holdings in drugs and pharmaceuticals and with two international subsidiaries.

MORLEY (*staring at* SPAATZ *as a tear slowly tracks down his cheek; in awe*). I have seen the face of God.

LANDAU. I don't like getting up with Frank Tosca.

SPAATZ. Jimmie assures me Tosca has at last found out there's a great deal more money to be made in legitimate business than in crime. Ever since the Apalachin Conference in 1957, he's been withdrawing from narcotics, extortion, gambling, policy and organized murder for more reputable rackets, a few restaurants, an interstate trucking company and a construction firm in California. (*He stands.*) Well, how do you feel about it, John? I'd like to get back to Jimmie Churchill and see if I can't sell him this package.

(MORLEY, *still numbed by the dazzling complexity of the arrangement, nods his head dazedly a few times.*)

LANDAU. I think Jimmie'll grab it.

SPAATZ. So do I.

(*He exits.* MORLEY *and* LANDAU *are alone onstage.* LANDAU *begins to gather up the files he had brought in.* MORLEY *remains sitting rigidly and blank of face for a moment.*)

MORLEY (*muttering*). It's the most frightening sensation. I feel quite faint.

LANDAU. I'm sorry, John, I didn't hear you.

MORLEY. I said I've just felt the strangest mythopoeic feeling. Do you know how, in Greek myths, heroes are forever being turned into trees and nymphs into waterfalls? Well, I swear to you, Arthur, I have the feeling as I sit here that some sort of physical reconstruction is going on in me. I'm changing into a *gesellschaft*. (LANDAU *smiles, turns his attention again to his files and papers.* MORLEY *stands, rather shakily; he has to hold on to the edge of the desk.*) Goddamnedest thing. (*He snickers nervously, carefully puts his Stetson back on, gathers his light topcoat off the back of the chair.*) If my wife calls, tell her I'm on my way. (*He exits, still shaky, knocking his elbow against the jamb as if he didn't have complete control of his faculties. His voice sounds from off.*) Good-bye, Arthur.

(LANDAU *is now alone onstage. He experiences an odd sensation of imbalance himself. He sits in* SPAATZ'S *swivel chair and frowns.*)

LANDAU (*calls back*). Good-bye, John.

(*The door opens, and* SPAATZ, CHURCHILL *and* DELANEY *come back in.*)

SPAATZ. Arthur, Jimmie's unhappy about using a publishing house. It doesn't give his principal enough leverage for future investment. They suggest forming a new parent corporation—Morley Associates, let's say—which would operate Morley House, Inc. as a division.

LANDAU. You've got a holding corporation.

SPAATZ. Jimmie suggests liquidating a couple of their own companies into the parent organization.

LANDAU. How are you going to split it, Jimmie?

CHURCHILL. Right down the middle.

LANDAU. I'm going to insist on a mutual buy-out clause.

CHURCHILL. That's okay with us.

LANDAU. Morley just left. I can probably still catch him at the elevators.

SPAATZ. No, let's get this thing worked out first. We can throw it at Morley later. What sort of gross do these companies have, Jimmie?

CHURCHILL. Four, five hundred thousand. As a matter of fact, I have figures on the construction company back in Mel's office.

SPAATZ. Let's have a look at them.

(*He exits, followed by* CHURCHILL *and* DELANEY. LANDAU *busies himself with his papers again. He suddenly looks up to the doorway and is startled to find* MORLEY's *head, seemingly suspended there, staring at him from the corridor.*)

LANDAU. I think you should know, John, that at this moment, you are a holding corporation called Morley Associates with three operating divisions in publishing, construction, and in interstate trucking.

MORLEY (*reflecting on this for a moment*). Listen, Arthur, how much did you say donating my library will save me in taxes?

LANDAU. About twenty-five thousand dollars.

MORLEY. Go ahead with it then. Send over the appraisers.

(*His head disappears.* LANDAU *is again left alone onstage, frowning, troubled, somehow surely aware that extraordinary things are to happen.*)

CURTAIN

Morley's marriage to Christine has kept him occupied and happy (in his own way) for six months—a period in which he has been conspicuously absent from the Spaatz office. That tax cathedral has been about its master's work, however, and expansions by way of more complex building programs have been explored. Morley's help is needed, and, like any good convert who has languished because his services are not required, he answers the priestly summons. His life has altered radically in the six-month period, his homosexuality (or impotence) vanishing in a surge of reasserted heterosexuality. The priests read his membership record as casually as they would read graffiti on a latrine wall—and with greater mirth. His own account of the six-month period provides them further delight which they conceal as he details the substitutes his life has supplied in lieu of his assumption of duties at the church. Dramatic enough, it has lacked the fire of participation within these walls however; so, asked to assume an active role, he immediately responds. Asked to make a new sacrifice (the library that is his only remaining link with the past), he refuses at first. Then, the prospects of his potential overwhelm him and he feels the stirrings of incorporation into the mystic body of his faith. Then, like a medieval peasant relinquishing his last doubt, Morley sacrifices his library. He has gone through the final door marked "forfeit."

If sadness seems to be setting in, you are not reading this comedy as the intellectual exercise it is. Remember Horace Walpole's observation to Sir Horace Mann in 1769: "The world is a comedy to those that think, a tragedy to those that feel."

SCENE FOUR

The conference room at Morley Associates, Inc., seven months later. There is a large modern conference table with large modern conference chairs distributed around it. At curtain's rise a secretary is placing pads, pencils, pens and ashtrays in front of each chair. The door opens and LANDAU *enters, carrying two briefcases and wearing a light coat and hat. The secretary smiles at* LANDAU, *takes his coat and hat.*

LANDAU. Thank you. (*The secretary exits.* LANDAU *begins to empty his briefcases of piles of files and documents. There is a knock on the door.* MRS. MORLEY *enters hesitatingly. She wears a fur stole and looks ravishing.* LANDAU *smiles benignly at her; she smiles shyly back. They nod at each other.* MRS. MORLEY *looks around the room.* LANDAU *turns back to his files and documents.*) Does your husband know you're here, Mrs. Morley? (*He reaches for the phone on the table.*)

CHRISTINE. His secretary says he's with Mr. Churchill, but they're both coming down here. (LANDAU *smiles, nods, turns back to his unpacking.* CHRISTINE *smiles, nods, finds a chair in the back of the room, sits and looks around.*) Well, they're very nice offices. Do they have the ninth floor too?

LANDAU (*unpacking away*). Yes. Haven't you been here before, Mrs. Morley?

CHRISTINE. No.

LANDAU. My dear Mrs. Morley, I've just realized you're no longer pregnant. May I offer congratulations? Is it a boy or a girl?

CHRISTINE. It was a boy, Mr. Landau, but it was stillborn. Five weeks ago tomorrow.

LANDAU. Oh, I am sorry. I didn't know. I've spoken to your husband a number of times, but he never said anything.

CHRISTINE. He doesn't like to talk about it.

LANDAU. Of course.

CHRISTINE. Has he seemed strange to you lately, Mr. Landau?

LANDAU. No. Subdued, but I wouldn't say strange. I haven't really seen him all that much. My business with him is usually over the phone. Is something wrong?

CHRISTINE (*muttering*). He hasn't been home in eight days.

LANDAU. I'm sorry, I didn't hear you, Mrs. Morley.

CHRISTINE. I said, he hasn't been home in eight days. He stays here in the office all the time. He sleeps here.

LANDAU. What do you mean he sleeps here?

CHRISTINE. He sleeps in his office. He must have a couch there or something. He has clothes down here, shaving equipment. He lives here, he never goes out. He hasn't even been to his analyst. I know because his analyst called this morning to find out why he's missed his last three sessions. I don't know what he does for food. I suppose he sends out for it. He sounds all right. I talk to him on the phone every day. I said to him last night: "What do you do down there, John?" He said: "Nothing. Reading. Sitting." Maybe he has a TV set in his office. I don't know.

LANDAU. I'm not sure I understand you, Mrs. Morley. Do you mean he literally lives here in his office?

CHRISTINE. His analyst says it's a hysterical reaction to the baby's stillbirth.

LANDAU. I didn't even know he was going to an analyst.

CHRISTINE. Oh, yes. About three months ago he stopped taking dope, just like that, and he started going to an analyst. He says he can't deduct the dope, but he can the analyst. Mr. Landau, I've known a few junkies in my time. I've even known one or two who kicked it. But this is the first junkie I've ever known who kicked it for tax purposes. Don't you think that's strange?

LANDAU. Well, if you need a reason for going off dope, a tax savings is as good as any.

CHRISTINE (*with urgency*). He also gave up writing. He hasn't written a word since last spring. He says it jeopardizes his company's tax position. Let me put it this way, Mr. Landau. When I first met my husband, he was a faggot, junkie, poet. Well, he stopped being a faggot, he kicked the junk, and he hasn't written a word since last spring. He's the husband of a whore, the father of a dead son. I mean, the only thing that's real to him any more is this corporation of his. He talks about it like it was alive.

LANDAU. I don't think you could call that strange, Mrs. Morley. To any good businessman, a corporation is a living thing. All of us are very fond of Morley Associates, not just your husband. As a corporation, it even has a sense of humor, having been born in ludicrous circumstances and having matured as something very close to a travesty on the American business structure. Its growth rate is phenomenal. We have to keep reducing the ratio of dividend income to gross income, you see. Your husband's partner has already liquidated three of his own companies into the corporation. One of these, a construction company in California, is building a senior citizens' development near the city of Riverside; so, not five months after Morley Associates was incorporated, it added to its corporate family a real-estate-development subsidiary and a real-estate-management subsidiary; and I don't know if your husband told you, but his own publishing company, Morley House, Inc., which has also been liquidated into Morley Associates and is being operated as a separate division, aside from its two foreign subsidiaries in Switzerland and Liechtenstein, has begun negotiations for the purchase of a local television station in Amarillo, Texas; and we are just now completing the purchase and sale of a luggage company in Saarbrücken, West Germany. You must admit your husband's corporation is a vigor- ous young lady. She takes up two floors of this building, a healthy, ruddy-complected, air-conditioned goddess with two hundred people on her various payrolls, her own finance department and this very well appointed conference room. I don't find it hard to understand your husband's infatuation for his corporation. She's a raving beauty.

CHRISTINE (*near tears*). He lives here, don't you understand? He's wrapping himself up inside this corporation. He's closing out the rest of the world, Mr. Landau.

LANDAU. Do you think he's going mad? Is that what you mean?

CHRISTINE. Yes, Mr. Landau, I think he's going mad.

LANDAU. What does his analyst say?

CHRISTINE. His analyst says this is a familiar withdrawal syndrome, John'll come out of it, and I just have to be patient.

LANDAU. Well—

CHRISTINE (*crying now*). I love him, Mr. Landau.

LANDAU. You mustn't cry, Mrs. Morley.

CHRISTINE (*standing*). I told him on the phone last night I was coming down to bring him home today. He said: "Don't intrude." I don't care what he says. I've got the Chrysler downstairs, double-parked, probably got a ticket by now, I'm going to take him home with me. I just can't watch him go mad, Mr. Landau.

(*The door opens, and* JIMMIE CHURCHILL *enters, followed by* MORLEY. *They are both dressed as corporate executives are expected to be dressed.* MORLEY *doesn't seem at all as strange as his wife had indicated. His left leg seems a bit game, and he's affecting the use of a gnarled walking stick, but on the whole he seems less eccentric than he had ever seemed. He crosses past his wife as if he didn't see her and makes for the chair at the upstage end of the conference table.* CHURCHILL, *on the other hand, turns to* MRS. MORLEY *and beams at her.*)

CHURCHILL. Well, this is nice. We don't see half enough of you, Mrs. M. Listen, why don't you and John have dinner with us tonight? (*Reaches for the phone.*) I'll give Florence a ring. She's very fond of both of you.

MORLEY (*to* CHRISTINE, *in glacial rage*). I told you to stay the hell away from here. I want to be left alone! Totally, artically alone! Get out!

(CHRISTINE *darts a brief, humiliated look at each of the other men; then turns, goes to the door and exits.* MORLEY *promptly sits at the head of the conference table, as expressionless as a statue.* CHURCHILL, *in the embarrassed silence, takes another chair, reaches for the phone.*)

CHURCHILL. How long's this going to take, Arthur?

LANDAU (*arranging the enormous piles of documents he's extracted from his briefcases*). Ten, fifteen minutes at the most.

CHURCHILL (*on phone*). This is Mr. Churchill. Get me my law office. (*Regards* MORLEY, *who is sitting stiffly, staring at the shimmering table top.*) John, I think I know you well enough to say you treat your wife brutishly. She's a damned nice woman and utterly devoted to you, aside from the fact she's one of the most beautiful sights in Christendom. Florence is nuts about her. When we were up to see you that last time—(*To* LANDAU.) Their kid, you know—

LANDAU. Yes, I know.

CHURCHILL. Damn it, John, your wife's a woman, and it doesn't demand much sensitivity to know an experience like the one she's gone through is a shocking blow to any woman's sense of femininity. And you kept asking her to tell funny stories about the men she used to know when she was on the town. I thought Florence was going to belt you over the head with that Egyptian samovar you've got in the middle of the kitchen. (*On phone*) Janet, this is Mr. Churchill. I'm still at Morley Associates. I'll be here another ten, fifteen minutes. . . . Yes. I know. Ask Mr. Whitcomb to hold the fort. I'm coming directly I finish here. (*He hangs up.*) My law partners are getting sore as hell. I spend more time here than I do at my own practice. (MORLEY *is now sitting in a formal executive posture at the head of the conference table, pen poised, waiting for* LANDAU *to lay the first document before him.*) I don't know why you make such a ritual out of this contract signing.

MORLEY. Because it's a ritual.

LANDAU (*leaning over and putting a document in front of* CHURCHILL). As a matter of fact, you first, Jimmie. (CHURCHILL *scrawls his signature.* LANDAU *retrieves the document, goes to* MORLEY's *side, lays the document in front of the rigid* MORLEY.) This, John, is the Secretary's Certificate, signed by Jimmie here as Secretary, which establishes the authority of the meeting of the Board of Directors of Morley Associates at which the motion to acquire the shares in the Steuben Leder Aktiengesellschaft of Saarbrücken was approved. You sign here as Chairman certifying the accuracy of Jimmie's signature. (MORLEY *signs.* LANDAU *takes that paper away, deposits a sheaf of onionskin in its place.*) Now, these are the minutes of that Board of Directors meeting I just spoke of, at which the acquisition of the stock was approved. Three copies, I'm afraid. Just sign here—as Chairman, John—(*he leafs through to the next copy*)—and here—(*he leafs through to the third copy*)—and again here—(*he transfers the sheafs to* CHURCHILL). Three copies, Jimmie— (CHURCHILL *sets about signing.* LANDAU *places more papers in front of* MORLEY.) This is the Waiver of Notice, John, in which you, as Chairman of the Board, waive the formal ten-day notice of the Board meeting you just signed the minutes of. Thank you, Jimmie. (MORLEY *signs. With one hand.* LANDAU *moves the Waiver of Notice over to* CHURCHILL: *with the other he selects a thick wad of contracts and sets them before* MORLEY.) Now, this, John, is the Contract of Purchase and Sale between Morley Associates and the Steuben Leder Aktiengesellschaft. Initial here, please—and here. (MORLEY *initials.* LANDAU *flips a page.*) And again here. (MORLEY *initials.* LANDAU *hands* CHURCHILL *a document.*) Opinion letter from the German lawyers, you might want to see that. (*Flips another page for* MORLEY. MORLEY *initials.* LANDAU *hands* CHURCHILL *another document.*) Financial reports and representations and their accountants' opinion letter. (*To* MORLEY.)

And here. (MORLEY *initials.*) The reason we're buying this company, John, as I think Jimmie's explained to you—(*flips a page.* MORLEY *initials*)—is because Nicholson and Mayer are marketing their contraceptive pill in March of next year, and they—yes, here—(MORLEY *initials.* LANDAU *flips a page.* MORLEY *initials*)—and they could conceivably declare a dividend this December on the strength of that.

CHURCHILL (*studying the documents handed to him*). They almost went bankrupt six months ago. If they declare anything, it will more likely be next June.

LANDAU (*flipping another page*). And your full signature as Chairman of the Board there.

(MORLEY *pens his signature. The process of signing has by now developed into a rhythmic ritual, in which* MORLEY'S *arm dips, he initials, the arm goes up, pauses, dips, initials, up, down, scrawl, up, down, scrawl, piston-like, mechanical.*)

CHURCHILL (*now scanning The New York Times*). You going ahead with that television station in Amarillo?

LANDAU. It provides us with offsets against profits. (*He removes the signed contract from before* MORLEY, *sets another in its place.*) Five copies, I'm afraid, John. Just initial wherever marked in the margins.

CHURCHILL (*stands, stretches*). My people in Texas tell me Vice-President Johnson has a hammerlock on the whole television business down there.

LANDAU (*examining other contracts*). Even if we run it at a loss, there'll be such appreciation we can still unload it as a capital gain at disposal. (*He flips the page for* MORLEY, *up, down, scrawl.*) These contracts conclude only the first stage of the negotiations, John. The actual closing—(*flips a page, up, down, scrawl*)—that is to say, the passing of title—(*flips a page, up, down, scrawl*)—the transference of the German company's stock to Morley Associates—(*flips a page, up, down, scrawl*)—will take place in about ten days; at which time, we will hold a Board of Directors meeting —(*flips a page, up, down, scrawl*)—in which Morley Associates, as principal stockholders in the German corporation, will vote out the old Board of Directors—(*flips page, up, down, scrawl*)—and vote in their own Board. At that same meeting, we'll conclude an ancillary bit of business—(*flips page*)—and your full signature as Chairman here. (*Up, down, signature.* LANDAU *sets new contract before* MORLEY, *up, down, scrawl.*) You may recall, we set up a Liechtenstein Corporation to take care of the foreign distribution of the publications of Morley House, Inc.—(*flips page, up, down, scrawl*)—on which we pay a fixed tax to the Liechtenstein government of two hundred dollars a year for the next seventeen years. (*Flips page, up, down, scrawl.*) What we want to do now, is to engage your Liechtenstein Corporation—(*flips page, up, down, scrawl*)—as the selling agents of the Steuben Leder Aktiengesellschaft—(*flips page, up, down, scrawl*)—so that the bulk of the Steuben company's gross—(*flips page, up, down, scrawl*)—which comes to nearly two million Deutsche Marks—(*flips page, up, down, scrawl*)—will be taxed on the fixed rate of the Liechtenstein subsidiary —(*flips page, up, down, scrawl*)—which, you recall, is only two hundred dollars a year—(*flips page, up, down, scrawl*)—providing an annual savings in taxes—(*flips* page, up, down, scrawl)—of some three hundred thousand dollars—(*flips page, up, down, scrawl*)—and your full signature there, as Chairman of the Board.

CHURCHILL (*looking out the window now*). Is Irving still down in Washington?

LANDAU (*setting another contract before* MORLEY). Yes. I just spoke to him. He says the Kennedy Administration is going to crack down on foreign corporations, but it'll be at least a year before they can push that through. In my opinion, it's well worth it. (*Flips the page for* MORLEY.) As marked in the margins, John. (*Comes down to* CHURCHILL *at the downstage end of the table, bearing a handful of documents.*) The minutes of the Board Meeting and the Waiver, Jimmie, and I think that's all for you. (CHURCHILL *sits, extracts his fountain pen, and quickly scrawls three copies of this and three copies of that. Behind them,* MORLEY's *piston-like ritual has now been enhanced to go up, flip page, down, scrawl, up, flip page, down, scrawl.* LANDAU *begins to stack the already signed material back into a briefcase. He glances at* MORLEY *mechanically signing away, then at* CHURCHILL *also scrawling his signature, frowns, then mutters to* CHURCHILL.) Mrs. Morley tells me Morley hasn't been home in eight days. He hasn't left this building. He sleeps in his office.

CHURCHILL (*signing away*). Maybe he's got a broad.

LANDAU. That would be too orthodox for Morley. No, this seems to be some form of agoraphobia, a terror of the outside world. According to Mrs. Morley, his analyst says it's only temporary. She's nevertheless worried about it.

CHURCHILL (*frowning, looking back to* MORLEY, *who is still initialing metronomically away*). John, have you been staying over in the office nights?

MORLEY (*without pausing—up, down, scrawl, flip*). Yes. I'm withdrawing into the sanctuary of my corporate identity which I find superior to my human identity. (*He pauses in his signing; his eyes are aglow with fervor.*) It is my belief that beyond the frayed little terrors of life, on the far side of despair, there is a perfect and permanent identity of each of us, a consummate essence. I've caught momentary refractions of this before in my life, induced by rigorous religious practices or psychedelic drugs, but I've never felt it so strongly as I do now. I am convinced that inside this corporate identity of mine, there is serenity.

CHURCHILL (*muttering to* LANDAU). He's putting us on, isn't he?

MORLEY. You've often asked me, Jimmie, what I do in my office all day. Well, I sit at my desk, hunched over the corporate accounts like a medieval sorcerer—the invoices, remittances, petty-cash receipts, manifests, bills of lading, ledgers, passbooks, balance sheets—balance sheets—it's in the balance sheets, you see. Somewhere in that infinite innocence of numbers lies the formula for ultimate unity.

(CHURCHILL *looks to* LANDAU *to see what he makes of this.* LANDAU, *who has been organizing all his papers and documents, merely smiles.*)

LANDAU (*to* CHURCHILL). I've drafted a letter to the Amarillo lawyers requesting additional financial information on the television station for Fifty-eight and Fifty-nine, Jimmie, and I've got the F.C.C. application with supporting documents and schedules with me, if you'd like to see those.

CHURCHILL. Hell, there's no hurry on that, is there?

LANDAU. None at all.

CHURCHILL (*muttering to* LANDAU). So what do you think we ought to do?

LANDAU (*shrugging*). I suppose we ought to let it ride, as long as his analyst is in touch with the situation.

CHURCHILL. He just can't live here, Arthur.

LANDAU. I'm sure he's tidy. Of course, the lease for these premises has no allocation for residential purposes, but I'm not sure he's actually violating that.

CHURCHILL (*to* MORLEY). For Christ's sake, John, what is it, the baby? Is that what this is all about? For God's sake, a blue baby isn't the end of the world. My niece had two. She didn't go into a morbid retreat like this. Go on home and give your wife a good bang in the sack and have another one, for Chrissakes. (MORLEY *doesn't seem to hear. Up, down, scrawl, flip page, up, down, scrawl, flip page.* CHURCHILL *mutters to* LANDAU.) Well, look, I've got a law practice to take care of. Am I finished here? (*He crosses to the door, pauses.*) Good-bye, John.

MORLEY (*up, down, scrawl, flip page*). Good-bye, Jimmie. See you in the morning.

CHURCHILL. I'll see you, Arthur.

(LANDAU *smiles, nods.* CHURCHILL *exits.* LANDAU *is already at* MORLEY's *elbow with a new batch of documents, the first of which he sets down before* MORLEY.)

LANDAU. Now, John, we're setting up a pension plan for the executives and nonunion personnel of the corporation. (*Up, down, scrawl.* LANDAU *flips page.*) This is a copy of the first agreement. (*Up, down, scrawl.*) Contributions to the pension fund are of course deductible—(*up, down, scrawl*)—so you get an annual deduction in your personal tax—(*up, down, scrawl*)—of twenty-five thousand dollars—(*up, down, scrawl*)—and at age sixty-five—(*up, down, scrawl*)—if you choose to collect your pension in a lump—(*up, down, scrawl*)—you are taxed at the minimal capital-gains rate. (*Up, down, scrawl.*) This one you also have to sign as one of the trustees. (MORLEY *scrawls his signature.*) And that, John, is that for today. (*He gathers the remaining documents and returns them to his briefcases. Behind him,* MORLEY *remains sitting rigidly, arm still stiffly poised, pen in hand.*) Did she take my hat and coat outside, do you know?

MORLEY (*expressionless, rigid*). Yes, I think I saw them hanging on the tree just outside the door. Is it cold enough to need a coat, Arthur?

LANDAU (*clamping the briefcases shut*). Not really. It's warm for September, but I'm one of those people who put on their coats the day after Labor Day and keep them on till the summer solstice. What's wrong with your leg, by the way?

MORLEY (*rigid, expressionless*). I think it's a muscular weakness of hysterical origin, part of this agoraphobia I seem to be caught up in. It just suddenly stiffened last night.

LANDAU (*moving to the door*). Well, take care of it.

MORLEY. I'm being very careful.

LANDAU (*at the door*). I'll see you, John.

MORLEY. Good-bye, Arthur. My best to Irving when you see him.

(LANDAU *smiles, nods his priestly little nod, and exits.*)

(MORLEY *is alone onstage, sitting in his frozen posture at the head of the conference table, arm rigidly up, pen poised like a dart. For a long moment, he simply sits this way. Then suddenly, despite the fact the polished table before him is desolate of any paper,* MORLEY'S *arm comes down, he scrawls with his pen, the arm goes up, a fractional pause, then down, scrawl, up, down, scrawl, up. Then as the whole mechanical ritual continues, tears begin to track down* MORLEY'S *cheeks and, in a moment, his shoulders shake with sobs. Grunts of anguish escape from the distraught man. And all the while he sobs and weeps, his right arm goes up, down, scrawl, up, down, scrawl.*)

(*The door to the room opens, and* MRS. MORLEY *slips back into the room. She closes the door softly behind her and stands for a moment silently regarding the singular spectacle of her husband at the table. Then she moves to a chair to the side of her husband, who, to all appearances, is not aware she is there or that her eyes are as filled with tears as his. Then, suddenly, the hysterogenic signature-signing ritual ends.* MORLEY'S *arm sinks slackly to his lap. The pen slips from his fingers and clinks on the vinyl floor.*)

(MRS. MORLEY *rises, goes to her husband, and, with some effort, manages to get him standing. She wraps his arm around her shoulders and they manage a step together toward the door.*)

MORLEY (*muttering*). My stick. Don't forget my stick. It cost seventeen bucks.

CHRISTINE (*reaching back for the stick*). What's happened to your leg, John?

MORLEY. I don't know what the hell it is. It just stiffened on me. (*They shuffle across the room to the door,* MORLEY *muttering.*) Seventeen dollars for a walking stick—I told the girl not to spend more than ten. . . .

(MRS. MORLEY *opens the door, and they shuffle out.* MRS. MORLEY *reaches back with her free hand and quietly closes the door behind them.*)

CURTAIN

Morley has sacrified everything to his new identity, his corporate Self. Even his child has not survived, though that sacrifice was not overtly made by him. Modernity, an impersonal kind of stark sterility, rests on the set, the characters seeming a part of the smooth, clean workings of the great economic cathedral. Morley is aware of the religious significance of the building, and of the activities. Signing the documents is a "ritual," and he, like some infallible Pope of an earlier day, follows the directions of his priests and cardinals. His church is too large for him to control; the many serfs dependent on his church are as remote and as unknown as those faceless thousands whose lives were guided by Pope Alexander VI, sire of Cesare Borgia and ruler of a spiritual empire deprived of spiritual leadership. Morley's explanation ("I'm withdrawing into the sanctuary of my corporate identity") is as reasonable as any self-effacing religious leader's reason for becoming a part of the mystic body of the faith. Between the governmental controls and the manipulations of his priesthood, John Morley is caught by circumstances that may or may not have meaning for him. He has set in motion a chain of events that far exceeded his original intention. In fact, the chain resulted from a lack of foresight rather than from premeditation. Now, utterly enmeshed in the events, he could not withdraw even if he cared to—which he does not. His early involvement eventually included Christine and, after his brief rejection of her in this scene, he submits with a kind of impotent docility to her ministering hand.

Vast and wealthy beyond comprehension though his empire may be, he is personally concerned with the small cost of his staff—an irony that is multiple in its possibilities as the joke begins to assume full proportions.

SCENE FIVE

MORLEY'S *house in Ardsley, nine months later, the afternoon of Monday, June 11, 1962. The sun shines down mercilessly on the old Hudson Valley mansion, its four floors of peeling grey paint, its rusty ironwork. The general vegetative effect is one of rankness. The trees are heavy with leaf, and the weeds and yellow wild flowers grow everywhere, even in the driveway and between the slate in the footpath.*

At curtain's rise, SPAATZ, *squat, indestructible, wearing a seersucker suit, is regarding the ramshackle house and its surroundings with a worried frown.* LANDAU, *bland, bespectacled, also in a seersucker suit, enters. He carries his inevitable attaché case.*

LANDAU. I thought I'd better bring the figures on the property arrangement.

SPAATZ. I'm not sure we should thrust everything at him at one time.

LANDAU. Jimmie insists he's lucid, and he seemed competent enough to me the last time I was here.

SPAATZ. Well, let's wait and see how it goes. What are those odd growths there?

LANDAU. I expect they're familiar local weeds and wild flowers, marguerites and daisies and the like.

SPAATZ. I don't mind telling you I have a feeling of foreboding about this afternoon.

CHURCHILL (*entering, wearing a summer suit*). She's gone up to tell Morley we're here.

LANDAU. Irving's worried about throwing the Liechtenstein business at him.

CHURCHILL. Stop fretting, Irving. You're not going to find a lunatic. He's simply an invalid. You've always found him all right, Arthur, haven't you?

LANDAU. Oh, yes.

CHURCHILL. By all means, tell him about the Liechtenstein ruling. He tends to drift occasionally if you just chat with him, but in matters of business he's as penetrating as ever, and the son of a bitch can be pretty penetrating, as you know. He's become reclusive, of course. He has that trouble with his leg, so he stays in his library mostly.

SPAATZ. I must say I'm looking forward to seeing that library.

LANDAU. It's been appraised and catalogued, Irving. It's no longer that jungle of literature he used to have. It looks like a public library now.

CHURCHILL. No mean sight, regardless.

LANDAU. No, indeed, still pretty impressive.

CHURCHILL. Ah! (*This last in reference to the fact* MRS. MORLEY *is entering. She is wearing Levis and a grey V-neck sweater but somehow manages to seem totally naked.*) Chris, you remember Mr. Spaatz.

CHRISTINE. Oh, yes.

(*The fact is,* MRS. MORLEY *gives the impression* SPAATZ *has never left her thoughts. She takes his hand, refuses to let it go and trains a look of a barely repressed rapture on him.*)

SPAATZ. Actually, Mrs. Morley, I don't think we've seen each other since you and your husband first met in my office, and that would be about a year and a half ago.

CHRISTINE (*breathlessly*). Yes.

(SPAATZ, *a little startled to find* MRS. MORLEY *has no intention of unclasping his hand, looks questioningly at her. She quickly releases his hand and looks guiltily away, as if she had been indiscreetly exposing their secret intimacy.*)

LANDAU. You look very well indeed, Mrs. Morley.

CHRISTINE. Thank you. You look very well too, Mr. Landau.

(SPAATZ *now finds she has taken his arm and is pressing against him.*)

CHURCHILL. You said John was edgy today.

CHRISTINE. Well, he hasn't been good all week really. (*She darts a quick ecstatic look at* SPAATZ *and lets her hand fall from his arm to take possession of his hand again.*) His hearing, which has been erratic for months now, faded out almost completely yesterday, and he complained that his eyes hurt this morning.

(SPAATZ *looks at the other two men to see if they're aware of the flagrant pass being made at him. Neither* LANDAU *nor* CHURCHILL *seems especially concerned.*)

CHURCHILL. It's very important we see him today, Chris. We wouldn't have driven all the way up here if it weren't.

CHRISTINE. Oh, listen, this visit's the best thing in the world for him. The one thing that perks him up is talking business. He's expecting you. Why don't we go up? I'll bring the coffee later. I brought some chairs from the kitchen so you can all sit.

(*As she turns smiling to lead the way, she slips her hand under the flap of* SPAATZ'S *seersucker jacket and shamelessly if briefly fondles him.* SPAATZ *gives a startled grunt and leaps back.*)

LANDAU. Did you say something, Irving? (SPAATZ *can only shake his head.*) She's an interesting woman, don't you agree? Jimmie tells me she takes tireless care of Morley. She dresses, bathes and feeds him as if he were a baby.

SPAATZ (*musing*). I think this will be an afternoon I will not readily forget. (*They exit after* MRS. MORLEY *and* CHURCHILL.)

(*The scrim rises on* MORLEY'S *library which indeed looks like a room in a public library. There are countless enfiladed rows of ten-foot-high wooden bookshelves, marked by category: Anthology, Biography, Fiction, History, Manuscripts, etc. The fiction is ticketed off alphabetically by little wooden markers reading H-L and so on. There are even wooden index cabinets, precisely like those in public libraries. The entire stage is filled with these racks of books, arranged in sections, except for the downstage right area,* MORLEY'S *work area—where* MORLEY *sits in a checked shirt and rumpled corduroy trousers, barefooted. He sits stiffly, his arms rigid on the armrests, his thin shanks shooting straight out, knee by knee. He is quite mad. This area of the enormous library room is the only one which isn't darkish; it is in fact over-illuminated by a blast of white summer sunshine bursting in through a window on the right wall.* MORLEY, *staring stiffly, blankly ahead, seems unaware that his wife, followed by* CHURCHILL *and* LANDAU *and, lastly,* SPAATZ, *have entered from upstage and are coming down the central aisle toward him.*)

CHRISTINE (*shouting from about five feet*). John! Mr. Spaatz and Mr. Landau and Jimmie Churchill are here!

(MORLEY *slowly turns his head just enough to acknowledge the three men standing in a silhouetted clump halfway down the aisle.*)

CHURCHILL (*booming out*). How are you, John?

(MORLEY *doesn't answer; he seems sullen, rebellious. The three men come further down the aisle.* MRS. MORLEY *has started back up.*)

CHRISTINE (*to* SPAATZ, *with a soft smile, somehow suggesting an assignation is being made*). I'm going down for the coffee and cakes now.

(SPAATZ *nods, smiles, and, protecting his crotch with his right hand, moves aside to let her pass.*)

LANDAU (*seating himself at the work table*). Well, how are you, John?

(MORLEY *doesn't seem to have heard.*)

CHURCHILL (*booming out*). I don't know whether Christine told you or not, John, but Frank Tosca was shot last night—

MORLEY. What are you yelling about?

CHURCHILL. I'm sorry. I thought you were having one of your deaf spells.

MORLEY. I'm not.

(SPAATZ *joins the men in the work area, slips onto a white kitchen chair.*)

SPAATZ (*smiling his serene smile*). Well, John, are you up to a conference? Or would you rather we came back another time? You seem to be in a temper. (MORLEY *says nothing.* SPAATZ *takes the silence to mean he should go on.*) John, Frank Tosca was shot around nine o'clock last night by three unidentified assailants in the lobby of his apartment house on Central Park West. He was taken to Roosevelt Hospital where he died less than an hour later without ever regaining consciousness. Jimmie was notified, and he called me at home, and this morning we conferred on what to do about Morley Associates. You know, of course, that in your original contract with Tosca, you had a mutual buy-out clause providing for the cross purchase of the stock of the deceased stockholder by the survivor, and we here all recommend strongly you exercise your repurchase option and buy Tosca's stock from his estate.

MORLEY (*murmuring*). Very well.

SPAATZ. The repurchase will be made at book value. I haven't determined that yet, but it will easily come to a couple of million dollars. However, it's the corporation that exercises the repurchase option; the money will come out of the corporation; it won't cost you anything personally.

MORLEY. Very well.

SPAATZ. Jimmie, here, who's executor, says Tosca's estate consists of his estranged wife and his two sisters who live in Naples. That's going to delay matters a little, but not very much. Jimmie'll have to draw up waivers of citation for the heirs to sign, and the waivers for the two sisters will have to be executed through the U.S. Consulate in Rome. But Jimmie says he should have all that done by the end of July.

CHURCHILL. First week in August at the latest.

MORLEY. Very well.

SPAATZ. At that point—is it sixty days, Arthur?

LANDAU. Yes.

SPAATZ. At that point, Morley Associates has sixty days to give notice to the estate of the deceased stockholder of its intention to exercise its repurchase option. That means that either at a stockholders' or a Board of Directors' meeting—(MRS. MORLEY *returns bearing a large tray of coffee, cups, plates and cakes.* LANDAU *leaps up to help her with it*)—you, John, as the surviving stockholder, vote your shares or cause the Board to purchase back Tosca's shares, which will make you the single stockholder in Morley Associates. In effect, you are now Morley Associates, John, and Morley Associates, Inc. is you.

(MRS. MORLEY *brings a plate with a piece of cake on it to her husband.*)

CHRISTINE (*in that admonitory tone one uses with children*). I want you to have some cake. You hardly ate breakfast and very little lunch. I've taken all the raisins out, so don't tell me you don't want it.

(MORLEY *sets the plate on his lap.*)

SPAATZ. At any rate, Jimmie has already started drawing up the petition to submit Tosca's will to probate, which will take a day or two. Thank you, Arthur. (*This last in reference to a cup of coffee poured and passed to him by* LANDAU.)

CHURCHILL. Let me call my office and push them on that. (*He exits back up the aisle.*)

CHRISTINE (*to her husband with motherly tut-tutting*). Now, just don't sit there with the plate on your knee. Eat it.

(MORLEY *nibbles at the cake. His wife strokes his hair affectionately, smiles at* LANDAU.)

LANDAU (*murmuring*). Shall I pour you a cup, Mrs. Morley?

CHRISTINE. Thank you, no. I'm going to leave you to talk. (*She smiles at* SPAATZ *with the extravagant shyness of a fawn and then at* LANDAU *and exits off up the aisle.*)

LANDAU. You're very lucky in your wife, John.

(MORLEY *stares down at his cake on his knee.*)

SPAATZ. Yes, a lovely woman, John. Obviously devoted to you. Arthur and I are now going to suggest you get a divorce. (MORLEY *looks up to regard* SPAATZ *briefly.* SPAATZ *smiles to reassure him the suggestion was not merely an idle remark.* MORLEY *pinches off a piece of cake, nibbles at it, makes a wry face and returns the piece to the plate on his lap.*) You remember we converted your Liechtenstein subsidiary John Morley S.A. into the selling agent for that German luggage company to get the benefit of the fixed tax rate; it saved us several hundred thousand dollars this year. Unfortunately, the Kennedy Administration is cracking down on foreign corporations. A new statute will be in effect within a few months. It'll require American corporations to report their foreign earnings and pay regular American taxes, which is at least a fifty-two-percent bite. The situation isn't totally irremediable however. This ruling applies only to foreign subsidiaries entirely owned by American companies. If the subsidiary is at least fifty percent owned by a non-American shareholder, the old tax situation continues to prevail. Mrs. Morley, we understand, still retains her Dutch citizenship. If you give her fifty percent of the stock of your Liechtenstein subsidiary, we can retain all the original tax benefits, which comes—let me repeat—to a few hundred thousand dollars every year, no mean consideration. However—(SPAATZ *uncrosses his legs and recrosses them the other way*)—however, we are now faced with another sticky business. If you make a gift to your wife of fifty percent of the Liechtenstein stock, she'll have to pay an enormous gift tax, vitiating most of the tax savings effected by the transfer. However—(SPAATZ *switches legs around again*)—Arthur informs me that if husband and wife enter a separation arrangement pursuant to a divorce, any such property arrangements are exempt from the gift tax. You get the point, I'm sure. If you were to settle fifty percent of your Liechtenstein stock on Mrs. Morley as part of the property arrangement in a divorce, you would not have to pay the government their tax on foreign subsidiaries, and Mrs. Morley would not have to pay a gift tax.

MORLEY. No.

LANDAU. The divorce itself is entirely technical, you understand, John. There is no actual separation.

SPAATZ. She continues to live right here with you, John. The whole thing is done overnight. Mrs. Morley simply flies down to El Paso.

LANDAU. As a matter of fact, American Airlines has a special divorce flight, which takes off daily at four in the afternoon, I think.

SPAATZ. Mrs. Morley simply crosses the border to Juárez, and the next morning she goes to the courthouse, picks up her decree, grabs the next flight back to Idlewild, and she's back home that day. The two of you can remarry the next morning, if you want to.

LANDAU. I think that would be pushing things, Irving.

SPAATZ. The government has to recognize the divorce, Arthur.

LANDAU. Yes, but I'm afraid they might disallow the settlement, which is, after all, the purpose of the divorce.

SPAATZ. What's the time on that sort of thing, anyway, three years?

LANDAU. From date of filing.

SPAATZ. When would that be?

LANDAU. April.

SPAATZ. Sixty-six then.

LANDAU. Yes.

SPAATZ (*turning back to* MORLEY *and smiling*). Arthur prefers you wait three years before remarrying. But that's only a technicality. Mrs. Morley will continue to live here all that while, and your lives will go on as they do now.

(MORLEY *lifts his right arm and with a backhand sweep sends the plate he has been holding crashing against the window on the wall, shattering it, the piece of raisinless cake crumbling to the floor.*)

MORLEY. No! (*He forces himself to stand on obviously incapable legs, clutches one of the chair's armrests for support.*) I will not separate from her!

SPAATZ. I'm not sure you understand, John. The only actual separation will be for the one night Mrs. Morley flies down to Mexico.

(*The strain of standing has spent* MORLEY, *and he's breathing heavily.*)

MORLEY (*gasping*). No! Not one night! Not one minute! She's my last sensation of sanity!

SPAATZ. Please, John, don't take on so. It was only a suggestion. We had no idea you'd feel so strongly about it.

MORLEY (*in a hoarse, hissing whisper*). Listen to me! I'm going insane—hideous! —it cannot be described! I am literally taking leave of my senses! I no longer hear —see—taste—smell—I no longer feel pain! I no longer feel hunger or desire—I can hardly walk, I can hardly stand! I'm being stripped of all my creature functions! I'm losing all those faculties that identify me as a human entity! I am being transformed by some hideous force! I am hardening! I am literally hardening into some abstract reality!

SPAATZ. I hope you've been seeing a doctor about this, John.

(MORLEY *exsufflates more air out of his constricted body and sits.*)

MORLEY (*himself again*). As a matter of fact, I have.

SPAATZ. Who?

MORLEY. Your Doctor Leverett. He's been my psychiatrist, off and on, for a year now.

SPAATZ. What'd he say?

MORLEY. He told my wife I was a psychogenic, not violent, but I should be institutionalized. He's been here several times. There's a sanatorium in the neighborhood to which he's connected in an advisory capacity, and he drops in here whenever he's by. He has, needless to say, been making a pass at my wife, and I told him the last time he was here that, if he patted my wife's ass one more time, he'd find me a good deal more violent than he had diagnosed. She's all I've got. If I lose her, the game's up with me. She's the only link with reality I retain. As you see, when I talk about her, I manage to be reasonably contained.

SPAATZ. Did Dr. Leverett say what he thought was wrong with you?

MORLEY. Irving, I know what's wrong with me. It's metaphysical, not medical. I'm being reified, disincarnated and converted into an abstract. I'm surrendering my human identity to take on the disembodied identity of my corporate identity. Everything human about me is atrophying. (*He leans toward* SPAATZ, *eyes glinting dementedly.*) There's something more than madness here, Irving. Something's being done to me. There's juju afoot. I'm being stripped of my senses—and, my God, when I think of all those Encratic practices I've pursued, the hours I've squatted under carob trees in Oriental meditation, chanting anagogic formulas—the books of ba, the fetal cauls and fern seeds I've incanted over at midnight, the madstones, periapts and pentacles I've hung about my neck—and all for the single purpose of surpassing the senses! Well, I'm surpassing them! It's happening! Hideous! I hear you now through yards of static! I see only boneless shades of you. I can't determine day from night or whether I'm asleep or awake. The hours pass in formless, shifting terrors. All sensation of substance—walls, chairs, tables, this floor—dissolve, exfoliate into deformed chemical complexities, dazzling, colorless, horrible, horribly incomprehensible images, burning braseros, screaming stones—I can't breathe! I can't breathe! (*He is standing again, gasping desperately for air, and at last succeeds. He cries out into the suddenly airless room.*) Oh, God Almighty, I don't want to go mad! (*His face is suddenly illuminated with terror as if by a flash of lightning. His jaw slumps slack. He strains to say something, and, after a moment, forces some lifeless words from the primeval rictus of his mouth.*) I—can't—talk—(*then he suddenly flings up an arm to protect himself against some invisible swooping thing and cries out a piteous and primitive moan.*) Hideous! Hideous! (*Abruptly he sits again, his arms riveted to the armrests, his long lean legs straight out, knees locked together, his sizable bare feet as rigid as stone.*)

LANDAU (*understandably disconcerted by all this, stands and addresses* MORLEY). Shall I get your wife? (*When* MORLEY, *immobilized, doesn't answer,* LANDAU *turns to* SPAATZ.) What do you think we ought to do?

SPAATZ (*frowns a moment, studying* MORLEY's *rigid form, and suddenly says to him*). There's a very strong possibility N & M may decide to make a public offering of their shares and be listed on the Exchange.

MORLEY (*crossing his long legs and saying in a normal voice, smiling even*). The New York Exchange?

SPAATZ. Yes.

MORLEY. I didn't think the governors allowed corporations on the Exchange which have nonvoting stockholders.

SPAATZ. That's just the point. They'll have to recapitalize and eliminate their nonvoting shares by converting them.

MORLEY. Nevertheless, I want you to destroy my corporate identity, Irving. I want Morley Associates liquidated.

SPAATZ. Well, it isn't all that easy, you know.

MORLEY. I want it liquidated and its assets strewn to the winds. I want it impaled at midnight through its heart. This monstrous deformity is devouring me and will devour us all in its maniacal maw. (SPAATZ *frowns.* MORLEY *stands, shouts.*) I want Morley Associates liquidated! I'm the sole stockholder, and I want the thing liquidated!

SPAATZ. It's a sizable corporation with various and complex interests! It has a life of its own! It's not so easily destroyed! (*Stands.*) My God, what am I arguing for? Frankly, John, I think Arthur and I ought to leave you now. We obviously overexcite you. We'll send Mrs. Morley up. It'd be better if we go, Arthur.

(*He hunches up the aisle,* LANDAU *following. When they get about halfway to the rear,* MORLEY *roars out, bringing them to a sudden halt.*)

MORLEY. My God, it's you, isn't it, Irving? You're the one who's doing this to me! All that numerological jabber, all those phylacteric incantations. You're a goddam son-of-a-bitching cabalist, aren't you?

SPAATZ (*murmuring to* LANDAU). You better get his wife.

MORLEY (*shouting*). The pair of you! The sorcerer and his apprentice!

LANDAU. John, please don't work yourself up into another state!

MORLEY. A year and a half ago I stumbled into your gingerbread office, a lost, frightened soul in terrified flight across the great yawning terror of doubt—a human being, in short!—and you chanted some hagridden formulas and dangled some fylfots and made the sign of the gammadion and turned me into a corporation! (LANDAU's *attention has been riveted by something in the upstage left corner of the room, obscured to us by all those racks of books. So aghast is he that he is at first unaware of the fact* MORLEY *has gone amok. The raging poet has lunged against one of the book-packed ten-foot shelves and sent it crashing to the floor, toppling another rack of shelves in the process, books scattering in every direction.*) My love triumphs over your sinister sacraments! I love her, and she loves me! The spell is broken, you wretched wizards! (*Crash! as he thrusts over a second rack, causing a small avalanche of books to come pouring in a spuming tumult onto the floor.*)

SPAATZ (*to* LANDAU). Get his wife.

(LANDAU, *however, while stepping back to avoid still another thundering torrent of books which* MORLEY, *raging with release, has sent crashing down, remains staring in mute astonishment at offstage left. Crash! and another swash of books comes tumbling down.* MORLEY, *standing knee-deep in surging books, suddenly calms.*)

MORLEY. There—I feel much better. Don't look so frightened, Irving. I'm not going berserk. I'm only restoring some disorder to my life. There were a few months just after my marriage when I think I was happy. I'm going to restore the conditions of those days. I'm going back to my heroin, my library and my wife. You liquidate that corporation of mine, Irving. I don't care how complicated it will be—you liquidate it. Watch out to the right!

(*He pushes mightily against another long shelf of books, sending Fiction A-D cascading to the floor in a new tidal wave of crashing bindings and pages and exposing, at least to* SPAATZ, *what* LANDAU, *shocked into muteness, has been and is still staring at. Indeed, now* SPAATZ *joins him in staring, mouth agape, at offstage left. Whatever cause for astonishment is going on offstage remains invisible to* MORLEY *and to the audience as well by those racks of books still standing.* JIMMIE CHURCHILL'S *voice rises suddenly from that direction.*)

CHURCHILL'S VOICE (*offstage left*). Oh, Christ, don't stop now—

MORLEY (*heading upstage, wading ankle-deep through the books, shouting happily*). Christine! Christine!

SPAATZ (*staring off*). Holy cow!

(*Now* MORLEY *is also staring aghast offstage left. The happy smile has been wiped from his face.*)

CHURCHILL'S VOICE (*offstage left*). Goddam, what the hell—

(MORLEY *suddenly stiffens like an epileptic and pitches forward onto the floor in a dead swoon.*)

SPAATZ (*calling to offstage left*). For God's sakes, Jimmie, are you out of your mind? With eleven rooms in this house, did you have to pick this one?

CHRISTINE (*entering on her knees from offstage left, staring at her husband's body*). Did he see?

LANDAU (*kneeling to examine* MORLEY). Of course he saw.

CHRISTINE. Is he dead?

LANDAU. No.

CHRISTINE. I have this compulsive attraction to impotent men, Mr. Spaatz. It's the only way I can affirm my femininity.

SPAATZ (*squatting beside* LANDAU). That seems a curiously unnecessary thing to say at this moment, Mrs. Morley.

CHURCHILL (*entering from offstage left, tucking his shirttail in*). I'm in love with this woman, Irving! She's the only woman I've responded to in fifteen years!

SPAATZ (*as they all struggle to raise* MORLEY'S *limp body*). Yeah, well, zipper your damn pants.

CHURCHILL (*staring at the book-strewn nightmare all around him*). What happened to all the books?

LANDAU. Maybe we better get a doctor.

(SPAATZ *and* LANDAU, *bearing* MORLEY'S *limp body between them, lumber back through the piles of books and manage to get* MORLEY *back on his chair. Petrifaction promptly sets in. No sooner are his arms restored to the armrest than* MORLEY'S *head, which had been lolling on his chest, slowly comes up, and his eyes open to stare as vacuously as a statue's.)*

CHRISTINE. John, can you hear me? *(She raises her voice.)* John! Can you hear me? *(She turns away on the verge of tears.)* Oh, boy—

(LANDAU shakes MORLEY by the shoulder, tentatively at first and then more vigorously. MORLEY sits stonily, his body renitent to the touch.)

LANDAU. He's in a catatonic condition.

CHURCHILL *(zippering his pants).* We better get a doctor.

CHRISTINE *(erupting into tears).* I can't take it anymore! You don't know what it's been like here. He's going crazy, and I'm going crazy with him. I've got to get away from him. But he'll never divorce me, never! Especially now. He's insanely jealous. He locked me in a room on the fourth floor because he thought I was flirting with that psychiatrist, which, God knows, I was. And now, I mean, now he's caught me, oh, my God, what's going to happen to me? And I just can't leave him! I have to take care of him, you see! Shall I call that psychiatrist, Mr. Spaatz?

(SPAATZ frowns over this for a moment. Then he cocks his head and regards MORLEY carefully.)

SPAATZ *(to MORLEY suddenly).* Well, you know, John, the government's position on these Liechtenstein corporations is understandable. They're upset by all that money being accumulated abroad by American corporations which is eventually brought back as a capital gain.

(The effect of this remark on MORLEY is extraordinary. He suddenly sighs, leans back comfortably in his chair, sets one long leg akimbo across the knee of the other, smiles.)

MORLEY. About how much money will this divorce save me, Irving?

SPAATZ. About two hundred thousand a year.

MORLEY. Well, what the hell are you waiting for? Take the lousy whore away.

(Saying this, he abruptly reverts to a petrified state, his legs uncrossing themselves like pistons and relocking themselves into the position SPAATZ first saw him in this afternoon, knee to knee, the arms concreting on the armrests, his eyes resuming the emmarbled vacuity of a statue. MORLEY has finally, for all general purposes, gone mad.)

CURTAIN

The home of the head of the vast organization is primitive and neglected on the outside. Nature has almost reclaimed it, in fact. Inside, however, it is well-tended and opulent, if old-fashioned. Presided over by Christine, it is *her* house, but the inner-sanctum, the holy-of-holies, the library, remains the exclusive domain of Morley. He has deteriorated. Passing time and the growing body of his multiple universes have weakened him until he is more dependent on his priests than ever, but his is still the ultimate authority. The familiarities between his bride and his priests have surfaced, however, and are no longer veiled.

Spaatz is startled by Christine's familiarity, and Churchill is thoroughly amenable, participating in utter disregard of the possibility of discovery. This Scene (a crucial one foreshadowing the punch line of Scene Six) is the most salacious (vulgar, if you will) of the lot. You may be shocked as you read it, but you will laugh if you read it with others. The explanation for your laughter is not simple, but it is understandable in terms of mass reaction. *Time* magazine profiled Ed Ames (of the Ames Brothers musical group, "Mingo" of television's *Daniel Boone* show) as the actor most likely to be remembered for his performance on a 1965 Johnny Carson *Tonight* show. Because he is Mingo, Ames (a natural athlete)

was to fling a tomahawk at an eight-foot-high cardboard cutout of a cowboy; during rehearsal, he hit the target in the heart 19 times straight. On the air, old Mingo took aim, let fly and ripped the cutout right in the crotch. Carson, his crew and the audience broke into a hysterical orgy of laughter that ran 3 min. 45 sec. on the tape—probably the longest sidesplitter in television history.°

If you cannot understand why Carson, crew, and crowd were reduced to "a hysterical orgy of laughter" for three minutes and forty-five seconds, it cannot be explained. Psychologists would be forced to defend their theories in massive volumes and no two would be in strict agreement. However, the incident provoked the laughter, and Scene Five is laugh-provoking for the same reasons.

Christine's major service to Morley Associates, Inc., is at an end. She will be phased out of the corporate body, but she will remain in residence in the house. The proposal is made in the heart of the house (the library) with its accumulation of centuries of man's knowledge, beliefs, and faith scientifically catalogued and methodically arranged on ordered shelves. But divorce is the one suggestion that restores Morley to his early, primitive strength, both mentally and physically. He will *not* divorce himself from Christine, and in his reasserted strength he begins to clear away the ecumenical neatness that has reduced him to taking orders from his own priests of high finance. In the struggle, surrounded by the debris of his violent outbreak, Morley sees the coarse act of Christine and Churchill. His bride and his priests are, in his very house, engaging in flagrant indelicacies.

Overwhelmed, he dismisses her as a "lousy whore." Then, surrendering himself utterly to his priests, he loses all remaining identity as the man he once was.

° "Show Business," September 29, 1967.

If you have followed the progress of the action and been aware of the growing story line, you may begin to anticipate the punch line, for it is Scene Six.

SCENE SIX

MORLEY'S *home, a year and a half later.* MORLEY'S *library, now stripped of all its books, is shatteringly empty. The only articles of furniture are a large bed with a golden coverlet and a wooden armchair of ancient elegance, a sort of curule with armrests. The general effect is one of cavernousness. Drawn Venetian blinds cover the windows, and the floor, clinically dustless, seems glazed in the subdued light. It is as bare as a madhouse.*

At curtain's rise MORLEY *is propped up in bed; he wears pale-blue pajamas; he is almost unrecognizable. He seems tiny, a fragile, porcelain old man with large, blue, blinded eyes, shocking in their expression of helplessness. His hair is entirely white. He sits absolutely motionless, emmarbled.*

A starchily white middle-aged matron of a nurse enters, carrying a red bathrobe and a hypodermic needle. She lays the bathrobe on the bed and efficiently administers the injection, to which MORLEY *reacts no more than would stone or any other inanimate substance. She sets the hypodermic down and begins the business of getting* MORLEY'S *lifeless arms into the sleeves of the bathrobe; it's like dressing a doll.*

THE NURSE. All right, let's get the robe on now. Your visitors have just come.

(*A hulking attendant enters carrying a chair.*)

THE ATTENDANT. Where do you want this? (*The nurse indicates by a motion of her head that she wants the chair set down beside the curule.*) Eddie's digging up some bushes. He said he'd be right up.

(*A hulking handyman appears in the doorway. He wears a mackinaw and holds a pair of pruning shears.*)

THE HANDYMAN. I'm here. What do you want?

THE NURSE. I want you to put him on the chair. (*The handyman and the attendant pick up the now bathrobed* MORLEY *and carefully carry the huge doll of a man to the curule, where they set him carefully down.*) I think we're going to need another chair.

DR. KLUNE. No, that'll be fine, Mary, thank you.

(SPAATZ *and a psychiatrist,* DR. KLUNE, *have entered.* SPAATZ *still has his winter coat on and carries an attaché case.* DR. KLUNE *carries his coat.* SPAATZ *stares appalled at the change in* MORLEY.)

THE NURSE (*to the doctor*). I just gave him a shot, but he hasn't been responding to the shots lately.

(*The attendant and the handyman exit.*)

SPAATZ (*to the doctor, in lowered voice*). Landau told me I'd be appalled at the deterioration, and indeed I am.

DR. KLUNE. You don't need to whisper. He can't hear you.

SPAATZ. Listen, is he capable of signing his name?

DR. KLUNE. I honestly don't know. He functions a little bit. I've been treating him with these new tranquilizers, but not very successfully. He has moments of rational behavior, but they're becoming more occasional.

SPAATZ. Are you sure he can't hear?

DR. KLUNE. He responds, as I've explained, only to stimuli affecting his corporation. That's the thing, you see. He has totally identified with his corporation. I'm sure if you talk to him about his corporation, he'll hear and understand you and might even talk to you. Otherwise he has no sensory faculties at all.

SPAATZ (*staring at* MORLEY). He's only forty-six years old, you know.

DR. KLUNE. Yes. Now, I'm a little anxious about this, Mr. Spaatz. As I understand it, you want to dissolve his corporation. (*A strange little sound escapes from* MORLEY, *causing everyone to turn to him.* DR. KLUNE *moves* SPAATZ *a few paces off.*) As you see, he responds to anything dealing with his corporation, which is just what concerns me—the possible pain your talk with him might cause him. If whatever you're going to say is painful to his corporation, he physically suffers in response. Do you understand what I'm saying?

SPAATZ. Yes.

DR. KLUNE. Is what you're going to say to him painful?

SPAATZ. Not necessarily. There are enormous tax benefits to be derived from a liquidation, the total tax bite in such an instance being only twenty-five percent.

DR. KLUNE. Presumably, that's good.

SPAATZ. Well, he's paying fifty-two percent on his separate corporations now, and a twenty-five percent tax is obviously more attractive than a fifty-two percent bite. The point is, something has to be done. Nicholson and Mayer decided last month to make a public offering, and we've got to decide whether to accept conversion on a one-to-one basis or sell our holdings at face value. Now, Morley's company, an indefatigable monster, has been expanding at a formidable rate. At the same time, Mr. Churchill, the de-facto executive, has decided to return to his own law practice, and so there's no one left to actually administer the company. We voted yesterday to liquidate; but we require Mr. Morley's signature, he being the single stockholder, on this document I told you about over the phone, called Stockholders' Consent to Corporate Action. So, in one sense, what I'm going to say to Mr. Morley will be agreeable in that he stands to make a number of millions out of it. On the other hand, let's not kid ourselves. I'm about to persuade Mr. Morley to liquidate the corporation, and, from what you say, that would seem to mean the liquidation of Morley's physical self as well.

DR. KLUNE. No, I don't think that would happen. It might even be therapeutic to strip him of his corporate identity. At least then we'll be able to deal with him and not his delusions.

SPAATZ. Does that nurse have to stand there like that?

DR. KLUNE. Well, he might topple over otherwise. He has absolutely no control of his faculties.

SPAATZ. I regard this whole business with considerable misgivings.

DR. KLUNE. You can only try, Mr. Spaatz. It's understood, of course, that if I ask you to stop, you must.

SPAATZ. Of course. (SPAATZ *frowns, slips out of his coat, drops it on the bed. He comes downstage to where* MORLEY *has been sitting stonily throughout all the preceding matters.* DR. KLUNE *remains watchfully upstage by the bed. The nurse retains her tutelary position at* MORLEY'S *elbow.* SPAATZ *pulls the other chair up with a scrape and sits. He unlatches the attaché case, looks up, tries a smile.*) Hello, John. (MORLEY, *of course, doesn't respond.* SPAATZ *extracts the necessary papers from his attaché case. He darts a look at* MORLEY *and erupts into his report.*) I have here, John, a financial statement, both consolidated and by individual divisions and subsidiaries, wholly or substantially owned, and statements also for our affiliated companies. I have a copy for you if you want to follow along. (*Obviously not.*) The significant figure on this consolidated statement is Earnings, Net, which, as you see, as of December Thirty-first, 1963, came to just short of forty-seven million dollars.

DR. KLUNE (*moving a step closer*). Ah—

(SPAATZ *looks up from his papers to see* MORLEY'S *blind blue eyes slowly blinking.*)

THE NURSE. His eyes blinked.

DR. KLUNE. Yes, I know.

(*The handyman appears in the doorway. Everybody looks toward him.*)

THE HANDYMAN. I left my pruning shears—

(*The doctor waves him off.*)

SPAATZ. Shall I go on?

DR. KLUNE. Yes.

SPAATZ. Our scope in operations has expanded considerably in the past year, mostly in the field of real estate, and, as you know, we have established a separate subsidiary, the Union Safety Security Title and Guaranty Company whose gross earnings—(*he holds a paper up for* MORLEY'S *steadily blinking eyes to see*)—marked Comparative Statement down near the bottom—passed over the six million mark in Sixty-three, a rise of four hundred thirty-two thousand and nine dollars over the previous year. We had that nonrecurring title loss there, as you see, but net earnings rose to two hundred seventy-six thousand, four hundred and thirteen dollars, and we are, of course, optimistic about the financing of quality high-rise residential units located in several Western states. (*A low, rusty, creaking sound escapes* MORLEY, *and* SPAATZ *looks up startled to find that* MORLEY *is now smiling—that is to say, the expression of a smile is now chiseled on* MORLEY'S *face.*) This item here—Mortgages Receivable and Construction Loan Advances—represents first and junior liens, principally on apartment houses and commercial properties in Santa Barbara, Anaheim and Carmel, all in California. In line with our basic long-term investment policies, our major effort has been in the acquisition of properties through sale-leaseback arrangements with builders, usually our own wholly or substantially owned subsidiaries and affiliates; and, if I may call your attention now to the balance sheet for Bello Construction Company of Pasadena, California, sixty-two percent of the capital stock of which was purchased in Sixty-two by our Tri-State Division, Trucking and Construction—

(*Here,* SPAATZ'S *words drift away into inaudibility, for he can only stare speechless at the transformation going on in* MORLEY. *The hunched over little puppet of a man to whom* SPAATZ *had first begun his report is now expanding visibly on the chair as if someone were pumping air into him. He is sitting erect and is once again recognizable as the six-foot man* SPAATZ *had known before. The vacuity in* MORLEY'S *eyes has been replaced by an intense concentration which he directs at* SPAATZ *and which makes* SPAATZ *squint as if he had been caught in a bright shaft of light.*)

NURSE. Well, is that something, or isn't it?

SPAATZ (*to* MORLEY). Shall I go on? (MORLEY'S *granite-like head nods.* SPAATZ *continues, unable to take his eyes from* MORLEY, *as fascinated as a mongoose by a cobra.*) I would like, John, to take each of the divisions, subsidiaries and affiliates separately with a view toward placing a marketable value on them in the event of a most profitable opportunity for a spin-off. We have every reason to expect I.G. Farben to pick up the bulk of our foreign companies; their German attorneys have twice made us offers. And we could readily spin off the Bello Construction Company, for example, to a syndicate representing the minority stockholders at book value which would—if you will examine the attached memorandum—come to a capital-gains profit of just short of six hundred thousand dollars. This money could then be invested in trusts and tax-exempt bonds. (*Again* SPAATZ *finds himself sinking into silence as* MORLEY *slowly, agonizingly rises from his seat, like man emerging from the primordial slime, to stand in terrifying height directly in front of* SPAATZ, *who, perched on the edge of his chair with papers spread out on his lap, goes nervously on.*) Generally speaking, just about all your divisions and subdivisions are prospering, and, if you were to spin off just the affiliates and partially owned subsidiaries, you could effect a profit in excess of seven million dollars, taxable, of course, at the minimal capital gains level.

(*Suddenly,* MORLEY'S *right arm shoots up to form a posture of rigid triumph, rather like the Statue of Liberty in pose, and at the same time there roars out of his grotesquely grinning mouth a grotesque cheer-like sound, as if he were trying to create the effect of a Nuremberg rally.*)

MORLEY. Aaaaaaaahhhhhh!!!!!!

(*Poor* SPAATZ *is startled into half-standing, sending the papers and his attaché case splashing to the floor.*)

SPAATZ (*muttering to the doctor*). Maybe I ought to quit. I'm frankly unnerved by this whole business.

DR. KLUNE. I'll be damned if I know what to advise you. (*He reaches up to the statue of* MORLEY *towering over him and probes* MORLEY'S *upraised arm; it is rigid.*)

Can you give him some mildly negative news so we can at least get him back on the chair? Right now, he's in a cataleptic state, and he'll hold that arm up there forever if we don't get it down for him.

(SPAATZ, *squatting to gather the fallen papers, nods nervously, leafs through the disordered papers, finally finds the one he wants, stands.*)

SPAATZ. Of course, John, that's the rosy end of the spectrum. We have one or two unhappy accounts to report. (*A grunt of pain escapes* MORLEY *but he retains his monstrous posture of grinning, forward-thrusting triumph.*) The fact is, your publishing division, Morley House, is very, very sick indeed. We've dumped over half a million dollars into that wretched television station in Amarillo, and we've been unable to get F.C.C. licensing. President Johnson seems to have all of Texas television tied up. Last year's winter list of books was a disaster, and we've got a four-hundred-thousand-dollar obligation held by West Texas Guaranty and Trust due in February. They might very well proceed against our other companies that guaranteed that loan.

(*The effect of this news on* MORLEY *is horrifying. A moan of anguish wrenches itself loose from him, and his posture of statuesque strength crumbles into one of contorted pain. The stiffly upraised arm comes plunging down to grasp at his stomach as if he had been struck there, and the grinning mask of elation is replaced in a staggering flash with an expression of excruciating agony. The nurse and DR. KLUNE get him slowly back onto his chair where, before* SPAATZ'S *astonished eyes, he slowly deflates, dissolves, collapses back into the tiny, mute mummy of a man* SPAATZ *had found waiting for him when he first came into the room.*)

DR. KLUNE (*to the nurse*). You'd better administer a sedative.

(*The nurse heads for the door. The doctor hurries after her to give her further instructions.* SPAATZ *left alone onstage with* MORLEY, *and upset and eager to get away, crushes all the papers back into his attaché case, grabs his coat from the bed, and makes for the door.*)

MORLEY (*in an intense whisper*). Irving—(SPAATZ, *at the door, looks quickly to the hallway for help, but there's no one immediately there.* MORLEY *slowly turns his head to stare at him with pitifully moist blue eyes*) Irving—

SPAATZ (*coming slowly back into the room*). Yes, John, what is it?

(MORLEY'S *white face contorts with the effort to talk.*)

MORLEY (*in an intense whisper*). I want to die. I would like very much to die. Please.

(*A stinging sensation of compassion shivers through* SPAATZ. *Tears well in his eyes. The doctor reappears in the doorway, shuffles downstage to* SPAATZ.)

DR. KLUNE. Did he say anything?

SPAATZ. Yes. He said he wanted to die. Is he in such great pain?

DR. KLUNE. Yes. I think he is. It's commonly thought insanity is a refuge from the pain of life, but it isn't really. If I had to describe Mr. Morley's condition, I would say he lives constantly exposed to the ultimate terror of life which is the existential state of all men. It must be insufferable.

SPAATZ. Why doesn't he kill himself?

DR. KLUNE. He lacks the locomotor faculty, don't you see? He's utterly helpless to do anything for or to himself.

(SPAATZ *nods. The two men make for the door.* SPAATZ *pauses.*)

SPAATZ. Could I talk to him for a moment?

DR. KLUNE. Yes, of course.

(SPAATZ *frowns in thought, then comes back downstage into the echoing room.* MORLEY *hasn't moved a muscle since his last words. He seems unaware of* SPAATZ'S *return.* SPAATZ *pulls the other chair up, sits, folds overcoat on his lap.*)

SPAATZ. The situation with Morley House is not unredeemable by any means, John. Our obligation to West Texas Guaranty and Trust is secured by your company's pension plan. West Texas Guaranty and Trust has been designated beneficiary. Your pension is, of course, covered by insurance, at the proportion of one hundred times your monthly pension, which, in this instance, is fifty thousand a year or four thousand a month, so you are carrying four hundred thousand dollars' worth of insurance for your pension. That's only good, of course, if you're dead, John. Do you understand what I'm saying? You could make a hell of a tax savings if you were to die, John. Can you hear me, John? It would be of great benefit to your corporation if you were to die.

(*There is no response from* MORLEY. *Indeed, he seems not to have heard a word. After a moment,* SPAATZ *stands and, feeling unbearably sad, shuffles back to the upstage door.*)

MORLEY (*in an intense whisper*). Irving—(SPAATZ *turns*) thank you, Irving.

(SPAATZ *nods and exits.*)

(*For a long moment,* MORLEY *remains stony and silent. Then, slowly, he rises from his chair, turns stiffly and slowly makes his way to the bed where he finds the pruning shears left by the handyman.* MORLEY *sinks slowly to his knees.*)

MORLEY. Did you ever hear the story of the man who got married to get the benefit of the joint declaration, got divorced to maintain his Liechtenstein tax status, and finally killed himself on the advice of his accountant? Well, there was once this poet—not a very good one, I'm sure—but possibly the very last of his kind—

(*So saying, he plunges the shears into his stomach, twisting it about with such a sureness of hand you would have thought he had committed ritual suicide many times before, his face adamantine, innocent of the pain of his disemboweling himself. With one last sigh, he sinks to the floor, just about dead, certainly beyond saving.*)

CURTAIN

Morley is as removed from the sensory life of man as he can be without ceasing to exist. His house is empty, but his grounds are well-kept. Spaatz, the highest of the priestly caste, has done his master's bidding; now he will help his master find release. It would, he assures Morley, be better for the corporate structure if its central authority were to cease to exist.

Morley-the-corporation and Morley-the-poet ("possibly the very last of his kind") die from a self-imposed wound. Giraudoux's concept of comedy is achieved: the pure has not compromised and lived on. The pure has died. Therefore, we have read a comedy.

Suggested Assignments. 1. On page 351 you were given paragraph one (the beginning) of "the joke." Now that you have read the play, write paragraphs two (the middle) and three (the end) of the joke. Your ability to create a surprising punch line will reveal your understanding of this comedy and the magnitude of your sense of humor. If you are still uncertain, count the number of months that pass in the play, consider each a century, and see the time progression.

2. If any play ever stripped the flesh from the bone of a problem, this one does. Brilliant comedy it is; brilliant satire it may also be. In a paper of whatever length is necessary, attempt to prove or disprove the possibility that *The Latent Heterosexual* is a satire.

CHAPTER VII

The Fates Are Laughing—Tragicomedy

Calling it a "mongrel," Sir Philip Sidney first used the term *tragicomedy* in his *Apology for Poetry* in 1595. His contemporaries, Francis Beaumont and John Fletcher, originated the form and used it so effectively that Shakespeare borrowed it from his young rivals for *Pericles, Cymbeline,* and *The Winter's Tale.* The form offered no great challenge to him, for such earlier plays as *The Merchant of Venice, Measure for Measure,* and *Troilus and Cressida* are a measured blend of the tragic and the comic, often being called "dark comedies."

Nor, actually, had the drama retained purity of form (if indeed it ever possessed it) in either tragedy or comedy from the time of the Greeks. Euripides included some comedy in several of his tragedies and (as H. D. F. Kitto observes in his study, *Greek Tragedy*) avoided both the tragic theme and the seriously-advocated intellectual theme in such plays as *Alcestis* and *Iphigenia in Tauris.* The inclusion of greater reality reduced the tragic to the pathetic in such plays and made possible a much wider range of emotional effects.

Curiously, in those historical periods most concerned with reality rather than with idealism, tragicomedy not only flourishes but becomes dominant. Tragedy and comedy, to qualify by either name, must follow a system of relatively logical rules. Structurally, *a tragedy* is plotted as a series of connected and causal incidents which create a beginning, a middle, and an end (á la Aristotle), whereas *a comedy* is a more loosely-knit series of incidents not necessarily related but occurring as a random pattern not unlike that of the picaresque novel. Such structures impose their own restraints on the author and the form, allowing him limited access to the highway of human emotions.

Man does laugh and cry simultaneously when he

is happy and when he is sad. His emotions are so intertwined that he is often incapable of judging whether he is happy or sad, so he registers both emotions. Such is the nature of reality, and it establishes the structure of *tragicomedy:* a series of loosely connected incidents which create a beginning, a middle, and an end, but which allow the insertion of seemingly unrelated and random interludes designed to lighten the heavy gloom. The awful and the humorous can be juxtaposed, much as they are in reality, and the third form emerges.

Those contemporaries of Shakespeare who originated the form as we know it, Beaumont and Fletcher, were actually more popular than Shakespeare in his day and for the following two hundred years. In the preface to his play *The Faithful Shepherdess,* Fletcher defined tragicomedy:

A tragi-comedie is not so called in respect of mirth and killing, but in respect it wants deaths, which is inough to make it no tragedie, yet brings some neere it, which is inough to make it no comedie: which must be a representation of familiar people with such kinde of trouble as no life be questioned, so that a God is as lawfull in this as in a tragedie, and meane people as in a comedie.

Many of Fletcher's Elizabethan contemporaries created plays which were, in the main plot, tragedies, but which also contained a subplot that was a comedy. The two actions were chronologically simultaneous, but they did not exert any real influence on each other. It would be easy enough to extract the comedy portions from these plays and to create two distinctly separate plays, neither being changed in the process nor needing the other to complete its general unity. Theoretically, the tragic elements appealed to the "serious" audience; the comic, to the groundlings (those poorer, common folk who voiced their displeasure or boredom by fighting or talking so loudly that the play was often disrupted).

Shakespeare is never unaware of the groundlings, sometimes making direct references to them in his plays, and weaving comic scenes through the tapestry of all his tragedies for their amusement. However, also aware of his more controlled audience, he made comic relief serve the tragic development, therefore not doing a disservice to the basic structure of the play. The porter's scene in *Macbeth*, for instance, is probably the most brilliantly interwoven comic scene in all of tragedy. Employed at that point where the reader's emotions are stretched almost to the breaking point, it provides *comic relief* (a humorous episode designed to make the tragic gloom lighter), not by lessening the tragic burden on the reader but by illuminating facets of the tragedy that would remain lusterless if the darkness were not dispelled long enough for the light of the commonplace to shine on them. The porter may be crude, but his comments are vulgar truth. Lacking refinement of intellect, he is the antithesis of Macbeth. That "cultured" noble refines his language even as his actions reduce him to utter coarseness. The porter's actions are "correct" because they meet expectation and his speech complements them, creating a near-perfect unit. That such perfection should exist in such a ludicrous picture moves us to laughter only when we compare the porter and the dark prince whose speech and conduct are so warped that they create a distorted canvas. Desiring to identify with dark Macbeth, we guiltily realize that the uncouth porter is the more honest, the more emulable—if less socially acceptable—figure. And we laugh in embarrassment at our preference. The forward movement of the play is not halted for this appraisal; no subplot emerges; but Macbeth stands more clearly revealed in the light that emanates from the "common" man and refracts in the distorted elements of the noble thane.

However, if we prefer to view the scene from a shallow perspective (as a groundling might), we are free to laugh at the porter, fancying ourselves his superior, or we may laugh with him, recognizing our own coarseness in him and delighting in our positions of undemanding service. After all, the porter does his job, drinks, fornicates, and sleeps. In competition with no one, he need worry about the present moment only. That others must worry about the world also allows us to laugh with gentle relief.

Such comic relief in no way detracts from the tragedy, however. It does intensify it, for we return our attention to Macbeth, with whom we have identified, and, for the space of the remaining scenes, we are once again responsible for large actions, for consequences. The comic relief has merely allowed us to take a deep breath, to renew our determination to see the whole distasteful business through to an end. Nor do such comic interludes reduce the tragedy or violate the Aristotelian edict that each action must contribute to the total effect in such a way that, removed, it would alter or change the total structure. Our understanding of Macbeth would be altered if we were not, at this point, reminded of our human ties to the common man as well as to the noble. The scene is, then, an integral part of the whole. *Macbeth* remains a tragedy, for this comic moment assumes no dominance. Once its function is served, it does not recur. The tragedy of Macbeth's disintegration moves forward, and comedy has merely served it, not become its equal.

Tragicomedy must mix the tragic and the comic in relatively equal portions, balancing one against the other, integrating them until, at times, their individual identity is lost and they become almost impossible to distinguish individually. Such moments of *pathos* (sympathy and pity so tempered by gentle humor that the reader cannot identify personally but retains his function as an observer) must be skillfully handled by the playwright or they become *bathos* (the excessively sentimental, the melo-dramatic that, commenting on the death of Little Nell in Dickens' *The Old Curiosity Shop,* Oscar Wilde once said could be read without laughing only by a man with a heart of stone). Such *melodramas* as *Uncle Tom's Cabin* and *East Lynne* dominated the nineteenth-century theater and are revived today for the pleasure of coffee-house and supper-club audiences who delight in cheering the hero and hissing the villain, contributing, after a fashion, their own Choric function.

An enjoyable reading of tragicomedy demands a greater understanding of the structure of reality than does the reading of tragedy or comedy. Each of those forms is an extreme. Sadness or the ludicrous dominates them, creating a set of contrived circumstances almost beyond reality. Tragicomedy recognizes the absence of subplots in life. A man's existence encompasses a series of simultaneous plots of equal importance, one illuminating the other and sometimes interacting with it, but each retaining its own unique importance. For instance, your life at home is one *plot* (a series of causal incidents closely related) with its own cast of characters (parents, brothers, sisters, and so on). Your academic life at school is another plot with a second cast of characters. Your social life at school is a third plot with its own cast. And your social life away from school and home is still another plot. From your viewpoint, you are the central character, and you recognize the overlappings of plot, but those plots do not have subservient importance to each other. They may influence, illuminate, or vie with each other, but they do not coalesce at any point to create one paramount, meaningful moment. No shattering climax occurs in any plot, though a series of minor explosions is constantly taking place.

If you can see the structure of your own life, you can understand the structure of tragicomedy. Unfortunately, looking at the structure of your life, you may conceive of it as a *problem play* rather than as a tragicomedy. Henrik Ibsen (1828–1906) became the "father of modern drama" by creating the problem play, a form of drama which is concerned less with the characters than with their central problem. This kind of play demands a structure that will illuminate the problem from as many angles as possible, and the characters, rather than coming into conflict with each other, are at constant odds with their environment, which merely includes the clash of wills.

In such plays as *A Doll's House, Hedda Gabler, Ghosts,* and *An Enemy of the People,* Ibsen did not consider himself a social doctor, concerning himself with suggested solutions to problems. Rather, he was a diag-nostician, presenting the problem, proving that it existed, examining its nature and causes, relating it to humanity to prove its pertinence, and leaving the reader with the disturbing realization that no cure had been suggested but that one had better be found quickly if the patient (society) were to survive. An air of immediacy results from the problem play and, once the problem is recognized, the play has served its purpose. It then becomes dated (no matter how great its craftsmanship) and becomes boring. *A Doll's House,* for instance, seems pallid stuff in our age when women have achieved a place in society. *Ghosts* seems hopelessly antique with its presentation of syphilis as a social problem of great danger. Each play served to arouse a lethargic public, but, once aroused, that public went on to other things, leaving us with the problem still to be solved. But the play had served its function: it started our awareness of the inheritance. The characters in the plays scarcely rise to the believable level, however, because the focus of the plays does not center on them. The problem is paramount.

Tragicomedy differs from the problem play primarily in its focusing on the characters rather than on their problem. Such a focus weds the form to comedy, which achieves its impact by presenting characters in ridiculous situations rather than by presenting ideas through the ridiculous behavior of characters. In tragedy, on the other hand, the dominant idea is a matter of urgency to the playwright. In tragicomedy, therefore, the idea may become so urgent that the playwright's view is, not infrequently, tinged with a bitterness that is alien to both tragedy and comedy.

In recent British tragicomedy, a unique new drama emerged in the 1950's with such plays as John Osborne's *Look Back in Anger* and Shelagh Delaney's *A Taste of Honey.* These plays balanced the comedy of life with the tragic consequences of living a comedy. The tragic characters in both plays are frighteningly real, their human condition a grimly-reflected image from a mirror that does not distort quite enough to force the reader to be objective. Realizing his subjective participation in the ridiculous reality, he becomes amused—even to the point of near-hysteria at times—but his laughter is hollow and mirthless. Frightened by his inability to be amused by the characters, the reader becomes uncertain about his response to the dominant idea of the play, and he becomes as angry with himself and the human condition as the playwright is.

The master playwright William Shakespeare flirted with such a form 350 years before Osborne and Delaney, but the romance did not develop. As his first undisputed masterpiece (possibly as early as 1594), Shakespeare created the romantic comedy *A Midsummer Night's Dream.* The central action revolves around lovers, the dominant idea being that love is completely irrational, "a fancy engendered in the eyes and fed with gazing." A classic example of such irrationality in the play is Titania's doting on the "translated" Bottom sporting the ears of an ass. Almost contemporaneously, Shakespeare penned *Romeo and Juliet* (1596), a tragedy so lyrical, so impassioned that the emphasis is on the situation (the fate of star-crossed lovers) rather than on the idea of love or on character. Standing almost midway between the romantic comedy and the romantic tragedy, Peter Quince's *The Most Lamentable Comedy and Most Cruel Death of Pyramus and Thisby* dominates *A Midsummer Night's Dream* and foreshadows *Romeo and Juliet*. It is (in its curious blending of tragedy, comedy, melodrama, and burlesque) a miniature tragicomedy within a comedy.

The story of Pyramus and Thisby is tragic, for the characters are as star-crossed as their counterparts, Romeo and Juliet. The presentation of the "lamentable comedy, the laughable tragedy" and the events of "tragical mirth" are imbued with all the dichotomies suggested by Peter Quince. Thisby's death is, by its physical and emotional nature, heartbreaking. As a result of the melodramatic language and deliberately humorous elements (*adieu* repeated three times, for example), it is marvelously funny. Such a blending creates superb tragicomedy:

> THISBY. Asleep, my love?
>> What, dead, my dove?
>> O Pyramus, arise!
>>> Speak, speak! Quite dumb?
>>> Dead, dead? A tomb
>> Must cover thy sweet eyes.
>>> These lily lips,
>>> This cherry nose,
>> These yellow cowslip cheeks,
>>> Are gone, are gone!
>>> Lovers, make moan.
>> His eyes were green as leeks.
>>> O Sisters Three,
>>> Come, come to me,
>> With hands as pale as milk;
>>> Lay them in gore,
>>> Since you have shore
>> With shears his thread of silk.
>>> Tongue, not a word!
>>> Come, trusty sword;
>> Come, blade, my breast imbrue! (*Stabs herself.*)
>>> And, farewell, friends;
>>> Thus, Thisby ends.
>> Adieu, adieu, adieu.   (*Dies.*)

> *A Midsummer Night's Dream,*
> *Act V, Scene 1*

The same blending is pervasive in Jean Giraudoux's *Sodom and Gomorrah,* which follows. Based on the biblical account, the play hurriedly departs from a slavish recreation of the "Genesis" recital. Before you begin to read Giraudoux's play, read the story of the destruction of the Cities of the Plain in a translation of the Bible of your choice. The tragedy, the religious mystery, the symbolism are all a part of Giraudoux's restatement and should be fresh in your mind.

By now you are quite accustomed to reading plays with interpolated material. Beginning with this play, you will find questions to guide your analysis—*you* will do all the work.

SODOM AND GOMORRAH

by Jean Giraudoux
A play in two acts, translated by Herma Briffault

CHARACTERS

THE GARDENER, *employed at the villa owned by John and Leah*
THE ARCHANGEL, *announcing the end of the world*
RUTH, *a discontented wife, guest of Leah at her villa*
LEAH, *highly intelligent, beautiful, and discontented wife*
THE ANGEL, *specially appointed to survey John and Leah*
JOHN, *husband of Leah, with his eyes on Ruth*
JAMES, *husband of Ruth, with his eyes on Leah*
DELILAH, *smug wife of Samson*
SAMSON, *henpecked husband of Delilah*
JUDITH
SALOME
ATHALIA
NAOMI } *all refugees from the Cities of the Plain*
MARTHA
PETER
LUKE

1. What expectations are generated by the title of the play? Why?
2. The cast of characters suggests many biblical allusions. *The Gardener* suggests what account? How does that allusion change your initial response to the names *John* and *Leah?*

3. Explain the irony of the description of Ruth as "a *discontented* wife."

4. Who is *Leah* in the Bible?

5. Why are the names *John* and *James* particularly apt for tragicomic reasons?

6. Explain the adjectives *smug* and *henpecked* as they change your first response to the names *Samson* and *Delilah*.

7. The "refugees from the Cities of the Plain" are chosen for various reasons. If you cannot recall the story of each, do a little research before continuing. Why is each a logical inhabitant of Sodom or Gomorrah?

8. Much of Giraudoux's attitude about humans is revealed in his choice of characters. What conclusions can you draw at this point?

PROLOGUE

The curtain rises on a darkened stage. Gradually a rosy light illuminates what looks like an enormous rose window of a cathedral; suspended against the rose window is an ARCHANGEL, *his great wings spread. In the foreground of what appears to be a flower garden stands the dark figure of an old* GARDENER, *his back to the audience, his face raised towards the* ARCHANGEL. *The* GARDENER *half turns towards the audience and speaks in an awed voice.*

9. Explain the function of the set. What is suggested by the curtain's rising on a "darkened" stage, for instance? Explain the use of the "rosy light" and the rose window. Why is the flower-garden setting effective?

10. What is suggested as the words *rose window* and *flower garden* are juxtaposed? Is the setting realistic, romantic, expressionistic, or symbolic? Explain.

THE GARDENER. This promises to be the most beautiful prologue that ever was or will be! The curtain rises, and the spectators behold—The Archangel of Archangels!

THE ARCHANGEL. Let them quickly take advantage of the sight. It won't last long. And the scene that follows will no doubt be horrifying!

THE GARDENER. I know. The prophets have announced it. The world is coming to an end!

THE ARCHANGEL. A world is coming to an end! And a most deplorable catastrophe!

11. Why does the Archangel correct the Gardener's statement, "The world is coming to an end!"?

THE GARDENER. They say that Sodom and Gomorrah are about to be destroyed! They say that the dominion of those cities which extends eastward to the Indies is condemned! Their vast world-wide empire will soon collapse in final ruin!

THE ARCHANGEL. That's not the worst of it! Nor is it the chief point of the story. Other empires have gone down in ruin. And also at a moment's notice. We've all seen the collapse of empires—the most solidly established, the most worthy to endure. At the height of their inventiveness and talent, with new and splendid armies, with granaries overflowing, with theatres humming with activity, they have ended! They have collapsed just when the dyers had discovered the deepest reds, the purest whites; when diamonds still filled their mines, when the atom in the cell was still untouched, when from the air the sweetest symphonies had just been caught, when a thousand systems had been thought out to protect pedestrians in the midst of traffic! Empires have gone down just when their scientists had found all kinds of ways to counteract darkness, ugliness, and cold, and discovered antidotes of every kind against such things as potato blight and insect bites! At the very time when even hailstorms could be anticipated and prevented or canceled out by law, suddenly, in a few hours, the insidious illness has attacked the healthiest and happiest of empires. And the sickness of empires is a mortal sickness. The vaults are full of gold; but the dollar and the penny become valueless. Cattle and sheep abound; but famine stalks. The empire is attacked at every point by everything—from the devouring worm to the hereditary enemy and the crushing mortgages of Jehovah. The sickness manifests itself in the very places from which, presumably, it had been forever banished: the jackal appears in the busiest city streets, the louse appears on the body of the millionaire. My colleague, that other archangel—the one who sours the milk and curdles the sauces—appears upon the scene, and all is finished! He is there, and rivers flood, armies retreat, blood grows thin, gold tarnishes; and in the general tumult, the catastrophe, and the war of wars, all is destroyed. Nothing remains but bankruptcy, the pinched faces of starving children, the wild shrieks of women in despair, and death, death.

12. Does the Archangel seem to be speaking of empires in general or of one empire in particular? Defend your answer with specific references.

13. Who is "My colleague, that other archangel"? Is there an historical chronology in his listed talents?

THE GARDENER. But they say that if one righteous man can be found in Sodom . . .

THE ARCHANGEL. Empty words! What have justice and righteousness to do with it? In the past, when God's creation was not in danger and He could afford to use such base metal as currency of the realm, the just man or the scapegoat did serve some purpose. The Lord allowed the gluttony of the world to go unpunished if one famous man lived on a handful of lentils; He permitted all the world's filth to go uncleansed if one heart remained pure; He winked at the world's lies if one man remained silent. Mankind has hailed this Divine indulgence and proclaimed the conditions acceptable and right. And indeed, one righteous man, with his lentils and his innocence, suffices for the day. And until the present, God's wrath was not very great; up to now, all world catastrophes have been little more serious than spankings administered to a naughty child; the Lord inflicted them upon mankind without any veritable wrath. But tonight, if the many sleuths of Heaven who are combing the roads of Sodom have not found what they are looking for, then mankind will face all the fire and death of punishment, God's wrath in all its terror. . . . Apparently you do not understand?

THE GARDENER. No. No, I don't understand why God should hate me.

14. The Archangel says God's creation has never before been in danger, but it is now. Why?

THE ARCHANGEL. Are you married?

THE GARDENER. No. I'm a bachelor, as are my brothers.

THE ARCHANGEL. And why?

THE GARDENER. We like being by ourselves.

THE ARCHANGEL. Do you have a sweetheart? Do you step out with the girls?

THE GARDENER. No. I like to step out alone.

THE ARCHANGEL. Then you are hateful to the Lord.

THE GARDENER. I do not understand. There are plenty of towns far worse than ours. The lies and lechery of Tyre and Sidon have become bywords! Here we have committed no sin that would make Sodom and Gomorrah bywords!

THE ARCHANGEL. Listen!

THE GARDENER. I hear. It's people, singing.

THE ARCHANGEL. What kind of singing is it?

THE GARDENER. Towards the North—those are men's voices. Towards the South—those are women's voices.

THE ARCHANGEL. And no duet?

THE GARDENER. What's the good of a duet?

THE ARCHANGEL. In Sodom and Gomorrah the evil and the infamy rest in the fact that each sex sins apart and on its own account. Up to now, in their misdeeds, men and women have at least respected the only basis God provided for their lives—that fundamental principle of their union. Until now, as couples men and women have brought upon themselves the sorrows and wrath of Heaven. The annals of humanity's sins against God, from the apple to the Deluge, are the annals of the male and female couple. Together they invented all the sins displeasing to the Lord and their union brought forth the first child, too, and the generations of mankind. And the Lord dealt harshly with them, but never did He wage a mortal war, for this coupling and this league against Him were also a sign and a promise. Do you understand, now?

15. What does the Archangel mean by "this coupling and this league against Him were also a sign and a promise"?

THE GARDENER. In Sodom there are still some happily married couples.

THE ARCHANGEL. You will presently tell me who they are. From on High, the view of those women in the South and those men in the North, each day more separated from each other, has become intolerable. The properties of the human couple, faults or virtues, are being greedily disputed by men and women, like the jewels and the furniture of a married couple on the eve of a divorce. This joint property of natural instincts, tastes, and prejudices is now being divided up and apportioned out. Pleasures, memories, objects, everything, now has a sexual connotation. No longer do men and women hold in common such things as joy, work, pleasures, flowers. Even wickedness has sex: female wickedness, male wickedness. And so, the world must be destroyed—

16. Why should such things as "joy, work, pleasures, flowers" be held in common by men and women?

THE GARDENER. There are still some happy couples in Sodom. If God requires a happy couple today, as in former times He needed a just and righteous man, we still have John and Leah, we still have Samson and Delilah.

THE ARCHANGEL. I know . . . And in them lies your only hope. All the huntsmen of Heaven have returned with empty game-bags, except the one in charge of those two couples. He's late. That's not a good sign. Samson and Delilah are away on a journey; will they return in time? As for John and Leah, your master and mistress, I have also spied upon them. The eyes of all eternity are upon them—everything concerned with the fate of ephemeral humanity. There was no sign of evil until this morning. They smiled when they spoke to each other, they buttered each other's bread, they slept in each other's arms. They still hold all creation as joint property between them. But suddenly each of them has begun to secrete his own light. Each of them is irritable—thus far within himself, but that's bad; they'll soon be irritated with each other. It may simply mean, as far as she is concerned, that she is expecting a baby—perhaps, as far as he is concerned, it simply means that he has money-worries. In which case, all the sins of the world can still be held in abeyance. But if it means that each of them has become infected with the virus of Sodom, by the consciousness of his own sex, then God Himself can't do anything about it. . . . Let us still have hope! You yourself, O Gardener, can render us assistance. Help us to keep anything nearby from pulling them apart. Put *their* tortoise under the lettuce in the garden; place *their* treefrog in a tree. These things belong to them, together. As for myself, I shall see to it that the sun and the moon and the earth shall work with all the forces of mass and magnetism to remain intact and not become split apart above their heads or beneath their feet.

17. Explain the intentional anachronism of "They still hold all creation as joint property between them." Anachronism not only abounds in this play, it is vital to the structure. Explain why.

18. Does the "virus of Sodom . . . the consciousness of [one's] own sex" suggest homosexuality or some other ill? If some other, is it a lesser or greater danger?

THE GARDENER. They are kind and generous. Couldn't someone warn them that their continued happiness and success in marriage would prevent all this threatened death and ruin?

THE ARCHANGEL. No. God's will is supreme. He does not demand a couple who are willing to sacrifice themselves; He is looking for a couple who are really happy . . .

THE GARDENER. But sacrifice sometimes brings happiness . . .

THE ARCHANGEL. Self-sacrifice is far too easy a way out. It's God's last solution. Save through His mercy, God never has been able to distinguish between self-sacrifice and suicide. No. On the contrary. The rumors of the city, the responsibility that weighs upon them must not, upon any account, reach the ears of John and Leah. The last happy couple in the world must fight it out in the strictest intimacy and among familiar things, they must settle their differences over breakfast, dinner, supper. . . . Well, now, I believe everything is ready. . . . Let them enter upon the scene. The usual blackbird is upon its usual bough. From the kitchen savory odors are being wafted. Now, all ye powers of air, hear my commands! Let there be for the moment around their home a zone of boiling mud which shall keep away any messenger of pity or misfortune. All the portholes of the sky and the Gardener's eye suffice to witness the end of the world.

(The ARCHANGEL vanishes. The GARDENER withdraws. Full light now upon the scene which, except for the light surrounding the ARCHANGEL, has been in semi-darkness.)

19. What is meant by "God never has been able to distinguish between self-sacrifice and suicide"?

20. The Prologue establishes the necessary conventions of the play at the same time as it supplies the expository matter. Is it humorous, tragic, serious, frightening? In short, what is the tone of the opening section? Is a social-problem play suggested? What is the tragedy that is suggested? (Do not confuse *tragedy* and *tragic event!*)

21. Are the Gardener and the Archangel employed as characters, as devices of exposition, or do they have a Choric function? Defend your answer.

ACT ONE

We see the terrace of a country home which stands upon a height above the Cities of the Plain. The door to the house, right, is sheltered from the blazing sun by a red silk awning. On the wall by the door hangs a gilt birdcage with a canary in it.

Standing on the terrace is a big white jar filled with a bouquet of enormous white feathers—from angels' wings, as we shall learn. At center, a pergola stretches away apparently into infinity. This will periodically be lit up with a bright blue light, whenever the ANGEL *appears framed in it. The scene portrays comfort, happiness, security. In the distance the blue mountains, and in the valley the white walls of the towns.*

1. Explain the use of color in the setting.
2. What things do you visualize in the setting that suggest "comfort, happiness, security"? Defend your reasons for such a visualization.

(LEAH *and* RUTH *come out upon the terrace, talking.*)

RUTH. What a lovely view you have here, Leah! How quiet and peaceful that little town looks, down there among the linden trees!

LEAH. Yes. That's Sodom.

RUTH. And that white city among the poplar trees—what a delight to the eyes!

LEAH. Yes. That's Gomorrah. And that path down the mountain, like a furrow ploughed by the sky, that's the path the angels follow when they come down here.

RUTH. And do they often come?

LEAH. Hordes of them, at this time of year. It's summer, and the path is dry.

3. What is the significance of the geography of Leah and John's home?

RUTH. Why do they come?

LEAH. For any and every reason. Whenever I tell the stupidest little white lie, or express the least feeling of envy—there they are! Like game-keepers when the shooting season opens. Turn over any little evil thought in your mind and there, where you angrily expected or hoped to find a demon, you find instead an angel. You know how I've always liked to be alone. Well, it's impossible now. The Angel of Solitude is always there, staring at me.

RUTH. They say he's quite good-looking?

LEAH. That's not the point. Solitude in company, even in the company of an angel, I assure you, it's intolerable.

RUTH. What do they say to you?

LEAH. Nothing. Not a word. But obviously they're simply bursting to talk. The Kingdom of Heaven is a great place for gossip. Their lips move and I stare at their lips. It upsets them. I suppose they're obeying orders. I'm hoping the orders will be lifted one day.

4. Explain Leah's statement: "Solitude in company . . . it's intolerable."
5. Account for the humor of "Like game-keepers when the shooting season opens" and "The Kingdom of Heaven is a great place for gossip."

RUTH. Any sign of reproach?

LEAH. Yes. The way they look at you, their angelic expressions! Mute faces of unearthly beauty. . . . Quite horrible! I used to get some enjoyment out of my sins. I used to enjoy looking at myself in a mirror to see what I looked like when I was doing something wrong. Nowadays, I look in vain for myself. An angel's face is always there, staring back at me, hiding my face like a mask!

RUTH. Does your husband see them?

LEAH. If so, he doesn't mention it. But then, he never mentions anything not officially recognized: he pretends to ignore boredom, fits of temper, little misunderstandings. He simply ignores them, and carries on as if conjugal bliss still existed.

RUTH. You're still in love with John, of course?

LEAH. Yes, of course, I adore him. And these angels aren't the kind that used to appear like lightning. These angels don't have wings. Quite different from the old days when we used to be visited by the cherubims! The minute we broke one law of God, the entire aviary of Heaven was set loose upon us! What scenes we had! The blows they gave us with their wings! Enough to knock down an elephant! But at least one could defend one's self. I certainly defended myself—with words, teeth, fists! And we said anything we liked, it didn't matter, as long as we spoke in anger. Look at that big jar there: it's filled with feathers I pulled out of their wings. . . . And suddenly they would fly away, up and off, while we stood there in their fluttering shadow. And it was over. The battle with the angels was over and I could pin up my hair again. . . . No, these angels that come nowadays are like wingless insects; they travel on foot, forever going up and down in the land.

6. Account for the humor of "The minute we broke one law of God, the entire aviary of Heaven was set loose upon us!"

RUTH. But you *are* still in love with John?

LEAH. I hate him! As you know quite well.

RUTH. The trouble is, you were too wildly in love with him!

LEAH. You're crazy. On the contrary, no bride and bridegroom ever began married life with more in their favor. We were quite calm and sensible. At least, I was. We took this house and began our married life without any of the festivity and flowers that usually surround newlyweds—and animals destined for the sacrifice. John was my mate, my stag, and I was his doe. I looked at him with clear eyes, seeing him for what he was. I never let my feeling of tenderness and devotion disguise his real self from me. And so, I never had to strip him of anything but his clothes!

7. Explain the impact of "I never let my feelings of tenderness and devotion disguise his real self from me. And so, I never had to strip him of anything but his clothes!" Is the statement humorous, serious, both, or neither? How is it related to the three statements in Questions 5 and 6?

RUTH. Lucky you! As for me, I was too much in love with James.

LEAH. John was my stag, I was his doe . . . and oh, how beautiful the world is to the doe! How real, how pure! Oh, it was marvellous and natural, our happiness. And it was entirely without what goes ordinarily by the name of love. Then suddenly, everything went wrong . . .

RUTH. What happened?

LEAH (*softly*). Wait a minute. Look behind you without seeming to. There's one of them now.

(*The* ANGEL *is standing watching them.*)

RUTH. An angel! Oh, which one is it?

LEAH. These angels don't even have names! The cherubims used to bellow out their names: "Karazobad!" Or "Elethradon!" They acted like door-to-door salesmen! But these angels wander about like stray dogs! (*She turns abruptly upon the* ANGEL.) You, there! What's your name?

RUTH. Oh, Leah!

LEAH (*still addressing the* ANGEL). Why are you here? Because I burnt the toast this morning? Or because I said I hate my husband?

(*The* ANGEL *goes off, pausing in the middle-distance.*)

RUTH. You've offended him!

LEAH. Heaven is horrible. Look at him! He's not scandalized, he's merely peeved. I've never been able to endure sulking. . . . It's enough to make one become righteous! What's he doing now, there at the foot of the tree? Apparently a sparrow has broken one of God's laws! He is looking at a sparrow with infinite sadness. (*She claps her hands bruskly.*)

RUTH. What are you doing? You've frightened the sparrow away.

LEAH. Maybe that will show the Angel what it's like to fly!

RUTH. He's very good-looking.

LEAH. Yes; he looks like your husband. So, if James won't have me, I'll flirt with the Angel!

RUTH. How odd! I was on the point of saying he looks like *your* husband!

LEAH. He looks like someone else's husband, no matter whose!

8. Is Leah humorous or cruel as she says "Maybe that will show the Angel what it's like to fly!"?

9. Explain the significance of Ruth and Leah's each saying that the Angel looks like the husband of the other.

RUTH. You and your husband just weren't made for each other.

LEAH. And I suppose you were made for yours?

RUTH. I was made for any man but him!

LEAH. That's what marriage teaches us. To begin with, the man you marry is endowed with every charm. He is like an elm tree full of song birds. Then, each week, one of his charms vanishes—flies off and perches upon another tree—another man!

And by the end of the year your husband is left devoid of any charm; or rather, his charms have all been scattered elsewhere . . .

RUTH. And all that's left of your husband is someone you don't recognize? Lucky Leah!

10. Explain Leah's simile: "[A husband] is like an elm tree full of song birds."
11. Explain the irony of Ruth's "Lucky Leah!"

LEAH. What do I still have of John? I'm thinking of his body, not his mind. I'm thinking of the very features which marked him out from other men and fascinated me. His voice, his eyes, his hands—I find them in other men now. Peter's voice, Andrew's eyes, my uncle's hands now have the attractions I once thought were exclusively John's.

RUTH. Don't complain. I'm much worse off than you!

LEAH. I might have been able to resign myself to the loss of his physical charms. Heaven knows, I did everything to keep his image alive in me. I tried religion, I tried witchcraft! It was no good. So I took myself in hand. In the depths of those nights when I faced the situation squarely, I told myself: Well, it's endurable. My arms are clasping a phantom, my breast is against a phantom's breast. Too bad, but I can stand it. I am a woman, and night is night. . . . But then this unreality in our physical relations began to permeate our souls. His qualities, his virtues, his faults—everything that made him so vivid in our honeymoon days—they vanished from my eyes. It was as though he had borrowed jewels for our wedding day, then gradually replaced them with less precious gems.

RUTH. What nonsense! John is exactly the same John. So frank and generous!

LEAH. Yes, I suppose he is frank. When it's a nice day he'll tell you it's a nice day. He accuses me of vanity. He's right—I am vain. What good is that? The fact is that we now see things differently. It's as though everything had two aspects—one for me, another for him. . . . Generous? Yes, he's generous. But it's meaningless to me. Oh, it's horrible, having a husband you can't share things with any more. . . . Sometimes, when he calls to me from a distance, I can still hear him. His reflection in a mirror—I can still recognize it as his. But it's senseless only to recognize him in an echo and a reflection. Him, flesh of my flesh!

12. Compare Leah's speech beginning "What do I still have of John" with the Elizabethan attitude that love is "a fancy engendered in the eyes and fed with gazing." Are they the same? How do they differ?
13. Leah agrees that John is generous but she adds "Oh, it's horrible, having a husband you can't share things with any more." If John is generous, why can they not share?

(*The* ANGEL *has once more approached.*)

THE ANGEL. Is there no fresh water here? I'm thirsty.

LEAH. We have only a cistern. The spring is at Segor.

THE ANGEL. Is that far off?

LEAH. Only three minutes, if you fly. On foot, an hour. Why don't you pick some oranges?

THE ANGEL. The day has come, Leah. Try to realize it . . .

LEAH. Realize what?

THE ANGEL. That the eye of God is resting upon Sodom and Gomorrah, and from this day onward He will not turn His eye aside. Night and day these cities and their inhabitants will be focussed beneath His magnifying glass . . .

LEAH. Did He commission you to tell us this?

THE ANGEL. My silence should have warned you. But it was not enough.

LEAH. I like it better when you talk. Even your angry voice is sweet. So! Humanity is being warned by Heaven?

RUTH. Leah, please. Don't blaspheme!

LEAH. Jesting with Heaven is called blasphemy? True! Well, the Angel made me do it. What wrong are we doing here, you and I? What were we talking about, Ruth? Clothes? Or about our husbands?

RUTH. You've hurt him. He's going away.

(*The* ANGEL *withdraws.*)

LEAH (*shouting after him*). The best oranges are on that tree in the hedge. . . . They're blood-oranges. . . . Why don't you come back? You're missing the most exciting part of our conversation. Ruth's going to tell us now all about *her* husband. . . . No, not those! They're sour! Look, Ruth! See how funny an angel looks when he makes a face!

RUTH. Why are you always flouting Heaven?

LEAH. Because Will is my middle name; as Submission is yours, Ruth. . . . Yes, he certainly does look like your husband. But of course, you'd be the last to notice it. I imagine you've forgotten what James looks like by now.

14. Is *Will* Leah's middle name? To what does she refer?

RUTH. Would to Heaven I could forget! But it's just the opposite in our case.

LEAH. You're still in love with him?

RUTH. Of course not. But it's not because James has changed. Nothing about him has changed. He's lost none of his charms.

LEAH. Is that so unpleasant?

RUTH. What could be more unpleasant? Every night for five years I've slept with a bridegroom! When you talked about how John had changed, I envied you.

LEAH. I remember your wedding. When James appeared, you stumbled.

RUTH. No, I almost fainted. I almost fainted from sheer joy and hope! Do you remember what James looked like then?

LEAH. Exactly as he is now: as handsome and sunny as the day.

RUTH. So I thought then. Yes, I thought I'd found a man as clear and warm as sunlight. He would be my stake in happiness, and my continual adventure. With him, through him, I would taste all the delights and pleasures of life which, till then, had been without taste or color. I believed I held in my arms the man who would love me and suffer for me. Life would leave its traces on him—for me to see, and I would shelter in him until death!

LEAH. Ah! you expected a show and there was none?

RUTH. There was nothing. Nothing happened. I thought he would express for me everything worth hearing, would be for me everything worth seeing. But not at all! He has his own unchanging ideas about everything. He is impervious to outside impressions. Everything, to him, keeps a frightful sameness. He always goes through the same motions to dress himself, to comb his hair, or to make love. He has a prodigious faculty for always seeing the same things and always in the same light. I surrendered my five senses to him. In despair, I have had to reclaim them, one by one. Now, all by myself I must eat, think, love, and suffer.

LEAH. Still, he's alive!

RUTH. And how alive! He breathes the air as if it were a foreign element in which he risked suffocation. Do you or I ever worry about breathing? A fish out of water does—and so does James. Filling his lungs, expanding his chest, he inhales and exhales deeply, regularly. One-two; one-two! Oh, for a husband who could occasionally be out of breath, as unheedful of life as a golden statue! But his life—his life is a battle to the end against asphyxia.

LEAH. You might get him to dye his hair, for a change.

RUTH. I did. I made him tint his hair, changing it from dark to fair. And he is taking dancing lessons. I have struggled to give his eyes another expression—of uncertainty and sorrow instead of that look of complacency. But never is he so much himself as when he tries to change. He struggles hopelessly to become the man I want him to be. At masked balls he disguises himself as a Chaldean or as a Pharaoh—but he never succeeds in stepping outside himself, not for a single minute!

15. Ruth has tired of James because he does not change. Did she love the man she married or did she marry a man she viewed as a mirage? How did she differ from Leah in her marriage choice?

16. Ruth's "improvements" in James suggest that she has tried to make him resemble what?

LEAH. It might help you to do as I do when I try to revive my love. Try to realize that one day he will die!

RUTH. As if I haven't done that! I have often wished for death, as all women do when they feel they are beginning to hate the man who is their husband. And I have not always yielded to his desire for love or sleep. But he ignores his own unhappiness, regarding it as something impersonal, as a universal suffering. At his side I have not been able to imagine his death, but have glimpsed the death of everyone. The idea of death. But the suffering that I was able to imagine on my wedding day at the prospect of his death—a suffering that would be sheer torture—no, I can no longer imagine it. It's all over. I know that I'll never die through him.

LEAH. We've all gone through that. We've all wanted a world where women didn't have to face life for themselves.

RUTH. I think it's simpler than that. It's just that you and I made a mistake. I have the destiny meant for you, and you have mine! You wanted security in love—I wanted change. I have what you wanted, you have what I wanted.

LEAH. Does he realize your state of mind?

RUTH. I don't know. Probably just as much as John realizes your state of mind. You know what men are. They make a parade of their frankness. They display the events of their lives like battle trophies. But underneath the trappings, no matter how bright they are, reserves and ruses scurry about like mice, at times. And then, there's silence.

LEAH. Yes. I detest their magic carpets.

RUTH. Their what?

LEAH. John has a magic carpet. Whenever something too disturbing happens between us, John simply gets on his magic carpet and flies away. And from high up he gazes down at me, replying to my pleadings or my fits of temper . . . presumably. But he sees nothing and understands nothing. He is safely settled on his magic carpet. From the calm sky where he securely sails he reaches down, sometimes, to give me a soothing kiss. But he abandons me alone, helpless, betrayed. And from above our evening meal he flies off on that magic carpet—on a non-stop flight which carries him into the very depths of sleep. Oh, he knows how to fly, does John! The angels could well take flying lessons from him!

RUTH. What shall we do? What can we do? Must we try a separation? Or murder?

LEAH. There's a third way out, as you're aware. Hush! Here they are . . .

17. Paraphrase Leah's concept of John's "magic carpet." What does she mean?

18. What is the "third way out" that Leah suggests?

(*Enter* JOHN *and* JAMES.)

JOHN. Hello, Ruth darling! Glad to see you! Lovely day, isn't it?

LEAH. No!

JOHN. My dear, I was speaking to Ruth.

LEAH. I'm tired of hearing you always talking about the weather. Surely, John, we're grown up enough to do without a man to tell us whether it's raining or not.

JOHN. Well, I'll go on talking about the weather. It's the only subject left to me if I'm to avoid a quarrel with you.

LEAH. And you haven't got that now. Anyway, you're wrong. For a summer day, I think the weather's awful. The sunshine is dim and everything is horrible.

JAMES. Except you.

LEAH. Since John never notices what I look like, I still win the argument.

JOHN. I can see what Ruth looks like, at any rate. She's lovely. And I'm sure she agrees with me that the weather is magnificent.

LEAH. Don't be a coward, Ruth. Say something.

RUTH. Say what?

LEAH. That you agree with me. That the weather is awful.

RUTH. But I don't agree. The sun is shining beautifully upon Sodom, and this breeze blowing from the direction of Gomorrah is delightful. I don't see anything wrong with this weather.

LEAH. In other words, you think John is wonderful?

RUTH. I certainly do. And you yourself agree to that.

LEAH. What about James? What's his opinion of today's weather in Sodom and Gomorrah?

JAMES. As to James, he's hungry. James would like to have some lunch.

JOHN. Good idea. Let's eat.

LEAH. Oh, what cowards! How typically men—every inch of them!

JOHN. You seem to be every inch a woman this morning, my dear Leah. . . . What's cowardly about wanting to eat? Ruth's a coward too, then; for I'm sure she's hungry, too.

LEAH. I never denied that Ruth's a coward. Of course she is. But she's cowardly in a woman's way and for a woman's reasons; probably because she wants to arouse some man's manly instincts. You're afraid to say the truth, confess it, Ruth. You're afraid of offending John. Well, that's your own affair. But they—they are cowards because of indifference, or because they want to triumph over us.

JOHN. So it's cowardly, is it, not to decide, before lunch, the momentous question of whether or not the sunshine over Sodom is beautiful?

LEAH. Yes.

RUTH. Come to lunch, Leah.

JOHN. Have it your way. The sunshine over Sodom is but shadow, the breeze wafted from Gomorrah is but stagnant air, and on the branches of the trees and bushes in the garden hang only sordid rags, without color or perfume, although they happen to be called jasmin and roses . . .

LEAH. So you're both dying to eat! All men are alike. Whenever an event or the hand of God leads them to the door of reality, they think it's a trap and they run away from it like mad!

JOHN. And upon what do you think the Door of Reality opens today?

LEAH. Upon the usual landscape: the battleground of sex, where men and women touch each other with distaste, look at each other with contempt, and where even their shadows mingle in mutual loathing. An open quarrel, a good fight might clear the air. But no. It's time for lunch! So everything's fine. So bring on the magic carpets which provide escape, the helmets which ensure deafness, the ring which bestows upon its wearer invisibility. The hunger which tortures the vitals of womankind must give way before a man's hunger for roast wild duck and green peas!

JOHN. Wild duck! Oh, is there wild duck for lunch?

RUTH. Don't tease her, John!

19. The weather and food are, ordinarily, safe topics for men to discuss. Do they run away from "the door of reality," as Leah suggests? If so, what is the refuge offered by weather and food?

20. Is Leah's concept of "the battleground of sex" correct or incorrect? Defend your choice.

LEAH. Let him alone. Men are always like that. On every day that might be a decisive one, when we think we'll have it out at last! Poor, deluded females that we are, we imagine we'll discover what a man's mind and soul are, just as we once found out what kind of leg he had or how he kissed! Well. At the very moment when we think we're going to make that great discovery, our man announces that it's time to eat, or there's work to do, or he has a headache, or he must wash his hands! A man will seize upon any pretext to be absent in the flesh. Men use their bodies as an alibi. They are never there when you want them. This physical absence, they think, is a clever way to disguise their perpetual absence from us. But we're not fooled by it any more than we are fooled by their love-making, which they sometimes resort to for the same reasons . . .

21. Explain Leah's "Men use their bodies as an alibi." Could she have as truthfully said "Women use their bodies as an alibi"? More truthfully? Less truthfully? Explain.

JOHN. I'd like to know what would happen to us if we didn't have some kind of protective armor against you!

LEAH. As for me, my body has never been anything but a voice calling to you. My breasts, my hair, my limbs have spoken the words of that language which, since Eden, may not be uttered by the lips. You acquired all your knowledge of nature and the universe that way, through me. But you! Your body is only an armor, an attitude, a silence. O, John! When, when will you really speak?

JOHN. Sh! Ruth and James must be wondering . . .

LEAH. Witnesses! The fear of what people will say! That's one more of your excuses for evading the issue. Whether it's Ruth and James or Peter and Mary, all married couples, if they're self-respecting, must fight behind closed doors. It's called "observing the proprieties" but it's really only another kind of cowardice. Why worry about Ruth and James? They're just like us and all the legions of married couples. Men have always, by the thousands, eluded women's questioning and no one has ever succeeded in unsealing men's lips, that is to say, violating their one and only virginity: the Word. Ruth, why did you move over towards John? Stay where you are, at my side. . . .

22. How can "the Word" be man's "one and only virginity"?

JOHN. All right! You asked for it, so here goes . . .

LEAH. Look over there, to your right.

JOHN. I know what you are, and I'm going to tell you . . .

LEAH. I told you to look to your right. You have a most distinguished witness. You have a fine new excuse to remain silent.

JOHN. You see! You've never understood! You've never had the least glimmering of understanding!

LEAH. What was there to understand?

JOHN. That I've been waiting for a proper judge to hear my case. When I objected to Ruth and James as witnesses, it was because I thought they'd be prejudiced. Ruth is devoted to me; James admires you. But if the Angel wants to hear us, let him approach. If the day has come for men and women to have it out at last . . .

RUTH. He's going away.

JOHN. Then I have nothing to say. Then I'll say what I'm in the habit of saying at such a time: I'm hungry. The roast duck appeals to me. Look, Leah: this is what you've never understood. Except in the presence of God, men never really speak.

23. How true is John's statement that "Except in the presence of God, men never really speak"? If it is untrue, is its epigrammatic quality good or bad? If it is true, is it a humorous or a tragic statement?

LEAH. Since men are made in His image, He, naturally, loves only men!

JOHN. Blasphemy is as good a way as any to bring back the Angel.

LEAH. You are like God and God is like you! He, too, knows how to dodge important issues! That the human beings He created are like gears that cannot mesh does not bother Him greatly. He, too, has His magic carpet—the Kingdom of Heaven. And He, too, has His alibi. Yours is your body and its needs; His, the wandering angels. The root of all evil is just this: God is a man.

JOHN. Call the Angel!

LEAH. The Angel hasn't any name.

RUTH (*calling*). Mael!

JOHN. Surely a woman should be able to invent names for angels.

RUTH. That's exactly what I'm trying to do. Alzoa! Gabriel! Michael! How strange!

From behind every bush and clump of trees and shrubbery, angels' heads are popping up!

LEAH. Yes. Apparently it's the open season. All God's gillies are at their posts!

JOHN. And there comes ours.

24. How many interpretations can you supply for Leah's declaration that "The root of all evil is just this: God is a man"?

25. The line "From behind every bush and clump of trees and shrubbery, angels' heads are popping up!" is well timed because it is needed at this point. Explain why.

(*The* ANGEL *approaches.*)

THE ANGEL. What do you want? What's wrong?

LEAH. We want you to settle an argument.

JOHN. We want you to judge men and women.

LEAH. Nothing of the sort! We want you to decide whether it's good or bad weather today in Sodom.

THE ANGEL. What is your opinion, Leah?

LEAH. The atmosphere is heavy and oppressive. My soul is weary unto death. During five long years I have struggled to possess this man. With all my force I've thrown myself upon him. I have been open and vulnerable. He has been encased in solid armor. So I had to be satisfied with merely living at his side. I tried to learn him by heart, I memorized his gestures and words and silences. But now I seem to have forgotten everything. He is facing me, I am quarreling with him . . . but in reality . . . he's ceased to exist for me.

THE ANGEL. You haven't answered my question.

JOHN. O Angel, I married this woman to have light and warmth and sparkle in my life. I was a lamp without a flame until our wedding day. The lamp was lighted. She was the flame. I was only the oil and the wick, but I was content, for I loved the light she gave me. Now, her light still flares—but not with or for me. I don't know what wind carried her away: perhaps her pride, perhaps her fill of me. I am still the lamp. But the lamp's flame is gone. It burns elsewhere according to unknown laws and moods. While I live in darkness.

LEAH. All this doesn't stop you from thinking that today's weather is magnificent.

THE ANGEL. Yes, let us settle that question. You, too, must answer, John. What sort of a day is it in Sodom?

JOHN. There's no room for argument. The sun is shining; the sky is cloudless.

LEAH. It's a horrible day!

JOHN. The swallows are flying high. The insects are flying at their highest.

LEAH. A storm is raging. The shutters are banging against the windows.

JOHN. The air is calm. The grain-fields stand motionless. Isn't that so, Ruth?

RUTH. Yes, John, and I am very happy.

LEAH. You're happy because you're absorbed in John. And John thinks the leaden sky is blue and the waving cornfields motionless because he, too, is happy. The horrible statue of a woman that has for some time lived at his side has become transformed and animated. It is a graceful body that moves and breathes. Ruth has become for him what I once was and no longer am: a language and a perfume.

JOHN. And you—I know what you've become for James. Isn't it true, James, that you see, as she does, a cloudy sky and swallows flying low, barely skimming the ground?

JAMES. No. I see motionless cornfields. I see a sky of clearest blue. But why pester Leah? She has the right to see Sodom in whatever light she chooses.

RUTH. Of course, James. Leah certainly has the right to be wrong.

26. Why does John see the day as it is (re-check the stage directions for this Act) while Leah sees it as the opposite? Does her unrealistic viewpoint nullify her belief that men escape reality? Why or why not?

JAMES. Oh! If Ruth says that Leah is wrong, then it's quite possible that Leah is right and that Ruth secretly agrees with her!

RUTH. What business is it of yours if I do?

JAMES. Let me contribute something to the squabble, O Angel. Here it is: I have never had anything from Ruth but fakery and falsehood. She has never spoken a word of truth either to me or to her dog. She doesn't take the trouble; it's easier to lie. She agrees with others, even when she knows they are wrong; she loves to live in the midst of other people's errors and mistakes. The real and the true have no use or meaning for Ruth.

RUTH. You're boring the Angel, James.

JAMES. In every house in Sodom and Gomorrah, I'll bet there's an angel witnessing a scene such as this between husbands and wives. I'll bet they came here just for that purpose.

RUTH. The Angel came to rub up against us. We are warm, living people, after all. What we say doesn't matter to him. The report he will make to Heaven will be made upon the basis of the amount of human warmth he will be able to take back.

JAMES. How typically Ruth! She manages to surround even an angel with ambiguity! What a little viper she is! What a little serpent!

JOHN. Don't drag in the serpent. It's just possible that the Angel may not like to hear such references. Anyway, it's a lovely day.

LEAH. It's a horrible day.

JOHN. Forgive her, Angel. She's out of her mind.

THE ANGEL. No. She is right.

JOHN. Even the Angel is joking and making fun of you . . .

THE ANGEL. I'm not joking. You are blind; whereas Leah can see. The atmosphere of Sodom is heavy, frightful. The children and the birds are still singing, but a horrible note has crept into their song, a note too low to be heard by human ears. It is the note of death. And the swallows are flying high, but it's not because the insects have risen in the tepid air, but because the earth today is a corpse and every winged creature is seeking to escape it. And the streams flow, bright and limpid, the spring gushes and sparkles, but I have tasted that water: it is the water of the Deluge. And the sun shines, but when I tested the warmth of the sunlight with my hand, I found it had the heat of boiling pitch. And God has allowed the earth to keep its fair garments and its wrappings, but never have they lain so thinly above the eruptions and the lava of damnation. And in the throat of the lark one may hear the unleashed thunders. And from the gashed pine tree flows not resin but tears for the end of the world. Leah is right.

27. Does the fact that the Angel agrees with Leah change your answer to Question 26 above? How?

JOHN. I'm leaving! Goodbye!

THE ANGEL. Why are you leaving?

JOHN. Because Leah is right. Because God is unjust. Because women are always in the right, always have the last word. Everything in them is ignorance, but they understand everything. They are a mass of vanities and trivialities, but they are simple before the problems of the heart. Everything in them is noise and distraction, but they contain within themselves the cage of silence where the last creaking and palpitation of the world may be heard. Everything in them is egotism and sensuality, yet they are the sextant of innocence, the compass of purity. Everything in them is fear, but they are courage itself. Their eyes are blinded by makeup and false lashes, but they can see what angels see.

JAMES. Yes. It isn't that Ruth saw blue sky. She simply lied about it.

RUTH. I didn't even bother to look! I just said what John said about it.

THE ANGEL. And I am to tell God for you that He is unjust?

JOHN. Yes. Tell Him that! O God, why were You so illogical and irresponsible? You created man. You went to a great deal of trouble to establish on earth the being best equipped to wage Your battles for You. He was the perfect inhabitant of the earth. You weighed and measured him with care so that he would not be found wanting in any of the roles You destined him to play. For each enigma which You set him to solve, there springs to his hand the necessary tool. There remained for You only to bestow upon him the qualities You have lavished upon some of Your other creatures: the faceted eye of the bee, the bratticed ear of the pigeon, the premonition of lurking danger which even the stupidest sheep possesses. But You refused to give him all this! Instead, You delegated Your force and intuitive powers to his weaker companion, endowing woman with these gifts. She is there, beside the man. And she bears upon her the real weapons of the man, as does the equerry beside the knight in battle. But the man cannot reclaim his armor. And so, behold the human couple: a man capable of everything, but without his weapons; a woman who has all the weapons but who, because of childishness and folly, wounds herself without profit and without glory.

28. John assumes that God favored women. Can you explain his ambiguous statements?

LEAH. Here: I will give you one of the weapons you covet: hatred.

THE ANGEL. I repeat: O God . . .

LEAH. And Ruth is preparing to hand you another: tenderness. But both weapons are a little too heavy for a man to carry.

RUTH. Leah, I assure you . . .

JAMES. Stop. You know your mind's full of John. But I'll say this for you: you've struggled against your desire and you continue to struggle. But, O Angel, Ruth's loyalty has become worse than treason. Whenever she has a stab of remorse, she treats me as if I were John. She makes me eat what he likes, she treats me as if I were as patient as he, whereas I am impatient; as if I were as energetic as he, whereas I am indolent. And at night she treats me as though I were fresh and new, whereas I feel like a centenarian. I can't stand it!

RUTH. You can't stand it because you're in love with Leah. And you behave the same with me. You've endowed me with Leah's form, locked me in it as in an armor. And when a part of my real self shows—if I cough, for example, when Leah would only have sneezed—you turn away in disgust.

THE ANGEL. I repeat: O God, behold the human couple; a man who is the husband of all other men's wives, a woman who is the wife of all men save her own.

29. How true is the Angel's definition of "the human couple"? *Why do you agree or disagree?*

LEAH. It took an angel to sum up the situation. It's up to us to find a way out. You, Angel, are the bailiff appointed to follow our bankruptcy to the very end. That's so, isn't it?

THE ANGEL. What are you getting at?

LEAH. At your solution to our problem. Would you like to have me as your wife, James?

JAMES. I admire you, Leah. But to live with you is a reward I don't deserve.

LEAH. Then you're lucky. The Angel will tell you that on earth we never have what we deserve. . . . And Ruth is lucky, too. For if there is anyone she does not deserve, it's John!

RUTH. Leah!

LEAH. John has a great soul. Ruth has none at all. John speaks elegantly, but simply. Ruth not only tells lies but she makes grammatical mistakes. . . . Be quiet,

RUTH. For once in our lives, miraculously, we are able to speak and act as we are doing now. I'm seizing the opportunity of telling you just what I think. You don't deserve John; therefore, you will have him.

JOHN. So you want action now, do you? You're getting ready to do something, aren't you?

LEAH. Yes. I have an intuition—and that is one of the weapons you will never own—that action of some sort is inevitable. Listen, and maybe you will also understand the presence of the Angel. The world, to the Celestial Powers, is a kaleidoscope. You and I, James and Ruth, are four of the many bits of colored glass inside that kaleidoscope. The Heavenly Hosts are tired of the present arrangement of our colors; they want to reassort us. So they are shaking the kaleidoscope. The Angel is here to consecrate that reassortment, to give it a Heavenly meaning, to make of it a holy experiment and to appear as the Will of God! Isn't that so, Angel?

THE ANGEL. No.

30. Explain the failure of Leah's vaunted intuition. Why did it fail her?

LEAH. Too bad. Then the experiment will be purely human. My decision has been made, John. I am leaving you for James. Are you ready, James?

JAMES. I love you, Leah. I will do whatever you wish.

LEAH. Whatever I wish! A nice master I've given myself once more!

JOHN. Go away, James. Go away, Ruth. Leave me alone with Leah.

LEAH. I haven't time to talk, John. I'm as much in a hurry as I used to be at school when the bell rang. Nothing could keep me in the school yard. The bell has rung, John!

THE ANGEL. Stay, Leah.

LEAH. But I'm late. I shall be punished!

THE ANGEL. You're not sure of yourself? You're running away? God demands a real divorce, Leah, with the case heard to the very end.

LEAH. Very well. He shall have it. (*Exeunt the* ANGEL, RUTH, *and* JAMES.)

LEAH. Farewell, John.

JOHN. You're leaving me? Really?

LEAH. I'm not leaving you, I'm being borne off. Earth, air, and water have conspired to drag me from your side . . .

JOHN. And you do love James?

LEAH. I am going to love him, yes.

JOHN (*with heavy irony*). You will doubtless fly to him on the line of flame and lightning traced 'midst the stars, the rainbows, and the sparkling dews!!

LEAH. No. I shall go afoot, quite simply.

JOHN. You shall not go!

LEAH. If I died still loving you, you would let me go. Despair would fill your heart; then, comforted, you would marry Ruth.

JOHN. You're leaving me because I'm in love with Ruth?

LEAH. Don't be naive. Don't resort at such a moment to the worst kind of masculine stupidity.

JOHN. Then it's because of consideration for me?

LEAH. I'm incapable of such hypocrisy. Don't worry. I'm not sacrificing myself in leaving you, and I don't expect you to sacrifice yourself by preventing me from leaving you.

JOHN. Are you insane, Leah?

LEAH. Unusually sane! As all women are at crucial moments. I haven't the luck to be like men or horses. With a bandage over their eyes they will go round and round in a meaningless circle forever.

JOHN. You're not only insane, you're cruel! And you're ugly! Ugly, beneath that splendid face of yours!

LEAH. You can't tell me anything about that. I have a looking-glass.

JOHN. You're not going away with James!

LEAH. You mean, with James in particular?

JOHN. Oh, to Hell with James. You might as well take him as any other.

LEAH. Then why should I stay?

JOHN. Because I command it.

LEAH. Oh, if you were really to command it, that would be wonderful. I would stay, I would obey you. But you do not command it.

JOHN. I do command you!

LEAH. You shout, you wave your arms, but you do not command. You have no power over me. You command for the sake of appearances, because of what people will say. And I'm finished with all that. The others don't count now.

31. Explain Leah's assertion that she would stay if John *could* "command." What, exactly, is a "command" as Leah employs the word?

JOHN. What others? Who has the right to hold you? Who and what, except this house and what it means to you?

LEAH. That's exactly what I mean. You're delegating to the house, now, the job of holding me. You're no longer strong enough. How like a man! So it's up to these things to hold me now: your house, your possessions, your memories. . . . You don't try to find what is left of our love in ourselves, but in the things which have served us. Stay, you say, on account of our garden. Stay, on account of the roast duck. And on account of that bed where, without us, every night our ghosts will embrace.

JOHN. No. You are being unjust.

LEAH. You are less affected by me now than by the things we own. My dress means more to you than my body beneath it. If my empty dress could stay, could walk about empty, could nestle against you, why, you could bear my absence. You could bear it, having my empty dress at your side, and with Ruth beside you, naked . . .

JOHN. You shall not go!

LEAH. But I am going. And without possessions or souvenirs. Once upon a time there was a poor little snake who collected all his skins. The snake was a man. The man was you. For you have kept every skin you've ever shed. Your present is but the past remembered. I, at least, have never shown you any skin but that of your wife, you have touched it only, caressed it only. It came to life beneath your hand. Below it surged my blood and all creation. I have suffered, John. It's horrible to live with someone who hides his heart beneath every object in his house.

32. Is Leah's accusation that "Your present is but the past remembered" true or false? Is it a comic or tragic statement?

JOHN. If you go, I leave the house, and everything in it shall be destroyed.

LEAH. You will leave it and you will destroy it because you love it. Oh, pitiful and stupid sacrifice! As for me, I leave this house because it is no longer mine. So, destroy the entire world as well, for it belongs to you. The world is the house in which you live. You have hidden our wedding ring in all the beauties of the world—like a magpie hiding things in its nest. This ring is not really here on my hand and hasn't been for some time. You've hidden it in the forests, in the early morning light, in the calling of that nightbird we heard that first night together. . . . Well, I swear it, I am leaving you with fresh eyes, ears open to new sounds. And in the arms of the man I am going to love, at my bedroom window, I shall hear the nightbird call as if for the first time.

JOHN. What shall I do? What will you do? We've given each other everything! How little we shall have left to give anyone now, and how terribly little shall we have left for ourselves!

LEAH. You have given me nothing but yourself—and how much of yourself you kept back! Even when your love was like a strong wind blowing, you protected your life from that wind by sealing it down with the weight of your work. Well, now, I have my revenge. You will retain forever the marks I made upon your life. You will not be able to rid yourself of them when you are living with Ruth. Whereas I, who gave myself utterly to you, shall be fresh and virginal for the man I shall choose.

33. Can a man protect his life from the wind of love by sealing it down with work? Defend your answer.

JOHN. Forget Ruth. I shall not marry Ruth.

LEAH. You're wrong not to. I like Ruth. There never has been a more literal translation of lying, a more slavish translation of independence, or a more terrifying translation of callousness. But I think she might be the right woman for you. She has always been near and close to us. She is almost an item of our common property, and as such is the one to console you. And also, she has no false hopes and illusions. She knows that a man never loves but once. That is the barrier, the lock and key to all men's hearts: the number one.

JOHN. Tell me the truth, Leah. Are you leaving just to be rid of me? Are you simply running away? Or is it because you're in love with James?

LEAH. My poor darling, I'm not running away from you. It's just that I no longer seem to know you. I can't see you any more. The universe has not narrowed for me; but. . . . How can I explain? It's as though a piece of it has been cut away, and the opening has your form, size, and shape. There's an emptiness where you were; an opening upon the light and upon the horizon. Standing here before you I do not see you at all. I merely see a window which has your shape, a window opening upon—nothingness.

JOHN. But James—is he real to you?

LEAH. How am I to fill that emptiness? I need a man to fill it. Too much wind comes through it, and ghosts, and the sound of crying. So, I must push James in front of it. And the vacancy is filled. He has just the right dimensions.

34. According to Giraudoux, with what does a woman seal out the wind of love? Agree or disagree.

JOHN. Give me your hand, Leah. Like all women on the day of divorce and separation, you are endowed with the word of God. Give me your hand.

LEAH. No. My body is at war with you.

JOHN. Yet only an hour or so ago, you belonged to me completely: from the nape of your neck to your little toes, you were mine. All mine.

LEAH. If you so much as touch me with the tips of your fingers, I'll scream!

JOHN. Oh, my darling Leah, if we had chosen each other of our own free will, then we would have the right to separate. But we did not. God planned it. Why be unduly modest? We were destined for each other. Have you ever known another man and woman with so much in common? We were patterned on the first couple, in every detail. You and I are products of the same artist's palette and brush. Weighed in the balance as human beings, you and I weigh exactly the same, to the ounce. I always had this voluptuous certainty of our identity and mutual understanding, and I offered up to it the burnt offerings of bad temper, bitterness, neglect, even. You see, Leah, I was so sure of you! Believe me, the first passionate needs and fires of love are doomed eventually to abate, to die down. But it is by such a couple as we were and are that God judges mankind, His handiwork, and finds it good.

LEAH. And so the fires have abated! We are no longer in love?

JOHN. You say so. But whether it is because you have become a thousand times more demanding, or whether you have indeed ceased to love me, I am the last one who could tell.

LEAH. Oh, my dear John. You see? We've always fallen far short of being the ideal couple, and I've forced you to admit it at last. We see things differently. For you, life is a parade in which men and women go by, two by two, hand in hand, holding their heads high. Maybe their proud and happy attitude conceals a lot. Maybe their smile is tight-lipped. That doesn't matter. The main thing is to fool God as to what His creatures are really like. Humanity is vile, behaves abominably, and we know it. But let a handsome couple appear on parade, a man and wife whose feet, mouths, and shoulders look well together, you and society rejoice and pay them tribute. Maybe that handsome couple loathe each other, maybe they remain together purely out of self-sacrifice. No matter. We owe them tribute. They mask humanity for the Creator. So, cursed be anyone who denies them respect! The frustrated wife is supposed to accept gratefully from the hands of the surfeited husband this role of Lady Benefactress to Society. That's the role you want me to play. Well, I refuse!

JOHN. I offer you a life of dignity.

LEAH. O Lord, there You have an example of the supreme vice of men! Like robots they go on making the gestures which You gave Adam when You first wound him up. Life has dignity when life is life! Love has dignity—not when it manufactures two human beings in the semblance of a model couple, but when it grinds them, as in a mortar, exceeding fine and from that dust molds a body which is one flesh. As long as I loved you, I was as if melted and absorbed into you, lost in you. But there came a day, a terrible day—I was doing my nails, it was in the morning—when suddenly I saw my hand as mine. It was no longer a part of you. . . . That was a frightful rebirth. Rebirth of myself as an individual. Then I realized that everything was over between us. And though we may be as graceful as the birch tree or as handsome as the oak, we are failures. We, as a couple, are deformed, and the shadow our marriage casts is monstrous.

JOHN (*taking her into his arms*). Leah.

LEAH. Let me alone. Don't touch me. Your gesture is purely conventional and automatic. Men always behave like this at a time like this. A woman wants to go away quite simply without any fuss and with very little baggage. And she has to contend with a man and all his rigmarole of conventions.

JOHN. I'm not just a man. I am John—you forget that.

LEAH. You have suddenly become to me just "a man." Don't touch me. We have already played this scene twenty times, without words. Everything that has happened to us today has happened before, but in silence. And I always gave in at last when you spoke that final word, "Leah!" I gave in, without honor or joy. And at night, afterwards, I suffered shame and remorse. Today, maybe we were right to speak out, maybe we were wrong. It doesn't matter. Everything is over between us.

JOHN. Kiss me!

LEAH. I tell you to let me alone! We can do without all this ritual-of-separation. You don't even really want me to kiss you. You just want to get the better of me. You want to bring to life in me something you think is numbed. I am not benumbed. I am simply another person. To kiss me now would get you nowhere.

JOHN. I want to kiss that other person.

LEAH. That other person doesn't belong to you. She's perhaps the only woman in the world who can never belong to you.

JOHN. Leah!

LEAH. You are a husband one no longer loves. You must now take your turn in line, behind all the other men in the world!

JOHN. Kiss me.

LEAH. Let me go, or I'll call Ruth.

JOHN. Call Ruth! But you shall kiss me!

LEAH. James! James!

(RUTH *enters. The* ANGEL *also enters, but remains in the background.*)

RUTH. Did you call James?

JOHN. Yes. But it's you *I* want. Let's go. (*Exeunt* JOHN *and* RUTH.)

35. Does John love Leah?
36. Has Leah ever loved John?
37. Does John *want* Ruth? If so, why? If not, why does he say he does?

LEAH. I love you . . .

THE ANGEL. How you talk! Others lose their voice. But you, apparently, have lost the ability to be silent!

LEAH. You have heard my words. That's something.

THE ANGEL. I heard. Worse still, I understood. The day bodes no good, Leah!

LEAH. The day when a woman speaks her mind?

THE ANGEL. The day when she bares her soul. The soul's nakedness is far worse than the body's nakedness.

LEAH. I needed that kind of nakedness today. The other is forbidden.

THE ANGEL. Once before this I heard a woman pour out such a torrent of words. Next day there was the Deluge.

LEAH. It took that much water to drown a voice so weak?

THE ANGEL. The voice was not drowned. Beneath the rushing Flood the voice could still be heard, arguing. God could hear nothing but that voice.

38. If, as the Angel asserts, "the soul's nakedness is far worse than the body's nakedness," why is baring the body forbidden but baring the soul allowed?

39. The woman who spoke as Leah does was drowned in the Deluge (the flood survived by Noah), but her voice was not drowned. Can you explain the Angel's symbolic meaning? Remember this passage, because it foreshadows the closing lines of the play.

LEAH. I have only three more words to say now in this world, "I love you."

THE ANGEL. Are you really going to leave John for James?

LEAH. Yes. I'm changing partners. God, I am aware, condones the divorce of sterile couples. Well, John's and my marriage was sterile. Nothing was born of it but a mortal weariness.

THE ANGEL. And what will now be born? Disgust?

LEAH. A long voyage. That voyage of exploration round the great peninsulas of tenderness—a voyage which can only be taken with a new lover.

THE ANGEL. But you don't love James.

LEAH. He loves me, though. I have his love. In other words, I have the vessel for the voyage.

THE ANGEL. Now, speak the truth! What is this suicide you're contemplating? Admit it: you are imagining at this moment the Cape of Sweetness which you once rounded with John, that night of your betrothal.

LEAH. No. Certainly not. Nor can I imagine it with James, while your eyes are upon me. But stop preaching! All I want to know is this: am I the first woman in the world you've ever laid your eyes upon?

40. In your own paraphrase, explain Leah's metaphor of the "voyage."
41. Why does the Angel call such a voyage "suicide"? Is he speaking of suicide of the body or suicide of the soul?

THE ANGEL. So, you renounce all this! All these leafy trees, these flowering fields, the animals of the fields and forests, nervous and fleet, all things which were given to man to divert him from his sins and solitude, all these voices of sparkling streams, these brightly colored birds, these trades and crafts and wagons on the roads, the things which have kept mankind from listening to his thoughts too much—you renounce them, you disdain them! What is your occupation? You are preoccupied with your own self, merely. What is life? You are concerned with your own life, solely. And all those names of innocence, diamond-pure names, with which humanity has cloaked itself, those names of flesh and blood, such as Leah, Naomi, Ruth, John, James—you renounce them! Is your name decay and rottenness?

LEAH. My name is Woman. My name is Love. (*She approaches him.*)

THE ANGEL. Stop! No human being has ever yet touched an angel.

LEAH. Nor has a human being ever yet touched another human being. I know that. But there is a lot more to be said on the subject.

42. Why has no human being ever yet touched an angel?
43. Is Leah correct in saying that no human has ever yet touched another human?

THE ANGEL. You, doubtless, could find much to say on any subject.

LEAH. Yes. On human stupidity and misery. I accept them. On glory and politeness, on food and wine, on death, on all the things that imprison mankind as if in a stifling room. It's never been worth my while to talk about them. I have always expressed but one thing, whether in my silence or in my wildest talk—as you grasped at my first word—and that is my longing to have for mate and companion some creature other than a man.

THE ANGEL. For instance, an angel?

LEAH. Yes, why not an angel? A darling, wingless, walking angel like you, that I could watch coming towards me from the distant horizon, circumventing the cornfields and the strawberry beds. Even an angel who would fall from on high before me, with half-bent knees. I would stretch all my carpets to catch him. You have no wings. But I would not be frightened by wings. I would fold them up and pleat them smoothly for the night.

THE ANGEL. Cease this wild talk! Stop mingling in an unholy mess things Heavenly and terrestrial!

LEAH. Aren't you doing just that by coming here? And Heaven and its inhabitants are mistaken. The celestial glaze which separates Heaven from earth is not completely impenetrable. Communication of a sort is possible. But the inhabitants of earth are most terribly separated from each other. Can't you realize that I could have been satisfied to possess just one man alone? To reach him, touch him—that was all I asked. I tried. But the invisible partition which separated me from John is still intact. As will be that of James. All I ever had of the one man was his name; and it is all I shall ever have of the next. Without their names they would be only phantoms. You have no name; yet all my body calls to you, calling you a name it knows. Don't hold it against me that I aspire to Heaven and that my body longs for celestial things.

THE ANGEL. For the last time I ask you: Have you finally chosen between those two men?

LEAH. I have chosen. But not between those two.

THE ANGEL. Whom have you chosen?

LEAH. You.

THE ANGEL. How typically feminine! I assume the voice of a man to speak to her, and already she sets traps for me as if I were a man. Next thing, she will be telling me that she has never known what love is!

LEAH. Nor have I, ever. I have only glimpsed and faintly heard from time to time things not of this earth. I have never loved, except occasionally, and the object of my love was always a glimmering phantom that resembled you.

THE ANGEL. Foolish creature! And now, she will certainly ask me, as women do, if she is pleasing to my eyes!

LEAH. I know that you find me attractive. And for the first time in my life I am truly glad to please!

THE ANGEL. How she glows with passionate animation! And she is sincere, she means it. And she has never been more beautiful! And she knows that she is offending Heaven, but the wheels of feminine machinations are turning now too rapidly to be stopped!

44. When the Angel anticipates Leah's avowals of love, does he speak to her or to the audience? If to the audience, why? Does he attempt to force audience participation? Or is his function Choric—that is, does he allow the audience to participate? If his words are addressed to Leah, why does he use the third person rather than the second? Can his words be understood to work at both levels simultaneously? If so, does Leah, then, assume a Choric function? Examine the exchange carefully before deciding. Defend your answer by arguing your case with a classmate who holds a divergent view.

LEAH. Why should you be offended? Why is Heaven trying to get the better of me today? What I want of my life with you, my only wish, is exactly this: a life that will make no demands. Oh, the demands I made upon John, and oh, the demands I shall make upon James! Just to give the bare semblance of union to our marriage, how often I pressed John's hands, laid my cheek against his, allowed myself in vain to be transported! What joy if I could think all that was over forever! I need not touch you; with you I do not need to have hands or breasts or lips. I have no need of them, for I am no longer crouching in the shadows calling for help. Now I stand in a brightness and all things are made clear. What I demand of you is nothing but to go on standing in your light . . .

THE ANGEL. Infamous! Infamous! It is not your love that shocks me, it is your deceit. You are looking for a victim.

45. Explain the Angel's charge, "You are looking for a victim."

LEAH. Won't you take me? Won't you let me be your companion? Oh, if you would, then there would be at last, here on earth, a veritable marriage!

THE ANGEL. Not another word! This is what you must do. You see the town of Segor over there? In it are some just and honest people . . .

LEAH. I'll be good! I won't talk to you. I won't approach you. I won't even watch you . . .

THE ANGEL. Silence! Listen to me!

LEAH. Will you have me or not?

THE ANGEL. I am here to save you. And you lay down conditions!

LEAH. There is only one way to save me. O Angel, I know in advance what my life with James will be! Every minute will be a profanation. His name instead of John's will stamp every hour and every action of the day. . . . The new name, and the echo of the old one . . . You are wrong if you think it is with a happy heart and a light foot that I go! Save me! You who are without a name, give me a world without baptism, a heart empty of all memories, a dawn which is a veritable beginning. O you who are without desire, give me the supreme happiness, which is to be without desire . . .

THE ANGEL. Listen to me. I command it. You will leave at once for Segor and safety.

LEAH. With you?

THE ANGEL. You are seeing me for the last time. You will leave alone!

LEAH. Then I'll stay here, and I'll stay with James.

THE ANGEL. O God, You were right! Fire and brimstone are the only possible remedies! Behold me, held in ransom for James now!

LEAH. At last you understand. It took you a long time. But I suppose it's quite natural for an angel to be naive.

46. Why does the Angel attempt to save Leah by sending her to Segor? Is he not violating God's commandment? Why?

47. Is it "quite natural for an angel to be naive"? Why?

THE ANGEL. James is weakness itself, uncertainty, ignorance. His lovemaking is brusk and brutal. I conjure you: Wait a little, at least. Another will come to replace him.

LEAH. Heaven still does not understand what women are if it thinks they can resign themselves to half-measures. I will have James—or you.

THE ANGEL. A choice between Heaven and Hell.

LEAH. Heaven forced me to it. I, personally, chose Heaven.

THE ANGEL. Your name is falsehood, Leah.

LEAH. And Heaven's name is obstinacy. And through that obstinacy I lose you. Will you not understand? Will you, like God, turn a deaf ear? The love I offer and the voice with which I make that offer are not mine, but those of the First Woman! Don't summon man between her and you! Hear me, Angel! Angel! Hear my prayer!

THE ANGEL. Go! Get out!

(JAMES *approaches*.)

JAMES. Did you call me, Leah?

LEAH. Yes. Loudly. Come . . . (*Exeunt* LEAH *and* JAMES.)

(*Enter the* GARDENER.)

THE ANGEL. Are you the Gardener?

THE GARDENER. By God's grace, yes.

THE ANGEL. By God's grace. Thank you. Now, hearken. We shall see if you are a good God's gardener. . . . It is ordained that before tomorrow dawns these cypress trees shall grow to giant height, reaching the sky; these jasmins shall turn into moss and lichens; these hedges shall become petrified forests. It is God's will that your carnations shall smell of death, your cedars howl with the wind, and all your roses become black as night. . . . What's wrong, good Gardener? You would perhaps like to save one from destruction?

THE GARDENER. In God's name, yes. Only one . . .

THE ANGEL. Very well. Keep one red rose. (*The* ANGEL *vanishes*.)

48. Why does the Gardener desire to keep one perfect plant? This is not a simple question!

49. Why does the Angel permit him to keep one red rose? This is less simple! Be specific!

(During the scene the light dims progressively.)

THE GARDENER. Now what am I going to do with this rose? What made me beg of the Angel to let one rose survive the death of the garden? The last rose of the world cannot be put in a vase or pressed and put in an herbarium. Nor worn in a buttonhole. The last rose is not just an ornament or a decoration. Nor is it a symbol of fragility, for it will live as long as we live, this rose. It is the first of my flowers that I shall not live to see withered. The wrath of God has changed my rose into an *immortelle*. Well, that's something! Once again the life of the rose is the symbol of human life. Which is flattering to humanity. I shall have to spade with one hand now, shall have to rake with one hand. By God's will and providence, everything I can say today, everything that I can possibly think or do or offer must be thought, done, offered, with this flower in my hand. On this sinister day of judgment, God has turned me into a kind of flowering bush, a walking rosebush. It is a privilege. I am as awkward and stupid as ever; but I am flowering, and with a flower that sheds perfume. I am fortunate to be chosen at a time when most men are burning bushes of sin and crime. I am grateful that the Angel made me a rosebush rather than a tulip or a zinnia or a wisteria. I would feel less comfortable and far more ridiculous were I condemned to walk about the entire last evening of the world with a zinnia in my hand. What would be the lesson in that case, and what would be the symbol? I'm sure I don't know what it means for an actor, and the most unimportant of actors, to walk about carrying a rose in the midst of these horrors and cataclysms, but it wasn't my idea. It was an idea that came from God, it was the crowning gift of God. Whether I carry the hope of God or God's malediction, He alone knows. It is for me to bear it. And see how easy it is! After a minute you acquire the habit, and you see that it is not in the nature of man to kill lambs or to break stones, but rather, to walk about with a rose in his hand. Look, it stays there even when I open my fingers! I stuck one of the thorns into my finger; it stays there, the drop of blood is the color of the rose. That must be why the Angel wanted it to be a red rose, not white or yellow. Ah! I think I understand my mission now. It is quite clear. It is like a promise: in the midst of this chaos when the blood of men will flow from wounds, will flow and clot and will fill the gutters—I am chosen to be the man from whom the blood gushes, flowering and perfumed . . . *(Exit* GARDENER.*)*

50. Symbolically, the Gardener expresses a profound truth when he says "It is the first of my flowers that I shall not live to see withered." If "the *life* of the rose is the symbol of human life," what victory has the Gardener won? Can "God's gardener" win such a victory? Is victory "the crowning gift of God"?

51. Does the Gardener arrive at an answer or an acceptable conclusion? Differentiate.

52. As the Gardener discusses the privilege of being a rosebush rather than a tulip or a zinnia or a wisteria, he is amazingly like the porter in *Macbeth*. Compare the structural functions of the two speeches. Are they similar or dissimilar?

ACT TWO

The terrace of JOHN'S and LEAH'S villa above the plain; but, though the setting is the same as in Act One, it no longer expresses security and happiness. The light is grey and threatening. Thin smoke rises from the Cities of the Plain in the distance. The house-front, right, shows neglect. The awning sags; the bird cage on the wall is open and the bird has flown; the big white jar that held the bouquet of angels' feathers has fallen on its side and the feathers are scattered. RUTH and JOHN enter from the left and lean over the balustrade. RUTH'S attitude shows fear and terror, JOHN'S, detachment.

1. Compare the set directions of Act Two with those of Act One. If you were staging this play, what would you do to create "security and happiness" and how would you indicate their absence? Lest you assume that "the bird" expresses such security and happiness, remember: he is *caged* in Act One; he is free in Act Two. The subtleties of stage directions are apparent here. You are given only basic features by the playwright. Explain the additions you make.

JOHN. Lovely, isn't it, this spectacle of the world coming to an end!

RUTH. For me, it is the end of the day spent with you. And it's horrible!

JOHN. How curious! Something strange about the air today. In spite of the distance, you can see people running down there and hear their cries. What panic! Come nearer. Come and see human beings at their most harmonious—in fear—at their most exalted—in full flight . . .

RUTH. No, no! I, too, am afraid!

2. Is John's opening comment serious, ironic, or satirical?

3. Are people "at their most harmonious" when they are bound by fear? Cite examples from your experience to prove your contention.

JOHN. The end of the world. At least, that's what it's called. I would say, rather, that God frees the world today of its hypocrisies. This frenzy, this rumbling and roaring, these conflagrations—what are they but the world's naked truths? And those stars breaking loose from their constellations and furrowing the sky in their flight like runaway horses—what are they but Heaven's naked truths? The end of the world is the moment when the world shows itself in its real light: explosive, submersible, combustible. In the same way, war is the moment when human nature reverts to its origins. We live in the midst of fire that burns, water that drowns, gas that suffocates. We live in the midst of hate and stupidity. Ruth, you're the one that brought me here. You have got your way, so take advantage of it . . .

4. Do you agree or disagree that "war is the moment when human nature reverts to its origins"? Defend your answer.

RUTH. I brought you here to save us and to save myself . . . and to bring Leah back to you.

JOHN. Leah will not come. You'll have plenty of time to see the show. Come! Come nearer!

RUTH. She will come. Knowing James as I do, I can be sure of it. Leah will come.

JOHN. To die at the end of the world and with the person one loves. That's quite a privilege, isn't it?

RUTH. Save me!

JOHN. How? By forsaking you?

RUTH. No, John darling. But by not forsaking Leah. By returning to her. Oh, my dearest . . .

JOHN. All the tender words that women use to hold a lover, you are using to drive me away.

RUTH. I'm only a living creature, John. I'm just one of those ordinary creatures who need perfection in such simple things as air and water. I need pure air to breathe, pure water to drink. Rather than die, I would do anything. I'm ready to disown you, lose you. Why do you force me to confess my cowardice? I love you more than anything in life; but ever since I heard that voice in the night declaring that only a perfect human couple, a happy man and wife could save us from destruction, I have felt that God was still thinking of you and Leah. Since that voice crying in the darkness I have done everything to force you of your own accord to leave me. I counted upon this dawn and this awakening. I thought when you found me at your side, instead of Leah, that you would reckon up your losses with disgust. I turned my face to the wall. I thought perhaps God would mistake me for Leah. I pretended to be asleep. I had left the door half open. Oh, why didn't you run away? You stayed. But not because you preferred me. Admit it: you stayed because you preferred death!

5. Why does Ruth insist that she loves John even as she tries to force his return to Leah? Whom does she love?

JOHN. No. I stayed for a very simple reason. Leah guessed it. That's why she hasn't come and won't come. The fact is, I woke up this morning entirely happy to find myself there at your side.

RUTH. Don't say that. The Heavens are listening. You'll bring us all to destruction. You don't love me. You despise me.

JOHN. You needn't shout so loud. You'll not fool the Angel, if he's listening, for he knows that I liked to be there beside you.

RUTH. You called out Leah's name in your sleep.

JOHN. That's not true. I didn't have a dream. I didn't need to dream. Come here, Ruth. Stand near me, my sweet. . . . Heaven has evidently ordained that at this world-shaking moment we should stand here, reciting the "Song of Songs" of the counterfeit married couple.

RUTH. I won't listen to you. It's sheer pride that's making you say such things.

JOHN. The "Song of Songs" of the false wife, the untruthful wife. That's the idea. Put your arms around me. I will chant it. . . .

RUTH. Hush! You're bringing destruction upon all of us.

JOHN. Your soul is false: so false that the very word "falseness" sits lightly, like a caress upon you, becoming praise. Ah, that makes you smile! Everything about you is suspect. But with me you have been frankness incarnate. I was the first to enjoy your candor. You have surrendered to me a virginity which ceaselessly renews itself. You fed your husband upon lies and infantilism. But everything you have given me has been branded with truth. I have heard your true adventures, shared your memories. Even the most trivial! That story you told me about the lame nightingale and the crutch you made for it with a tooth of your tortoise-shell comb—well, I believe it.

RUTH. It wasn't a nightingale—it was a sparrow. And my comb wasn't genuine tortoise shell; it was imitation.

JOHN. James knew nothing of you but lies, lies, lies. You pretended to enjoy everything you loathed, everything that revolted you. Your real joys you buried in silence. With me you have been sincere. When you were sleepy you yawned. And in your dreams you talked, you called my name.

RUTH. What are you getting at?

JOHN. I'll tell you. I left a woman whom, for five years as my wife, I adored and esteemed and regarded with delight because her loyalty to me seemed Divine, incredible. But at your side, my beloved of one short day, I at last found reality in all its peacefulness. There you have my balance sheet; that satisfies me.

RUTH. Why do you say such things? Why do you pretend you've not always known that the maximum of truth and tenderness and virtue can only be revealed to you by women who are insincere, egotistic, and undisciplined? You've always known, as all men know, that the best way to appreciate what silence and submission can be is to live for a week or a day with a talkative and stubborn woman.

JOHN. You have given me all the things that you withheld from your husband. For this, I thank you . . .

RUTH. What have I to give? By comparison with you and Leah, James and I are very small indeed. That's why you two have made a very bad bargain. Leah is frank and generous; she could never conceal her real feelings, her contempt, from James.

Just as you, who are naturally strong and gentle, have had to be weak and brutal in your dealings with me. Anyway, it's all over. I can't stand it any longer. Call Leah: save us, John. The city will be spared only through you and Leah! All the prophets have said so. All the echoes have repeated it. Oh! Don't you believe them?

JOHN. I wish I could believe them. I know that God takes pleasure in tying up the destiny of the world and the destiny of each human being with small things, conditions, passwords, details. He forces us to employ, like token coins or counters, words and acts which seem irrelevant. Up to now I have always obeyed these sham orders. When I go downstairs, I always start off on the left foot; I don't walk on the cracks of the sidewalks; I break apples in two instead of cutting them, and so on. It is just possible, as you say, that our life today hangs in the balance because of some such formality. Perhaps Leah and I have only to take each other by the hand and call out, "Present!" and all the world would right itself again. But I cannot. I don't feel as though I were present in this world which is coming to an end. I feel more like shouting, "Absent!" with all my heart. And apparently Leah feels the same. For, as you see, she is still absent. I came up here to please God and to please Ruth, because men are always dutiful just as women are always right! Yes, Leah is right not to come. By staying away she is avoiding making a scene and a scandal. Since our quarrel—which she started yesterday—it would be impossible for us to meet as we formerly did. Our meeting would be more like a confrontation.

RUTH. She will come. . . . Listen! She is coming. . . . Call out to her!

JOHN. No part of me calls out to her, except my voice.

RUTH. That is enough. Call her! Shout!

6. Were you reminded of Ruth's avowal to Naomi in *The Book of Ruth* ("Whither thou goest I will go") as you read this section? If so, why? However, the Ruth of this play is not Ruth the Moabitess—or is she?

7. Does John accuse God of forcing man to live with superstition? Or does he accuse man of being superstitious as a formality that encompasses God?

(*Sound of voices, offstage. Enter some* YOUNG GIRLS, *talking excitedly. The* GARDENER *follows, but remains at left, a silent spectator.*)

YOUNG GIRLS. They've come! They're here! We are saved!

A GIRL. Behold the only happy couple, the only truly happy married couple!

RUTH. What couple?

A GIRL. Samson and Delilah! Some messengers have seen them nearby. They heard the prophecy. And of their own accord, they have come!

A SECOND GIRL. Martha is bringing them. We will all escort them to Sodom in triumph!

JUDITH. They've come just in time. The earth down there is boiling hot. It's impossible now for anyone to run away. People are managing somehow. They stand on tripods, they have placed boardwalks everywhere as if for a heavy rain. But the boardwalks are now burning.

RUTH. How did you manage to get here?

JUDITH. Three or four of us don't seem to mind the heat very much. So we volunteered to act as messengers.

(SALOME *appears.*)

SALOME. O John, it's horrible! All the animals have collapsed and are now burning. Only one animal is still alive, a horse. That horse apparently has hooves insensible to heat. And he gallops, gallops in the town.

8. Explain the irony of Salome's discussing the galloping horse with John. (Recall *The Book of Revelations.*)

(DELILAH *and* LEAH *appear from the door of the villa, right, and advance a short way upon the terrace, remaining apart from the others. They stand there, as if upon a stage within a stage.*)

SALOME. They're here! Behold Delilah!

ATHALIA. Thanks be to Heaven!

JUDITH. What luck! She's talking with Leah. Listen. She's going to tell us her secret of how to make a successful marriage!

(*The* GARDENER *throws his rose to* DELILAH, *who pins it to the bosom of her dress.*)

9. What is the irony of Judith's wishing to hear "the secret of how to make a successful marriage"? (Recall the story of Judith and Holofernes here.)

10. Why does the Gardener relinquish his rose? In the structure of the play, his act represents what?

JOHN. Give me your hand again, Ruth. Your perfect couple has been found.

RUTH. Horrible! But listen . . .

(RUTH, JOHN, *and the* GARDENER *remain standing aside, left, as spectators.*)

DELILAH. As for me, I chose the strongest man. I chose Samson.

LEAH. Your names go well together.

DELILAH. A man is strength, first and foremost. Like all women, I was born timid. At the sight of the least little insect or animal, I have a fit. I could not feel safe against mice and mosquitoes except with a husband who could strangle a lion with his two hands if necessary. And all you women are exactly like that. You're afraid of a little brook unless you know your husband can dam a river; you're afraid of a trembling leaf unless you know he could uproot an oak tree. Samson does such things so easily! I'm no longer frightened at the squalling of infants, for Samson has already killed about two thousand adults. John, I believe, hasn't killed anyone yet?

LEAH. As yet, no one.

11. How "human" is Delilah when she says "John, I believe, hasn't killed anyone yet?"

DELILAH. They say he's very intelligent and learned. Is he learned in magic? Does he know how to read signs and portents?

LEAH. Yes, and he even invents some of his own.

DELILAH. As for me, I chose the stupidest man for a husband. An intelligent husband is always sitting in judgment, always comparing you with other women and especially with all the other women you yourself have ever been. He is like a spy, investigating your past and standing guard over your future. Such a man makes any woman feel guilty—guilty even of being alive! But when Samson looks at me, I feel as if I were made of solid platinum. What does John do?

LEAH. Do? Oh, nothing. He has plenty of time just to attend to me.

DELILAH. Well, as for me, I intentionally picked a very busy man. I didn't want a man who'd always be underfoot. I wanted plenty of time to attend to myself. A husband who occupies himself with you simply distracts you from the important business of your own life. I think a woman needs to attend to herself, to get acquainted with herself. Just see what happens when a woman goes one hour without inspecting herself in a looking-glass! She loses track of things. Samson's away from home a lot. He's always being called upon to do something—wherever there's vengeance being wreaked or a massacre going on or a temple collapsing or lions that need exterminating. He has a lot to do, and his work never keeps him at home. So, while he's away, Delilah takes care of Delilah, day and night. And very good care she takes, with pumice stone and emery board and all the rest. I never lose sight of myself for five minutes. . . . They say John was quite a Don Juan, once upon a time?

LEAH. Women say so.

DELILAH. As for me, I intentionally picked a man who is a man's man, who never knew any woman but me. I was very friendly with his mother; and she simply handed him over to me, with all his souvenirs, his first fights, his first trousers, and with a list of his likes and dislikes, the food he prefers, etc. All I have to do is to preserve that little boy, for he will always be a little boy all his life. You might say my job is to keep him forever in clean diapers. How could he ever manage to be unfaithful to me? To make doubly sure, I refer to every iniquity as though it were female. I don't talk to him about the Amalekites or the Philistines, but of the detestable *women* of those tribes. I make him think of women as the symbols of everything he should avoid, and of me as the living symbol of everything attractive— charm, intelligence, social position and—and—candor. Delilah's middle name is Candor.

LEAH. What's he like?

DELILAH. The type I detest. But that's an advantage. It leaves me free of all those little sensations of weakness and tenderness we have at the sight of a charmingly handsome man. Samson is like all men: he needs above everything to be kept well in hand. All his muscles simply cry out for that. Before I came along, he was already trained in obedience, but to God only. He obeyed visions, signs, and portents—such as letters of fire on a wall. God's orders, however, were rarely issued—three or four times a year only—whereas Samson needs to be made to obey every second of the time. Now, in the intervals of God's commands, I am there, a constant sign, a continual demand.

LEAH. When God is silent, Delilah speaks . . .

DELILAH. And also, when God speaks, Delilah interprets. Women forget that they were created to act as intermediaries between their husbands and the rest of the world, and that is why their husbands slip out of their hands. If a wife does not interpret for her husband nature's laws and Heaven's inspiration, then he takes them directly without her intervention, and she finds herself outside his life. So, Leah, there's my formula. You see how easy it is to follow . . .

JUDITH (*calling out from the group of* GIRLS). And that's all you've got to say?

DELILAH. I might add that for my part, I chose the richest, most famous, and the least talkative man in the world. And one who sleeps more soundly than any other. My only complaint is that he talks in his sleep in a language I don't understand—that no one can understand.

SALOME. Ah, so other people you know have watched him as he slept?

DELILAH. And so there you have the picture of the perfect married couple, Leah. I will add that it's not a bad idea for a woman to choose as husband the kindest possible man, the most generous and just. In these difficult times it's perhaps one of the best guarantees against the wrath of God. Whenever there's a menace from on high, I seize Samson in my arms, and I'm saved!

12. Is Delilah's method of choosing a husband, generally speaking, the rule or the exception? Defend your answer.

MARTHA. O Leah, how awful! We are lost!

SALOME. O Leah, is this the kind of marriage we must resign ourselves to?

DELILAH. What do these girls want? Who are they?

MARTHA. We are the little beasts and things you need Samson to protect you from! Oh, here he is! Come, Salome, let's get out of here!

(SAMSON *has entered from the house.*)

DELILAH. What have you been doing, Samson? We're late.

SAMSON. I was in the game-room looking at John's collection of weapons. The bludgeons are particularly fine. Light as feathers.

DELILAH. Apparently John shares my tastes. Weapons should be light, jewels heavy. But this is not the moment to talk about trifles. Sodom awaits us!

MARTHA *and the other* GIRLS. Tell us, poor unhappy Samson, what virtues you chose in your mate?

SAMSON. Me? I chose the love, the loyalty, the bosom and the eyes of Delilah. I chose the generosity, the hand and heart of Delilah. I chose the sympathy and the cheek down which flow the tears of Delilah. I chose the passion and softness of her lips. There is a certain moonstone which at night turns everything to frosty and resplendent beauty: it is Delilah when she sleeps.

SALOME. Poor blind mouse of a man, who thinks he has ever seen a tear on those cheeks!

MARTHA. How do you fight her off? With the jawbone of an ass?

DELILAH. What did you say, you hussy?

SAMSON. I chose the woman all other women hate and envy. When they see Delilah they are blinded by her beauty. They can't stand it . . .

JUDITH. You chose a weasel and a viper.

SAMSON. Shut up, you girls!

MARTHA. O God, let Samson die before our very eyes! So much the worse for Sodom! But let us, before we perish, have the pleasure of seeing Delilah a widow!

(SAMSON *collapses as if dead upon the ground.*)

13. Explain the humor of Martha's question to Samson, "How do you fight her off? With the jawbone of an ass?"

14. Why does Martha pray to see Delilah a widow?

DELILAH. You fools, what have you done?

ATHALIA. He's dead. His heart's stopped beating.

DELILAH. You, there, hold his head up! Here, you, get some vinegar and a sponge!

MARTHA. Just look at her! You'd think she was the manager of a prize fighter!

DELILAH. There, there, Samson, it's all right . . . Here, you, rub his chest.

MARTHA. There, there, Samson, it's nothing. It's only the hand of God.

SALOME. What a woman! She won't admit defeat until she has to, even in a fight with God!

DELILAH. You, there, stroke his forehead. While I rub his legs . . .

(DELILAH *rubs* SAMSON'S *legs vigorously, while the others obey her instructions.* SAMSON, *still prone, gives evidence of reviving.*)

SAMSON. Oh, what sweet soft hands upon my forehead!

DELILAH. They are Delilah's hands, my love.

MARTHA. Liar.

SAMSON. Oh, sweet soft breath upon my face!

DELILAH. The breath of Delilah, my love. (To SALOME.) Where do you buy your toothpaste, you?

SALOME. In Sodom.

15. Why is "Where do you buy your toothpaste, you?" funny?

SAMSON. Oh, lovely perfume, the sweetest I have ever smelt!

DELILAH. It's mine. You're familiar with it, darling. You've smelt it before.

SAMSON. No, never.

DELILAH (*to* ATHALIA). Where do you buy that perfume? Speak up.

ATHALIA. In Segor.

DELILAH. It's the perfume I buy in Segor. If you like, I'll use it exclusively from now on. Now, get up! You're much better now!

SAMSON (*with difficulty rising to his feet*). I was just taking a little rest.

DELILAH. In the arms of Death, stupid man! Stand up!

SAMSON. I'm quite all right now.

MARTHA. She raised him up when God had struck him down! That shows you the power of a wife who does not know the meaning of love!

SAMSON. As for me . . . I have chosen . . .

DELILAH. Everyone knows what you have chosen! Come on now, let's go!

MARTHA. Yes, and when she wants him to die, she'll kill him herself!

DELILAH. Let's get away from these crazy creatures. . . . Farewell, Leah! Come, my beauty . . .

SAMSON. I come, my strength . . .

(SAMSON *and* DELILAH *exeunt. The* GIRLS *retire to back, left, peering over the balustrade.* LEAH, RUTH, JOHN, *and* JAMES *remain as spectators with the* YOUNG GIRLS *and the* GARDENER. *The* GARDENER *recovers the red rose that has fallen to the ground.*)

16. Explain the significance of the return of the rose to the Gardener.

RUTH. Leah, here's John. He's been looking for you.

LEAH. What does he want?

JOHN. I wasn't looking for you. I merely, once again, run into you. We seem to be fated to have such collisions, in life as in death.

LEAH. As for life, I wonder. As for death, we shall find out very soon. What do you want?

JOHN. Nothing. A terrace from which to view the show. Our terrace happens to be the highest above the Cities of the Plain. If our presence bothers you, we'll go.

RUTH. He came here to tell you that you are his wife, that you are still his wife.

JAMES. Leah was looking for you, John.

LEAH. Oh, was I? I would certainly be a fool to hope to catch him. I might find him anywhere else, but never when he's standing right before me, in the flesh.

RUTH. O Lord, they're beginning again!

JOHN. You doubtless expected to find me in James! Leave us, you girls. Go!

LEAH. No, don't go. Stay. But you might as well be forewarned. You're not going to witness one of those big reconciliation scenes, in which the male and female rend each other and say terrible things before kissing and making up. No, nothing of the sort.

JOHN. Are you quite sure?

LEAH. I think I may say I am sure.

JAMES. Leah, time's flying. You seem to forget why we came here!

LEAH. I have forgotten nothing. I do not forget the prophecy. Since daybreak the blackbirds have been chanting it. The spider wrote it on his web in letters of fire. This is the fatal hour, and I'm aware of it. Yes, indeed: just one happy couple may save Sodom from destruction! Samson and Delilah have not passed the test. It's again up to Leah and John. Otherwise, everyone will be destroyed. Otherwise, Ruth will perish and all the young girls will perish. That, at least, is the prophecy . . .

JAMES. And you don't believe it!

LEAH. Yes, I do believe it. And I am full of despair. For the evil is without remedy. The problem the Lord has set and which must be solved is not that of Sodom and Gomorrah, but the problem of Leah and John. All the brightness of the universe is now focussed upon us so that God may clearly see just what kind of human couple He has created. We're the victims of God's blackmail!

RUTH. Leah!

LEAH. He is putting us to the torture to get us to betray that secret which has hitherto eluded him.

JOHN. What secret?

LEAH. The secret defect in His handiwork. He wants to find out what's wrong with the couple intended to be the most loving, sane, healthy, and loyal. He doesn't understand why we don't get along better than we do. Why did this crack appear in the edifice of our happiness? Why do I quarrel with the only man who has understood me, why do I hate the only man I love, why do I run away from the only man for whom I have no aversion? Do you understand now, John?

17. Is Leah's "We're the victims of God's blackmail" blasphemy, a lie, or truth?

JAMES. Don't answer her, John. Be quiet.

JOHN. No, I don't understand! Not at all. You are what I most admire in the world, Leah. Yet your words have only filled me with discouragement. You are what I love most, and yet your love inspires me now only with something like disgust.

LEAH. You prefer the Angel to me. Isn't that so?

JOHN. Yes, I prefer the Angel. Although I haven't had the nerve to go right to him and say so, as you did, I admit that I prefer the Angel.

LEAH. You're wrong to be so shy with him. He has refused a woman. Perhaps a man might be more to his liking!

JOHN. I can wait. In Ruth I have found a fragment of the Angel.

18. How can Ruth be "a fragment of the Angel" for John? Compare him with Morley in *The Latent Heterosexual*.

RUTH. Leah, open your eyes. Listen! Save us! Take John by the hand. The Lord wills it!

LEAH. If God wills it, His strength is enough to obtain it in spite of ourselves. He has bonds that can bind two human beings, magnets that can draw together two bodies and two pairs of lips . . . I will submit to nothing else.

RUTH. We have them in our power now! Come, use your strength, girls!

(*The* GIRLS *push* JOHN *and* LEAH *together and make them join their hands.*)

RUTH (*helping them*). Salome, take charge of their hands! Judith, move Leah's head over to the left! Athalia, pay attention to John's chin!

LEAH. Charming names. . . . Sweet promises . . .

RUTH. And now, let's leave them alone together! Come! O God, behold them! Behold them quickly! (*Exeunt all save* JOHN *and* LEAH.)

19. The girls force John and Leah to assume a traditional lovers' pose, hoping God will "behold them quickly." What is indicated about human nature by this scene?

LEAH. Of course you realize as I do that we can't help them? We can do nothing!

JOHN. Nothing.

LEAH. The battle is between us, isn't it? The world coming to an end is nothing more than a stage-setting, isn't it?

JOHN. Merely a detail of the setting for the tragedy of marriage.

LEAH. Then release me. And go!

JOHN. You must first release me.

LEAH. No. You know better than I how to do it. You always knew how to free yourself from me at night, when I felt that you and I were one, when I thought my legs and arms were chains to hold you.

JOHN. All right then. There, you are free.

LEAH. Thank you. . . . This time you didn't even waken me. . . . Now go. Go at once! (JOHN *goes out slowly.*)

20. Why does Leah insist that John free her? Did Eben free Abbie in the same way in *Desire Under the Elms?*

LEAH. O Lord God, look at him! Men do not experience their feelings! They only act them out, and think that's enough. Look at John! He is not going away; he is merely acting the part of going away. He is acting his departure just as he acted his presence a few minutes ago, when Ruth stood beside him. If he were leaving me as I am leaving him, soaring straight up into the Heavens, plunging straight down into Hell, or by staying as I do, why then, one could believe in his sincerity. Oh, if he really left me, I would fly, I would run after him to be with him forever, in life or death. But just look: when he left me it didn't occur to him to strike out across the lawn. Instead, he is following all the winding paths of the garden. And he will certainly not climb over the wall. . . . See? He is opening the gate. He is closing the gate. When his father sent him away from the table, that's the way he left it, and no passion of any kind will ever make him abandon the pattern set in childhood. Whereas I have a new and fresh approach to every change in my life, he only follows the routine his first nurse set for him. O Lord, if You desire never again to hear a woman's voice raised in complaint, then create a man who is completely adult! What are we supposed to do with these lunatic sons whom we have neither borne nor suckled? O John, I beg of you: for once in your life, take the clear road of anger, of destruction! Let my body bring you back, let my heart draw you! Forget paths, walk on the grass! Come back like leaping flames, like raging torrents! I want only that to be conquered!

21. As John leaves, Leah's monolog is addressed to God. How honest is it? Is there reason for her to be deceitful? Does the monolog recall any earlier statements Leah has made? In short, how consistent is Leah?

THE ANGEL'S VOICE. Leah!

LEAH. Who's there?

THE ANGEL (*appearing*). It's I, Leah. The Angel.

LEAH. Oh, what a relief! I feared the worst!

THE ANGEL. You can guess what I have come to command you to do.

LEAH. He is God's messenger, he is as without wings as a travelling salesman, and he loves me. The world wails with death like a newborn babe; the world is agonizing in a new birth. It is necessary to kill and be killed, to fight in armor or naked and defenseless, to put a tourniquet on the burst arteries of the world—and the Angel asks me, as a deed of heroism, to lay down my arms and to return to my husband!

THE ANGEL. I offer you no feats of arms, no deeds of heroism. But I do offer you a human heart.

LEAH. Other women are luckier than I. For instance, that woman who was commanded to seduce the enemy chief, waylay him in his tent, and cut off his head. How exciting it would be, to look through all the shops for a dagger to suit my hand, and to practice with it on my way to the tents, by cutting off a few heads of poppy and rye . . .

THE ANGEL. It's a little too easy to be a Judith. All you need is pride.

LEAH. Or, for another example, consider the woman commanded by God to leave the husband she adores. Why, how good it would be to choose the desert in which to flee the beloved, to choose the sand on which to throw the last souvenirs, one by one—the necklace, the ring! To do so there, in the heart of solitude and death!

THE ANGEL. You only seem to think of your own satisfactions obtainable in your heroic deeds?

LEAH. I am glad you have chosen me. But that I should have been spied by the Lord and selected by His agents to carry through to the end the heroism required by marriage! That the Divine choice should be me, that the Heavenly incense should burn for me, the tongues of Heaven flatter my body and soul in an effort to persuade me to return to my husband whom I detest and who no longer loves me! I cannot obey these orders. I cannot accept this mission.

THE ANGEL. Bravo! We have got to the heart of the matter, at last. It is when the soul is set in total abhorrence against a thing that heroism begins!

22. Explain "It is when the soul is set in total abhorrence against a thing that heroism begins."

LEAH. I don't understand.

THE ANGEL. I never asked you to understand, did I? Obey: Go back to John.

LEAH. To obey a Divinity that speaks to me like a mother-in-law—I don't see the sense of it. You could take John away for a few months or years. There are wars in nearby countries, and men invented war to get away from us and to be amongst themselves . . . Let him be killed then. Let him come back without legs and arms. I shall only find my husband alive and complete again in death and mutilation.

THE ANGEL. Leah, it's not a matter of years, but of seconds. God has allowed you but a moment's grace—the moment's grace accorded a naughty child by a wise mother. God, like such a mother, has averted His eyes until you recover your self-control. He, like the wise mother, pretends not to have seen your grimace.

LEAH. What grimace?

THE ANGEL. The worst one. Stubbornness. A grimace with a fair, unwrinkled face.

LEAH. Did God turn His eyes away when I kissed John that last time? Will He look upon us again when we kiss and make up? Will He have seen nothing in the interval? When God is not looking, may mankind commit any amount of mischief? God the Father is a mother, then?

23. Explain Leah's indictment, "God the Father is a mother, then?" Explain the humorous seriousness of it. Does Iocastê's behavior in *Oedipus Rex* follow Leah's reasoning?

THE ANGEL. Leah, my dear Leah!

LEAH. So then, God's eye is like the revolving beam of a lighthouse? And when the light is upon us I must love John and make him happy? And when the beam of light moves off, I may insult and betray him?

THE ANGEL. You'll not upset me. In Heaven, at this very moment, there is a mounting fury against mankind. Well, you shall not succeed in diverting it upon yourself for your own personal benefit. In this impotent and worn-out century, it is only simple courtesy towards God for the soul to perform its acts of duty, if only to go through the motions.

LEAH. God will not hate us all the more for our hypocrisy?

THE ANGEL. When a man continues to make the ritual gestures of a faith his mind rejects, he has not necessarily abjured it; his mind and heart have merely delegated an office to his hand, as to a servant. Indeed, as he delegates his life to his body during sleep.

LEAH. Then, instead of all these deluges and conflagrations, why not put a heavy sleep upon the world? Oh, I would willingly lie down at your feet and sleep forever.

THE ANGEL. The dormouse and the hibernating bear are enough for Him. Human sleep has always been a last expedient. Even for one night, Heaven is perturbed at the sight of humanity lying there without consciousness, and each morning at dawn Heaven's anxiety regarding mankind begins again.

24. Does any religious group agree with the statement made by the Angel beginning "When a man continues to make the ritual gestures of a faith his mind rejects, he has not necessarily abjured it . . ."?

25. "Human sleep has always been a last expedient" is ambiguous. Define "sleep" within the context of the speech.

LEAH. If I agree to see John again, you will know why. It will be out of weakness and cowardice. Don't you prefer strength to weakness in those you have chosen?

THE ANGEL. No. Be cowardly. Thank you, Leah.

LEAH. And partly out of curiosity, and for the love of scandal. To see what marks Ruth has left upon him.

THE ANGEL. Be scandalous, Leah. Thank you, Leah.

LEAH. And to humiliate what I hold most sacred. And in wrath. And to double our profanations.

THE ANGEL. Blaspheme if you will. And if you will, be profane. Thank you, Leah.

LEAH. And out of love for you. As you well know. Blackmailer!

THE ANGEL. Thank you, Leah.

LEAH. And out of my lack of faith in God, because of my contempt for God!

THE ANGEL. I thank you in His name, Leah.

LEAH. All right then, I'll see John. But it's a mystery to me how I shall know when God's beacon light is upon us. I'll have to take the risk. But if He sees me spit in John's face in that beam of light, and if I kiss him in the darkness, then it's your fault. I hold you responsible. That will teach God to hold the sanctity of marriage above the happiness of the individual!

26. What feelings has the Angel for Leah? Prove your contention.

THE ANGEL. Leah, try to understand. God created no single, individual creature. With man, as with the lower animals, God created the male and female couple. He created twin bodies, united by a band of flesh which later, in an access of confidence, He severed. That was done on the day when He created tenderness. And, on the day when He created harmony, He endowed each of those two almost identical bodies with dissonance and harmony. And finally, on the day when God had His only access of joy, when He wished to praise Himself, He created liberty and delegated to the human couple the power to establish the two rewards, the two Divine prizes: constancy and human intimacy. Nothing could compensate Him for the loss of these, His favorite children. He delights in other things: the twilight in the cedars of Lebanon, the snow and the dawn upon the snow. These He delights in, but they are no compensation. So if, because of your and John's failure and disunity, God must renounce His true firmament, it is something He will never forgive.

LEAH. What firmament?

THE ANGEL. The only constellations that are visible from Heaven are those made by the fires of happy human couples. In olden times the whole firmament shone and sparkled. Each star was the light shed by a happy marriage. Now, one by one, those fires have gone out. In Sodom there is not one left. Your fires still seemed to burn, this morning, seen from on high . . . as the fires of dead stars shine long after their extinction. I descended a thousand times more swiftly than light so as to reach you before Heaven could see that you were only dead embers and grey ashes.

27. The Angel's explanation of God's creation of the male and female couple suggests certain Platonic concepts in "The Symposium" and "Phaedrus." Can you point out the similarities?

28. The Angel "descended a thousand times more swiftly than light so as to reach you before Heaven could see that you were only dead embers and grey ashes." Does this statement change your conception of his feelings for Leah? If so, how? If not, why?

LEAH. I know the human couple better than you do. I know marriage from the inside and not just by appearances. Well, it is a barren and completely sterile thing.

ANGEL. Sterile as the double fountain-head; sterile as the double rose. From on high we chiefly see the desert, which covers three-quarters of the earth. A desert is indeed a desert when a man alone or a woman alone ventures forth upon it. But let a couple wander there, the desert is turned into an oasis, a flowering field. And perhaps that couple has only one beast of burden. Yet it is worth more than all the caravans that carry treasures and rare spices. And perhaps, searching for water, they find only slime and ooze—because they are together, it is enough. And from on high the most sparkling fountains and cascades appear muddy by comparison. And suppose they get lost and die there in the desert. Their very bones, scattered upon the sands, will be as precious ivory set with emeralds. Because they are the remains of what was once a happy couple, they will shimmer with a light that will shine, through the black night of eternity, forever.

LEAH. Yes, that's the way I tried to think of our marriage! What an illusion!

THE ANGEL. No, what a defeat! You had no need to call upon imagination. One does not "try to think" of one's wife or husband. He is there. She is there. That's all. You know it, and that's enough. A husband is not a toy that you wind up each morning. He needs no disguise. He is there. You don't imagine your husband, you don't judge him, you don't esteem him: he can see and be seen, hear and be heard, touch and be touched. His presence gives reality and beauty to the day and night. And in his absence, nothing and no one will replace him. The emptiness made by his absence is a terrible void which nothing can fill. It does no good to try to fill it with his memory or his favorite possessions; nor, as you have tried to do, with another man. Or, as John has tried to do, with another woman.

LEAH. Well, then, let God reunite the bodies of mankind, male and female, with that band of flesh you spoke of, so that John and I can open the morning and shut the evening like a book. I mistrust any other kind of union. For, beloved Angel, my heart is hard. I am as though changed into stone, from head to heels, dear Angel. Were I to speak a tender word on this day when the lips are speaking the heart's most secret thoughts, why, the words would burn me like a flame. And John, too, is hard. The human being worthy of the name is strengthened by suffering. But he is also hardened. . . . Tell me to kill John, I would try to do it. Tell me to kill myself! I would prefer that to what you ask of us. If you must have this perfect and happy pair which alone can save Sodom and Gomorrah, take Abraham and his good Sarah. Those two weep, they embrace, they are full of tenderness and pity. You are well used to saving the world from floods and fire by such tear-ducts and sponges.

THE ANGEL. Obey me. Be my accomplice. This is our little plot against God. . . . We want him to spare the world through Leah and not through Abraham.

29. Leah suggests that the Angel present Abraham and Sarah as the perfect pair. Why are they not considered?

30. Why should the Angel plot against God "to spare the world through Leah and not through Abraham"?

LEAH. All right, if you will. But I want my recompense.

THE ANGEL. You shall have it. God is preparing it.

LEAH. Something unsuitable, I'm sure. God has never known what I want and need.

THE ANGEL. You will never again be happy.

LEAH. Thank you, Angel.

THE ANGEL. Your beauty will fade and vanish.

LEAH. Thank you, Angel.

THE ANGEL. All these men and women you detest will multiply, will swarm like insects.

LEAH. Thank you, Angel.

THE ANGEL. And I shall forget you. I have already forgotten you.

LEAH. Thank you. He has understood.

THE ANGEL. And you will forget me.

LEAH. I will not forget you. I will forget everything else but you.

THE ANGEL. From this evening on, you will forget me.

LEAH. Very well. Let John come now.

31. How do the two "thank you" passages of dialog in this section parallel each other? Why does Leah refuse to thank the Angel when he says she will forget him?

(JOHN *appears.*)

LEAH. Forgive me, John.

JOHN. Forgive you for what?

LEAH. For having loved you. For having hated you. For having left you.

JOHN. From the expression on your face, you're ready to begin again!

LEAH. Yes. From the beginning.

JOHN. Heaven and I could do with far less!

32. Is John's "Heaven and I could do with far less" irony, comedy, satire, burlesque, or what?

LEAH. I wouldn't be surprised. I have always been more demanding than either you or God. But I feel incapable of taking up my life again with you, except with love.

JOHN. Love? Does our love still exist?

LEAH. Perhaps not. But Love exists. Maybe I don't love you any more. But you look absolutely like the man I loved. Looking at you, I can see him again. You have his hands and eyes. Don't draw away. Maybe I could touch him by touching you.

JOHN. Oh, no! To be in love with Love, instead of with a human being—no, that's not for me.

LEAH. How much you look like him just now! Your face full of hatred reminds me of your face alight with joy as you came towards me on our wedding day. How right I was, during those nights when I lay wakefully beside you and gazed down at your sleeping face, memorizing every feature in case I should ever lose you! That wrinkle on the forehead, that mole at the corner of your nose, I remember them, and there they are, even now. O, John, sleep tonight in my arms! Let us begin our new life together with an awakening . . .

JOHN. And this is all you learned from James?

LEAH. Yes. That's what James taught me. I wondered why God had suggested that exchange, why He had allowed it and watched over us so we could make that exchange. Now I know. It was to make us lose our pride. We are no longer, you and I, a couple on display; we are just a pitiful couple who have failed, who have between us now, like another dowry, the agony of remembrance and repentance. But it was also to teach me that there is no one in the world except you, the man I loved. All other men are only an echo, and everything that does not come from you is only mockery.

33. Is Leah's knowledge (learned from James) the knowledge of all women, of some women, or of just a few women?

JOHN. I learned no such things from Ruth.

LEAH. Hush, John. Everything's finished if you tell me what you learned from Ruth.

JOHN. I learned from Ruth that one woman is as good as another. I had thought you possessed unique gifts of devotion and tenderness, that you alone knew the secrets of love, of abandoning yourself completely and of conquering completely. I learned from Ruth that every woman possesses those gifts and can turn them to account, at will.

LEAH. You lie! When I left you I had ceased to love you. Yet every minute I spent with James degraded me.

JOHN. I was still in love with you. Yet these days spent with Ruth have been a triumphant success. That's why I've left her. I wanted to preserve the memory of my first happiness. But already it seems to be worn threadbare, I can see through it. And what I see beyond is night and death.

34. Is John's knowledge (learned from Ruth) the knowledge of all men, of some men, or of just a few men?

LEAH. Oh! It's ended! Goodbye . . .

JOHN. Leah, enough of words! Time is short. We have other things to do than to stand here talking about ourselves. The point is this: Do you agree?

LEAH. It's amusing how much fuss a man can make over the world coming to an end!

JOHN. I asked you a question. Are you in accord?

LEAH. In accord with what? That we shall obey the Angel? That we shall embrace in the beacon-light of God? No. I no longer agree to it.

JOHN. I don't know what your angel told you. I don't quite know how it is that we are standing here, side by side, like a host and hostess ready to receive invited guests. The guests tonight are plague, fire, and cataclysm. And those angels and prophets who have talked all that drivel about our being able to save the cities from destruction are merely raving. Let the people of Sodom perish! I don't give a damn! And I feel the same about my own death! I am here neither out of fear nor obedience. But since Divine punishment there is, since fire and flood there are, since the world is coming to an end for a fact, I want to receive them on my doorstep, with my wife at my side.

LEAH. How destitute of originality! That's the way all men behave when they have a duty to perform! You saw God's lightning; your wife comes to you, hurt, begging, repenting of her adultery; and you have nothing to say or ask of her but this: to pose with you for a final tableau which will prove to unseen witnesses that Leah and John knew how to meet death. So that's what you want me to be, and what all men want to be: a figure in a dignified family portrait!

JOHN. You won't get tired of posing. I very much fear that you won't have time to get tired.

35. When John says "You won't get tired of posing. I very much fear that you won't have time to get tired," you probably laughed. The tragedy is overwhelming at this moment, and yet the line is almost hysterically funny. Tragicomedy functions completely here. Explain how.

LEAH. I no longer have a face of my own; mine is only the face of all women in agony and catastrophe. But just look at him! All his features have become more distinct. That's the way all men are when confronting death. Women sink, vanish, and dissolve in the general chaos . . . a man keeps his individuality to the last.

JOHN. You're mistaken. I'm not trying to give my Creator one more of those childish lessons in heroism with which history overwhelms us. Although that would perhaps be a better employment of our last hour on earth than a family squabble. But I don't want to be alone when the last armies of God come charging down upon me. I beg of you, Leah: stay here with me!

LEAH. Why me, particularly? Why not Ruth? Why not Martha?

JOHN. Because I know that with my dying breath I would call out the name of Leah, no matter what woman stood at my side. Because my arms would not be able to encompass any other form but yours for my last embrace. Because a man's first wife is the only one that gives his world its dimensions, the taste of the air he breathes. She is the one who adjusts to his ears, once and for all, the acoustics of the dome of Heaven. Then, too, I do not want to die with a stranger beside me, a person borrowed from someone else. A man may find that living with his wife is horrible; but the only way to die is at her side.

LEAH. When death comes to me, if death comes today to me, I do not want to be at the side of the man I loved, but with the man I love.

JOHN. Who forbids you to love me? Why, oh why since yesterday have we been quarreling? Can't you love me? Do you love me?

LEAH. Why drag that in? Yes, I have loved you! Rather, I thought I had found in you the Prince Charming we hear about from the cradle, that man who doesn't in fact exist. That epitome of chivalry with his biceps and his valor dedicated to every virgin! I now know that such strength is weakness, and such valor only indolence, and such dedication nothing but vanity. Mankind has failed to produce a real man. At least, I've never seen one.

36. Is it true that "Mankind has failed to produce a real man"? If you think so, why? If you think not, name "a real man" and defend your choice.

JOHN. My poor dear Leah! You are trying to unmask humanity. But in tearing off the mask you are tearing off the face!

LEAH. I tried in vain to lift your mask, to crack the abominable shell in which you are encased. I killed myself doing that, and in vain.

JOHN. What about you? Have you no mask? Do you think you are perfect?

LEAH. I have this advantage over you: I believe in myself.

JOHN. So you believe in yourself, do you? I suppose you still believe in that creature called "Woman" which has been made up by men out of scraps? You believe in those faults and virtues that men have hung around your neck and which are really no more a part of you than your necklace?

LEAH. What a time to bring that up! You're more typically Man than I thought! Now that you know the ground is sterile, swampy, and unhealthy, why, you suddenly want to build upon it a house that would stand, our house, a perfect house.

JOHN. You're right. I am a man. And I long for one minute of human repose before I sink into eternal sleep!

LEAH. Well, I'm a woman. And I want eternal sleep to catch me fully alive.

JOHN. You mean, flayed alive. Do you want to know what you are?

LEAH. Doubtless everything but what I think I am!

JOHN. Yes. You have none of the qualities you think you have, none of the qualities all women think they have. Oh, how naive you are! All your man-made attributes—you believe in them. And they're false!

LEAH. Why did they endow me with those attributes? No doubt, out of simple generosity.

JOHN. No. Simply because men didn't give a damn. While they were about it, they thought they might as well adorn you with the flashiest of gems! Oh, poor unchanging woman, none of those gems is real!

LEAH. Unchanging, am I? You do admit I am not inconstant?

JOHN. You are not inconstant. You are not Inconstancy, either. Nor are you any element or breeze or eddy. You are a stockade. You are a weight. You are habit and prejudice incarnate. A crazy idea comes to you one evening: you let it govern your acts for the rest of your life! You talk twaddle. You repeat yourself. You're a bore! Your constancy is enough to drive anyone wild!

LEAH. Go on with your list of my virtues. I suppose I have no foresight?

JOHN. You have neither vision nor foresight. You are always mistaken. That supposed sixth sense of yours! Those supposed marvellous antennae! You have no more antennae than men have. Your ear is no more attuned to the universe than ours is. You are as blind as a bat. What do you know of the universe? You have never glimpsed it, you have only touched its outer trappings. You are only affected by the sum total of truths; you have never grasped the meaning of Truth itself. You have the most wonderful capacity for finding interest in someone devoid of interest, of ascribing generosity to the most miserly, of finding elegance in the most sordid, seeing splendor in the ugliest of things. For five years you have lived with a man that you thought was the most malleable of men, the most courteous and self-controlled. In reality, he is willful and insolent and undisciplined . . .

LEAH. We were talking about me, not you. Go on. I suppose there's no truth in me?

JOHN. In the absolute sense of the word—no. For you have no real openness. You have none of those freedoms and impulses that a truly naked being has. Your nakedness is a travesty: the nakedness of a flashy burglar who steals from hotel rooms. With that nakedness you used a pass-key to open up the doors of our nights together. And that's all.

LEAH. But I suppose you will let men keep all the medals and decorations they have bestowed upon themselves? Their goodness, their courage, their loyalty!

JOHN. I'm not sure. But of this I am sure: men are inconstant, because they regulate their lives by the magnetic needles of the universe. They're the ones who speak not only for themselves, but for every inarticulate thing in nature—and that includes women. I'm the one that put all the words into your mouth that you have spoken today. I'm the one who can see and foresee.

LEAH. Can you see what kind of weather it is . . . Gomorrah had wonderful weather, yesterday, didn't it?

JOHN. Wonderful.

LEAH. Nothing but skylarks and sunshine?

JOHN. It was the most beautiful day I have ever seen. As today is the most sinister.

LEAH. Oh, my poor John! We'll never be able to agree!

JOHN. I suppose you think today is the most beautiful day possible?

LEAH. It doesn't matter. Stop. Leave me . . .

JOHN. But say what you think! It *is* the most beautiful day possible, isn't it?

LEAH. Yes. It is the most beautiful day the world has ever seen, the most beautiful day of my life!

JOHN. You're mad!

37. Why does Leah say "It is . . . the most beautiful day of my life"?

(The ANGEL enters.)

THE ANGEL. Enough, enough!! Be quiet and get out of here! We can't stand any more of this!

LEAH. I noticed there wasn't any thunder to drown our voices.

THE ANGEL. It will come. And fire and brimstone to blot out your effrontery . . . and asphyxiation to check your blasphemy . . .

LEAH. Oh, how the little angels without wings are going to run from the flaming oil and the boiling pitch!

JOHN. It's of no use to go on trying, is it, Angel? Our efforts can change nothing now.

THE ANGEL. Nothing.

LEAH. Yes, there's still hope. Good old Abraham and his good wife Sarah were endowed by God with feet insensitive to heat and they are hurrying now, this minute, through the ruins, carrying their canary cage, they are hurrying towards Segor.

JOHN. And no one among us will be spared?

THE ANGEL. No one.

LEAH. Oh yes, there'll be. Lot, the righteous man, in a long frock coat, will be able to ford the raging fires, carrying his daughters pickaback.

38. Why do Abraham and Sarah carry "their canary cage" to Segor?
39. Why does Leah characterize Lot as wearing "a long frock coat" and "carrying his daughters pickaback"?

JOHN. Leah, let us stop quarreling. It's no longer a question of making the right gestures or posing for a show. Nor of winning a respite for that humanity we despise. Come, stand at my side, close to me. Let us forget who we are.

LEAH. No. I have forgotten who I am. But I remember who you are.

JOHN. Let us just be one man and one woman, together.

LEAH. No. If God saw all the women facing death together on one side, and all the men on the other, at war even in the face of death, He would understand at last. The Deluge taught God nothing. For He saw the floating corpses of men and women, embracing even in death.

JOHN. And you will face this horror alone?

LEAH. Not alone. I have just told you. . . . Are you there, Ruth?

RUTH (*running forward*). Yes, Leah. Where are the men?

LEAH (*drawing* RUTH *aside, to the left*). For us, Ruth my dearest, men no longer exist. That is why the air is so soft, that is why you are so soft and sweet, so light, so free. The weight of men has been lifted from our bodies and souls. We are rid of men's sufferings, which we pretended to feel, of men's defeats, which we pretended to share—we have shed all those things. Finished all this false display of our weakness and their strength, of our soft skins and their rough beards, of our carelessness and their zeal! What a relief that they are no longer there to hand us non-inflammable garments, fireproof and waterproof shoes, and a farewell kiss and all their other childish inventions. What a relief that they will let us go without their usual fuss to an eternity of indolence. . . . Are you shivering, my dear Ruth? Are you cold? No, it's fear. So much the better! I have always wanted to have my feelings not just inside myself but beside me, incorporated in someone like myself! Come here, Naomi, the other women are now with us. . . . This way, Martha; we are all here together. . . .

Do I believe this is the end of everything? Yes. The world is coming to an end. And marvellously . . . terribly . . .

(RUTH, JUDITH, MARTHA, *and* NAOMI, *along with the other* YOUNG GIRLS *are now standing in a group around* LEAH, *upon whom they seem more or less to lean. At the right, another group—of* MEN—*is forming around* JOHN. *The* ANGEL *stands alone, impassively, between the two groups. Refugees, men and women, constantly appear from below the terrace, back, and silently range themselves according to sex.*)

LEAH. Look at our dear little Angel standing there, between us. He looks as though he were still expecting me to capitulate, to forget, to forget him. It's touching, really: an angel waiting for a miracle from mankind! And when he can no longer hope for anything from me, when he has at last understood that men and women no longer know each other, have repulsed each other and now despise each other, then he will raise his arms, he will shout his signal in his angel voice, and all will be over!

JOHN. Is that you, James?

JAMES. Yes. Where are the women?

JOHN. What did you say? Whom are you talking about?

JAMES. Where are the women? Leah, Ruth, Martha, Judith!

(*The light is becoming very obscured. In the sky, smoke and flames appear.*)

JOHN. Thousands of leagues away, beyond reach. God be praised, there will be no more women in our lives, James. Never again will we have to put up with that talkative statue of Silence, that perfidious portrait of Loyalty. No longer in our beds will there be that voluptuous incarnation of insensitivity. Everything will be quite simple and easy from now on, James, as it was in our childhood, simple, easy and pure as when you and I first learned to skip flat pebbles in the Dead Sea. Look! In the plain below, the trees are moving. All Creation is dividing itself finally, between us. Look, the birds and snakes and all the felines have already surrounded the women, and the orchid already grows in their cypress trees, and their wind of death is perfumed! And just see! The wild ass and the bee and the buffalo are coming to range themselves on our side, in our tempest and our keen biting air. You are shivering. Are you afraid? No, you are cold. Here, take this coat, old fellow. We must meet death all warm and full of strength—as men must be when they tackle a job. Death is our job from now on. Come here, Peter. Come here, Luke. . . . We have been promised that Death will have a man's face. And you, Gardener. Sit here with us. Why! You again have your beautiful red rose! Throw it to the women. It will be our final farewell.

(*The* GARDENER *throws the rose to* LEAH.)

LEAH. Thank you for the rose.

THE ANGEL. Be silent, Leah.

40. Why must the sexes meet death apart?
41. Why does the Gardener throw the rose to Leah?

LEAH. Is it all right over there with you men? Is everything just as you like it?

JOHN. Perfect. Men and women at last have what they always wanted.

THE ANGEL. I tell you to be quiet!

LEAH. And is the honest buffalo all right? And does the proud wild ass flick away with his tail the fly of death while continuing to stamp in his own dung? Do you plan to yoke the two together and plow furrows in the void?

JOHN. What is that hissing sound over there?

LEAH. The snakes. They are arriving now. They are wrapping themselves around our bodies and limbs and hearts.

JOHN. Are you afraid—all of you?

LEAH. What do you men by "all"? Here we are but one woman. We are Everywoman.

JOHN. So much the worse for you. Here we are thousands of men, millions of men.

LEAH. Do you want to know the answer to the riddle? I've found it.

JOHN. No. Allow me the pleasure of dying without understanding.

LEAH. God allowed an angel to argue. The result was Satan. Men allowed their wives to argue. And the result was Woman.

JOHN. With the first word spoken by a woman, all was lost.

LEAH. My first words were "I love you."

JOHN. What a cheapening of your final silence!

(*The* REFUGEES *continue to arrive and in the gathering gloom sink down, exhausted. The* WOMEN *range themselves with* LEAH, *the* MEN *with* JOHN.)

MARTHA. Is the air still pure over there, Gardener?

THE GARDENER. It's impossible to breathe. And the wind is dreadful, the black cinders are falling like hailstones . . .

LEAH. Oh? Over here it's lovely.

JOHN. What a liar you are, Leah!

LEAH. Here, there's not a breath of wind, not a cloud in the sky. Congratulate God for us, Angel. The world is coming to an end in great style!

MARTHA. I'm suffocating, Leah.

JUDITH. Leah, I'm dying.

LEAH. You hear? We're suffocating with the pure air.

JOHN. Leah!

LEAH. What do you want?

JOHN. Be quiet, you liar! Oh, what darkness!

LEAH. What sunshine!

THE ANGEL. Now, Heaven, let your wrath descend!

(*Thunder and lightning. The world comes to an end. The groups of* MEN *and* WOMEN *are reduced to piles of ashes in a grey-blue light.*)

JOHN'S VOICE. Forgive us, Heaven! What a night!

LEAH'S VOICE. Praised be Heaven! What a dawn!

(*The* ARCHANGEL *of Archangels appears.*)

THE ARCHANGEL. Will they never be quiet? Will they never die?

THE ANGEL. They are dead.

THE ARCHANGEL. Who is talking, then?

THE ANGEL (*the curtain descends slowly as he is speaking, his voice asserting itself above the confused sound of* JOHN'S *and* LEAH'S *voices, still quarreling*). They are. Death was not enough. The quarrel goes on and on . . . and on . . . □

42. Why does the final, bitter argument lack humor? Why can you not laugh now?

43. As "the quarrel goes on and on . . . and on . . ." the woman's voice from the Deluge recalls itself. Why?

44. As the men and women are reduced to ashes in grey-blue light, does the rose also crumble? Is it one spot of red as the curtain descends? Explain the rose.

Suggested Assignments. 1. Read Plato's *Symposium* and *Phaedrus* carefully. Then, in a carefully considered paper, compare the Angel's statements about love with Plato's philosophy.

2. Read Shakespeare's *A Midsummer Night's Dream* and compare the love chain with the wife-swapping in *Sodom and Gomorrah,* considering both as dramatic structural devices.

3. In a detailed paper, describe the set you would create for Act One of *Sodom and Gomorrah,* then describe the set as it would appear in Act Two. Be *very* specific!

4. In a composition of whatever length you need, compare the opening lines of Shakespeare's Sonnet 73

> That time of year thou mayst in me behold
> When yellow leaves, or none, or few, do hang
> Upon those boughs which shake against the cold,
> Bare ruin'd choirs where late the sweet birds sang

with

To begin with, the man you marry is endowed with every charm. He is like an elm tree full of song birds. Then, each week, one of his charms vanishes—flies off and perches upon another tree—another man! And by the end of the year your husband is left devoid of any charm; or rather, his charms have all been scattered elsewhere . . .

5. Each human is a giver and a receiver of emotional or spiritual gifts. It is easier to be a generous giver than to be a generous receiver. In a paper, discuss a stingy receiver in this play, revealing your own capacity for generous receiving.

CHAPTER VIII

The Mask and the Lyre—Poetic Drama

If any one thing can be said to dominate man's life, it is rhythm. Certainly rhythm pervades his life. By its simplest definition, *rhythm* is measured motion, and life is seldom, if ever, at rest or motionless. Seasons come and go with a regular recurrence of months, weeks, days, hours, minutes, and seconds—all measured by natural laws, all measured by man's technology. Hearts beat with a regularity so predictable that any irregularity suggests disease. The sun rises and sets with such constancy that its exact second of appearance and disappearance can be accurately predicted. Tides rise and fall with equal reliability. Wheels are constructed to achieve maximum efficiency in motion, and man even hopefully measures such infinite things as eternity and love (who has not asked "How much do you love me?").

Primitive man observed the same immutable laws at work and, seemingly, perhaps because he was a thinking creature, patterned his existence after them. He learned to walk by balancing one part of his body against another part. He learned to speak by causing sounds to recur meaningfully. He learned to construct weapons and tools by joining unrelated objects in rhythmical patterns. And, consciously or unconsciously, he learned to control rhythm, to refine it, to employ it for his own satisfaction and pleasure. Speeding or slowing his balanced body movements, he learned to creep, to walk, to run, and to dance. Speeding or slowing his breathing, he found he could whisper, speak, sing, and yell. Juxtaposing the motion of lines, he created the visual arts of sculpture and painting. His understanding of such concepts as time, tempo, and meter grew as he observed, experimented, and imitated the harmonies and disharmonies of the rhythmical world around him. Observing balance in those rhythms (the sun followed by the moon, land and water and sky complementing each other), primitive man also observed tension in them: sunny days and violent storms creating contrasting harmonies; light allowing sight of concrete elements in nature; dark creating abstract visions in his own inner nature. He lived with the hyperbole of nature (the sun in its glaring, unbearable heat) and its litotes (the no-sun of an eclipse). He heard iambs in the "tŭ-wīt, tŭ-woo" of the owl, the spondee of the dog's "bow-wow." In short, poetry surrounded primitive man and he employed poetry naturally long before he formulated it consciously, for poetry is merely the control of rhythm in sound. Unfortunately, history has not recorded the order of man's formulations. Scholars argue such questions as "Did description in words follow description in visual form?" Actually, *which* imitation came first isn't really important. But that man imitated is.

One thing we can say with certainty: the drama came after all other rhythms had been formulated, for it employed them all in a conscious arrangement. The rhythm of language was juxtaposed (in both balance and tension) against emotions, body movements, musical sounds (notes), and visual rhythms (dress, masks, and architecture). Poetry dominated drama from its dim, distant beginnings until June 22, 1731, when George Lillo presented the first prose drama at Drury Lane. Titled *The London Merchant; or, The History of George Barnwell,* it abandoned the poetry that had held drama captive through the centuries and allowed prose its first audience. Nor was the change in language form its only innovation. Its characters are not of the nobility; therefore, it is a bourgeois domestic tragedy—a sentimental one. Its genesis lay in an old ballad, however, and it contains a poetic prologue. Standing as a gigantic landmark, *George Barnwell* points the way to Henrik Ibsen, that pioneer of modern drama who followed the path first walked by Lillo.

Many scholars and critics have said that there is no modern tragedy, only modern drama. They hold that tragedy died after the Elizabethan period in England and after Racine in France. If, indeed, it died, Lillo's prose domestic tragedy was the executioner, for great poetic tragedy *was* dealt a mortal blow by *George Barnwell.* Others contend that tragedy was merely given an enchanted kiss by the warlock Lillo, that it fell into a deep slumber disturbed now and again by those playwrights still concerned with poetic truth rather than with bold reality: John Millington Synge, T. S. Eliot, and William Butler Yeats in England; Tennessee Williams with his rich southern free verse and Arthur Miller with his Yiddish cadences in America. Tragedy still awaits, these critics add, the kiss that will restore it to complete awakening to be the vital, alive, beautiful queen of the arts it once was when poetic truth was man's only truth.

Poetic truth results when man is explored in his human condition with his environment as a contributing factor. *Realistic truth* (for who could safely use the term "real truth"?) explores man in his environment with the human condition as a contributing factor. Realism cannot unequivocally state that there is or is not a God, that love is blind or keen-sighted, that beauty is truth and truth, beauty. Lacking scientific or observable evidence, realism must state its position with some equivocation. Poetic truth, on the other hand, can assume man's immortality, his ability to love with Dante's "love that moves the sun and other stars," and his innate capacity for truth.

Through metaphor, poetry can create analogies at many levels, endowing them with vitality and beauty merely because man seems to need his rich symbols. Asked by their alarmed elders, "What do you want out of life?" young American revolutionaries of our time may offer a flower to the even more alarmed interrogator—and smile. Poetically, the flower is an answer, its truth so rich in symbolic accretion that it defies an organized answer in twenty-five well-chosen words.

Thomas Jefferson, a realistic man himself, could not frame the Declaration of Independence in prose truth. For the most important statement made by our infant nation, he departed from prose and intellectual truth to declare: "We hold these truths to be self evident; that all men are created equal; that they are endowed by their creator with certain unalienable rights; that among these rights are life, liberty, and the pursuit of happiness." Two hundred years have passed since those words were cast in their lilting iambs and anapests (those joyous, happy measures that defy sad doubt), and generations of realists have attempted to reduce them to acceptable prose. All have failed, but the poetic logic of the words is understood by every schoolchild—understood and aspired to, even to the point of riot in recent times. Americans understand their response to the words without being able to explain their literal meaning— and that response is poetic truth.

Perhaps *intense* emotion—not necessarily intellectual, logical, or scientifically realistic—accounts for man's need of poetry with its rhythms so directly traceable to the natural order of things rather than to the imposed laws of civilized society. Certainly, in times of greatest stress, man reverts to primitive poetic rhythms. In iambs, he says "Be mine"; in anapests, "Be my love"; in trochees, "Don't go"; in dactyls, "Please don't go"; in spondees, "Shut up"; or, combining rest spondees (for determination) with trochees (for sadness that such must be), "Burn, baby, burn." Using hyperbole, he says "Drop dead" to a friend—and poetic logic allows a correct interpretation.

The *tempo* of poetry more successfully evokes an emotional response than does the tempo of prose. And it implies a great deal that must be stated in exposition or built through description in prose. For instance, in prose, a character might say, "That isn't what she had in mind," and you can neither assess the mood and tone of the speaker nor supply any details of the scene. Poetically stated, the line might read "Not so! Not so. Not from her mind." The initial iambs of "Nŏt sō! Nŏt sō," poetically repeated, impel you to repeat the iambic rhythm in *Not from* and *her mind*. But the sense will not allow that tempo, so you do not stress *from*—an act that literally forces stress onto the next word *her,* creating a decided response. Whoever she may be, whatever the situation, this woman is distinguished from other women or other people in general. The common mental pattern is not hers. One word is left, *mind,* and it must receive stress, so the metrical pattern of the whole line becomes

$$\text{Nŏt sō! } \| \text{ Nŏt sō. } \| \text{ Nŏt frŏm } | \text{ hĕr mīnd.}$$

There is a pattern of unwilling protest in the rapid iambs separated by enforced pauses (the caesuras) and an almost unseemly haste in the pyrrhic that creates a tone of absolute, unarguable finality in the spondee. Contrasted with the simple exposition of prose, the poetic line demands to be understood, to be read with many implications that could not be defended intellectually.

The *caesura* (that enforced pause which exists between the three phrases of the poetic line above) serves further to control *timing* (the pace of dramatic delivery of lines), an element that is vital to suspense in tragedy and to humor in comedy. Timing and tempo work smoothly together when the poetic dramatist understands the possibilities, possibilities denied to the prose dramatist, for he must always be concerned with levels of usage in the prose line, ensuring that they are consistent. Rhythm (and the caesura is a rhythmical device, creating a voiceless accent to fill a space of time) conspires with such elements of rhyme as assonance, consonance, and alliteration to allow a blurring of the rules of language consistency in poetry.

Diction, idiom, argot, slang—all may be blended into one acceptable line of dialog in a poetic play without destroying character verisimilitude. Because poetry is a definite convention in drama, the reader accepts the necessity (and, actually the desirability) of enriching the language with as much license as the author needs. Because poetic drama cannot be realistic or naturalistic, it need not strive for direct imitation such as those limiting adjectives demand.

Having accepted the convention of poetry in the first place, the reader is willing to suspend any other reality the dramatist desires. For example, Oedipus may not seem very bright if you examine him clinically. He should have discovered his own identity before the play began, in fact. But the poetic form permits such intellectual considerations to be suspended and, as poetry assumes command of the emotions, you are simply unconcerned with such doubts as "Life isn't that complex." In a prose play, the witches of *Macbeth* would seem utterly ridiculous, and anyone carrying on a conversation with such impossibilities would automatically be elected inmate of an asylum rather than future king of Scotland. Poetry allows the impossible to become a symbol via the uncharted route of poetic truth and we travel the road happily, knowing that reality is too limited to allow such a journey in prose.

That journey, however, is merely afforded by poetry as a form. It serves as the conveyance alone. An automobile or airplane is the conveyance we use to take a trip; they are not the trip itself. Spanning time and space, they create the possibility of expanding experience, of encompassing more of life than we could if they didn't exist. Poetry, then, is the mode of travel; the poetic drama is the expanded experience allowed by such a convenient conveyance. Together, they allow far longer trips than prose and prose drama, for they are not confined by the observable, the provable, or the defensible.

One of the princes who kissed the sleeping beauty of poetic drama in the twentieth century was T. S. Eliot. His *Murder in the Cathedral* stirred the slumbering princess but failed to awaken her. Speaking of Shakespeare's happy life with that vital lady before Lillo's enchantment slowed her to dreams, Eliot observed:

A verse play is not a play done into verse, but a different kind of play: in a way more realistic than 'naturalistic drama,' because, instead of clothing nature in poetry, it should remove the surface of things, expose the underneath, or the inside, of the natural surface appearance. It may allow the characters to behave inconsistently, but only with respect to a deeper consistency. It may use any device to show their real feelings and volitions, instead of just what, in actual life, they would normally profess or be conscious of; it must reveal, underneath the vacillating or infirm character, the indomitable unconscious will; and underneath the resolute purpose of the planning animal, the victim of circumstance and the doomed or sanctified being. So the poet with ambitions of the theatre, must discover the laws, both of another kind of verse and of another kind of drama.*

The originators of "expressionistic" drama attempted that "different kind of a play" by seeking the expanded experience of poetic truth through prose. Whether the originator of the form was Alice Gerstenberg in her

* Introduction to S. L. Bethell's *Shakespeare and The Popular Dramatic Tradition,* 1944.

one-act *Overtones* or August Strindberg in his *The Dream Play* and *The Spook Sonata* (critics argue endlessly for their favorite contender), it was Eugene O'Neill who perfected the formula in such plays as *The Great God Brown, The Emperor Jones,* and *A Long Day's Journey into Night.* His consistent failure to achieve great tragedy may be laid to many reasons, but one of the most obvious is his failure to achieve those poetic rhythms employed by the predecessors of Lillo.

Aristotle, in *The Poetics,* reasoned that the basic ingredients of drama were poetry, music, and the dance—all imitations of life through the medium of rhythm. If those rhythms seemed unreal or not true-to-life, he argued further, the poet does not merely attempt to imitate life as it is but life as it is, was, or should be (the present, the past, the ideal). Agreeing with Aristotle, Eliot added his belief that a great juggler (he cited Rastelli) creates greater catharsis than does a performance of Ibsen's *A Doll's House* because the rhythm of the former works on the total experience of man while the lack of rhythm in the latter is a limiting factor.[°]

Always at verbal war with Eliot, William Butler Yeats accused[°] him of levity in calling Rastelli "cathartic." Yet, in *The Cutting of an Agate,* Yeats stated his belief that character (that is, the completely created person, so real onstage that he could be recognized as a human offstage) is realized only in poetic drama when the lyric quality (impassioned, intense, singing poetry) is absent. He cites the comedy figure of Falstaff and the oratorical Henry the Fifth as characters completely defined into reality. Those touched with lyric poetry (Oedipus and Macbeth, for example) become "ourselves that we see upon the stage." In short, Yeats seems to argue, it is the lack of lyricism that creates the photograph, the presence of lyricism that paints the abstraction which we view as the reality of Self.

More recently, Eugene Ionesco has accused the anti-poetic theater of alienating man's "unfathomable third dimension," a dimension Ionesco believes necessary to make a "whole man."[°] Perhaps the non-metaphysical world, the scientific period in which we live, has, as Ionesco believes, destroyed the mystery of life. Comedy and tragedy merge and blend, for the poetic truths (such as the *necessity* for good) are lost; man becomes alienated merely by living in a world that is neither good nor bad, and he grows hopelessly bored. Testifying to the strength of the poetic line and poetic truth, Ionesco cries out, "And all great drama is unbearable," a belief he supports—much as Yeats did—by an example: "When

[°] "The Beating of a Drum," *The Nation and Athenaeum,* October 6, 1923.

[°] F. O. Matthiessen, *The Achievement of T. S. Eliot* (Oxford, 1958).

[°] "The World of Ionesco," *International Theatre Annual No. 2* (1957), ed. Harold Hobson.

Richard II is killed in his cell, I see the death of all kings on earth, I witness the agonizing desecration and downfall of all values and civilizations. It is beyond our control, and therefore it is true. I am myself a dying King."*

A leader in the avant-garde theater and the theater of the absurd (which you will explore in the next chapter), Ionesco affirms his own return to classical (ergo poetic) forms by stating that "I believe that the aim of the 'avant-garde' should be to rediscover—not invent—in their purest state, the permanent forms and forgotten ideals of the theatre."°

Ionesco's *The Chairs,* for example, is a relatively successful expressionistic drama that is more poetic in concept than in achievement. It concerns an old couple who live alone on an island (and, remember, a symbol is vital to any poetic concept, so an island here equals another reality). Wanting desperately to communicate the husband's knowledge of life to others, the couple hire an orator to deliver the message to a group of guests at a large party. As each guest seems to arrive, the old couple speak with and provide a chair for each. Slowly, the stage and the orchestra pit fill with empty chairs, for no one actually comes, though the orchestra chairs slowly join the audience to the stage as the orchestra did in Greek tragedy. The orator does eventually arrive—but he is a deaf-mute. Overcome by shock and the final frustration of non-communication, the old couple commit suicide, and the orator attempts to fulfill his part of the bargain by writing the message on a blackboard. Ironically, he produces only meaningless scribblings before fleeing in frustration. Abandoned, the stage retains only the empty chairs—which suddenly give voice to embarrassed laughter, coughings, and sputterings as the play ends. The audience, usually filing out of the theater a little stunned, also laugh and cough and sputter—often without knowing why.

Whatever his message, Ionesco's form is startlingly similar to that of an anonymous fifteenth-century playwright of great poetic skill, skill which he exhibited in *The Moral Play of Everyman.* Realistic in setting, *Everyman's* setting differs from the realism of its poetic predecessor *Oedipus,* which was set on the steps of the palace at Thebes. It differs too from the realistic moor and castle settings of *Macbeth.* But *Everyman* is still realistic because it exists even today. It exists in your mind as you read, because the setting is the mind of a man, Everyman, and you are that man.

The physical properties of the world, the dramatist seems to say, are illusory. They do not exist as eternal realities. Reality is, on the other hand, the Self, the consciousness of the Self as a God-created soul. And

* Ibid.
° Ibid.

that soul, after a fleeting moment on Earth, must return to its Creator for final judging.

The characters in the play are:

MESSENGER	GOOD DEEDS
GOD: *Adonai*	KNOWLEDGE
DEATH	CONFESSION
EVERYMAN	BEAUTY
FELLOWSHIP	STRENGTH
COUSIN	DISCRETION
KINDRED	FIVE WITS
GOODS	ANGEL
	DOCTOR

Each character is an *abstraction* (an embodiment of a thought or an idea, a non-concrete entity lacking physical substance) given human form, therefore a *personification*. The play, then, is immediately classifiable as an *allegory* (a narrative employing abstractions to communicate a moral). In a very real sense, then, *Everyman* is an extended narrative sermon designed to reveal (dramatically rather than intellectually) the medieval Christian beliefs about man and his transient world.

As a dramatic sermon, *Everyman* is a remarkably effective device, for the poetry appeals to the emotional rather than to the intellectual man. Observing someone else, the reader is slowly led to identify with Everyman, then to become Everyman in such a fashion that he does not watch something happen to a character—he becomes the character to whom it is happening.

The dramatic structure of the play will become obvious as you read. Broken roughly into four main parts, it creates character and conflict in the first part, reveals the weaknesses of man in the second part, raises hope through complication which creates suspense in the third, and intensifies complication before resolving the drama in the fourth or last part of the play.

As you read *Everyman,* you should ask yourself certain questions. Is this a tragedy in the classical sense that *Oedipus* is—that is, does Everyman go to his death defeated by a flaw? Or is it a tragedy in the romantic sense of *Macbeth*—is there promise in the defeat of Everyman? Or is it a tragedy in the modern sense of *Desire Under the Elms*—that is, is death release rather than defeat? You may well be surprised at the answer. Read the play first in its entirety; then, on rereading, attempt to answer the questions which have been inserted at various points.

EVERYMAN

Here beginneth a treatise how the High Father of Heaven sendeth Death to summon every creature to come and give account of their lives in this world, and is in manner of a moral play.

MESSENGER. I pray you all give your audience,
And hear this matter with reverence,
By figure a moral play—
The *Summoning of Everyman* called it is,
That of our lives and ending shows   *5*
How transitory we be all day.
This matter is wondrous precious,
But the intent of it is more gracious,
And sweet to bear away.
The story saith: Man, in the beginning,   *10*
Look well, and take good heed to the ending,
Be you never so gay!
Ye think sin in the beginning full sweet,
Which in the end causeth the soul to weep,
When the body lieth in clay.   *15*
Here shall you see how Fellowship and Jollity,
Both Strength, Pleasure, and Beauty,
Will fade from thee as flower in May.
For ye shall hear how our Heaven King
Calleth Everyman to a general reckoning.   *20*
Give audience, and hear what he doth say.   *(Exit.)*

1. There can be no doubt of the moral, theme, or meaning of this play. It is stated by the Messenger (lines 1–21). Restate it in one prose sentence.

(GOD *speaketh.*)
GOD. I perceive, here in my majesty,
How that all creatures be to me unkind,
Living without dread in worldly prosperity.
Of ghostly sight the people be so blind,   *25*

3. **By figure,** in form.   6. **How . . . day,** the life span is one day in eternal time.   23. **unkind,** unnatural.   25. **ghostly,** spiritual.

Drowned in sin, they know me not for their God.
In worldly riches is all their mind,
They fear not my rightwiseness, the sharp rod;
My love that I showed when I for them died
They forget clean, and shedding of my blood red;   *30*
I hanged between two, it cannot be denied;
To get them life I suffered to be dead;
I healed their feet, with thorns hurt was my head.
I could do no more than I did, truly;
And now I see the people do clean forsake me.   *35*
They use the seven deadly sins damnable,
As pride, covetise, wrath, and lechery,
Now in the world be made commendable;
And thus they leave of angels the heavenly company.
Every man liveth so after his own pleasure,   *40*
And yet of their life they be nothing sure.
I see the more that I them forbear
The worse they be from year to year;
All that liveth appaireth fast.
Therefore I will, in all the haste,   *45*
Have a reckoning of every man's person;
For, and I leave the people thus alone
In their life and wicked tempests,
Verily they will become much worse than beasts;
For now one would by envy another up eat;   *50*
Charity they all do clean forget.
I hoped well that every man
In my glory should make his mansion,
And thereto I had them all elect;
But now I see, like traitors deject,   *55*
They thank me not for the pleasure that I to them meant,
Nor yet for their being that I them have lent.
I proffered the people great multitude of mercy,
And few there be that asketh it heartily;
They be so cumbered with wordly riches,   *60*
That needs on them I must do justice,
On every man living without fear.
Where art thou, Death, thou mighty messenger?
   (*Enter* DEATH.)

44. **appaireth,** decays.   47. **and,** if.

DEATH. Almighty God, I am here at your will,
Your commandment to fulfil.   65
    GOD. Go thou to Everyman,
And show him, in my name,
A pilgrimage he must on him take,
Which he in no wise may escape;
And that he bring with him a sure reckoning   70
Without delay or any tarrying.   (*Exit* GOD.)

2. God as Trinity speaks in lines 22–71. Is any one element of the
Trinity more obvious than another? Is any one element less obvious than
the other two? Give reasons for your answer and attempt to explain why
a fifteenth-century monk or clerk writing for an unsophisticated, illiterate
audience might choose to exaggerate or minimize any part of the three-
personed God.
    3. God enumerates several reasons for sending Death to Everyman.
What is the most important one? Why?
    4. State God's attitude toward the Doctrine of the Elect as it is
suggested in *Everyman.* How does it differ from later Calvinism?

DEATH. Lord, I will in the world go run over all,
And cruelly out search both great and small.
Every man will I beset that liveth beastly
Out of God's laws, and dreadeth not folly.   75
He that loveth riches I will strike with my dart,
His sight to blind, and from heaven to depart,
Except that alms be his good friend,
In hell for to dwell, world without end.
    (*Enter* EVERYMAN.)
Lo, yonder I see Everyman walking;   80
Full little he thinketh on my coming.
His mind is on fleshly lusts and his treasure,
And great pain it shall cause him to endure
Before the Lord, Heaven King.
Everyman, stand still! Whither art thou going   85
Thus gaily? Hast thou thy Maker forgot?
    EVERYMAN. Why askest thou?
Wouldst thou wete?

69. **wise,** way.   77. **depart,** separate.   78. **alms,** charity.   88. **wete,** know.

DEATH. Yea, sir, I will show you:
In great haste I am sent to thee   *90*
From God out of his Majesty.
  EVERYMAN. What, sent to me?
  DEATH. Yea, certainly.
Though thou have forgot him here,
He thinketh on thee in the heavenly sphere,   *95*
As, ere we depart, thou shalt know.
  EVERYMAN. What desireth God of me?
  DEATH. That shall I show thee:
A reckoning he will needs have
Without any longer respite.   *100*
  EVERYMAN. To give a reckoning, longer leisure I crave.
This blind matter troubleth my wit.

5. Do God and Death speak in the same tone and manner? If not,
who seems more compassionate? More dispassionate? More businesslike?
More emotionally involved? More intellectual? Characterization begins
to emerge in the play through their dialog. Account for it.

6. Is line 78 ambiguous in any way?

7. Everyman's tone changes radically between lines 87 and 102.
Why?

DEATH. On thee thou must take a long journey;
Therefore thy book of count with thee thou bring;
For turn again thou can not by no way.   *105*
And look thou be sure of thy reckoning,
For before God thou shalt answer and show
Thy many bad deeds, and good but a few,
How thou hast spent thy life, and in what wise,
Before the Chief Lord of paradise.   *110*
Have ado that we were in that way,
For, wete thou well, thou shalt make none attorney.

8. Line 112 has been stated in song and story for many centuries.
List three or four recent examples from memory. Poetry frequently causes
other literary counterparts to suggest themselves. If none do, you may
be less well-read than you should be.

102. **blind,** obscure.   **troubleth my wit,** disturbs my thought.   104. **count,** accounts.   111.
Have . . . way, prepare to go.   112. **make,** have.

EVERYMAN. Full unready I am such reckoning to give.
I know thee not. What messenger art thou?
    DEATH. I am Death, that no man dreadeth.   *115*
For every man I 'rest, and no man spareth;
For it is God's commandment
That all to me should be obedient.
    EVERYMAN. O Death! thou comest when I had thee least in mind!
In thy power it lieth me to save.   *120*
Yet of my goods will I give thee, if thou will be kind;
Yea, a thousand pound shalt thou have,
If thou defer this matter till another day.
    DEATH. Everyman, it may not be, by no way!
I set not by gold, silver, nor riches,   *125*
Nor by pope, emperor, king, duke, nor princes.
For, and I would receive gifts great,
All the world I might get;
But my custom is clean contrary.
I give thee no respite. Come hence, and not tarry.   *130*

9. Everyman's tone changes again in line 119. Why?
10. Compare lines 124–130 with "Ozymandias" by Percy Bysshe Shelley and "Thanatopsis" by William Cullen Bryant. Do they differ in basic attitude? Compare the final lines of "Thanatopsis" and Dylan Thomas' "Do Not Go Gentle Into That Good Night" with Everyman's evasions. Which poet is more like Everyman?

EVERYMAN. Alas! shall I have no longer respite?
I may say Death giveth no warning.
To think on thee, it maketh my heart sick,
For all unready is my book of reckoning.
But twelve year and I might have abiding,
My counting-book I would make so clear,   *135*
That my reckoning I should not need to fear.
Wherefore, Death, I pray thee, for God's mercy,
Spare me till I be provided of remedy.
    DEATH. Thee availeth not to cry, weep, and pray;
But haste thee lightly that thou were gone that journey,   *140*

115. that . . . dreadeth, that fears no man.   116. 'rest, arrest (note the pun).   125. set not by, care not for.   135. But . . . abiding, if I could remain for only twelve years.   139. of remedy, with aid.   141. lightly, quickly.

And prove thy friends if thou can.
For wete thou well the tide abideth no man;
And in the world each living creature
For Adam's sin must die of nature.   *145*
    EVERYMAN. Death, if I should this pilgrimage take,
And my reckoning surely make,
Show me, for saint charity,
Should I not come again shortly?
    DEATH. No, Everyman; and thou be once there,   *150*
Thou mayst never more come here,
Trust me verily.
    EVERYMAN. O gracious God, in the high seat celestial,
Have mercy on me in this most need!
Shall I have no company from this vale terrestrial   *155*
Of mine acquaintance that way me to lead?

11. What pleas does Everyman make of Death that he be spared momentarily?

12. When pleas are unavailing, he asks "Should I not come again shortly?" What theological doctrine is he pleading?

13. When all pleas fail, where does Everyman turn? Is this both theologically desirable and psychologically sound? Explain your answer in some detail.

    DEATH. Yea, if any be so hardy,
That would go with thee and bear thee company.
Hie thee that thou were gone to God's magnificence,
Thy reckoning to give before his presence.   *160*
What! weenest thou thy life is given thee,
And thy worldly goods also?
    EVERYMAN. I had weened so, verily.
    DEATH. Nay, nay; it was but lent thee;
For, as soon as thou art gone,   *165*
Another a while shall have it, and then go therefrom
Even as thou hast done.
Everyman, thou art mad! Thou hast thy wits five,
And here on earth will not amend thy life;
For suddenly I do come.   *170*
    EVERYMAN. O wretched caitiff! whither shall I flee,
That I might 'scape endless sorrow?

159. **Hie . . . gone,** hasten.   161. **weenest,** think.

Now, gentle Death, spare me till tomorrow,
That I may amend me
With good advisement.   *175*
    DEATH. Nay, thereto I will not consent,
Nor no man will I respite,
But to the heart suddenly I shall smite
Without any advisement.
And now out of thy sight I will me hie;   *180*
See thou make thee ready shortly,
For thou mayst say this is the day
That no man living may 'scape away.   (*Exit* DEATH.)

14. Why is Death so willing to allow Everyman the company of any friend who will volunteer to share the journey? Explain one irony of this situation.

15. If you were staging this for a group and you wished to make it believable and clear, how would you costume Everyman and Death? How would you represent God? Check your theater of the mind to see if you have visualized the characters as you would present them on a stage. Account for any differences.

16. By now, Everyman should have a definite character—as should Death. How has the dramatist created such believable characters?

17. Rhyme scheme, prosody, all the elements of poetry are curiously akin to the freedoms from convention employed by poets of the twentieth century. Explain the extreme liberties taken in the structural form of this play. Are they a result of mediocre versification, deliberate effort to avoid monotony, or sheer accident? Defend your answer with concrete illustrations.

    EVERYMAN. Alas! I may well weep with sighs deep.
Now have I no manner of company   *185*
To help me in my journey and me to keep;
And also my writing is full unready.
How shall I do now for to excuse me?
I would to God I had never been get!
To my soul a full great profit it had be,   *190*
For now I fear pains huge and great.
The time passeth; Lord, help, that all wrought.
For though I mourn it availeth naught.
The day passeth, and is almost a-go;

175. advisement, warning.   187. writing, record.   189. get, born.

I wot not well what for to do.   195
To whom were I best my complaint to make?
What if I to Fellowship thereof spake,
And showed him of this sudden chance?
For in him is all mine affiance,
We have in the world so many a day   200
Been good friends in sport and play.
I see him yonder, certainly;
I trust that he will bear me company;
Therefore to him will I speak to ease my sorrow.
Well met, good Fellowship, and good morrow!   205

18. Everyman shares a wish (line 189) with what other dramatic
characters you have studied?

(FELLOWSHIP *speaketh.*)
FELLOWSHIP. Everyman, good morrow, by this day!
Sir, why lookest thou so piteously?
If any thing be amiss, I pray thee me say,
That I may help to remedy.
EVERYMAN. Yea, good Fellowship, yea,   210
I am in great jeopardy.
FELLOWSHIP. My true friend, show to me your mind.
I will not forsake thee to my life's end
In the way of good company.
EVERYMAN. That was well spoken, and lovingly.   215
FELLOWSHIP. Sir, I must needs know your heaviness;
I have pity to see you in any distress;
If any have you wronged, ye shall revenged be,
Though I on the ground be slain for thee,
Though that I know before that I should die.   220
EVERYMAN. Verily, Fellowship, gramercy.
FELLOWSHIP. Tush! by thy thanks I set not a straw!
Show me your grief, and say no more.
EVERYMAN. If I my heart should to you break,
And then you to turn your mind from me,   225
And would not me comfort when you hear me speak,
Then should I ten times sorrier be.
FELLOWSHIP. Sir, I say as I will do, indeed.

195. wot, know.   199. affiance, trust.   221. gramercy, great thanks.   224. break, reveal.
225. to, were to.

EVERYMAN. Then be you a good friend at need;
I have found you true here before.   *230*
FELLOWSHIP. And so ye shall evermore;
For, in faith, and thou go to hell,
I will not forsake thee by the way!
EVERYMAN. Ye speak like a good friend. I believe you well;
I shall deserve it, and I may.   *235*
FELLOWSHIP. I speak of no deserving, by this day!
For he that will say and nothing do
Is not worthy with good company to go;
Therefore show me the grief of your mind,
As to your friend most loving and kind.   *240*

19. Explain the irony of Fellowship's protestations up to this point.
Is "Fellowship" synonymous with "Friend" or with "Fair-weather
Friend"? Can you state the difference? If he is only one of these, why
is there no counterpart for the other?

EVERYMAN. I shall show you how it is:
Commanded I am to go a journey,
A long way, hard and dangerous,
And give a strait count without delay
Before the high judge, Adonai.   *245*
Wherefore, I pray you, bear me company,
As ye have promised, in this journey.
FELLOWSHIP. That is matter indeed! Promise is duty;
But, and I should take such a voyage on me,
I know it well, it should be to my pain.   *250*
Also it maketh me afeared, certain.
But let us take counsel here as well as we can,
For your words would fright a strong man.
EVERYMAN. Why, ye said if I had need,
Ye would me never forsake, quick nor dead,   *255*
Though it were to hell, truly.
FELLOWSHIP. So I said, certainly,
But such pleasures be set aside, the sooth to say.
And also, if we took such a journey,
When should we come again?   *260*

---

229. **at,** in.   235. **deserve,** repay.   **and I may,** if I can.   244. **strait count,** strict accounting.   258. **But . . . say,** but such pleasantries are, truly, only a manner of speech.

EVERYMAN. Nay, never again till the day of doom.

FELLOWSHIP. In faith, then will not I come there!
Who hath you these tidings brought?

EVERYMAN. Indeed, Death was with me here.

FELLOWSHIP. Now, by God that all hath bought,   *265*
If Death were the messenger,
For no man that is living today
I will not go that loath journey—
Not for the father that begat me!

EVERYMAN. Ye promised otherwise, pardie.   *270*

FELLOWSHIP. I wot well I said so, truly;
And yet if thou wilt eat, and drink, and make good cheer,
Or haunt to women the lusty company,
I would not forsake you while the day is clear,
Trust me verily!   *275*

EVERYMAN. Yea, thereto ye would be ready.
To go to mirth, solace, and play,
Your mind will sooner apply
Than to bear me company in my long journey.

FELLOWSHIP. Now, in good faith, I will not that way.   *280*
But and thou wilt murder, or any man kill,
In that I will help thee with a good will!

EVERYMAN. O, that is a simple advice indeed!
Gentle fellow, help me in my necessity;
We have loved long, and now I need,   *285*
And now, gentle Fellowship, remember me!

FELLOWSHIP. Whether ye have loved me or no,
By Saint John, I will not with thee go.

20. Why does Fellowship swear by Saint John rather than by Saint Christopher?

EVERYMAN. Yet I pray thee, take the labor, and do so much for me
To bring me forward, for saint charity,   *290*
And comfort me till I come without the town.

FELLOWSHIP. Nay, and thou would give me a new gown,
I will not a foot with thee go;
But, and thou had tarried, I would not have left thee so.
And as now God speed thee in thy journey,   *295*
For from thee I will depart as fast as I may.

---

265. **bought,** redeemed.   270. **pardie,** *par dieu,* by God.   289. **take,** undertake.   290. **To . . . forward,** to accompany me.

EVERYMAN. Whither away, Fellowship? Will you forsake me?
FELLOWSHIP. Yea, by my fay, to God I betake thee.
EVERYMAN. Farewell, good Fellowship! For thee my heart is sore;
Adieu for ever! I shall see thee no more.   *300*
FELLOWSHIP. In faith, Everyman, farewell now at the end!
For you I will remember that parting is mourning.   (*Exit* FELLOWSHIP.)
EVERYMAN. Alack! shall we thus depart indeed
(Ah, Lady, help!) without any more comfort?
Lo, Fellowship forsaketh me in my most need.   *305*
For help in this world whither shall I resort?
Fellowship here before with me would merry make,
And now little sorrow for me doth he take.
It is said, "In prosperity men friends may find,
Which in adversity be full unkind."   *310*
Now whither for succor shall I flee,
Sith that Fellowship hath forsaken me?
To my kinsmen I will, truly,
Praying them to help me in my necessity;
I believe that they will do so,   *315*
For "kind will creep where it may not go."
I will go say, for yonder I see them go.
Where be ye now, my friends and kinsmen?

21. Why, specifically, does Everyman pray to the "Lady" (line 304)? Reconsider your answer to Question 2, if necessary.

(*Enter* KINDRED *and* COUSIN.)
KINDRED. Here be we now, at your commandment.
Cousin, I pray you show us your intent   *320*
In any wise, and do not spare.
COUSIN. Yea, Everyman, and to us declare
If ye be disposed to go any whither,
For, wete you well, we will live and die together.
KINDRED. In wealth and woe we will with you hold,   *325*
For over his kin a man may be bold.

22. Kindred and Cousin speak as ironically as Fellowship did before he knew the request. Explain the logic employed by the dramatist.

298. fay, faith. betake, commend. 302. For you, because of you. 312. Sith, since. 313. will, will go. 316. "kind . . . go," "kinship will creep where it may not walk." 317. say, attempt. 320. Cousin, any relative, except brother or sister. 321. wise, case.

EVERYMAN. Gramercy, my friends and kinsmen kind.
Now shall I show you the grief of my mind.
I was commanded by a messenger
That is a high king's chief officer;   330
He bade me go a pilgrimage, to my pain,
And I know well I shall never come again;
Also I must give a reckoning straight,
For I have a great enemy that hath me in wait,
Which intendeth me for to hinder.   335
    KINDRED. What account is that which ye must render?
That would I know.
    EVERYMAN. Of all my works I must show
How I have lived, and my days spent;
Also of ill deeds that I have used   340
In my time, sith life was me lent;
And of all virtues that I have refused.
Therefore I pray you go thither with me,
To help to make mine account, for saint charity.
    COUSIN. What, to go thither? Is that the matter?   345
Nay, Everyman, I had liefer fast bread and water
All this five year and more.
    EVERYMAN. Alas, that ever I was bore!
For now shall I never be merry
If that you forsake me.   350
    KINDRED. Ah, sir, what! Ye be a merry man!
Take good heart to you, and make no moan.
But one thing I warn you, by Saint Anne,
As for me, ye shall go alone.
    EVERYMAN. My Cousin, will you not with me go?   355
    COUSIN. No, by our Lady! I have the cramp in my toe.
Trust not to me, for, so God me speed,
I will deceive you in your most need.

23. Why does Kindred swear by Saint Anne? A pattern should begin to emerge with this second oath. How is the pattern similar to that of classical tragedy?

24. How believable is Cousin's excuse in line 356?

    KINDRED. It availeth not us to tice.
Ye shall have my maid with all my heart;   360

334. **hath . . . wait,** watches me.   335. **hinder,** harm.   346. **had liefer,** would rather.
359. **tice,** entice.

She loveth to go to feasts, there to be nice,
And to dance, and abroad to start,
I will give her leave to help you in that journey,
If that you and she may agree.
    EVERYMAN. Now show me the very effect of your mind.   *365*
Will you go with me, or abide behind?
    KINDRED. Abide behind? Yea, that will I, and I may!
Therefore, farewell till another day.   (*Exit* KINDRED.)
    EVERYMAN. How should I be merry or glad?
For fair promises men to me make,   *370*
But when I have most need, they me forsake.
I am deceived; that maketh me sad.
    COUSIN. Cousin Everyman, farewell now,
For verily I will not go with you;
Also of mine own life an unready reckoning   *375*
I have to account; therefore I make tarrying.
Now, God keep thee, for now I go.   (*Exit* COUSIN.)

25. Is Cousin's farewell excuse (375–376) ironic? Why or why not?
26. Why is Everyman less ambiguous with Kindred and Cousin than
he was with Fellowship? Why is the scene only half as long?

    EVERYMAN. Ah, Jesus! is all come hereto?
Lo, fair words maketh fools fain;
They promise and nothing will do, certain.   *380*
My kinsmen promised me faithfully
For to abide with me steadfastly,
And now fast away do they flee.
Even so Fellowship promised me.
What friend were best me of to provide?   *385*
I lose my time here longer to abide.
Yet in my mind a thing there is:
All my life I have loved riches;
If that my good now help me might,
He would make my heart full light.   *390*
I will speak to him in this distress.
Where art thou, my Goods and riches?
    GOODS (*to one side*). Who calleth me? Everyman? What, hast thou haste?
I lie here in corners, trussed and piled so high,
And in chests I am locked so fast,   *395*

---

361. **nice,** wanton.   362. **abroad to start,** travel about.   379. **fain,** happy.

Also sacked in bags—thou mayest see with thine eye—
I cannot stir; in packs low I lie.
What would ye have? Lightly me say.
EVERYMAN. Come hither, Goods, in all the haste thou may.
For of counsel I must desire thee.   *400*
(*Enter* GOODS.)
GOODS. Sir, and ye in the world have sorrow or adversity,
That can I help you to remedy shortly.
EVERYMAN. It is another disease that grieveth me;
In this world it is not, I tell thee so.
I am sent for another way to go,   *405*
To give a strict count general
Before the highest Jupiter of all;
And all my life I have had joy and pleasure in thee,
Therefore I pray thee go with me,
For, peradventure, thou mayst before God Almighty   *410*
My reckoning help to clean and purify;
For it is said ever among,
That "money maketh all right that is wrong."

27. Goods (earthly possessions) seems an obviously poor choice for
Everyman to consult. Is the dramatist guilty of anticlimax or is he
employing anticlimax to good effect?

28. Everyman is almost abrupt in announcing his request to Goods.
What about man does the author reveal in speeding the request each
time it is made?

GOODS. Nay, Everyman; I sing another song,
I follow no man in such voyages;   *415*
For, and I went with thee,
Thou shouldst fare much the worse for me;
For because on me thou did set thy mind,
Thy reckoning I have made blotted and blind,
That thine account thou cannot make truly;   *420*
And that hast thou for the love of me.
EVERYMAN. That would grieve me full sore,
When I should come to that fearful answer.
Up, let us go thither together.
GOODS. Nay, not so! I am too brittle, I may not endure;   *425*
I will follow no man one foot, be ye sure.
EVERYMAN. Alas! I have thee loved, and had great pleasure
All my life-days on goods and treasure.

GOODS. That is to thy damnation, without lesing!
For my love is contrary to the love everlasting.   *430*
But if thou had me loved moderately during,
As to the poor to give part of me,
Then shouldst thou not in this dolor be,
Nor in this great sorrow and care.

29. Goods refuses to accompany Everyman, stating as his reasons the three that have become so common as to be trite. State the clichés he avoids.

30. Again a subtle bit of brainwashing is employed. Explain lines 431–434 as a type of psychological warfare.

EVERYMAN. Lo, now was I deceived ere I was ware,   *435*
And all I may wyte my spending of time.
    GOODS. What, weenest thou that I am thine?
    EVERYMAN. I had weened so.
    GOODS. Nay, Everyman, I say no;
As for a while I was lent thee,   *440*
A season thou hast had me in prosperity.
My condition is man's soul to kill;
If I save one, a thousand I do spill;
Weenest thou that I will follow thee
From this world? Nay, verily.   *445*
    EVERYMAN. I had weened otherwise.
    GOODS. Therefore to thy soul Goods is a thief;
For when thou art dead, this is my guise,
Another to deceive in the same wise
As I have done thee, and all to his soul's reprief.   *450*
    EVERYMAN. O false Goods, curséd may thou be!
Thou traitor to God, that hast deceived me
And caught me in thy snare.
    GOODS. Marry! thou brought thyself in care,
Whereof I am right glad.   *455*
I must needs laugh, I cannot be sad.
    EVERYMAN. Ah, Goods, thou hast had long my heartly love;
I gave thee that which should be the Lord's above.
But wilt thou not go with me indeed?
I pray thee truth to say.   *460*

---

429. **lesing,** lying.   431. **during,** at the time.   435. **ware,** aware.   436. **And all . . . time,**
and I may blame all on the way I spent my time.   443. **spill,** destroy.   448. **guise,** custom.
450. **reprief,** reproof.

GOODS. No, so God me speed!

Therefore farewell, and have good day. (*Exit* GOODS.)

31. Line 440 is almost a repetition of what earlier line? Is there a theological contradiction? If so, what is it? If not, why not?

32. Goods does not equivocate. He is honest in his refusal as Fellowship, Kindred, and Cousin were not. From his opening speech he is honest, yet the statement *seems* dishonest. Are lines 401–402 verbal or dramatic ambiguity or both or neither? Explain.

33. Abandoned by friends, relatives, and possessions, Everyman is in the depths of despair. Such elaborate characterization goes far beyond mere sermonizing. By now, you probably see yourself as Everyman. The point at which such transference took place will not be the same for everyone. Compare the point at which you identified completely with Everyman with the point of some of your classmates. Why is there a variance? What is revealed to you by the variance?

EVERYMAN. O, to whom shall I make my moan
For to go with me in that heavy journey?
First Fellowship said he would with me gone;   *465*
His words were very pleasant and gay,
But afterward he left me alone.
Then spake I to my kinsmen, all in despair,
And also they gave me words fair,
They lacked no fair speaking,   *470*
But all forsook me in the ending.
Then went I to my Goods, that I loved best,
In hope to have comfort, but there had I least;
For my Goods sharply did me tell
That he bringeth many into hell.   *475*
Then of myself I was ashamed,
And so I am worthy to be blamed;
Thus may I well myself hate.
Of whom shall I now counsel take?
I think that I shall never speed   *480*
Till that I go to my Good Deeds.
But alas! she is so weak
That she can neither go nor speak.
Yet will I venture on her now.
My Good Deeds, where be you?   *485*

480. **speed,** prosper.   483. **go,** walk.

(GOOD DEEDS *speaks from below.*)

GOOD DEEDS. Here I lie, cold in the ground.
Thy sins hath me sore bound,
That I cannot stir.

EVERYMAN. O Good Deeds, I stand in fear!
I must you pray of counsel,   490
For help now should come right well.

GOOD DEEDS. Everyman, I have understanding
That ye be summoned account to make
Before Messias, of Jerusalem King;
And you do by me, that journey with you will I take.   495

EVERYMAN. Therefore I come to you my moan to make;
I pray you that ye will go with me.

GOOD DEEDS. I would full fain, but I cannot stand, verily.

EVERYMAN. Why, is there anything on you fall?

GOOD DEEDS. Yea, sir, I may thank you of all;   500
If ye had perfectly cheered me,
Your book of count full ready had be.
Look, the books of your works and deeds eke.
Behold how they lie under the feet,
To your soul's heaviness.   505

EVERYMAN. Our Lord Jesus help me!
For one letter here I can not see.

GOOD DEEDS. There is a blind reckoning in time of distress!

EVERYMAN. Good Deeds, I pray you, help me in this need,
Or else I am for ever damned indeed.   510
Therefore help me to make my reckoning
Before the Redeemer of all thing,
That King is, and was, and ever shall.

GOOD DEEDS. Everyman, I am sorry of your fall,
And fain would I help you, and I were able.   515

EVERYMAN. Good Deeds, your counsel I pray you give me.

GOOD DEEDS. That shall I do verily;
Though that on my feet I may not go,
I have a sister that shall with you also,
Called Knowledge, which shall with you abide,   520
To help you to make that dreadful reckoning.

---

491. **come right well,** be welcome.   495. **And . . . me,** and if you will follow my advice.
498. **fain,** willingly.   500. **of all,** for everything.   501. **cheered,** cared for.   503. **eke,** also.
520. **Knowledge,** knowledge of sin.

34. The redemption of Everyman begins with line 476. Explain why.

35. What is the irony of Everyman's going to Good Deeds who, of all his possibilities, is the weakest yet the strongest?

36. What is the symbolic significance of the "cold ground" that binds Good Deeds?

37. Explain Good Deeds' knowing, in advance, of Everyman's revelation, what it is.

38. Why does Good Deeds volunteer to accompany Everyman without his asking?

39. Good Deeds is too weak, however, to accompany Everyman. Is this an excuse or a valid explanation?

(*Enter* KNOWLEDGE.)

KNOWLEDGE. Everyman, I will go with thee, and be thy guide,
In thy most need to go by thy side.

EVERYMAN. In good condition I am now in every thing,
And am wholly content with this good thing;   *525*
Thanked be God my Creator.

GOOD DEEDS. And when he hath brought thee there,
Where thou shalt heal thee of thy smart,
Then go you with your reckoning and your Good Deeds together
For to make you joyful at heart   *530*
Before the blesséd Trinity.

EVERYMAN. My Good Deeds, gramercy!
I am well content, certainly,
With your words sweet.

40. Knowledge could not have come without Everyman's awareness in line 476. Explain why.

KNOWLEDGE. Now go we together lovingly   *535*
To Confession, that cleansing river.

EVERYMAN. For joy I weep; I would we were there!
But I pray you, give me cognition
Where dwelleth that holy man, Confession.

KNOWLEDGE. In the house of salvation,   *540*
We shall find him in that place,
That shall us comfort, by God's grace.

(KNOWLEDGE *leads* EVERYMAN *to* CONFESSION.)

Lo, this is Confession. Kneel down and ask mercy,
For he is in good conceit with God almighty.

528. **smart,** pain.   544. **conceit,** esteem.

EVERYMAN. O glorious fountain, that all uncleanness doth clarify,   *545*
Wash from me the spots of vice unclean,
That on me no sin may be seen.
I come, with Knowledge, for my redemption,
Redempt with hearty and full contrition,
For I am commanded a pilgrimage to take,   *550*
And great accounts before God to make.
Now, I pray you, Shrift, mother of salvation,
Help my Good Deeds for my piteous exclamation.
    CONFESSION. I know your sorrow well, Everyman.
Because with Knowledge ye come to me,   *555*
I will you comfort as well as I can,
And a precious jewel I will give thee,
Called penance, voider of adversity.
Therewith shall your body chastised be
With abstinence and perseverance in God's service.   *560*
Here shall you receive that scourge of me
    (*Gives* EVERYMAN *a scourge.*)
Which is penance strong that ye must endure
To remember thy Savior was scourged for thee
With sharp scourges and suffered it patiently.
So must thou ere thou 'scape that painful pilgrimage.   *565*
Knowledge, keep him in this voyage,
And by that time Good Deeds will be with thee.
But in any wise be sure of mercy,
For your time draweth fast, and ye will saved be;
Ask God mercy, and He will grant truly;   *570*
When with the scourge of penance man doth him bind,
The oil of forgiveness then shall he find.   (*Exit* CONFESSION.)
    EVERYMAN. Thanked be God for his gracious work!
For now I will my penance begin;
This hath rejoiced and lighted my heart,   *575*
Though the knots be painful and hard within.

41. Explain the significance of Confession as symbolized by a river.

42. How can a river be "in the house of salvation"? (Remember, this is symbolism!)

43. Theologically, why would Confession have been powerless to cleanse Everyman had he not been accompanied by Knowledge?

44. Why is scourging necessary, according to Confession?

552. Shrift, Confession.   **565. 'scape,** complete.   **569. fast,** to an end.

45. Everyman seems pleased with scourging and penance. Does this seem strange? Why or why not?

KNOWLEDGE. Everyman, look your penance that ye fulfil,
What pain that ever it to you be,
And Knowledge shall give you counsel at will
How your account ye shall make clearly.   *580*
  EVERYMAN. O eternal God! O heavenly figure!
O way of rightwiseness! O goodly vision!
Which descended down in a virgin pure
Because he would Everyman redeem,
Which Adam forfeited by his disobedience.   *585*
O blesséd Godhead! elect and high divine,
Forgive me my grievous offence;
Here I cry thee mercy in this presence.
O ghostly treasure! O ransomer and redeemer!
Of all the world hope and conductor,   *590*
Mirror of joy, and founder of mercy,
Which illumineth heaven and earth thereby,
Hear my clamorous complaint, though it late be.
Receive my prayers; unworthy in this heavy life.
Though I be a sinner most abominable,   *595*
Yet let my name be written in Moses' table.
O Mary! pray to the Maker of all thing,
Me for to help at my ending,
And save me from the power of my enemy,
For Death assaileth me strongly.   *600*
And, Lady, that I may by means of thy prayer
Of your Son's glory to be partner,
By the means of his passion I it crave.
I beseech you, help my soul to save.
Knowledge, give me the scourge of penance.   *605*
My flesh therewith shall give a quittance.
I will now begin, if God give me grace.

46. Explain the order of prayer in lines 581–607, remembering that the author was a Roman Catholic writing for Roman Catholics. If you are not a Catholic, is the joy lessened? Why or why not? Consider carefully before answering.

---

596. in Moses' table, in the list of saved souls.   **606. quittance,** complete payment.

KNOWLEDGE. Everyman, God give you time and space.
Thus I bequeath you in the hands of our Savior,
Now may you make your reckoning sure.   610
  EVERYMAN. In the name of the Holy Trinity,
My body sore punished shall be. (*Scourges himself.*)
Take this, body, for the sin of the flesh.
Also thou delightest to go gay and fresh,
And in the way of damnation thou did me bring;   615
Therefore suffer now strokes of punishing.
Now of penance I will wade the water clear,
To save me from purgatory, that sharp fire.
  (GOOD DEEDS *rises from below.*)
  GOOD DEEDS. I thank God, now I can walk and go,
And am delivered of my sickness and woe.   620
Therefore with Everyman I will go, and not spare;
His good works I will help him to declare.
  KNOWLEDGE. Now, Everyman, be merry and glad!
Your Good Deeds cometh now, ye may not be sad.
Now is your Good Deeds whole and sound,   625
Going upright upon the ground.
  EVERYMAN. My heart is light, and shall be evermore.
Now will I smite faster than I did before.

47. That the body should be physically scourged and the pain enjoyed
may seem psychologically unsound (or at least unhealthy) to you.
Remembering, however, that we are a nation of high suicide and ulcer
rates, explain the pleasure of such pain in contemporary as well as
fifteenth-century terms. You will find them dissimilar in terminology
only.

48. Why could Good Deeds not leave the cold ground before the
scourging? This should now be easy to answer. What is the "cold
ground"?

  GOOD DEEDS. Everyman, pilgrim, my special friend,
Blesséd be thou without end.   630
For thee is prepared the eternal glory.
Ye have me made whole and sound,
Therefore I will bide by thee in every stound.
  EVERYMAN. Welcome, my Good Deeds; now I hear thy voice,
I weep for very sweetness of love.   635

633. **stound,** moment of trial.

KNOWLEDGE. Be no more sad, but ever rejoice;
God seeth thy living in his throne above.
Put on this garment to thy behoof,
　(*Handing* EVERYMAN *a cloak.*)
Which is wet with your tears,
Or else before God you may it miss,　　　　　　　　640
When you to your journey's end come shall.
　　EVERYMAN. Gentle Knowledge, what do ye it call?
　　KNOWLEDGE. It is the garment of sorrow;
From pain it will you borrow;
Contrition it is　　　　　　　　　　　　　　　645
That getteth forgiveness;
It pleaseth God passing well.

49. Is there a seeming contradiction in "sorrow" shielding Everyman from "pain"? Distinguish between sorrow and pain, remembering *physical* pain (scourging) is past. "Pain" assumes a nonphysical meaning here.

　　GOOD DEEDS. Everyman, will you wear it for your heal?
　　(EVERYMAN *puts on the cloak.*)
　　EVERYMAN. Now blesséd be Jesu, Mary's Son,
For now have I on true contrition.　　　　　　　650
And let us go now without tarrying;
Good Deeds, have we clear our reckoning?
　　GOOD DEEDS. Yea, indeed I have it here.
　　EVERYMAN. Then I trust we need not fear.
Now, friends, let us not part in twain.　　　　　655
　　KNOWLEDGE. Nay, Everyman, that will we not, certain.
　　GOOD DEEDS. Yet must thou lead with thee
Three persons of great might.
　　EVERYMAN. Who should they be?
　　GOOD DEEDS. Discretion and Strength they hight,　　660
And thy Beauty may not abide behind.
　　KNOWLEDGE. Also ye must call to mind
Your Five Wits as for your counselors.
　　GOOD DEEDS. You must have them ready at all hours.
　　EVERYMAN. How shall I get them hither?　　　　665
　　KNOWLEDGE. You must call them all together,
And they will hear you incontinent.

---

638. behoof, benefit.　　644. borrow, ransom.　　660. hight, are called.　　663. Wits, senses.
667. incontinent, immediately.

EVERYMAN. My friends, come hither and be present,
Discretion, Strength, my Five Wits, and Beauty.
(*Enter* DISCRETION, STRENGTH, FIVE WITS, *and* BEAUTY.)

50. Why should Discretion, Strength, and Beauty stand with Everyman before his God?
51. Why does he need his Five Wits (or Senses) at that time?
52. Look at the stage direction following line 669. Read it before continuing with this question. STOP. Read it! All right, how did you visualize the eight personifications? Did you have an emotional visualization that refused concreteness? Or did you see clearly describable characters? Your response may surprise you. Poetic truth explains your response while intellectual truth seems as absent as Goods.

BEAUTY. Here at your will we be all ready.   *670*
What will ye that we should do?
GOOD DEEDS. That ye would with Everyman go,
And help him in his pilgrimage.
Advise you, will ye with him or not in that voyage?
STRENGTH. We will bring him all thither,   *675*
To his help and comfort, ye may believe me.
DISCRETION. So will we go with him all together.
EVERYMAN. Almighty God, lovéd may thou be!
I give thee laud that I have hither brought
Strength, Discretion, Beauty, and Five Wits. Lack I naught.   *680*
And my Good Deeds, with Knowledge clear,
All be in company at my will here.
I desire no more to my business.
STRENGTH. And I, Strength, will by you stand in distress,
Though thou would in battle fight on the ground.   *685*
FIVE WITS. And though it were through the world round,
We will not depart for sweet nor sour.
BEAUTY. No more will I, unto death's hour,
Whatsoever thereof befall.
DISCRETION. Everyman, advise you first of all,   *690*
Go with a good advisement and deliberation.
We all give you virtuous monition
That all shall be well.
EVERYMAN. My friends, hearken what I will tell:
I pray God reward you in his heavenly sphere.   *695*

679. laud, praise.   692. monition, admonition.

Now hearken, all that be here,
For I will make my testament
Here before you all present:
In alms half my goods I will give with my hands twain
In the way of charity, with good intent,   700
And the other half still shall remain,
I it bequeath to be returned there it ought to be.
This I do in despite of the fiend of hell,
To go quite out of his peril
Ever after and this day.   705
   KNOWLEDGE. Everyman, hearken what I say;
Go to Priesthood, I you advise,
And receive of him in any wise
The holy sacrament and ointment together;
Then shortly see ye turn again hither;   710
We will all abide you here.

53. Everyman has two parcels of goods to dispose of. The first he
leaves "in the way of charity" (the Church). How have you been prepared for this through careful foreshadowing? If you are unsure, reread
line 78 and lines 431–434. The second parcel shall be returned (to the
Church) when it ought to be. What is the second parcel? Remember,
Everyman has given all his material possessions in the first bequest. Would
the second bequest be accepted without the first? This dramatist is clever
indeed.

54. How do the two bequests free Everyman from Satan's power?

55. Everyman could not go for Communion and Extreme Unction
before this time. Why not?

   FIVE WITS. Yea, Everyman, hie you that ye ready were.
There is no emperor, king, duke, nor baron,
That of God hath commission
As hath the least priest in the world being;   715
For of the blessèd sacraments pure and benign
He beareth the keys, and thereof hath the cure
For man's redemption—it is ever sure—
Which God for our soul's medicine
Gave us out of his heart with great pain,   720
Here in this transitory life, for thee and me.

702. **there,** when.   704. **peril,** perilous power.   709. **holy sacrament and ointment,** Communion and Extreme Unction.   712. **hie,** hasten.

The blesséd sacraments seven there be:
Baptism, confirmation, with priesthood good,
And the sacrament of God's precious flesh and blood,
Marriage, the holy extreme unction, and penance.   *725*
These seven be good to have in remembrance,
Gracious sacraments of high divinity.
    EVERYMAN. Fain would I receive that holy body
And meekly to my ghostly father I will go.
    FIVE WITS. Everyman, that is the best that ye can do.   *730*
God will you to salvation bring,
For priesthood exceedeth all other thing;
To us Holy Scripture they do teach,
And converteth man from sin, heaven to reach;
God hath to them more power given,   *735*
Than to any angel that is in heaven.
With five words he may consecrate
God's body in flesh and blood to make,
And handleth his Maker between his hands.
The priest bindeth and unbindeth all bands,   *740*
Both in earth and in heaven.
Thou, ministers all the sacraments seven,
Though we kissed thy feet, thou wert worthy;
Thou art the surgeon that cureth sin deadly:
No remedy we find under God   *745*
But all only priesthood.
Everyman, God gave priests that dignity,
And setteth them in his stead among us to be;
Thus be they above angels, in degree.   (*Exit* EVERYMAN.)

56. Lines 712–749 constitute sermon and preachment. It is for these lines the unknown author penned the allegory; yet he was too conscious a craftsman not to make the sermon serve a dramatic function. These lines are comparable to that point in *Oedipus* and *Macbeth* wherein the kings seem about to attain their goals, the falling action. You can expect further reversals for Everyman if you are following the drama carefully.

    KNOWLEDGE. If priests be good, it is so, surely.   *750*
But when Jesus hanged on the cross with great smart,
There he gave out of his blesséd heart

---

737. **five words**, the five words being *Hoc est enim corpus meum.*   740. **bands**, agreements.
748. **stead**, place.

The same sacrament in great torment.
He sold them not to us, that Lord omnipotent.
Therefore Saint Peter the Apostle doth say   755
That Jesus' curse hath all they
Which God their Savior do buy or sell,
Or they for any money do take or tell.
Sinful priests giveth the sinners example bad;
Their children sitteth by other men's fires, I have heard;   760
And some haunteth women's company
With unclean life, as lusts of lechery.
These be with sin made blind.
    FIVE WITS. I trust to God no such may we find.
Therefore let us priesthood honor,   765
And follow their doctrine for our souls' succour.
We be their sheep, and they shepherds be
By whom we all be kept in surety.
Peace! for yonder I see Everyman come,
Which hath made true satisfaction.   770
    GOOD DEEDS. Methinketh it is he indeed.

57. The worldly or external aspects of the world (friends, family, possessions) deserted Everyman at the onset of death. Accepting the inevitable, he made his peace with the Church and has gone to assign his property and body to that institution. He momentarily takes leave of Good Deeds, Strength, Beauty, Knowledge, Discretion, and Five Wits. Symbolically, are they not the internal man, the Self? At what point in his physical death process is Everyman when Knowledge questions the total goodness of the princes of the Church and their preoccupation with the things of the world? Why does Five Wits place trust in God and priests?

58. Does the doubt of Knowledge serve a dramatic function?

59. Returning from receiving Extreme Unction, Everyman is at what point in his death process?

(*Re-enter* EVERYMAN.)
    EVERYMAN. Now Jesu be your alder speed.
I have received the sacrament for my redemption,
And then mine extreme unction.
Blesséd be all they that counseled me to take it!   775
And now, friends, let us go without longer respite.

758. tell, count.   772. your alder speed, everyone's help.

I thank God that ye have tarried so long.
Now set each of you on this rood your hand,
And shortly follow me.
I go before, there I would be. God be our guide.   *780*
   STRENGTH. Everyman, we will not from you go,
Till ye have done this voyage long.
   DISCRETION. I, Discretion, will bide by you also.
   KNOWLEDGE. And though this pilgrimage be never so strong,
I will never part you fro.   *785*
Everyman, I will be as sure by thee
As ever I did by Judas Maccabee.
   (*They go to a grave.*)
   EVERYMAN. Alas! I am so faint I may not stand,
My limbs under me do fold.
Friends, let us not turn again to this land,   *790*
Not for all the world's gold;
For into this cave must I creep
And turn to earth, and there to sleep.

60. Free of worldly externals, Everyman assumes a calm attitude of acceptance, volunteering to lead the way. As a character, how great has his character change been? Has it been logical?

61. Why do Strength, Discretion, and Knowledge reaffirm their constancy? Why do Beauty and Five Wits not?

62. At what point in dying is Everyman in lines 788–794?

   BEAUTY. What, into this grave? Alas!
   EVERYMAN. Yea, there shall you consume, more and less.   *795*
   BEAUTY. And what, should I smother here?
   EVERYMAN. Yea, by my faith, and never more appear.
In this world live no more we shall,
But in heaven before the highest Lord of all.
   BEAUTY. I cross out all this; adieu, by Saint John!   *800*
I take my cap in my lap and am gone.
   EVERYMAN. What, Beauty, whither will ye?
   BEAUTY. Peace! I am deaf. I look not behind me,
Not and thou would give me all the gold in thy chest.   (*Exit* BEAUTY.)

63. What is indicated by Everyman's counseling Beauty in this dread hour?

---

778. rood, cross.   795. more and less, utterly.   800. all this, all my former promises.   801. I take . . . lap, take off my cap and bow.

64. Beauty deserts Everyman at the lip of the grave. Explain the symbolic meaning and/or reason for this.

65. Which of the *external* aspects of Everyman deserted him first in the same fashion that Beauty, first of the internal aspects, does? Both invoke Saint John. What ironic parallel is suggested?

EVERYMAN. Alas, whereto may I trust?   *805*
Beauty goeth fast away from me;
She promised with me to live and die.
   STRENGTH. Everyman, I will thee also forsake and deny.
Thy game liketh me not at all.
   EVERYMAN. Why, then ye will forsake me all?   *810*
Sweet Strength, tarry a little space.
   STRENGTH. Nay, sir, by the rood of grace,
I will hie me from thee fast,
Though thou weep till thy heart to-brast.
   EVERYMAN. Ye would ever bide by me, ye said.   *815*
   STRENGTH. Yea, I have you far enough conveyed.
Ye be old enough, I understand,
Your pilgrimage to take on hand.
I repent me that I hither came.
   EVERYMAN. Strength, you to displease I am to blame;   *820*
Yet promise is debt, this ye well wot.
   STRENGTH. In faith, I care not!
Thou art but a fool to complain.
You spend your speech and waste your brain.   *824*
Go, thrust thee into the ground.   (*Exit* STRENGTH.)

66. With as flimsy an excuse as Cousin's "I have the cramp in my toe," Strength deserts saying "Thy game liketh me not at all." What ironic parallel is here suggested?

67. Explain Strength's statement: "Ye be old enough." What ambiguities are involved in the words? There are more than one.

   EVERYMAN. I had weened surer I should you have found.
He that trusteth in his Strength
She him deceiveth at the length.
Both Strength and Beauty forsaketh me,
Yet they promised me fair and lovingly.   *830*
   DISCRETION. Everyman, I will after Strength be gone;
As for me I will leave you alone.

814. to-brast, break.

EVERYMAN. Why, Discretion, will ye forsake me?

DISCRETION. Yea, in faith, I will go from thee;
For when Strength goeth before   *835*
I follow after evermore.

EVERYMAN. Yet, I pray thee, for the love of the Trinity,
Look in my grave once piteously.

DISCRETION. Nay, so nigh will I not come.   *839*
Farewell, every one!   (*Exit* DISCRETION.)

68. Discretion scarcely outlasts Strength. What is the implication?
Does his desertion parallel that of Goods? Why or why not?

EVERYMAN. O all thing faileth, save God alone,
Beauty, Strength, and Discretion;
For when Death bloweth his blast,
They all run from me full fast.

FIVE WITS. Everyman, my leave now of thee I take;   *845*
I will follow the other, for here I thee forsake.

EVERYMAN. Alas! then may I wail and weep,
For I took you for my best friend.

FIVE WITS. I will no longer thee keep;   *849*
Now farewell, and there an end.   (*Exit* FIVE WITS.)

69. Five Wits deserts Everyman at what point in his dying? Why is
there no external parallel to Five Wits?

EVERYMAN. O Jesu, help! All hath forsaken me!

GOOD DEEDS. Nay, Everyman; I will bide with thee,
I will not forsake thee indeed;
Thou shalt find me a good friend at need.

EVERYMAN. Gramercy, Good Deeds! Now may I true friends see.   *855*
They have forsaken me, every one;
I loved them better than my Good Deeds alone.
Knowledge, will ye forsake me also?

KNOWLEDGE. Yea, Everyman, when ye to death shall go;
But not yet, for no manner of danger.   *860*

EVERYMAN. Gramercy, Knowledge, with all my heart.

KNOWLEDGE. Nay, yet I will not from hence depart
Till I see where ye shall be come.

EVERYMAN. Methink, alas, that I must be gone
To make my reckoning and my debts pay,   *865*
For I see my time is nigh spent away.

Take example, all ye that this do hear or see,
How they that I loved best do forsake me,
Except my Good Deeds that bideth truly.
    GOOD DEEDS. All earthly things is but vanity.   *870*
Beauty, Strength, and Discretion do man forsake,
Foolish friends and kinsmen, that fair spake,
All fleeth save Good Deeds, and that am I.

70. Is there a parallel between Shakespeare's line "The evil that men do lives after them,/The good is oft interred with their bones" (*Julius Caesar,* III:ii:79) and Good Deeds' statement in lines 870–873? Is the parallel complete?

    EVERYMAN. Have mercy on me, God most mighty;
And stand by me, thou Mother and Maid, holy Mary!   *875*
    GOOD DEEDS. Fear not, I will speak for thee.
    EVERYMAN. Here I cry God mercy!
    GOOD DEEDS. Short our end, and 'minish our pain.
Let us go and never come again.
    EVERYMAN. Into thy hands, Lord, my soul I commend.   *880*
Receive it, Lord, that it be not lost.
As thou me boughtest, so me defend,
And save me from the fiend's boast,
That I may appear with that blesséd host
That shall be saved at the day of doom.   *885*
In manus tuas—of might's most
For ever—*commendo spiritum meum.*
                (EVERYMAN *and* GOOD DEEDS *go into the grave.*)
    KNOWLEDGE. Now hath he suffered that we all shall endure;
The Good Deeds shall make all sure.
Now hath he made ending.   *890*
Methinketh that I hear angels sing
And make great joy and melody
Where Everyman's soul received shall be.
    ANGEL. Come, excellent elect spouse to Jesu!
Here above thou shalt go   *895*
Because of thy singular virtue.
Now the soul is taken the body fro,
Thy reckoning is crystal clear.

878. Short . . . pain, shorten our deaths and diminish our pain.   886. *In manus tuas,* into Thy hands.   887. *commendo spiritum meum,* I commend my spirit.

Now shalt thou into the heavenly sphere,
Unto the which all ye shall come   900
That liveth well before the day of doom.
(*Exit* KNOWLEDGE. *Enter* DOCTOR.)

71. Knowledge is steadfast to what point in Everyman's earthly existence? Why does Knowledge not accompany him into the grave?
72. Though Knowledge did not accompany Everyman into the grave, he did not desert him. Explain the seeming paradox.
73. At what point in Everyman's process of dying does the Angel speak, declaring the salvation of Everyman?

DOCTOR. This moral men may have in mind;
Ye hearers, take it of worth, old and young,
And forsake Pride, for he deceiveth you in the end,
And remember Beauty, Five Wits, Strength, and Discretion,   905
They all at the last do Everyman forsake,
Save his Good Deeds there doth he take.
But beware, and they be small
Before God he hath no help at all.
None excuse may be there for Everyman.   910
Alas, how shall he do then?
For, after death, amends may no man make,
For then mercy and pity doth him forsake.
If his reckoning be not clear when he doth come,
God will say, "*Ite, maledicti, in ignem aeternum.*"   915
And he that hath his account whole and sound,
High in heaven he shall be crowned.
Unto which place God bring us all thither,
That we may live body and soul together.
Thereto help the Trinity!   920
Amen, say ye, for saint charity.

THUS ENDETH THIS MORAL PLAY OF EVERYMAN.

74. Who or what is "saint charity"? Why are the words not capitalized? What does the Doctor (teacher) mean by his command "Thereto help the Trinity"? Is inversion employed in the line? If so, would not the verb be *helps* since the Trinity is a three-personed God rather than three persons? Compare the word *charity* with its other uses in the play, remembering that this play is a sermon.

902. DOCTOR, teacher.   915. *"Ite, . . . aeternum,"* "Hence, accursed one, into eternal fire."

Suggested Assignments. 1. *Everyman* is a sermon, therefore a kind of propaganda developed to a single end which may be at odds with its apparent purpose. It is also a poetic drama of apparent elaborate artistry. Decide which aspect (sermon or drama) was primary in the unknown author's heart as he wrote the allegory. In a brief paper, defend your answer with intellectual rather than emotional arguments.

2. *Everyman* is a tragedy in that the subject is of high seriousness and the protagonist dies. It is not a tragedy in that he dies without being defeated. Is it then a comedy because it ends happily? (The promise of salvation for the Christian soul is the epitome of happiness.) Or is *Everyman* both a tragedy and a comedy (with Cousin and Strength supplying humorous lines), therefore a tragicomedy? In a carefully considered paper, defend *your* classification of this poetic drama.

3. *Everyman* and *Macbeth* are comparable in many ways. Choose one way that occurs to you and develop it in a paper of whatever length you need.

Folk Drama

There are relatively few dramatic subjects in man's amazingly large world. Love, fear, hate, communication with Self and others, ambition, religion—and the list is pretty well finished. Limited though it may be, however, it is incapable of being exhausted. Centuries of writers have attacked it from every conceivable angle, yet it continues to provide the material to keep the world's presses rolling at a rate that sets new records daily. Not all of the books are literary, of course. Science and technology create the necessity for new books steadily, for, as William Lyon Phelps once pointed out, science books have to be revised every few years to stay abreast of new discoveries while the truths expressed in poetry remain the same centuries later. So the old books come out in new editions and new poetic treatments of old poetic truths are written by new writers in varying degrees of dissatisfaction with the communications of old authors. Each age needs new assessments of old truths just as much as it needs the old assessments, loved because they are familiar and because they, at least, suggest some constancy in an inconstant world.

In poetic drama, the search for constancy frequently turns back to *the folk*—those less sophisticated, more primitive people who have either resisted change (the Quakers, Mennonites, and the Amish, for instance) or who have been so geographically cut off from the highroads of progress that they have escaped the blessings of dehumanizing science. There are many reasons that modern dramatists look to the folk for illuminative material. Realistically, the folk reflect their environments in ways more readily explorable because they are less complex than those of city dwellers. Bounded by tradition and relatively static conditions, the folk reflect life more as a group than as individuals. Collective peculiarities or idiosyncracies emerge, and the person who violates accepted patterns is so starkly emphasized that he becomes a ready-made, clinical specimen for the writer.

In this limited area, then, the folk seem interestingly unique, quaint, and different. Actually, however, they are probably more representative of man than their urban counterparts, for they live and respond in a more natural habitat than the one so changed by technology. Their responses are more basic, less studied, and more honest because they have not been conditioned by forces outside the human condition. Clinically interesting they are, but they are even more humanly interesting. The playwright and the audience look at them with nostalgia and with a sense of loss. A touch of envy for the simple life may attend such an examination, but technology has worked its insidious wonder and the reader knows that he will not trade his complex and agonized existence for the primitive pleasures of the folk. Still, that less artificial life calls and he responds by vicariously shedding the protective layers of civilization as he identifies with the created characters of the folk drama. When the final speech is done and the reader returns to his convenient world, he has had a kind of spiritual refurbishing, a vacation from the demands imposed by machines and densely populated areas. Briefly, he has recalled something of his own past—even if he is Irish and the folk drama was Jewish or he is Jewish and the folk drama was Spanish.

An ethnic patina always overlays the folk drama, for it attempts to reproduce the essential spirit, the feel, the flavor of a group whose customs and conduct are pronounced enough to create a cultural oasis bounded on all sides by the vast desert of humanity. Contemporary American literature seems to be focusing on the Jew of the self-imposed ghettos of the land, but that movement is too young to be assessed as yet. The last (and greatest) folk drama movement occurred as an adjunct to the Irish national movement at the turn of this century. Centering in the Abbey Theatre (Dublin, 1904), Irish drama was a conscious and deliberate effort to create a national theater by exploring the culture of the fabled green island—not for world consideration but for Ireland's consumption, to awaken the slumbering pride of its Celtic descendants.

No more dramatic location could have been chosen. The vivid colors, the barren coasts, the earth-bound folk with their soaring speech—a poetic idiom rich in tradition, lyrical in structure, and strong in linguistic pride—all conspired to create a brilliant interlude in the long history of drama rivaled only by the American Negro folk drama that included

Marc Connelly's *The Green Pastures,* Dorothy and DuBose Heyward's *Porgy,* and Paul Green's *In Abraham's Bosom.*

Brilliant Irish plays include Lennox Robinson's *The White Headed Boy* and Sean O'Casey's *Juno and the Paycock,* but the youthful genius John Millington Synge was to add the three-act comedy *Playboy of the Western World* and the undisputed masterpiece of poetic folk drama, the one-act *Riders to the Sea.*

The value of poetic language is nowhere more apparent than in this prose drama that is a poem, this prose poem that is a drama. So blended are the two forms you will probably find yourself reading the play as both. That probability alone justifies the poetic drama as a form—if justification is needed—but one further justification seems desirable before you read *Riders to the Sea.*

Christopher Fry is one of the few playwrights to approach the brilliance of Elizabethan poetic comedy. If the realism of the contemporary stage had not forced him to mingle the good and bad, the tragic and the comic so that love triumphs—but barely—his *The Lady's Not for Burning* would have achieved Elizabethan poetic excellence. At any rate, he is a remarkable poetic dramatist and he explains the value of poetry well in his essay

Why Verse?

There are many people to whom verse in the theatre is an irritating, or boring, or distracting, or pretentious flight of fashion; and in certain moods I can pish and tush with the best of them. This point is not held so strongly about literature in general. It isn't often said that there should be no such thing as poetry at all. When Wordsworth writes:

Felt in the blood, and felt along the heart

we should think twice, perhaps, before we asked him why he didn't write the passage in prose. "Felt in the blood, and felt along the heart" is a good example, by the way, of the speed and economy with which poetry can express what would take prose far longer.

What reason is there for limiting the theatre to one form of communication? It is even believed that the prose play and the verse play are in opposition, or that the one precludes the other; there appears to be a kind of color bar in the matter. Such rivalry is nonsense. Indeed, prose and verse existing side by side counter each other's dangers. If they pass altogether out of each other's reach they cease to be themselves, becoming on the one hand journalese, official cant, or any other string of sentences; and on the other a vagueness, an abstraction, a preciousness. This interplay of difference, one touching the hand of the other as it separates, like men and women dancing the Grand Chain, is what keeps each in its own state of grace.

One explanation of our impatience with a verse play is that the spring of theatre is action, and any insistence upon words is felt to hang like heavy clothes on the body of an athlete. When we go to the theatre we go to be interested by a story of lives living out their conflicts in a concentration of time. We do not go to hear them discuss the matter; we go to see and hear them live it.

But we know that words and actions are not unrelated. One illuminates the other; and the full significance of action can be explored only by words. If we compare the murder of Maria Marten in the Red Barn, with the murder of Duncan in Macbeth's castle, we see that in each the physical action is roughly the same, but the significance of the action is entirely different. The one is merely done, the other is experience, and the experience is in the words. What is more, the experience is the true nature of the action. The experience ultimately is the action. The action is not the dagger in Duncan's breast, or the blood on Macbeth's hand, but rather the limitless experience of the words arising out of them: the experience of:

> Macbeth does murder sleep!

of:

> . . . this my hand will rather
> The multitudinous seas incarnadine,
> Making the green one red.

The three words "this my hand," in the context, so deepen our thoughts about the human hand and what it performs, that the action is not only true of this one human, and this one deed; it becomes also an elemental action, done in the beginning of the fallen world. In sounds alone, "multitudinous," which heaves like a wilderness of molten lava, set against the three monosyllables "this my hand," gives us, or should give us, an experience of being. We begin to feel there is not one action, but two, not two, but twenty in the course of a speech.

You may be prepared to agree with me that words give us a larger, or deeper, experience of action, but still you may say, "Why verse? Why this formality of syllables? Why this unnatural division of sentences into lines?"

I suggest we forget the questions, and go on as though verse plays, like wasps, are apparently with us for some reason which they don't reveal. I only ask you to allow me to suppose an organic discipline, pattern, or proportion in the universe, evident in all that we see, which is a government uniting the greatest with the least, form with behavior, natural event with historic event, which stamps its mark through us and through our perceptions, as the name of Brighton is marked through a stick of rock candy. When Milton says: "Elephants endors'd with towers," or when Wordsworth says: "A noticeable man with large gray eyes," they are not being so true to that organic discipline as, for instance, Chaucer, when he says:

> Now with his love, now in the colde grave
> Allone, withouten any companye.

I ask you to allow me to suppose a shaping but undogmatical presence "felt in the blood, and felt along the heart," which is of a kind with the law of gravity, and the moral law, and the law which gives us two legs and not six.

From the way I am going on you would think I was talking about the Eleusinian mysteries, not about a theatre in which you propose to spend an entertaining evening. It is the fault of the question "Why verse?" I should really write a play which would be so good that the question would never arise, a play which would please not some of the people some of the time, but all of the people all of the time, which would be both the immediate appearance of things and the eternal nature of things, combined with felicity.

I wish I could promise any such thing. Every few generations have to shape afresh the language which will express both these things together; and some of us find, like the donkey, that communication with our fellow being is something not easily achieved. We may think we have avoided all misconception, and then overhear a member of the audience making his comment, as after a performance of *The Dark Is Light Enough* (a play about the Austro-Hungarian war, taking place near Vienna) when a gentleman said with charitable resignation, "I never can understand these Russian plays."

It is no good asking poetry to tell us what it says; it simply *is* what it says. In the theatre it must have a direct surface meaning, an immediate impact of sense, but half its work should be going on below that meaning, drawing the ear, consciously or unconsciously, into a certain experience of being.

This has been an age of signposts, of ideologies, of patent cures, of battle cries; we must take up our positions, draw clear lines between this or that, label, analyze, dissect; we must live the letter, for the letter is the law. But we have been looking at the possibility that poetry has another, deeper law. The truth of poetry deepens under your eye. It is never absolute. There is no moment when we can trumpet it abroad as finally understood.

In a play I wrote called *A Sleep of Prisoners*, Cain and Abel throw dice together, and Abel prays as he shakes the dice:

> Deal me high, deal me low.
> Make my deeds
> My nameless needs.
> I know I do not know.

In our anxiety to be in the know we defend our scraps of knowledge and decision so passionately that over the centuries we have burned, tortured, imprisoned, shot, and blown up those who contradicted or doubted us. But the spirit of our scrap of knowledge was in the contradiction and doubt, as much as in the belief. What we were torturing and blowing up was the spirit of truth.

Poetry in the theatre is the action of listening. It is an unrolling exploration, following your nose, or it would be better to say following your ear, for sound itself, pure sound, has logic, as we know in music, and what does that logic accord to if not the universal discipline felt along the heart? What part this logic plays in our life here on the earth is beyond calculation. If it wakens harmony, modulation, and the resolving discord in us, we are nearer to our proper natures.

> The man that hath no music in himself,
> Nor is not moved with concord of sweet sounds,
> Is fit for treasons, stratagems and spoils;
> The motions of his spirit are dull as night,
> And his affections dark as Erebus:
> Let no such man be trusted.
> Mark the music.

Mark the music. Even in the broad give-and-take of the theatre our ears should be able to accept the interplay of the vowel sounds of a line of poetry, and know them as indications of the universal discipline, and consider the comma in the line with almost as much purpose as the comma on the underwing of the butterfly. But this precision has to exist within the broad and tough character of the theatre; it has to hold its own against distractions of many kinds: against coughs in the auditorium, failings in the author, even—on rare occasions—against irregularities of the actor's memory; just as in life our awareness of our larger natures has to hold its own against a host of distractions within and without.

So the general lines of the play, the shape of the story, the disposition of the characters, should point and implicate by their actions and their wider uses the texture of the poetry. The large pattern of the action should have a meaning in itself, above and beyond the story; the kind of meaning which gives everlasting truth to myths and legends, and makes the fairy story into a sober fact; a meaning not so conscious as a parable or so contrived as an allegory, but as it were tracing a figure which the poetry can naturally and inevitably fill.

This is all very well, you may now say, this fine theory; but we have to put up with verse plays as they are, not as ideally they should be; it seems to us that a good deal of these plays could be written at least as well, and more honestly, in prose. Why, for instance, should you present to us as verse a speech such as this:

> I sometimes think
> His critical judgement is so exquisite
> It leaves us nothing to admire except his opinion.
> He should take into account
> The creative value of the fault.

I have no answer to satisfy you if you believe that human nature, or human personality, is divided into two parts, of whatever proportion, the prosaic and the poetic. I think we live always with a foot in each camp, or rather, that there is no moment when we can safely say that we belong entirely to one or the other. There is no moment when we can certainly say that even our apparently most insignificant actions have not a significance greatly beyond ourselves.

It is this tension between two meanings which verse conveys, favoring sometimes one, sometimes the other. The prosaic or colloquial can be rhythmically just sufficiently charged to resolve into the implication of verse at a moment's notice, even halfway through a sentence, and back again, without disturbing the unity of the speech, in the way that the spirit and the flesh work in ourselves without noticeably sawing us in half. The writer's responsibility is to know when he can safely break free of this, and relax for contrast into the rhythms of prose.

In *The Dark Is Light Enough* there comes a moment when the situation reduces everyone to silence; when there seems no way of the scene going on without bringing the curtain down. And then the Countess begins to speak. I will tell you what she says, not because the verse does what I want it to do, but it says something to our purpose.

> How shall we manage, with time at a standstill?
> We can't go back to where nothing has been said;
> And no heart is served, caught in a moment
> Which has frozen. Since no words will set us free—
> Not at least now, until we can persuade
> Our thoughts to move—
> Music would unground us best,
> As a tide in the dark comes to boats at anchor
> And they begin to dance. My father told me
> How he went late one night, a night
> Of some Hungarian anxiety,
> To the Golden Bull at Buda, and there he found
> The President of your House of Deputies
> Alone and dancing in his shirtsleeves
> To the music of the band, himself
> Put far away, bewitched completely
> By the dance's custom; and so it went on,
> While my father drank and talked with friends,
> Three or four hours without a pause:
> The weighty man of seventy, whose whole
> Recognition of the world about him
> During those hours, was when occasionally
> He turned his eyes to the gipsy leader
> And the music changed, out of a comprehension
> As wordless as the music.
> It was dancing that came up out of the earth
> To take the old man's part against anxiety.

A comprehension as wordless as the music. It is this comprehension which poetry tries to speak, this revelation of discipline that comes up out of the earth, or is felt along the heart; it is this which verse has to offer. ☐

"Poetry in the theater is," indeed, "the action of listening." *Riders to the Sea* illustrates the point remarkably well. The plot is so slight it seems trivial when stated in prose. Maurya is an old Irish woman who has waged a long struggle with the uncompromising sea. It has been victorious, claiming her father-in-law, her husband, and four of her six sons. The play covers the last day of the unfair competition, a day in which her fifth son is identified as a drowning victim and her sixth is also lost. It is Maurya's tragedy. Yet Maurya is never a fully-developed character. The play is too brief, the language too poetically essential to allow such development. Maurya remains a type, a representative of the Irish peasant woman in conflict with indifferent, awesome natural forces. But therein lies the brilliance of the play, a brilliance that lifts it to the front rank of great tragedy—for Maurya is not just a character in a poetic drama. She is a towering symbol in her struggle, her defeat, and her acceptance of defeat. In her final speech, Maurya becomes all women who would be mothers, all mothers who would be women, and her tragedy is the tragedy of the race for it includes the death of her men.

Such a short play to achieve so much! In prose, it would, of necessity, be much longer and it would, almost assuredly, lose its tragic force and become sentimental drama if not outright melodrama. The tightly-knit poetic lines are not confined to the conveyance of a single idea or emotion, however, but are free to define reality—poetic reality—by lifting language from the literal level and permitting it to function symbolically, metaphorically, and literally all at the same time.

Every word of the play, every detail of each scene, every character, and every action is woven into the taut emotional frame of poetry so that your intellect reads the words but your emotions respond simultaneously, creating a complex admixture of truth and poetic truth that is more apt to motivate you in the future than allow you to explain it in the present. To test your complete understanding of *Riders to the Sea,* it would be necessary to wait twenty-five or thirty years. Then, having experienced the scientific realities that are the counterparts of the poetic truths of the play, you could possibly state the meaning of the play. Denied such leisurely activity, however, it were well we got on with the play itself.

Seeking material, inspiration, background—call it what you will—John Millington Synge, at the suggestion of William Butler Yeats, journeyed in 1898 to "The Last Fortress of the Celt": the Aran Islands of Inishmaan and Inisheer, lying off the west coast of Ireland, about a hundred miles south of Donegal, separated by Gregory Sound. So barren that upthrust boulders or a bush serve as landmarks, the islands support life grudgingly. Seaweed (kelp) is gathered by the islanders, piled in ricks (mounds) until it has dried out enough to burn. The ashes are hardened into blocks and sold for their iodine content. Animals (especially cattle and horses) are bred and raised to be sold in Connemara, the mountainous district due north of Aran, where the horses are grazed from June through August or September (the islands being too barren to support grass for the animals) and sold or shown in competition at the Galway Fair.

Life is hard in Aran, money is scarce, and everything needed by the islanders (lumber, cloth, manufactured goods such as knives, and even the dried peat, called turf, used as fuel for heat and cooking) must be imported from Connemara. Nor is it easy to bring goods into or take livestock off of the islands. Cruel surf, harsh coasts, treacherous shallows, and dangerous currents force sea-going vessels to anchor offshore for loading and unloading trade goods which are transported to and from the shore in *curaghs,* fragile but agile boats made of tarred canvas over lath frames. Curaghs will not support such cargo as livestock, however, so horses and cattle must be ridden into the sea and towed behind the light boats to the larger vessels. It is a dangerous business, for animals panic in the treacherous waters, crush the fragile boats, and send men to certain death in the churning sea.

But it is the way of life in these islands where a strong people, geographically isolated, have retained much of their Celtic heritage in language, vigor, and determination. The indestructible spirit of man, the refusal to desert his land and flee to kinder shores, the determination to fight to whatever death awaits him rather than bow before expediency—these human strengths are embodied in the Aran Islanders Synge lived among. Later, in quiet Wicklow, he reflected on his observations, selected his materials, and arranged them into *Riders to the Sea,* which was published in 1903.

Living among the folk, he had learned to understand their dark superstitions. If a star seemed to touch the moon, bad fortune would surely come. Parting without invoking the blessing of God would grant the Devil leave to do his ugly work. Devout Catholics, the islanders knew the priests were the representatives of God. But the Church was a spiritual institution a little too intellectual for the priests to ward off evil effectively, for they were out of touch with the harsh realities of earth and sea—those elements that, possessed of their own truths, operated by natural laws far removed from God's moral considerations.

Listening through chinks in the floor of the inn where he stayed, talking to the people and remembering their words and phrases, Synge stored up the experiences he could later acknowledge thus: "In countries where the imagination of the people, and the language they use, is rich and living, it is possible for a writer to be rich and copious in his words, and at the same time to give the reality, which is the root of all poetry, in a comprehensive and natural form." The five years of observing and listening were well-spent years, for out of them came

RIDERS TO THE SEA

by John Millington Synge

CHARACTERS

MAURYA, *an old woman*
BARTLEY, *her son*
CATHLEEN, *her daughter*
NORA, *a younger daughter*
MEN AND WOMEN

SCENE—*An Island off the West of Ireland. Cottage kitchen, with nets, oil-skins, spinning wheel, some new boards standing by the wall, etc.* CATHLEEN, *a girl of about twenty, finishes kneading cake, and puts it down in the pot-oven by the fire; then wipes her hands, and begins to spin at the wheel.* NORA, *a young girl, puts her head in at the door.*

1. Your visualization of the scene probably comes from movies, television, and so on—which is fine. Do not be hasty, however, and visualize a *general* scene. Where are the nets hanging or lying? What color are the oil-skins? What do Cathleen's hands look like as she finishes kneading the bread (*cake*) she will bake in the pot-oven by the fire? What does the fireplace look like? Is it in the wall or flush with the floor? What is the sound of the spinning wheel, if it makes a sound? Are there odors in the kitchen? Do the "new boards" seem strange or natural in a kitchen? Why?

2. Your attention has been carefully called to the "new boards." Good writers introduce no object without a reason; everything mentioned in the setting is included to establish atmosphere or to be utilized at a later time. Cloth is made from the yarn spun on a wheel, so cloth will have

attention. Bread feeds man (even though he cannot live by it alone), so the bread will be needed later. Boards are expensive luxuries here, so they *would* be sheltered in the dry kitchen, but what will they be used for? Because their presence is inexplicable *now,* you can expect them to be central to the play. They are literal boards, but they will serve throughout as a symbol. What color are they in your visualization of the scene? This color may change in the course of the play, but you should be conscious of it now so the change will have meaning.

> NORA (*in a low voice*). Where is she?
> CATHLEEN. She's lying down, God help her, and may be sleeping, if she's able.

3. The opening speeches of Nora and Cathleen are intensely poetic. They scan: NORA: Whĕre ĭs shē? CATHLEEN: Shē's lȳĭng dōwn, ‖ Gŏd hĕlp hĕr, ‖ ănd mȳ | bĕ slēepĭng, | ĭf shē's āble.

Nora's speech is an *amphibrach,* a foot that combines speed with dignity, a rhythm that overlays her question with two urgencies. "She" must not be present, but the words are not conspiratorial; there is simply need of haste in the matter before "she" comes.

The first foot of Cathleen's response is a *diamb* (two iambs joined as a single foot to indicate speed and relief, rather than happiness). Note the difference had Synge written "Rĭght nōw, | shĕ's lȳ | ĭng dōwn." The initial iamb forces the next two feet to be read as separate iambs, accenting "*ly*ing" to create a subtle suggestion of falsity. Synge's diamb cannot be read as two iambs, and the rising accent on the falling denotative meaning of *down* suggests the weariness in Cathleen's voice, a weariness that becomes visually evident in her carriage. The caesuras surrounding "God help her" set the phrase apart as a traditional cliché and force stress onto *help,* creating a second amphibrach which hastes with dignity, emphasizing the form of the blessing rather than the intent. The iamb of *and may* emphasizes doubt in the stressed syllable, the amphibrach of *be sleeping* suggesting the weariness of *she* as well as the weary hope of Cathleen. The final foot is a *ditrochee* (two trochees joined as a single foot to indicate wistful doubt tempered with hope). The rhythm and the words are so harmonious that they cannot be misread or misunderstood.

So perfect is the poetic accomplishment of these lines that, even though the words are scannable as metered verse, they fall into the cadences of natural speech and seem recorded rather than arranged. Any rearrangement destroys the total effect. Notice, for instance, the loss of emotional tone in:

God help her, she's lying down and may be sleeping, if she's able.
She's lying down and may be sleeping, God help her, if she's able.
She's lying down and may be sleeping, if she's able, God help her.

Examining the poetry of the whole play would be profitable to you (as one who needs to use language effectively); however, it would require more time and effort than can be justified here. On the other hand, dialog that seems particularly effective could well be examined in such a fashion. Such demands the student makes on himself, however.

(NORA *comes in softly, and takes a bundle from under her shawl.*)

CATHLEEN (*spinning the wheel rapidly*). What is it you have?

NORA. The young priest is after bringing them. It's a shirt and a plain stocking were got off a drowned man in Donegal.

(CATHLEEN *stops her wheel with a sudden movement, and leans out to listen.*)

NORA. We're to find out if it's Michael's they are, some time herself will be down looking by the sea.

CATHLEEN. How would they be Michael's, Nora. How would he go the length of that way to the far north?

NORA. The young priest says he's known the like of it. "If it's Michael's they are," says he, "you can tell herself he's got a clean burial° by the grace of God, and if they're not his, let no one say a word about them, for she'll be getting her death," says he, "with crying and lamenting."

4. What is indicated by Cathleen's spinning the wheel "rapidly"? What is indicated by Cathleen's stopping the wheel "with a sudden movement"? Explain the dramatic reason for the parallel stage directions. Is this not also poetry; does not one act balance the other perfectly? Note the poetic quality of the stage directions throughout the play.

5. Michael's identity is not yet made clear but suspense is already high when his name is first mentioned. Why does Synge not tell us outright that Michael is Maurya's son? Why is his name used before hers in the play?

(*The door which* NORA *half closed is blown open by a gust of wind.*)

CATHLEEN (*looking out anxiously*). Did you ask him would he stop Bartley going this day with the horses to the Galway fair?

NORA. "I won't stop him," says he, "but let you not be afraid. Herself does be saying prayers half through the night, and the Almighty God won't leave her destitute," says he, "with no son living."

° Has received ritual Catholic burial

6. The door blown open by a gust of wind foreshadows what? Is it effective?

7. Why should the priest be asked to stop Bartley's departure? Caution, there is more than one answer.

8. The priest's statement that God will not take Maurya's last son is a kind reassurance, but the irony of such an assurance is immediately apparent and will become more so later. Explain the irony as it exists now.

CATHLEEN. Is the sea bad by the white rocks, Nora?

NORA. Middling bad, God help us. There's a great roaring in the west, and it's worse it'll be getting when the tide's turned to the wind. (*She goes over to the table with the bundle.*) Shall I open it now?

CATHLEEN. Maybe she'd wake up on us, and come in before we'd done. (*Coming to the table.*) It's a long time we'll be, and the two of us crying.

NORA (*goes to the inner door and listens*). She's moving about on the bed. She'll be coming in a minute.

CATHLEEN. Give me the ladder, and I'll put them up in the turf-loft, the way she won't know of them at all, and maybe when the tide turns she'll be going down to see would he be floating from the east.

(*They put the ladder against the gable of the chimney;* CATHLEEN *goes up a few steps and hides the bundle in the turf-loft.* MAURYA *comes from the inner room.*)

9. Explain the accumulation of stormy details (the wind, the door, and the sea by the white rocks).

10. What is the significance of "the tide turned to the wind" (that point in time when the outgoing tide is against the incoming wind)?

11. Does Cathleen know that the clothes belong to Michael before she has seen them? Prove your answer.

12. The drama of Maurya's entrance is carefully built. Explain how this first part of the play convinces you that she is the central character.

MAURYA (*looking up at* CATHLEEN *and speaking querulously*). Isn't it turf enough you have for this day and evening?

CATHLEEN. There's a cake baking at the fire for a short space (*throwing down the turf*) and Bartley will want it when the tide turns if he goes to Connemara.

(NORA *picks up the turf and puts it round the pot-oven.*)

MAURYA (*sitting down on a stool at the fire*). He won't go this day with the wind rising from the south and west. He won't go this day, for the young priest will stop him surely.

NORA. He'll not stop him, mother, and I heard Eamon Simon and Stephen Pheety and Colum Shawn saying he would go.

MAURYA. Where is he itself?

NORA. He went down to see would there be another boat sailing in the week, and I'm thinking it won't be long till he's here now, for the tide's turning at the green head, and the hooker's° tacking from the east.

CATHLEEN. I hear some one passing the big stones.

NORA (*looking out*). He's coming now, and he in a hurry.

13. Maurya's entrance has been so superbly prepared that her querulousness may come as a shock. She seems a crabby, dislikable old woman in her opening speech. Justify Synge's decision to make her complain.

14. Cathleen does not lie to her mother, neither does she tell her the truth. How do you explain her answer, which is more than simple evasion?

15. Nora overtly shares in the deception. Explain how.

16. What is the dramatic effect of your having heard in advance that the priest will not stop Bartley? Irony becomes artful as Maurya places her word-faith in the priest. What is Synge suggesting to his audience? Remember: This play was written as part of the Irish National Movement to make Irishmen aware and proud of their cultural past! Eamon Simon, Stephen Pheety, and Colum Shawn are named for what two reasons?

17. How do the weather and tide reports generate suspense and foreshadow future action?

18. The landmarks (*stones*) create a picture almost as clearly realized as if you were looking out a window. Explain how. The stones also serve as a foreshadowing element. Explain.

19. Nora's statement "He's coming now, and he in a hurry" creates tempo within the line by the omission of a single consonant—'s after the second *he*. The inconsistency of language is apparent but it is not bothersome. Why?

BARTLEY (*comes in and looks round the room; speaking sadly and quietly*). Where is the bit of new rope, Cathleen, was bought in Connemara?

CATHLEEN (*coming down*). Give it to him, Nora; it's on a nail by the white boards. I hung it up this morning, for the pig with the black feet was eating it.

NORA (*giving him a rope*). Is that it, Bartley?

MAURYA. You'd do right to leave that rope, Bartley, hanging by the boards. (BARTLEY *takes the rope.*) It will be wanting in this place, I'm telling you, if Michael is washed up tomorrow morning, or the next morning, or any morning in the week, for it's a deep grave we'll make him by the grace of God.

° A single-masted fishing smack for transporting livestock

20. Bartley greets no one. He speaks "sadly and quietly" as he asks for the "new rope." Interpret his behavior (but be assured he is *not* being rude). What does the word *new* contribute?

21. Cathleen does not descend from the turf-loft until Bartley arrives. Why not?

22. The "new" boards become "white" boards now. Why? What are the reasons for including *black* and *white* in Cathleen's speech? If you can see the *many* effects achieved by this line, you are understanding the beauty of poetry in drama.

23. Cathleen makes the decision that Bartley shall have the rope. Should the decision not have been Maurya's? Why does Cathleen usurp her mother's prerogative?

24. Is Nora too stupid to recognize new rope? If not, why does she ask Bartley "Is that it?"

25. Maurya's statement that "You'd do right to leave that rope . . ." has several meanings, all centering in the word *right*. What are they?

26. Is Bartley unaware that the rope was bought to lower Michael's coffin into the ground? Why does Maurya remind him? Is she merely stating an obvious truth or has she a less obvious reason for the words?

BARTLEY (*beginning to work with the rope*). I've no halter the way I can ride down on the mare, and I must go now quickly. This is the one boat going for two weeks or beyond it, and the fair will be a good fair for horses I heard them saying below.

MAURYA. It's a hard thing they'll be saying below if the body is washed up and there's no man in it to make the coffin, and I after giving a big price for the finest white boards you'd find in Connemara. (*She looks round at the boards.*)

27. Is Bartley going to Galway Fair because he selfishly wants to have a good time or are there other reasons?

28. Is Maurya being penurious in mentioning the "big price" of the boards? Is it an arbitrary statement or is it an answer to Bartley's reasons for going to Connemara?

29. What is achieved in the stage direction "She looks round at the boards"?

BARTLEY. How would it be washed up, and we after looking each day for nine days, and a strong wind blowing a while back from the west and south?

MAURYA. If it wasn't found itself,° that wind is raising the sea, and there was a star up against the moon, and it rising in the night. If it was a hundred horses, or

° Even if the body hasn't been found

a thousand horses you had itself, what is the price of a thousand horses against a son where there is one son only?

30. Bartley's question about the failure of Michael's body to appear seems reasonable. Is he trying to tell Maurya anything about his trip to Connemara?

31. Maurya finally reveals her true reason for wanting Bartley to remain at home. Why did she use such a circuitous route? Does she love Bartley? How emotional is she? Would an avowal of concern have been realistic, sentimental, neither, or both?

BARTLEY (*working at the halter, to* CATHLEEN). Let you go down each day, and see the sheep aren't jumping in on the rye, and if the jobber° comes you can sell the pig with the black feet if there is a good price going.

MAURYA. How would the like of her get a good price for a pig?

BARTLEY (*to* CATHLEEN). If the west wind holds with the last bit of the moon let you and Nora get up weed enough for another cock for the kelp.° It's hard set we'll be from this day with no one in it but one man to work.

MAURYA. It's hard set we'll be surely the day you're drownd'd with the rest. What way will I live and the girls with me, and I an old woman looking for the grave?

32. Why does Bartley not answer his mother? Why does he direct his orders to Cathleen? Why does he tell her to sell "the pig with the black feet" rather than some other animal?

33. Does Maurya suggest that Cathleen lacks good sense or business acumen in the line "How would the like of her get a good price for a pig?" Or is she offering Bartley another plea to stay home?

34. Bartley still does not answer his mother. Why?

35. Why does Bartley remind Cathleen that life will be harder with only one man to do the work? Is he telling Cathleen anything she doesn't already know or is he attempting to make Maurya understand something?

36. Does Maurya understand? Is her answer designed to elicit Bartley's sympathy and bend him to her will? Do not be hasty in your judgment.

(BARTLEY *lays down the halter, takes off his old coat, and puts on a newer one of the same flannel.*)

BARTLEY (*to* NORA). Is she coming to the pier?

NORA (*looking out*). She's passing the green head and letting fall her sails.

° Livestock dealer
° Rake up enough seaweed to dry for iodine

BARTLEY (*getting his purse and tobacco*). I'll have half an hour to go down, and you'll see me coming again in two days, or in three days, or maybe in four days if the wind is bad.

MAURYA (*turning round to the fire, and putting her shawl over her head*). Isn't it a hard and cruel man won't hear a word from an old woman, and she holding him from the sea?

CATHLEEN. It's the life of a young man to be going on the sea, and who would listen to an old woman with one thing and she saying it over?

BARTLEY (*taking the halter*). I must go now quickly. I'll ride down on the red mare, and the gray pony'll run behind me. . . . The blessing of God on you. (*He goes out.*)

37. Explain the significance of Bartley's changing coats.

38. The hooker's progress has been reported with regularity. Why?

39. Bartley makes a final preparation to leave and Maurya delivers her final argument. Is it easy for her?

40. Bartley does not answer Maurya. Why?

41. Why does Cathleen answer for her brother? Would he have said exactly the same thing had he answered?

42. Why have stage directions been directed at the halter so consistently? There is more than one reason.

43. In the old ballads known to all Irishmen, the color "red" signifies life, the color "gray" signifies death. Explain the symbols and foreshadowing here.

MAURYA (*crying out as he is in the door*). He's gone now, God spare us, and we'll not see him again. He's gone now, and when the black night is falling I'll have no son left me in the world.

CATHLEEN. Why wouldn't you give him your blessing and he looking round in the door? Isn't it sorrow enough is on every one in this house without your sending him out with an unlucky word behind him, and a hard word in his ear?

(MAURYA *takes up the tongs and begins raking the fire aimlessly without looking round.*)

NORA (*turning towards her*). You're taking away the turf from the cake.

CATHLEEN (*crying out*). The Son of God forgive us, Nora, we're after forgetting his bit of bread. (*She comes over to the fire.*)

NORA. And it's destroyed° he'll be going till dark night, and he after eating nothing since the sun went up.

CATHLEEN (*turning the cake out of the oven*). It's destroyed he'll be, surely. There's no sense left on any person in a house where an old woman will be talking forever.

(MAURYA *sways herself on her stool.*)

° Exhausted

44. Does Maurya withhold her blessing in anger or is there another explanation?

45. Maurya scatters the fire as if to put it out. Explain the symbolism. Explain the significance of Maurya's act reminding Cathleen that she did not give Bartley the bread.

46. Is Cathleen being disrespectful to Maurya in anger or has she another reason for her unkind reference to Maurya's incessant talk?

47. What is Maurya's reaction to Cathleen's words? (Assess the stage direction "Maurya sways herself on her stool," paying particular attention to *herself*.)

CATHLEEN (*cutting off some of the bread and rolling it in a cloth; to* MAURYA). Let you go down now to the spring well and give him this and he passing. You'll see him then and the dark word will be broken, and you can say "God speed you," the way he'll be easy in his mind.

MAURYA (*taking the bread*). Will I be in it as soon as himself?°

CATHLEEN. If you go now quickly.

MAURYA (*standing up unsteadily*). It's hard set I am to walk.

CATHLEEN (*looking at her anxiously*). Give her the stick, Nora, or maybe she'll slip on the big stones.

NORA. What stick?

CATHLEEN. The stick Michael brought from Connemara.

MAURYA (*taking a stick* NORA *gives her*). In the big world the old people do be leaving things after them for their sons and children, but in this place it is the young men do be leaving things behind for them that do be old. (*She goes out slowly.*)

48. Explain Cathleen's several reasons for directing Maurya to deliver the bread.

49. What does the stick symbolize? Remember, these people are Catholic and Maurya will carry bread.

50. In Maurya's last speech, *do be* is used three times. Why?

51. Maurya goes out slowly though she must hurry if she is to intercept Bartley. Explain Synge's reasons for the direction.

(NORA *goes over to the ladder.*)

CATHLEEN. Wait, Nora, maybe she'd turn back quickly. She's that sorry, God help her, you wouldn't know the thing she'd do.

NORA. Is she gone round by the bush?

CATHLEEN (*looking out*). She's gone now. Throw it down quickly, for the Lord knows when she'll be out of it again.

° Will I have time to intercept him?

NORA (*getting the bundle from the loft*). The young priest said he'd be passing tomorrow, and we might go down and speak to him below if it's Michael's they are surely.

CATHLEEN (*taking the bundle*). Did he say what way they were found?

NORA (*coming down*). "There were two men," says he, "and they rowing round with poteen° before the cocks crowed, and the oar of one of them caught the body, and they passing the black cliffs of the north."°

CATHLEEN (*trying to open the bundle*). Give me a knife, Nora, the string's perished* with the salt water, and there's a black knot on it you wouldn't loosen in a week.

NORA (*giving her a knife*). I've heard tell it was a long way to Donegal.

CATHLEEN (*cutting the string*). It is surely. There was a man in here a while ago—the man sold us that knife—and he said if you set off walking from the rocks beyond, it would be seven days you'd be in Donegal.

NORA. And what time would a man take, and he floating?

52. Is Cathleen's opening speech spoken in the same tone that her speech on p. 500 was? Account for the difference.

53. Why does Synge dwell on the difficulties of opening the bundle?

54. Explain the dramatic function of the knife (it becomes plain in Nora's question about floating-time).

(CATHLEEN *opens the bundle and takes out a bit of a stocking. They look at them eagerly.*)

CATHLEEN (*in a low voice*). The Lord spare us, Nora! isn't it a queer hard thing to say if it's his they are surely?

NORA. I'll get his shirt off the hook the way we can put the one flannel on the other. (*She looks through some clothes hanging in the corner.*) It's not with them, Cathleen, and where will it be?

CATHLEEN. I'm thinking Bartley put it on him in the morning, for his own shirt was heavy with the salt in it (*pointing to the corner*). There's a bit of a sleeve was of the same stuff. Give me that and it will do.

(NORA *brings it to her and they compare the flannel.*)

CATHLEEN. It's the same stuff, Nora; but if it is itself aren't there great rolls of it in the shops of Galway, and isn't it many another man may have a shirt of it as well as Michael himself?

NORA (*who has taken up the stocking and counted the stitches, crying out*). It's Michael, Cathleen, it's Michael; God spare his soul, and what will herself say when she hears this story, and Bartley on the sea?

° Illegal whiskey
° The high, north cliffs of Donegal Bay
* Contracted and stiffened

55. What previous stage direction foreshadowed the absence of Michael's coat? Is the reason clear to you yet?

56. Is Cathleen dubious, hopeful, or fearful when the flannel matches? Is her doubt intellectual or emotional?

57. Is Nora's greatest agony for Michael or for Maurya's response to proof of Michael's death when she knows the stocking is Michael's?

CATHLEEN (*taking the stocking*). It's a plain stocking.

NORA. It's the second one of the third pair I knitted, and I put up three score stitches, and I dropped four of them.

CATHLEEN (*counts the stitches*). It's that number is in it. (*Crying out*) Ah, Nora, isn't it a bitter thing to think of him floating that way to the far north and no one to keen° him but the black hags° that do be flying on the sea?

NORA (*swinging herself round, and throwing out her arms on the clothes*). And isn't it a pitiful thing when there is nothing left of a man who was a great rower and fisher, but a bit of an old shirt and a plain stocking?

CATHLEEN (*after an instant*). Tell me is herself coming, Nora? I hear a little sound on the path.

NORA (*looking out*). She is, Cathleen. She's coming up to the door.

CATHLEEN. Put these things away before she'll come in. Maybe it's easier she'll be after giving her blessing to Bartley, and we won't let on we've heard anything the time he's on the sea.

NORA (*helping CATHLEEN to close the bundle*). We'll put them here in the corner.

(*They put them into a hole in the chimney corner. CATHLEEN goes back to the spinning-wheel.*)

NORA. Will she see it was crying I was?

CATHLEEN. Keep your back to the door the way the light'll not be on you.

(NORA *sits down at the chimney corner, with her back to the door.*)

58. Cathleen's anguish is a stated regret that Michael was unkeened, Nora's that his accomplishments are so inadequately represented by the possessions he left. Which girl is more conscious of Michael, which of herself? Which girl is more human, which more humanitarian? What lines in *Everyman* state similar truths?

59. Account for the poetic addition of the Irish idiom of "black hags" for cormorants.

60. Wherein lies Cathleen's strength? Wherein lies Nora's? Are such strengths representative of anything more encompassing than the two characters?

° Ritual lamentation chanted for the dead
° Cormorants, sea birds

61. Cathleen returns to the spinning wheel again. Is this stage business inserted just to keep her busy or does the act indicate something about Cathleen? About all women?

(MAURYA *comes in very slowly, without looking at the girls, and goes over to her stool at the other side of the fire. The cloth with the bread is still in her hand. The girls look at each other, and* NORA *points to the bundle of bread.*)

62. The silent action in the stage directions that open this section is as poetic as any of the words in the play. Motion and motionlessness are balanced in harmony and in tension. The picture created by the women includes the flickering lights of the fire and the shadows of the room. Masses are juxtaposed and balanced in the geometric arrangement of the women, and the pantomimic gesture of Nora seems subtle enough to be suggested by an artist's brush rather than by an actual hand. Considering Synge's careful planning, explain the function of setting in relation to non-verbal and verbal statement in the drama. You will find no better example than this one in all literature.

63. Three symbols dominate the scene before any words are spoken— the cloth-wrapped bread, the spinning wheel, and the white boards. Explain the harmony of symbols as they are placed in tension in this scene to create balance.

CATHLEEN (*after spinning for a moment*). You didn't give him his bit of bread?

(MAURYA *begins to keen softly, without turning round.*)

CATHLEEN. Did you see him riding down?

(MAURYA *goes on keening.*)

CATHLEEN (*a little impatiently*). God forgive you; isn't it a better thing to raise your voice and tell what you seen, than to be making lamentation for a thing that's done? Did you see Bartley, I'm saying to you?

MAURYA (*with a weak voice*). My heart's broken from this day.

CATHLEEN (*as before*). Did you see Bartley?

MAURYA. I seen the fearfulest thing.

64. Is Cathleen's question about the bread an accusation or a plea for an explanation?

65. When Maurya answers with keening, how do Nora and Cathleen assess her grief? Do you assess it the same way?

66. Cathleen's question "Did you see him riding down?" almost creates the title of the play. Explain the ambiguities in the line.

67. Cathleen's impatience with Maurya's keening rises from what reasons?

CATHLEEN (*leaves her wheel and looks out*). God forgive you; he's riding the mare now over the green head, and the gray pony behind him.

MAURYA (*starts, so that her shawl falls back from her head and shows her white tossed hair; with a frightened voice*). The gray pony behind him.

CATHLEEN (*coming to the fire*). What is it ails you, at all?

MAURYA (*speaking very slowly*). I've seen the fearfulest thing any person has seen, since the day Bride Dara seen the dead man with the child in his arms.

CATHLEEN and NORA. Uah. (*They crouch down in front of the old woman at the fire.*)

NORA. Tell us what it is you seen.

MAURYA. I went down to the spring well, and I stood there saying a prayer to myself. Then Bartley came along, and he riding on the red mare with the gray pony behind him. (*She puts up her hands, as if to hide something from her eyes.*) The Son of God spare us, Nora!

CATHLEEN. What is it you seen.

MAURYA. I seen Michael himself.

CATHLEEN (*speaking softly*). You did not, mother. It wasn't Michael you seen, for his body is after being found in the far north, and he's got a clean burial by the grace of God.

68. Explain the poetic and dramatic effect of Maurya's white hair being suddenly exposed. Where is she sitting in relation to the white boards?

69. What rides behind Bartley in Maurya's mind as Cathleen reports his progress?

70. As Nora and Cathleen crouch down before Maurya, it is as if a second painting has emerged. The artist employs the same visual elements, but he changes the composition of the painting by rearranging masses. How has the lighting changed in the newly-created picture? Is there more or less sound now?

71. Explain Cathleen's telling Maurya of Michael's death while Bartley is in the water, even though she had told Nora that they would say nothing while Bartley was on the sea.

MAURYA (*a little defiantly*). I'm after seeing him this day, and he riding and galloping. Bartley came first on the red mare; and I tried to say "God speed you," but something choked the words in my throat. He went by quickly; and "the blessing of God on you," says he, and I could say nothing. I looked up then, and I was crying, at the gray pony, and there was Michael upon it—with fine clothes on him, and new shoes on his feet.

CATHLEEN (*begins to keen*). It's destroyed we are from this day. It's destroyed, surely.

72. Explain Maurya's vision of Michael. Do not be hasty. Examine the words "with fine clothes on him, and new shoes on his feet."

73. Compare Maurya's inability to say "God speed you" with Macbeth's inability to pronounce "Amen." How do superstition and psychological reason seem to complement each other in these instances?

74. Cathleen and Nora understand the symbols of Maurya's vision (Bartley on the *red* mare followed by Michael on the *gray* pony) and accept the inevitability of its truth even though Cathleen has just seen Bartley alive and passing the green head. Beginning to keen, Cathleen says "It's destroyed we are from this day." Does *destroyed* mean "exhausted" in the sense of "fatigued" here or is it the standard English meaning? Has the word gained poetic power to convey connotative meanings through its earlier usage? What can you deduce about "poetic language" from this cumulative usage?

NORA. Didn't the young priest say the Almighty God wouldn't leave her destitute with no son living?

MAURYA (*in a low voice, but clearly*). It's little the like of him knows of the sea. . . . Bartley will be lost now, and let you call in Eamon and make me a good coffin out of the white boards, for I won't live after them. I've had a husband, and a husband's father, and six sons in this house—six fine men, though it was a hard birth I had with every one of them and they coming to the world—and some of them were found and some of them were not found, but they're gone now the lot of them. . . There were Stephen, and Shawn, were lost in the great wind, and found after in the Bay of Gregory of the Golden Mouth, and carried up the two of them on the one plank, and in by that door.

(*She pauses for a moment, the girls start as if they heard something through the door that is half open behind them.*)

NORA (*in a whisper*). Did you hear that, Cathleen? Did you hear a noise in the north-east?

CATHLEEN (*in a whisper*). There's some one after crying out by the seashore.

MAURYA (*continues without hearing anything*). There was Sheamus and his father, and his own father again, were lost in a dark night, and not a stick or sign was seen of them when the sun went up. There was Patch after was drowned out of a curagh that turned over. I was sitting here with Bartley, and he a baby, lying on my two knees, and I seen two women, and three women, and four women coming in, and they crossing themselves, and not saying a word. I looked out then, and there were men coming after them, and they holding a thing in the half of a red sail, and water dripping out of it—it was a dry day, Nora—and leaving a track to the door.

(*She pauses again with her hand stretched out towards the door. It opens softly and old women begin to come in, crossing themselves on the threshold, and kneeling down in front of the stage with red petticoats over their heads.*)

75. Is Nora's reminder of the priest's promise made with conviction?
76. Explain Maurya's dismissal of the Catholic priest in the words "It's little *the like of him* knows of the sea." What is Synge suggesting about the Celtic heritage and the Catholic church? Are they two separate cultures? Are they integrated in Maurya's mind in this fatal moment? What is Synge suggesting about the human condition—if anything?
77. Out of her lifetime of grieved loss, Maurya recalls vividly the long procession of death through this cottage. Explain the tightly-knit poetic structure of her account and the entrance of the old women. Does the scene seem natural or contrived? Why?
78. The color red has become dominant at this moment: red mare, red sail, red petticoats. Red symbolizes life, but it is inextricably bound to death in this scene. Explain the irony that creates the power of this fusion.

MAURYA (*half in a dream, to* CATHLEEN). Is it Patch, or Michael, or what is it at all?

CATHLEEN. Michael is after being found in the far north, and when he is found there how could he be here in this place?

MAURYA. There does be a power° of young men floating round in the sea, and what way would they know if it was Michael they had, or another man like him, for when a man is nine days in the sea, and the wind blowing, it's hard set his own mother would be to say what man was it.

CATHLEEN. It's Michael, God spare him, for they're after sending us a bit of his clothes from the far north.

(*She reaches out and hands* MAURYA *the clothes that belonged to* MICHAEL. MAURYA *stands up slowly, and takes them in her hands.* NORA *looks out.*)

NORA. They're carrying a thing among them and there's water dripping out of it and leaving a track by the big stones.

CATHLEEN (*in a whisper to the women who have come in*). Is it Bartley it is?

ONE OF THE WOMEN. It is surely, God rest his soul.

(*Two younger women come in and pull out the table. Then men carry in the body of* BARTLEY, *laid on a plank, with a bit of a sail over it, and lay it on the table.*)

CATHLEEN (*to the women, as they are doing so*). What way was he drowned?

ONE OF THE WOMEN. The gray pony knocked him into the sea, and he was washed out where there is a great surf on the white rocks.

79. Maurya knows it cannot be Patch. What is Synge's purpose in putting this question in her mouth?
80. Nora's report of Bartley's cortege includes phrases which Maurya

° Large number

has just used in describing the death of Patch ("a thing," "water dripping out of it," and "leaving a track") and a reference to the big stones (the last time Bartley came by them he was in a hurry). Poetry is the distillation of emotion, a form of brevity creating limitless vision, and this fact is nowhere more apparent than here. Can you explain Synge's power in achieving so much?

81. You knew that Bartley's body was being returned and Cathleen knew it. Why then does she ask the old women? Does the question seem unnecessary? Why or why not?

82. The *white* rocks, the *gray* pony, the *red* mare begin to complete the pattern of color symbolism. What do white rocks and white boards now suggest? How has your response changed in the course of the play?

(MAURYA *has gone over and knelt down at the head of the table. The women are keening softly and swaying themselves with a slow movement.* CATHLEEN *and* NORA *kneel at the other end of the table. The men kneel near the door.*)

MAURYA (*raising her head and speaking as if she did not see the people around her*). They're all gone now, and there isn't anything more the sea can do to me. . . . I'll have no call now to be up crying and praying when the wind breaks from the south, and you can hear the surf is in the east, and the surf is in the west, making a great stir with the two noises, and they hitting one on the other. I'll have no call now to be going down and getting Holy Water in the dark nights after Samhain,° and I won't care what way the sea is when the other women will be keening. (*To* NORA) Give me the Holy Water, Nora, there's a small sup still on the dresser.

(NORA *gives it to her.*)

MAURYA (*drops* MICHAEL'S *clothes across* BARTLEY'S *feet, and sprinkles the Holy Water over him*). It isn't that I haven't prayed for you, Bartley, to the Almighty God. It isn't that I haven't said prayers in the dark night till you wouldn't know what I'd be saying; but it's a great rest I'll have now, and it's time surely. It's a great rest I'll have now, and great sleeping in the long nights after Samhain, if it's only a bit of wet flour we do have to eat, and maybe a fish that would be stinking. (*She kneels down again, crossing herself, and saying prayers under her breath.*)

83. The sea has taken Maurya's last male child and has therefore defeated her. Explain the tragic irony employed. Remember: the sea is usually a symbol of life, the great womb image from which all things came.

84. In defeating Maurya, the sea has freed her. Explain the irony of her acceptance.

° All Souls Day celebrated in the Catholic church with the feast of the dead. Pronounced Sów•in, the word sounds like winds blowing softly through dead trees.

CATHLEEN (*to an old man*). Maybe yourself and Eamon would make a coffin when the sun rises. We have fine white boards herself bought, God help her, thinking Michael would be found, and I have a new cake you can eat while you'll be working.

THE OLD MAN (*looking at the boards*). Are there nails with them?

CATHLEEN. There are not, Colum; we didn't think of the nails.

ANOTHER MAN. It's a great wonder she wouldn't think of the nails, and all the coffins she's seen made already.

CATHLEEN. It's getting old she is, and broken.

(MAURYA *stands up again very slowly and spreads out the pieces of* MICHAEL'S *clothes beside the body, sprinkling them with the last of the Holy Water.*)

85. Bread (cake) assumes its full poetic irony as Cathleen speaks to Colum. Explain.

86. Colum's inquiry after nails for the coffin adds a common, natural touch that momentarily seems to break the tragic mood. However, consider "when the sun rises" in conjunction with "white boards," Cathleen's description of Maurya as "broken," the nails, and Michael's garments, and you will see powerful poetic symbols creating the end of this finely-wrought play. In her moment of earthly defeat, Maurya silently states her resigned acceptance. She accepts the will of God. What other powerful scene is overlaid on this one?

NORA (*in a whisper to* CATHLEEN). She's quiet now and easy; but the day Michael was drowned you could hear her crying out from this to the spring well. It's fonder she was of Michael, and would any one have thought that?

CATHLEEN (*slowly and clearly*). An old woman will be soon tired with anything she will do, and isn't it nine days herself is after crying and keening, and making great sorrow in the house?

MAURYA (*puts the empty cup mouth downwards on the table, and lays her hands together on* BARTLEY'S *feet*). They're all together this time, and the end is come. May the Almighty God have mercy on Bartley's soul, and on Michael's soul, and on the souls of Sheamus and Patch, and Stephen and Shawn (*bending her head*); and may He have mercy on my soul, Nora, and on the soul of every one is left living in the world.

(*She pauses, and the keen rises a little more loudly from the women, then sinks away.*)

MAURYA (*continuing*). Michael has a clean burial in the far north, by the grace of the Almighty God. Bartley will have a fine coffin out of the white boards, and a deep grave surely. What more can we want than that? No man at all can be living for ever, and we must be satisfied.

(*She kneels down again and the curtain falls slowly.*) ☐

87. What is the significance of Maurya's nine days of grief and her tenth day of acceptance?

88. After emptying the holy-water cup, Maurya turns it mouth downward on the table. In this one action, she repeats her two speeches preceding the action. Explain the balanced rhythm of the act and the words.

89. It can be argued that Maurya's greatest tragedy is not in the loss of her sons—it lies in her human necessity to speak the final lines of the play. Do you agree or disagree? Defend your belief.

90. Job, in the Old Testament, accepted the decisions of God in a way similar to and dissimilar from Maurya's. Compare her acceptance of fate with Job's.

91. How does Maurya's final speech complete the cathartic act of the play?

92. Maurya is present in only two of the four scenes of this one-act play, yet she dominates those from which she is absent. Explain how her absence from the stage contributes to the starkness and the drama of the play, making it more tragic.

Suggested Assignments. 1. Choose that portion of *Riders to the Sea* that seems most poetic and discuss the poetic technique as it is discussed in Question 3, p. 500.

2. In a brief paper, discuss the poetic contributions of the stage directions of the play. See Question 4, p. 501.

3. This masterpiece of tragedy could easily have become sentimental. In a three-paragraph paper, explain how Synge avoided the pitfalls that would have reduced it to melodrama.

4. Maurya's final statement ("No man at all can be living for ever and we must be satisfied") is comparable to the closing lines of *Oedipus Rex,* to the final speech in Voltaire's *Candide* (*Il faut cultiver notre jardin* —"we must cultivate our garden"), and Don Quixote's speech in Part I, Book IV of Cervantes' novel:

I would be absolute; and who but I? Now, he that is absolute can do what he likes; he that can do what he likes, can take his pleasure; he that can take his pleasure, can be content; and he that can be content, has no more to desire. So the matter's over; and come what will come, I am satisfied.

In a paper of some length, compare the four situations to discover if the authors mean the same thing in all four works.

CHAPTER IX

The Muse in the Laboratory—
The Theater of the Absurd

At Sarajevo on June 28, 1914, all the world became
a stage whereon the tragic hero Man stood exposed
to an audience he could not see, in a play for which
he had no script. Improvising, he moved without
stage diagrams, ad-libbed lines desperately, and prayed
that the producer of his drama would not close the
show even though his one actor was ill-prepared,
afflicted with stage fright, and helpless without
supporting actors. World War I was merely the first
act of our tragedy, however, and it is axiomatic in
the theater that actors may recover their stage presence
and give great performances later in the play if the
audience will only be patient. Indeed, a thoroughly
bad Act One may be followed by superb Acts Two
and Three.

Whatever the audience of our tragedy, it waited
in some unseen lobby during the intermission—an
intermission furiously active for Man. Assembling the
existing playwrights, the poets, the novelists—in short,
the writers of the 1920's—he demanded a workable
script for the next act. Poet T. S. Eliot composed *The
Waste Land;* novelist Ernest Hemingway penned *The
Sun Also Rises;* dramatist Eugene O'Neill offered *The
Great God Brown;* and the list goes on and on. In
the 1930's, John Steinbeck suggested *The Grapes of
Wrath* and Luigi Pirandello wrote his most tragic
drama *One Doesn't Know How.* Movements and experimentation abounded, because the second act had
to be interesting, show promise, and keep the unseen
audience in its chairs while the future dramatists
worked on the third act.

In 1933, the second-act curtains parted. And, sure
enough, World War II buffeted the lone actor with
the most awesome effects possible, leaving him broken,
burned, and bleeding in the rubble of Hiroshima and
Nagasaki. Romanticism had brought Man to World
War I. But Realism and Naturalism had not pre-

pared him for World War II. How could he look at the grim spectacle of his bombed-out world realistically, naturalistically? Mercifully, the curtains finally closed on Act Two, and the silent audience withdrew to the eternal lobby, obviously interested by the spectacle, if not the script or acting, to await the third act.

We are working on the script now. It has incorporated John Hersey's *The Wall*, Arthur Miller's *Death of a Salesman,* and Ezra Pound's *Pisan Cantos.* The greatest impetus has come from Expressionism, however, to create *the theater of the absurd,* a term coined by Martin Esslin, foremost critic of the movement. Stretching back to the allegorical *Everyman,* the theater of the absurd is in a process of formulation and experimentation because playwrights of the form are as yet uncertain about the cast. The personifications of *Everyman* are old hat, and the new identifications of Freud will not create a cohesive cast because they fragment the basic man into several parts: Ego, Id, Libido, and Superego. Experience itself provides the central convention in our experiment, but we are unsure about the nature of experience. Acts One and Two left us dazed and doubting. Experience seems surrealistic rather than real, bizarre rather than ordinary. Is life what happens on the street and in the home, or is that the shadow play, merely the projection of the reality which exists only within us? Do the senses perceive or are metaphors, similes, and symbols the reality? Is what we have called "life" the dream?

If, as Nietzsche declared in *The Gay Science,* God is dead, we are beginning to get the message. When it is thoroughly transmitted and received, an agonizing awareness attends it: If there is no God, God did not create the world. If the world was not created by divine plan, it has little meaning and less purpose. Man merely exists amid the shattered wreckage of his symbols which have lost their power to evoke the expanded concept.

Sweden's August Strindberg is the old master of this newest form. In 1902, he gave the world *The Dream Play,* a pageant in fifteen scenes of the absurdity that is man. A poet (the heart of man) sees a vision in which the daughter of Indra comes to Earth to experience human life. In strange settings (for instance, the grotto of the human ear), she meets such representational characters as a Lawyer (the mind) and an Officer (the physical body) only to find them victim or victimized, oppressed or oppressor. Strindberg explained:

The characters split, double, multiply, vanish, solidify, blur, grow clear. But one consciousness reigns above them all—that of the dreamer; and before it, there are no secrets, no incongruities, no scruples, no laws. There is neither judgment nor exoneration, merely narration. And as the dream is for the most part painful, rarely pleasant, a note of melancholy and of pity for all living things runs all through the wobbly tale. Sleep, the liberator, often plays a dismal part; but when the pain is at its worst, the awakening comes and reconciles the sufferer to reality, which, however distressful it may be, seems nevertheless happy in comparison with the torments of the dream.°

Setting is vital in the play; and colors which are almost psychedelic in concept dominate from the opening view of a castle crowned with a bud behind hundreds of rainbow hollyhocks, through such effects as a door with a clover-leaf opening, to the breaking of the castle bud into a giant chrysanthemum. The play does not act well. This kind of reality cannot be staged with realistic conventions. But the play acts superbly in the theater of the mind where physical limitations do not exist.

Germany's Georg Kaiser called his *From Morn to Midnight* a "think-play," for it is a *monodrama* (seen through the eyes of one character only) that recreates an idea in much the same way James Joyce's stream-of-consciousness novel *Ulysses* does. The protagonist of *From Morn to Midnight* is a bank cashier who spends one day with 60,000 embezzled marks. He pursues a seductive woman who becomes a mother, finds himself at a seven-day bicycle race which is his life, and progresses to an all-night cabaret via the Salvation Army. Illusion after illusion rises, is shattered, and is replaced by a new illusion until he recognizes the futility of living and shoots himself before the police arrive to arrest him. It too reads better than it acts for the same reasons noted about *The Dream Play.*

Ireland's Samuel Beckett lives in France where he wrote *Waiting for Godot,* a play that electrified world audiences with its seeming pessimism, its nihilistic air of hopelessness. On a stage containing only a stunted tree, two characters wait for Godot. They do not really know his name, whether he plans to come, or if, in fact, he exists. Still they wait. Angering some audiences, frustrating others who found it incomprehensible, *Waiting for Godot* was enthusiastically received by 1400 convicts at San Quentin penitentiary. Reporting their reception, Martin Esslin says that various convicts identified Godot as society and the outside. A teacher at the prison explained that the convicts understood the play because they understood waiting. Further, they knew that Godot would be a disappointment if he ever did come.°

° Quoted in Joseph T. Shipley, *Guide to Great Plays* (Washington, D.C., 1956), pp. 755–756.
° See "The Absurdity of the Absurd," *The Theatre of the Absurd* by Martin Esslin (New York, 1961).

Ionesco's *The Chairs,* as we have noted, also presents its version of a nightmare: man's inability to communicate. Similarly, in Harold Pinter's *The Birthday Party,* Stanley asks Lulu to go away with him and, when she asks where they will go, he answers, "Nowhere." She says they might as well stay here, but he reminds her that "here" is "no good." "Well, where else is there?" she asks, and he responds, "Nowhere." Communication is impossible because nothing is worth communicating. Life is meaningless but must be lived. Brendan Behan sums it up in *The Quare Fellow* when a convict, asked how one can live through eleven years in prison, answers "a minute at a time." Jean Paul Sartre sees the world as a hell from which there is *No Exit* even after death unless, like Orestes in his *The Flies,* man refuses to feel either guilt or remorse for his actions.

Busy writing man's third act, today's dramatists are often accused of speaking for the intellectual only—not for man as a whole. Their critics claim it is ironic that man is offered absurdity when he most desperately needs hope or optimism or a return to the "eternal verities." Ward Hooker, writing in *The Kenyon Review* (a journal for intellectuals rather than for the common man), has observed that the avant-garde theater is a kind of confusion in a vacuum.° By this, Mr. Hooker and other critics of the theater of the absurd mean that man is, at least, admitting he has no answers, that the meaning of existence is either absent or hopelessly incomprehensible. In short, such critics argue, such drama is thoroughly nihilistic, the drama of negation. They may be right—we haven't seen the outcome of the third act yet—but poets, novelists, playwrights would generally disagree, for is not every literary work, regardless of its most negative feature, an act of faith on the part of the author, his personal affirmation that man will survive and, surviving, read? A man who reads, thinks. A man who thinks, progresses. And a man who progresses eventually gets somewhere.

Certainly the avant-garde dramatists are experimenting with form, with content, with philosophy. But, then, were not the Greek tragedians avant-garde by those standards? Was not Shakespeare? Is not every author who is worth reading? Slavish imitation and endless repetitions are utterly deadly. Free verse, so recently avant-garde, is today a respectable member of the poetic family, and its most recent offerings seem unpleasantly repetitive.

The theater of the absurd is a vital experiment, creating new forms as it goes. Yet Sartre, Ionesco, Strindberg—all the experimenters have retained the traditions of their past, building on them, changing and

---

° "Irony and Absurdity in the Avant-Garde Theatre," Vol. XXII.

shaping them to create a statement of their individual talent. T. S. Eliot defended such practice in "Tradition and the Individual Talent," saying:

Yet if the only form of tradition, of handing down, consisted in following the ways of the immediate generation before us in a blind or timid adherence to its successes, "tradition" should positively be discouraged. We have seen many such simple currents soon lost in the sand; and novelty is better than repetition. Tradition is a matter of much wider significance. It cannot be inherited, and if you want it you must obtain it by great labour. It involves, in the first place, the historical sense, which we may call nearly indispensable to any one who would continue to be a poet beyond his twenty-fifth year; and the historical sense involves a perception, not only of the pastness of the past, but of its presence; the historical sense compels a man to write not merely with his own generation in his bones, but with a feeling that the whole of the literature of Europe from Homer and within it the whole of the literature of his own country has a simultaneous existence and composes a simultaneous order. This historical sense, which is a sense of the timeless as well as of the temporal and of the timeless and of the temporal together, is what makes a writer traditional. And it is at the same time what makes a writer most acutely conscious of his place in time, of his own contemporaneity.°

And William Faulkner, in a *Paris Review* interview, projected today's writer into the future, into the growing, steady stream of tradition:

FAULKNER: Life is not interested in good and evil. Don Quixote was constantly choosing between good and evil, but then he was choosing in his dream state. He was mad. He entered reality only when he was so busy trying to cope with people that he had no time to distinguish between good and evil. Since people exist only in life, they must devote their time simply to being alive. Life is motion, and motion is concerned with what makes man move—which is ambition, power, pleasure. What time a man can devote to morality, he must take by force from the motion of which he is a part. He is compelled to make choices between good and evil sooner or later, because moral conscience demands that from him in order that he can live with himself tomorrow. His moral conscience is the curse he had to accept from the gods in order to gain from them the right to dream.

INTERVIEWER: Could you explain more what you mean by motion in relation to the artist?

FAULKNER: The aim of every artist is to arrest motion, which is life, by artificial means and hold it fixed so that a hundred years later, when a stranger looks at it, it moves again since it is life. Since man is mortal, the only immortality possible

° *Selected Essays;* New Edition (New York, 1960).

for him is to leave something behind him that is immortal since it will always move. This is the artist's way of scribbling "Kilroy was here" on the wall of the final and irrevocable oblivion through which he must someday pass.°

The symbols Faulkner employs to explain the author's affirmation of hope are immediately understandable at the emotional level, for they are intellectually conceived and effectively employed. Long a basic tool of the dramatist, such symbols exist as the rock to which Prometheus is bound by Aeschylus, as the swollen foot of Oedipus, as the witches of Macbeth. Even realism could not abandon the poetic symbol: Henrik Ibsen employed it brilliantly in *Hedda Gabler.* If you have read that play, you will remember that Hedda commits suicide with a gun left by her father, a gun she views as a memento of her former meaningless existence in a reasonless society. Her death, then, results from a concrete representation of that society and indicts it harshly. Anton Chekhov's masterpiece of realism, *The Cherry Orchard,* combines symbol and theme in the title to create a poetic response in the final moments of the play. Expressionism, as we have seen, creates its total effect from symbols, and the theater of the absurd is an offshoot if not a part of the expressionist movement.

A sadly neglected play in the expressionistic theater of the absurd is Tennessee Williams' *Camino Real.* Probably the least commercially successful play he ever wrote, it is completely non-representational of him as a dramatist. And yet he has written no finer play. *The Glass Menagerie* alternates between expressionism, realism, and the poetic drama to create one of the distinctive modern tragedies, but it lacks the soaring imagination, the brilliance of verse that abounds in *Camino Real.* If an affirmation of faith in man were ever penned, this play is that affirmation. Perhaps that alone explains its Broadway failure. It is no *Camelot;* its truths are stark and ugly, its characters the scurvy scum of the literary earth. Yet therein lies its great beauty. When the lost, the hopeless, the alienated, the abandoned speak truth, it comes from that area "along the heart" and must be felt there if it is to succeed as a communication. *Camino Real* succeeds as a communication with those who wish to hear truth. Rather than being structured in acts and scenes, the play is dramatically structured in "Blocks," the action intermingling and overlapping, each incident coloring what comes before it and what follows it to re-create the pattern of truth.

The first necessity of any play is to catch and hold the attention of the reader. Conflict, tension, suspense, and satisfying familiarity must be

° *Writers at Work,* ed. Malcolm Cowley (New York, 1957), pp. 138–139.

interwoven to create that interest. Beginning *in medias res* (as Aristotle said), it is well for conflict to be suggested from the opening moment. Relying on Greek tradition, Williams brings his first characters down *through* the audience, involving that group and posing conflict as the well-known Don Quixote and Sancho argue and part. The potential conflict initiated, the dramatist can openly suggest the *major dramatic question* (the primary question the play will attempt to answer) and proceed with the *attack* (that point at which the major dramatic question is posed and which must culminate in an answer before the play ends). *Minor dramatic questions* (ones contributing in some way to the major question) are posed and a *resolution* (the point at which the major dramatic question is answered) reached. Between the attack and the resolution, a point of *crisis* (the turning point of the play) occurs—a standard structure that centuries of dramatists have found to be the most functional. Williams does not violate that structure; he violates only the expository approach. His symbols—but let him tell you about his symbols:

FOREWORD*

It is amazing and frightening how completely one's whole being becomes absorbed in the making of a play. It is almost as if you were frantically constructing another world while the world that you live in dissolves beneath your feet, and that your survival depends on completing this construction at least one second before the old habitation collapses.

More than any other work that I have done, this play has seemed to me like the construction of another world, a separate existence. Of course, it is nothing more nor less than my conception of the time and world that I live in, and its people are mostly archetypes of certain basic attitudes and qualities with those mutations that would occur if they had continued along the road to this hypothetical terminal point in it.

A convention of the play is existence outside of time in a place of no specific locality. If you regard it that way, I suppose it becomes an elaborate allegory, but in New Haven we opened directly across the street from a movie theatre that was showing *Peter Pan* in Technicolor and it did not seem altogether inappropriate to me. Fairy tales nearly always have some simple moral lesson of good and evil, but that is not the secret of their fascination any more, I hope, than the philosophical import that might be distilled from the fantasies of *Camino Real* is the principal element of its appeal.

To me the appeal of this work is its unusual degree of freedom. When it began

* Written prior to the Broadway premiere of *Camino Real* and published in the New York *Times* on Sunday, March 15, 1953.

to get under way I felt a new sensation of release, as if I could "ride out" like a tenor sax taking the breaks in a Dixieland combo or a piano in a bop session. You may call it self-indulgence, but I was not doing it merely for myself. I could not have felt a purely private thrill of release unless I had hope of sharing this experience with lots and lots of audiences to come.

My desire was to give these audiences my own sense of something wild and unrestricted that ran like water in the mountains, or clouds changing shape in a gale, or the continually dissolving and transforming images of a dream. This sort of freedom is not chaos nor anarchy. On the contrary, it is the result of painstaking design, and in this work I have given more conscious attention to form and construction than I have in any work before. Freedom is not achieved simply by working freely.

Elia Kazan was attracted to this work mainly, I believe, for the same reason—its freedom and mobility of form. I know that we have kept saying the word "flight" to each other as if the play were merely an abstraction of the impulse to fly, and most of the work out of town, his in staging, mine in cutting and revising, has been with this impulse in mind: the achievement of a continual flow. Speech after speech and bit after bit that were nice in themselves have been remorselessly blasted out of the script and its staging wherever they seemed to obstruct or divert this flow.

There have been plenty of indications already that this play will exasperate and confuse a certain number of people which we hope is not so large as the number it is likely to please. At each performance a number of people have stamped out of the auditorium, with little regard for those whom they have had to crawl over, almost as if the building had caught on fire, and there have been sibilant noises on the way out and demands for money back if the cashier was foolish enough to remain in his box.

I am at a loss to explain this phenomenon, and if I am being facetious about one thing, I am being quite serious about another when I say that I had never for one minute supposed that the play would seem obscure and confusing to anyone who was willing to meet it even less than halfway. It was a costly production, and for this reason I had to read it aloud, together with a few of the actors on one occasion, before large groups of prospective backers, before the funds to produce it were in the till. It was only then that I came up against the disconcerting surprise that some people would think that the play needed clarification.

My attitude is intransigent. I still don't agree that it needs any explanation. Some poet has said that a poem should not mean but be. Of course, a play is not a poem, not even a poetic play has quite the same license as a poem. But to go to *Camino Real* with the inflexible demands of a logician is unfair to both parties.

In Philadelphia a young man from a literary periodical saw the play and then cross-examined me about all its dream-like images. He had made a list of them while he watched the play, and afterward at my hotel he brought out the list and asked me to explain the meaning of each one. I can't deny that I use a lot of those things called symbols but being a self-defensive creature, I say that symbols are nothing but the natural speech of drama.

We all have in our conscious and unconscious minds a great vocabulary of images, and I think all human communication is based on these images as are our dreams; and a symbol in a play has only one legitimate purpose which is to say a thing more directly and simply and beautifully than it could be said in words.

I hate writing that is a parade of images for the sake of images; I hate it so much that I close a book in disgust when it keeps on saying one thing is like another; I even get disgusted with poems that make nothing but comparisons between one thing and another. But I repeat that symbols, when used respectfully, are the purest language of plays. Sometimes it would take page after tedious page of exposition to put across an idea that can be said with an object or a gesture on the lighted stage.

To take one case in point: the battered portmanteau of Jacques Casanova is hurled from the balcony of a luxury hotel when his remittance check fails to come through. While the portmanteau is still in the air, he shouts: "Careful, I have—" —and when it has crashed to the street he continues—"fragile—mementoes . . ." I suppose that is a symbol, at least it is an object used to express as directly and vividly as possible certain things which could be said in pages of dull talk.

As for those patrons who departed before the final scene, I offer myself this tentative bit of solace: that these theatregoers may be a little domesticated in their theatrical tastes. A cage represents security as well as confinement to a bird that has grown used to being in it; and when a theatrical work kicks over the traces with such apparent insouciance, security seems challenged and, instead of participating in its sense of freedom, one out of a certain number of playgoers will rush back out to the more accustomed implausibility of the street he lives on.

To modify this effect of complaisance I would like to admit to you quite frankly that I can't say with any personal conviction that I have written a good play, I only know that I have felt a release in this work which I wanted you to feel with me.

In expressionistic drama and the theater of the absurd, symbols are intensely personal. A rose to one reader may suggest pure love; to another, blood drawn by the thorn, and therefore war. For that reason, there are no right answers, no wrong ones to the questions you will find posed after each Block. They are asked only to help you examine the inner recesses of your unconscious, to suggest ways in which you may join symbol to symbol to reach an answer to the major dramatic question. Even here, the question is a personal one. Mr. Williams' answer is not necessarily the only one—it may not be the right one at all for you. Your fund of experience will determine your response to each symbol; your pattern of emotional and intellectual growth will predispose you to follow your own reaction pattern. The answer to the question may be the words of the dying Gertrude Stein: when Alice B. Toklas asked,

"What is the answer?" Stein answered, "What is the question?" And if that makes little sense to you now, remember, you are reading from the theater of the absurd.

CAMINO REAL

by Tennessee Williams

for Elia Kazan

> "In the middle of the journey of our life I came to myself
> in a dark wood where the straight way was lost."
>
> Canto I, Dante's Inferno

CHARACTERS

GUTMAN	WAITER
SURVIVOR	LORD BYRON
ROSITA	NAVIGATOR OF THE FUGITIVO
FIRST OFFICER	PILOT OF THE FUGITIVO
JACQUES CASANOVA	MARKET WOMAN
LA MADRECITA DE LOS PERDIDOS	SECOND MARKET WOMAN
HER SON	STREET VENDOR
KILROY	LORD MULLIGAN
FIRST STREETCLEANER	THE GYPSY
SECOND STREETCLEANER	HER DAUGHTER, ESMERALDA
ABDULLAH	NURSIE
A BUM IN A WINDOW	EVA
A. RATT	THE INSTRUCTOR
THE LOAN SHARK	ASSISTANT INSTRUCTOR
BARON DE CHARLUS	MEDICAL STUDENT
LOBO	DON QUIXOTE
SECOND OFFICER	SANCHO PANZA
A GROTESQUE MUMMER	PRUDENCE DUVERNOY
MARGUERITE GAUTIER	OLYMPE
LADY MULLIGAN	STREET VENDORS, GUESTS, PASSENGERS, etc.

1. Pronounced *Cá*-mino *Ré*-al, the title means "Real (or) True Road"; the abandoned Spanish pronunciation (Ca-*mino* Re-*ál*) meant "Royal (or) King's Highway." The general theme of the play is established in the title which is then combined with a headnote, the opening lines of Dante's

Inferno, wherein Dante states that he came to a place of confusion about life and its values when he was thirty-five years old. From that confusion came his vision of eternality. Williams began to write his play when he was about thirty-five; it was produced when he was thirty-nine and financially secure, critically established, and lionized by the intelligentsia. What do such considerations lead you to conclude about the play?

2. In the "Foreword," Williams said that the characters are "mostly archetypes [original patterns or prototypes] of certain basic attitudes and qualities with those mutations that would occur if they had continued along the road [of time] to this hypothetical terminal point in it." Some of the characters are Williams' creations for the play, others are historical-literary figures. The names of created characters establish their archetypal personalities (A. Ratt, for instance, owns the flophouse, therefore breeds in poverty and filth). The historical-literary characters are noted for certain characteristics, as follows:

ROSITA: "Little Rose," slang term for the female genital organs

JACQUES CASANOVA: Amorous Italian adventurer (1725–1798) whose *Memoirs* record unbelievable sexual success in excess: the "ladies' man"

LA MADRECITA DE LOS PERDIDOS: Little Mother of the Hopeless or Doomed Ones

KILROY: The ubiquitous, anonymous American soldier of World War II who recorded his having passed through by scrawling "Kilroy was here" on walls, fences, and any other surface that would support graffiti: the unimportant wayfarer who desires to leave an historical record of himself but lacks the distinguishing characteristics such as history records

ABDULLAH: A son of the Prophet (Muhammad), fearless and bold

BARON DE CHARLUS: A major character in Marcel Proust's *Remembrance of Things Past,* protagonist of Book IV, *Cities of the Plain;* a social lion, the Baron is haughty and proud, concealing his homosexual depravities as he slowly goes insane

LOBO: The human wolf of literature (sometimes a werewolf) who preys on the weak, following them to exhaustion, then killing them; a cowardly predator

MARGUERITE GAUTIER: Heroine of *La Dame aux Camelias* by Alexandre Dumas *fils;* also, Camille, heroine of the opera *La Traviata* by Verdi; the tubercular, beautiful courtesan who falls in love but is denied happiness until the moment of death

LORD BYRON: Creator and exemplar of the "Byronic hero," a melancholy but beautiful young man always brooding about some unidentified mysterious evil in his past; the young rebel against convention, always seeking new horizons of experience and encouraging gossip about himself to keep his name in public fancy

ESMERALDA: A beautiful gypsy in Victor Hugo's *Notre Dame de Paris* who dances in front of the cathedral and is accused of witchcraft; protected by the hunchback Quasimodo, she is given sanctuary in the cathedral until it is attacked and she is hanged: beauty and the beast

DON QUIXOTE: Protagonist of Cervante's novel of the same name: an impractical dreamer, slightly mad, a frustrated idealist in a materialistic world

SANCHO PANZA: Don Quixote's squire, a rustic exemplar of all things material and "practical"

PRUDENCE DUVERNOY: Companion to Marguerite Gautier, arranger of trysts, female pimp

OLYMPE: Camille's fellow-courtesan who did not make the mistake of falling in love

3. If the characters are archetypes who inhabit a world, what might characterize that world? Would you care to live in it? Do you?

PROLOGUE

As the curtain rises, on an almost lightless stage, there is a loud singing of wind, accompanied by distant, measured reverberations like pounding surf or distant shellfire. Above the ancient wall that backs the set and the perimeter of mountains visible above the wall, are flickers of a white radiance as though daybreak were a white bird caught in a net and struggling to rise.

The plaza is seen fitfully by this light. It belongs to a tropical seaport that bears a confusing, but somehow harmonious, resemblance to such widely scattered ports as Tangiers, Havana, Vera Cruz, Casablanca, Shanghai, New Orleans.

On stage left is the luxury side of the street, containing the façade of the Siete Mares hotel and its low terrace on which are a number of glass-topped white iron tables and chairs. In the downstairs there is a great bay window in which are seen a pair of elegant "dummies," one seated, one standing behind, looking out into the plaza with painted smiles. Upstairs is a small balcony and behind it a large window exposing a wall on which is hung a phoenix painted on silk: this should be softly lighted now and then in the play, since resurrections are so much a part of its meaning.

Opposite the hotel is Skid Row which contains the GYPSY'S gaudy stall, the LOAN SHARK'S establishment with a window containing a variety of pawned articles, and the "Ritz Men Only" which is a flea-bag hotel or flophouse and which has a practical window above its downstairs entrance, in which a bum will appear from time to time to deliver appropriate or contrapuntal song titles.

Upstage is a great flight of stairs that mount the ancient wall to a sort of archway that leads out into "Terra Incognita," as it is called in the play, a wasteland between the walled town and the distant perimeter of snow-topped mountains.

Downstage right and left are a pair of arches which give entrance to dead-end streets.

Immediately after the curtain rises a shaft of blue light is thrown down a central aisle of the theatre, and in this light, advancing from the back of the house, appears DON QUIXOTE DE LA MANCHA, *dressed like an old "desert rat." As he enters the aisle he shouts, "Hola!", in a cracked old voice which is still full of energy and is answered by another voice which is impatient and tired, that of his squire,* SANCHO PANZA. *Stumbling with a fatigue which is only physical, the old knight comes down the aisle, and* SANCHO *follows a couple of yards behind him, loaded down with equipment that ranges from a medieval shield to a military canteen or Thermos bottle. Shouts are exchanged between them.*

1. Sounds and sights, changing colors, and daybreak create what kind of atmosphere at this point?

2. Divisions are sharply marked. The time is between daylight and dark. A wall separates the town from the outside. A street separates the luxury side of the street from the Skid Row side. What do such divisions indicate? How realistic is the device? How expressionistic? Which is more "true"?

3. What do the dawn, the dummies, the phoenix painted on silk, and the singing bum symbolize?

QUIXOTE *(ranting above the wind in a voice which is nearly as old).* Blue is the color of distance!

SANCHO *(wearily behind him).* Yes, distance is blue.

QUIXOTE. Blue is also the color of nobility.

SANCHO. Yes, nobility's blue.

QUIXOTE. Blue is the color of distance and nobility, and that's why an old knight should always have somewhere about him a bit of blue ribbon . . . *(He jostles the elbow of an aisle-sitter as he staggers with fatigue; he mumbles an apology.)*

SANCHO. Yes, a bit of blue ribbon.

QUIXOTE. A bit of faded blue ribbon, tucked away in whatever remains of his armor, or borne on the tip of his lance, his—unconquerable lance! It serves to remind an old knight of distance that he has gone and distance he has yet to go . . .

*(*SANCHO *mutters the Spanish word for excrement as several pieces of rusty armor fall into the aisle.* QUIXOTE *has now arrived at the foot of the steps onto the forestage. He pauses there as if wandering out of or into a dream.* SANCHO *draws up clanking behind him.)*

4. What effect does Don Quixote's arrival through the theater audience create in you? Is it *your* seat he stumbles against? Has Quixote any relationship to the Greek Chorus concept?

5. What is the meaning of the color "blue" as it is applied to distance? What visual images did you see in your mind that seem irrelevant? (Do not dismiss them as "incorrect." There is no right or wrong reaction!)

6. Is the stage itself "a dream" or reality? Is this at variance with your concept of the play's setting? Does the stage as "a dream" make expressionistic sense or realistic sense? Explain.

(MR. GUTMAN, *a lordly fat man wearing a linen suit and a pith helmet, appears dimly on the balcony of the Siete Mares, a white cockatoo on his wrist. The bird cries out harshly.*)

GUTMAN. Hush, Aurora.

QUIXOTE. It also reminds an old knight of that green country he lived in which was the youth of his heart, before such singing words as *Truth!*

SANCHO (*panting*). —Truth.

QUIXOTE. Valor!

SANCHO. —Valor.

QUIXOTE (*elevating his lance*). Devoir!

SANCHO. —Devoir . . .

QUIXOTE. —turned into the meaningless mumble of some old monk hunched over cold mutton at supper!

(GUTMAN *alerts a pair of* GUARDS *in the plaza, who cross with red lanterns to either side of the proscenium where they lower black and white striped barrier gates as if the proscenium marked a frontier. One of them, with a hand on his holster, advances toward the pair on the steps.*)

7. Such poetic lines as "the meaningless mumble of some old monk hunched over cold mutton at supper" will be employed throughout the play. Emotionally, you know what the line means. But can you explain the meaning intellectually? Try.

8. Explain the use of color in your visualized production.

GUARD. Vien aquí. (SANCHO *hangs back but* QUIXOTE *stalks up to the barrier gate. The* GUARD *turns a flashlight on his long and exceedingly grave red face,* "*frisks*" *him casually for concealed weapons, examines a rusty old knife and tosses it contemptuously away.*) Sus papeles! Sus documentos!

(QUIXOTE *fumblingly produces some tattered old papers from the lining of his hat.*)

GUTMAN (*impatiently*). Who is it?

GUARD. An old desert rat named Quixote.

GUTMAN. Oh!—Expected!—Let him in.

(*The* GUARDS *raise the barrier gate and one sits down to smoke on the terrace.* SANCHO *hangs back still. A dispute takes place on the forestage and steps into the aisle.*)

QUIXOTE. Forward!

SANCHO. Aw, naw. I know this place. (*He produces a crumpled parchment.*) Here it is on the chart. Look, it says here: "Continue until you come to the square of a walled town which is the end of the Camino Real and the beginning of the Camino Real. Halt there," it says, "and turn back, Traveler, for the spring of humanity has gone dry in this place and—"

QUIXOTE (*he snatches the chart from him and reads the rest of the inscription*). "—there are no birds in the country except wild birds that are tamed and kept in—" (*he holds the chart close to his nose*)—Cages!

SANCHO (*urgently*). Let's go back to La Mancha!

QUIXOTE. Forward!

SANCHO. The time has come for retreat!

QUIXOTE. The time for retreat never comes!

SANCHO. I'm going back to La Mancha! (*He dumps the knightly equipment into the orchestra pit.*)

QUIXOTE. *Without me?*

SANCHO (*bustling up the aisle*). With you or without you, old tireless and tiresome master!

QUIXOTE (*imploringly*). Saaaaaan-chooooooooo!

SANCHO (*near the top of the aisle*). I'm going back to La Maaaaaaaaan-chaaaa-aaa . . .

(*He disappears as the blue light in the aisle dims out. The* GUARD *puts out his cigarette and wanders out of the plaza. The wind moans and* GUTMAN *laughs softly as the Ancient Knight enters the plaza with such a desolate air.*)

9. Why does Sancho, the materialist, the realist, refuse to leave the Royal Highway and enter the Real Road? Is a dramatic question posed here?

QUIXOTE (*looking about the plaza*). —Lonely . . . (*To his surprise the word is echoed softly by almost unseen figures huddled below the stairs and against the wall of the town.* QUIXOTE *leans upon his lance and observes with a wry smile—*) —When so many are lonely as seem to be lonely, it would be inexcusably selfish to be lonely alone. (*He shakes out a dusty blanket. Shadowy arms extend toward him and voices murmur.*)

VOICE. Sleep. Sleep. Sleep.

QUIXOTE (*arranging his blanket*). Yes, I'll sleep for a while, I'll sleep and dream for a while against the wall of this town . . . (*A mandolin or guitar plays "The Nightingale of France."*) —And my dream will be a pageant, a masque in which old meanings will be remembered and possibly new ones discovered, and when I wake from this sleep and this disturbing pageant of a dream, I'll choose one among its shadows to take along with me in the place of Sancho . . . (*He blows his nose between his fingers and wipes them on his shirttail.*) —For new companions are not as familiar as old ones but all the same—they're old ones with only slight differences of face and figure, which may or may not be improvements, and it would be selfish of me to be lonely alone . . . (*He stumbles down the incline into the Pit below the stairs where most of the* STREET PEOPLE *huddle beneath awnings of open stalls.*)

(*The white cockatoo squawks.*)

GUTMAN. Hush, Aurora.

QUIXOTE. And tomorrow at this same hour, which we call madrugada, the loveliest of all words, except the word alba, and that word also means daybreak—Yes, at daybreak tomorrow I will go on from here with a new companion and this old bit of blue ribbon to keep me in mind of distance that I have gone and distance I have yet to go, and also to keep me in mind of—(*The cockatoo cries wildly.* QUIXOTE *nods as if in agreement with the outcry and folds himself into his blanket below the great stairs.*)

10. Is Quixote's defense of loneliness humor, wit, epigram, or what?

GUTMAN (*stroking the cockatoo's crest*). Be still, Aurora. I know it's morning, Aurora. (*Daylight turns the plaza silver and slowly gold.* VENDORS *rise beneath white awnings of stalls. The* GYPSY'S *stall opens. A tall, courtly figure, in his late middle years* (JACQUES CASANOVA) *crosses from the Siete Mares to the* LOAN SHARK'S, *removing a silver snuff box from his pocket as* GUTMAN *speaks. His costume, like that of all the legendary characters in the play (except perhaps* QUIXOTE) *is generally "modern" but with vestigial touches of the period to which he was actually related. The cane and the snuff box and perhaps a brocaded vest may be sufficient to give this historical suggestion in* CASANOVA'S *case. He bears his hawklike head with a sort of anxious pride on most occasions, a pride maintained under a steadily mounting pressure.*)
—It's morning and after morning. It's afternoon, ha ha! And now I must go downstairs to announce the beginning of that old wanderer's dream . . .

(*He withdraws from the balcony as old* PRUDENCE DUVERNOY *stumbles out of the hotel, as if not yet quite awake from an afternoon siesta. Chattering with beads and bracelets, she wanders vaguely down into the plaza, raising a faded green silk parasol, damp henna-streaked hair slipping under a monstrous hat of faded silk roses; she is searching for a lost poodle.*)

PRUDENCE. Trique? Trique?

(JACQUES *comes out of the* LOAN SHARK'S *replacing his case angrily in his pocket.*)

JACQUES. Why, I'd rather give it to a street beggar! This case is a Boucheron, I won it at faro at the summer palace, at Tsarskoe Selo in the winter of—

(*The* LOAN SHARK *slams the door.* JACQUES *glares, then shrugs and starts across the plaza. Old* PRUDENCE *is crouched over the filthy gray bundle of a dying mongrel by the fountain.*)

PRUDENCE. Trique, oh, Trique!

(*The* GYPSY'S *son,* ABDULLAH, *watches, giggling.*)

JACQUES (*reproving*). It is a terrible thing for an old woman to outlive her dogs. (*He crosses to* PRUDENCE *and gently disengages the animal from her grasp.*) Madam, that is not Trique.

PRUDENCE. —When I woke up she wasn't in her basket . . .

JACQUES. Sometimes we sleep too long in the afternoon and when we wake we find things changed, Signora.

PRUDENCE. Oh, you're Italian!

JACQUES. I am from Venice, Signora.

PRUDENCE. Ah, Venice, city of pearls! I saw you last night on the terrace dining with—Oh, I'm so worried about her! I'm an old friend of hers, perhaps she's mentioned me to you. Prudence Duvernoy? I was her best friend in the old days in Paris, but now she's forgotten so much . . . I hope you have influence with her! (*A waltz of* CAMILLE'S *time in Paris is heard.*) I want you to give her a message from a certain wealthy old gentleman that she met at one of those watering places she used to go to for her health. She resembled his daughter who died of consumption and so he adored Camille, lavished everything on her! What did she do? Took a young lover who hadn't a couple of pennies to rub together, disinherited by his father because of her! Oh, you can't do that, not now, not any more, you've got to be realistic on the Camino Real!

(GUTMAN *has come out on the terrace: he announces quietly—*)

GUTMAN. Block One on the Camino Real.

11. Is a dramatic question posed in Prudence's presence on the Camino Real?

12. Explain the humor of the name *Trique*. What does it foreshadow?

13. Why is Gutman chosen to announce the Blocks, and what do the Blocks represent?

14. In Cervantes' novel, the "mad" Quixote eventually found "sanity." Is this pageant symbolic of insanity, divine madness (vision as a gift of the gods), or sanity? Justify your answer.

BLOCK ONE

PRUDENCE (*continuing*). Yes, you've got to be practical on it! Well, give her this message, please, Sir. He wants her back on any terms whatsoever! (*Her speech gathers furious momentum.*) Her evenings will be free. He wants only her mornings, mornings are hard on old men because their hearts beat slowly, and he wants only her mornings! Well, that's how it should be! A sensible arrangement! Elderly gentlemen have to content themselves with a lady's spare time before supper! Isn't that so? Of course so! And so I told him! I told him, Camille isn't well! She requires delicate care! Has many debts, creditors storm her door! "How much does she owe?" he asked me, and, oh, did I do some lightning mathematics! Jewels in pawn, I told him, pearls, rings, necklaces, bracelets, diamond ear-drops are in pawn! Horses put up for sale at a public auction!

JACQUES (*appalled by this torrent*). Signora, Signora, all of these things are—

PRUDENCE. —What?

JACQUES. Dreams!

(GUTMAN *laughs. A woman sings at a distance.*)

PRUDENCE (*continuing with less assurance*). —You're not so young as I thought when I saw you last night on the terrace by candlelight on the—Oh, but—Ho ho!—I bet there is one old fountain in this plaza that hasn't gone dry!

(*She pokes him obscenely. He recoils.* GUTMAN *laughs.* JACQUES *starts away but she seizes his arm again, and the torrent of speech continues.*)

1. What is the effect of changing Blocks in the middle of a character's speech?

2. How does Gutman's laugh serve as an emphatic effect?

3. Fountains are employed throughout the play. Explain the relationship of the dry public fountain and the "fountain" Prudence jokes about. Is it realistic that Casanova should recoil from her obscenity? Remember time distortions before you decide.

PRUDENCE. Wait, wait, listen! Her candle is burning low. But how can you tell? She might have a lingering end, and charity hospitals? Why, you might as well take a flying leap into the Streetcleaners' barrel. Oh, I've told her and told her not to live in a dream! A dream is nothing to live in, why, its gone like a—Don't let her elegance fool you! That girl has done the Camino in carriages but she has also done it on foot! She knows every stone the Camino is paved with! So tell her this. You tell her, she won't listen to me!—Times and conditions have undergone certain changes since we were friends in Paris, and now we dismiss young lovers with skins of silk and eyes like a child's first prayer, we put them away as lightly as we put away white gloves meant only for summer, and pick up a pair of black ones, suitable for winter . . .

(*The singing voice rises: then subsides.*)

4. Explain Prudence Duvernoy's ambivalence toward Camille.

JACQUES. Excuse me, Madam. (*He tears himself from her grasp and rushes into the Siete Mares.*)

PRUDENCE (*dazed, to* GUTMAN).—What block is this?

GUTMAN. Block One.

PRUDENCE. I didn't hear the announcement . . .

GUTMAN (*coldly*). Well, now you do.

(OLYMPE *comes out of the lobby with a pale orange silk parasol like a floating moon.*)

OLYMPE. Oh, there you are, I've looked for you high and low!—mostly low . . .
(*They float vaguely out into the dazzling plaza as though a capricious wind took them, finally drifting through the Moorish arch downstage right. The song dies out.*)
GUTMAN (*lighting a thin cigar*). Block Two on the Camino Real.

5. Explain the significance of Prudence's green parasol and Olympe's orange one.

6. Prudence and Olympe enter one of the dead-end streets as though taken on a capricious wind. Explain the symbolism.

7. What is the dramatic function of Block One in the structure of the play?

BLOCK TWO

After GUTMAN'S *announcement, a hoarse cry is heard. A figure in rags, skin blackened by the sun, tumbles crazily down the steep alley to the plaza. He turns about blindly, murmuring: "A donde la fuente?" He stumbles against the hideous old prostitute ROSITA who grins horribly and whispers something to him, hitching up her ragged, filthy skirt. Then she gives him a jocular push toward the fountain. He falls upon his belly and thrusts his hands into the dried-up basin. Then he staggers to his feet with a despairing cry.*

THE SURVIVOR. La fuente está seca!
(ROSITA *laughs madly but the other* STREET PEOPLE *moan. A dry gourd rattles.*)
ROSITA. The fountain is dry, but there's plenty to drink in the Siete Mares!
(*She shoves him toward the hotel. The proprietor,* GUTMAN, *steps out, smoking a thin cigar, fanning himself with a palm leaf. As the* SURVIVOR *advances,* GUTMAN *whistles. A man in military dress comes out upon the low terrace.*)
OFFICER. Go back!
(*The* SURVIVOR *stumbles forward. The* OFFICER *fires at him. He lowers his hands to his stomach, turns slowly about with a lost expression, looking up at the sky, and stumbles toward the fountain. During the scene that follows, until the entrance of* LA MADRECITA *and her* SON, *the* SURVIVOR *drags himself slowly about the concrete rim of the fountain, almost entirely ignored, as a dying pariah dog in a starving country.* JACQUES CASANOVA *comes out upon the terrace of the Siete Mares. Now he passes the hotel proprietor's impassive figure, descending a step beneath and a little in advance of him, and without looking at him.*)
JACQUES (*with infinite weariness and disgust*). What has happened?
GUTMAN (*serenely*). We have entered the second in a progress of sixteen blocks on the Camino Real. It's five o'clock. That angry old lion, the Sun, looked back once and growled and then went switching his tail toward the cool shade of the Sierras. Our guests have taken their afternoon siestas . . .

(*The* SURVIVOR *has come out upon the forestage, now, not like a dying man but like a shy speaker who has forgotten the opening line of his speech. He is only a little crouched over with a hand obscuring the red stain over his belly. Two or three* STREET PEOPLE *wander about calling their wares: "Tacos, tacos, fritos . . ."—Lotería, lotería"—*ROSITA *shuffles around, calling "Love? Love?"—pulling down the filthy décolletage of her blouse to show more of her sagging bosom. The* SURVIVOR *arrives at the top of the stairs descending into the orchestra of the theatre, and hangs onto it, looking out reflectively as a man over the rail of a boat coming into a somewhat disturbingly strange harbor.*)

1. What does the public fountain gone dry symbolize?
2. Who or what is the Survivor?
3. Time is again "between time," between afternoon and evening. Why?
4. Why does the Survivor not descend the stairs into the orchestra?

GUTMAN (*continuing*). —They suffer from extreme fatigue, our guests at the Siete Mares, all of them have a degree or two of fever. Questions are passed amongst them like something illicit and shameful, like counterfeit money or drugs or indecent postcards— (*He leans forward and whispers.*) —"What is this place? Where are we? What is the meaning of—Shhhh!"—Ha ha . . .

THE SURVIVOR (*very softly to the audience*). I once had a pony named Peeto. He caught in his nostrils the scent of thunderstorms coming even before the clouds had crossed the Sierra . . .

VENDOR. Tacos, tacos, fritos . . .

ROSITA. Love? Love?

LADY MULLIGAN (*to waiter on terrace*). Are you sure no one called me? I was expecting a call . . .

GUTMAN (*smiling*). My guests are confused and exhausted but at this hour they pull themselves together, and drift downstairs on the wings of gin and the lift, they drift into the public rooms and exchange notes again on fashionable couturiers and custom tailors, restaurants, vintages of wine, hair-dressers, plastic surgeons, girls and young men susceptible to offers . . . (*There is a hum of light conversation and laughter within.*) —Hear them? They're exchanging notes . . .

JACQUES (*striking the terrace with his cane*). I asked you what has happened in the plaza!

GUTMAN. Oh, in the plaza, ha ha!—Happenings in the plaza don't concern us . . .

5. Why are the archetypal patrons of the Siete Mares ashamed of their questions? They are adept at social exchange over drinks. Explain the dichotomy.

6. What is the plaza? Remember: happenings there, according to Gutman, "don't concern us" (in the Siete Mares).

JACQUES. I heard shots fired.

GUTMAN. Shots were fired to remind you of your good fortune in staying here. The public fountains have gone dry, you know, but the Siete Mares was erected over the only perpetual never-dried-up spring in Tierra Caliente, and of course that advantage has to be—protected—sometimes by—martial law . . .

(*The guitar resumes.*)

THE SURVIVOR. When Peeto, my pony, was born—he stood on his four legs at once, and accepted the world!—He was wiser than I . . .

VENDOR. Fritos, fritos, tacos!

ROSITA. Love!

THE SURVIVOR. —When Peeto was one year old he was wiser than God! (*A wind sings across the plaza; a dry gourd rattles.*) "Peeto, Peeto!" the Indian boys call after him, trying to stop him—trying to stop the wind!

(*The SURVIVOR'S head sags forward. He sits down as slowly as an old man on a park bench. JACQUES strikes the terrace again with his cane and starts toward the SURVIVOR. The GUARD seizes his elbow.*)

7. What is the significance of the Survivor's memory of Peeto?

JACQUES. Don't put your hand on *me!*

GUARD. *Stay here.*

GUTMAN. Remain on the terrace, please, Signor Casanova.

JACQUES (*fiercely*). —Cognac!

(*The WAITER whispers to GUTMAN. GUTMAN chuckles.*)

GUTMAN. The Maître 'D' tells me that your credit has been discontinued in the restaurant and bar, he says that he has enough of your tabs to pave the terrace with!

JACQUES. What a piece of impertinence! I told the man that the letter that I'm expecting has been delayed in the mail. The postal service in this country is fantastically disorganized, and you know it! You also know that Mlle. Gautier will guarantee my tabs!

GUTMAN. Then let her pick them up at dinner tonight if you're hungry!

JACQUES. I'm not accustomed to this kind of treatment on the *Camino Real!*

GUTMAN. Oh, you'll be, you'll be, after a single night at the "Ritz Men Only." That's where you'll have to transfer your patronage if the letter containing the remittance check doesn't arrive tonight.

JACQUES. I assure you that I shall do nothing of the sort!—Tonight or ever!

GUTMAN. Watch out, old hawk, the wind is ruffling your feathers! (*JACQUES sinks trembling into a chair.*) —Give him a thimble of brandy before he collapses . . . Fury is a luxury of the young, their veins are resilient, but his are brittle . . .

8. Explain Gutman's assertion that "Fury is a luxury of the young."

JACQUES. Here I sit, submitting to insult for a thimble of brandy—while directly in front of me—(*The singer,* LA MADRECITA, *enters the plaza. She is a blind woman led by a ragged* YOUNG MAN. *The* WAITER *brings* JACQUES *a brandy.*)—a man in the plaza dies like a pariah dog!—I take the brandy! I sip it!—My heart is too tired to break, my heart is too tired to—break . . .

(LA MADRECITA *chants softly. She slowly raises her arm to point at the* SURVIVOR *crouched on the steps from the plaza.*)

GUTMAN (*suddenly*). Give me the phone! Connect me with the Palace. Get me the Generalissimo, quick, quick, quick! (*The* SURVIVOR *rises feebly and shuffles very slowly toward the extended arms of "The Little Blind One."*) Generalissimo? Gutman speaking! Hello, sweetheart. There has been a little incident in the plaza. You know that party of young explorers that attempted to cross the desert on foot? Well, one of them's come back. He was very thirsty. He found the fountain dry. He started toward the hotel. He was politely advised to advance no further. But he disregarded this advice. Action had to be taken. And now, and now—that old blind woman they call "La Madrecita"?— She's come into the plaza with the man called "The Dreamer" . . .

SURVIVOR. Donde?

THE DREAMER. Aquí!

GUTMAN (*continuing*). You remember those two! I once mentioned them to you. You said "They're harmless dreamers and they're loved by the people."—"What," I asked you, "is harmless about a dreamer, and what," I asked you, "is harmless about the love of the people?—Revolution only needs good dreamers who remember their dreams, and the love of the people belongs safely only to you—their Generalissimo!"—Yes, now the blind woman has recovered her sight and is extending her arms to the wounded Survivor, and the man with the guitar is leading him to her. . . (*The described action is being enacted.*) Wait one moment! There's a possibility that the forbidden word may be spoken! Yes! The forbidden word is about to be spoken!

(*The* DREAMER *places an arm about the blinded* SURVIVOR, *and cries out.*)

THE DREAMER. Hermano!

(*The cry is repeated like springing fire and a loud murmur sweeps the crowd. They push forward with cupped hands extended and the gasping cries of starving people at the sight of bread. Two* MILITARY GUARDS *herd them back under the colonnades with clubs and drawn revolvers.* LA MADRECITA *chants softly with her blind eyes lifted. A* GUARD *starts toward her. The People shout "NO!"*)

LA MADRECITA (*chanting*). "Rojo está el sol! Rojo está el sol de sangre! Blanca está la luna! Blanca está la luna de miedo!"

(*The crowd makes a turning motion.*)

GUTMAN (*to the waiter*). Put up the ropes! (*Velvet ropes are strung very quickly about the terrace of the Siete Mares. They are like the ropes on decks of steamers in rough waters.* GUTMAN *shouts into the phone again.*) The word was spoken. The crowd is agitated. Hang on! (*He lays down instrument.*)

JACQUES (*hoarsely, shaken*). He said "Hermano." That's the word for brother.

GUTMAN (*calmly*). Yes, the most dangerous word in any human tongue is the word for brother. It's inflammatory.—I don't suppose it can be struck out of the language altogether but it must be reserved for strictly private usage in back of soundproof walls. Otherwise it disturbs the population . . .

9. Why is La Madrecita blind? Who is her son "The Dreamer"?

10. Why does the word *Hermano* (brother) agitate the crowd? Would it be a powerful word if it were "reserved for strictly private usage in back of soundproof walls"?

JACQUES. The people need the word. They're thirsty for it!

GUTMAN. What are these creatures? Mendicants. Prostitutes. Thieves and petty vendors in a bazaar where the human heart is a part of the bargain.

JACQUES. Because they need the word and the word is forbidden!

GUTMAN. The word is said in pulpits and at tables of council where its volatile essence can be contained. But on the lips of these creatures, what is it? A wanton incitement to riot, without understanding. For what is a brother to them but someone to get ahead of, to cheat, to lie to, to undersell in the market. Brother, you say to a man whose wife you sleep with!—But now, you see, the word has disturbed the people and made it necessary to invoke martial law!

11. Why can pulpits and tables of council contain the "volatile essence" of *Hermano?* Do you agree or disagree?

12. Intellectually (not emotionally) defend or attack Gutman's argument that *Hermano* is merely an "incitement to riot, without understanding" when the people speak it.

(*Meanwhile the* DREAMER *has brought the* SURVIVOR *to* LA MADRECITA, *who is seated on the cement rim of the fountain. She has cradled the dying man in her arms in the attitude of a* Pietà. *The* DREAMER *is crouched beside them, softly playing a guitar. Now he springs up with a harsh cry.*)

THE DREAMER. *Muerto!*

(*The* STREETCLEANERS' *piping commences at a distance.* GUTMAN *seizes the phone again.*)

GUTMAN (*into phone*). Generalissimo, the Survivor is no longer surviving. I think we'd better have some public diversion right away. Put the Gypsy on! Have her announce the Fiesta!

LOUDSPEAKER (*responding instantly*). Damas y Caballeros! The next voice you hear will be the voice of—the Gypsy!

GYPSY (*over loudspeaker*). Hoy! Noche de Fiesta! Tonight the moon will restore the virginity of my daughter!

13. Explain Gutman's and the Generalissimo's reasoning concerning the need for "public diversion." Does Gutman understand the people in this case?
14. Is "virginity" restoration of interest? To whom? Why? Is a dramatic question posed?

GUTMAN. Bring on the Gypsy's daughter, Esmeralda. Show the virgin-to-be!

(ESMERALDA *is led from the* GYPSY'S *stall by a severe duenna, "*NURSIE,*" out upon the forestage. She is manacled by the wrist to the duenna. Her costume is vaguely Levantine.* GUARDS *are herding the crowd back again.*)

GUTMAN. Ha ha! Ho ho ho! Music! (*There is gay music.* ROSITA *dances.*) Abdullah! You're on!

(ABDULLAH *skips into the plaza, shouting histrionically.*)

ABDULLAH. Tonight the moon will restore the virginity of my sister, Esmeralda!

GUTMAN. Dance, boy!

(ESMERALDA *is led back into the stall. Throwing off his burnoose,* ABDULLAH *dances with* ROSITA. *Behind their dance, armed* GUARDS *force* LA MADRECITA *and the* DREAMER *to retreat from the fountain, leaving the lifeless body of the* SURVIVOR. *All at once there is a discordant blast of brass instruments.* KILROY *comes into the plaza. He is a young American vagrant, about twenty-seven. He wears dungarees and a skivvy shirt, the pants faded nearly white from long wear and much washing, fitting him as closely as the clothes of sculpture. He has a pair of golden boxing gloves slung about his neck and he carries a small duffle bag. His belt is ruby-and-emerald-studded with the word CHAMP in bold letters. He stops before a chalked inscription on a wall downstage which says: "Kilroy Is Coming!" He scratches out "Coming" and over it prints "Here!"*)

GUTMAN. Ho ho!—a clown! The Eternal Punchinella! That's exactly what's needed in a time of crisis! Block Three on the Camino Real.

15. Why does Gutman call Kilroy "a clown" and suggest that clowns are needed in time of crisis. Do you agree with Gutman? Do you agree partially, completely, or do you disagree?

BLOCK THREE

KILROY (*genially, to all present*). Ha ha! (*Then he walks up to the* OFFICER *by the terrace of the Siete Mares.*) Buenas dias, señor. (*He gets no response—barely even a glance.*) Habla Inglesia? Usted?

OFFICER. What is it you want?

KILROY. Where is Western Union or Wells-Fargo? I got to send a wire to some friends in the States.

OFFICER. No hay Western Union, no hay Wells-Fargo.

KILROY. That is very peculiar. I never struck a town yet that didn't have one or the other. I just got off a boat. Lousiest frigging tub I ever shipped on, one continual hell it was, all the way up from Rio. And me sick, too. I picked up one of those tropical fevers. No sick-bay on that tub, no doctor, no medicine or nothing, not even one quinine pill, and I was burning up with Christ knows how much fever. I couldn't make them understand I was sick. I got a bad heart, too. I had to retire from the prize ring because of my heart. I was the light heavyweight champion of the West Coast, won these gloves!—before my ticker went bad.—Feel my chest! Go on, feel it! Feel it. I've got a heart in my chest as big as the head of a baby. Ha ha! They stood me in front of a screen that makes you transparent and that's what they seen inside me, a heart in my chest as big as the head of a baby! With something like that you don't need the Gypsy to tell you, "Time is short, Baby—get ready to hitch on wings!" The medics wouldn't okay me for no more fights. They said to give up liquor and smoking and sex!—To give up sex!—I used to believe a man couldn't live without sex—but he can—if he wants to! My real true woman, my wife, she would of stuck with me, but it was all spoiled with her being scared and me, too, that a real hard kiss would kill me!—So one night while she was sleeping I wrote her good-bye . . . *(He notices a lack of attention in the* OFFICER: *he grins.)* No comprendo the lingo?

1. Is Kilroy's dialog expressionistic or realistic? Defend your belief.
2. Do you believe Kilroy's stated reason for leaving his wife? Is your answer a result of realism or romanticism or expressionism?

OFFICER. What is it you want?

KILROY. Excuse my ignorance, but what place is this? What is this country and what is the name of this town? I know it seems funny of me to ask such a question. Loco! But I was so glad to get off that rotten tub that I didn't ask nothing of no one except my pay—and I got short-changed on that. I have trouble counting these pesos or Whatzit-you-call-'em. *(He jerks out his wallet.)* All-a-this-here. In the States that pile of lettuce would make you a plutocrat!—But I bet you this stuff don't add up to fifty dollars American coin. Ha ha!

OFFICER. Ha ha.

KILROY. Ha ha!

OFFICER *(making it sound like a death-rattle)*. Ha-ha-ha-ha-ha.

3. Why does the Officer laugh at Kilroy's joke about money? Why does the laughter become a death-rattle?

(He turns and starts into the cantina. KILROY *grabs his arm.)*

KILROY. Hey!

OFFICER. What is it you want?

KILROY. What is the name of this country and this town? (*The* OFFICER *thrusts his elbow in* KILROY'S *stomach and twists his arm loose with a Spanish curse. He kicks the swinging doors open and enters the cantina.*) Brass hats are the same everywhere.

(*As soon as the* OFFICER *goes, the* STREET PEOPLE *come forward and crowd about* KILROY *with their wheedling cries.*)

STREET PEOPLE. Dulces, dulces! Lotería! Lotería! Pasteles, café con leche!

KILROY. No caree, no caree!

(*The* PROSTITUTE *creeps up to him and grins.*)

ROSITA. Love? Love?

KILROY. What did you say?

ROSITA. *Love?*

KILROY. Sorry—I don't feature that. (*To audience*) I have ideals.

4. Why does Kilroy tell *the audience,* "I have ideals"? Do you believe him? Do you believe he believes himself?

(*The* GYPSY *appears on the roof of her establishment with* ESMERALDA *whom she secures by handcuffs to the iron railing.*)

GYPSY. Stay there while I give the pitch! (*She then advances with a portable microphone.*) Testing! One, two, three, four!

NURSIE (*from offstage*). You're on the air!

GYPSY'S LOUDSPEAKER. Are you perplexed by something? Are you tired out and confused? Do you have a fever? (KILROY *looks around for the source of the voice.*) Do you feel yourself to be spiritually unprepared for the age of exploding atoms? Do you distrust the newspapers? Are you suspicious of governments? Have you arrived at a point on the Camino Real where the walls converge not in the distance but right in front of your nose? Does further progress appear impossible to you? Are you afraid of anything at all? Afraid of your heartbeat? Or the eyes of strangers! Afraid of breathing? Afraid of not breathing? Do you wish that things could be straight and simple again as they were in your childhood? Would you like to go back to Kindy Garten?

(ROSITA *has crept up to* KILROY *while he listens. She reaches out to him. At the same time a* PICKPOCKET *lifts his wallet.*)

KILROY (*catching the whore's wrist*). Keep y'r hands off me, y' dirty ole bag! No caree putas! No loteria, no dulces, nada—so get away! Vamoose! All of you! Quit picking at me! (*He reaches in his pocket and jerks out a handful of small copper and silver coins which he flings disgustedly down the street. The grotesque people scramble after it with their inhuman cries.* KILROY *goes on a few steps—then stops short—feeling the back pocket of his dungarees. Then he lets out a startled cry.*) Robbed! My God, I've been robbed! (*The* STREET PEOPLE *scatter to the walls.*) Which of you got my wallet? *Which* of you dirty—? Shh—Uh! *(They mumble with gestures of incomprehension. He marches back to the entrance to the hotel.)* Hey! Officer! Official!—General! *(The* OFFICER *finally lounges out of the hotel entrance and glances at* KILROY.*)* Tiende? One of them's got my wallet! Picked it out of my pocket while that old whore there was groping me! Don't you comprendo?

OFFICER. Nobody rob you. You don't have no pesos.

KILROY. Huh?

OFFICER. You just dreaming that you have money. You don't ever have money. Nunca! Nada! *(He spits between his teeth.)* Loco . . .

(The OFFICER *crosses to the fountain.* KILROY *stares at him, then bawls out.)*

KILROY *(to the* STREET PEOPLE*).* We'll see what the American Embassy has to say about this! I'll go to the American Consul. Whichever of you rotten spivs lifted my wallet is going to jail—calaboose! I hope I have made myself plain. If not, I will make myself plainer! *(There are scattered laughs among the crowd. He crosses to the fountain. He notices the body of the no longer* SURVIVOR, *kneels beside it, shakes it, turns it over, springs up and shouts.)* Hey! This guy is dead! *(There is the sound of the* STREETCLEANERS' *piping. They trundle their white barrel into the plaza from one of the downstage arches. The appearance of these men undergoes a progressive alteration through the play. When they first appear they are almost like any such public servants in a tropical country; their white jackets are dirtier than the musicians' and some of the stains are red. They have on white caps and black visors. They are continually exchanging sly jokes and giggling unpleasantly together.* LORD MULLIGAN *has come out upon the terrace and as they pass him, they pause for a moment, point at him, snicker. He is extremely discomfited by this impertinence, touches his chest as if he felt a palpitation and turns back inside.* KILROY *yells to the advancing* STREETCLEANERS.*)* There's a dead man layin' here! *(They giggle again. Briskly they lift the body and stuff it into the barrel; then trundle it off, looking back at* KILROY, *giggling, whispering. They return under the downstage arch through which they entered.* KILROY, *in a low, shocked voice.)* What is this place? What kind of a hassle have I got myself into?

5. Do the people understand the concept of *Hermano* as Kilroy is robbed and they scramble after the coins?

6. Explain the man with "ideals" (Kilroy) calling the people "rotten spivs."

LOUDSPEAKER. If anyone on the Camino is bewildered, come to the Gypsy. A poco dinero will tickle the Gypsy's palm and give her visions!

ABDULLAH *(giving* KILROY *a card).* If you got a question, ask my mama, the Gypsy!

KILROY. Man, whenever you see those three brass balls on a street, you don't have to look a long ways for a Gypsy. Now le' me think. I am faced with three problems. One: I'm hungry. Two: I'm lonely. Three: I'm in a place where I don't know what it

is or how I got there! First action that's indicated is to—cash in on something—Well
. . . let's see . . .

(*Honky-tonk music fades in at this point and the Skid Row façade begins to
light up for the evening. There is the* GYPSY'S *stall with its cabalistic devices, its
sectional cranium and palm, three luminous brass balls overhanging the entrance to
the* LOAN SHARK *and his window filled with a vast assortment of hocked articles for
sale: trumpets, banjos, fur coats, tuxedos, a gown of scarlet sequins, loops of pearls
and rhinestones. Dimly behind this display is a neon sign in three pastel colors, pink,
green, and blue. It fades softly in and out and it says: "Magic Tricks Jokes." There
is also the advertisement of a flea-bag hotel or flophouse called "Ritz Men Only."
This sign is also pale neon or luminous paint, and only the entrance is on the street
floor, the rooms are above the* LOAN SHARK *and* GYPSY'S *stall. One of the windows
of this upper story is practical. Figures appear in it sometimes, leaning out as if
suffocating or to hawk and spit into the street below. This side of the street should
have all the color and animation that are permitted by the resources of the production.
There may be moments of dancelike action* [*a fight, a seduction, sale of narcotics,
arrest, etc.*]*)

7. Explain the several levels of ambiguity in the words of the pawnshop
sign.

KILROY (*to the audience from the apron*). What've I got to cash in on? My golden
gloves? Never! I'll say that once more, never! The silver-framed photo of my One True
Woman? Never! Repeat that! Never! What else have I got of a detachable and a
negotiable nature? Oh! My ruby-and-emerald-studded belt with the word CHAMP on
it. (*He whips it off his pants.*) This is not necessary to hold on my pants, but this
is a precious reminder of the sweet used-to-be. Oh, well. Sometimes a man has got
to hock his sweet used-to-be in order to finance his present situation . . .
(*He enters the* LOAN SHARK'S. *A* DRUNKEN BUM *leans out the practical window of
the "Ritz Men Only" and shouts.*)
BUM. O Jack o' Diamonds, you robbed my pockets, you robbed my pockets of
silver and gold! (*He jerks the window shade down.*)
GUTMAN (*on the terrace*). Block Four on the Camino Real!

8. Again Kilroy speaks to the audience. Why? Is this the conventional
soliloquy or is it something else?
9. Explain Kilroy's final line before entering the pawnshop.
10. What does the title of the song shouted by the Bum suggest?
Has it anything to do with the present situation? The "sweet used-
to-be"? Both? Neither?

BLOCK FOUR

There is a phrase of light music as the BARON DE CHARLUS, *an elderly foppish sybarite in a light silk suit, a carnation in his lapel, crosses from the Siete Mares to the honky-tonk side of the street. On his trail is a wild-looking young man of startling beauty called* LOBO. CHARLUS *is aware of the follower and, during his conversation with* A. RATT, *he takes out a pocket mirror to inspect him while pretending to comb his hair and point his moustache. As* CHARLUS *approaches, the Manager of the flea-bag puts up a vacancy sign and calls out:*

A. RATT. Vacancy here! A bed at the "Ritz Men Only"! A little white ship to sail the dangerous night in . . .

THE BARON. Ah, bon soir, Mr. Ratt.

A. RATT. Cruising?

THE BARON. No, just—walking!

1. Why does A. Ratt speak in such eloquent imagery? What is your emotional response to his definition of a bed?

2. Compare the diction and idiom of A. Ratt (*cruising* means "looking for a pickup for sexual purposes"). Does the sharp change in language usage strengthen or weaken verisimilitude?

A. RATT. That's all you need to do.

THE BARON. I sometimes find it suffices. You have a vacancy, do you?

A. RATT. For you?

THE BARON. And a possible guest. You know the requirements. An iron bed with no mattress and a considerable length of stout knotted rope. No! Chains this evening, metal chains. I've been very bad, I have a lot to atone for . . .

A. RATT. Why don't you take these joy-rides at the Siete Mares?

THE BARON (*with the mirror focused on* LOBO). They don't have Ingreso Libero at the Siete Mares. Oh, I don't like places in the haute saison, the alta staggione, and yet if you go between the fashionable seasons, it's too hot or too damp or appallingly overrun by all the wrong sort of people who rap on the wall if canaries sing in your bed-springs after midnight. I don't know why such people don't stay at home. Surely a Kodak, a Brownie, or even a Leica works just as well in Milwaukee or Sioux City as it does in these places they do on their whirlwind summer tours, and don't look now, but I think I am being followed!

A. RATT. Yep, you've made a pickup!

THE BARON. Attractive?

A. RATT. That depends on who's driving the bicycle, Dad.

THE BARON. Ciao, Caro! Expect me at ten. (*He crosses elegantly to the fountain.*)

A. RATT. Vacancy here! A little white ship to sail the dangerous night in!

3. Who is more degenerate, the Baron de Charlus or Lobo? Defend your answer.

4. In this time distortion the Baron de Charlus has become sadistic and has also become scornful of opinion. Casanova has grown into "late middle years." What do such extensions suggest?

5. Do you resent or agree with the Baron's assessment of tourists? Why?

(*The music changes.* KILROY *backs out of the* LOAN SHARK'S, *belt unsold, engaged in a violent dispute. The* LOAN SHARK *is haggling for his golden gloves.* CHARLUS *lingers, intrigued by the scene.*)

LOAN SHARK. I don't want no belt! I want the gloves! Eight-fifty!

KILROY. No dice.

LOAN SHARK. Nine, nine-fifty!

KILROY. Nah, nah, nah!

LOAN SHARK. Yah, yah, yah.

KILROY. I say nah.

LOAN SHARK. I say yah.

KILROY. The nahs have it.

LOAN SHARK. Don't be a fool. What can you do with a pair of golden gloves?

KILROY. I can remember the battles I fought to win them! I can remember that I used to be—CHAMP!

(*Fade in Band Music: "March of the Gladiators"—ghostly cheers, etc.*)

LOAN SHARK. You can remember that you *used to be*—Champ?

KILROY. Yes! I used to be—CHAMP!

THE BARON. Used to be is the past tense, meaning useless.

KILROY. Not to me, Mister. These are my gloves, these gloves are gold, and I fought a lot of hard fights to win 'em! I broke clean from the clinches. I never hit a low blow, the referee never told me to mix it up! And the fixers never got to me!

LOAN SHARK. In other words, a sucker!

KILROY. Yep, I'm a sucker that won the golden gloves!

LOAN SHARK. Congratulations. My final offer is a piece of green paper with Alexander Hamilton's picture on it. Take it or leave it.

KILROY. I leave it for you to *stuff* it! I'd hustle my heart on this street, I'd peddle my heart's true blood before I'd leave my golden gloves hung up in a loan shark's window between a rusted trombone and some poor lush's long ago mildewed tuxedo!

LOAN SHARK. So you say but I will see you later.

THE BARON. The name of the Camino is not unreal!

6. Explain Kilroy's willingness to sell the proof of his victories but not the means of them. Do you agree or disagree with his thinking?

7. Explain the statement "The name of the Camino is not unreal!"

(*The* BUM *sticks his head out the window and shouts.*)

BUM. Pa dam, Pa dam, Pa dam!

THE BARON (*continuing the* BUM'S *song*). Echoes the beat of my heart! Pa dam, Pa dam—*hello!* (*He has crossed to* KILROY *as he sings and extends his hand to him.*)

KILROY (*uncertainly*). Hey, mate. It's wonderful to see you.

THE BARON. Thanks, but why?

KILROY. A normal American. In a clean white suit.

THE BARON. My suit is pale yellow. My nationality is French, and my normality has been often subject to question.

KILROY. I still say your suit is clean.

8. Explain Kilroy's logic about the clean white suit. Is he representative of American logic?

THE BARON. Thanks. That's more than I can say for your apparel.

KILROY. Don't judge a book by the covers. I'd take a shower if I could locate the "Y."

THE BARON. What's the "Y"?

KILROY. Sort of a Protestant church with a swimmin' pool in it. Sometimes it also has an employment bureau. It does good in the community.

THE BARON. Nothing in this community does much good.

KILROY. I'm getting the same impression. This place is confusing to me. I think it must be the aftereffects of fever. Nothing seems real. Could you give me the scoop?

THE BARON. Serious questions are referred to the Gypsy. Once upon a time. Oh, once upon a time. I used to wonder. Now I simply wander. I stroll about the fountain and hope to be followed. Some people call it corruption. I call it—simplification . . .

BUM (*very softly at the window*). I wonder what's become of Sally, that old gal of mine? (*He lowers the blind.*)

KILROY. Well, anyhow . . .

THE BARON. Well, anyhow?

KILROY. How about the hot-spots in this town?

THE BARON. Oh, the hot-spots, ho ho! There's the Pink Flamingo, the Yellow Pelican, the Blue Heron, and the Prothonotary Warbler! They call it the Bird Circuit. But I don't care for such places. They stand three-deep at the bar and look at themselves in the mirror and what they see is depressing. One sailor comes in—they faint! My own choice of resorts is the Bucket of Blood downstairs from the "Ritz Men Only."—How about a match?

KILROY. Where's your cigarette?

THE BARON (*gently and sweetly*). Oh, I don't smoke. I just wanted to see your eyes more clearly . . .

KILROY. Why?

THE BARON. The eyes are the windows of the soul, and yours are too gentle for someone who has as much as I have to atone for. (*He starts off.*) Au revoir . . .

9. In a country where birds are caged, why are the nightclubs named after birds?

KILROY. —A very unusual type character . . . (CASANOVA *is on the steps leading to the arch, looking out at the desert beyond. Now he turns and descends a few steps, laughing with a note of tired incredulity.* KILROY *crosses to him.*) Gee, it's wonderful to see you, a normal American in a—(*There is a strangulated outcry from the arch under which the* BARON *has disappeared.*) Excuse me a minute! (*He rushes toward the source of the outcry.* JACQUES *crosses to the bench before the fountain. Rhubarb is heard through the arch.* JACQUES *shrugs wearily as if it were just a noisy radio.* KILROY *comes plummeting out backwards, all the way to* JACQUES.) I tried to interfere, but what's th' use?!

JACQUES. No use at all!

(*The* STREETCLEANERS *come through the arch with the* BARON *doubled up in their barrel. They pause and exchange sibilant whispers, pointing and snickering at* KILROY.)

KILROY. Who are they pointing at? At me, Kilroy? (*The* BUM *laughs from the window.* A. RATT *laughs from his shadowy doorway. The* LOAN SHARK *laughs from his.*) Kilroy is here and he's not about to be there!—If he can help it . . . (*He snatches up a rock and throws it at the* STREETCLEANERS. *Everybody laughs louder and the laughter seems to reverberate from the mountains. The light changes, dims a little in the plaza.*) Sons a whatever you're sons of! Don't look at me, I'm not about to take no ride in the barrel!

(*The* BARON, *his elegant white shoes protruding from the barrel, is wheeled up the Alleyway Out. Figures in the square resume their dazed attitudes and one or two* GUESTS *return to the terrace of the Siete Mares as*—)

GUTMAN. Block Five on the Camino Real! (*He strolls off.*)

10. Why does Kilroy try to involve himself in protecting the Baron? Why does he then return and say "What's the use?!"
11. Explain the significance of the Streetcleaners and their barrel.
12. Why are the inhabitants of *Tierra Caliente* so cold in their disinterest? Is irony involved?

BLOCK FIVE

KILROY (*to* JACQUES). Gee, the blocks go fast on this street!
JACQUES. Yes. The blocks go fast.

KILROY. My name's Kilroy. I'm here.
JACQUES. Mine is Casanova. I'm here, too.

1. Why do blocks go fast on the Camino Real?

KILROY. But you been here longer than me and maybe could brief me on it. For instance, what do they do with a stiff picked up in this town? (*The* GUARD *stares at them suspiciously from the terrace.* JACQUES *whistles "La Golondrina" and crosses downstage.* KILROY *follows.*) Did I say something untactful?

JACQUES (*smiling into a sunset glow*). The exchange of serious questions and ideas, especially between persons from opposite sides of the plaza, is regarded unfavorably here. You'll notice I'm talking as if I had acute laryngitis. I'm gazing into the sunset. If I should start to whistle "La Golondrina" it means we're being overheard by the Guards on the terrace. Now you want to know what is done to a body from which the soul has departed on the Camino Real!—Its disposition depends on what the Streetcleaners happen to find in its pockets. If its pockets are empty as the unfortunate Baron's turned out to be, and as mine are at this moment—the "stiff" is wheeled straight off to the Laboratory. And there the individual becomes an undistinguished member of a collectivist state. His chemical components are separated and poured into vats containing the corresponding elements of countless others. If any of his vital organs or parts are at all unique in size or structure, they're placed on exhibition in bottles containing a very foul-smelling solution called formaldehyde. There is a charge of admission to this museum. The proceeds go to the maintenance of the military police. (*He whistles "La Golondrina" till the* GUARD *turns his back again. He moves toward the front of the stage.*)

2. Why is communication between persons from "opposite sides of the plaza" regarded unfavorably?
3. Relate Jacques' explanation of the disposition of corpses to reality.

KILROY (*following*). —I guess that's—sensible . . .
JACQUES. Yes, but not romantic. And romance is important. Don't you think?
KILROY. Nobody thinks romance is more important than me!
JACQUES. Except possibly me!
KILROY. Maybe that's why fate has brung us together! We're buddies under the skin!
JACQUES. Travelers born?
KILROY. Always looking for something!
JACQUES. Satisfied by nothing!
KILROY. Hopeful?
JACQUES. Always!

OFFICER. Keep moving!

(*They move apart till the* OFFICER *exits.*)

4. Is it ironic that Kilroy and Jacques are "buddies under the skin"? Explain.

KILROY. And when a joker on the Camino gets fed up with one continual hassle—how does he get *off* it?

JACQUES. You see the narrow and very steep stairway that passes under what is described in the travel brochures as a "Magnificent Arch of Triumph"?—Well, that's the Way Out!

KILROY. That's the way out? (KILROY *without hesitation plunges right up to almost the top step; then pauses with a sound of squealing brakes. There is a sudden loud wind.*)

JACQUES (*shouting with hand cupped to mouth*). Well, how does the prospect please you, Traveler born?

KILROY (*shouting back in a tone of awe*). It's too unknown for my blood. Man, I seen nothing like it except through a telescope once on the pier on Coney Island. "Ten cents to see the craters and plains of the moon!"—And here's the same view in three dimensions for nothing! (*The desert wind sings loudly:* KILROY *mocks it.*)

JACQUES. Are you—ready to cross it?

KILROY. Maybe sometime with someone but not right now and alone! How about you?

JACQUES. I'm not alone.

KILROY. You're with a party?

JACQUES. No, but I'm sweetly encumbered with a—lady . . .

KILROY. It wouldn't do with a lady. I don't see nothing but nothing—and then more nothing. And then I see some mountains. But the mountains are covered with snow.

JACQUES. Snowshoes would be useful! (*He observes* GUTMAN *approaching through the passage at upper left. He whistles "La Golondrina" for* KILROY'S *attention and points with his cane as he exits.*)

KILROY (*descending steps disconsolately*). Mush, mush.

(THE BUM *comes to his window.* A. RATT *enters his doorway.* GUTMAN *enters below* KILROY.)

BUM. It's sleepy time down South!

GUTMAN (*warningly as* KILROY *passes him*). Block Six in a progress of sixteen blocks on the Camino Real.

5. Why is Kilroy unwilling to cross *Tierra Incognita?* Would he cross it with the wife he loved but abandoned?

6. Why does Gutman announce the next Block "warningly"?

7. Has a dramatic question been posed in Block Five?

8. Can you state your concept of conflict in the play now?

BLOCK SIX

KILROY (*from the stairs*). Man, I could use a bed now.—I'd like to make me a cool pad on this camino now and lie down and sleep and dream of being with someone—friendly . . . (*He crosses to the "Ritz Men Only."*)

A. RATT (*softly and sleepily*). Vacancy here! I got a single bed at the "Ritz Men Only," a little white ship to sail the dangerous night in.

(KILROY *crosses down to his doorway.*)

KILROY. —You got a vacancy here?

A. RATT. I got a vacancy here if you got the one-fifty there.

KILROY. Ha ha! I been in countries where money was not legal tender. I mean it was legal but it wasn't tender. (*There is a loud groan from offstage above.*) —Somebody dying on you or just drunk?

A. RATT. Who knows or cares in this pad, Dad?

KILROY. I heard once that a man can't die while he's drunk. Is that a fact or a fiction?

A. RATT. Strictly a fiction.

VOICE ABOVE. *Stiff in number seven! Call the Streetcleaners!*

A. RATT (*with absolutely no change in face or voice*). Number seven is vacant. (STREETCLEANERS' *piping is heard. The* BUM *leaves the window.*)

KILROY. Thanks, but tonight I'm going to sleep under the stars.

(A. RATT *gestures "Have it your way" and exits.* KILROY, *left alone, starts downstage. He notices that* LA MADRECITA *is crouched near the fountain, holding something up, inconspicuously, in her hand. Coming to her, he sees that it's a piece of food. He takes it, puts it in his mouth, tries to thank her but her head is down, muffled in her rebozo and there is no way for him to acknowledge the gift. He starts to cross.* STREET PEOPLE *raise up their heads in their Pit and motion him invitingly to come in with them. They call softly, "Sleep, sleep . . ."*)

1. Is Kilroy humorous? Does he consider himself so?

2. Is A. Ratt's way of speaking deliberately geared to any particular group? (Remember, this play was produced in 1953.)

3. Why does La Madrecita feed Kilroy?

GUTMAN (*from his chair on the terrace*). Hey, Joe.

(*The* STREET PEOPLE *duck immediately.*)

KILROY. Who? Me?

GUTMAN. Yes, you, Candy Man. Are you disocupado?

KILROY. —That means—unemployed, don't it? (*He sees* OFFICERS *converging from right.*)

GUTMAN. Jobless. On the bum. Carrying the banner!

KILROY. —Aw, no, aw, no, don't try to hang no vagrancy rap on me! I was robbed on this square and I got plenty of witnesses to prove it.

GUTMAN (*with ironic courtesy*). Oh? (*He makes a gesture asking "Where?"*)

4. A "Candy Man" is a dope peddler. Is Gutman calling Kilroy a pusher?

KILROY (*coming down to apron left and crossing to the right*). Witnesses! Witness! Witnesses! (*He comes to* LA MADRECITA.) You were a witness! (*A gesture indicates that he realizes her blindness. Opposite the* GYPSY'S *balcony he pauses for a second.*) Hey, Gypsy's daughter! (*The balcony is dark. He continues up to the Pit. The* STREET PEOPLE *duck as he calls down.*) You were witnesses!

(*An* OFFICER *enters with a Patsy outfit. He hands it to* GUTMAN.)

GUTMAN. Here, Boy! Take these. (GUTMAN *displays and then tosses on the ground at* KILROY'S *feet the Patsy outfit—the red fright wig, the big crimson nose that lights up and has horn rimmed glasses attached, a pair of clown pants that have a huge footprint on the seat.*)

KILROY. What is this outfit?

GUTMAN. The uniform of a Patsy.

KILROY. I know what a Patsy is—he's a clown in the circus who takes prat-falls but *I'm no Patsy!*

GUTMAN. Pick it up.

KILROY. Don't give me orders. Kilroy is a free agent—

GUTMAN (*smoothly*). But a Patsy isn't. Pick it up and put it on, Candy Man. You are now the Patsy.

KILROY. So you say but you are completely mistaken. (*Four* OFFICERS *press in on him.*) And don't crowd me with your torpedoes! I'm a stranger here but I got a clean record in all the places I been, I'm not in the books for nothin' but vagrancy and once when I was hungry I walked by a truck-load of pineapples without picking one, because I was brought up good— (*Then, with a pathetic attempt at making friends with the* OFFICER *to his right*) and there was a cop on the corner!

OFFICER. Ponga selo!

KILROY. What'd you say? (*Desperately to audience he asks*) What did he say?

OFFICER. Ponga selo!

KILROY. What'd you say? (*The* OFFICER *shoves him down roughly to the Patsy outfit.* KILROY *picks up the pants, shakes them out carefully as if about to step into them and says very politely*) Why, surely. I'd be delighted. My fondest dreams have come true. (*Suddenly he tosses the Patsy dress into* GUTMAN'S *face and leaps into the aisle of the theatre.*)

GUTMAN. Stop him! Arrest that vagrant! Don't let him get away!

LOUDSPEAKER. Be on the lookout for a fugitive Patsy. The Patsy has escaped. Stop him, stop that Patsy!

5. In what Block was Kilroy's being chosen the Patsy foreshadowed? Exactly what is a Patsy? Does Kilroy understand the term fully?

(A wild chase commences. The two GUARDS rush madly down either side to intercept him at the back of the house. KILROY wheels about at the top of the center aisle, and runs back down it, panting, gasping out questions and entreaties to various persons occupying aisle seats, such as)

KILROY. How do I git out? Which way do I go, which way do I get out? Where's the Greyhound depot? Hey, do you know where the Greyhound bus depot is? What's the best way out, if there is any way out? I got to find one. I had enough of this place. I had too much of this place. I'm free. I'm a free man with equal rights in this world! You better believe it because that's news for you and you had better believe it! Kilroy's a free man with equal rights in this world! All right, now, help me, somebody help me find a way out, I got to find one, I don't like this place! It's not for me and I am not buying any! Oh! Over there! I see a sign that says EXIT. That's a sweet word to me, man, that's a lovely word, EXIT! That's the entrance to paradise for Kilroy! Exit, I'm coming, Exit, I'm coming!

6. As Kilroy flees through the theater of your mind, what is your audience doing? What are you doing? Do you want to help Kilroy? Why do you sit grimly reading, unwilling to involve yourself? If your answer is, "It's only a play," you are a non-involved spectator, a safe liver of life. If you wrote in an extra scene wherein you tried to help Kilroy but were thwarted, what is suggested?

(The STREET PEOPLE have gathered along the forestage to watch the chase. ESMERALDA, barefooted, wearing only a slip, bursts out of the GYPSY'S establishment like an animal broken out of a cage, darts among the STREET PEOPLE to the front of the Crowd which is shouting like the spectators at the climax of a corrida. Behind her, NURSIE appears, a male actor, wigged and dressed austerely as a duenna, crying out in both languages.)

NURSIE. Esmeralda! Esmeralda!
GYPSY. Police!
NURSIE. Come back here, Esmeralda!
GYPSY. Catch her, idiot!
NURSIE. Where is my lady bird, where is my precious treasure?

7. Why is Nursie a male actor, wigged and dressed as a duenna?
8. "Where is my lady bird, where is my precious treasure?" was written before America was aware of the wife of the 36th President of the United States. The line has lost none of its original meaning, but it has accrued additional meaning with the passing of time. What literary conclusion can you draw from such accretion?

GYPSY. Idiot! I told you to keep her door locked!

NURSIE. She jimmied the lock, Esmeralda!

(*These shouts are mostly lost in the general rhubarb of the chase and the shouting* STREET PEOPLE. ESMERALDA *crouches on the forestage, screaming encouragement in* Spanish to the fugitive. ABDULLAH *catches sight of her, seizes her wrist, shouting.*)

ABDULLAH. Here she is! I got her!

(ESMERALDA *fights savagely. She nearly breaks loose, but* NURSIE *and the* GYPSY *close upon her, too, and she is overwhelmed and dragged back, fighting all the way, toward the door from which she escaped.*)

9. Account for Esmeralda's attempt to aid Kilroy. Is "love" involved? Is something else?

(*Meanwhile—timed with the above action—shots are fired in the air by* KILROY'S *Pursuers. He dashes, panting, into the boxes of the theatre, darting from one box to another, shouting incoherently, now, sobbing for breath, crying out*)

KILROY. Mary, help a Christian! Help a Christian, Mary!

ESMERALDA. Yankee! Yankee, jump! (*The* OFFICERS *close upon him in the box nearest the stage. A dazzling spot of light is thrown on him. He lifts a little gilded chair to defend himself. The chair is torn from his grasp. He leaps upon the ledge of the box.*) Jump! Jump, Yankee!

(*The* GYPSY *is dragging the girl back by her hair.*)

KILROY. Watch out down there! Geronimo!

(*He leaps onto the stage and crumples up with a twisted ankle.* ESMERALDA *screams demoniacally, breaks from her mother's grasp and rushes to him, fighting off his pursuers who have leapt after him from the box.* ABDULLAH, NURSIE *and the* GYPSY *seize her again, just as* KILROY *is seized by his pursuers. The* OFFICERS *beat him to his knees. Each time he is struck,* ESMERALDA *screams as if she received the blow herself. As his cries subside into sobbing, so do hers, and at the end, when he is quite helpless, she is also overcome by her captors and as they drag her back to the* GYPSY'S *she cries to him.*)

ESMERALDA. They've got you! They've got me! (*Her mother slaps her fiercely.*) Caught! Caught! We're caught!

(*She is dragged inside. The door is slammed shut on her continuing outcries. For a moment nothing is heard but* KILROY'S *hoarse panting and sobbing.* GUTMAN *takes command of the situation, thrusting his way through the crowd to face* KILROY *who is pinioned by two* GUARDS.)

GUTMAN (*smiling serenely*). Well, well, how do you do! I understand that you're seeking employment here. We need a Patsy and the job is yours for the asking!

KILROY. I don't. Accept. This job. I been. Shanghied! (KILROY *dons Patsy outfit.*)

GUTMAN. Hush! The Patsy doesn't talk. He lights his nose, that's all!

GUARD. Press the little button at the end of the cord.

GUTMAN. That's right. Just press the little button at the end of the cord!
(KILROY *lights his nose. Everybody laughs.*)
GUTMAN. Again, ha ha! Again, ha ha! Again!
(*The nose goes off and on like a firefly as the stage dims out. The curtain falls. There is a short intermission.*)

10. Gutman's defeat of Kilroy brings an intermission. Is the defeat a complication, a climax, or what?
11. Assess the meaning of the Prologue and the first six Blocks before continuing. Also, have a Coke, a cup of coffee, or some other refreshment. Intermissions are as valuable in reading a play as in seeing one. And they serve the same purposes. Refreshment stands and restrooms play their part, but it is the unimportant part. An intermission affords you time to reflect on the drama as it has unfolded so that you are prepared to understand the next unfolding more fully.

BLOCK SEVEN

The DREAMER *is singing with mandolin, "Noche de Ronde." The* GUESTS *murmur, "cool—cool . . ."* GUTMAN *stands on the podiumlike elevation downstage right, smoking a long thin cigar, signing an occasional tab from the bar or café. He is standing in an amber spot. The rest of the stage is filled with blue dusk. At the signal the song fades to a whisper and* GUTMAN *speaks.*

GUTMAN. Block Seven on the Camino Real—I like this hour. (*He gives the audience a tender gold-toothed smile.*) The fire's gone out of the day but the light of it lingers . . . In Rome the continual fountains are bathing stone heroes with silver, in Copenhagen the Tivoli gardens are lighted, they're selling the lottery on San Juan de Latrene . . .
(*The DREAMER advances a little, playing the mandolin softly.*)
LA MADRECITA (*holding up glass beads and shell necklaces*). Recuerdos, recuerdos?
GUTMAN. And these are the moments when we look into ourselves and ask with a wonder which never is lost altogether: "Can this be all? Is there nothing more? Is this what the glittering wheels of the heavens turn for?" (*He leans forward as if conveying a secret.*) —Ask the Gypsy! Un poco dinero will tickle the Gypsy's palm and give her visions!

1. Explain "this hour" on the Camino Real.
2. Are Gutman's poetic musings surprising? Should they be?
3. Is Gutman heartless, compassionate, erratic? Explain him as an archetype.

(ABDULLAH *emerges with a silver tray, calling.*)

ABDULLAH. Letter for Signor Casanova, letter for Signor Casanova!

(JACQUES *springs up but stands rigid.*)

GUTMAN. Casanova, you have received a letter. Perhaps it's the letter with the remittance check in it!

JACQUES (*in a hoarse, exalted voice*). Yes! It is! The letter! With the remittance check in it!

GUTMAN. Then why don't you take it so you can maintain your residence at the Siete Mares and so avoid the more somber attractions of the "Ritz Men Only"?

JACQUES. My hand is—

GUTMAN. Your hand is paralyzed? . . . By what? *Anxiety? Apprehension?* . . . Put the letter in Signor Casanova's pocket so he can open it when he recovers the use of his digital extremities. Then give him a shot of brandy on the house before he falls on his face!

(JACQUES *has stepped down into the plaza. He looks down at* KILROY *crouched to the right of him and wildly blinking his nose.*)

JACQUES. Yes. I know the Morse code. (KILROY'S *nose again blinks on and off.*) Thank you, brother. (*This is said as if acknowledging a message.*) I knew without asking the Gypsy that something of this sort would happen to you. You have a spark of anarchy in your spirit and that's not to be tolerated. Nothing wild or honest is tolerated here! It has to be extinguished or used only to light up your nose for Mr. Gutman's amusement . . . (JACQUES *saunters around* KILROY *whistling "La Golondrina." Then satisfied that no one is suspicious of this encounter* . . .) Before the final block we'll find some way out of here! Meanwhile, patience and courage, little brother! (JACQUES *feeling he's been there too long starts away giving* KILROY *a reassuring pat on the shoulder and saying*) Patience! . . . Courage!

4.   Why is "anarchy in your spirit" not to be tolerated on the Camino Real in Tierra Caliente?

5.   Dramatically, why does Jacques assure Kilroy that they will eventually escape?

LADY MULLIGAN (*from the* MULLIGANS' *table*). Mr. Gutman!

GUTMAN. Lady Mulligan! And how are you this evening, Lord Mulligan?

LADY MULLIGAN (*interrupting* LORD MULLIGAN'S *rumblings*). He's not at all well. This . . . climate is so enervating!

LORD MULLIGAN. I was so weak this morning . . . I couldn't screw the lid on my tooth paste!

LADY MULLIGAN. Raymond, tell Mr. Gutman about those two impertinent workmen in the square! . . . These two idiots pushing a white barrel! Pop up every time we step outside the hotel!

LORD MULLIGAN. —point and giggle at me!

LADY MULLIGAN. Can't they be discharged?

GUTMAN. They can't be discharged, disciplined nor bribed! All you can do is pretend to ignore them.

LADY MULLIGAN. I can't eat! . . . Raymond, stop stuffing!

LORD MULLIGAN. *Shut up!*

GUTMAN (*to the audience*). When the big wheels crack on this street it's like the fall of a capital city, the destruction of Carthage, the sack of Rome by the white-eyed giants from the North! I've seen them fall! I've seen the destruction of them! Adventurers suddenly frightened of a dark room! Gamblers unable to choose between odd and even! Con men and pitchmen and plume-hatted cavaliers turned baby-soft at one note of the Streetcleaners' pipes! When I observe this change, I say to myself: "Could it happen to ME?"—The answer is "YES!" And that's what curdles my blood like milk on the doorstep of someone gone for the summer!

6. Lord and Lady Mulligan are archetypes of what? Explain the humor of their names.

7. Gutman's speech about "When the big wheels crack" is similar to Prufrock's statement beginning "For I have known them all already" in T. S. Eliot's "The Love Song of J. Alfred Prufrock." An interesting paper could result from a comparison.

(*A* HUNCHBACK MUMMER *somersaults through his hoop of silver bells, springs up and shakes it excitedly toward a downstage arch which begins to flicker with a diamond-blue radiance; this marks the advent of each legendary character in the play. The music follows: a waltz from the time of* CAMILLE *in Paris.*)

GUTMAN (*downstage to the audience*). Ah, there's the music of another legend, one that everyone knows, the legend of the sentimental whore, the courtesan who made the mistake of love. But now you see her coming into this plaza not as she was when she burned with a fever that cast a thin light over Paris, but changed, yes, faded as lanterns and legends fade when they burn into day! (*He turns and shouts.*) Rosita, sell her a flower!

(MARGUERITE *has entered the plaza. A beautiful woman of indefinite age. The* STREET PEOPLE *cluster about her with wheedling cries, holding up glass beads, shell necklaces and so forth. She seems confused, lost, half-awake.* JACQUES *has sprung up at her entrance but has difficulty making his way through the cluster of vendors.* ROSITA *has snatched up a tray of flowers and cries out.*)

ROSITA. Camellias, camellias! Pink or white, whichever a lady finds suitable to the moon!

GUTMAN. That's the ticket!

MARGUERITE. Yes, I would like a camellia.

ROSITA (*in a bad French accent*). Rouge ou blanc ce soir?

MARGUERITE. It's always a white one, now . . . but there used to be five evenings out of the month when a pink camellia, instead of the usual white one, let my admirers know that the moon those nights was unfavorable to pleasure, and so they called me—Camille . . .

8. Explain the pathos of Marguerite's "It's always a white one now" as she buys a camellia. Is it irony or poetic justice that Rosita sells it to her? Before you answer, consider Rosita's question. Was it mocking or kind?

JACQUES. Mia cara! (*Imperiously, very proud to be with her, he pushes the* STREET PEOPLE *aside with his cane.*) Out of the way, make way, let us through, please!

MARGUERITE. Don't push them with your cane.

JACQUES. If they get close enough they'll snatch your purse. (MARGUERITE *utters a low, shocked cry.*) What is it?

MARGUERITE. *My purse is gone! It's lost! My papers were in it!*

JACQUES. Your passport was in it?

MARGUERITE. My passport and my permiso de residencia! (*She leans faint against the arch during the following scene.*)

(ABDULLAH *turns to run.* JACQUES *catches him.*)

JACQUES (*seizing* ABDULLAH'S *wrist*). Where did you take her?

ABDULLAH. Oww!—P'tit Zoco.

JACQUES. The Souks?

ABDULLAH. The Souks!

JACQUES. Which cafés did she go to?

ABDULLAH. Ahmed's, she went to—

JACQUES. Did she smoke at Ahmed's?

ABDULLAH. Two kif pipes!

JACQUES. Who was it took her purse? Was it *you?* We'll see! (*He strips off the boy's burnoose. He crouches whimpering, shivering in a ragged slip.*)

MARGUERITE. Jacques, let the boy go, he didn't take it!

JACQUES. He doesn't have it on him but knows who does!

ABDULLAH. No, no, I don't know!

JACQUES. You little son of a Gypsy! Senta! . . . You know who I am? I am Jacques Casanova! I belong to the Secret Order of the Rose-colored Cross! . . . Run back to Ahmed's. Contact the spiv that took the lady's purse. Tell him to keep it but give her back her papers! There'll be a large reward. (*He thumps his cane on the ground to release* ABDULLAH *from the spell. The boy dashes off.* JACQUES *laughs and turns triumphantly to* MARGUERITE.)

9. A disrobing-in-public scene is usually humorous, usually slapstick. Is there humor in Abdullah's divesture?

10. Why does Jacques tell Abdullah that he belongs to "the Secret

Order of the Rose-colored Cross"? What supreme irony is involved? Is your reaction today the same as it would have been in 1953? Why or why not? What is revealed about you in your answer?

LADY MULLIGAN. Waiter! That adventurer and his mistress must not be seated next to Lord Mulligan's table!

JACQUES (*loudly enough for* LADY MULLIGAN *to hear*). This hotel has become a mecca for black marketeers and their expensively kept women!

LADY MULLIGAN. Mr. Gutman!

11. What is the humor, pathos, or irony of Lady Mulligan's refusal to sit next to Casanova and Marguerite?

MARGUERITE. Let's have dinner upstairs!

WAITER (*directing them to terrace table*). This way, M'sieur.

JACQUES. We'll take our usual table. (*He indicates one.*)

MARGUERITE. Please!

WAITER (*overlapping* MARGUERITE'S *"please!"*). This table is reserved for Lord Byron!

JACQUES (*masterfully*). This table is always our table.

MARGUERITE. I'm not hungry.

JACQUES. Hold out the lady's chair, cretino!

GUTMAN (*darting over to* MARGUERITE'S *chair*). Permit me!

(JACQUES *bows with mock gallantry to* LADY MULLIGAN *as he turns to his chair during seating of* MARGUERITE.)

LADY MULLIGAN. We'll move to *that* table!

JACQUES. —You must learn how to carry the banner of Bohemia into the enemy camp.

(*A screen is put up around them.*)

MARGUERITE. Bohemia has no banner. It survives by discretion.

12. Defend or attack Casanova's statement: "You must learn how to carry the banner of Bohemia into the enemy camp."

13. Marguerite's statement that Bohemia "survives by discretion" may seem foolish. It is not. Can you find arguments to defend it?

JACQUES. I'm glad that you value discretion. *Wine list!* Was it discretion that led you through the bazaars this afternoon wearing your cabochon sapphire and diamond ear-drops? You were fortunate that you lost only your purse and papers!

MARGUERITE. Take the wine list.

JACQUES. Still or sparkling?

MARGUERITE. Sparkling.

GUTMAN. May I make a suggestion, Signor Casanova?

JACQUES. Please do.

GUTMAN. It's a very cold and dry wine from only ten metres below the snowline in the mountains. The name of the wine is Quando!—meaning when! Such as "When are remittances going to be received?" "When are accounts to be settled?" Ha ha ha! Bring Signor Casanova a bottle of Quando with the compliments of the house!

JACQUES. I'm sorry this had to happen in—your presence . . .

MARGUERITE. That doesn't matter, my dear. But why don't you *tell* me when you are short of money?

JACQUES. I thought the fact was apparent. It is to everyone else.

MARGUERITE. The letter you were expecting, it still hasn't come?

JACQUES (*removing it from his pocket*). It came this afternoon—Here it is!

MARGUERITE. You haven't opened the letter!

JACQUES. I haven't had the nerve to! I've had so many unpleasant surprises that I've lost faith in my luck.

MARGUERITE. Give the letter to me. Let me open it for you.

JACQUES. Later, a little bit later, after the—wine . . .

MARGUERITE. Old hawk, anxious old hawk! (*She clasps his hand on the table: he leans toward her: she kisses her fingertips and places them on his lips.*)

JACQUES. Do you call that a kiss?

MARGUERITE. I call it the ghost of a kiss. It will have to do for now. (*She leans back, her blue-tinted eyelids closed.*)

14. What truth does Marguerite express in calling Jacques an "old hawk"?

JACQUES. Are you tired? Are you tired, Marguerite? You know you should have rested this afternoon.

MARGUERITE. I looked at silver and rested.

JACQUES. You looked at silver at Ahmed's?

MARGUERITE. No, I rested at Ahmed's, and had mint-tea.

(*The* DREAMER *accompanies their speech with his guitar. The duologue should have the style of an antiphonal poem, the cues picked up so that there is scarcely a separation between the speeches, and the tempo quick and the voices edged.*)

JACQUES. You had mint-tea downstairs?

MARGUERITE. No, upstairs.

JACQUES. Upstairs where they burn the poppy?

MARGUERITE. Upstairs where it's cool and there's music and the haggling of the bazaar is soft as the murmur of pigeons.

JACQUES. That sounds restful. Reclining among silk pillows on a divan, in a curtained and perfumed alcove above the bazaar?

MARGUERITE. Forgetting for a while where I am, or that I don't know where I am. . .

JACQUES. Forgetting alone or forgetting with some young companion who plays the lute or the flute or who had silver to show you? Yes. That sounds very restful. And yet you do seem tired.

MARGUERITE. If I seem tired, it's your insulting solicitude that I'm tired of!

JACQUES. Is it insulting to feel concern for your safety in this place?

MARGUERITE. Yes, it is. The implication is.

JACQUES. What is the implication?

MARGUERITE. You know what it is: that I am one of those *aging—voluptuaries—* who used to be paid for pleasure but now have to pay!—Jacques, I won't be followed, I've gone too far to be followed!—*What is it?*

(*The* WAITER *has presented an envelope on a salver.*)

WAITER. A letter for the lady.

MARGUERITE. How strange to receive a letter in a place where nobody knows I'm staying! Will you open it for me? (*The* WAITER *withdraws.* JACQUES *takes the letter and opens it.*) Well! What is it?

JACQUES. Nothing important. An illustrated brochure from some resort in the mountains.

MARGUERITE. What is it called?

JACQUES. Bide-a-While. (*A chafing dish bursts into startling blue flame at the* MULLIGANS' *table.* LADY MULLIGAN *clasps her hands and exclaims with affected delight, the* WAITER *and* MR. GUTMAN *laugh agreeably.* MARGUERITE *springs up and moves out upon the forestage.* JACQUES *goes to her.*) Do you know this resort in the mountains?

MARGUERITE. Yes. I stayed there once. It's one of those places with open sleeping verandahs, surrounded by snowy pine woods. It has rows and rows of narrow white iron beds as regular as tombstones. The invalids smile at each other when axes flash across valleys, ring, flash, ring again! Young voices shout across valleys Hola! And mail is delivered. The friend that used to write you ten-page letters contents himself now with a postcard bluebird that tells you to "Get well Quick!" (JACQUES *throws the brochure away.*) —And when the last bleeding comes, not much later nor earlier than expected, you're wheeled discreetly into a little tent of white gauze, and the last thing you know of this world, of which you've known so little and yet so much, is the smell of an empty ice box.

15. Is the antiphonal dialog effective? Why or why not?

16. What irony resides in the proximity of Marguerite's *"aging— voluptuaries"* and "Bide-a-While"?

17. Is Marguerite's description of Bide-a-While merely pathos? If not, what saves it?

(*The blue flame expires in the chafing dish.* GUTMAN *picks up the brochure and hands it to the* WAITER, *whispering something.*)

JACQUES. You won't go back to that place.

(*The* WAITER *places the brochure on the salver again and approaches behind them.*)

MARGUERITE. I wasn't released. I left without permission. They sent me this to remind me.

WAITER (*presenting the salver*). You dropped this.

JACQUES. We threw it away!

WAITER. Excuse me.

JACQUES. Now, from now on, Marguerite, you must take better care of yourself. Do you hear me?

MARGUERITE. I hear you. No more distractions for me? No more entertainers in curtained and perfumed alcoves above the bazaar, no more young men that a pinch of white powder or a puff of gray smoke can almost turn to someone devoutly remembered?

JACQUES. No, from now on—

MARGUERITE. What "from now on," old hawk?

JACQUES. Rest. Peace.

MARGUERITE. Rest in peace is that final bit of advice they carve on gravestones, and I'm not ready for it! Are you? Are *you* ready for it? (*She returns to the table. He follows her.*) Oh, Jacques, when are we going to leave here, how are we going to leave here, you've got to tell me!

JACQUES. I've told you all I know.

MARGUERITE. Nothing, you've given up hope!

JACQUES. I haven't, that's not true.

(GUTMAN *has brought out the white cockatoo which he shows to* LADY MULLIGAN *at her table.*)

GUTMAN (*his voice rising above the murmurs*). Her name is Aurora.

LADY MULLIGAN. Why do you call her Aurora?

GUTMAN. She cries at daybreak.

LADY MULLIGAN. Only at daybreak?

GUTMAN. Yes, at daybreak only.

(*Their voices and laughter fade under.*)

18. Compare Marguerite's wistful defense of heroin and opium with current arguments for marijuana. Are there parallels?

19. Why does Aurora cry only at daybreak?

MARGUERITE. How long is it since you've been to the travel agencies?

JACQUES. This morning I made the usual round of Cook's, American Express, Wagon-lits Universal, and it was the same story. There are no flights out of here till further orders from someone higher up.

MARGUERITE. Nothing, nothing at all?

JACQUES. Oh, there's a rumor of something called the Fugitivo, but—

MARGUERITE. The What!!!?

JACQUES. The Fugitivo. It's one of those non-scheduled things that—

MARGUERITE. When, when, when?

20. How does mention of "the Fugitivo" add complication? Suspense?

JACQUES. I told you it was non-scheduled. Non-scheduled means it comes and goes at no predictable—

MARGUERITE. Don't give me the dictionary! I want to know how does one get on it? Did you bribe them? Did you offer them money? No. Of course you didn't! And I know why! You really don't want to leave here. You *think* you don't want to go because you're brave as an old hawk. But the truth of the matter—the real not the royal truth—is that you're terrified of the Terra Incognita outside that wall.

JACQUES. You've hit upon the truth. I'm terrified of the unknown country inside or outside this wall or any place on earth without you with me! The only country, known or unknown that I can breathe in, or care to, is the country in which we breathe together, as we are now at this table. And later, a little while later, even closer than this, the sole inhabitants of a tiny world whose limits are those of the light from a rose-colored lamp—beside the sweetly, completely known country of your cool bed!

MARGUERITE. The little comfort of love?

JACQUES. Is that comfort so little?

MARGUERITE. Caged birds accept each other but flight is what they long for.

JACQUES. I want to stay here with you and love you and guard you until the time or way comes that we both can leave with honor.

MARGUERITE. "Leave with honor"? Your vocabulary is almost as out-of-date as your cape and your cane. How could anyone quit this field with honor, this place where there's nothing but the gradual wasting away of everything decent in us . . . the sort of desperation that comes after even desperation has been worn out through long wear! . . . Why have they put these screens around the table? (*She springs up and knocks one of them over.*)

LADY MULLIGAN. There! You see? I don't understand why you let such people stay here.

GUTMAN. They pay the price of admission the same as you.

LADY MULLIGAN. What price is that?

GUTMAN. Desperation!—With cash here! (*He indicates the Siete Mares.*) Without cash there! (*He indicates Skid Row.*) Block Eight on the Camino Real!

21. Examine Casanova's love avowal to Marguerite (beginning "You've hit upon the truth"). Is he being sincere or affecting the great-lover technique? Examine his words carefully before deciding.

22. Consider the line "Caged birds accept each other but flight is what

they long for." In light of your own experience, is this true or false of "love" and marriage?

23. Apply Marguerite's speech beginning "Leave with honor?" to recent American military involvements. Are there parallels?

24. Why were the screens placed around the table? What moral implication is raised?

25. Explain why (structurally) Block Seven is so long.

BLOCK EIGHT

There is the sound of the loud desert wind and a flamenco cry followed by a dramatic phrase of music.

A flickering diamond blue radiance floods the hotel entrance. The crouching, grimacing HUNCHBACK *shakes his hoop of bells which is the convention for the appearance of each legendary figure.*

LORD BYRON *appears in the doorway readied for departure.* GUTMAN *raises his hand for silence.*

GUTMAN. You're leaving us, Lord Byron?

BYRON. Yes, I'm leaving you, Mr. Gutman.

GUTMAN. What a pity! But this is a port of entry and departure. There are no permanent guests. Possibly you are getting a little restless?

BYRON. The luxuries of this place have made me soft. The metal point's gone from my pen, there's nothing left but the feather.

GUTMAN. That may be true. But what can you do about it?

BYRON. Make a departure!

GUTMAN. From yourself?

BYRON. From my present self to myself as I used to be!

GUTMAN. *That's the* furthest *departure a man could make!* I guess you're sailing to Athens? There's another war there and like all wars since the beginning of time it can be interpreted as a—struggle for *what?*

BYRON. —For *freedom!* You may laugh at it, but it still means something to *me!*

GUTMAN. Of course it does! I'm not laughing a bit, I'm beaming with admiration.

BYRON. I've allowed myself many distractions.

GUTMAN. Yes, indeed!

BYRON. But I've never altogether forgotten my old devotion to the—

GUTMAN. —To the *what,* Lord Byron? (BYRON *passes nervous fingers through his hair.*) You can't remember the object of your one-time devotion?

(*There is a pause.* BYRON *limps away from the terrace and goes toward the fountain.*)

BYRON. When Shelley's corpse was recovered from the sea . . . (GUTMAN *beckons the* DREAMER *who approaches and accompanies* BYRON'S *speech.*) —It was burned on the beach at Viareggio.—I watched the spectacle from my carriage because the stench was revolting . . . Then it—fascinated me! I got out of my carriage. Went nearer, holding a handkerchief to my nostrils!—I saw that the front of the skull had broken away in the flames, and there—(*He advances out upon the stage apron, followed by* ABDULLAH *with the pine torch or lantern.*) And there was the brain of Shelley, indistinguishable from a cooking stew!—boiling, bubbling, hissing!—in the blackening—cracked—pot—of his skull! (MARGUERITE *rises abruptly.* JACQUES *supports her.*)—Trelawney, his friend, Trelawney, threw salt and oil and frankincense in the flames and finally the almost intolerable stench—(ABDULLAH *giggles.* GUTMAN *slaps him.*)—was *gone* and the burning was *pure!*—as a man's burning should be . . . A man's burning *ought* to be pure!—not like mine—(a crepe suzette— burned in brandy . . .) *Shelley's* burning was finally very *pure!* But the body, the corpse, split open like a grilled pig! (ABDULLAH *giggles irrepressibly again.* GUTMAN *grips the back of his neck and he stands up stiff and assumes an expression of exaggerated solemnity.*) —And then Trelawney—as the ribs of the corpse unlocked—reached into them as a baker reaches quickly into an oven! (ABDULLAH *almost goes into another convulsion.*) —And snatched out—as a baker would a biscuit!—the *heart* of Shelley! Snatched the heart of Shelley out of the blis- tering corpse!—Out of the purifying—blue-flame . . . (MARGUERITE *resumes her seat;* JACQUES *his.*)—And it was *over!*—I thought—(*He turns slightly from the audi- ence and crosses upstage from the apron. He faces* JACQUES *and* MARGUERITE.) —I thought it was a disgusting thing to do, to snatch a man's heart from his body! What can one man do with another man's heart?

1. The violent, beautiful description of the cremation of Shelley creates what ambivalences in you? Why?

(JACQUES *rises and strikes the stage with his cane.*)
JACQUES (*passionately*). He can do this with it! (*He seizes a loaf of bread on his table, and descends from the terrace.*) He can twist it like this! (*He twists the loaf.*) He can tear it like this! (*He tears the loaf in two.*) He can crush it under his foot! (*He drops the bread and stamps on it.*) —And kick it away—like this! (*He kicks the bread off the terrace.*)
(LORD BYRON *turns away from him and limps again out upon the stage apron and speaks to the audience.*)
BYRON. That's very true, Señor. But a poet's vocation, which used to be my vocation, is to influence the heart in a gentler fashion than you have made your mark on that loaf of bread. He ought to purify it and lift it above its ordinary level. For what is the heart but a sort of—(*He makes a high, groping gesture in the air.*)—A sort of—instrument!—that translates *noise* into *music,* chaos into—order . . . (ABDULLAH *ducks almost to the earth in an effort to stifle his mirth.* GUTMAN *coughs to cover his own amusement.*) —a mysterious order! (*He raises his voice till it fills the*

plaza.) —That was my vocation once upon a time, before it was obscured by vulgar plaudits!—Little by little it was lost among gondolas and palazzos!—masked balls, glittering salons, huge shadowy courts and torch-lit entrances!—Baroque façades, canopies and carpets, candelabra and gold plate among snowy damask, ladies with throats as slender as flower-stems, bending and breathing toward me their fragrant breath—Exposing their breasts to me! Whispering, half-smiling!—And everywhere marble, the visible grandeur of marble, pink and gray marble, veined and tinted as flayed corrupting flesh,—all these provided agreeable distractions from the rather frightening solitude of a poet. Oh, I wrote many cantos in Venice and Constantinople and in Ravenna and Rome, on all of those Latin and Levantine excursions that my twisted foot led me into—but I wonder about them a little. They seem to improve as the wine in the bottle—dwindles . . . *There is a passion for declivity in this world!* And lately I've found myself listening to hired musicians behind a row of artificial palm trees—instead of the single—pure-stringed instrument of my heart . . . Well, then, it's time to leave here! (*He turns back to the stage.*)—There is a time for departure even when there's no certain place to go! I'm going to look for one, now. I'm sailing to Athens. At least I can look up at the Acropolis, I can stand at the foot of it and look up at broken columns on the crest of a hill—if not purity, at least its recollection . . . I can sit quietly looking for a long, long time in absolute silence, and possibly, yes, *still* possibly—The old pure music will come to me again. Of course on the other hand I may hear only the little noise of insects in the grass . . . But I am sailing to Athens! *Make voyages!—Attempt them!*—there's nothing else . . .

2. Why does Williams have Byron address his definition of poetry "to the audience"? (Williams himself has published two volumes of poetry—good poetry.)

3. Explain *"There is a passion for declivity in this world!"*

4. Compare Byron's "There is a time for departure even when there's no certain place to go!" with Stanley and Lulu's exchange in *The Birthday Party* (p. 520) Are Stanley and Byron in agreement or disagreement?

MARGUERITE (*excitedly*). *Watch where he goes!* (LORD BYRON *limps across the plaza with his head bowed, making slight, apologetic gestures to the wheedling* BEGGARS *who shuffle about him. There is music. He crosses toward the steep Alleyway Out. The following is played with a quiet intensity so it will be in a lower key than the later Fugitivo Scene.*) Watch him, watch him, see which way he goes. Maybe he knows of a way that we haven't found out.

JACQUES. Yes, I'm watching him, Cara.

(LORD *and* LADY MULLIGAN *half rise, staring anxiously through monocle and lorgnon.*)

MARGUERITE. Oh, my God, I believe he's going up that alley.

JACQUES. Yes, he is. He has.

LORD and LADY MULLIGAN. Oh, the fool, the idiot, he's going under the arch!

MARGUERITE. Jacques, run after him, warn him, tell him about the desert he has to cross.

JACQUES. I think he knows what he's doing.

MARGUERITE. I can't look! (*She turns to the audience, throwing back her head and closing her eyes.*)

(*The desert wind sings loudly as* BYRON *climbs to the top of the steps.*)

BYRON (*to several porters carrying luggage—which is mainly caged birds*). THIS WAY!

(*He exits.* KILROY *starts to follow. He stops at the steps, cringing and looking at* GUTMAN. GUTMAN *motions him to go ahead.* KILROY *rushes up the stairs. He looks out, loses his nerve and sits—blinking his nose.* GUTMAN *laughs as he announces—*)

GUTMAN. Block Nine on the Camino Real! (*He goes into the hotel.*)

5. Why is Byron's luggage "caged birds"? What do they represent?

6. Why has Byron got the nerve to go into Terra Incognita? Why does Kilroy lack it? (Remember, these are archetypes!) Is a dramatic question posed?

7. Byron's escape is an escape to what? How did he die historically?

BLOCK NINE

ABDULLAH *runs back to the hotel with the billowing flambeau. A faint and far away humming sound becomes audible . . .* MARGUERITE *opens her eyes with a startled look. She searches the sky for something. A very low percussion begins with the humming sound, as if excited hearts are beating.*

MARGUERITE. Jacques! I hear something in the sky!

JACQUES. I think what you hear is—

MARGUERITE (*with rising excitement*). —No, it's a plane, a great one, I see the lights of it, now!

JACQUES. Some kind of fireworks, Cara.

MARGUERITE. Hush! LISTEN! (*She blows out the candle to see better above it. She rises, peering into the sky.*) I see it! I see it! There! It's circling over us!

LADY MULLIGAN. Raymond, Raymond, sit down, your face is flushed!

HOTEL GUESTS (*overlapping*). —What is it?—The FUGITIVO!—THE FUGITIVO! THE FUGITIVO!—Quick, get my jewelry from the hotel safe!—Cash a check!—Throw some things in a bag! I'll wait here!—Never mind luggage, we have our money and papers!—Where is it now?—There, there!—It's turning to land!—To go like this?— Yes, go anyhow, just go anyhow, just go!—Raymond! Please!—Oh, it's rising again! —Oh, it's—SHH! MR. GUTMAN!

(GUTMAN *appears in the doorway. He raises a hand in a commanding gesture.*)

GUTMAN. Signs in the sky should not be mistaken for wonders! (*The Voices modulate quickly.*) Ladies, gentlemen, please resume your seats! (*Places are resumed at tables, and silver is shakily lifted. Glasses are raised to lips, but the noise of concerted panting of excitement fills the stage and a low percussion echoes frantic heart beats.* GUTMAN *descends to the plaza, shouting furiously to the* OFFICER.) Why wasn't I told the Fugitivo was coming?

1. Who is Gutman that his "guests" fear him so much?

(*Everyone, almost as a man, rushes into the hotel and reappears almost at once with hastily collected possessions.* MARGUERITE *rises but appears stunned. There is a great whistling and screeching sound as the aerial transport halts somewhere close by, accompanied by rainbow splashes of light and cries like children's on a roller-coaster. Some incoming* PASSENGERS *approach the stage down an aisle of the theatre, preceded by* REDCAPS *with luggage.*)

PASSENGERS. —What a heavenly trip!—The scenery was thrilling!—It's so quick!— The only way to travel! Etc., etc.

(*A uniformed man, the* PILOT, *enters the plaza with a megaphone.*)

PILOT (*through the megaphone*). Fugitivo now loading for departure! Fugitivo loading immediately for departure! Northwest corner of the plaza!

MARGUERITE. Jacques, it's the Fugitivo, it's the non-scheduled thing you heard of this afternoon!

PILOT. All out-going passengers on the Fugitivo are requested to present their tickets and papers immediately at this station.

MARGUERITE. He said "out-going passengers"!

PILOT. Out-going passengers on the Fugitivo report immediately at this station for customs inspection.

MARGUERITE (*with a forced smile*). Why are you just standing there?

JACQUES (*with an Italian gesture*). Che cosa possa fare!

MARGUERITE. Move, move, do something!

JACQUES. *What!*

MARGUERITE. Go to them, ask, find out!

JACQUES. I have no idea what the damned thing is!

MARGUERITE. I do, I'll tell you! It's a way to escape from this abominable place!

JACQUES. Forse, forse, non so!

MARGUERITE. It's a way *out* and *I'm* not going to miss it!

2. Why is Jacques unwilling even to attempt passage on the Fugitivo?

PILOT. Ici la Douane! Customs inspection here!

MARGUERITE. Customs. That means luggage. Run to my room! Here! Key! Throw a few things in a bag, my jewels, my furs, but hurry! Vite, vite, vite! I don't believe there's much time! No, everybody is—(*Out-going* PASSENGERS *storm the desk and table.*)—Clamoring for tickets! There must be limited space! Why don't you do what I tell you? (*She rushes to a man with a rubber stamp and a roll of tickets.*) Monsieur! Señor! Pardonnez-moi! I'm going, I'm going out! I want my ticket!

PILOT (*coldly*). Name, please.

MARGUERITE. Mademoiselle—Gautier—but I—

PILOT. Gautier? Gautier? We have no Gautier listed.

MARGUERITE. I'm—*not* listed! I mean I'm—traveling under another name.

TRAVEL AGENT. What name are you traveling under?

(PRUDENCE *and* OLYMPE *rush out of the hotel half dressed, dragging their furs. Meanwhile* KILROY *is trying to make a fast buck or two as a Redcap. The scene gathers wild momentum, is punctuated by crashes of percussion. Grotesque mummers act as demon custom inspectors and immigration authorities, etc. Baggage is tossed about, ripped open, smuggled goods seized, arrests made, all amid the wildest importunities, protests, threats, bribes, entreaties; it is a scene for improvisation.*)

3. Explain Kilroy's making "a fast buck or two as a Redcap." Remember: he is an archetype!

PRUDENCE. Thank God I woke up!

OLYMPE. Thank God I wasn't asleep!

PRUDENCE. I knew it was non-scheduled but I *did* think they'd give you time to get in your girdle.

OLYMPE. Look who's trying to crash it! I know damned well *she* don't have a reservation!

PILOT (*to* MARGUERITE). What name did you say, Mademoiselle? Please! People are waiting, you're holding up the line!

MARGUERITE. I'm so confused! Jacques! What name did you make my reservation under?

OLYMPE. She has no reservation!

PRUDENCE. *I have, I got mine!*

OLYMPE. *I got mine!*

PRUDENCE. *I'm next!*

OLYMPE. Don't push *me*, you old bag!

MARGUERITE. I was here first! I was here before anybody! Jacques, quick! Get my money from the hotel safe!

(JACQUES *exits.*)

AGENT. *Stay in line!*

(*There is a loud warning whistle.*)

PILOT. Five minutes. The Fugitivo leaves in five minutes. Five, five minutes only! (*At this announcement the scene becomes riotous.*)

TRAVEL AGENT. *Four minutes! The Fugitivo leaves in four minutes!* (PRUDENCE *and*

OLYMPE *are shrieking at him in French. The warning whistle blasts again.) Three minutes, the Fugitivo leaves in three minutes!*

4. Explain the device of announcing the minutes to departure of the Fugitivo. Is this more or less effective than it was in 1953? Why?

MARGUERITE (*topping the turmoil*). Monsieur! Please! I was here first, I was here before anybody! Look! (JACQUES *returns with her money.*) I have thousands of francs! Take whatever you want! Take all of it, it's yours!

PILOT. Payment is only accepted in pounds sterling or dollars. Next, please.

MARGUERITE. You don't accept francs? They do at the hotel! They accept my francs at the Siete Mares!

PILOT. Lady, don't argue with me, I don't make the rules!

MARGUERITE (*beating her forehead with her fist*). Oh, God, Jacques! Take these back to the cashier! (*She thrusts the bills at him.*) Get them changed to dollars or—Hurry! *Tout de suite!* I'm—going to faint . . .

JACQUES. But Marguerite—

MARGUERITE. *Go! Go! Please!*

PILOT. Closing, we're closing now! The Fugitivo leaves in two minutes!

(LORD *and* LADY MULLIGAN *rush forward.*)

LADY MULLIGAN. Let Lord Mulligan through.

PILOT (*to* MARGUERITE). You're standing in the way.

(OLYMPE *screams as the* CUSTOMS INSPECTOR *dumps her jewels on the ground. She and* PRUDENCE *butt heads as they dive for the gems: the fight is renewed.*)

MARGUERITE (*detaining the* PILOT). Oh, look, Monsieur! Regardez ça! My diamond, a solitaire—two carats! Take that as security!

PILOT. Let me go. The Loan Shark's across the plaza!

(*There is another warning blast.* PRUDENCE *and* OLYMPE *seize hat boxes and rush toward the whistle.*)

MARGUERITE (*clinging desperately to the* PILOT). You don't understand! Señor Casanova has gone to change money! He'll be here in a second. And I'll pay five, ten, twenty times the price of—*JACQUES! JACQUES! WHERE ARE YOU?*

VOICE (*back of auditorium*). We're closing the gate!

MARGUERITE. You can't close the gate!

PILOT. Move, Madame!

MARGUERITE. I won't move!

LADY MULLIGAN. I tell you, Lord Mulligan is the Iron & Steel man from Cobh! Raymond! They're closing the gate!

LORD MULLIGAN. I can't seem to get through!

GUTMAN. Hold the gate for Lord Mulligan!

PILOT (*to* MARGUERITE). Madame, stand back or I will have to use force!

MARGUERITE. Jacques! Jacques!

LADY MULLIGAN. Let us through! We're clear!

PILOT. Madame! Stand back and let these passengers through!

MARGUERITE. No, No! I'm first! I'm next!

LORD MULLIGAN. Get her out of our way! That woman's a whore!

LADY MULLIGAN. How dare you stand in our way?

PILOT. Officer, take this woman!

LADY MULLIGAN. Come on, Raymond!

MARGUERITE (*as the* OFFICER *pulls her away*). Jacques! Jacques! Jacques! (JACQUES *returns with changed money.*) Here! Here is the money!

PILOT. All right, give me your papers.

MARGUERITE. —My papers? Did you say my papers?

PILOT. Hurry, hurry, your passport!

MARGUERITE. —Jacques! He wants my papers! Give him my papers, Jacques!

JACQUES. —The lady's papers are lost!

MARGUERITE (*wildly*). No, no, no, THAT IS NOT TRUE! HE WANTS TO KEEP ME HERE! HE'S LYING ABOUT IT!

JACQUES. Have you forgotten that your papers were stolen?

MARGUERITE. I gave you my papers, I gave you my papers to keep, you've got my papers.

5. Could any other character create the suspense Marguerite does in her frustrated attempt to board the plane? Explain why or why not.

(*Screaming,* LADY MULLIGAN *breaks past her and descends the stairs.*)

LADY MULLIGAN. Raymond! Hurry!

LORD MULLIGAN (*staggering on the top step*). I'm sick! I'm sick!

(*The* STREETCLEANERS *disguised as expensive morticians in swallowtail coats come rapidly up the aisle of the theatre and wait at the foot of the stairway for the tottering tycoon.*)

LADY MULLIGAN. You cannot be sick till we get on the Fugitivo!

LORD MULLIGAN. Forward all cables to Guaranty Trust in Paris.

LADY MULLIGAN. Place de la Concorde.

LORD MULLIGAN. Thank you! All purchases C.O.D. to Mulligan Iron & Steel Works in Cobh—Thank you!

LADY MULLIGAN. Raymond! Raymond! Who are these men?

LORD MULLIGAN. I know these men! I recognize their faces!

LADY MULLIGAN. Raymond! They're the Streetcleaners! (*She screams and runs up the aisle screaming repeatedly, stopping half-way to look back. The two* STREET-CLEANERS *seize* LORD MULLIGAN *by either arm as he crumples.*) Pack Lord Mulligan's body in dry ice! Ship Air Express to Cobh care of Mulligan Iron & Steel Works, in Cobh! (*She runs sobbing out of the back of the auditorium as the whistle blows repeatedly and a Voice shouts.*) I'm coming! I'm coming!

6. Explain characterization of the Mulligans in his death and her departure.

MARGUERITE. Jacques! Jacques! Oh, God!

PILOT. The Fugitivo is leaving, all aboard! (*He starts toward the steps.* MARGUERITE *clutches his arm.*) Let go of me!

MARGUERITE. You can't go without me!

PILOT. Officer, hold this woman!

JACQUES. Marguerite, let him go!

(*She releases the* PILOT'S *arm and turns savagely on* JACQUES. *She tears his coat open, seizes a large envelope of papers and rushes after the* PILOT *who has started down the steps over the orchestra pit and into a center aisle of the house. Timpani build up as she starts down the steps, screaming—*)

MARGUERITE. Here! I have them here! Wait! I have my papers now, I have my papers!

(*The* PILOT *runs cursing up the center aisle as the Fugitivo whistle gives repeated short, shrill blasts; timpani and dissonant brass are heard. Out-going* PASSENGERS *burst into hysterical song, laughter, shouts of farewell. These can come over a loud-speaker at the back of the house.*)

VOICE IN DISTANCE. Going! Going! Going!

MARGUERITE (*attempting as if half-paralyzed to descend the steps*). NOT WITHOUT ME, NO, NO, NOT WITHOUT ME!

(*Her figure is caught in the dazzling glacial light of the follow-spot. It blinds her. She makes violent, crazed gestures, clinging to the railing of the steps; her breath is loud and hoarse as a dying person's, she holds a blood-stained handkerchief to her lips. There is a prolonged, gradually fading, rocketlike roar as the Fugitivo takes off. Shrill cries of joy from departing* PASSENGERS; *something radiant passes above the stage and streams of confetti and tinsel fall into the plaza. Then there is a great calm, the ship's receding roar diminished to the hum of an insect.*)

GUTMAN (*somewhat compassionately*). Block Ten on the Camino Real.

7. Why did Jacques prevent Marguerite's escape? What does this imply about the nature of love (at least Casanova's love)? Is a dramatic question posed?

8. What is the Fugitivo's destination?

9. Why does Gutman make his announcement "somewhat compassionately"?

BLOCK TEN

There is something about the desolation of the plaza that suggests a city devastated by bombardment. Reddish lights flicker here and there as if ruins were smoldering and wisps of smoke rise from them.

LA MADRECITA (*almost inaudibly*). Donde?

THE DREAMER. Aquí. Aquí, Madrecita.

MARGUERITE. Lost! Lost! Lost! Lost! (*She is still clinging brokenly to the railing of the steps.*)

(JACQUES *descends to her and helps her back up the steps.*)

JACQUES. Lean against me, Cara. Breathe quietly, now.

MARGUERITE. Lost!

JACQUES. Breathe quietly, quietly, and look up at the sky.

MARGUERITE. Lost . . .

JACQUES. These tropical nights are so clear. There's the Southern Cross. Do you see the Southern Cross, Marguerite? (*He points through the proscenium. They are now on the bench before the fountain; she is resting in his arms.*) And there, over there, is Orion, like a fat, golden fish swimming North in the deep clear water, and we are together, breathing quietly together, leaning together, quietly, quietly together, completely, sweetly together, not frightened, now, not alone, but completely quietly together . . . (LA MADRECITA, *led into the center of the plaza by her son, has begun to sing very softly; the reddish flares dim out and the smoke disappears.*) All of us have a desperate bird in our hearts, a memory of—some distant mother with— wings . . .

1. Why does the plaza seem "devastated"? Through whose eyes is the plaza portrayed?

2. As Marguerite is soothed by Jacques, and as La Madrecita sings, the devastation vanishes. Explain why.

3. What does Jacques mean when he says we remember a "distant mother with—wings"? Is the statement poetic, scientific, neither, or both?

MARGUERITE. I would have—left—without you . . .

JACQUES. I know, I know!

MARGUERITE. Then how can you—still—?

JACQUES. Hold you? (MARGUERITE *nods slightly.*) Because you've taught me that part of love which is tender. I never knew it before. Oh, I had—mistresses that circled me like moons! I scrambled from one bed-chamber to another bed-chamber with shirttails always aflame, from girl to girl, like buckets of coal-oil poured on a conflagration! But never loved until now with the part of love that's tender . . .

MARGUERITE. —We're used to each other. That's what you think is love . . . You'd better leave me now, you'd better go and let me go because there's a cold wind blowing out of the mountains and over the desert and into my heart, and if you stay with me now, I'll say cruel things, I'll wound your vanity, I'll taunt you with the decline of your male vigor!

JACQUES. Why does disappointment make people unkind to each other?

MARGUERITE. Each of us is very much alone.

JACQUES. Only if we distrust each other.

MARGUERITE. We have to distrust each other. It is our only defense against betrayal.

JACQUES. I think our defense is love.

MARGUERITE. Oh, Jacques, we're used to each other, we're a pair of captive hawks caught in the same cage, and so we've grown used to each other. That's what passes for love at this dim, shadowy end of the Camino Real . . . What are we sure of? Not even of our existence, dear comforting friend! And whom can we ask the questions that torment us? "What is this place?" "Where are we?" — a fat old man who gives sly hints that only bewilder us more, a fake of a Gypsy squinting at cards and tea-leaves. What else are we offered? The never-broken procession of little events that assure us that we and strangers about us are still going on! Where? Why? and the perch that we hold is unstable! We're threatened with eviction, for this is a port of entry and departure, there are no permanent guests! And where else have we to go when we leave here? Bide-a-While? "Ritz Men Only"? Or under that ominous arch into Terra Incognita? We're lonely. We're frightened. We hear the Streetcleaners' piping not far away. So now and then, although we've wounded each other time and again—we stretch out hands to each other in the dark that we can't escape from—we huddle together for some dim-communal comfort—and that's what passes for love on this terminal stretch of the road that used to be royal. What is it, this feeling between us? When you feel my exhausted weight against your shoulder—when I clasp your anxious old hawk's head to my breast, what is it we feel in whatever is left of our hearts? Something, yes, something—delicate, unreal, bloodless! The sort of violets that could grow on the moon, or in the crevices of those far away mountains, fertilized by the droppings of carrion birds. Those birds are familiar to us. Their shadows inhabit the plaza. I've heard them flapping their wings like old charwomen beating worn-out carpets with gray brooms . . . But tenderness, the violets in the mountains—can't break the rocks!

JACQUES. The violets in the mountains can break the rocks if you believe in them and allow them to grow!

4. Marguerite and Jacques do not define love alike. Is his an archetypical man's view? Is hers an archetypical woman's?

5. What is "this dim, shadowy end of the Camino Real" that Marguerite mentions?

6. What are the "violets" that Marguerite refers to?

(*The plaza has resumed its usual aspect.* ABDULLAH *enters through one of the downstage arches.*)

ABDULLAH. Get your carnival hats and noisemakers here! Tonight the moon will restore the virginity of my sister!

MARGUERITE (*almost tenderly touching his face*). Don't you know that tonight I am going to betray you?

JACQUES. —Why would you do that?

MARGUERITE. Because I've out-lived the tenderness of my heart. Abdullah, come here! I have an errand for you! Go to Ahmed's and deliver a message!

ABDULLAH. I'm working for Mama, making the Yankee dollar! Get your carnival hats and—

MARGUERITE. Here, boy! *(She snatches a ring off her finger and offers it to him.)*

JACQUES. —Your cabochon sapphire?

MARGUERITE. Yes, my cabochon sapphire!

JACQUES. Are you mad?

MARGUERITE. Yes, I'm mad, or nearly! The specter of lunacy's at my heels tonight! *(JACQUES drives ABDULLAH back with his cane.)* Catch, boy! The other side of the fountain! Quick! *(The guitar is heard molto vivace. She tosses the ring across the fountain. JACQUES attempts to hold the boy back with his cane. ABDULLAH dodges in and out like a little terrier, laughing. MARGUERITE shouts encouragement in French. When the boy is driven back from the ring, she snatches it up and tosses it to him again, shouting.)* Catch, boy! Run to Ahmed's! Tell the charming young man that the French lady's bored with her company tonight! Say that the French lady missed the Fugitivo and wants to forget she missed it! Oh, and reserve a room with a balcony so I can watch your sister appear on the roof when the moonrise makes her a virgin! *(ABDULLAH skips shouting out of the plaza. JACQUES strikes the stage with his cane. She says, without looking at him.)* Time betrays us and we betray each other.

JACQUES. Wait, Marguerite!

MARGUERITE. No! I can't! The wind from the desert is sweeping me away!

(A loud singing wind sweeps her toward the terrace, away from him. She looks back once or twice as if for some gesture of leave-taking but he only stares at her fiercely, striking the stage at intervals with his cane, like a death-march. GUTMAN watches, smiling, from the terrace, bows to MARGUERITE as she passes into the hotel. The drum of JACQUES' cane is taken up by other percussive instruments, and almost unnoticeably at first, weird-looking celebrants or carnival mummers creep into the plaza, silently as spiders descending a wall. A sheet of scarlet and yellow rice paper bearing some cryptic device is lowered from the center of the plaza. The percussive effects become gradually louder. JACQUES is oblivious to the scene behind him, standing in front of the plaza, his eyes closed.)

GUTMAN. Block Eleven on the Camino Real.

7. Why does Marguerite plan to betray Jacques? Why does she hurt him with the knowledge?

8. What do the "wind" and "percussive" effects signify? The "rice paper"?

9. The major dramatic question of the play is posed in this Block. State it.

BLOCK ELEVEN

GUTMAN. The Fiesta has started. The first event is the coronation of the King of Cuckolds.

(*Blinding shafts of light are suddenly cast upon* CASANOVA *on the forestage. He shields his face, startled, as the crowd closes about him. The blinding shafts of light seem to strike him like savage blows and he falls to his knees as*—*The* HUNCHBACK *scuttles out of the* GYPSY'S *stall with a crown of gilded antlers on a velvet pillow. He places it on* JACQUES' *head. The celebrants form a circle about him chanting.*)

JACQUES. What is this?—a crown—

GUTMAN. A crown of horns!

CROWD. Cornudo! Cornudo! Cornudo! Cornudo! Cornudo!

GUTMAN. Hail, all hail, the King of Cuckolds on the Camino Real!

(JACQUES *springs up, first striking out at them with his cane. Then all at once he abandons self-defense, throws off his cape, casts away his cane, and fills the plaza with a roar of defiance and self-derision.*)

JACQUES. Si, si, sono cornudo! Cornudo! Cornudo! Casanova is the King of Cuckolds on the Camino Real! Show me crowned to the world! Announce the honor! Tell the world of the honor bestowed on Casanova, Chevalier de Seingalt! Knight of the Golden Spur by the Grace of His Holiness the Pope . . . Famous adventurer! Con man Extraordinary! Gambler! Pitch-man par excellence! Shill! Pimp! Spiv! And—great—lover . . . (*The crowd howls with applause and laughter but his voice rises above them with sobbing intensity.*) Yes, I said GREAT LOVER! The greatest lover wears the longest horns on the Camino! GREAT! LOVER!

1. Explain the complex layers of symbolism in the line "A crown of horns!" If you become hopelessly confused in your explanation even though you are sure that you know the answer, what are you discovering about the nature of symbolism? Of poetry?

2. Has Casanova understood himself in accepting the crown? Can you explain what he understands?

GUTMAN. Attention! Silence! The moon is rising! The restoration is about to occur!

(*A white radiance is appearing over the ancient wall of the town. The mountains become luminous. There is music. Everyone, with breathless attention, faces the light.* KILROY *crosses to* JACQUES *and beckons him out behind the crowd. There he snatches off the antlers and returns him his fedora.* JACQUES *reciprocates by removing* KILROY'S *fright wig and electric nose. They embrace as brothers. In a Chaplinesque dumb-play,* KILROY *points to the wildly flickering three brass balls of the* LOAN SHARK *and to his golden gloves: then with a terrible grimace he removes the gloves from about his neck, smiles at* JACQUES *and indicates that the two of them together will take flight over the wall.* JACQUES *shakes his head sadly, pointing to his heart and then to the Siete Mares.* KILROY *nods with regretful understanding of a human and manly folly. A* GUARD *has been silently approaching them in a soft shoe dance.* JACQUES *whistles "La Golondrina."* KILROY *assumes a very nonchalant pose. The* GUARD *picks up curiously the discarded fright wig and electric nose. Then glancing suspiciously at the pair, he advances.* KILROY *makes a run for it. He does a baseball slide into the* LOAN SHARK'S *welcoming doorway. The door slams. The* COP *is about to crash it when a gong sounds and* GUTMAN *shouts.)*

GUTMAN. SILENCE! ATTENTION! THE GYPSY!

3. Explain the need of Kilroy and Casanova to become brothers. Does the act agitate them?

GYPSY *(appearing on the roof with a gong).* The moon has restored the virginity of my daughter Esmeralda!

(The gong sounds.)

STREET PEOPLE. Ahh!

GYPSY. The moon in its plenitude has made her a virgin!

(The gong sounds.)

STREET PEOPLE. Ahh!

GYPSY. Praise her, celebrate her, give her suitable homage!

(The gong sounds.)

STREET PEOPLE. Ahh!

GYPSY. Summon her to the roof! *(She shouts.)* ESMERALDA! *(Dancers shout the name in rhythm.)* RISE WITH THE MOON, MY DAUGHTER! CHOOSE THE HERO!

*(*ESMERALDA *appears on the roof in dazzling light. She seems to be dressed in jewels. She raises her jeweled arms with a harsh flamenco cry.)*

ESMERALDA. OLE!

DANCERS. OLE!

(The details of the Carnival are a problem for director and choreographer but it has already been indicated in the script that the Fiesta is a sort of serio-comic, grotesque-lyric "Rites of Fertility" with roots in various pagan cultures. It should not be over-elaborated or allowed to occupy much time. It should not be more than three minutes from the appearance of ESMERALDA *on the* GYPSY'S *roof till the return of* KILROY *from the* LOAN SHARK'S.)*

4. Why does Williams leave the details of the fertility rite to the director and choreographer—that is, to you?

5. Is Esmeralda's virginity restored by the moon? Why do the people assume that it is? Religion is explored here. Explain.

*(*KILROY *emerges from the Pawn Shop in grotesque disguise, a turban, dark glasses, a burnoose and an umbrella or sunshade.)*

KILROY (*to* JACQUES). So long, pal, I wish you could come with me.

(JACQUES *clasps his cross in* KILROY'S *hands.*)

ESMERALDA. Yankee!

KILROY (*to the audience*). So long, everybody. Good luck to you all on the Camino! I hocked my golden gloves to finance this expedition. I'm going. Hasta luega. I'm going. I'm gone!

ESMERALDA. Yankee!

(*He has no sooner entered the plaza than the riotous women strip off everything but the dungarees and skivvy which he first appeared in.*)

KILROY (*to the women*). Let me go. Let go of me! Watch out for my equipment!

ESMERALDA. Yankee! Yankee!

(*He breaks away from them and plunges up the stairs of the ancient wall. He is half-way up them when* GUTMAN *shouts out.*)

GUTMAN. Follow-spot on that gringo, light the stairs!

(*The light catches* KILROY. *At the same instant* ESMERALDA *cries out to him.*)

ESMERALDA. Yankee! Yankee!

GYPSY. What's goin' on down there? (*She rushes into the plaza.*)

KILROY. Oh, no, I'm on my way out!

ESMERALDA. Espere un momento!

(*The* GYPSY *calls the police, but is ignored in the crowd.*)

KILROY. Don't tempt me, baby! I hocked my golden gloves to finance this expedition!

ESMERALDA. Querido!

KILROY. Querido means sweetheart, a word which is hard to resist but I must resist it.

ESMERALDA. Champ!

KILROY. I used to be Champ but why remind me of it?

ESMERALDA. Be champ again! Contend in the contest! Compete in the competition!

GYPSY (*shouting*). *Naw, naw, not eligible!*

ESMERALDA. Pl-eeeeeeze!

GYPSY. Slap her, Nursie, she's flippin'.

(ESMERALDA *slaps* NURSIE *instead.*)

ESMERALDA. Hero! Champ!

KILROY. I'm not in condition!

ESMERALDA. You're still the Champ, the undefeated Champ of the golden gloves!

KILROY. Nobody's called me that in a long, long time!

ESMERALDA. Champ!

KILROY. My resistance is crumbling!

ESMERALDA. Champ!

KILROY. It's crumbled!

ESMERALDA. Hero!

KILROY. GERONIMO! (*He takes a flying leap from the stairs into the center of the plaza. He turns toward* ESMERALDA *and cries*) DOLL!!

(KILROY surrounded by cheering STREET PEOPLE goes into a triumphant eccentric dance which reviews his history as fighter, traveler and lover. At finish of the dance, the music is cut off, as KILROY lunges, arm uplifted towards ESMERALDA, and cries) KILROY. *Kilroy the Champ!*

ESMERALDA. *KILROY the Champ!* (She snatches a bunch of red roses from the stunned NURSIE and tosses them to KILROY.)

CROWD (sharply). OLE!

(The GYPSY, at the same instant, hurls her gong down, creating a resounding noise. KILROY turns and comes down towards the audience, saying to them) KILROY. *Y'see?*

(Cheering STREET PEOPLE surge towards him and lift him in the air. The lights fade as the curtain descends.)

CROWD (in a sustained yell). OLE!

(The curtain falls. There is a short intermission.)

6. Why does Esmeralda choose Kilroy?
7. Would Kilroy have gone into Terra Incognita had Esmeralda not chosen him?
8. Explain Esmeralda's triumph over Kilroy.
9. How is the Marguerite-Jacques scene in Block Ten poetically balanced against this Block?
10. Is the major dramatic question answered in any way in this Block? Partially or completely?
11. Why is an intermission desirable at this point?

BLOCK TWELVE

The stage is in darkness except for a spot light which picks out ESMERALDA on the GYPSY'S roof.

ESMERALDA. Mama, what happened? —Mama, the lights went out!—Mama, where are you? It's so dark I'm scared!—MAMA!

(The lights are turned on displaying a deserted plaza. The GYPSY is seated at a small table before her stall.)

GYPSY. Come on downstairs, Doll. The mischief is done. You've chosen your hero!

GUTMAN (from the balcony of the Siete Mares). Block Twelve on the Camino Real.

NURSIE (at the fountain). Gypsy, the fountain is still dry!

GYPSY. What d'yuh expect? There's nobody left to uphold the old traditions! You raise a girl. She watches television. Plays be-bop. Reads *Screen Secrets*. Comes the Big Fiesta. The moonrise makes her a virgin—which is the neatest trick of the week! And what does she do? Chooses a Fugitive Patsy for the Chosen Hero! Well, show him in! Admit the joker and get the virgin ready!

NURSIE. You're going through with it?

GYPSY. Look, Nursie! I'm operating a legitimate joint! This joker'll get the same treatment he'd get if he breezed down the Camino in a blizzard of G-notes! Trot, girl! Lubricate your means of locomotion!

1. The Gypsy says that the public fountain is dry because "There's nobody left to uphold the old traditions." What does she mean? Does "the public fountain" still seem to symbolize what you earlier thought?
2. Is the glib slang of the Gypsy appropriate to her character? To the setting? Is it amusing to you? Decide carefully why it is or is not.

(NURSIE *goes into the* GYPSY'S *stall. The* GYPSY *rubs her hands together and blows on the crystal ball, spits on it and gives it the old one-two with a "shammy" rag . . . She mutters "Crystal ball, tell me all . . . crystal ball tell me all" . . . as* KILROY *bounds into the plaza from her stall . . . a rose between his teeth.)*

GYPSY. Siente se, por favor.

KILROY. No comprendo the lingo.

GYPSY. Put it down!

NURSIE *(offstage).* Hey, Gypsy!

GYPSY. Address me as Madam!

NURSIE *(entering).* Madam! Winchell has scooped you!

GYPSY. In a pig's eye!

NURSIE. The Fugitivo has *"fftt . . ."!*

GYPSY. In Elizabeth, New Jersey . . . ten fifty seven P.M. . . . Eastern Standard Time—while you were putting them kiss-me-quicks in your hair-do! Furthermore, my second exclusive is that the solar system is drifting towards the constellation of Hercules: Skiddoo! (NURSIE *exits. Stamping is heard offstage.)* Quiet, back there! God damn it!

NURSIE *(offstage).* She's out of control!

3. What happened to the Fugitivo? What is the irony? What makes the accident seem unimportant?

GYPSY. Give her a double-bromide! *(To* KILROY*)* Well, how does it feel to be the Chosen Hero?

KILROY. I better explain something to you.

GYPSY. Save your breath. You'll need it.

KILROY. I want to level with you. Can I level with you?

GYPSY *(rapidly stamping some papers).* How could you help but level with the Gypsy?

KILROY. I don't know what the hero is chosen for.

(ESMERALDA *and* NURSIE *shriek offstage.)*

GYPSY. Time will brief you . . . Aw, I hate paper work! . . . NURSEHH! (NURSIE *comes out and stands by the table.*) This filing system is screwed up six ways from Next Sunday . . . File this crap under crap!— (*To* KILROY) The smoking lamp is lit. Have a stick on me! (*She offers him a cigarette.*)

KILROY. No thanks.

GYPSY. Come on, indulge yourself. You got nothing to lose that won't be lost.

KILROY. If that's a professional opinion, I don't respect it.

GYPSY. Resume your seat and give me your full name.

KILROY. Kilroy.

GYPSY (*writing all this down*). Date of birth and place of that disaster?

KILROY. Both unknown.

GYPSY. Address?

KILROY. Traveler.

GYPSY. Parents?

KILROY. Anonymous.

GYPSY. Who brought you up?

KILROY. I was brought up and down by an eccentric old aunt in Dallas.

GYPSY. Raise both hands simultaneously and swear that you have not come here for the purpose of committing an immoral act.

ESMERALDA (*from offstage*). Hey, Chico!

GYPSY. *QUIET!* Childhood diseases?

KILROY. Whooping cough, measles and mumps.

GYPSY. Likes and dislikes?

KILROY. I like situations I can get out of. I don't like cops and—

GYPSY. Immaterial! Here! Signature on this! (*She hands him a blank.*)

4. Evaluate the archetypal Kilroy's answers to the Gypsy's questionnaire.

KILROY. What is it?

GYPSY. You always sign something, don't you?

KILROY. Not till I know what it is.

GYPSY. It's just a little formality to give a tone to the establishment and make an impression on our out-of-town trade. Roll up your sleeve.

KILROY. What for?

GYPSY. A shot of some kind.

KILROY. What kind?

GYPSY. Any kind. Don't they always give you some kind of a shot?

KILROY. "They"?

GYPSY. Brass-hats, Americanos! (*She injects a hypo.*)

KILROY. I am no guinea pig!

GYPSY. Don't kid yourself. We're all of us guinea pigs in the laboratory of God. Humanity is just a work in progress.

KILROY. I don't make it out.

GYPSY. Who does? The Camino Real is a funny paper read backwards! (*There is weird piping outside.* KILROY *shifts on his seat. The* GYPSY *grins.*) Tired? The altitude makes you sleepy?

KILROY. It makes me nervous.

5. Agree or disagree (stating clear, logical reasons) with the Gypsy's statement that: "We're all of us guinea pigs in the laboratory of God. Humanity is just a work in progress." Compared with her breezy, slangy approach to other matters, is the statement more or less impressive? Why?

6. Compare the above statement with "The Camino Real is a funny paper read backwards!" Which statement is more challenging to you? Do they make the same observation, nearly the same, or totally different observations? Does one minimize the other? Speculate on the reason for Williams' inclusion of both statements so close together. Is a major dramatic question posed here?

GYPSY. I'll show you how to take a slug of tequila! It dilates the capillaries. First you sprinkle salt on the back of your hand. Then lick it off with your tongue. Now then you toss the shot down! (*She demonstrates.*) —And then you bite into the lemon. That way it goes down easy, but what a bang! —You're next.

KILROY. No, thanks, I'm on the wagon.

GYPSY. There's an old Chinese proverb that says, "When your goose is cooked you might as well have it cooked with plenty of gravy." (*She laughs.*) Get up, baby. Let's have a look at yuh!—You're not a bad-looking boy. Sometimes working for the Yankee dollar isn't a painful profession. Have you ever been attracted by older women?

KILROY. Frankly, no, ma'am.

GYPSY. Well, there's a first time for everything.

KILROY. That is a subject I cannot agree with you on.

GYPSY. You think I'm an old bag? (KILROY *laughs awkwardly. The* GYPSY *slaps his face.*) Will you take the cards or the crystal?

KILROY. It's immaterial.

GYPSY. All right, we'll begin with the cards. (*She shuffles and deals.*) Ask me a question.

KILROY. Has my luck run out?

GYPSY. Baby, your luck ran out the day you were born. Another question.

KILROY. Ought I to leave this town?

GYPSY. It don't look to me like you've got much choice in the matter . . . Take a card.

(KILROY *takes one.*)

GYPSY. Ace?

KILROY. Yes, ma'am.

GYPSY. What color?

KILROY. Black.

GYPSY. Oh, oh—That does it. How big is your heart?

KILROY. As big as the head of a baby.

GYPSY. It's going to break.

KILROY. That's what I was afraid of.

GYPSY. The Streetcleaners are waiting for you outside the door.

KILROY. Which door, the front one? I'll slip out the back!

GYPSY. Leave us face it frankly, your number is up! You must've known a long time that the name of Kilroy was on the Streetcleaners' list.

KILROY. Sure. But not on top of it!

GYPSY. It's always a bit of a shock. Wait a minute! Here's good news. The Queen of Hearts has turned up in proper position.

KILROY. What's that mean?

GYPSY. Love, Baby!

KILROY. Love?

GYPSY. The Booby Prize! —Esmeralda!

7. Is Kilroy's "reading" by the Gypsy symbolism, humor, satire, or all three?

(*She rises and hits a gong. A divan is carried out. The* GYPSY'S DAUGHTER *is seated in a reclining position, like an odalisque, on this low divan. A spangled veil covers her face. From this veil to the girdle below her navel, that supports her diaphanous bifurcated skirt, she is nude except for a pair of glittering emerald snakes coiled over her breasts.* KILROY's *head moves in a dizzy circle and a canary warbles inside it.*)

KILROY. WHAT'S—WHAT'S *HER* SPECIALTY?—Tea-leaves?

8. Esmeralda as "an odalisque" is borrowed from a number of paintings. Why?

9. Explain the humor of Kilroy's "WHAT'S—WHAT'S *HER* SPECIALTY?—Tea-leaves?"

(*The* GYPSY *wags a finger.*)

GYPSY. You know what curiosity did to the tom cat!—Nursie, give me my glamour wig and my forty-five. I'm hitting the street! I gotta go down to Walgreen's for change.

KILROY. What change?

GYPSY. The change from that ten-spot you're about to give me.

NURSIE. Don't argue with her. She has a will of iron.

KILROY. I'm not arguing! (*He reluctantly produces the money.*) But let's be *fair* about this! I hocked my golden gloves for this saw-buck!

NURSIE. All of them Yankee bastids want something for nothing!

KILROY. I want a receipt for this bill.

NURSIE. No one is gypped at the Gypsy's!

KILROY. That's wonderful! How do I know it?

GYPSY. It's in the cards, it's in the crystal ball, it's in the tea-leaves! Absolutely no one is gypped at the Gypsy's! (*She snatches the bill. The wind howls.*) Such changeable weather! I'll slip on my summer furs! Nursie, break out my summer furs!

NURSIE (*leering grotesquely*). Mink or sable?

GYPSY. Ha ha, that's a doll! Here! Clock him! (NURSIE *tosses her a greasy blanket, and the* GYPSY *tosses* NURSIE *an alarm clock. The* GYPSY *rushes through the beaded string curtains.*) Adios! Ha ha!! (*She is hardly offstage when two shots ring out.* KILROY *starts.*)

10. The conversation between Nursie and the Gypsy as she prepares to go for change is pure vaudeville slapstick. Account for the humor if you are amused. Account for your failure to be amused if you are not.

ESMERALDA (*plaintively*). Mother has such an awful time on the street.

KILROY. You mean that she is insulted on the street?

ESMERALDA. By strangers.

KILROY (*to the audience*). I shouldn't think acquaintances would do it. (*She curls up on the low divan.* KILROY *licks his lips.*)—You seem very different from—this afternoon . . .

11. Kilroy's "I shouldn't think acquaintances would do it" is a conventional aside. Is it effective? Why or why not?

ESMERALDA. This afternoon?

KILROY. Yes, in the plaza when I was being roughed up by them gorillas and you was being dragged in the house by your Mama! (ESMERALDA *stares at him blankly.*) You don't remember?

ESMERALDA. I never remember what happened before the moonrise makes me a virgin.

KILROY. —That—comes as a shock to you, huh?

ESMERALDA. Yes. It comes as a shock.

KILROY (*smiling*). You have a little temporary amnesia they call it!

ESMERALDA. Yankee . . .

KILROY. Huh?

ESMERALDA. I'm glad I chose you. I'm glad that you were chosen. (*Her voice trails off.*) I'm glad, I'm very glad . . .

NURSIE. Doll!

ESMERALDA. —What is it, Nursie?

NURSIE. How are things progressing?

ESMERALDA. Slowly, Nursie—

(NURSIE *comes lumbering in.*)

NURSIE. I want some light reading matter.

ESMERALDA. He's sitting on *Screen Secrets.*

KILROY (*jumping up*). Aw. Here. (*He hands her the fan magazine. She lumbers back out, coyly.*) —I—feel——self-conscious . . . (*He suddenly jerks out a silver-framed photo.*) —D'you—like pictures?

ESMERALDA. Moving pictures?

KILROY. No, a—motionless—snapshot!

ESMERALDA. Of you?

KILROY. Of my—real—true woman . . . She was a platinum blonde the same as Jean Harlow. Do you remember Jean Harlow? No, you wouldn't remember Jean Harlow. It shows you are getting old when you remember Jean Harlow. (*He puts the snapshot away.*) . . . They say that Jean Harlow's ashes are kept in a little private cathedral in Forest Lawn . . . Wouldn't it be wonderful if you could sprinkle them ashes over the ground like seeds, and out of each one would spring another Jean Harlow? And when spring comes you could just walk out and pick them off the bush! . . . You don't talk much.

12. Why does Nursie lumber in for a magazine? Careful, this is subtle.
13. Why does Kilroy show Esmeralda the photograph of his wife?

ESMERALDA. You want me to *talk?*

KILROY. Well, that's the way we do things in the States. A little vino, some records on the victrola, some quiet conversation—and then if both parties are in a mood for romance . . . Romance—

ESMERALDA. Music! (*She rises and pours some wine from a slender crystal decanter as music is heard.*) They say that the monetary system has got to be stabilized all over the world.

KILROY (*taking the glass*). Repeat that, please. My radar was not wide open.

ESMERALDA. I said that *they* said that—uh, skip it! But we couldn't care less as long as we keep on getting the Yankee dollar . . . plus federal tax!

KILROY. That's for surely!

ESMERALDA. How do you feel about the class struggle? Do you take sides in that?

KILROY. Not that I—

ESMERALDA. Neither do we because of the dialectics.

KILROY. Who! Which?

ESMERALDA. Languages with accents, I suppose. But Mama don't care as long as they don't bring the Pope over here and put him in the White House.

KILROY. Who would do that?

ESMERALDA. Oh, the Bolsheviskies, those nasty old things with whiskers! *Whiskers scratch!* But little moustaches tickle . . . (*She giggles.*)

KILROY. I always got a smooth shave . . .

ESMERALDA. And how do you feel about the Mumbo Jumbo? Do you think they've got the Old Man in the bag yet?

KILROY. The Old Man?

ESMERALDA. God. We don't think so. We think there has been so much of the Mumbo Jumbo it's put Him to sleep!

(KILROY *jumps up impatiently.*)

KILROY. This is not what I mean by a quiet conversation. I mean this is no where! *No where!*

14. Why is Kilroy alarmed at Esmeralda's first attempt at "quiet conversation"? Is a dramatic question posed?

ESMERALDA. What sort of talk do you want?

KILROY. Something more—intimate sort of! You know, like—

ESMERALDA. —Where did you get those eyes?

KILROY. *PERSONAL! Yeah* . . .

ESMERALDA. Well,—where did you get those eyes?

KILROY. Out of a dead cod-fish!

NURSIE (*shouting offstage*). DOLL!

(KILROY *springs up, pounding his left palm with his right fist.*)

ESMERALDA. What?

NURSIE. Fifteen minutes!

KILROY. I'm no hot-rod mechanic. (*To the audience.*) I bet she's out there holding a stop watch to see that I don't over-stay my time in this place!

ESMERALDA (*calling through the string curtains*). *Nursie, go to bed, Nursie!*

KILROY (*in a fierce whisper*). That's right, go to bed, Nursie!!

(*There is a loud crash offstage.*)

ESMERALDA. —Nursie has gone to bed . . . (*She drops the string curtains and returns to the alcove.*)

15. Is Kilroy more or less comfortable with Esmeralda's second attempt at "quiet conversation"? Why?

KILROY (*with vast relief*). —Ahhhhhhhhhh . . .

ESMERALDA. What've you got your eyes on?

KILROY. Those green snakes on you— what do you wear them for?

ESMERALDA. Supposedly for protection, but really for fun. (*He crosses to the divan.*) What are you going to do?

KILROY. I'm about to establish a beach-head on that sofa. (*He sits down.*) How about—lifting your veil?

ESMERALDA. I can't lift it.

KILROY. Why not?

ESMERALDA. I promised Mother I wouldn't.

KILROY. I thought your mother was the broadminded type.

ESMERALDA. Oh, she is, but you know how mothers are. You can lift it for me, if you say pretty please.

KILROY. Aww——

ESMERALDA. Go on, say it! Say pretty please!

KILROY. No!!

ESMERALDA. Why not?

KILROY. It's silly.

ESMERALDA. Then you can't lift my veil!

KILROY. Oh, all right, Pretty please.

ESMERALDA. Say it again!

KILROY. Pretty please.

ESMERALDA. Now say it once more like you meant it. (*He jumps up. She grabs his hand.*) Don't go away.

KILROY. You're making a fool out of me.

ESMERALDA. I was just teasing a little. Because you're so cute. Sit down again, please—*pretty* please!

(*He falls on the couch.*)

KILROY. What is that wonderful perfume you've got on?

ESMERALDA. Guess!

KILROY. Chanel Number Five?

ESMERALDA. No.

KILROY. Tabu?

ESMERALDA. No.

KILROY. I give up.

ESMERALDA. It's *Noche en Acapulco!* I'm just dying to go to Acapulco. I wish that you would take me to Acapulco. (*He sits up.*) What's the matter?

KILROY. You gypsies' daughters are invariably reminded of something without which you cannot do—just when it looks like everything has been fixed.

ESMERALDA. That isn't nice at all. I'm not the gold-digger type. Some girls see themselves in silver foxes. I only see myself in Acapulco!

KILROY. At Todd's Place?

ESMERALDA. Oh, no, at the Mirador! Watching those pretty boys dive off the Quebrada!

KILROY. Look again, Baby. Maybe you'll see yourself in Paramount Pictures or having a Singapore Sling at the Statler bar!

ESMERALDA. You're being sarcastic?

KILROY. Nope. Just realistic. All of you gypsies' daughters have hearts of stone, and I'm not whistling "Dixie"! But just the same, the night before a man dies, he says, "Pretty please—will you let me lift your veil?"—while the Streetcleaners wait for him right outside the door!—Because to be warm for a little longer is life. And love?—that's a four-letter word which is sometimes no better than one you see printed on fences by kids playing hooky from school!—Oh, well—what's the use of complaining? You gypsies' daughters have ears that only catch sounds like the snap of a gold cigarette case! Or, pretty please, Baby,—we're going to Acapulco!

ESMERALDA. *Are we?*

KILROY. See what I mean? (*To the audience.*) Didn't I tell you?! (*To* ESMERALDA.) Yes! In the morning!

ESMERALDA. Ohhhh! I'm dizzy with joy! My little heart is going pitty-pat!

KILROY. My big heart is going boom-boom! Can I lift your veil now?

ESMERALDA. If you will be gentle.

KILROY. I would not hurt a fly unless it had on leather mittens. (*He touches a corner of her spangled veil.*)

ESMERALDA. Ohhh . . .

KILROY. What?

ESMERALDA. Ohhhhhh!!

KILROY. Why! What's the matter?

ESMERALDA. You are not being gentle!

KILROY. I *am* being gentle.

ESMERALDA. You are *not* being gentle.

KILROY. What was I being, then?

ESMERALDA. Rough!

KILROY. I am *not* being rough.

ESMERALDA. Yes, you *are* being rough. You have to be gentle with me because you're the first.

KILROY. Are you kidding?

ESMERALDA. No.

KILROY. How about all of those other fiestas you've been to?

ESMERALDA. Each one's the first one. That is the wonderful thing about gypsies' daughters!

KILROY. You can say that again!

ESMERALDA. I don't like you when you're like that.

KILROY. Like what?

ESMERALDA. Cynical and sarcastic.

KILROY. I am sincere.

ESMERALDA. Lots of boys aren't sincere.

KILROY. Maybe they aren't but I am.

ESMERALDA. Everyone says he's sincere, but everyone isn't sincere. If everyone was sincere who says he's sincere there wouldn't be half so many insincere ones in the world and there would be lots, lots, lots more really sincere ones!

KILROY. I think you have got something there. But how about gypsies' daughters?

ESMERALDA. Huh?

KILROY. Are they one hundred percent in the really sincere category?

ESMERALDA. Well, yes, and no, mostly no! But some of them are for a while if their sweethearts are gentle.

KILROY. Would you believe I am sincere and gentle?

ESMERALDA. I would believe that you believe that you are . . . For a while . . .

KILROY. Everything's for a while. For a while is the stuff that dreams are made of, Baby! Now?—Now?

ESMERALDA. Yes, now, but be gentle!—*gentle* . . .

(*He delicately lifts a corner of her veil. She utters a soft cry. He lifts it further. She cries out again. A bit further . . . He turns the spangled veil all the way up from her face.*)

KILROY. I am sincere.

ESMERALDA. I am sincere.

KILROY. I am sincere.

ESMERALDA. I am sincere.

KILROY. I am sincere.

ESMERALDA. I am sincere.

KILROY. I am sincere.

ESMERALDA. I am sincere. (KILROY *leans back, removing his hand from her veil. She opens her eyes.*) Is that all?

KILROY. I am tired.

ESMERALDA. —Already?

(*He rises and goes down the steps from the alcove.*)

KILROY. I am tired, and full of regret . . .

ESMERALDA. Oh!

KILROY. It wasn't much to give my golden gloves for.

ESMERALDA. You pity yourself?

KILROY. That's right, I pity myself and everybody that goes to the Gypsy's daughter. I pity the world and I pity the God who made it. (*He sits down.*)

ESMERALDA. It's always like that as soon as the veil is lifted. They're all so ashamed of having degraded themselves, and their hearts have more regret than a heart can hold!

KILROY. Even a heart that's as big as the head of a baby!

ESMERALDA. You don't even notice how pretty my face is, do you?

KILROY. You look like all gypsies' daughters, no better, no worse. But as long as you get to go to Acapulco, your cup runneth over with ordinary contentment.

ESMERALDA. —I've never been so insulted in all my life!

KILROY. Oh, yes, you have, Baby. And you'll be insulted worse if you stay in this racket. You'll be insulted so much that it will get to be like water off a duck's back! (*The door slams. Curtains are drawn apart on the* GYPSY. ESMERALDA *lowers her veil hastily.* KILROY *pretends not to notice the* GYPSY'S *entrance. She picks up a little bell and rings it over his head.*) Okay, Mamacita! I am aware of your presence!

16. Is the act of lifting Esmeralda's veil humor, symbolism, or what? Explain the implied criticism (Kilroy is archetypal—Esmeralda is archetypal) and state reasons for agreeing or disagreeing with it. You will need to rely on your vicarious and actual experience.

17. Restate in less symbolic terms Kilroy's statement that "It wasn't much to give my golden gloves for." (This can be done without crudity!)

GYPSY. Ha-ha! I was followed three blocks by some awful man!

KILROY. Then you caught him.

GYPSY. Naw, he ducked into a subway! I waited fifteen minutes outside the men's room and he never came out!

KILROY. Then you went in?

GYPSY. No! I got myself a sailor!—The streets are brilliant! . . . Have you all been good children? (ESMERALDA *makes a whimpering sound.*) The pussy will play while the old mother cat is away?

18. Why does Williams bring the Gypsy back onstage with a washroom joke? There is a structural reason.

KILROY. Your sense of humor is wonderful, but how about my change, Mamacita?

GYPSY. What change are you talking about?

KILROY. Are you boxed out of your mind? The change from the ten-spot you trotted over to Walgreen's?

GYPSY. Ohhhhh—

KILROY. *Oh, what?*

GYPSY (*counting on her fingers*). Five for the works, one dollar luxury tax, two for the house percentage and two more pour la service!—makes ten! Didn't I tell you?

KILROY. —What kind of a deal is this?

GYPSY (*whipping out a revolver*). A rugged one, Baby!

ESMERALDA. Mama, don't be unkind!

GYPSY. Honey, the gentleman's friends are waiting outside the door and it wouldn't be nice to detain him! Come on—Get going—Vamoose!

KILROY. Okay, Mamacita! Me voy! (*He crosses to the beaded string curtains: turns to look back at the* GYPSY *and her daughter. The piping of the* STREETCLEANERS *is heard outside.*) Sincere?—Sure! That's the wonderful thing about gypsies' daughters! (*He goes out.*)

(ESMERALDA *raises a wondering fingertip to one eye. Then she cries out.*)

ESMERALDA. Look, Mama! Look, Mama! A tear!

GYPSY. You have been watching television too much . . . (*She gathers the cards and turns off the crystal ball as—Light fades out on the phony paradise of the* GYPSY'S.)

GUTMAN. Block Thirteen on the Camino Real. (*He exits.*)

19. What is the significance of Esmeralda's one tear? Remember the fairy tales you have read about females who cannot cry and what happens when they learn to. Is a dramatic question posed here?

20. John van Druten's *Bell, Book and Candle* is resolved with the witch's tears which indicate her human ability to love. An interesting comparative paper could result from a study of the device in the two plays.

21. The Prologue, Block Six, and Block Twelve are the lengthiest portions of the play. State structural and dramatic reasons for this proportion.

22. The humor of Block Twelve works rhythmically against the pathos (or is it tragedy?) of Block Ten. Why should the first love affair be so tender, the second so brutal? Which is more realistic? Which more romantic? Why do you think so?

BLOCK THIRTEEN

In the blackout the STREETCLEANERS *place a barrel in the center and then hide in the Pit.*

KILROY, *who enters from the right, is followed by a spot light. He sees the barrel and the menacing* STREETCLEANERS *and then runs to the closed door of the Siete Mares and rings the bell. No one answers. He backs up so he can see the balcony and calls.*

KILROY. Mr. Gutman! Just gimme a cot in the lobby. I'll do odd jobs in the morning. I'll be the Patsy again. I'll light my nose sixty times a minute. I'll take prat-falls and assume the position for anybody that drops a dime on the street . . . Have a heart! Have just a LITTLE heart. Please!

1. Is Kilroy archetypal in his opening speech?

(There is no response from GUTMAN'S *balcony.* JACQUES *enters. He pounds his cane once on the pavement.)*

JACQUES. Gutman! Open the door!—*GUTMAN! GUTMAN!*

*(*EVA, *a beautiful woman, apparently nude, appears on the balcony.)*

GUTMAN *(from inside).* Eva darling, you're exposing yourself! *(He appears on the balcony with a portmanteau.)*

JACQUES. What are you doing with my portmanteau?

GUTMAN. Haven't you come for your luggage?

JACQUES. Certainly not! I haven't checked out of here!

GUTMAN. Very few do . . . but residences are frequently terminated.

JACQUES. Open the door!

GUTMAN. Open the letter with the remittance check in it!

JACQUES. In the morning!

GUTMAN. Tonight!

JACQUES. Upstairs in my room!

GUTMAN. Downstairs at the entrance!

JACQUES. I won't be intimidated!

GUTMAN (*raising the portmanteau over his head*). What?!

JACQUES. Wait!— (*He takes the letter out of his pocket.*) Give me some light. (KILROY *strikes a match and holds it over* JACQUES' *shoulder.*) Thank you. What does it say?

GUTMAN. —Remittances?

KILROY (*reading the letter over* JACQUES' *shoulder*). —discontinued . . .

(GUTMAN *raises the portmanteau again.*)

JACQUES. Careful, I have— (*The portmanteau lands with a crash. The* BUM *comes to the window at the crash.* A. RATT *comes out to his doorway at the same time.*) —fragile—mementoes . . . (*He crosses slowly down to the portmanteau and kneels as . . .* GUTMAN *laughs and slams the balcony door.* JACQUES *turns to* KILROY. *He smiles at the young adventurer.*) —"And so at last it has come, the distinguished thing!"

2. Explain your reaction to the crashing portmanteau. Does the scene do what Williams hoped it would in his discussion in the Foreword?

3. Explain the irony of the words "the distinguished thing!"

(A. RATT *speaks as* JACQUES *touches the portmanteau.*)

A. RATT. Hey, Dad—Vacancy here! A bed at the "Ritz Men Only." A little white ship to sail the dangerous night in.

JACQUES. Single or double?

A. RATT. There's only singles in this pad.

JACQUES (*to* KILROY). Match you for it.

KILROY. What the hell, we're buddies, we can sleep spoons! If we can't sleep, we'll push the wash stand against the door and sing old popular songs till the crack of dawn! . . . "Heart of my heart, I love that melody!" . . . You bet your life I do. (JACQUES *takes out a pocket handkerchief and starts to grasp the portmanteau handle.*) —It looks to me like you could use a Redcap and my rates are non-union! (*He picks up the portmanteau and starts to cross towards the "Ritz Men Only." He stops at right center.*) Sorry, buddy. Can't make it! The altitude on this block has affected my ticker! And in the distance which is nearer than further, I hear—the Streetcleaners'—piping!

(*Piping· is heard.*)

JACQUES. COME ALONG! (*He lifts the portmanteau and starts on.*)

KILROY. NO. Tonight! I prefer! To sleep! Out! Under! The stars!

JACQUES (*gently*). I understand, Brother!

KILROY (*to* JACQUES *as he continues toward the "Ritz Men Only"*). Bon Voyage! I hope that you sail the dangerous night to the sweet golden port of morning!

JACQUES (*exiting*). Thanks, Brother!

KILROY. Excuse the *corn!* I'm sincere!

BUM. Show me the way to go home! . . .

GUTMAN (*appearing on the balcony with white parakeet*). Block Fourteen on the Camino Real.

4. Have Kilroy and Jacques become "brothers"? "Buddies under the skin"? Prove your contention using their stated and unstated communication.

5. Why does Kilroy prefer to sleep out under the stars?

BLOCK FOURTEEN

At opening, the BUM *is still at the window.*

The STREETCLEANERS' *piping continues a little louder.* KILROY *climbs, breathing heavily, to the top of the stairs and stands looking out at Terra Incognita as . . .*

MARGUERITE *enters the plaza through alleyway at right. She is accompanied by a silent* YOUNG MAN *who wears a domino.*

MARGUERITE. Don't come any further with me. I'll have to wake the night porter. Thank you for giving me safe conduct through the Medina. (*She has offered her hand. He grips it with a tightness that makes her wince.*) Ohhhh . . . I'm not sure which is more provocative in you, your ominous silence or your glittering smile or— (*He's looking at her purse.*) What do you want? . . . Oh! (*She starts to open the purse. He snatches it. She gasps as he suddenly strips her cloak off her. Then he snatches off her pearl necklace. With each successive despoilment, she gasps and retreats but makes no resistance. Her eyes are closed. He continues to smile. Finally, he rips her dress and runs his hands over her body as if to see if she had anything else of value concealed on her.*) —What else do I have that you want?

THE YOUNG MAN (*contemptuously*). Nothing. (*The* YOUNG MAN *exits through the cantina, examining his loot.*)

(*The* BUM *leans out his window, draws a deep breath and says*)

BUM. Lonely.

MARGUERITE (*to herself*). Lonely . . .

KILROY (*on the steps*). Lonely . . .

(*The* STREETCLEANERS' *piping is heard.*)

1. Does Marguerite "get what she deserves" here? Are you sorry for her? Why or why not?

(MARGUERITE *runs to the Siete Mares and rings the bell. Nobody answers. She crosses to the terrace.* KILROY, *meanwhile, has descended the stairs.*)

MARGUERITE. Jacques!

(*Piping is heard.*)

KILROY. Lady?

MARGUERITE. What?

KILROY. —*I'm—safe* . . .

MARGUERITE. I wasn't expecting that music tonight, were you?

(*Piping.*)

KILROY. It's them Streetcleaners.

MARGUERITE. I know.

(*Piping.*)

KILROY. You better go on in, lady.

MARGUERITE. No.

KILROY. GO ON IN!

MARGUERITE. NO! I want to stay out here and I do what I want to do! (KILROY *looks at her for the first time.*) Sit down with me please.

2. Kilroy, the archetype, looks at Marguerite "for the first time" only after she has said "I do what I want to do!" Explain his reaction.

KILROY. They're coming for me. The Gypsy told me I'm on top of their list. Thanks for. Taking my. Hand.

(*Piping is heard.*)

MARGUERITE. Thanks for taking mine.

(*Piping.*)

KILROY. Do me one more favor. Take out of my pocket a picture. My fingers are. Stiff.

MARGUERITE. This one?

KILROY. My one. True. Woman.

MARGUERITE. A silver-framed photo! Was she really so fair?

KILROY. She was so fair and much fairer than they could tint that picture!

MARGUERITE. Then you have been on the street when the street was royal.

KILROY. Yeah . . . when the street was royal!

3. Explain Marguerite's statement: "Then you have been on the street when the street was royal." Has she learned anything from her recent experience?

(*Piping is heard.* KILROY *rises.*)

MARGUERITE. Don't get up, don't leave me!

KILROY. I want to be on my feet when the Streetcleaners come for me!

MARGUERITE. Sit back down again and tell me about your girl.

(*He sits.*)

KILROY. Y'know what it is you miss most? When you're separated. From someone. You lived. With. And loved? It's waking up in the night! With that—warmness beside you!

MARGUERITE. Yes, that *warmness* beside you!

KILROY. Once you get used to that. *Warmness!* It's a hell of a lonely feeling to wake up without it! Specially in some dollar-a-night hotel room on Skid! A hot-water bottle won't do. And a stranger. Won't do. It has to be some one you're used to. And that you. *KNOW LOVES* you! (*Piping is heard.*) Can you see them?

MARGUERITE. I see no one but you.

KILROY. I looked at my wife one night when she was sleeping and that was the night that the medics wouldn't okay me for no more fights . . . Well . . . My wife was sleeping with a smile like a child's. I kissed her. She didn't wake up. I took a pencil and paper. I wrote her. Good-bye!

MARGUERITE. That was the night she would have loved you the most!

KILROY. Yeah, *that* night, but what about *after* that night? Oh, Lady . . . Why should a beautiful girl tie up with a broken-down champ?—The earth still turning and her obliged to turn with it, not out—of dark into light but out of light into dark? Naw, naw, naw, naw!—Washed up!—Finished! (*Piping.*) . . . that ain't a word that a man can't look at . . . There ain't no words in the language a man can't look at . . . and know just what they mean. And be. And act. And go! (*He turns to the waiting* STREETCLEANERS.) Come on! . . . Come on! . . . COME ON, YOU SONS OF BITCHES! KILROY IS HERE! HE'S READY!

(*A gong sounds.* KILROY *swings at the* STREETCLEANERS. *They circle about him out of reach, turning him by each of their movements. The swings grow wilder like a boxer. He falls to his knees still swinging and finally collapses flat on his face. The* STREETCLEANERS *pounce but* LA MADRECITA *throws herself protectingly over the body and covers it with her shawl. Blackout.*)

MARGUERITE. Jacques!

GUTMAN (*on balcony*). Block Fifteen on the Camino Real.

4. How does Kilroy's conversation with Marguerite give him the strength to resist the Streetcleaners?

5. Is the major dramatic question advanced in this Block?

BLOCK FIFTEEN

LA MADRECITA *is seated: across her knees is the body of* KILROY. *Up center, a low table on wheels bears a sheeted figure. Beside the table stands a* MEDICAL INSTRUCTOR *addressing* STUDENTS *and* NURSES, *all in white surgical outfits.*

INSTRUCTOR. This is the body of an unidentified vagrant.

LA MADRECITA. This was thy son, America—and now mine.

INSTRUCTOR. He was found in an alley along the Camino Real.

LA MADRECITA. Think of him, now, as he was before his luck failed him. Remember his time of greatness, when he was not faded, not frightened.

INSTRUCTOR. More light, please!

LA MADRECITA. More light!

INSTRUCTOR. Can everyone see clearly?

LA MADRECITA. Everyone must see clearly!

INSTRUCTOR. There is no external evidence of disease.

LA MADRECITA. He had clear eyes and the body of a champion boxer.

INSTRUCTOR. There are no marks of violence on the body.

LA MADRECITA. He had the soft voice of the South and a pair of golden gloves.

INSTRUCTOR. His death was apparently due to natural causes.

(*The* STUDENTS *make notes. There are keening voices.*)

LA MADRECITA. Yes, blow wind where night thins! He had many admirers!

INSTRUCTOR. There are no legal claimants.

LA MADRECITA. He stood as a planet among the moons of their longing, haughty with youth, a champion of the prize-ring!

INSTRUCTOR. No friends or relatives having identified him—

LA MADRECITA. You should have seen the lovely monogrammed robe in which he strode the aisles of the Colosseums!

INSTRUCTOR. After the elapse of a certain number of days, his body becomes the property of the State—

LA MADRECITA. Yes, blow wind where the night thins—for laurel is not everlasting . . .

INSTRUCTOR. And now is transferred to our hands for the nominal sum of five dollars.

LA MADRECITA. This was thy son,—and now mine . . .

INSTRUCTOR. We will now proceed with the dissection. Knife, please!

LA MADRECITA. Blow wind! (*Keening is heard offstage.*) Yes, blow wind where night thins! You are his passing bell and his lamentation. (*More keening is heard.*) Keen for him, all maimed creatures, deformed and mutilated—his homeless ghost is your own!

INSTRUCTOR. First we will open up the chest cavity and examine the heart for evidence of coronary occlusion.

LA MADRECITA. His heart was pure gold and as big as the head of a baby.

INSTRUCTOR. We will make an incision along the vertical line.

LA MADRECITA. Rise, ghost! Go! Go bird! "Humankind cannot bear very much reality."

(*At the touch of her flowers,* KILROY *stirs and pushes himself up slowly from her lap. On his feet again, he rubs his eyes and looks around him.*)

VOICES (*crying offstage*). Olé! Olé! Olé!

KILROY. Hey! Hey, somebody! Where am I? (*He notices the dissection room and approaches.*)

INSTRUCTOR (*removing a glittering sphere from a dummy corpse*). Look at this heart. It's as big as the head of a baby.

KILROY. My heart!

INSTRUCTOR. Wash it off so we can look for the pathological lesions.

KILROY. Yes, siree, that's my heart!

GUTMAN. Block Sixteen!

(KILROY *pauses just outside the dissection area as a* STUDENT *takes the heart and dips it into a basin on the stand beside the table. The* STUDENT *suddenly cries out and holds aloft a glittering gold sphere.*)

INSTRUCTOR. Look! This heart's solid gold!

1. Who is La Madrecita?
2. Why does she say the archetypal Kilroy was America's son, now hers?
3. La Madrecita's lines are pure poetry and, freed of the inserted dialog of the Instructor, can be read as a poem. What does the poem state? How is its statement made more effective by the interpolated lines of the Instructor?
4. Explain La Madrecita's references to "the wind." What does the wind symbolize?
5. Remember Hans Christian Anderson's "Little Tin Soldier" and speculate on reasons for Kilroy's heart being "solid gold." How does such symbolism advance the major dramatic question? Is this the climax of the play?

BLOCK SIXTEEN

KILROY (*rushing forward*). That's mine, you bastards!

(*He snatches the golden sphere from the* MEDICAL INSTRUCTOR. *The autopsy proceeds as if nothing had happened as the spot of light on the table fades out, but for* KILROY *a ghostly chase commences, a dreamlike re-enactment of the chase that occurred at the end of Block Six.* GUTMAN *shouts from his balcony.*)

GUTMAN. Stop, thief, stop, corpse! That gold heart is the property of the State! Catch him, catch the golden-heart robber!

(KILROY *dashes offstage into an aisle of the theatre. There is the wail of a siren: the air is filled with calls and whistles, roar of motors, screeching brakes, pistol-shots, thundering footsteps. The dimness of the auditorium is transected by searching rays of light—but there are no visible pursuers.*)

KILROY (*as he runs panting up the aisle*). This is my heart! I don't belong to no State, not even the U.S.A. Which way is out? Where's the Greyhound depot? Nobody's going to put my heart in a bottle in a museum and charge admission to support the rotten police! Where are they? Which way are they going? Or coming? Hey, somebody, help me get out of here! Which way do I—which way—which way do I—go! go! go! go! go! (*He has now arrived in the balcony.*) Gee, I'm lost! I don't know where I am! I'm all turned around, I'm *confused,* I don't understand—what's—happened, it's like a—*dream,* it's—just like a—dream . . . Mary! Oh, Mary! Mary! (*He has entered the box from which he leapt in Act One. A clear shaft of light falls on him. He looks up into it, crying*) Mary, help a Christian!! Help a Christian, Mary!—It's like a dream . . .

1. Are you more or less surprised than you were in Block Six by Kilroy's dash past your chair? Why?

(ESMERALDA *appears in a childish nightgown beside her gauze-tented bed on the* GYPSY'S *roof. Her Mother appears with a cup of some sedative drink, cooing . . .*)

GYPSY. Beddy-bye, beddy-bye, darling. It's sleepy-time down South and up North, too, and also East and West!

KILROY (*softly*). Yes, it's—like a—dream . . .(*He leans panting over the ledge of the box, holding his heart like a football, watching* ESMERALDA.)

GYPSY. Drink your Ovaltine, Ducks, and the sandman will come on tip-toe with a bag full of dreams . . .

ESMERALDA. I want to dream of the Chosen Hero, Mummy.

GYPSY. Which one, the one that's coming or the one that is gone?

ESMERALDA. The *only* one, *Kilroy! He* was *sincere!*

KILROY. That's *right! I was*, for a while!

GYPSY. How do you know that Kilroy was sincere?

ESMERALDA. He said so.

KILROY. That's the truth, I *was!*

GYPSY. When did he say that?

ESMERALDA. When he lifted my veil.

GYPSY. Baby, they're always sincere when they lift your veil; it's one of those natural reflexes that don't mean a thing.

KILROY (*aside*). What a cynical old bitch that Gypsy mama is!

GYPSY. And there's going to be lots of other fiestas for you, baby doll, and lots of other chosen heroes to lift your little veil when Mamacita and Nursie are out of the room.

ESMERALDA. No, Mummy, never, I mean it!

KILROY. I *believe* she means it!

GYPSY. Finish your Ovaltine and say your Now-I-Lay-Me.

(ESMERALDA *sips the drink and hands her the cup.*)

2. Has Esmeralda learned more or less than Marguerite? Have they learned equally little? Is the tone of her dialog ironic or pathetic here? Neither?

3. Is the Gypsy "a cynical old bitch" or is Kilroy naive, defensive, or sincere in assessing her so? Why is the line delivered as an aside?

KILROY (*with a catch in his voice*). I had one true woman, which I can't go back to, but now I've found another. (*He leaps onto the stage from the box.*)

ESMERALDA (*dropping to her knees*). Now I lay me down to sleep, I pray the Lord my soul to keep. If I should die before I wake, I pray the Lord my soul to take.

GYPSY. God bless Mummy!

ESMERALDA. And the crystal ball and the tea-leaves.

KILROY. Pssst!

ESMERALDA. What's that?

GYPSY. A tom-cat in the plaza.

ESMERALDA. God bless all cats without pads in the plaza tonight.

KILROY. Amen! (*He falls to his knees in the empty plaza.*)

ESMERALDA. God bless all con men and hustlers and pitch-men who hawk their hearts on the street, all two-time losers who're likely to lose once more, the courtesan who made the mistake of love, the greatest of lovers crowned with the longest horns, the poet who wandered far from his heart's green country and possibly will and possibly won't be able to find his way back, look down with a smile tonight on the last cavaliers, the ones with the rusty armor and soiled white plumes, and visit with understanding and something that's almost tender those fading legends that come and go in this plaza like songs not clearly remembered, oh, sometime and somewhere, let there be something to mean the word *honor* again!

QUIXOTE (*hoarsely and loudly, stirring slightly among his verminous rags*). Amen!

KILROY. Amen . . .

GYPSY (*disturbed*). —That will do, now.

ESMERALDA. And, oh, God, let me dream tonight of the Chosen Hero!

GYPSY. Now, sleep. Fly away on the magic carpet of dreams!

(ESMERALDA *crawls into the gauze-tented cot. The* GYPSY *descends from the roof.*)

4. Explain your reaction to Esmeralda's prayer. Would you be too embarrassed to explain your reaction fully to a class? Why or why not?

KILROY. *Esmeralda! My little Gypsy sweetheart!*

ESMERALDA (*sleepily*). Go away, cat.

(*The light behind the gauze is gradually dimming.*)

KILROY. This is no cat. This is the chosen hero of the big fiesta, Kilroy, the champion of the golden gloves with his gold heart cut from his chest and in his hands to give you!

ESMERALDA. Go away. Let me dream of the Chosen Hero.

KILROY. What a hassle! Mistook for a cat! What can I do to convince this doll I'm real? (*Three brass balls wink brilliantly.*) —Another transaction seems to be indicated! (*He rushes to the* LOAN SHARK'S. *The entrance immediately lights up.*) My heart is gold! What will you give me for it? (*Jewels, furs, sequined gowns, etc., are tossed to his feet. He throws his heart like a basketball to the* LOAN SHARK, *snatches up the loot and rushes back to the* GYPSY'S.) Doll! Behold this loot! I gave my golden heart for it!

ESMERALDA. Go away, cat . . .

(*She falls asleep.* KILROY *bangs his forehead with his fist, then rushes to the* GYPSY'S *door, pounds it with both fists. The door is thrown open and the sordid contents of a large jar are thrown at him. He falls back gasping, spluttering, retching. He retreats and finally assumes an exaggerated attitude of despair.*)

KILROY. Had for a button! Stewed, screwed and tattooed on the Camino Real!

Baptized, finally, with the contents of a slop-jar!—Did anybody say the deal was rugged?!

5. Why does Kilroy not give Esmeralda his heart? Why does he trade it for the worthless merchandise of the Loan Shark?
6. In Voltaire's *Candide,* the young hero says that love is "a kiss in the bushes and twenty kicks in the ass." Compare Kilroy's "Had for a button!" speech with Candide's assessment. What are the similarities? Do you agree or disagree?

(QUIXOTE *stirs against the wall of Skid Row. He hawks and spits and staggers to his feet.*)

GUTMAN. Why, the old knight's awake, his dream is over!

QUIXOTE (*to* KILROY). Hello! Is that a fountain?

KILROY. —Yeah, but—

QUIXOTE. I've got a mouthful of old chicken feathers . . .

(*He approaches the fountain. It begins to flow.* KILROY *falls back in amazement as the Old Knight rinses his mouth and drinks and removes his jacket to bathe, handing the tattered garment to* KILROY.)

7. Why does the fountain begin to flow?

QUIXOTE (*as he bathes*). Qué pasa, mi amigo?

KILROY. The deal is rugged. D'you know what I mean?

QUIXOTE. Who knows better than I what a rugged deal is! (*He produces a tooth brush and brushes his teeth.*) —Will you take some advice?

KILROY. Brother, at this point on the Camino I will take anything which is offered!

QUIXOTE. Don't! Pity! Your! Self! (*He takes out a pocket mirror and grooms his beard and moustache.*) The wounds of the vanity, the many offenses our egos have to endure, being housed in bodies that age and hearts that grow tired, are better accepted with a tolerant smile—like *this!*—You see? (*He cracks his face in two with an enormous grin.*)

GUTMAN. Follow-spot on the face of the ancient knight!

QUIXOTE. Otherwise what you become is a bag full of curdled cream—*leche mala,* we call it!—attractive to nobody, least of all to yourself! (*He passes the comb and pocket mirror to* KILROY.) Have you got any plans?

KILROY (*a bit uncertainly, wistfully*). Well, I was thinking of—going on from—here!

QUIXOTE. Good! Come with me.

KILROY (*to the audience*). Crazy old bastard. (*Then to the Knight.*) Donde?

QUIXOTE (*starting for the stairs*). Quien sabe!

8. Is Kilroy a good or bad replacement for Sancho Panza? Remember, Quixote will continue to tilt with windmills; however, he constantly moves toward sanity.

(The fountain is now flowing loudly and sweetly. The STREET PEOPLE *are moving toward it with murmurs of wonder.* MARGUERITE *comes out upon the terrace.)*

KILROY. Hey, there's—!

QUIXOTE. Shhh! Listen!

(They pause on the stairs.)

MARGUERITE. Abdullah!

*(*GUTMAN *has descended to the terrace.)*

GUTMAN. Mademoiselle, allow me to deliver the message for you. It would be in bad form if I didn't take some final part in the pageant. *(He crosses the plaza to the opposite façade and shouts "Casanova!" under the window of the "Ritz Men Only." Meanwhile* KILROY *scratches out the verb "is" and prints the correction "was" in the inscription on the ancient wall.)* Casanova! Great lover and King of Cuckolds on the Camino Real! The last of your ladies has guaranteed your tabs and is expecting you for breakfast on the terrace!

*(*CASANOVA *looks first out of the practical window of the flophouse, then emerges from its scabrous doorway, haggard, unshaven, crumpled in dress but bearing himself as erectly as ever. He blinks and glares fiercely into the brilliant morning light.* MARGUERITE *cannot return his look, she averts her face with a look for which anguish would not be too strong a term, but at the same time she extends a pleading hand toward him. After some hesitation, he begins to move toward her, striking the pavement in measured cadence with his cane, glancing once, as he crosses, out at the audience with a wry smile that makes admissions that would be embarrassing to a vainer man than* CASANOVA *now is. When he reaches* MARGUERITE *she gropes for his hand, seizes it with a low cry and presses it spasmodically to her lips while he draws her into his arms and looks above her sobbing, dyed-golden head with the serene, clouded gaze of someone mortally ill as the mercy of a narcotic laps over his pain.)*

*(*QUIXOTE *raises his lance in a formal gesture and cries out hoarsely, powerfully from the stairs.)*

QUIXOTE. The violets in the mountains have broken the rocks!

*(*QUIXOTE *goes through the arch with* KILROY.*)*

GUTMAN *(to the audience).* The Curtain Line has been spoken! *(To the wings.)* Bring it down! *(He bows with a fat man's grace as—The curtain falls.)* □

9. Does Marguerite send for Jacques because she has no bird to share her cage or for some other reason?

10. Why was it necessary for the public fountain to flow before the violets could break the rocks?

11. If Gutman's final two speeches seem anticlimactic to you, cover them and reread Block Sixteen with Quixote's line as the last words before the curtain. Now explain the structural necessity of Gutman's lines.

12. Is Block Sixteen the climax or the denouement of the play? Defend your answer.

13. Attempt a statement of the major dramatic question now.

14. Does Williams seem to attempt an answer to the major dramatic question? If so, what do you understand his answer to be? Do you agree or disagree with Williams?

15. Do you feel that "the theater of the absurd" is an adequate or inadequate name for plays such as *Camino Real?* Defend your answer.

Tragedy effects a catharsis, the catharsis being, according to Aristotle, a purgation through pity and fear. Beyond purgation lies purification, and some few dramas achieve a kind of purification that allows the reader to close the book, pleased that life is desirable, that it is not hopeless and utterly defeating. In such dramas, man is not noble, he is not great, but he does approach nobility, he does brush greatness without knowing it is at his elbow. Because man is unsure of the question, he misses the answer.

Man's failure to understand the question may be absurd, even as he may be. "God is dead," however, as one example, becomes a doubt rather than an unprovable, arbitrary statement when a man raises his voice rather than lowers it on the word *dead*. The "answer" becomes a "question." That language should be so whimsical is, on the one hand, an absurdity; on the other hand, it is the richest element of our remarkable instrument.

When a man questions blindly, he progresses toward his blue distances; if he finds answers, he has reached the distance. But journey's ends are often terribly disappointing, and perhaps we should be grateful we are merely on the road. Sophocles, Shakespeare, O'Neill, Williams—they and their fellow playwrights are well-trained guides for our journey. And if they do not know all the answers to our questions, the Travel Agency has probably failed to provide them with adequate training. Of course, you could always write a letter to the President of the Organization— unfortunately, the address seems to have been mislaid. . . .

Suggested Assignments. 1. Voltaire's novel *Candide* would be labeled as theater of the absurd if it were a drama. Read it and compare Candide and Kilroy as they are developed by the two authors.

2. Compare the structure of *Candide* and *Camino Real*. What have they in common?

3. In a brief paper, analyze *Camino Real* as a poetic drama. The poetry of the play is, in many ways, comparable to the poetry of T. S. Eliot's *The Waste Land* and Hart Crane's *Voyages I–VI*. You might wish to make comparisons.

4. In a three-paragraph paper, explain the geography of *Camino Real* in terms comparable to the geography of *Everyman*.

CHAPTER X

You and Your Muse— Writing a One-Act Play

Dramatic writing is a learned craft, based (hopefully) on genuine talent. Genuine talent, however, seems to result when a craft is learned unconsciously from infancy. Therefore, if you have already developed an ear that distinguishes basic speech patterns in people, an eye that observes unique mannerisms, and an awareness of people that allows you to understand their motives, you have cleared the most difficult hurdles in writing plays. If you have, further, learned to reproduce speech in a way that sounds realistic or have learned to write poetry that is well-structured and richly evocative, you may well write a readable play. In other words, the craft of dramatic writing covers so broad a field that, for the moment, we must assume certain accomplishments on your part and proceed from there. Narrative skills are also of vital importance because a plot, theme, and descriptive elements are all a part of the structure of a play. However, a basic mastery of those ingredients must also be assumed. Should you need help in such areas, see *The Discovery of Poetry* and *The Discovery of Fiction,* two earlier volumes in this series.

Beginning Your Play

Because the one-act play is shorter, it is well to start learning dramaturgy by working with it rather than with the three-act form. Compressed, structured very much like a three-act play, the one-act play forces you to learn to establish character rapidly, work with a tightly-knit and cohesive plot, and reveal the basic theme with some clarity. For these reasons, however, it demands more of the playwright than does the three-act play. You are denied the possibility of a dull first act—one act is all you have. Everything must work together well from the title to the final line.

Every dramatic work (poem, story, novel, or play)

must have some sort of theme. Oversimplified, the *theme* is the "meaning" of the work. Usually a cliché, it can be stated as something like "Love always finds a way" or "Man's strongest opponent is himself." Reducing a successful play to a theme becomes a suspect occupation, however, for the complexities of a literary work resist oversimplification. *Riders to the Sea,* for instance, could be said to embody the theme "Defeat must precede acceptance which is man's greatest victory." That statement is an oversimplification, and it does an obvious disservice to a great play. Reducing the final work to a theme is merely one of the methods we employ in attempting to understand a play completely.

Playwrights do, on the other hand, work from a general theme as they set about the job of structuring a play. They are not attempting the presentation of great new truths—there probably are none undiscovered. Working from an accepted truth or from a personally conceived poetic truth, they decide what general message they wish to convey to the audience, then seek a plot and characters that will project that truth. Sometimes, the playwright finds an interesting plot and sets about working it toward an understandable theme. Or he might become interested in certain characters and cast about for a theme which they illustrate and a plot that will support the ideas. In short, a play may start from any idea or chance remark, but, once the initial step (possibly the only "inspiration" of the play) is taken, conscious, deliberate craft must be called to work.

Because plot, characters, and theme are the basic necessities of a play, let's look at them one at a time. Whether you attempt a tragedy, a comedy, or a tragicomedy, the basic considerations will be the same. At the heart of the play, humans must be motivated to behave in certain ways because they are in *conflict* with something or someone. Their major conflict may be intensified by any number of *complications,* each producing a *minor conflict* which must have a direct or indirect bearing on the *major conflict,* thereby moving it toward a final or suggested *resolution.* That total movement *from motive to conflict to complication to resolution* creates a series of *scenes* wherein people enter and leave the depicted action until it reaches a point of intense emotion called the *climax.* And that total movement is the *plot.*

The plot will revolve around a *hero* or *protagonist* (the emulable or likable character with whom the reader identifies). The protagonist will be motivated to some action (to save the farm or to get the girl) by his own desires. Opposing him, creating problems he must surmount, is an *antagonist* (a villain or unlikable person or force with whom we least identify) who attempts to thwart the protagonist. As they do battle (physical, mental, spiritual, social) the resulting *suspense* (who will win?)

must be maintained until a satisfactory outcome can be achieved logically and naturally without obvious contrivance or dubiously employed coincidence. At that point, some conception of the theme should manifest itself to your reader.

Such structure is more readily apparent in *Desire Under the Elms* and *Riders to the Sea* than in the other plays you have studied. O'Neill's play contains a series of *subplots* in addition to the main one. The *primary plot* is, of course, the account of Ephraim's bitter conflict with everyone as he achieves submission to his God. Subplots exist in the love affair of Abbie and Eben as well as in the contest of wills between the brothers. Those two subplots are thoroughly interesting in themselves, but they are interwoven into the fabric of the major plot to give it a depth and substance it would not otherwise have. Subplots are much like the flesh of the human body: they make the skeleton (the primary plot) more interesting, less shocking to behold in its bare form.

Riders to the Sea is a primary plot without subplots of any kind. Its tense, lean frame is adorned only by the poetic language and the intensity of characterization. A subplot would have made the gaunt skeleton voluptuous, exotic, and disagreeable, for the beauty of the spare structure is like a sea-washed skeleton, whitened to luster and sanded to perfection by the abrasive action of the playwright's revisionary process. Until you have learned to handle a primary plot adequately, it would be advisable for you to avoid the complexities of subplotting.

An over-ambitious project often creates stormy seas for a beginning writer. You should learn to construct an accomplished couplet before aspiring to the epic. Once you have learned the craft of the one-act play, you may find, as Eugene O'Neill and Tennessee Williams did, material in your early efforts that can be expanded into three-act plays. Until that time, however, content yourself with perfecting your miniature; at least you can see the total picture and work out the necessary fine details.

Those fine details become most challenging in *characterization*. Your first attempts will probably founder on the rocks of excess. Identifying yourself with a character, allowing him to be your voice, you will make him unbelievably sympathetic. He will be too handsome, too good, too misunderstood, too victimized. The antagonist, on the other hand (whether it be a person, God, or society), may be equally excessive in depicted bad qualities. He may be utterly evil, horribly ugly, or outrageously devoted to defeating the protagonist. Remember this, however: the person you see as your antagonist in the drama of your personal life is the protagonist of the drama that is his life. In *his* script, *you* are the antagonist! Look at your antagonist objectively, and you may find that he is about to get the girl because he is more handsome than you, more sensitive to her needs, more capable of love. He may merely have a newer car, however, but that will probably not influence her to the exclusion of other traits. The playwright doesn't take sides; he creates them.

Credibility in life results not from combinations of good plus good or bad plus bad. It does result from an interesting admixture of both. The generous giver of gifts all too frequently is a stingy receiver, lacking humility and graciousness when he is a recipient. The outwardly beautiful girl frequently has an insipid, uninteresting personality. A teenager who hates his mother with murderous intensity may love an animal or a friend with equal intensity. Such complexity of human character makes us interesting, and that complexity should be the basic material of your dramatic creations. Oedipus, for instance, was a good king and an adequate father, but a poor citizen and a murderer. Had he been merely a good king, an adequate father, and an undistinguished citizen, he would lack dramatic interest of any kind. Because Eben Cabot was young and rangy, sensitive and rebellious, his violent treatment of Min was believable. Because he had "taken" her, his being "taken" by Abbie Putnam is believable. If he were a twenty-five year old virgin, free of taint, unsullied by anything but his desire, you might pity him and hate Abbie for corrupting him. But you wouldn't identify with either of them because, in their singular social responses, they would lack dramatic interest. The complexity of their natures makes them interesting.

Some interest can usually be created with description and exposition in short stories and the novel. Denied those two aids in drama, you must be utterly reliant on *dialog* to create the exposition of plot and any description that affects characters. Settings supply a small forum, but it is often forgotten, so dialog must remind the reader. Think how many times, for instance, characters commented on the "purty" sky in *Desire Under the Elms*. Or remember Eben's verbal description of the pasture hill touched with the gold of a setting sun. In supplying such details through dialog, you must remember that people are seldom extemporaneously eloquent. You do not incorporate descriptions of any length in your own conversation. If you make characters falsely eloquent, the result will be thoroughly unbelievable. Notice the falsity of the following dialog, for example. John and Mary are in love. He has taken her to the country to escape the crowded city where they live in the slums. On a high hill, amid grass and flowers and trees, they speak their dreams:

MARY. It's so good to be out of the apartment. Those little rooms and all the kids falling over each other. . . .

JOHN. Soon we'll be out of it forever. See that little farmhouse over there? The fields stretch away from it all the way to the sky and nothing touches the walls except those two big trees and that climbing rose. . . .

MARY. You could send the kids down to that stream that flows along the west edge of the barn and forget you had them.

Even highly educated, verbally eloquent people do not talk like that! Certainly slum-dwelling young lovers don't. A more realistic exchange would be:

MARY. Boy, no kids!
JOHN. We'll get out someday.
MARY. Imagine! Room to send the kids *somewhere!*

Unfortunately, the reader of this last exchange can't follow the conversation; he has no descriptive frame of reference. So it must be supplied unrealistically, but in such a fashion that it *seems* realistic:

MARY. All that *space!* You could lose every kid on Mallory Street in those hills!
JOHN. And only *one* family lives in that farmhouse! You just wait! Someday we won't have to listen to Maggie Pulaski holler at her old man! We'll own land like all the way down to those trees there!
MARY. When they got loud, I'd send the kids down to drown each other in that stream. . . .

This kind of conversation moves a play along, but it does more. It reveals John and Mary's dreary daily existence, their hopes, their ambitions. It also reveals their resentments, their selfishness, their shortsightedness. Mary will be free of the kids she hates in the slum, but she anticipates having children of her own. However, she assumes that they will be burdensome, so she will send them to the stream without supervision. She is vaguely aware that they may drown. . . .

Mary's character stands mercilessly revealed, yet the author has not presented her weaknesses as indictments made by another character. The reader is forced to evaluate Mary's character as her own words reveal it—without her awareness. Will she be a good wife? A good mother? Why does John love her? What does he expect of her? Is she not merely someone to escape with, someone who also hungers for freedom? She is forewarned not to raise her voice! Old man Pulaski may need to be hollered at, but John indicts only Mrs. Pulaski. That indicates something about John as a potential husband.

Characters must be molded to fit the needs of a plot, so John and Mary will be developed in relation to the basic formula used by the dramatist. *Formula* means recipe or pattern, but it does not imply dozens of products all alike. The most common formula, for instance, is the *love formula,* wherein boy meets girl, boy loses girl, boy gets girl.

Shakespeare's *Romeo and Juliet* is the classic of this formula. Paddy Chayefsky's remarkable television play *Marty* is a recent minor triumph. In Shakespeare's story, Romeo and Juliet are denied the right to love by their politically oriented families. Love conquers all, however, and they are married, only to lose each other in death—a death that binds them more closely together than life could have. Chayefsky's Marty is a butcher from the Bronx who falls in love with a homely girl at a dance. His family persuades him that she is old, ugly, and undesirable. When he realizes she is all of those things but she is also his only possibility for happiness, he dismisses the superficial judgments of his family and returns to the girl. The formula is the same in both plays; the characters, theme, plot, and treatment create plays that are related in formula only.

Closely allied to the love formula is the *triangle formula,* which places two characters in open conflict for the love or allegiance of a third. One of the "characters" may be an idea, an ideal, or an ambition, however. *Riders to the Sea* places Maurya and the sea at two points of the triangle; Bartley occupies the third. He must decide between duty to himself and devotion to Maurya. A lesser dramatist would have made Bartley the central character and reduced the importance of the play. In *A Streetcar Named Desire,* Tennessee Williams places Stella Kowalski between her husband Stanley and her sister Blanche DuBois. Struggling for Stella's allegiance, Stanley rapes Blanche, destroys her chance for happiness with Mitch, and forces Stella to reject her sister—a rejection Stella and Stanley cannot survive. The romantic triangle exists in thousands of television scripts and in such Hollywood fluff as *The Bachelor and the Bobbysoxer* or the Andy Hardy films. A perennial favorite, it can always succeed if the characters are interesting enough, for romantic intrigue and jealousy appeal to the average reader and viewer.

Not infrequently, a dramatic change occurs in a character to make him appealing; this is called *The Ugly Duckling formula.* It may be physical as in the fairy tale which gives the formula its name, or it may be completely pervasive as in George Bernard Shaw's *Pygmalion* (the musical comedy *My Fair Lady*) wherein the Cockney flowergirl, Eliza Doolittle, is transformed into a cultured young lady to become the darling of London society. Working in reverse, this formula can be used to reveal beauty disintegrating into ugly evil (Oscar Wilde's *Picture of Dorian Gray,* for instance).

The *success formula* involves a character in pursuit of some ambitious goal or ideal. Mystery plays and science-fiction scripts follow this pattern. Actual success may or may not be achieved (the murderer is caught, the mad scientist does not destroy the world), but suspense mounts steadily until the final minutes which reveal attainment or defeat. Such scripts as *Dial M for Murder* rest completely on the question "Will the murder succeed before time runs out?" Such tragedies as *Macbeth, Hamlet,* and *Oedipus* are basically success formula plays.

In the final moments of *Oedipus,* however, the play assumes characteristics of the *sacrifice formula.* The sacrifice formula employs a noble person willing to give his life for another, or one who will forgo his own ambitions so another person may attain happiness. The classic example of the sacrifice formula is *Camille* by Alexandre Dumas *fils.* Elements of this formula provide the basic characterization devices of Lady Macbeth and of Geoffrey in Shelagh Delaney's *A Taste of Honey.*

Helen, in *A Taste of Honey,* is a *return formula* character—one who comes back unexpectedly to create problems. Tennessee Williams' *The Glass Menagerie* is return formula even though Tom Wingfield does not return physically. That his memory leads him back to Laura and her glass animals establishes the formula successfully. W. Somerset Maugham's *The Circle* is another brilliant example. In this comedy of manners, a wife returns to the husband whom she fled thirty years before, bringing her lover with her. The classic return-formula play is usually combined with a sacrifice-formula ending—such as in Tennyson's *Enoch Arden,* a long narrative poem chronicling the return, after some years, of Arden, a seaman wrecked on a desert island; finding his wife happily remarried, he sadly leaves and dies of a broken heart rather than bring new grief to her.

The most complex dramatic formula is the *community formula,* which assembles members of a family (as in the novel *Swiss Family Robinson* or Clarence Day's *Life With Father*), a military group (Thomas Heggen's *Mr. Roberts*), a social or geographical community (Lynn Riggs' *Green Grow the Lilacs* which became the musical *Oklahoma!*), or a heterogenous group brought together for dramatic purposes (Thornton Wilder's *Bridge of San Luis Rey* or William Inge's *Bus Stop*). The interrelationships of the members of the group provide the dramatic framework. The motion picture *Stage Coach* brought the formula to near-perfection as a motion picture form, though mystery writers had long employed it in that medium: a favorite plot found the enemies of a killer invited to an isolated estate where they were locked in for the night and then murdered methodically. Agatha Christie's *Ten Little Indians* remains a suspenseful classic of this type.

In plotting your play, you may employ only one of the basic formulas or you might prefer to combine two or more. O'Neill's *Desire Under the Elms* combines the love formula (Abbie and Eben), the triangle formula (Abbie, Eben, and Ephraim), the success formula (Eben rids himself of his brothers and sires the son who will inherit if he doesn't), the community formula (the Cabot family), the sacrifice formula (Abbie proves her love by her sacrifice) and, finally, the *redemption formula*. In this last one, an evil or misguided person finds partial or complete salvation through some character change: Eben attains manhood in realizing that his love for Abbie transcends his greed for the farm. Other redemption-formula works are Christopher Marlowe's *The Tragical History of Doctor Faustus* and Charles Dickens' *A Christmas Carol*.

The single-formula play is more simple to plot, but characterization and dialog must be more skillfully handled to create vividness. *Riders to the Sea* is a remarkable example of the single-formula play that comes to greatness through superior characterization, dialog, and atmosphere. The mixed-formula play calls forth superior plotting skill because it must utilize subplots which may seem independent of the main plot unless their structural pattern is clearly defined. If your strength as a writer lies in characterization and dialog, then, you should begin with the single-formula play. If plot is your forte, attempt the mixed-formula approach at first.

Once you have decided upon a theme, established your cast of characters, and outlined your plot, you are ready to begin writing a play. Actually, about half of the work should be done before you begin writing the dramatic form itself. Now you are ready to work with the sequential parts of the play.

Title and Cast of Characters

You should know your characters thoroughly—know them far better than your reader ever will. You may engage a character in the action when he is thirty years old, but you should know everything about him from his infancy. You should understand his actions and reactions to many things that are not included in the play, for he must be consistent in everything he does in the play. Your initial description of him, however, must be relatively brief, revealing only his most important facets as a character to your reader. Ibsen's character descriptions are excellent models. In *Rosmersholm*, for instance, he describes Johannes Rosmer as "owner of Rosmersholm; a former clergyman," establishing Rosmer's economic importance, the importance of the house, and a definite reader response in *former* clergyman. Rebekka West's name follows with the suggestive "a member of the household," which attains no great importance until the remaining four characters (one Rosmer's brother-in-law and another his housekeeper) are listed and the reader realizes there is no Mrs. Rosmer in the play. Rebekka immediately assumes an interest that is speculative, and suspense is established even before the opening lines wherein Rebekka orders the housekeeper to lay the table for Mr. Rosmer's return. In Giraudoux's *The Madwoman of Chaillot,* on the other hand, only the four madwomen are so described, the remaining twenty-six characters merely being listed by name or profession. That the madwomen of Passy, St. Sulpice, and LaConcorde are all titled *Mlle.* while the Madwoman of Chaillot is a countess creates certain reader expectations. Also, in both Ibsen's and Giraudoux's play, the title directs the reader's attention to the central character to supply additional identification. Attempt, then, to arouse reader interest from the opening words of the title and cast. Also attempt to limit your cast at first. As a beginner, you should beware of parading characters in and out. Assess the contribution of each to the total plot and, if that contribution is not great, find a way to pare your script of the character for whom you will have a limited use.

Scene

The movie camera can encompass a great panoramic sweep in setting scenes, but the stage is a confined and limited space where elaborate detail seems distinctly unreal. A house may be employed as it is in O'Neill's *Desire Under the Elms;* a city may be suggested by looming, angry shapes towering over the skeletal suggestion of a house as in Arthur Miller's *Death of a Salesman.*

Limited details can be exceedingly effective (as in *Riders to the Sea,* for instance), allowing the reader or audience to supply additional properties. Poetic presentation of scene can endow it with a kind of wonderful enchantment that supplies any number of effects. Oscar Wilde's scene for *Salome* is a lyrical paragraph of great suggestive power as the cadencial verse creates massive stone walls and towers thrusting their tops toward heaven while the cistern drops away to the bowels of hell itself:

SCENE.—*A great terrace in the Palace of* HEROD, *set above the banqueting-hall. Some soldiers are leaning over the balcony. To the right there is a gigantic staircase, to the left, at the back, an old cistern surrounded by a wall of green bronze. The moon is shining very brightly.*

If it suits the mood of your play, a more elaborate scene may be employed. James M. Barrie becomes positively chatty as he prepares you for his one-act play *The Twelve-Pound Look:*

If quite convenient (as they say about cheques) you are to conceive that the scene is laid in your own house, and that HARRY SIMS *is you. Perhaps the ornamentation of the house is a trifle ostentatious, but if you cavil at that we are willing to re-decorate: you don't get out of being* HARRY SIMS *on a mere matter of plush and dados. It pleases us to make him a city man, but (rather than lose you) he can be turned with a scrape of the pen into a K.C., fashionable doctor, Secretary of State, or what you will. We conceive him of a pleasant rotundity with a thick red neck, but we shall waive that point if you know him to be thin.*

It is that day in your career when everything went wrong just when everything seemed to be superlatively right.

In HARRY'S *case it was a woman who did the mischief. She came to him in his great hour and told him she did not admire him. Of course he turned her out of the house and was soon himself again, but it spoilt the morning for him. This is the subject of the play, and quite enough too.*

HARRY *is to receive the honor of knighthood in a few days, and we discover him in the sumptuous "snuggery" of his home in Kensington (or is it Westminster?), rehearsing the ceremony with his wife. They have been at it all the morning, a pleasing occupation.* MRS. SIMS *(as we may call her for the last time, as it were, and strictly as a good-natured joke) is wearing her presentation gown, and personates the august one who is about to dub her* HARRY *knight. She is seated regally. Her jewelled shoulders proclaim aloud her husband's generosity. She must be an extraordinarily proud and happy woman, yet she has a drawn face and shrinking ways as if there were someone near her of whom she is afraid. She claps her hands, as the signal to* HARRY. *He enters bowing, and with a graceful swerve of the leg. He is only partly in costume, the sword and the real stockings not having arrived yet. With a gliding motion that is only delayed while one leg makes up on the other, he reaches his wife, and, going on one knee, raises her hand superbly to his lips. She taps him on the shoulder with a paper-knife and says huskily, "Rise, Sir Harry." He rises, bows, and glides about the room, going on his knees to various articles of furniture, and rises from each a knight. It is a radiant domestic scene, and* HARRY *is as dignified as if he knew that royalty was rehearsing it at the other end.*

Atmosphere must be established in the initial description of the set, and that atmosphere should lead into the dominant mood that you seek to develop in the play. Consider the great elms of O'Neill or the heath of Shakespeare's *Macbeth*. If music is to be utilized, it should be introduced now, its presence in the play seeming natural rather than intrusive because the audience is unprepared. Further, if a telephone is to ring, the existence of that telephone should be made known; if a rifle is to be fired onstage, hang it prominently on a wall.

Opening Exposition

The term *opening exposition* is a little misleading, for the first exposition of your play is the set. *Exposition* is a "revealing" or "exposing," and it is immediately vital if your audience is to be interested in the characters and caught up in the promised action. The king, the priest, and Creon present that background in *Oedipus*. Witches create atmosphere and the dialog of the major characters establishes background in *Macbeth*. Eben's limited dialog and revelatory action accomplish the job in *Desire Under the Elms*. Probably no single portion of the play is more important than this exposition; so do not fall into the easy traps of telephone conversations, loquacious servants, or gossipy neighbors to "tell" the audience what it must know. Examine the opening lines of many plays to see which ones impel you to continue reading. When a play is immediately gripping, discover why. Then either modify the technique to your own use or create the same urgency in an approach that is equally good.

Building Suspense

Tension (that suspenseful buildup to conflict between two characters) must be generated almost immediately. If your play opens on a weeping woman, men fighting, or a couple arguing, tension sparks the audience to awareness. Oedipus plunges into a description of plague. Maurice Maeterlinck challenges the audience of *Pelléas and Mélisande* with maidservants *inside* the castle walls shouting "Open the gate! Open the gate!" Tension hangs on the words. Tennessee Williams' Stanley bellows at his wife and heaves a bloody package of meat at her in *A Streetcar Named Desire*. In each case, the reader or audience wants to know why, what the action means, or what will happen next.

Once created, tension should mount steadily, stretching the scene (*tension* suggests the tensile and stretchable) until it is relaxed and a new scene builds new tensions. The entrances and exits of characters serve to relax or intensify suspense which, once established, may be relaxed for longer periods of time if new exposition or complicating material needs to be introduced. Once you have captured the interest of your audience by generating adequate suspense, it will allow you to develop characters, strengthen mood, or intensify atmosphere.

Logic must overlay the action at all times. If a character does or says anything, his action or words must contribute to the forward flow of the plot. And they must be paced so they come at the right time—that is, exactly when their contribution is the greatest. Sometime within the first half of the play, a major dramatic question must be posed. It will probably be suggested by the major dilemma that faces the protagonist. The second half of the play will intensify the conflict resulting from that dilemma and finally resolve it. Notice: *resolve,* not *solve.* Playwrights seldom solve problems—even God seems hesitant to do that. They do resolve the action. It must come to a conclusion that leaves the audience either satisfied or disturbed enough to reconsider the meaning of life as a result of the play.

CHAPTER XI

The Muse Reviewed—
Writing About the Play

At various times, you may be required to write about a play—either from the written script or from an acted version. The form of your paper may range anywhere from a critical, academic essay to a chatty, personal response. Between the two extremes, a large number of possibilities are open to you, all valid, all effective in achieving definite ends. At the most formal level, your paper might include a relatively complete examination of an author's life, his total works, and his position in the history of drama. At the least formal level, it might be a witty critique of an actor's lack of talent. Whatever the level, however, you will reveal a great deal about your educational and cultural background, your developed taste (or the lack of it), and the extent of your powers of observation.

Discussing the play from a printed script or from a performance demands that you make one or more of the following value judgments:

(1) Why did the playwright create this play? Is it merely an attempt to entertain the reader for a couple of hours or is it a vehicle to convey his philosophy of life to the reader? How seriously does the playwright take himself, and how seriously should the reader respond? In short, is the play important because it amuses, instructs, disturbs, or confuses the reader? Or is it unimportant because it attempts little and succeeds not at all?

(2) Is the plot convincing? The question, you will notice, is *not* "Is the plot true to life?" Chances are, it can't be. Drama is, after all, an imitation of life, a mirrored image of selected portions, therefore not true. If the drama could be true to life, it would be unbearably tedious and utterly dull. The elements of a convincing plot must be present and plausible if you are to get an illusion of reality as you read. The witches in *Macbeth,* for instance, are scarcely believable in a scientific age, but they remain con-

vincing because they are such a rational extension of Macbeth's dark mind that we can view them as hallucinations grown from battle fatigue in both Macbeth and Banquo. Abbie Putnam's irrational act of murder is not necessarily convincing just because such things often happen in life to create lurid headlines; it is convincing because Abbie is a woman controlled by passions that have made her behavior consistently irrational, and that consistency is convincing. *Camino Real* is thoroughly unrealistic since it peoples the plaza with fictional and historical characters, but it is convincing in that it establishes a believable cross-section of contemporary society whose members behave with fidelity to their natures.

(3) Do the characters exist as distinct entities even though they function as representational types? Kilroy, for example, in *Camino Real* is a person you might know because he is noble and kind on the one hand, selfish and dull on the other. He could be the boy next door or an aggregate of all the boys next door who have fought wars they did not understand in alien places for reasons they dared not examine. Their follies and their compassion make them pink-cheeked disseminators of social plague among conquered peoples, and they embrace incident not because it is experience but because it has the blue haze of distance about it. Kilroy's representational behavior creates you and me, and we see him as a distinct person who is legion in himself. His illogical behavior is the illogic of the sundered; his speech is the curious blend of stupidity and poetry that we speak. He is as romantic as a golden-hearted hero and as tawdry as the patsy he emulates so well. Verisimilitude grows from the artful blend of desirable and undesirable traits, and Kilroy's actions are consistent in their inconsistency for they suit his character.

(4) When the author's reason for writing the play becomes clear and the plot and the characters emerge as believable possibilities to depict that reason, the theme emerges. The next question, then, is "What is the theme and what is its pertinence?" The inclination to ask "What is its value?" should be curtailed until later, for value in itself demands careful analysis. If a play refuses to yield a theme, it is beyond critical consideration, for any literary work rests on an exploration of beliefs that remain universal and timelessly interesting even as reaction to them changes. Man's constant search for happiness (Maeterlinck's *The Blue Bird*), the necessity of paying attention to a man merely because he is human (Miller's *Death of a Salesman*), woman's inherent right to exist as a human being (Ibsen's *A Doll's House*)—all such themes are important to man and must be restated again and again as generations roll by. A "good" theme does not ensure a good play, but a play cannot be good without a discoverable theme.

(5) Is the dramatic technique adequate to the play? Does the plot

seem defensibly structured? Are the characters suitable to that plot? Is the pace of the play right or does the action drag in places? Even such masters as Shakespeare could write agonizingly dull acts. How suitable and interesting is the dialog? Do the rising action and the falling action seem proportionately effective? Is the climax truly climactic or is it merely structurally present? To what degree has the dramatist developed a literary style that stamps the play with his uniqueness?

(6) Finally, what is the value of the play to you? This question is the most critically demanding of the lot. First, what constitutes *value* in a literary work? If the abstraction *value* can be considered an equivalent, your time and effort are invested in the play on the assumption that your return will be at least equal in worth to the time expended. And you will judge value according to your own scale, a scale which is unique in its entirety. Your value scale may include such common acceptances as "The possibility of love is worth the probability of disappointment" or "Four college years gambled against a lifetime of greater economic, cultural, and social ease constitutes pretty fair odds," but the total scale is yours alone. Time is usually the determining factor when we assess the value of any activity in our brief life spans. Therefore, what potential values does the play offer if your time is to be the price? Here are three such potential values:

a. *Entertainment.* Is the play entertaining enough to keep you in suspense, amused, titillated, therefore worth the time you might otherwise spend at a party, on the beach, or in a bar?

b. *Instruction.* Does the play offer insight that may help you understand yourself and your world better than something else that requires the same expenditure of time?

c. *Therapy.* Are your emotions immersed in the cleansing agitation generated by the play so that your emotional body is purged and renewed as a result of your vicarious involvement in the lines of the characters?

Certain other observable values in the play should also be considered:

a. *Structural values.* Because life, however chaotic it seems at times, follows a formal pattern beginning with birth and ending in death, it is structured in some fashion. That structure is artistically reproduced in the basic framework of a play and is analogous to actual experience. If you analyze or outline a play, its structure should emerge to reveal the time relationships of the actions as well as the emotional relationships of the characters. Depending on the style and technique of the author, the theme will emerge from the observable structural pattern and you will understand something of the structure of reality.

b. *Psychological values.* You behave in your unique pattern as a result of the total past and present response of your five senses. A drama creates memory patterns from the images, symbols, emotions, and sensory perceptions you have stored in your intellectual warehouse on one of its three floors: conscious, unconscious, or subconscious. If the play acts as an agent to select, combine, and arrange a new experiential room where you can gain new perspectives, its psychological value becomes apparent. If your tolerance, understanding, empathy, or sympathy are expanded (singly or simultaneously), a play possesses value beyond immediate assessment.

c. *Ideational values.* The philosophical attitudes of Tennessee Williams and John Millington Synge are clearly revealed in *Camino Real* and *Riders to the Sea.* The religious concepts of O'Neill illumine every line of *Desire Under the Elms* with as much intensity as the unknown author's do in *Everyman.* Ethical considerations abound in *Oedipus Rex, Macbeth,* and *Sodom and Gomorrah.* At their simplest level, these values are a stateable theme; at their more complex levels, they are explicit and implicit ideas that abound to weave a brilliant tapestry of reaction and response in you, to shape your ultimate judgments of the play.

After you have read or seen the play and considered the value judgments you wish to discuss, you must decide upon the approach you will take in your paper. Nothing is less interesting than an unadorned plot summary, so reject that possibility from the beginning unless you can make it a revealing analysis of the strengths or weaknesses of the playwright. Notice as you read the following review of the motion picture *Privilege,* that the technical aspects of cinematography are largely ignored and the script is subjected to a value-judgment treatment:

A Phony Fable of a Pop Faust°

by Richard Schickel

If I were in charge of archives housing significant cultural artifacts of our times, I would run out tomorrow and buy several prints of a desperately chic English movie called *Privilege.* It is a pretty rotten film, but it is going to be invaluable to future historians, for it conveniently summarizes our most contradictory attitudes about popular culture and its effect on those who purvey it.

° *Life,* August 25, 1967.

The time is 1970 and our non-hero, Steve Shorter, has reached unprecedented heights as a pop singer—a sort of super-Beatle. Steve is, naturally, a simple soul, defenseless against the shameless manipulation by the management group which controls his destiny. He senses something wrong with the setup and goes around uttering small cries of pain into the ear of The Girl Who Understands. He also indulges in sullen little tantrums like forcing his handlers to drink hot chocolate with their lobsters instead of wine—ugh! But what, exactly, is it that's wrong?

Poor Steve, he doesn't know a neo-fascist when he sees one. That's too bad, for "they" are all around him (and us, if you can accept the film's thin premise). They have promoted Steve as a symbol of youthful rebellion all these years not merely to make money, but so that they can convert him—when the time is right—into a full-scale godhead, capable of leading his pimply flock out of the discothèques and back into Winchester Cathedral. Steve at length suffers martyrdom in an atmosphere redolent of Hitler's Germany—a torch-lit stadium full of supernumeraries giving the Nazi salute.

Finally, of course, he breaks. Accepting some phony award, he suddenly finds himself muttering that he is a person, not a symbol. Before you know it he's telling his fans and manipulators, "I hate you, I hate you, I hate you!" This their tiny, well-washed brains cannot accept and so they turn riotously against him.

Does all this sound familiar? Certainly. It is a blending of two basic mass-media myths, the stuff that has informed dozens of novels and films with much simple-minded social commentary. The first posits the inevitable loss of spiritual values when self-respect is bartered for the money and power that go with fame. Someday someone may give us a fiction that makes this bargain look somewhat less stringent than the one Faust inked with the devil, more like the kind of deal a clever agency makes for a hot client. I fear, however, that the resulting products will not be accepted, for most of us like to believe that successful people cannot possibly be enjoying themselves. Without this moral Miltown, I doubt that the majority of us losers could stand the rigors of the success ethic.

But it is the second myth in *Privilege* that shatters credulity. This is the fantasy of omnipotence with which people professionally engaged in mass media titillate themselves. They have put over some lulus—nonsinging singers, nonacting actors, *Valley of the Dolls*—and the occasional willingness of an audience to be gulled leads them first to contempt and then to the wild delusion that, given the right property, promotional technique could take over the world.

I suppose it's possible. But these self-confessed masterminds have a way of forgetting that the ratio of flops to hits is consistently three or four to one, and that for every Marilyn Monroe there is at least one Maria Montez. The frantic ineptness with which the business is ruled constitutes the best guarantee that the future predicted in *Privilege* will never come to pass.

This movie's makers, for instance, ask us to believe that a young singer named

Paul Jones can play "the biggest star in the last 500 years" (let's see, who was that guy who was so big in 1467?) when he can scarcely bring himself to move or to speak before a camera. Then we are asked to pay for the privilege of watching Jean Shrimpton, the well-known model, learn to act. The swing from satire to preachment, moreover, is so violent that you are in danger of laughing when you should be scared. Finally, Director Peter Watkins has been permitted to run riot with his flashy, fashionable style, a blend of semidocumentary and *cinéma vérité* techniques that never conveys a sense of menacing truth. This worked in his *The War Game* because atomic holocaust is truly frightening. It fails here because pop culture can't, or shouldn't, scare anyone. *Privilege* is a glib child's recital of a dream about the bogeyman, full of sensational inventions that melt away like patches of fog in the morning sun. □

Walter Kerr, one of Broadway's most influential critics, uses the form of the personal essay (a conversational, fluid procession of thought growing from thought) to discuss structure, language, dramatic philosophy, and printed as well as acted versions of Christopher Fry's poetic comedies:

Christopher Fry°

by Walter Kerr

It is possible to respect the "natural" poetic imagery of a man like Tennessee Williams and still yearn for the day when this shall grow, stage by stage through action and character, into language that is admittedly, and powerfully, verse. Christopher Fry has, in a sense, overleaped our time. He has come out for verse now; it has got him into trouble, but it has also made our eyes pop and our ears perk up.

The most striking thing Mr. Fry has accomplished is to have discovered a twentieth-century verse form for comedy—of all things. Matters had got to the point where it was almost impossible to convince anyone that comedy *could* be written in verse, so strong is the stranglehold of prose upon our age. Lip service was still paid to the notion of verse tragedy, because both verse and tragedy seemed equally remote to us; but prose comedy had been galloping along at a successful rate and there seemed no reason to wish for anything better. Mr. Fry has given us something better—has found both an imagery and a rhythm for comedy which increases the intellectual and emotional range of things to be laughed at—and his work comes as a genuine surprise.

Broadway had to wait for Mr. Fry's second American showing to take his work to heart. The first Fry venture to appear here, *A Phoenix Too Frequent*, was apparently so ruinously directed and acted as to conceal completely the quality of the play. On the printed page *A Phoenix Too Frequent* seems to me the most perfect thing of

° From *Pieces At Eight* (New York, 1957).

its kind since *The Importance of Being Earnest* and, within its limited intention and shorter length, superior to *The Lady's Not for Burning*. It has a sharply defined narrative that is developed with alacrity and precision. By comparison, *The Lady's Not for Burning* seems talky and meandering. But the play has its own virtues and they represent an experimental advance for Fry. He has tried for more complexity and got a richer texture out of it. He has tried for a slightly more rounded characterization and picked up a bit of human warmth. Where the earlier play was a perfect joke, intellectual to the core, the new one is an imperfect but possibly more appealing attempt to capture nature on its own vexing, complicated, and fulsome terms. It keeps shifting gears, and pulling back into first rather too often, but when it gets where it is going you feel you have been with the people all the way. *A Phoenix Too Frequent* is an exercise in detachment; *The Lady's Not for Burning* is an experiment in participation. Fry asks you to accompany the characters rather than observe them.

There is a perpetual danger of Fry's becoming too fulsome. In one of his plays he has a character settle back and sigh happily, "It's nice that anyone can say anything at all."

And it is nice, now that verse has made it possible. But drama is still limited by the singleness of its action and the things said must have some relation to this singleness. Occasionally Mr. Fry forgets this and indulges himself in the pure delight of all that can be said. I am so grateful for the method of saying it that I am willing to indulge him his indulgence, but the audience isn't likely to, and he will do well to brake his verbal exuberance every now and then.

The effect of talkiness was accented by John Gielgud's performance in the production of *The Lady's Not for Burning* that was imported from England. Where the rest of the company, under Mr. Gielgud's own direction, read contemporary verse as though it were contemporary verse, Gielgud himself was frequently guilty of chanting. The immediate result was that Fry's verse was compared to Shakespeare's in some quarters, whereas the author's chief distinction is that he has found a new form instead of echoing an old one. If Fry is like anything, he is like Shaw in verse.

In a later and less successful play *Venus Observed*, the stuffy Dominic is informing his sister Perpetua that their charming father is a crook and likely to go to jail. Dominic expects his sister to be shocked, but she is a pleasant realist:

> PERPETUA. . . . . I was able to believe you at once.
> Poppadillo has the most beguiling
> Jackdaw look about him. But you think
> He wouldn't be happy in prison?
> DOMINIC. He wouldn't, but what
> Difference does that make? Would you be able
> To look anyone in the face, with a father jailed?
> PERPETUA. Oh, yes, if he were comfortable.

That is like a dozen passages in Shaw, and Fry has much of the impudent love of paradox, the passion for plain sense, and the hopeful irony of his prose forbear. He has neither the romanticism of Shakespearean high comedy nor the lowness of Shakespearean bumpkin comedy. Even when, in *The Lady's Not for Burning*, he introduces two brothers who seem on the bumpkin side, they turn out to have the intellectual facility and emotional disillusionment of a couple of Shavian Caesars.

That third play, *Venus Observed*, did shake a number of Fry fans in various ways. By the time it appeared in America, in a rather sluggish production staged by Sir Laurence Olivier, two schools of thought about Fry had formed: one which held that the fanciful young comic poet had brought about a joyous rediscovery of the English language, and another which stubbornly held that his verbal dexterity was mere vaudeville, and difficult vaudeville at that.

I remain a Fry man myself, but I must confess that *Venus Observed* gave aid and comfort to the enemy. In the process of dazzling his contemporaries with the rare and rich antics through which obedient words can be put, Mr. Fry had apparently bedazzled, and perhaps even blinded, himself. The language was once more sent sailing through hoops; but it finally tumbled in a little clutter about the feet of some paper-thin people whose behavior was sometimes amusing, sometimes ingratiating, but almost always uncomfortably contrived.

No one should ask that a verse comedy, least of all the kind of fanciful conceit that Mr. Fry so pleasantly invents, be entirely level-headed about its people. And we should have been willing, momentarily at least, to accept as heroine a young lady who had spent a few years in America destroying such public objects as offended her aesthetic sense. We were, in fact, mildly entertained by the notion that she had spent some time in jail, making restitution. We may have been a little bewildered that she should suddenly draw a gun in a living room and shoot an apple out of a young man's hand, but we expected that Fry would sooner or later have some delectable point to make of the episode. And it was pleasant enough to watch the Duke of Altair, an aging rake who believed himself to have renounced all further conquests, fall in love with her.

But, having accepted all of the author's introductory whimsy, and having finally arrived at the moment of intimacy between Duke and girl, we were dismayed to discover that Mr. Fry had conceived no real relationship for them. No emotion fluttered upward to disturb the glossy verbal surface. Instead, the girl stood prettily in the center of the room and delivered a sparkling apostrophe to the glories of syntax. The speech ran on for forty-one lines, and while it was delivered (by Lilli Palmer) with some gaiety and some invention, it gave the whole show away. Mr. Fry had assembled his unlikely figures only to parse them.

At about the time that *Venus Observed* was being poorly received in this country, Mr. Fry was jotting down some thoughts of his own—for a small book called *An Experience of Critics*—on the creative processes, the behavior and misbehavior of words, and, of course, the critics who had been commenting on his work.

Most playwrights who turn on their tormentors do so in the heat of passion. Smarting under the immediate sting of a set of bad notices, they tend to cast both caution and coherence to the winds, erupting into a breathless invective that is quite as unpersuasive as the play which has preceded it.

Mr. Fry was cannier. He permitted his critics to go on to new targets, fully frocked; he caused his own rancor, if he ever had any, to relax into the graceful coil of the sleeping serpent; he seemed to have taken his hemlock in small daily doses so as to build up a splendid tolerance for the stuff. Then, in his quiet and almost jolly way, he let us have it.

An Experience of Critics may have been only a temporary victory for Mr. Fry, but it was a juicy one. For one thing, Mr. Fry writes better than the people who write about his writing. And for another, he had thought long enough, calmly enough and trenchantly enough to have found some true and tellings things to say.

On the critical treatment of still budding talent: "The newly sprouting acorn is dug up several times a week and solemnly told that whatever it may think to the contrary, it is not an oak tree."

On one of the occupational hazards of criticism, noted when Mr. Fry himself attempted to review a play: "I could scarcely hear a word of the play for the noise of my own mind wondering how I should write about it."

On the inadvisability of having infallible criticism: "No man in his senses expects a critic always to be right—indeed, it would be very disconcerting if he were: we should have to believe him."

On the howls that go up when critical thumbs go down: "An artist's sensitiveness to criticism is, at least in part, an effort to keep unimpaired the zest, or confidence, or arrogance, which he needs to make creation possible."

On the vision of versifier Fry at work, as conjured up by the newspaper notices: "I see a man reeling intoxicated with words; they flow in a golden—or perhaps pinchbeck—stream from his mouth; they start out at his ears; they burst like rockets and jumping crackers and Catherine-wheels round his head . . . his typewriter continues to chatter long after it has been put back in the case. Words will grow out of him, like finger-nails, for some time after his death."

The poet's morose account of how he turns from this sort of journalistic analysis of his work to the work itself, sitting like an ancient Indian for silent hour after silent hour until at last he is able to type out an inspired "How," is not only deliciously funny reading; it is also a sharp comment on the easy nonsense which critics often substitute for an accurate reading of a complex creative problem.

Meanwhile, our author was at work on the problem. Shortly thereafter he came up with a fourth major play, the "winter comedy" called *The Dark Is Light Enough*, in which one character turned to another at a fairly heated point in the verbal clamor and cried, "But that's only a word!"

"Still," replied someone who was obviously a friend of the playwright's, "a word stays in the mind—and has its children, too."

And at long last—and in spite of certain very real difficulties in the play—it did seem as though Mr. Fry's words were ready to give up philandering, settle down, and perhaps produce grandchildren. Until now, except for the hint of amiably rooted character in *The Lady's Not for Burning,* the unexpected poet had been having fun with the language—testing it, tormenting it, making it laugh in a manner to which it had been unaccustomed, and sometimes skyrocketing it right over the garden wall. If it had often been exhilarating, it had sometimes been irrepressible to the point of irresponsibility.

In *The Dark Is Light Enough*—my enthusiasm for this play is based on the British rather than the softer and sleepier American production—language was ready to come home and stay with people, even belong to them. As an Austrian countess of the 1860s chose to risk her life and endanger her loved ones in order to perform an entirely quixotic act of mercy, she spoke now with a quiet self-confidence ("I am always perfectly guilty of what I do"), now with tartness ("People are always ready to die for what death will take away from them"), now with humor ("Are you military by nature or misfortune?"). And each of the lines belonged not to a free flight of Mr. Fry's more errant invention but to the woman who was thinking it.

Elsewhere in this melodramatic poem in praise of human generosity there were further evidences of the author's beginning tryst with reality, his beginning fondness for dimension in addition to dexterity. Much of the second act was concerned with an elusive, tantalizing yet thoroughly alive relationship between a good-for-nothing deserter and a woman—the Countess' daughter—who had loved him, lost him, and was now risking the destruction of her second marriage by giving him the time of day and the kindness of her heart. As these two moved clumsily, then impulsively, toward each other, we were never quite certain what this lingering affection meant, or where it was going to lead. But it existed. For the moment something very concrete, thoroughly clothed in flesh, was seen to be working out its peculiar destiny before us—and the moment meant that Mr. Fry had begun to see his characters in terms of their secrets rather than their syntax.

Thus, toward the end of the evening, when one of the puzzled people whose lives had been turned topsy-turvy by a meaningless war paused to remark that he knew a certain truth "in the still of my mind," it was possible to believe that these figures did have still reservoirs, places of rest, behind their bright and eager phrasemaking.

Mr. Fry was slowly and patiently putting flesh on those dancing bones. □

Life magazine's theater editor Tom Prideaux discusses *The Homecoming* less as a play than as a springboard into consideration of the dangers besetting serious drama in America. Still, the reader is more aware of the values of the play than he would be if it were reviewed merely as another Broadway offering:

The Adventurous Play—Stranger to Broadway°

by Tom Prideaux

Is the philosopher's wife a prostitute or an enigmatic Mona Lisa who is all things to all men?

This is only one of the tantalizing questions that arise from Broadway's strange new drama by Harold Pinter. *The Homecoming* is an absorbing piece of modern theater, magnificently acted by England's Royal Shakespeare Company. And yet *Homecoming* stands almost no chance of Broadway success. Why? Because it is a serious play. And that by itself is nearly enough to relegate it to the graveyard where every other serious and adventurous play this season has gone.

The Homecoming is not a safe play. It doesn't take you where you expect to go. It has the same dreamlike illogic of Harold Pinter's *The Caretaker* and his well-known shorter works, *The Lover, A Slight Ache, The Collection.*

Seeing it in London two years ago, I had one of the rare theatrical experiences of a lifetime. Usually at any play I have some hunch about what future developments will be, at least within certain limits of probability. But halfway through *The Homecoming* I realized that I was in the hands of a maniac driver who followed no road map and was breaking free into his own dream landscape. Anything could happen.

Pinter sets his play in a London dwelling, bleak as a warehouse, inhabited by a brawling old widower and his two younger sons, an oafish pugilist and a sarcastic little Soho pimp. Into their murky sub-world arrives the oldest son, Teddy, who has been teaching philosophy in an American university for six years. With him is his wife Ruth. At once, for no apparent reason at all, she is menaced by the pimp, and venomously insulted by the father, who calls her "a stinking slut." The philosophic son is blandly indifferent to this nightmare tirade, and his wife remains calm.

In the end, the philosopher returns to his cloistered campus, and his subtly erotic wife opts to remain with the earthy household, serving each man according to his needs and desires: as sweetheart to the pugilist, hustler for the pimp, housekeeper for the father.

Taken literally, her decision is shocking. But she is acted with such serene dignity by Vivien Merchant—Pinter's wife—that she stands quite apart from the common definition of prostitute. "I look on her," says Pinter, "as a splendid woman."

Pinter is so adept at creating unfamiliar and otherworldly patterns of behavior that he seems at times to be writing science-fiction of the psyche. But behind his startling permutations of character is his own steadfastly moral attitude, his

° *Life*, March 3, 1967.

implied hatred of brutality, his implied compassion for mankind. "I always hesitate to mention moral considerations," he says, "but there are always one or two knocking about."

Audiences who at first are put off by Pinter's unorthodoxy might gain a little enlightenment by knowing about his unorthodox way of writing. He begins with no mapped-out plot or characters. Instead, he sits down with a pencil until, out of the blue, a snatch of dialogue strikes him, a string of words that evokes a situation and then suggests a sequence of events. *The Homecoming* grew out of a simple opening line, spoken by an old man rummaging through a drawer and asking, "What have you done with my scissors?"

Pinter then lets his characters do and say more or less what they please. "People seem to feel that I go with everything that happens in my plays, that I push things forward in an approving way. That is not the case. I have to give my characters their own rope and life."

Sometimes, he says, things get out of hand, and upstart characters barge in where he doesn't want them. While he was writing *The Caretaker*, for example, an unexpected visitor named Mick blew in at the close of Act I and asked, "What's the game?" Flabbergasted, Pinter found out he was the younger brother of a principal character, and took Mick into the plot. Later on, however, a stray girl popped in and blurted out six lines before Pinter recovered from his shock and kicked her out forever. "You have to do it soon," he says, "or you can't get rid of them."

"Once I know what's going on in a play," he adds firmly, "I take meticulous control." But because he starts without knowing what is coming next, Pinter's works build up a strong mood of suspense. "Suspense," he says, with a happy grin, "that's the joy of it."

The Pinter play is having a struggle to stay alive here chiefly because it can't pay its way according to Broadway's tough commercial terms. In London the terms are more sensible. The play was an important literary hit but it played only three or four nights a week in a repertory company. Thus, over a long period of time, *The Homecoming*, which is certainly not everybody's dish of tea, had a chance gradually to build up an audience that would appreciate it. It is as idiotic to suppose that all good drama should play to full houses eight times a week—as it must on Broadway in order to survive—as it is to suppose that all good books must be best-sellers.

Under the present system, serious drama gets to Broadway only if a brave producer like *Homecoming*'s Alexander Cohen is willing to risk almost certain financial disaster. But how long will such producers keep coming back for punishment? And how long will theatergoers have an appetite for serious drama when they get so little to whet it on?

The cause of this shameful state of things is complex and diffuse. It lies partly in the theater's economic mess which enables only surefire hits to survive. It lies in a long-standing disinclination among American intellectuals to support theater of any kind. And it lies in the revolution in serious drama, a swing toward more jolt-ing and imaginative forms that are often hard to take, harder to understand, and seem at times to be deliberately planned for the public's obfuscation.

That isn't all. Near the end of *The Homecoming,* the philosopher's wife chooses to forsake the safe academic world and join his disreputable family. When her husband leaves her without anger but without even a goodby, she calls after him, "Don't become a stranger."

That is really what threatens the serious drama—the danger of indifference, the danger of the public becoming strangers. ☐

If Prideaux is correct (and there is no reason to argue with him), you are in a rather enviable position as a student of drama. By now, it is not an unfamiliar form. It should be a vital, challenging literary genre promising you a lifetime of enjoyment. If you are indifferent to it, your loss is incalculable. If you are interested, however, you have joined the ranks of the bacchantes and a wild, wonderful, mystic experience is yours anytime you care to sit down for a couple of hours, open a book, and let the curtains part in the theater of your mind. On that vast stage, three thousand years of drama await your participation, your criticism, and your pleasure.

Suggested Assignment. The theater of your mind is a fantastically conceived architectural marvel. It is designed and equipped to house the great plays of the world with all the excitement and brilliance which they demand. Attend it often.

Index